D1226610

One Vast Winter Count

HISTORY OF THE AMERICAN WEST

Richard W. Etulain, Series Editor

One Vast Winter Count

The Native American West before Lewis and Clark

Colin G. Calloway

UNIVERSITY OF NEBRASKA PRESS
LINCOLN AND LONDON

Publication of this volume was assisted by The Virginia Faulkner Fund, established in memory of Virginia Faulkner, editor-in-chief of the University of Nebraska Press.

Manufactured in the United States of America

∞

Library of Congress Cataloging-in-Publication Data
Calloway, Colin G. (Colin Gordon), 1953–
One vast winter count: the Native American West before Lewis and Clark / Colin G. Calloway.
p. cm.—(History of the American West)
Includes bibliographical references and index.
ISBN 0-8032-1530-4 (cloth: alk. paper)
1. Indians of North America—West (U.S.)—History.
I. Title. II. Series.
E78.W5C43 2003
978'.01—dc21
2003044757

To Marcia, Graeme, and Megan, as usual,
and in memory of my father,
Ronald Keith Calloway (1920–2003)

Contents

Illustrations

Maps

Series Editor's Preface

Historical writing about the American West has undergone dramatic changes in the past half century. Specifically, western historians have moved away from the frontier thesis of Frederick Jackson Turner and turned in new directions: Authors such as Henry Nash Smith and Earl Pomeroy have helped us understand how mythic Wests and western imitations of European and eastern American traditions have shaped the history of the region. Other recent western histories highlight the roles of racial and ethnic groups, women and families, and urbanization in the development of the West. And widely recognized today is a New Western History that treats the darker, more complex sides of the region's past.

These historiographical shifts compel us to ask new questions about the history of the American West and to reexamine the past in light of our experiences in the late twentieth and early twentieth-first centuries. Fresh sociocultural, demographic, and environmental topics are being addressed; for many specialists in the field, the regional West has supplanted the frontier West, with *place* being emphasized more than *process.*

It's time for a new comprehensive history of the American West, one that reflects new scholarship without overlooking past perspectives. The History of the American West series does just that. A history of the region in six volumes, it builds on these recent historiographical developments of gender, ethnicity, and the environment. The volumes reflect current thought about the West as a region, provide a judicious blend of old and new subject matter, and offer narratives that appeal to specialists and general readers.

Colin Calloway meets all these goals in this initial volume of the series. He has produced an exhaustively researched and smoothly written study of the Native American West from prehistory to 1800. Beginning his volume with what he calls the "ancient history" of the human past, Calloway traces the first evidences of Paleo-Indian existence on the frontier and in the trans-Mississippi West up to the contact era. The following sections of his volume address contacts, conflicts, and sometimes combinations within individual tribes, among Native American groups, and between Native and European peoples.

Several of Calloway's achievements deserve specific mention. First, through apt use of telling quotations, he gives voices to many individual Native Americans as well as to several Native groups. Likewise, his diligent, wide-reaching research (and full notes) covers a variety of viewpoints on major controversies among historians, ethnographers, and archaeologists. Equally important, the author furnishes substantial discussions of human impact on the natural environment and extensive coverage of the tragic effects of disease on Native societies.

For all of these reasons, Calloway's volume will quickly become recognized as the best and most thorough source on the early history of Native Americans west of the Appalachians. It is an ideal study with which to launch this multivolume history of the American West.

I wish to thank two groups for helping me with the planning and preparation of this series: first, the historians who have agreed to author these important volumes, and second, the editors at the University of Nebraska Press who have encouraged my work and that of the volume authors.

Richard W. Etulain

Acknowledgments

I have lived in the West for part of my life, and, as far as I can remember, I have been thinking and reading about the West for all of my life. But I am not, by any stretch of the imagination, a westerner, unless spending my first twenty-eight years in West Yorkshire counts. I was invited to write this book because of my interest in American Indian history between 1500 and 1800. I balked. How could this, the first volume in a new six-volume history of the American West, begin in 1500, so close to the end of American history? To do its job, I argued, the book would have to stretch back thousands of years before Europeans arrived. Series editor Dick Etulain and Daniel Ross, former director of the University of Nebraska Press, agreed. And how could a book about the West before 1800 ignore the area between the Appalachians and the Mississippi, the territory that constituted "the West" for generations of colonial Anglo-Americans? Etulain and Ross agreed, again. Having let me talk myself into a mammoth project, Etulain and Ross gave me plenty of latitude in how to handle it. I am grateful to both of them.

This book would not have been possible without the research of countless scholars and the expertise of many friends and colleagues. They will recognize their influence on the pages that follow, and I have recognized their scholarship in the notes. I was fortunate to be at the Newberry Library at a time when Frederick Hoxie and Peter Nabokov were both working on Crow history and culture and when Helen Tanner was completing her monumental *Atlas of Great Lakes Indian History*. At the University of Wyoming, I was privileged to have the opportunity to know George Frison, even though our work together revolved around the American Heritage Center and academic administration rather than Clovis points and buffalo jumps. At Dartmouth, I am grateful to my colleagues in the Native American studies program: Deborah L. Nichols read the first two chapters, pointed me to many sources, and explained many things about the archaeology of the Southwest; Sergei Kan's work on Alaska enriched my view of history on the Northwest Coast; Dennis "Dan" Runnels deepened my understanding of Native history in the Northwest; Dale Turner provided endless discussions on Indian sovereignty and daily doses of Anishinabe humor; Elaine Jahner shared some of her last writings with me. Linda M. Welch dealt with my routine computer snags. Darren Ranco helped with preliminary research into the literature on the archaeology of the Southwest. Dartmouth's president, James Wright, himself a historian of the American West, supported my scholarship and my work as chair of the Native American studies program. Presidential student scholars Cat McCarthy, Kim Jorgensen, Jennifer Tlumak, Kathryn Ritcheske, and Robert Karl each contributed to a piece of the project. Kathryn Ritcheske in particular took a sustained interest in the book. She helped with the microfilm reels from the Spanish Archives of New Mexico, found and translated materials for me at Southern Methodist University De Golyer Library, and assisted with fact checking. Jennifer Ain helped wrestle the massive notes into the beginnings of a bibliography.

I am grateful to the dean of faculty of arts and sciences for the award of the Gordon W. Russell 1955 fellowship, which covered the cost of index preparation, and to the Nelson A. Rockefeller Center for the Social Sciences at Dartmouth College for a "small grant" that helped meet the cost of preparing the maps.

Roger Echo-Hawk pushed my thinking about how historians can, and must, make better use of oral traditions. Willard Rollings has been a good friend over the years, has engaged me in endless conversations about the southern plains, and has given someone who grew up in Old England an inkling of what it means to grow up in New Mexico. Joseph Key read portions of the manuscript. Elizabeth Fenn and I found we were both researching the same epidemic, but her research has been more intensive and covered a much broader canvas than mine, and I am grateful to her for sharing her work with me prior to its publication.

Many individuals assisted me in obtaining records and photographs. In particular, I wish to thank Lou Stancari at the National Museum of the American Indian; Joyce M. Raab at the National Park Service Chaco archives at the University of New Mexico; Arthur Olívas at the Palace of the Governors, Museum of New Mexico; Brian Leigh Dunnigan at the Clements Library at the University of Michigan; and George Miles, curator of the Western Americana Collection at Yale's Beinecke

Library for showing me the Bacstrom drawings. The staff of Dartmouth's Baker/Berry Library were invariably helpful, and I benefited from the efficient service provided by interlibrary loan and document delivery.

Five scholars read the manuscript for the University of Nebraska Press: Dick Etulain, David Rich Lewis, Donna Roper, David J. Weber, and Elliott West were all constructive in their comments, tolerant of my forays into their individual areas of expertise, and generous in their support of my efforts to cover large amounts of time and space in a single volume. I am grateful to Mary M. Hill for her meticulous copyediting.

When a book is published, reviews and royalties matter, but not very much. For its author, a book is a memory of when it was written, the experiences that surrounded it, and the things learned doing it. *Winter Count* holds memories of thinking about Native trade networks while pushing children on swings, putting off research trips, negotiating time to write with promises of late-afternoon trips to the pool, leaving paragraphs unfinished to deal with little crises or appeals for justice. The interruptions, frustrations, and demands that delayed the work probably made it a better book in the end; they certainly made me a better person. Researching and writing a book of this magnitude while raising two children with both parents working was made easier by having a highly efficient arrangement in my life: my toughest critic is also my best friend and the woman I love. As usual, she and my children share the dedication.

A Note on Terminology

I have used the terms *Indian* and *Native American* interchangeably. Indian peoples have their own names for themselves and sometimes find offensive the names used by outsiders in historical records and literature. I have indicated how some of these names came to be applied but generally have used those names that seemed most easily recognizable to most readers. The University of Nebraska Press normally employs the American rather than the Canadian form for tribal names, for example, *Ojibwe* rather than *Ojibwa*. While it is generally recognized that *Blackfeet* applies to the people who live in the United States and *Blackfoot* applies to the people who live in Canada, it made little sense and created much confusion to alternate between these terms depending upon whether a group happened to be in northern Montana or southern Saskatchewan during an era when the U.S.-Canadian border did not exist. I have used the term *Sioux* when referring to the people of that nation in general; I have used *Lakota* when referring to the western branch of the nation. *Algonkian* refers to the language family and its constituent tribes; *Algonkin* refers to the specific tribe. I have used *Pueblos* when referring to the people, *pueblos* when referring to the towns they inhabited. Since capitalization is generally used for the Northern Arapahos, Eastern Shoshones, and Western Apaches, that procedure has been followed consistently when referring to branches of other nations.

One Vast Winter Count

Prologue

Land and History in the American West

The Sioux used to keep winter counts, picture writings on buffalo skin, which told our people's story from year to year. Well, the whole country is one vast winter count. You can't walk a mile without coming to some family's sacred vision hill, to an ancient Sun Dance circle, an old battleground, a place where something worth remembering happened.

Mary Crow Dog, *Lakota Woman*

Oh, what a vast heathendom!

Father Francisco Garcés,
after his journey from Tubac to Monterey, 1774

In January 1804, while the men of the Lewis and Clark expedition were in winter camp at Camp DuBois at the mouth of the Wood River in Illinois, William Clark stumbled upon "an Indian Fortification" and a circle of nine mounds. He found "great quantities of Earthen ware & flints." Clark was on the northwestern edge of the Cahokia mounds, about eight miles north of Cahokia, the great Indian city that had flourished eight hundred years before. President Thomas Jefferson, who had dispatched Lewis and Clark with instructions to gather information on the Indians of the West, was especially interested in vanished civilizations—he had excavated an Indian burial mound near his home at Monticello. Jefferson would have been fascinated to learn of the Indian city, but Clark and his companions pushed west on their epic "voyage of discovery" without seeing the great mound of Cahokia, known today as Monks Mound. There would be much more of the Native American past and presence that eluded Lewis and Clark as they trekked across the West, much that they did not see, did not understand, and could never know. Knowledge of Cahokia's importance and history would come well over a century and a half later, when construction of Interstates 55 and 70 around St. Louis in the 1960s prompted archaeological excavations at the site.[1]

In many histories of the American West, the Lewis and Clark expedition marks the beginning of recorded history, with the captains' journals constituting a baseline of information about the region before the United States took possession. Their voyage ushers in a new "American" future for the West and serves as a launchpad for the real story; earlier history of the region is relegated to prelude. In most dramas of western history, the light shines so brightly on the Corps of Discovery that it blinds us to the storylines of previous acts and to what is occurring simultaneously elsewhere on the stage. The Lewis and Clark expedition was a momentous event and a heroic achievement, but it was only a subplot in a historical drama of time, place, and people that had been playing for thousands of years. The "new lands" Lewis and Clark explored were in fact very old. The West they saw had been shaped by many other histories—and ways of understanding history—involving other peoples and recorded not only in writing but in song and story and earth and memory.[2] Lewis and Clark did not bring the West into U.S. history, they brought the United States into western history.

In this book, the American West is not a canvas for a single national narrative; it is a series of Indian homelands. It is also a series of frontiers, zones of interaction that formed, overlapped, and re-formed around those homelands as Indian communities moved, mingled, and adjusted to new environments, other Indians, and, eventually, Europeans. Each community existed at the center of a kaleidoscopic world and had to hold its place as surrounding pieces rearranged themselves in response to outside influences and internal pressures. In the eighteenth century, Indian lands in the trans-Appalachian West were being wrested from Indians by war and whiskey, trade and treaty and transformed by massive deforestation and ecological change. West of the Mississippi, the land, with few exceptions, remained Indian country, but its inhabitants were feeling reverberations of what was happening on the eastern borders.

This book does not try to provide complete histories of the many Indian peoples and several European peoples who inhabited the Old West and shaped its history, nor does it give balanced coverage to all regions. Occasionally within the chapters, which are largely overviews, the text zeros in on a particular area or region. Based primarily on records generated by Europeans and concentrating on centers of action and interaction, the story focuses more, for example, on the Ohio Valley—very much "the West" to French and English colonists of the eighteenth century—than on the Great Basin. Different Indian and European nations enter and reenter the story where their experiences intersect with and illustrate the themes of the broader narrative.

In the summer of 1978, my Ph.D. freshly under my belt, I spent a month traveling around the West by Greyhound bus. I had flown from London to New York, and sleeping on buses allowed me to see as much country as possible before I flew home from Los Angeles. In California, the parents of a friend's friend opened their home to me, and the father insisted on driving me around. I saw missions, vineyards, and Disneyland. The old gentleman was an Anglophile. He loved our cathedrals and castles and the fact that we "had so much history over there." He apologized for the lack of history in the West. I asked him if he had ever seen Mesa Verde. (I had not.) He had, and he described it to me in detail and with appropriate expressions of awe. Then he went back to talking about the cathedrals of Europe. The conversation puzzled me. It may have puzzled him too. In retrospect, I realized that he did not intend to dismiss Mesa Verde; he just did not think of it as "history" in the same way that the monumental architecture of Europe constituted history.

This book, in part, is about the histories the old gentleman did not consider "history."

When Crazy Horse surrendered in 1877, an eighty-four-year-old man in his band carried "a stick about six feet long, covered with notches, thousands of them." An American officer asked him what it was; "he said it was the history of the world from the beginning, handed down by his fathers." With deliberate irony, anthropologist Eric Wolff called those who were absent from European written records of the past "people without history." History is a remembered interplay of time, space, and human experience, but these things hold different meanings for different people, and they record these meanings in different ways.[3]

Time and again in the history of the West we are reminded that human history and natural history are intertwined; we cannot understand one without the other.[4] The West is a land of grand scenery, magnificent distances, endless skies, and limited water. The landscape today is punctuated by national parks, small towns, and sprawling desert cities and crisscrossed by highways. Roadside markers point out the supposed or actual locations of historic events—pioneer experiences, Indian fights, explorers' debacles, fur trappers' campsites, first schoolhouses, and so on. But the West is also a land of intaglios, petroglyphs, earth mounds, ruins abandoned long before Europeans ventured there, tipi rings, buffalo jumps, sacred sites, and natural markers to human triumphs and tragedies. On and in the ground lie glimpses of different stories and ancient histories. Some are long forgotten or incompletely understood. Others can be read out of the land by people who see not the "empty wilderness" that daunted Europeans but a world alive with the spirits of ancestors, etched with the experiences of generations, and holding "memories of the past with which they coexist."[5] For Native peoples, the landscape, with its markers and stories, could be read like an historical text, or like a winter count, the calendar of events by which Lakotas recorded their histories.[6]

For nineteenth-century pioneers, the American West offered new lands in a new world. Geologists looking at those same lands see history stretching back millions of years. They figure out stories in rocks and construct a record of change over time that dwarfs human presence. In John McPhee's words, it is "detective work on a scale unimaginable to most detectives."[7] Mountain ranges were formed, flattened, re-formed, and moved. The Colorado River excavated the Grand Canyon quite recently. Canyon walls in the Llano Estacado of western Texas and eastern New Mexico reveal six major geologic periods, the Permian, Triassic, Jurassic, Cretaceous, Tertiary, and Quaternary, "crafting in detail a record of more than 260 million years." The rocks of Wyoming, the Dakotas, and Montana provide "a comprehensive record of the 13 million years following the extinction of the dinosaurs." In Wyoming "every period in the history of the world" is represented; there are places where Interstate 80 cuts through strata that record millions of years of history, and one can see quite clearly that even the landscape is temporary. Tourists to Grand Teton National Park see a dramatic and unchanging landscape; a geologist born and raised in Wyoming who has spent most of his life studying the complex geologic history of the Teton landscape sees it rather differently: "After half a century with the story assembling in his mind he can roll it like a Roman scroll. From the Precambrian beginnings, he can watch the landscape change, see it move, grow, collapse, and shuffle itself in an intricate, imbricate manner, not in spatial chaos but by cause and effect through time. He can see it in motion now."[8]

Rock art—petroglyphs and pictographs etched or painted on outcrops, cliff faces, and boulders—also chronicle histories that reach back

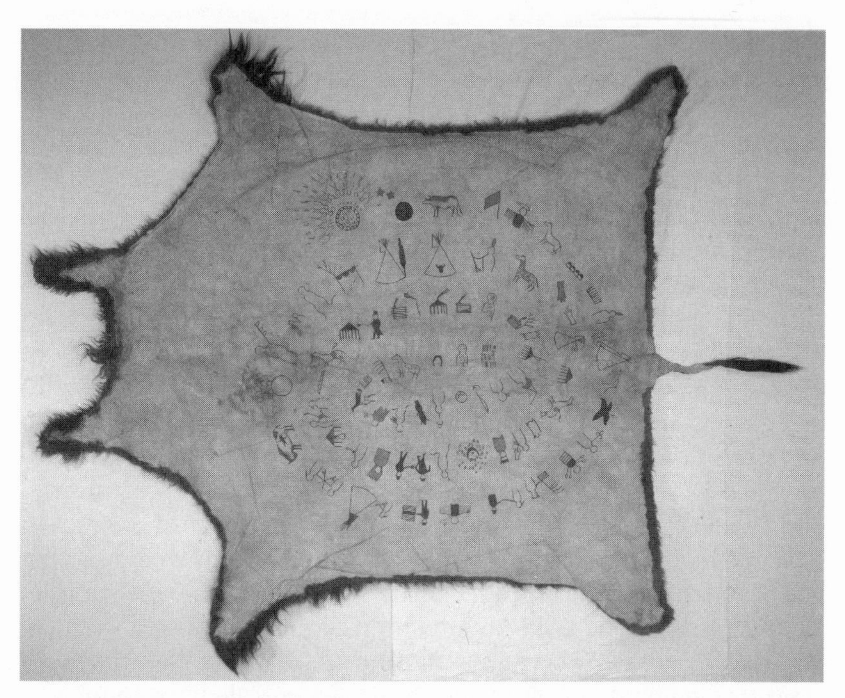

1. A Lakota winter count. Winter counts were read from the center outward, with symbols serving as mnemonic devices to recall the events of each year. This one, done by the Sicangu or Brulé Shunka Ishnala, Lone Dog, around 1870 begins several years before Lewis and Clark went west and shows the smallpox epidemic of 1801, the effects of which were still visible when the American captains arrived. (Courtesy, National Museum of the American Indian, Smithsonian Institution, neg. no. T010617. Photo by Janine Jones.)

hundreds and sometimes thousands of years. Often created in spectacular settings and sacred places, rock carvings and paintings reflect the connection between Native peoples and their natural and spirit worlds. Lewis and Clark provided the first written record of rock art on the northwestern plains, but more than twelve thousand rock art sites have been located across Alberta, Saskatchewan, Montana, and Wyoming as well as in California, Nevada, Utah, and the Southwest. Their images span at least five thousand years, with some possibly dating as far back as twelve thousand years. Some rock art scenes, with abstract designs and anthropomorphic beings representing supernatural power, convey "only enigmatic messages from an unknown past" and provide glimpses of a complex cosmography. Other scenes depict hunting ceremonies, battles with enemies, and, in some cases, the arrival of horses. Some scenes can "be read almost like a simple sentence," dated to a particular time, and attributed to a specific people; in other cases, traditional knowledge held by Indian people, past and present, is key to understanding the images. Many rock art sites are sacred places to modern Indian communities.[9]

"There is something stirring about finding evidence of human labor and care in the soil of an empty country," wrote western writer Willa Cather. "It comes to you as a sort of message, makes you feel differently about the ground you walk over every day."[10] From scattered fragments uncovered from the ground archaeologists read whole social structures, life patterns, and even ideologies. Projectile points and pottery shards, mounds and middens, ruins and burial sites hold clues about cultural developments, settlement patterns, subsistence strategies, migrations, alliances, the growth and disintegration of societies, exchange networks, wars, relationships between "cores" and "peripheries," ritual complexes, social structures, the emergence and nature of elites and chiefdoms, symbols of wealth and power, architecture, technologies and art styles, rituals and religions. People left behind faint traces of their lives; the people who analyze and decipher those traces often produce widely divergent interpretations of those lives. New scholars enter the field, new evidence emerges, and new technology gleans new answers from old evidence. As a result, archaeological literature on Cahokia or the Anasazi Southwest often seems to revolve around recurrent, heated, and sometimes acrimonious controversies about, well, practically everything.[11]

Scholars who view archaeology as science may be inclined to dismiss Native oral traditions as a means of understanding human history. But oral traditions can complement, illuminate, and breathe life into dry archaeological data.[12] Through oral traditions we may hear, however faintly, times that are beyond written record but not beyond collective memory. Through oral narratives knowledge and belief are handed down across the generations. Oral traditions contain echoes of how ancient people understood their origins, themselves, and the world into which they came. Calvin Martin describes these narratives as "stories out of step with time and history" through which we may begin to perceive what he calls "the way of the human being—the way of the world of those people who beheld the first Europeans splash ashore five hundred years ago, and yet who did not regard time or reality or even words themselves in the way those newcomers did then or we do now, and who have struggled mightily with this strange new western philosophy ever since."[13]

Place is often more important than time in recalling history. The past, anthropologist Peter Nabokov reminds us, is anchored in place. For

Western Apaches, writes Keith Basso, the past "lies embedded in features of the earth—in canyons and lakes, mountains and arroyos, rocks and vacant fields—which together endow their lands with multiple forms of significance that reach into their lives and shape the way they think."[14]

Land and lives are inseparable. "We have lived upon this land from days beyond history's records, far past any living memory, deep into the time of legend," said an elder from Taos Pueblo. "The story of my people and the story of this place are one single story."[15] As revealed in the works of contemporary Native American writers, homeland is both source and shaper of identity. "We are the land," writes Paula Gunn Allen. "To the best of my understanding, that is the fundamental idea embedded in Native American life and culture in the Southwest."[16] After three years working with the ninety-year-old Maria Chona in the 1930s, anthropologist Ruth Underhill realized that the Tohono O'odham, or Papagos, did not think of themselves as possessing the land; "it is the land that possesses the people."[17]

Mythic tales linked to specific places contained morals and teachings that enabled people to live as true human beings. At Bear Butte in South Dakota, for example, the Cheyenne culture hero Sweet Medicine received the Sacred Arrows and directions on how his people should live. From a Sioux perspective, asserts anthropologist Raymond DeMallie, myth is sacred history and "the only true history" because it explains the moral framework within which Lakota culture developed.[18] The lands people inhabited held stories about the interdependence of people, animals, and the natural world.[19] Tied to place by clan and family memories, stories connected the people to an ancient world whose lessons they must not forget and to the natural world in which they could survive only by maintaining proper relations with other forms of life. The landscape reinforced the continuity and accuracy of the narratives.[20] Storied places pulled the people to them. Hidatsa Indians told anthropologist Alfred Bowers in the twentieth century that they remembered the ancient villages on the Knife River. The villages had been abandoned before they were born, but "it was the custom for many families to return to these sites and to point out to the younger people the depressions of lodges where certain relatives had lived, their graves, or earth rings on the prairies where various ceremonies such as the Naxpike or Wolf ceremonies were held." Bowers's informants pointed out many of the features to him, identified other, earlier sites, "and explained many things that might have otherwise gone unrecognized."[21]

Among the things unrecognized by newcomers were the sacred meanings in the storied landscapes. Pawnee Indians in Nebraska learned that their people "were made by the stars." When the time comes for the world to end the stars will again fall to the earth. "They will mix among the people, for it will be a message to the people to get ready to be turned into stars." Through an elaborate round of ceremonies, the people kept the cosmic order in its course, moved the universe through its seasonal round, and maintained the earth and its life processes. Pawnees drew charts of the stars on elk skins and arranged their villages so that their earth lodges reflected the positions of the stars. People who studied the stars had detailed knowledge of their terrestrial landscape as well. They knew every aspect of the land they crossed on their annual migration to hunt buffalo on the plains. "Its topography," wrote anthropologist Gene Weltfish, "was in their minds like a series of vivid pictorial images, each a configuration where this or that event had happened in the past to make it memorable." Like many Americans today, Americans who crossed Nebraska in the nineteenth century saw the landscape as endless and tedious. Pawnees saw a landscape pinpointed with sacred sites.[22]

At first glance, rock carvings on the Colorado River Reservation in Arizona—home to members of the Mohave, Chemehuevi, Hopi, and Navajo tribes—appear to have been left haphazardly in the desert. The petroglyphs are part of an ancient system of markers that pointed runners to a network of trails covering vast distances. Ancient trails also linked intaglios, geometric figures of humans and animals etched on the desert floors. The desert, barren and unrevealing to European and American newcomers, and the rock carvings that have made prime targets for collectors of "Indian curiosities" may thus constitute "a map of the sacred world" and the ways in which ancient people connected with that world.[23] For Kiowa writer N. Scott Momaday, sacred sites do more than mark history; they define the earth. "If you would learn the earth for what it really is," he says, "learn it through its sacred places."[24]

Storied landscapes are surely not unique to the Native American West. They are common, for instance, in the Celtic regions of the British Isles. But, as Richard White points out, landscapes do not speak to strangers.[25] In the American West, non-Indians were newcomers; relatively speaking, they still are. "The man from Europe is still a foreigner and an alien," Lakota writer Luther Standing Bear said in the 1930s. "Men must be born and reborn to belong. Their bodies must be formed of the dust of their forefathers' bones."[26] Landscape becomes etched on the mind as a result of experiences and their retellings over generations. "People in the northern Great Plains know that narrative about the landscape is as necessary to their survival as water," wrote Elaine Jahner, who grew up in North Dakota. The Sioux lived on the plains long enough to develop narratives that relate to the landscape. European immigrants had their own narratives related to landscape in the Old Country; but "without narratives to place themselves in the vast seemingly empty landscape often faced madness [,] and immigrant literature chronicles their attempts to find ways to live with the natural forces that seemed to threaten their very humanity."[27] In O. E. Rölvaag's novel *Giants in the Earth*, the Norwegian pioneer woman Beret Hansen, "who could not take root in new soil," sits brooding in her Dakota sod house, fearful of the land and the constant wind.[28]

Native place-names, like some of the names applied by non-Indians, described location, natural features, and local animal life. Some names recorded where plants, herbs, minerals, and other natural resources might be gathered for food, medicine, ceremonial, and craft materials. At Celilo Falls on the Columbia River (now immersed under the waters of The Dalles Dam), for instance, Indians named almost every place suitable for fishing: places where people cast gill nets when the river ran normally; places where they cast when it was high; places where men could stand above the rushing torrents with dip nets; places where flat stones under clear water made spear fishing easy.[29] Other place-names alluded to events that occurred in legend and history. Indian place-names scattered across the West are so common that modern residents often fail to recognize them, let alone appreciate them as "tatters of the rich fabric of native geography."[30] And it was not just the tribal story that was embedded in landscape but also the histories of clans and families and individual experience and memory.

Indian peoples knew their homelands intimately. Many of them knew their continent as well. When Europeans arrived, some Indians participated in the European rediscovery of America. Drawing on knowledge derived from extensive travels, they pointed the way along rivers and trails, interpreted the landscape, and provided information on tribes the Europeans had yet to meet. Explorers and fur traders followed Indian canoe routes into the heart of the continent. Indians traced maps on the ground with their toes and fingers, etched them on birch bark, and drew them on deerskins and buffalo hides. They showed Frenchmen the way from the St. Lawrence River to the Great Lakes, to the Mississippi, and out onto the Great Plains. They showed Spaniards the way across the Southwest and from Florida to the Mississippi and led them out onto the Great Plains. In 1540 a Yuma Indian made a chart of the lower Colorado River for Hernando de Alarcón, the first white man to ascend the river; in return the Indian asked Alarcón to make a map of the country the Spaniards came from. In 1602 Miguel, an Indian from the plains captured during Juan de Oñate's expedition and taken to Mexico City for interrogation, made a map during the course of a long and carefully recorded interrogation. The map embraced a vast territory, probably more than one hundred thousand square miles of the central or southern plains, showed routes, rivers, and Indian settlements, and indicated the distances between places in terms of days of travel.[31] Indian maps guided Oñate across the Arizona desert in 1605 and René-Robert Cavelier, sieur de La Salle, down the Mississippi River in 1681.

Spanish and French expeditions across Texas followed Indian guides along ancient trails. Traveling with Indian guides up the Red River in 1718–20, Jean-Baptiste Bénard de la Harpe observed that the Indians "do not make any mistake when they show the part of the world where the nation dwells of which they have knowledge, and that, taking the bearing of the places with the compass, one is certain of their situation." James Isham, factor at York post on Hudson Bay who regularly employed Indian guides to lead wintering parties into the interior, said, "The Natives are Seldom at a loss in their travelling." On the northern plains in the late eighteenth century, French-Canadian trader Jean-Baptiste Truteau saw Indians make accurate skin maps of the countries with which they were familiar. "Nothing is wanting but the degrees of latitude and longitude," he said. A Chipewyan chief named Matonabee guided Samuel Hearne northwest from Hudson Bay to the Coppermine River in 1770–72 and drew him a map of the route. Scotsman Alexander Mackenzie, the first white man to cross the continent north of Mexico, more than a decade before Lewis and Clark, used Indian guides and maps on both his Arctic and his Pacific voyages.[32]

In 1801 and during the winter of 1802, three Blackfeet men named Ackomokki, Kioocus, and Ackoweeak and an unnamed "Fall Indian" (a Gros Ventre, or Atsina) visited the Hudson's Bay Company trading post at Chesterfield House on the South Saskatchewan River. At the request of trader and surveyor Peter Fidler, they drew maps of the region. The Gros Ventre drew a map depicting the western plains all the way south to New Mexico. The first map, drawn by Ackomokki (known to the traders as Old Swan or Feathers) and probably in the snow, showed the Red Deer and Saskatchewan Rivers coming from the west, the Rocky Mountains to the south, the tributaries of the Missouri River in the east. Beyond the Rockies it showed the Snake and Columbia Rivers and the Pacific Coast. Ackomokki provided information about the landscape, including the number of days' travel between prominent features of the Rockies, and also about the locations of different peoples—he drew circles indicating thirty-two bands. The result was "a detailed picture of more than two hundred thousand square miles of North America." Fidler committed a smaller copy of the map to paper, with annotations and information from other Indian informants, and sent it off to Hudson's Bay Company headquarters in London. A year later the information it contained was being added to British cartographer Aaron Arrowsmith's map of the West; three years later Lewis and Clark would be using Arrowsmith's map and following Ackomokki's directions, although since Arrowsmith lacked any familiarity with Blackfeet cartographic traditions to help him translate the map, his information probably did the captains little good.[33]

During their two and a half years in the West, Lewis and Clark themselves solicited thirty maps, sketches, and "cartographic devices" from Indian informants. The Mandan villages on the upper Missouri, where the expedition spent the winter of 1804–5, were a busy trade rendezvous and gave the American explorers access to knowledge and information about routes and peoples as far west as the Rocky Mountains. When the expedition reached those mountains, Cameahwait, leader of a Northern Shoshone band camped along the Lemhi River in present-day Idaho, created a three-dimensional map, forming piles of sand to depict the daunting topography of the mountains they were about to cross. Like their European predecessors, Lewis and Clark depended on Indians to point the way across the continent. Armed with the information the Indian maps conveyed, they began the process of rethinking, renaming, and remaking the West. But the knowledge of the West was already there. It was extensive in scope and deep in history.[34]

To people who have lived there for generations, homelands are not blank space, terra incognita, awaiting someone else's knowledge and charting. Indians had their own cartographic conceptions, maps that conveyed accumulated knowledge of place and were stored in the memories of individuals who could communicate the information by speech, gesture, and depiction in response to specific needs and requests. Native American maps did not rely on fixed points within a bounded space but on patterns of intersected lines. Euro-Americans never fully succeeded in tapping this knowledge or in fully translating Native maps into their own

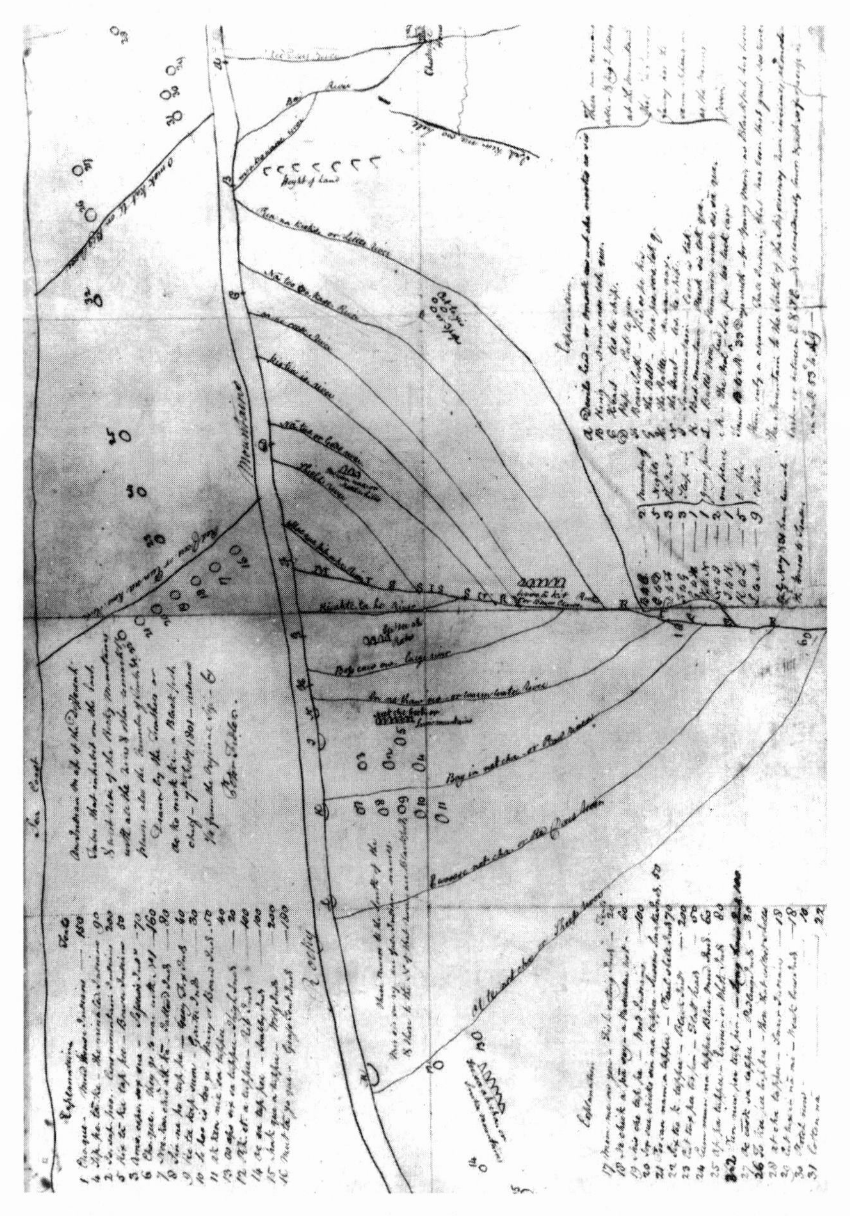

1. *An Indian map of the Different Tribes that inhabit on the East & West Side of the Rocky Mountains with all the rivers & other remarkbl. Places, also the number of Tents etc. Drawn by the Feathers or ac ko mok-ki—a Blackfoot chief—7th February 1801.* Peter Fidler's redrawn map. (Courtesy, Hudson's Bay Company Archives, Provincial Archives of Manitoba, G.1/25 [N4157])

maps. Native mapping used different cartographic conventions. European maps employed scale, direction, and latitude and longitude; Indian maps were "pictures of experience" and probably reflected dimensions that Europeans could neither grasp nor chart. As Peter Nabokov explains, Indians who drew maps knew the land in ways Europeans did not: "Before representing it, for instance, some native traditions expected you first to listen to its stories and learn its names, to follow it with your feet or to find a way to dream at its most propitious locations. Only after practicing a range of such knowledge-engendering practices *with* the landscape might you be truly able to depict it on a flat surface." Unlike European maps, Indian maps were not intended to be permanent documents. The map that Ackomokki drew, like other Indian maps made to help Europeans get where they were going, was, as Mark Warhus says, "an illustration of the Native American's oral landscape."[35]

Native American mapping patterns may have conferred spiritual significance on a region, but Indian people were not and are not the only people to possess spiritual relationships with the land.[36] During their long tenure in New Mexico, Hispanic communities have developed a profound attachment to place and ceremonies, songs, and traditions related directly to the landscape they have inhabited.[37] For some non-Indians in the twenty-first century whose families have lived in the West for generations, the land is alive with stories, memories, and experiences as it has always been for many Indian people. Europeans who invaded Indian country in the sixteenth and seventeenth centuries came with intimate memories of their own homelands, and they too saw the landscape as a spiritual as well as a physical space. When they drew maps of it, planted crosses on it, and built churches on sites held sacred by Indian peoples, they attempted to give it new meaning and transform it from a wilderness where they feared Satan's influence held sway to an ordered place where God was present, Christ was worshiped, and "civilization" could grow.[38] Struggles for the West were—and still are—not just about who should own and occupy the land but also about what the land should mean, the kind of lives that should be lived there, and, ultimately, the kind of stories it would hold. The stories that Indian people read in rivers, rocks, and canyons are not often the histories that make it into books, much less into American culture. But the new stories told by the invaders have not erased the old ones. They are the most recent chapters in a book and the most familiar, because most readers peruse the final pages first and rarely make it back to the opening chapters.

Anyone reading or thinking about or living and traveling in the American West encounters a dizzying array of opinions, perspectives, and insights on the specialness of place there. But one finds little agreement on where the West actually is. The West has always defied easy definition. For historic Indian peoples the term as we know it was probably meaningless; wherever they lived, they were at the center of their own universe. Indeed, terms like *West* and *frontier* can be seen as exerting "conceptual violence" on Indian peoples. These are "colonial constructs that erase Indian organizations and experiences of space."[39] The international border established between the United States and Mexico in 1848 has distorted Native American historical geography and obscured the Southwest's place as the northern edge of an Indian world that reached out from Mexico. Even from an Anglo-American perspective and experience, there have been many Wests. In one sense, the West as it is generally understood today—that part of the United States west of the Mississippi or Missouri River—was not "American" until Thomas Jefferson obtained Louisiana Territory and Lewis and Clark led their expedition across it. For Anglo-America before 1800, the West lay *east* of the Mississippi, albeit west of the Appalachian Mountains. Lewis and Clark shifted the idea of the West westward. Much of this book focuses on North America west of the Mississippi, but it also includes histories from the trans-Appalachian region, because for many people and for a long time that was the West, and because events there determined developments in other, later Wests.

No attempt has been made to pay equal attention to areas north and south of the present boundaries of the United States, but histories from what is now Canada and Mexico are included where they enrich the story. French presence and experiences in the West make little sense without considering events in Canada, notably, tracing Franco-Indian relations through Huronia; Spanish presence and experiences in the Southwest make little sense without considering events in northern Mexico and placing the Pueblo Revolt in a broader context of ongoing resistance. Much of what is now the Midwest was once part of New France; the Southwest was once part of New Spain. In U.S. history, New Mexico is often portrayed as the heartland of the Spanish Southwest, but it was actually the extreme northern tip—or the tail end—of a corridor of Spanish expansion that pushed north from the basin of Mexico. Always seen as remote from the rest of New Spain, Nuevo Mexico was not the big square territory encompassed by the modern state; it was a long, narrow colony of vulnerable settlements perched along the Rio Grande. Present-day Arizona lay at the northern edge of a corridor of expansion that reached up the coast of the Gulf of California through Sinaloa and Sonora. Texas lay at the northeastern frontier, beyond Coahuila and Nuevo León.[40] Likewise, French activities in the western Great Lakes, at the mouth of the Mississippi, and in Texas occurred at points remote from and tenuously connected to the core of France's North American empire—the settlements that hugged the St. Lawrence far to the northeast. For Russian fur traders, North America's Pacific Northwest Coast represented the farthest limit of Russia's *eastern* expansion.

This broad embrace is not intended to present the West as process rather than place and revert to a Turnerian view of American history as expansion along sequential frontiers—at the Appalachians in the mid-eighteenth century, at the Rockies a hundred years later. Rather, it recognizes that the term *West* meant different things to different people at different times. Nevertheless, it does echo Turner in viewing the history of "the West" as the history of the whole nation.[41] In large measure, all of America has been "the West" at some point, and the West has stood for all of America. To cut through these complex connections, exclude the trans-Appalachian West, and concentrate solely on the trans-Mississippi or trans-Missouri West would ignore many historical experiences that were, in their own way and time, "western" and to simplify and distort the meaning and place of the West in American history. Ralph Waldo Emerson once wrote that "Europe stretches to the Alleghenies; America lies beyond."[42] Substitute "the West" for "America," and his point helps define the geographic scope of this book.

Wallace Stegner, who spent most of his life writing and thinking about the West, described it as half a dozen different subregions with "every sort of topography and landform," from alpine mountains, plateaus, and mesas to short-grass plains, geyser basins, and deserts. What unifies and defines these various regions, said Stegner, is climate; what gives the landscape its special character is aridity. Aridity makes the air dry and clear, gives the light its unique brilliance, makes the stars appear bigger and brighter, shapes the earth through erosion, and governs the nature of the animal life and vegetation.[43] Aridity not only describes the geography of the West, it has also, always, defined how people lived there. Water, writes Elaine Jahner, "is perceived in an elementary equation with thirst." On the northern plains, "as the tree rings tell us, the cycles of ample or scarce rainfall are longer than the cycles of human lives so

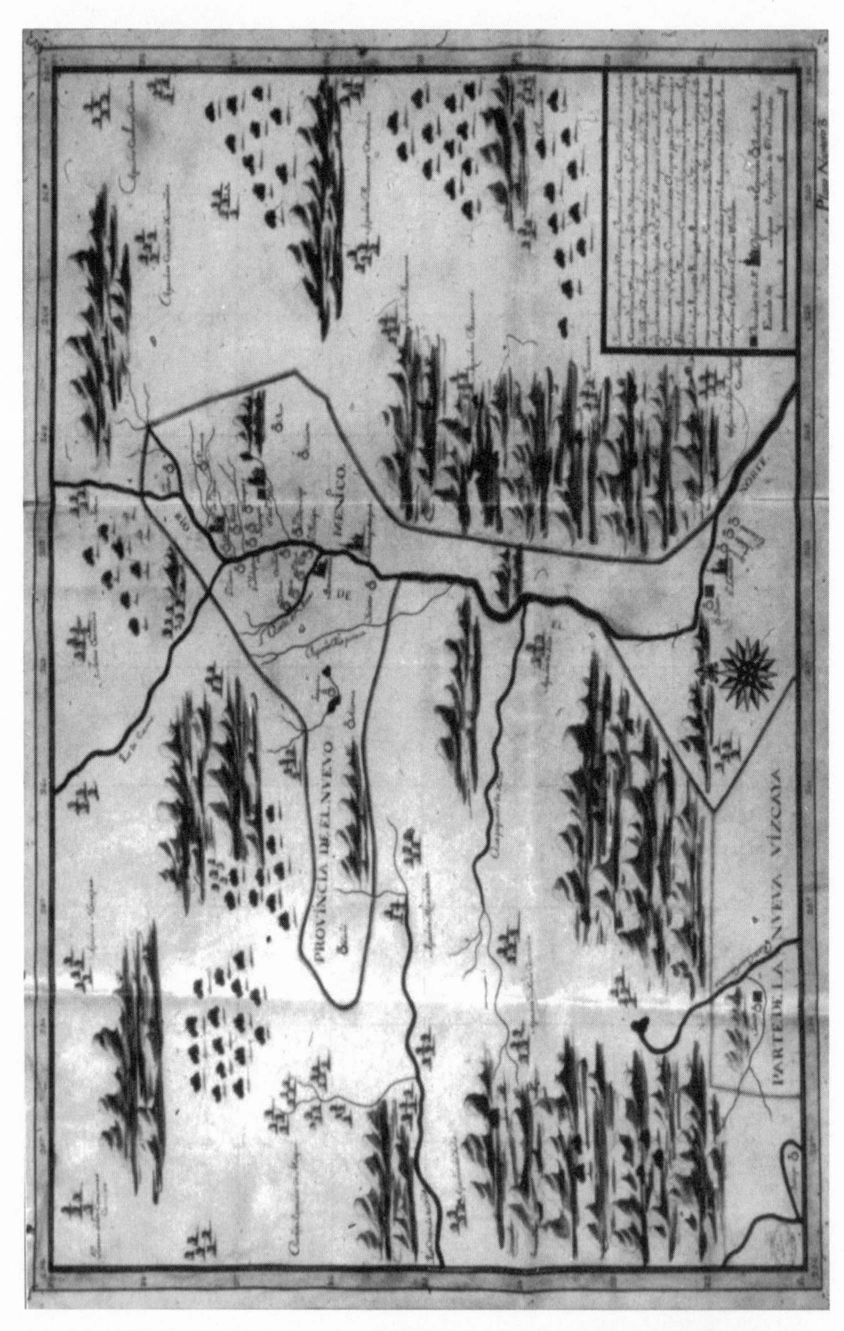

2. *Plano corográfico del reino y la provincia del Nuevo México* (Ministerio de Educación, Cultura y Deporte, Archivo General de Indias)

that the collective memory of living through a capricious rationing of life's resources is always there . . . [H]umans must learn to submit to the capricious availability of moisture or live in useless, angry rebellion against the very landscape of their lives."[44]

But aridity hardly describes the climate of the Pacific Northwest Coast or the trans-Appalachian West, lands that receive ample rainfall and, before Euro-American axes cut into them, were characterized by forests. For many Europeans and perhaps for easterners, space—vast distances and enormous skies—rather than aridity characterizes the West. For others, it may be the volatility of the climate: extreme swings in temperature (Spearfish, South Dakota, holds the record, jumping from two degrees below zero to thirty-eight degrees above in two minutes), tornadoes (90 percent of the world's tornadoes occur in North America, most originating between the Mississippi and the Rockies), parching summers, and freezing winters are common.[45]

For most of history, this huge amount of territory—the West from the Appalachians to the Pacific—was all Indian country, a vast buffalo hide on which the spiraling events of human experience have been recorded in one way or another for thousands of years. Pondering on the impression the vast West made on Europeans coming from communities of congestion and confinement, Scott Momaday suggests that "the West was beyond dreaming," limitless in its scope and its possibilities, at once beautiful and threatening, and "wild, definitely wild." It was inhabited by people who seemed "altogether alien and inscrutable, who were essentially dangerous and deceptive, often invisible, who were savage and unholy—and who were perfectly at home."[46]

They may have been perfectly at home, but home was rarely perfect. Sometimes it was a hard place to live, threatened by climatic change and human incursion. Those whose home it was were not a single people, and not all of them had always lived there. The West has always been a region of movement and migration, of peopling and repeopling; this was so in the fourteenth and eighteenth centuries as it still is in the twenty-first. For hundreds of years, Indian peoples explored, pioneered, settled, and shaped the West.

Even in a country notorious for its historical myopia, the so-called history of the West is short. In popular culture, a romanticized history still governs and is often invoked to justify continuing exploitation of places and peoples.[47] Professional historians are much more critical in their views of western history, but their length of treatment is often equally short. As Patricia Limerick observes, the western landscape has a number of layers, human as well as geologic, and telling the complete story requires paying attention to all the participants: "With anything less, the meaning of the landscape is fragmented and truncated." Scholars such as Limerick have cast their nets wide to embrace indigenous people as well as invaders, eastward-moving Asian Americans as well as westward-moving Euro-Americans. But the nets rarely sink very deep in time. The keys to understanding the meanings of the West, it seems, are still to be found in the histories that occurred after 1800, rarely in the those before 1800, before 1500, or before 1000.[48] The vast majority of books on western history and of panels at meetings of the Western History Association focus on the nineteenth and twentieth centuries. Richard White, a preeminent ethnohistorian, devoted only about fifty pages in the first edition of his six-hundred-page history of the American West to the period before 1821; Walter Nugent's *Into the West,* touted by its dust jacket as "a full scale history of the American West," skips "From Time Immemorial to 1848," in thirty-five pages.[49] Earlier works, published in the mid-twentieth century by Ray Allen Billington and Bernard DeVoto, reached farther back in time but only to chart the westward advance of the Anglo-American frontier. French and Spanish presences were treated as "barriers" (Billington), and Indians existed primarily to be pushed aside. Neither author had much interest in the West before Europeans contested it.[50]

Appreciation of the long history of the West and the United States requires acknowledging that the nation has precolonial roots running deep in America as well as in Europe. The events of recent centuries are part of an ongoing American saga rather than just the culmination of Europe's westward adventure. In the mid-nineteenth century, Henry David Thoreau traveled with Penobscot guides through the forests of Maine—"a new world, far in the dark of a continent." He was struck by the realization that though he and his guide shared the present, the Indian lived "three thousand years deep into time." Thoreau sensed a history "still more ancient," a dim past "obscured by the aeons that lie between the bark canoe and the batteau."[51] Like Thoreau, we cannot, most of us, see far enough back through the mists of time or sufficiently rethink the present to fully grasp America as it once was—what Calvin Martin describes as "the real world we do not perceive in this so-called New World."[52]

But we can rethink notions of time and the periodizations of American history. In America, events before 1776 are considered old; in Europe, they would be early modern. American archaeologists describe twelfth-century settlements in the Southwest as "prehistoric." Roger Echo-Hawk rightly rejects the term, pointing out that it not only ignores centuries of human experience but also suggests that oral traditions preserve something other than "history." Echo-Hawk urges replacing "prehistory" with "ancient history" as a conceptual framework that would include oral traditions as records of history.[53] Ancient history is now widely used by Native people, by scholars, and even by the authors of coffee table books on the Indian Southwest, but it does not adequately convey the many layers of time in the West. Many of the developments and sites labeled "ancient" in America would, in Europe, belong to the Middle Ages or even the early modern period. The point is not to subordinate Native American histories to some Old World time scale but to recognize change over time and the full depth of time in the Old West. The American West has a history that is truly ancient, but between "ancient" and "contact" lie histories that span centuries. The West was not the same in 1500 as it had been in 500 or in 1500 B.C.. To describe it all as ancient still separates most of America's past from America's sense of itself: anything that happened before Europeans arrived is, as the saying goes, "ancient history," that is, irrelevant.

But that history is neither irrelevant nor separate; it is part of a long and unbroken continuum that shaped the West as it was by the time Europeans arrived and even as it is today. For instance, in the fall of 1064, just a couple of years before the Norman conquest of England, a volcano erupted near present-day Flagstaff, Arizona. A fissure ten miles long split the earth, and a lava flow five miles wide spilled out. Fire and plumes of smoke filled the air, and hot cinders covered an area of about fifteen square miles. The Sinagua people who lived around the volcano's base may have anticipated the eruption and seem to have escaped. There may have been a second eruption in 1066 or 1067, and more lava flows occurred in 1150 and 1220. The volcanic eruptions literally shook the Sinagua world, but they did not produce an empty wasteland. In the wake of the eruptions, volcanic cinders enriched the soil and made it attractive to farmers, and Native peoples gravitated to a site they may now have regarded as sacred. Peoples from distant areas moved into the region, mingling with the original inhabitants. Population grew in some areas that previously had been sparsely settled, and large pueblos and cliff dwellings such as those at Walnut Canyon and Wupatki National Monument were built between 1150 and 1220.

But after about 1220 things changed again. Villages became smaller, and many were abandoned; farming seems to have declined in scale. Between 1300 and 1450, most of what had been traditional Sinagua territory was abandoned. The people probably moved north to Hopi country, where a new cycle of adjustment and community building began. European and American newcomers could hardly fathom the centuries of change that lay beneath the places and the peoples they saw. When John Wesley Powell visited the volcano in 1885, he named it Sunset Crater because of its red cinders.[54]

Without taking account of the long history of Native peoples on the continent, the history of the American West and America as a whole resembles the kind of history that Ralph Waldo Emerson dismissed as "a shallow village tale."[55] Without its long Indian past, America's story is a blip on the screen of human existence and experience. Only by considering America as Indian country can we get a sufficiently long span of history to recognize that civilizations here have risen and fallen as they have elsewhere in the world. Native peoples were pioneering the West while the civilizations of ancient Greece and Rome flourished and fell; Europeans arrived late—truly in the early modern era—in the history of the Native American West.

This book provides glimpses into that world. It does not presume or attempt to provide a complete narrative. It focuses on Indian country, and it emphasizes conflict and change. It highlights some stories, some parts of the past, from an area of the world that usually receives attention *after* Lewis and Clark arrived. For some people, history lies in the archives; for others, it lies in the earth; for others, it rests in the memories of families. I have read much work by archaeologists, and I hope my work has benefited from listening to Indian people. Anyone who has spent more than five minutes talking with Indian people will recognize the reaction of Richard White's Irish relatives to the history he wrote: "Compared to my mother's memories, my history is flat and its authority tentative."[56] But if I have any expertise it is in working with historical documents and synthesizing the published research of other scholars. That is the basis of this history, but this is only one of many histories in the history-laden West.

Readers of western histories that focus on the nineteenth century will be accustomed to a narrative of events that flows from east to west; readers of the histories in this book will find that important developments more often follow a south to north direction and chronology. The book is loosely organized into eight large chapters that embrace various stories and developments under a large, umbrella theme: the first pioneers; the diffusion of corn across much of Indian America and the transformations it produced; Spanish invasion; Indian resistance to Spanish colonialism; French-Indian relations in the heart of the continent; the diffusion of horses and horse cultures; the collision of rival European empires and the experiences of Indian peoples whose homelands became imperial borderlands; and the dramatic events between the American Revolution and the arrival of Lewis and Clark. The first two chapters survey developments over thousands of years; the final three chapters focus on a single century, with the last chapter covering a mere twenty-five to thirty years. The imbalance reflects the richness of the sources, my own interests and expertise, and the gathering momentum of change that culminated in the last quarter of the eighteenth century and set the stage for what was to follow. Sailors navigated and traded along the Pacific Northwest Coast, thereby completing the Euro-American encirclement of the West. European disease devastated most of the Indian communities in the West. A new American nation emerged independent of the British Empire, took over much of the trans-Mississippi West, and began to expand its own empire based on the concept of liberty and the acquisition of Indian land.

The West is not a land of empty spaces with a short history; it is a vast winter count, where many peoples etched their histories continuously from times beyond memory. These histories of the Native American West are part of American history, and American history is part of them, a linear or cyclical story of human experiences that stretches back thousands of years, dwarfs our recent endeavors, and perhaps adds urgency to our current concerns.[57]

Part 1

The West before 1500

Chapter 1

Pioneers

They buried their children and moved on. Gravestones at the foot of Register Cliff in eastern Wyoming give poignant reminder of a scene reenacted many times on the Oregon Trail: parents interred their little ones at the trailside, erected tiny grave markers, and pressed on with broken hearts. It was a common tragedy as pioneers struggled to make new lives for themselves, but it was an old scene in the West. Indian pioneers had moved into and across the West long before Europeans arrived. Twelve or thirteen thousand years before the Oregon Trail, parents buried two children on a tributary of the Yellowstone River near present-day Willsall, Montana. They covered the bodies in red ocher and interred them with more than one hundred artifacts to help the children on their journey to the next world. Then they moved on.[1] A dozen thousand years and immeasurable cultural distances separated the parents who grieved at Register Cliff from those who had grieved on the banks of the Yellowstone, but their profoundly human experience bound them together as pioneers in the West.

Origins and Emergences

In 1645, writing his huge *History of the Triumphs of Our Holy Faith amongst the Most Barbarous and Fierce Peoples of the New World,* Andrés Pérez de Ribas, a Jesuit missionary who had lived and worked among the Indian peoples of northwestern Mexico, touched briefly on the question of where the Native inhabitants of America came from. "Much has been studied and written concerning how these peoples reached the New World, separated as it is from the Old by such immense seas," he wrote. "I will not pause here to relate the ideas and debates on this subject. These can be reduced to the most likely opinion, which is that these people arrived from Asia overland to the north or crossed some narrow stretch of sea that was easy to cross and remains as yet undiscovered."[2]

Native peoples told about the creations of successive worlds and tribal migrations, but early Europeans usually preferred to draw on the Bible and classical mythology to create their own explanations of how these people came to be in America.[3] The sixteenth-century Jesuit José de Acosta was probably the first to conjecture that they had migrated as hunters from Asia across the Bering Strait. Scholarly opinion now generally regards migration to America as the last stage in a process of human dispersal across the globe that began ninety thousand years ago in Africa and the Near East, spread slowly across Europe and Asia, reached Australia, and finally pushed into the Americas. The "most likely opinion" has not changed much since Pérez de Ribas's day, but it is by no means the only opinion, and it is undergoing significant revision.

A million and a half years ago the world's climate chilled. Great sheets of ice formed and pushed south, covering much of North America for tens of thousands of years. An estimated seven million square miles of glacier covered North America (more than covers Antarctica today), and the Laurentide ice sheet alone contained about thirty-five million cubic yards of frozen water. When the climate warmed, ice melted and the glaciers retreated, churning up rocks and soil and unleashing massive floodwaters. The process has occurred at least four times in the past million and a half years. About twenty thousand years ago the ice sheets of the most recent glaciation, the Wisconsin (which occurred between 122,000 and 10,000 years ago), reached their greatest extent in North America. As the ice sheets began to melt, about eighteen thousand years ago, the environment changed, and the land became volatile and "active" in a way that has had no parallel in modern times. Immense volumes of meltwater produced huge glacial lakes that were constantly changing shape. When ice dams broke, torrential floods rushed across the land, shifting huge boulders; enormous rivers changed course abruptly; fierce winds whipped up sand and dust exposed by retreating ice sheets and created deserts. As the ice retreated, plants and animals moved in. Seeds spread north and germinated; different species of trees "migrated" until vast evergreen forests covered what is now the Great Plains.[4]

Lake Missoula and Lake Columbia formed south of the Cordilleran ice sheet more than fifteen thousand years ago. Over the next fifteen hundred years, Lake Missoula, which was about the size of present-day Lake Ontario, alternately filled and emptied about forty times, amassing meltwater, unleashing it in catastrophic floods, and filling up again. Lake Agassiz (named after the nineteenth-century Swiss naturalist, Louis Agassiz, who "discovered" the Ice Age),[5] the largest proglacial lake in North America, developed about twelve thousand years ago. More than four times the size of Lake Superior, it lasted for more than forty centuries, continually changing its size, shape, and location until it finally drained away, leaving modern lakes Winnipeg, Manitoba, and Winipegosis. Northwest of Lake Agassiz, glacial Lake McConnell ten thousand years ago was longer than any freshwater lake in the world today. As its waters drained away it separated into Great Bear Lake, Great Slave Lake, and Lake Athabasca.[6] Lake Bonneville once covered the Bonneville Salt Flats and the Great Salt Lake Desert; the Great Salt Lake is a shrinking remnant of a Pleistocene lake that once covered almost twenty thousand square miles. Lake Lahontan at its maximum covered more than eight thousand square miles of western and northwestern Nevada and reached into California.[7]

Falling water levels during the Ice Age exposed a huge area of land across what is now the Bering Strait. According to the "most likely opinion," people moved across it from Asia. As the continental glaciers retreated, an ice-free corridor developed between the Laurentide and Cordilleran ice sheets, opening a passage between interior Alaska and the rest of North America through which people are believed to have migrated and in subsequent millennia fanned out to fill the Americas. People may have come in phases, perhaps some twenty to twenty-five thousand years ago and again between ten and fourteen thousand years ago, with glaciers blocking migration during the last ice age about twelve or fourteen thousand years ago.

D'Arcy McNickle portrayed the Beringian migration as an epic human drama and an Ice Age tale of discovery. McNickle was an enrolled member of the Flathead tribe. After a stint at the Chemawa boarding school in Oregon, he sold his land allotment to finance his studies at Oxford University, returned to the United States, and worked as a BIA official implementing John Collier's Indian New Deal in the 1930s. He was a founding member of the National Congress of American Indians and the founding director of the Center for the History of the American Indian at the Newberry Library in Chicago, which was renamed in his honor after his death in 1977.[8] He was also a novelist and historian and a gifted storyteller. "The world was full of rumors just then, a marvelous thing had happened: a new land had been discovered, and just when it was needed. The people had wandered to the end of the world, in quest of food and safety." The rumors told of a new land where meat was plentiful and life was easy. "The older people, sitting in their crudely made tents of skin, their eyes blinded by smoke and snow-gazing, were inclined to shrug their shoulders. They had heard of such things before." But the young people would not be put off. Pushed by hunger, they drifted on. "Like sand in an hourglass, pouring grain by grain. Over many thousands of years, wandering bands of people drifted toward the end of one world and crossed over into another."[9]

Kiowa author N. Scott Momaday also related the standard line that the ancestors of Indian people came from Asia by means of Beringia, then pushed south through a corridor between ice sheets and dispersed across the Americas over the next seven thousand years.[10] Yet Momaday knows other, Kiowa stories of the peopling of America: "The Kiowas came one by one into this world through a hollow log. There were many more than now, but not all of them got out. There was a woman whose body was swollen up with child, and she got stuck in the log. After that, no one could get through, and that is why the Kiowas are a small tribe in number. . . . They called themselves *Kwuda,* 'coming out.'"[11]

The peoples who pioneered the West had their own stories of how it, and they, came into existence. Some peoples had priests who "recited memorized liturgies recounting tribal origins"; others had multiple accounts of the origins of the world.[12] A century ago, Tawakoni Jim told anthropologist George A. Dorsey the Wichitas' story of the creation: "When the earth was created it was composed of land and water, but they were not yet separated. The land was floating on the water, and darkness was everywhere." Man Never Known on Earth (Kinnekeasus) was the only man that existed, and he created all things. He made a man whose name was Having Power to Carry Light (Kiarsidia) and a woman named Bright Shining Woman (Kashatskihakatidise). "After the man and the woman were made they dreamed that things were made for them and when they woke they had the things of which they had dreamed." Having Power to Carry Light traveled east to a grass lodge, where he found light. New villages sprang up; there were more people, but the people "knew neither where they had come from nor how to live." Having Power to Carry Light and Bright Shining Woman went from village to village, teaching the inhabitants how to use the things they had. Having Power to Carry Light taught the men to make bows and arrows and to hunt, then disappeared to become the early morning star. Bright Shining Woman showed the women how to plant and raise corn, then disappeared into the sky and became the moon.[13]

Pawnees on the east-central plains said they came from the stars and would return to them. According to Pawnee origin traditions, "the world was sung into being by a chorus of powerful voices." Tirawahat, the most powerful sky power, spoke to the other powers by means of Thunder and placed the sun, moon, and stars of the four directions in their proper places to provide structure to the universe. As the sky powers sang, water appeared, the earth emerged, plants and animals were created. Morning Star and Evening Star copulated, and a female child was born; then Sun and Moon copulated, and a male child was born. The children were transported to earth on a whirlwind, and from them all Pawnee human beings were born.[14] Osages, who lived between the Missouri and Arkansas River when they first met Europeans, related stories of migration to that place and ultimately traced their origins to a meeting of heaven and earth. They divided themselves into two moieties and twenty-four patrilineal clans, each divided into several subclans. The nine clans of the Sky (Tsi-zhu) moiety came from the stars; with the help of Wah'-Kon-Tah, the guiding force of the universe, they found the fifteen clans of the Earth (Hon-ga) moiety and merged with them to become the Ni-U-Ko'n-Ska, the Children of the Middle Waters.[15]

Navajos remember it differently. "Alk'ídáá jiiní" [Of a time long, long ago these things are said]: people emerged into this world from several lower worlds. "First Man stood on the eastern side of the First World. He represented the Dawn and was the Life Giver. First Woman stood opposite in the West. She represented Darkness and Death." First Man burned a crystal, and First Woman went to live with him. The beings in the First World were Mist People, with no definite form. In each world they fought, squabbled, and behaved badly, causing a breakdown of *hozoho* (harmony). Each time, they fled to a higher world, where they met new people. Antisocial behavior and conflict produced misfortune; proper relationships between the sexes, with other peoples, and with other living things were crucial to social harmony. Finally, they reached the present world. Dinétah, the Navajo homeland, took shape, bounded by four sacred mountains: Dook'o'oosłííd (Abalone Shell Mountain, or San Francisco Peaks) to the west, Sis Naajiní (Dawn or White Shell Mountain, Blanca Peak) to the east, Tsoodził (Blue Bead or Turquoise Mountain, Mount Taylor) to the south, and Dibé Nitsaa (Obsidian Mountain, or Hesperus Peak) to the north. Changing Woman, also known as White

Shell Woman, was found as a baby on top of Ch'ool'į́'í (Gobernador Knob) and raised by First Man and First Woman. Changing Woman grew up, experienced her first Kinaaldá (puberty ceremony), and raised twin sons, Monster Slayer and Child Born for Water. She went to live with her husband, the Sun, in the western ocean and created four clans who then returned to Dinétah, met the other Navajos living there, and found they spoke the same language. The People had moved from lower worlds of chaos and strife into a higher world of beauty and harmony and came together in a sacred place.[16]

Among northern Plains peoples, origin stories often revolved around the actions of creator/trickster figures who often took animal form and other powers such as Sun and Wind, Moon and Stars. Creator figures differed, but stories often contained a common "earth diver" theme, in which animals or birds retrieved earth from below the surface of primal waters and the creator figures used it to bring the world into being. The people who told and heard the stories were culturally related to the creator figures and other characters, so the stories shaped identity as well as explained the world.[17] Crow accounts, for example, portrayed the formation of the world before the Crows existed as a people but linked them with a uniquely Crow creator figure, Old Man Coyote. Together with his little coyote brother, Cirape, Old Man Coyote created the earth and placed plants, animals, and human beings on it. He taught human beings how to live, eat plants, make weapons, hunt animals, and cook food.[18] Blackfeet told how Napi, or Old Man, whose father was the Sun and mother the Moon, "came from the south, making the mountains, the prairies, and the forests as he passed along . . . arranging the world as we see it today." He made the birds and animals and covered the plains with grass for the animals to feed on. Then he molded a woman and child out of clay, told them "You must be people," and taught them how to fend for themselves.[19]

The idea that Indians came from Asia, filtering across Beringia like some ancient Ellis Island immigrants, angers many Native people, who dispute that "science can tell them where they came from." Lakota scholar Vine Deloria Jr. dismisses the Beringian theory as a "white lie," something that "exists and existed only in the minds of scientists" and allows Euro-Americans to portray Indians as "latecomers who had barely unpacked before Columbus came knocking on the door."[20] Disconnected in this scenario from their American roots, first Americans become relegated to the status of first immigrants.

Most scholars are more concerned with finding evidence than with perpetuating lies. Archaeological, dental, biological, and faunal evidence all suggest ancient links between Asia and America, though that is no guarantee that traffic was one way across Beringia or that this was the only migration route. If humans were here all along, they would, presumably, have left evidence of a presence that predated the retreat of the ice sheets. A reading of current archaeological literature suggests a drive to find this evidence rather than a conspiracy to defend a lie.[21] But the strongest and most prolific evidence comes from the era when the Ice Age was in the last stages of retreat and Pleistocene mammals were becoming extinct.

In 1927, near Folsom, New Mexico, paleontologists from the Denver Museum of Natural History uncovered human artifacts near the bones of fossil bison believed to have been extinct for thousands of years, clear evidence that people had lived in the West since the late Pleistocene. Five years later, a road construction crew near Clovis, New Mexico, on the western edge of the Llano Estacado, or Staked Plain, unearthed a stone tool not far from a huge animal tooth. Archaeologists began excavations at the site, which became known as Blackwater Draw. They found distinctive fluted projectile points—"Clovis points"—mingled with mammoth bones. Other Clovis points were uncovered at sites throughout North America, providing the first well-documented culture and consistent evidence of human occupation in the West as much as 11,500 radiocarbon years (more than 13,000 calendar years) ago.[22] Much of the evidence for an earlier human presence has been equivocal, and most scholars are reluctant to accept evidence that will not "stand up in court," but the assumption that the Clovis point people were the very first Americans is under increasing assault.[23]

At Monte Verde in Chile, a group of people lived for a time on the banks of a stream as much as fifteen thousand years ago. In 1976 archaeologists excavated the wooden foundations of a dozen pole-frame houses, the oldest known village in the Americas. Among other evidence of human habitation they also found a child's footprint embedded in clay. Monte Verde is generally accepted as a pre-Clovis site. The new evidence from South America raised intriguing questions about North America and challenged the notion that Clovis points represented the work of the earliest inhabitants. If the first Americans came from Asia and pushed south as the ice sheets receded, how did these people happen to be in Chile so early? New climatic data and new radiocarbon calibrations for dating the Ice Age have now pushed back the whole timescale for first settlement.[24]

Ancient America becomes a more complex place with each new discovery. In 1996 the skeleton of an adult male age between forty and fifty-five was discovered near the junction of the Snake and Columbia Rivers at Kennewick in Washington State. The skeleton showed evidence of violence, including a stone projectile point lodged in the left hip, and was estimated to be about 9,500 years old. But when physical archaeologists reported that the skeleton exhibited Caucasoid features, "Kennewick Man" became the center of a storm of controversy. Some people suggested the man was European rather than Native American; others argued he was too ancient to be clearly affiliated with any modern Indian group; the Nez Perce, Umatilla, Wanapum, Yakima, and Colville tribes claimed him as their ancestor and demanded the return of the remains under the terms of the Native American Graves Protection and Repatriation Act of 1990. The Interior Department ordered the remains to be given to the tribes for reburial, but in August 2002, Justice John Jelderks, justice magistrate of the United States District Court in Portland, Oregon, found that scientists must be allowed access to the skeletal remains. The controversy and the questions continue.[25]

Perhaps humans came long before the ice caps retreated. Perhaps they came by sea, plying skin boats along the Aleutian Islands across the Gulf of Alaska and then south along the deglaciated Pacific Coast before the first Clovis hunters and before the continental glaciers melted.[26] They would have found numerous locations for habitation where coastal wildlife refuges offered easily exploitable resources of fish, birds, and sea mammals. Recent discoveries of two fishing and seabird-hunting campsites on the coast of Peru have been radiocarbon dated to as early as thirteen thousand years ago. Some scholars explain the remarkable diversity of Native languages—143 different languages—along the Pacific coast of North and Central America as the product of a process of successive splinterings from a common language that could have taken as long as thirty-five thousand years.[27]

Oral traditions of origin and emergence may not necessarily be in conflict with archaeological data and scientific wisdom about ancient America. They may be metaphors. Stories that survived for thousands of years may, as Roger Echo-Hawk suggests, "preserve glimpses and echoes of the long-vanished Pleistocene world of our ancestors." Stories of emergence from a dark underworld may be ancient memories of the Arctic

Circle and Beringia; stories of encounters with great bodies of water may recall giant glacial lakes; stories of monsters may describe long-extinct megafauna; stories of human encounters with animals who taught them how to build lodges may refer to the development of earth lodge architecture and animal lodge ceremonialism among the ancestors of the Pawnees on the central plains after A.D. 1000.[28]

Often in history what we think we know turns out to need revision and what we dismiss as nonsense proves to make a lot of sense. "Other" stories of coming into America—whoever may be telling them—may not be any more or less "accurate" than those we think we know to be true. Indian peoples had many stories to explain their presence in the West. In recent years, scholars committed to the Beringian explanation have had to consider other stories. Perhaps the first pioneers did not come to the West; perhaps they were made in the West.

Hunters and Hunted

To survive in the Old West, the people now known as Paleo-Indian had to be resourceful and resilient. They lived close to the land and close to the edge. They survived by developing hunting and gathering economies suited to their environments. Some of what we think we know about these ancient people is necessarily inferential, based on the lifestyles and experiences of hunting peoples in similar environments in historic times. Hunting was not an unchanging practice (hunters adapted, adopted, and adjusted over time), but some aspects of the hunting tradition persisted, and the relationship between hunters and hunted remained fundamental to the way of life. Skilled hunters depended upon exceptional knowledge of animal behavior and environment—they were professional hunters in the real sense of the word. To be successful hunters—indeed, to be human—also meant assuming proper relations with the other-than-human powers of the world, including the animals.[29]

Clovis people depended for survival on the weapons and tools they made from stone, bone, and wood. They searched out the best sources of fine-grained stone such as chert, jasper, and chalcedony and meticulously fashioned elegantly lethal projectile points. They flaked each spear point on both sides to give it greater penetration and etched out a channel or flute that allowed them to tie the point more securely to its shaft. University of Wyoming Professor Emeritus George Frison tested the penetrating potential of the Clovis projectile point on elephant carcasses culled from the herds in Zimbabwe and pronounced it "a model of efficiency in terms of inflicting lethal wounds on large animals."[30] Bone piles at the Colby site in northern Wyoming, where the remains of at least seven mammoths associated with several Clovis points have been interpreted as "insurance caches," suggest that Clovis hunters were able to kill more meat than they immediately needed and stored portions of carcasses for future use.[31]

As Clovis people pioneered their way into the West, some three dozen animal species became extinct. Mammoths, mastodons, camels, giant sloths, giant beavers the size of modern bears, saber-toothed cats, dire wolves, American lions and cheetahs, and short-faced bears—twice the size of the grizzly—all disappeared. Horses, which seem to have evolved in North America and crossed into Asia via Beringia, became extinct in America at the end of the Pleistocene, roughly ten thousand years ago. In the opinion of the eminent ecologist E. C. Pielou, this great wave of extinctions "is one of the most important and mysterious ecological events in the last 100,000 years."[32]

The fact that Clovis points have been found in the same location and strata as the skeletons of extinct megafauna has persuaded some paleontologists to blame the destruction on newly arrived two-legged predators wielding deadly weapons. Paul Martin attributed the die-offs to a Clovis "blitzkrieg." In his scenario, Clovis hunters moved rapidly through an ice-free corridor east of the Canadian Rockies and emerged south of the glacial ice into a vast hunter's paradise. Numerous large mammals with no previous experience of human predators made easy prey, and the skilled Clovis hunters blazed a trail of extinction. Moose, elk, musk ox, grizzly bear, bison, and other species survived, although some scholars point out that these were Eurasian "invaders" and may have been previously conditioned to man the hunter. Pronghorn antelope also survived. But the large mammals of North America disappeared in a relatively short space of time, said Martin, "not because they lost their food supply, but because they became one."[33]

Clovis hunters may have helped push some species to the brink, but most scientists now reject Martin's "Overkill Hypothesis." They attribute the extinction of the megafauna to changing climate and see human agency as only a contributory factor in the extinction of species that were already "unfit" for survival in the new world that was emerging. Winters grew colder, summers grew hotter, and precipitation became more seasonably varied. Warm-weather short grasses from the south and southwest may have gradually replaced taller-grass prairies on which mammoths and horses subsisted. Smaller mammals were able to adapt to changing conditions by adjusting their ranges, but larger, slow-moving herbivores and carnivores with low reproductive rates and inflexible mating habits were pushed into extinction. Radiocarbon dates now suggest that some species were on the road to extinction before the human predators were supposed to have arrived.[34]

Hunters pioneered new technology and adapted to changing conditions by diversifying their hunting and living styles. Whereas Clovis points have been found across North America, Folsom points were limited to the high plains. The Folsom people crafted more delicately chipped projectile points for hunting bison, including the now extinct species *Bison antiquus* and *Bison occidentalis,* which were larger than the modern *Bison bison.* They fashioned more elaborate tool kits for skinning and scraping animal hides and producing higher-quality weapons. Hunters who camped at the Lindenmeier site in northern Colorado apparently traveled or traded to quarry sites as far afield as what is now Yellowstone Park and New Mexico to obtain supplies of obsidian. By about 8000 B.C. the widespread Folsom tradition and technique of fluted projectile points had died out. In its place emerged a variety of regional cultures that archaeologists collectively refer to as Plano, whose craftsmen fashioned points without flutes. Around seventy-five hundred years ago, they developed the atlatl, an extension that hooked onto the end of a spear shaft and enabled the thrower to unleash the projectile with much greater velocity.

The atlatl in turn was generally replaced for hunting by the bow and arrow, although the Aztecs, who gave the weapon its name, used atlatls against invading Spaniards. Documented in Africa, northern Europe, and Asia by around 9000 B.C., bows and arrows may have been present in the North American Arctic between 9000 and 6000 B.C.; they were certainly present by five thousand years ago. Traced by the reduced size of projectile points, the new bow and arrow technology spread south slowly, its adoption tied to changes in hunting strategies. Bows and arrows reached the northern plains of Saskatchewan and Alberta by about A.D. 200, the southern plains of Texas between A.D. 500 and 600, and California around A.D. 500; they appear to have replaced the atlatl in the Southwest between A.D. 575 and 700.[35] A petroglyph at Little Petroglyph Canyon in California's Coso Range depicts an atlatl being used to hunt bighorn sheep, but Coso Range petroglyph hunting scenes typically show hunters using bows and arrows.[36]

In the era of global warming and faunal and floral change that marked the end of the Pleistocene, Indian peoples intensified their hunting and gathering techniques over several thousand years, a transitional period for humans and environments alike. In some areas people began to shift from a subsistence economy based on hunting and gathering by small itinerant bands to one that relied more heavily on the domestication of plant foods. This change allowed and required larger groups to live in more fixed settlements during an era that archaeologists and anthropologists call the Archaic. At the same time, hunters maintained a way of life based on ritual hunting and reciprocal relations with animals. Popular notions in the modern world often assume that hunting and gathering peoples lived a precarious hand-to-mouth existence, never quite knowing where their next meal was coming from, but Native peoples developed an intimate knowledge of animal habitats and behavior patterns, accumulated wisdom passed down by generations of experience and observation, and learned and perfected hunting skills and techniques over time. "The accomplished prehistoric hunter served a long apprenticeship with his elders before he absorbed enough knowledge and experience to almost instinctively know what strategy to apply in any given animal procurement situation," explained George Frison. Hunters needed to understand how weather, terrain, time of year, time of day, herd composition, and other factors affected animal behavior.[37] Hunters who understood animal behavior patterns knew where to find animals, and animals fell to generous hunters who behaved in accordance with the proper rituals and displayed proper respect. Hunting peoples managed their environment, mastered the skills to harvest animals, and developed the techniques to process and store their meat. For them it was a way of life that was predictable, not precarious. It was a way of life that humans everywhere practiced for thousands of years—and in some places still do—and a way of life whose beliefs, practices, and system of information became central to Native American cultures throughout the hemisphere.[38]

Hunting was a religious as well as an economic activity, a way of living in relation to other forces and the living environment. In anthropologist Robin Ridington's words, hunters "touched the spirits as well as the bodies of the animals that gave them life."[39] Animals possessed their own spiritual power and had to be treated with respect if they were to continue giving themselves so that humans might live. Hunters danced to prepare themselves and the animals for hunting, and they prayed to the spirits of their prey. They butchered the kill in a ritual manner lest the animal spirit take offense. Ritual hunting and adherence to the obligations established with animal kin guaranteed success in the short term and ensured renewal of the animals for the future, so that the ancient relationship recounted in stories could be continued. Knowledge and ritual served as a manual and provided symbolic meaning for the harvesting of animal meat, skins, and body parts on which the people depended for food, shelter and clothing, tools and utensils. Indian pioneers may not have merited description as the "first ecologists," and since they were human there were no doubt many occasions when they failed to live up to their own ideals, but they understood that ritual and relationship were more important than spears and arrows in ensuring a sustained food supply.[40] Stories that told of hoarding game animals—and the dire consequences of such action—and setting the world to rights by releasing them were told by hunting peoples from the Athapaskan north of Canada, down through the plateau and plains, in the Great Basin and Southwest, and in the northeastern woodlands.[41]

Hunting peoples lived with as well as on animals. They existed in such close relation that the lines between animal and human often became blurred. In traditional narratives, animals figured prominently in bringing the world into being as well as marrying and becoming kin with humans. People inscribed animal figures on drums, shields, and tipi covers, wore animal masks and parts in ceremony, mimicked animal movements in dance, sang songs that connected them to the animals and their ancestors, and sought contact with animals in dreams and visions. Animals imparted their powers, their wisdom, and their characteristics and spoke to humans. Stories were told of hunters who had sexual intercourse with animals and of humans who had animal wives and husbands.[42] In time, northern plains peoples developed buffalo-calling ceremonies in which women performed ritual sexual intercourse with men who had assumed the identity of buffalo. The ceremony stimulated the fecundity of the buffalo, transferred their power to humans, and perpetuated the hunter-hunted relationship.[43] Animals could transform themselves into human shape, humans into animal shape. Native American hunting peoples imagined and inhabited a world that few Europeans could see or understand.

Many peoples believed the buffalo herds emerged from the earth, and they might return there if they were offended by the people to whom they gave food and shelter. In some Blackfeet creation stories, the first people "were poor and naked and did not know how to get a living." Buffalo had power over them and ate them. But Old Man armed the ancient Blackfeet with bows and arrows, gave them the buffalo for food, and taught them how to get power through dreams. "Whatever these animals tell you to do you must do, you must obey them, as they appear to you in your sleep," he advised. "Be guided by them. If anybody wants help, if you are alone and travelling, and cry aloud for help, your prayer will be answered. It may be by the eagles, perhaps by the buffalo, or by the bears. Whatever animal answers your prayer, you must listen to him." Old Man showed the ancient Blackfeet how to call the buffalo so that the herds would come and allow themselves to be killed.[44]

While most of North America's Ice Age animals were dying off, buffalo or bison adapted well to the postglacial environment and prospered. Buffalo habitat extended from Georgia in the Southeast to Great Slave Lake and beyond in the Northwest and from Durango and Chihuahua to Lake Erie.[45] Nowhere did the herds thrive like they did on the Great Plains, the largest grassland in the world, stretching from northwestern Canada to the Gulf of Mexico in the rain shadow east of the Rocky Mountains. The short grasses of the western plains retained moisture at their roots and provided year-round forage and nutrients for grazing animals whose hooves could scrape away snow. A steadily warming climate permitted a longer breeding season. In the wake of the Ice Age, without hoofed competitors, buffalo herds flourished until they dominated the plains.[46]

The northwestern plains were a particularly good buffalo environment, and the vast buffalo herds were critical to the plains ecosystem, trampling mature vegetation, stimulating new plant growth, and returning precious nutrients as fertilizer for the grasses through their urine and feces.[47] Northwestern grasses were less productive than those of the northeastern plains, but they were more nutritious during the critical winter months, when the quality and quantity of forage determined the size of the herds and warm chinook winds helped keep the forage accessible.[48] On the southern and central plains, buffalo populations fluctuated with changing climates. Buffalo appear to have been scarce in south and central Texas between about 6000–5000 to 2500 B.C. and again between A.D. 500 to 1200–1300, but then buffalo populations grew and expanded into the region.[49] By the sixteenth century the southern plains teemed with buffalo. On the basis of his observations in the 1520s, Álvar Núñez Cabeza de Vaca said that buffalo herds ranged over more than four hundred leagues, from the north to the Gulf Coast of Texas, and "along this entire route throughout the valleys through which they come, the people who inhabit them come down and sustain themselves on them."[50]

The sheer number of buffalo may have discouraged some of the peoples who had been driven out by drought in the mid-fifteenth century from returning: earth lodge dwelling horticulturalists built their villages and planted their fields in regions where the vast buffalo herds posed less of a threat to their houses and fields and traveled long distances to hunt the buffalo.[51] But in general, increased precipitation around 1500 and consequent increases in buffalo population brought more people onto the plains for longer durations, in larger groups, and practicing more regular and organized communal buffalo hunts.[52] Even though the plains probably supported no more than thirty million buffalo (and not the seventy-five million suggested by some estimates), the herds represented an enormous resource of energy and protein.[53] As central plains archaeologist Waldo Wedel pointed out, killing even a single buffalo would have provided small groups of hunting peoples with a fairly steady supply of meat: "The biweekly killing of a 900-pound animal in reasonably good condition, with a yield of perhaps 400 pounds of fresh meat, would have provided a household or hamlet of 12–15 persons with 15.2 pounds of meat per person per day, with an estimated energy value of 1,500 to 2,000 calories." Buffalo meat remained an important source of protein for peoples whose daily diet depended on crops of protein-deficient corn.[54] About forty-eight hundred years ago, Indians began producing pemmican—dried meat ground between stones, mixed with hot melted fat and sometimes with berries, packed into bags made from buffalo hide or gut, and preserved for use during lean winter months.[55]

Buffalo generally came together in large herds during the summer; during the rest of the year, they dispersed in small groups to forage in an unpredictable environment. Herd movements varied according to local or abnormal weather conditions, but the search for grazing and water was sufficiently regular that pedestrian hunters, who were physically incapable of following migratory herds, could predict where herds would be at different times of the year. Hunters also influenced the animals' movements by the selective burning of grasslands. Armed with knowledge about the herds' likely movements, hunters could position themselves for a kill.[56]

Indian hunters on foot and using stone-tipped spears and arrows pioneered a variety of techniques to harvest buffalo meat more efficiently and with less risk to themselves. Communal hunting in arroyos, corrals, traps, pounds, and jumps goes back thousands of years.[57] At the Cooper site in northwestern Oklahoma, archaeologists in the 1990s documented three bison kills at the same place, each one occurring between 10,200 and 10,900 years ago. The animals had been herded into a dead-end arroyo, trapped, and killed by hunters on the rim of the gully using Folsom-style projectile points. Analysis of skeletal remains revealed information on the age and sex profiles of the extinct bison. Patterned distribution of cut marks gave evidence of selective "gourmet" butchering and processing techniques. All three kills occurred in the late summer or early fall. The most dramatic find was a bleached white buffalo skull with a single red ocher zigzag design painted on it. The skull had apparently been taken from an animal from the first kill, painted, repositioned to face straight down the arroyo in the direction of the oncoming animals, and trampled by the animals in the second kill. Some of the archaeologists interpreted this oldest painted artifact in North America as a lightning bolt to draw the herds. It provides clear evidence of a spiritual dimension to the hunting site and the slaughter. Ten thousand years ago, ritual accompanied and perhaps explained successful hunting.[58]

Excavations at the Olson-Chubbock buffalo kill site in eastern Colorado between 1958 and 1960 provided evidence of both the productivity of the trap technique and the social organization and coordination of ancient hunters. In just one day, around 8500 B.C., Indians killed almost 200 animals at this arroyo, fully butchered 150 of them, and obtained about 55,000 pounds of usable meat plus 10,000 pounds of tallow, marrow, and other meat, enough to sustain 100 people for a month. An estimated 150–200 people participated in the harvest.[59]

Early Hunting Tradition rock art, dated between 5800 and 500 B.C., depicts hunting scenes that frequently include loop lines, indicating corrals or fences, and sometimes show humans brandishing weapons or waving their arms, driving the animals toward a trap or toward waiting hunters. Such scenes may also represent hunting medicine, ensuring the success of the hunt and propitiating the spirits of the animals. Abstract petroglyphs on a group of boulders at Atlatl Rock in Nevada's Valley of Fire may reflect the spiritual dimensions of hunting at a site used by hunters to ambush mountain sheep or antelope at a watering place.[60]

At the Ruby site in Wyoming's Powder River Basin, second-century hunters using wooden and bone digging sticks constructed a corral some forty feet in diameter on a low-lying streambed in such a way that the buffalo could not see it as they were steered toward the pen. It could have taken twenty hunters as long as two weeks to build the corral and drive lane, and the corral was reused and strengthened over time. A nearby structure may have been used by a shaman whose songs and prayers lured the herd toward the corral. The burial and placement of buffalo bones and skulls in relation to the corral again indicate that these early hunters understood buffalo killing as a sacred activity.[61] At the Vore site in the Black Hills in northeastern Wyoming, hunters stampeded the buffalo into a deep, steep-sided sinkhole and slaughtered them. The site was used repeatedly from around 1450 to 1800, and between ten and twenty thousand buffalo died there. The site investigators concluded: "If ever there was a site that fits the northern Plains Indian term for a buffalo jump—'pishkun' or 'deep blood-kettle'—this is that site." Again, circular arrangements of buffalo skulls indicate ritual features and ceremonial activities associated with the kill.[62]

The buffalo jump was the most dramatic form of communal hunting. Buffalo jumping entailed more than simply stampeding a herd over a cliff; it required planning, coordinating, and orchestrating a communal drive that took advantage of natural features in the landscape to move animals toward the selected precipice and generate the momentum to carry them over the edge. Archaeologist David Hurst Thomas describes it as a "delicate art." After medicine men and women performed the rituals or songs necessary to "call" the buffalo and offered prayers for a successful hunt, runners went out to locate the herd. Disguising themselves in buffalo or wolf skins, they began to lure or nudge the herd slowly and precisely in the direction of the jump. Hudson's Bay Company trader Matthew Cocking heard Blackfeet in the Eagle Hills country of Saskatchewan "singing their Buffalo Pound songs" in the fall of 1772 and reported that the hunters "set off in the Evening; & drive the cattle all night." As the herd neared the kill site, the runners steered it between lines of obstacles or piles of stones that had been erected to funnel toward the edge of a cliff. The hunters had to time their movements perfectly to maneuver the herd into the lanes. People who had been watching the herd's approach now waved buffalo robes and shouted, panicking the animals until their gathering momentum sent them plummeting over the cliff.[63]

More than one hundred buffalo jump sites have been identified, the most famous at Head Smashed In, a sandstone escarpment on the edge of the Porcupine Hills in southern Alberta just north of the modern Peigan reserve.[64] (Blackfeet named the site Estipah-skikikini-kots—"where we got our heads smashed" or "where he got his head smashed in"—after a young man was caught under the cliff and crushed by falling buffalo.) The site was used for more than five thousand years until the nineteenth century. The jump's sixty-foot-high cliff faces east, opposite the prevailing winds, and a large basin of grassland to the west seems to have served as a natural gathering area for grazing herds. Hunters gradually drove them into one of several lanes marked by thousands of small piles of stones and extending as much as eight miles from the cliff. The drive to the jump itself might have taken several days. More than one hundred thousand buffalo died there over the centuries.[65]

Crow legend tells how Old Man Coyote first taught the people how to kill many buffalo at once by tricking a herd over a hidden cliff. Running Coyote, a contemporary of No Vitals who led part of the tribe west, was credited with originating the technique of stampeding buffalo over embankments. Relating information handed down to him by Charles Ten-Bear, a Crow historian who died in the early 1960s, tribal historian Joe Medicine Crow said that a medicine man officiated in the drive and jump: "Early in the morning, this Medicine Man would stand on the edge of the upper cliff, facing up the ridge. He would take a pair of bison hind quarters and, pointing the feet along the line of stones, would sing his sacred songs and call upon the Great Spirit to make the operation a success." He then gave the two head drivers a pouch of incense, which they would burn on the ground four times along the drive lines as they and their helpers headed up the ridge to begin the animal drive. Animals trying to escape from the drive would veer away from the areas where the incense was burned.[66]

Communal buffalo hunting produced surpluses for storage and may have been carried out most often in the fall or winter, when surplus meat could be frozen and cached.[67] Women usually performed the onerous tasks of butchering and processing the meat, an operation that also required knowledge of the animal, awareness of the effects of different conditions, and skill in the use of stone tools. As George Frison explains (and he would know), stone knives require the use of muscles and motor skills very different from those required by metal knives, but once mastered they can be just as effective skinning tools. Basic butchering techniques and technology seem to have changed very little over more than eleven thousand years on the northern plains.[68]

Communal kill sites represent only the most archaeologically visible aspects of a broad range of subsistence activities practiced by Paleo-Indian peoples and may create a skewed picture of the life they led. Large-scale kill sites reveal more "hard evidence" than do small kill sites, and both reveal more evidence than does plant gathering, but tools and lithic points can convey only a partial picture of the society that left them behind. Mammoths and buffalo constituted only a part of the Paleo-Indian diet. The "big game hunters" of the high plains were also foragers and gatherers, just as most foragers also hunted. They lived in small bands, engaged in noncommunal hunting as well as mass kills, and followed a mobile seasonal round that included but did not depend entirely upon harvesting the meat of large animals. Winters on the high plains, then as now, were not predictable. Storms and severe cold affected both the availability of feed for animals and the animals' behavior, and people had to be prepared for the worst. Women gathered a variety of plants, including grasses, roots, tubers, berries, and seeds, many of which were harvestable at different times and different elevations. Plants and berries served medicinal and ceremonial as well as dietary purposes. In addition to buffalo, hunters took mountain sheep, pronghorn antelope, mule deer, and smaller mammals such as rabbits and rodents.[69]

Lewis and Clark introduced the pronghorn to science when they collected a specimen on their western voyage, but Plains Indians appear to have hunted pronghorns for ten thousand years. They exploited the pronghorns' curiosity and predictable movements, used a variety of hunting methods, including communal drives of antelope herds into corrals, and, as in hunting buffalo, seem to have imbued hunting practices with ceremony and ritual. In the Great Basin, where Native peoples used drives to hunt antelope and jackrabbits as part of their seasonal round, communal antelope hunts were led by a shaman who had power over the animals.[70]

Because archaeology devotes so much attention to the recovery, analysis, and dating of artifacts, it is often criticized for losing sight of the people who produced the artifacts and relegating them to a passive role in a world shaped by larger processes over which they had little or no control.[71] In addition, archaeologists working on big game kill sites have perpetuated a "man the hunter" image that ignores women and children and portrays Paleo-Indian life in one-dimensional terms. Focus on what is assumed to be an exclusively male activity limits understanding of women's roles in everyday decision making, interactions, and activities. Women as well as men were involved in locating the herds, in making decisions about campsites and movements, in planning both practical and ritual preparations, and in butchering, processing, and distributing the meat. Victorian assumptions about gender roles and the rigid sexual division of labor may have blinded earlier generations of archaeologists and anthropologists to the possibility that things were different in Paleo-Indian societies. Modern ethnohistoric and feminist studies suggest a broader definition of hunting in which males and females performed a wide range of roles that were far more flexible and interdependent and in which plant gathering as often as hunting may have dictated the seasonal round and selection of site locations. Blades that are routinely called "projectile points" were likely used for other purposes than just killing game, and women may have fashioned many of the points attributed to big game hunters. It is unlikely that women relied on men to make and sharpen the knife blades and other tools they used, just as men who were off hunting were unlikely to have gone hungry just because women were not there to cook for them. As Alice Kehoe has pointed out, Blackfeet myths hardly convey the idea that women in ancient times occupied subordinate status; *iniskim* (bison fetishes), which called buffalo herds into a pound, were first revealed to a woman. A full picture of Paleo-Indian life should include "woman the hunter" and portray people pulling up wild plants more often than bringing down hairy mammoths.[72]

Only recently in the long span of western history did Indians hunt buffalo from horseback. They adopted the latest technology—the horse—as their ancestors had adopted the atlatl and the bow and arrow and had fine-tuned their hunting tool kits and strategies. But the horseback hunters were heirs to traditions, practices, and ways of knowing that had evolved over thousands of years in a changing and changeable environment where people on foot ate the animals whose world they shared.

Fishers and Foragers

Poverty Point on Maçon Ridge in northeastern Louisiana received its name in the nineteenth century because it was considered a poor site for a plantation, but three thousand years ago it was one of the busiest, largest, and most prosperous places in North America. It was a town with six mounds, the largest in the shape of a bird. Six concentric C-shaped earth rings encircled an open plaza. The earth works stretched almost four miles from north to south and contained almost one million cubic yards of dirt, constructed by the coordinated efforts of people who worked with stone tools and baskets. Smaller peripheral communities lay up to four miles beyond the rings. In the town's heyday as many as one thousand people may have lived there, with more on the outskirts or gathering there periodically, a population sustained by fishing, hunting, and collecting wild food. It stood at a crossroads of exchange for the whole lower Mississippi Valley.[73] Trading for raw materials for ceremonial use, burial goods, and personal adornments, the people of Poverty Point exchanged items with peoples in the Ouachita Mountains and as distant as Florida and the Missouri Valley. Transporting heavy and bulky goods by dugout, they seem to have exported stone and clay items, and they imported copper from the Great Lakes, flint from the Ohio Valley, chert from the Tennessee Valley and the Ozarks, steatite from the Appalachians, and galena (a lead sulphide ore usually ground into a powder and used to make white body paint) from the upper Mississippi Valley and southern Missouri.

Poverty Point puzzled archaeologists. They found no evidence of agriculture at the site. Conventional wisdom maintained that only societies that had "developed" to the level of agriculturalists living in large permanent villages could mobilize the resources and manpower necessary to construct such complex monumental projects. Yet radiocarbon dates ranging between 1700 and 1300 B.C. and the absence of agriculture meant that Poverty Point must have been constructed by hunter-gatherers and fishers, peoples widely assumed to lack the social and political organization necessary to mount such a building project as well as the stable economic base necessary to sustain it. Then, in the 1990s, other discoveries put Poverty Point in context. At Watson Brake on the Ouachita River about sixty miles from Poverty Point, archaeologists found an oval-shaped enclosure 920 feet in diameter containing eleven mounds connected by ridges. Radiocarbon dates indicate it was built between five thousand and fifty-four hundred years ago, almost two millennia before Poverty Point. Poverty Point was no longer the exception to the rule. Hunter-gatherers, living seasonally mobile lifestyles without an agricultural base or the coercive power normally associated with hierarchical societies, possessed the motivation, the means, and the manpower to construct impressive earthworks.[74]

On the Northwest Pacific Coast too early travelers and later anthropologists encountered communities that confounded their assumptions about how human societies developed. The coastal peoples were hunters and gatherers, fishers and foragers, not farmers, yet they lived in sedentary villages, owned property, practiced economic and craft specialization, developed an elaborate material culture, built monumental architecture, held slaves, and measured rank by wealth and heredity. Community populations ranged from less than one hundred to more than two thousand, and population densities were among the highest in Native North America. Hundreds of years before Europeans arrived, Northwest Coast peoples had become "affluent foragers."[75]

The many diverse peoples who inhabited the coast that stretches from the Gulf of Alaska to Cape Mendocino in northern California built villages facing out to the vast northern Pacific Ocean and drew life from the sea.[76] Around seven thousand years ago, the climate became cooler and more moist, especially during the summers, and sea levels seem to have reached their current positions in most areas by about five thousand years ago. Geological research and oral traditions record earthquakes in the area. An earthquake in the Puget Sound region between around A.D. 950 and 1000 caused land to drop as much as three feet in some places and to rise as much as twenty-three feet elsewhere and unleashed a tsunami, or tidal wave, that crashed against the coast. A bigger earthquake hit the coast from Cape Mendocino to Vancouver Island about three hundred years ago. Changes in climate and stabilizing sea levels brought changes in human subsistence and settlement patterns. People made greater use of intertidal resources such as shellfish and adopted a less mobile way of life. As they improved their technology and increased their exploitation of marine resources, their communities grew in size, wealth, and complexity.[77] Archaeological evidence from San Juan Island in the Strait of Georgia (which separates present-day Washington State and Vancouver Island) indicates that people were living there at least five thousand years ago. Shell middens, fish bones, and other artifacts from summer campsites confirm Native accounts that their ancestors harvested shellfish more than two thousand years ago and supplemented a diet of fish and shellfish with birds and land mammals. They harvested fat sockeye salmon, perhaps by reef netting, as they followed their migration routes through the Strait of Georgia back to the Fraser and Skagit Rivers.[78]

Coastal peoples fished for five species of salmon, halibut, herring, cod, smelt, eulachon, and rockfish and gathered shellfish. Men hunted for whales, seals, sea otters, and other sea mammals from dugouts. Women gathered strawberries, cranberries, blueberries, huckleberries, roots, and wild plants. Moving between the coast in the summer and more sheltered inland locations in the winter, people enjoyed a rich diet based on their management of huge fisheries and their exploitation of marine and river resources. On the Olympic Peninsula of present-day Washington State, at the westernmost point in the continental United States, sometime between three and five hundred years ago a mud slide engulfed several cedar-plank longhouses at Ozette, a Makah whaling village. Most of the people escaped, but their material culture was buried and preserved. During eleven years of excavation, archaeologists and Makah students recovered some sixty thousand artifacts from the site, providing a detailed portrait of life at Ozette and the sea mammal–hunting culture that had developed in the area in the thousand years before the mud slide. Northwest Coast peoples developed increasingly efficient ways of harvesting marine resources. They made more elaborate tool kits for fishing and sea mammal hunting, such as steam-bent wooden hooks with bone barbs and bone-tipped harpoons with long wooden shafts. They felled tall straight red cedar trees with finely ground stone adzes and carved out large (sometimes more than forty feet long) yet maneuverable canoes for whaling, sealing, fishing, and trading voyages. Effective exploitation of their resource base and accumulated surpluses provided the foundation for complex social structures and rich cultural traditions that included elaborate woodworking, cedar-bark clothing, basketry, and large cedar-plank lodgings in permanent village sites.[79] Competition for resources also provided motivation for warfare, as did revenge and the capture of slaves for labor and status.[80]

In the Pacific Northwest and Columbia River Plateau salmon were as central to Indian life and culture as buffalo were on the Great Plains. The plateau fisheries constituted "one of the world's leading inland aquatic food resources."[81] Many plateau peoples followed a seasonal round that included gathering wild plants, digging roots, and harvesting camas bulbs as well as hunting. They employed fire to manage and shape the environment—to control and promote plant growth and to preserve and generate habitat suitable for root crops and berries—and used fire drives to hunt deer and elk.[82] Sometimes they ventured across the mountains to take buffalo on the plains. But the seasonal round revolved around salmon runs. Salmon pervaded diets, trade networks, and rituals. Gathering at places where the tremendous power of the Northwest's great rivers was most concentrated, people harvested the caloric energy the salmon had stored in the ocean in preparation for their long battle back up the river of their birth to spawn. People on the lower Fraser River in British Columbia were eating salmon at least nine thousand years ago. At The Dalles, a site at the upstream end of the Long Narrows where the Columbia River rushed for miles through a rocky channel, archaeologists recovered between 150,000 and 200,000 salmon vertebrae and evidence that Indian people were harvesting salmon runs at the narrows as early as 5800 B.C. Lewis and Clark, who saw The Dalles before it was inundated by a dam in the twentieth century, described it as a terrifying place, "an agitated gut Swelling, boiling & whorling in every direction," but for hundreds of generations of Indians it was a fishing paradise. Lewis and Clark reported "an abundance of dry and pounded Sammon" stacked up on the riverbanks.[83]

Estimates of annual salmon runs on the Columbia vary between eight and twenty-five million. Salmon came in the spring, summer, and fall, but the largest run of chinook salmon reached The Dalles in late spring and carried on into the summer, making it the finest salmon fishery in North America if not the world. Men caught the salmon with harpoons, dip nets, weirs, and traps; women butchered, dried, smoked, and stored the catch. Fishing stations became sites of social and ceremonial activity when the salmon were running. Upper Chinookan peoples, primarily the Wacos and Wishrams, occupied the banks of the Columbia around The Dalles, but each summer thousands of Columbia River people gathered, socialized, and caught millions of pounds of salmon there. Dried fish were packed in baskets for eating or for trading. Located where Chinookan-speaking peoples from downriver met Sahaptian speakers from upstream, The Dalles became one of the largest trade fairs in western North America, linked to trade routes that extended south to California, east to Yellowstone, and, ultimately, all the way across the continent. The Columbia became the channel through which Northwest Coast and plains influences met, as plateau peoples traded at The Dalles for the products of the coast, which they exchanged for the products of the plains at other rendezvous farther east.[84]

Elsewhere in North America, invading armies and expeditions depended on supplies of Indian corn to keep them going; on the Columbia, the Lewis and Clark expedition depended on supplies of dried salmon, although men accustomed to eating meat had a hard time adjusting to a diet of dried fish. For the people who lived on its banks and fished its rapids, the Columbia River was both an economic resource and a spiritual force, the dwelling place of spirits who provided the bounty that sustained their lives and cultures.[85]

But fishing peoples did not take their bounty for granted. Changing climatic conditions could cause changes in fisheries and sea mammal migration patterns. Earthquakes and landslides occasionally blocked salmon runs on the Columbia River; changes in water temperature and mineral content could discourage the fish from returning to their spawning grounds. Around 1250 a mountainside collapsed into the river near the present site of the Bonneville Dam, temporarily impeding the waters until they broke through and flooded the valley below, destroying many settlements, permanently altering the floodplain topography, and creating the Cascades of the Columbia.[86] Stories explained how such things came about. In one, Beaver trapped the salmon behind a huge dam until the trickster hero, Coyote, freed them. In a Sanpoil story the lecherous Coyote freed the salmon from two women who had trapped them. He then followed the salmon, giving them as gifts to the villages he passed. But wherever women resisted his sexual advances, Coyote created waterfalls that kept the salmon away.[87] Haida stories from the Queen Charlotte Islands told how Raven released the salmon from a beaver house where they had been trapped.[88]

Salmon were as fundamental to world order as they were to diet. On the Northwest Coast, art and legends taught that success in hunting, survival, and ultimately identity as a people were all inextricably linked to relationships with the sea and with the fish and mammals harvested from it. They portrayed salmon as immortals who gave their bodies so that humans could live. Personal experiences with salmon were passed down in the oral traditions and art of clans. Salmon featured in clan crests. Vital rituals accompanied the start of the spring salmon runs. In northern California, people recited traditions recounting the origins and travels of the first salmon, thereby honoring the fish and inducing it to allow itself to be caught. The first salmon was ritually prepared and eaten. Only after the ceremonies were completed was the fishing season open.[89] Lewis and Clark witnessed the start of the spring salmon run near The Dalles in April 1806. The Indians were overjoyed when the first salmon was caught: "This was the harbinger of good news to them. They informed us that these fish would arrive in great quantities in the course of about 5 days. This fish was dressed and being divided into small pieces was given to each child in the village. This custom is founded in a superstitious opinion that it will hasten the arrival of the salmon."[90] People threw salmon bones back into the water to allow the spirit of the salmon to return to the sea and ensure that the endless cycle of abundance would continue. But bones from other animals polluted the salmon's waters, as did scales and bowels from cleaned fish. Taboos limited women's contact with salmon and water, especially during menstruation, when their blood had the power to jeopardize the salmon run.[91]

For whale-hunting peoples like the Haidas, killer whales embodied the power of the sea.[92] As migratory whales approached, whale hunters and their wives ritually purified themselves in preparation for the hunt; a whale would only surrender itself to a hunter who had rigorously observed the necessary restraints and rituals. Northwest Coast chiefs played a leading role in hunting whales. After a successful hunt, the whale leader distributed the first cuts of blubber, the villagers butchered the carcass for meat, bone, and oil, and women prayed for the spirit of the whale.[93]

On the twelve-hundred-mile-long California coast, people were harvesting fish and marine mammals ten thousand years ago. After about 3000 to 200 B.C., California's climate became much like it is today, and its coastal waters constituted one of the world's richest marine environments.[94] Men fished the rivers and ocean shores for salmon and hunted deer and smaller mammals. Women harvested acorns, stored them in granaries, and dried, shelled, and pounded them into flour using bedrock mortars. They then leached the flour to remove tannic acid and cooked it in a variety of soups, gruels, mushes, and breads. Women constructed, maintained, and apparently owned the milling sites and storage facilities. People ate acorns year-round and over the centuries came to depend on them for a major portion of their dietary needs. That dependence generated population growth, influenced settlement patterns, and determined labor roles of women and men.[95] Chumash Indians in the Santa Barbara region followed an annual cycle of subsistence that allowed them to harvest and store mammals, fish, and shellfish from the sea and acorns, pine nuts, and other wild plants from the land. Chumash villages sometimes housed a thousand people. California was one of the most heavily populated areas of ancient North America, with three hundred thousand people living there as late as 1769, when Spanish colonization began in earnest, and a great diversity of languages and cultures.[96]

But California was no Garden of Eden whose occupants feasted effortlessly on the natural bounty. Periodic El Niño events, unpredictable fluctuations in ocean temperatures, and shifts in rainfall and drought could disrupt coastal fisheries, affect sea mammal behavior, and render food supplies precarious. A prolonged dry period appears to have settled on the coast between A.D. 200 and 1300, reaching drought conditions during the last two hundred years of the cycle. Native peoples developed intensive and often highly specialized strategies of hunting, gathering, and fishing in order to ensure a regular and reliable food supply.[97] They took an active role in managing oak trees and the acorn crop. Like the buffalo economy of the plains and the salmon economy of the rivers, the acorn economy of California rested on a reciprocal relationship: people needed the plants in order to live; the plants needed the care and prayers of the people. Regular and respectful use of the plants ensured good crops. Elders say that the plants became less healthy after the people stopped using them.[98] Native peoples employed fire to encourage plant growth, eliminate competing plants under acorn trees, maintain fruit production, destroy insects and parasites, get rid of dead wood, and attract deer and other game by creating better browse. The earliest Spanish expeditions to the San Diego region, led by Juan Rodríguez Cabrillo in 1542 and Sebastián Vizcaíno in 1602, reported numerous fires burning on the mainland.[99]

Writing to his king the next year, Vizcaíno reported: "I have traveled more than eight hundred leagues along the coast and kept a record of all the people I encountered. The coast is populated by an endless number of Indians who said there were large settlements in the interior."[100] But the Spaniards did less well in explaining how these large populations fed themselves. Spaniards (and later Americans) were accustomed to fields cleared for a single crop and familiar with Native domesticates like corn, squash, and beans. They saw no evidence of agriculture in California and assumed that the inhabitants simply gathered what nature provided. But the newcomers saw little or no untouched "wilderness"; they described grasslands, plants growing so evenly they looked to have been sowed, and clear evidence of human management of vegetational and faunal resources. Native peoples practiced intensive plant husbandry, protecting, pruning, encouraging, and interplanting. Kumeyaay people developed and harvested a semidomesticated grass grain (now extinct) that they cut and gathered into sheaves. They scattered seeds over burned areas and produced interplanted areas that Europeans did not recognize as "fields." They developed a complex knowledge of plant biology and ecology and planted desired species of medicinal and plant foods near their village sites. They harvested multiple food resources, from season to season, valley to valley. The California landscape was both cultivated and cultural.[101] California Indians redistributed resources within their own societies through networks of kinship and rituals of reciprocity; they redistributed resources outside the community along long-distance exchange networks that carried shell beads over immense distances and into the Great Basin.[102]

The Great Basin—John Charles Frémont's term for the arid West's area of internal drainage—encompasses some four hundred thousand square miles between the Rocky Mountains and the Sierra Nevada and embraces tremendous environmental and topographical diversity. Between ten and twelve thousand years ago, lakes in the region shrank, rivers dried up, and the lusher vegetation retreated to higher elevations and to the north. Temperatures rose until five or six thousand years ago, and arid conditions and high temperatures continued to characterize the area into historic times. The diverse environments of the Great Basin underwent constant change, and populations moved regularly to take advantage of unevenly distributed and often precarious food resources to survive in a hard land. People gathered, processed, and stored nutritious piñon nuts that were abundant in higher elevations during the fall, collected in villages and subsisted on stored food sources in the winter, and dispersed again in family bands during the spring, when new foods became available. The well-watered and resource-rich Owens Valley supported larger populations and permanent villages. In areas like the shores of Pyramid Lake and Walker River in Nevada, people lived in sedentary communities for most of the year, supplementing a staple diet of fish with game and plants. In other areas such as the desert regions of southern Utah and Nevada, people traveled on foot, living primarily on wild plants and small game, and congregated only when rabbit population or piñon productivity permitted. Everywhere, Great Basin peoples pursued subsistence strategies that required intimate knowledge of the land and its animals, regular movement to take advantage of seasonal diversity and changing conditions, and careful exploitation of the environment. Men took larger animals such as deer, antelope, mountain sheep, and, in some areas, buffalo, often in communal hunts. Women hunted smaller game and gathered plants in lightweight baskets. They crafted close-twined baskets for gathering food, for winnowing seeds, for cooking, as bowls and water bottles, and for general utility purposes.[103]

Hunting and gathering functioned and endured as a way of life for ten thousand years, but the population of the Great Basin, like the Basin itself, underwent changes. Between about A.D. 400 and 1300, horticultural communities appeared in Utah, eastern Nevada, western Colorado, and southern Idaho, growing corn, beans, and squash, making pottery, and living in relatively sedentary villages. Their ways of life clearly differed from those of the people who were there before them and who came after them. Whether this "Fremont culture" was an in situ development or was introduced by immigrants from the Southwest, it proved short-lived in Great Basin terms—a mere nine hundred years.[104] Great Basin peoples interacted with peoples beyond their region. Shells from the Pacific Coast and obsidian (volcanic glass) from southern Idaho that may have been present in the Great Basin as early as 5000 B.C. were traded over vast areas along with food, hides, and other perishable items.[105]

Throughout the West, over thousands of years, Indian hunters and gatherers, fishers and foragers developed techniques and strategies, ceremonies and social structures, knowledge of the land, and relationships with the animal world. They pioneered ways of life that enabled them to live—and sometimes to live well—in places that Europeans and later Americans regarded as formidable and inhospitable. In time, some became farmers. Some did not, although often they supplemented their diet by trading with those who did. The hunting and gathering pioneers adapted to changing conditions and had no need to abandon their way of life until outside forces threatened the sources on which they had built.

People and Identities in Motion

Western history is often portrayed as synonymous with westward movement, and mobility is often regarded as a quintessentially western trait. Nineteenth-century European migrants moved predominantly from east to west, but in the Old West, as in the modern West, people moved often and in many directions. When Europeans penetrated the West, they encountered peoples whose roots in their homelands stretched back beyond memory. They also encountered peoples who had arrived relatively recently in their current locations and peoples who were still on the move. Archaeological evidence, together with tribal migration stories and glimpses of the past accorded to the first European chroniclers, make it clear that, then as later, population movements in the West usually meant people edging into areas already inhabited by other people rather than moving into empty spaces, and that movement was often an important part of the process by which groups became "a people." Many of these migrations were still going on when Europeans first saw the West, and the repercussions of European contact stimulated a new round of migrations.

George Frison, in his now classic survey of northwestern plains hunting cultures, divided twelve thousand years of history from the end of the Pleistocene to the arrival of Europeans into half a dozen overlapping time periods based on cultural complexes and developments in lithic technology: Paleo-Indian, Early Plains Archaic, Middle Plains Archaic, Late Plains Archaic, Late Prehistoric, and Protohistoric. Other, more chronologically and regionally specific culture "phases" and "complexes" are associated with particular characteristics in projectile points. The Besant complex on the northern plains, for example, associates thirteen hundred years of human activity and experience between 500 B.C. and A.D. 800 with a characteristic atlatl dart point with shallow side notches and round shoulders; the Avonlea complex of side-notched projectile points associated with the introduction of the bow and arrow embraces more than a thousand years from A.D. 100 to 1200.[106] Identifying entire eras and areas with specific traits in a projectile point or a style of pottery provides archaeological signposts in mapping change over time, but it cannot convey the full range of human experience and may even strengthen an impression of stasis in the minds of modern-day readers accustomed to frenetic change—change happened, but it was so slight and slow that it hardly seems to constitute change at all. Though Indian pioneers left scant archaeological evidence of their migrations, they did more than make additions and refinements to their tool kits.

Looking back hundreds or thousands of years, it is rarely possible and often misleading to try and assign "tribal" designations to the peoples who moved in or out of a particular region or to expect that discrete groups moved unchanged over time and space. Population movements entailed changes in sociopolitical organization and intertribal relationships as well as shifts in location and utilization of different environmental niches. Archaeological evidence and oral traditions alike point to complex social histories and dynamic population interactions. Many movements are shrouded by time and memory, contain apparent contradictions in the retelling, and elude precise tracking and dating. But oral traditions tell how, as people moved from place to place in search of new homes, they encountered other peoples and created new societies through ongoing processes of separation and amalgamation. They learned new things and sometimes became or redefined themselves as new people who would later be known as Navajos, Choctaws, or Cheyennes. People developed and expressed their cohesion as a group on the basis of shared kinship, language, residency, worldviews, and ceremonies. Boundaries of identity were fluid and flexible, not firm and fixed. Migrations produced genesis as well as exodus.[107]

Like pioneers and migrants in different times and places, Indian people in the Old West moved for various reasons. The rapid environmental change that swept the continent at the end of the Pleistocene did not occur at the same rate in every region, and early Paleo-Indians escaped periodic resource stress by switching to different resources within the territory they occupied or by moving to other territories where vegetation and animal life were richer.[108] Some peoples pursued a mobile hunting and gathering lifestyle that revolved around the movement of the herds and the seasonal exploitation of varied resources. People moved to take advantage of new opportunities; to increase or reduce contact with other peoples; to find a better, safer, warmer, or cooler way of life. Periodic and prolonged shifts in weather conditions propelled people into motion. On the Great Plains, for example, between A.D. 300–400 and 700–750 strong westerly winds produced drier and warmer conditions than exist today, especially on the northern plains. For the next four hundred years, until about 1150–1200, warm conditions continued, an influx of tropical air brought increased summer rains, and the prairie expanded westward. Over the next three or four hundred years, stronger westerly winds again brought seasonally dry air and reduced temperatures and precipitation, resulting in a retreat of the prairie by 1500. Hunting and gathering peoples who also grew crops followed the prairie as it pushed west and then receded from the edge of the plains.[109]

People left traces where they lived. Brushing away the dust of centuries, archaeologists document the presence and movements of people who used certain styles of arrowheads, tools, and ceramics or shared certain ways of living on the land. In some cases, changes in pottery styles and hunting techniques represent in situ cultural developments among the peoples who inhabited the area; in other cases, they reflect intrusion by other peoples.[110] For instance, the peoples archaeologists designate as the Upper Republican phase were farmers who penetrated the central plains of Kansas and Nebraska beyond the one hundredth meridian after 1100 but moved away during the Pacific climate conditions that followed. Hundreds of panhandle sites identified as belonging to the Antelope Creek phase (1200–1500) reveal a people who lived on the upper Canadian River by farming, hunting, and gathering: they ate corn, beans, buffalo, deer, antelope, and smaller animals. Their lithic tool kit included beveled diamond-shaped knives, scrapers, and T-shaped drills. They fashioned knives, hoes, digging sticks, and other implements out of buffalo bone. Many of their villages contain the ruins of stone-slab houses. They appear to have abandoned farming over time and become more reliant on hunting and gathering. They also participated in exchange networks that brought trade items from the northeastern plains and from the Southwest. The Antelope Creek people descended from earlier groups in the region and may have been embraced by later "phases" or "complexes." By the time of Coronado's expedition in the 1540s, the Antelope Creek villages were in ruins, and only buffalo hunters inhabited the panhandle.[111] Archaeologists identify the way of life of these hunting people as the Tierra Blanca complex. Their arrowheads and pottery shards suggest they were Athapaskan migrants—Apaches whom the first Spaniards onto the plains called Querechos.[112]

Over the course of about five hundred years, the southern plains had shifted from an area predominantly occupied by sedentary villagers pursuing a mixed economy based on hunting, gathering, and farming to a region dominated by mobile buffalo hunters.[113] The bewildering array of regional and temporal "phases," "traditions," "complexes," "variants," and "foci" that archaeologists have identified hint at the kaleidoscope of population movements and interactions in the Old West.

Peoples' stories often included not only how they came to be but also how they came to be in a particular place, stories of migration as well as emergence. Many origin stories refer to "multiple locations as stopping points in the journey of an ancestral group," or what Roger Echo-Hawk calls "rest areas along a migration superhighway." Narratives of movement may represent people coming together or separating over time rather than a single "tribal" migration. In-migration by one group might come to be remembered as the formative experience of the whole people. Traditions that seem inconsistent or even contradictory within one historic tribe may in fact accurately reflect the movements and merging of several groups that eventually came together to form one people. Different tribes may share migration stories from a time before groups separated and went their different ways.[114]

Anishinabe oral tradition relates that the Ojibwes, Ottawas, and Potawatomis were once a single people living near the "Great Salt Sea" in the Northeast, possibly near the Gulf of the St. Lawrence. For reasons "buried in uncertainty," they moved west until they reached the Straits of Mackinac, where Lakes Huron and Michigan come together, at which point the people separated into three groups.[115] Climatic changes causing a retreat of the boreal forest around Hudson Bay, perhaps seventeen hundred years ago, may have prompted Eskimo peoples to follow the expanding tundra southward and triggered migrations among Algonkian-speaking groups. Formerly moose- and caribou-hunting forest dwellers, some of these people eventually moved south of the Great Lakes, the ancestors of the historic Potawatomis, Menominees, Miamis, Illinois, Sauks, Foxes, Kickapoos, and Shawnees. Others eventually arrived on the northern plains to become the ancestors of historic Blackfeet and Cheyennes.[116]

Cheyenne traditions recall that their ancestors inhabited a country in the Far North across a great body of water. In the early twentieth century, George Bent, son of trader William Bent and Owl Woman, said that before the Cheyennes had bows and arrows they lived on the shore of great lakes in the Far North. The late John Stands in Timber, Northern Cheyenne tribal historian and keeper of oral traditions, said they lived "in another country, where great waters were all around them." Subsisting mainly on fish and fowl and pressed by more powerful enemies, they set out "to find a better country." Following buffalo herds or guided by a medicine man carrying a long staff, they moved onto the grasslands. As they did so, they became transformed as a people.[117]

Athapaskan peoples also moved south. Linguistic relatives of the Chipewyan, Sarcee, Beaver, and other caribou-hunting peoples in northwestern Canada appear to have begun a southward migration around A.D. 200, a gradual movement by family bands in successive waves that lasted for at least a millennium. Arriving on the northwestern plains by about the seventh century at a time when buffalo populations were expanding, Athapaskan migrants appear to have brought with them bow and arrow technology and techniques of communal hunting such as the pound, which they had used farther north in harvesting caribou. They appear to have introduced the Avonlea projectile point, a distinctive triangular arrowhead with side notches and finely serrated edges. Avonlea sites have been found clustered in southern Alberta (including Head Smashed In buffalo jump), southern Saskatchewan, and Montana, with a few in Wyoming and South Dakota. The dates of the sites indicate a gradual shift southward: Athapaskan migrants had abandoned Saskatchewan by about A.D. 700 but occupied sites in Montana and Wyoming until around A.D. 1000. They would have met and perhaps intermarried with other peoples on the move. Pushing south, they may have begun to infiltrate the Gobernador Canyon area of northwestern New Mexico as early as A.D. 700.[118]

The Athapaskan migrants were ancestors of the historic Apaches and Navajos. The dates and routes of their arrival in the Southwest have long been hotly debated. Different migration paths—through the high plains, along the borders of the plains, through the Rocky Mountains, and along intermontane routes—have been hypothesized. Limited archaeological evidence, fragmentary documentation, and uncertainties as to the identities of different peoples mentioned in early Spanish records complicate the picture. Some scholars say the first migrants arrived five or six hundred years before the Spaniards arrived.[119] Others insist they arrived no more than a hundred years before the Spaniards or even after the first Spanish contacts. Many scholars have favored the interpretation that migrating Athapaskans first reached the southern plains relatively recently, not long before the Spanish invasion, and that from there bands fanned out west into New Mexico and Arizona.[120]

Oral tradition and other evidence support the theory that Athapaskans were in the Southwest well before the Spaniards arrived. Western Apaches appear to have been living in northern Arizona, in the Mogollon Rim and Little Colorado River area, by 1400.[121] The people who became known as Navajos, the Diné, settled in the Colorado Plateau country of what is now northeastern Arizona, northwestern New Mexico, and southeastern Utah. Navajo stories place their emergence into this world and the first events of creation in the Gobernador Canyon area, and archaeological work has placed Navajos there by the late 1400s or early 1500s. Excavations at a dozen sites in northwestern New Mexico suggest that ancestral Navajo groups were living in the upper San Juan drainage in the mid-sixteenth century and that they might have entered the area a hundred years before that. Navajos may have occupied the Chama Valley during the seventeenth century, although some Navajos appear to have migrated as far west as Black Mesa in northern Arizona by the early 1600s. As Navajos moved from place to place, their origin stories say, they left behind in different places people who eventually became the different groups of Apaches. Across the southern regions of New Mexico and Arizona moved ancestors of the Lipan, Mescalero, Chiricahua, and Western Apaches.[122] In some versions of the emergence story, in the Fourth World the Diné met "a strange race of men, who cut their hair square in front, who lived in houses in the ground and cultivated fields." These Kisáni (Pueblos) treated them kindly, fed them, and gave them corn and pumpkins.[123] But Hopis remembered the coming of the Navajos as the arrival of the Tasavuh, or Head Pounders.[124]

Athapaskans may have introduced shields and shield pictographs into the northern plains. Markers of Athapaskan presence and movement can be found in the rock art motif of the shield-bearing warrior, showing the large round body shields used in Plains Indian warfare before the arrival of the horse. Shield-bearing warrior images have been recorded in Alberta, Montana, Wyoming, the Black Hills region, and the Fremont area of the Great Basin. At the Valley of the Shields in south-central Montana, sixteen different places contain panels of rock drawings, and one panel displays the remnants of ten separate shields or shield-bearing warrior figures. The shield-bearing warrior figures have often been attributed to Shoshonean peoples, who were known for their use of large shields, but radiocarbon dating indicates the figures were done about nine hundred years ago, two to four centuries before Shoshonean speakers migrating out of the Great Basin are thought to have reached the area. The pictographs may have been produced by southward-moving Athapaskans associated with the Avonlea culture who appear to have been in the Valley of the Shields area between 650 and 1100.[125]

The Shoshonean migration was just one of a series of population movements from the Great Basin. People began to move from the Great Basin into the Rocky Mountains as much as ninety-five hundred years ago in response to changing environmental conditions. The "Mountain Tradition" they established may have endured in Wyoming and Montana for five thousand years but farther south appears to have lasted until about 1300. Around that time, drought struck the Great Basin, triggering a series of population movements. Numic-speaking peoples—ancestors of the historic Utes and Shoshones—moved in, and the people of the Mountain Tradition either moved out or merged with the newcomers.[126] Other Shoshonean people seem to have migrated from the southern Sierra Nevada across the Great Basin sometime after 1000 and probably did not reach southern Wyoming until the fifteenth century.[127] By the time Europeans arrived, the Great Basin was inhabited by Numic-speaking peoples—Paiutes and Gosiutes—who, unlike the people of the Fremont culture who preceded them, did not grow corn, beans, and squash and who crafted very different styles of basketry, pottery, and projectile points. It is widely believed that Numic peoples expanded across the Great Basin around one thousand years ago, although where and how such an expansion actually occurred remains open to debate.[128] Southern Paiutes appear to have been pushing into the San Juan Basin in the Four Corners region by about 1300.[129]

Athapaskan Kiowa Apaches and Tanoan Kiowas were also on the move. The Kiowas' Tanoan language suggests an affiliation with some of the Puebloan peoples of the Southwest, but Kiowa people may have been in Wyoming's Big Horn Basin when Athapaskan-speaking Avonlea hunters began to move in during the fifth century. Kiowas appear to have moved from the mountains of western Montana in the fourteenth or fifteenth century and occupied lands around the Black Hills, where they stayed until the eighteenth century. At some point Kiowas created a legend around Devils Tower that related them to the stars.[130]

Members of the Siouan language family seem to have once occupied large areas of the East, South, and Midwest. The Western Siouans moved northwest, ultimately reaching the northern plains and becoming the Mandans, Hidatsas, and, eventually, Crows. The Eastern Siouans moved south and east. The Central Siouan group consisted of three subgroups, Dakota, Dhegiha, and Chiwere-Winnebago, who, in a series of schisms, migrations, and amalgamations, emerged as the Siouan tribes of the prairies met by Europeans. Tribal legends suggest that Chiwere Siouan peoples split when groups who became Ioways, Missouris, and Otos separated from the people who became Winnebagos near Green Bay, Wisconsin, and moved southwest to the Mississippi. The Ioways stopped at the Iowa River; the people who became Otos and Missouris moved south to the Missouri. The Dhegiha Siouans—the Osages, Omahas, Poncas, and Kansas—had roots reaching back to the Ohio Valley. According to tribal traditions, they were once a single people living near the Ohio River. Sometime before 1673, when Father Marquette jotted down their locations on a crude map, these people had followed the river to its mouth, crossed the Mississippi, and undergone successive separations and relocation. When they reached the junction of the Ohio and the Mississippi, the Quapaws, the "downstream people," turned south and eventually settled on the lower Arkansas River. The other Dhegihas moved north and west up the Mississippi and then followed the Des Moines and Missouri Rivers. According to tradition, the people who became the Osages crossed the Mississippi first, but a heavy mist arose and prevented the rest of the migrants from crossing. At the mouth of the Osage River, this group split off and followed the tributary south to become the Osages. The Kaws or Kansas first settled in the Missouri Valley and moved to the Kaw River late in the eighteenth century. The Omahas and Poncas moved farther up the Missouri. Dhegihan and Chiwerean traditions convey a picture of recurrent splintering and regrouping. Clans spread out over large areas as people dispersed to hunt and gather food, fled from natural disasters, followed new leaders, or separated after a quarrel. As they moved, they sometimes amalgamated with other Dhegihan-speaking peoples, as evidenced by the presence of a Kansa clan in the Omaha tribe, an Osage clan among the Poncas, and a Ponca clan among the Kansas, Osages, and Quapaws. They retained aspects of the cultures from which they emerged and absorbed some of the cultures of the people they met: Quapaws demonstrated Mississippian cultural influences, Kansas incorporated Oneotan influences, Osages took over elements of both, and Poncas and Omahas adopted traits from the Caddoan-speaking Pawnees and Arikaras who were there before them.[131] Archaeological evidence regarding the timing of such separations and migrations is inconclusive.[132]

Pawnee traditions as recorded in the late nineteenth century told that they came from the Southwest (other traditions said the Southeast). Along the way, some people split off and remained on the southern plains, ancestors of the Wichitas. Other groups continued and made their homes in eastern Nebraska or moved up the Missouri River.[133] The expansion of these Northern Caddoan groups up the Missouri beginning in the thirteenth century and their emergence there as the Arikaras contributed to a shunting of Mandan groups into the area between the Knife and Heart Rivers.

Mandan traditions include two distinct accounts of their origins. In one version they originated in their historic Heart River homeland. In another they emerged from the earth, carrying corn with them, on the right or western bank of the Mississippi at its mouth near the ocean. They then migrated north until they reached the Missouri, crossed it, and lived on the northern bank for a time. They resumed their northward migration up the Mississippi into present-day Minnesota, where they headed southwest away from the river and settled near the pipestone quarries. One clan moved to an area north of the Turtle Mountains, then later moved west to the Missouri River. The rest of the Mandans moved south, back to the Missouri River, which they ascended, and built a village on the eastern bank opposite the White River. At this time the Awigaxa band disappeared. Some of them returned later, but by that time they spoke differently from the other Mandans, who moved north along the Missouri until they reached the Heart River. A southern subgroup of the Mandans moved west to the Black Hills and then back to the Missouri, establishing villages at the mouths of the Cheyenne, Moreau, and Grand Rivers by about 1500 or soon after.[134]

Mandan tradition, as reported by Prince Maximilian zu Wied, who visited their upper Missouri villages in the 1830s, provided additional explanation for settling on the western bank. God shared the work of shaping the landscape with first man. God made the western bank of the Missouri a rich and variegated landscape of trees, hills, and valleys, but first man made the eastern bank flat and bare. Seeing first man's work, God saw that it would be impossible to surprise game on the eastern bank. "Men will not be able to live there," he said. But west of the Missouri God had created hills, valleys, streams, and trees and added all kinds of animals: "Here men will be able to live by the chase, and feed on the flesh of those animals."[135]

Hidatsas also had varied explanations of how they came to be in the area between the Heart and Knife Rivers. The Awatixa group said they came to the earth from the sky and never lived anywhere else. The Awaxawi group said they emerged from the earth in the Southeast long ago and then moved north, first to Devils Lake and then on to the Missouri, where they found the Mandans and a village of Awatixas already established. The Hidatsas proper separated from the Awaxawis in western Minnesota and moved north and then south to Devils Lake. They found the Mandans soon afterward and settled north of them and the Knife River.[136]

Sometime during or after these movements, some Hidatsas separated and through their migrations began the process of transforming themselves into Crows. Anthropologists and historians have dated the split anywhere between 1450 and 1700, and evidence from Crow pottery sites suggests Crows may have reached the Big Horn Mountains by the sixteenth century. Hidatsa tradition asserts that the Crows split off from them and divided into the Mountain and River bands *before* they reached the Missouri. The Mountain Crows may have reached the northwestern plains as much as two hundred years before their River band relatives. Arikara tradition attributes the split to a hunting dispute over a buffalo paunch.[137] According to Joseph Medicine Crow, the migration story of the River Crows, as related by sixteen generations of Crow historians, told that in the long ago times the ancestors of the Crows and Hidatsas lived in the "tree country" to the east, near the western shores of the Great Lakes. But when drought struck, hunters searched far and wide for buffalo, returning empty-handed. Only the hunters who had gone west were successful, returning with "huge packs of jerked buffalo meat." They told of open grasslands and rolling hills where buffalo ranged in great herds. Soon after, the people moved west into what may have been northern Minnesota and southern Manitoba. Later, perhaps around the mid-sixteenth century, they moved southwestward into what is now North Dakota. By the turn of the seventeenth century they had reached the Missouri River and built earth lodge villages near the confluence of the Knife and Missouri Rivers, upstream from the Mandans.

Sometime early in the seventeenth century, a Crow chief named No Vitals who had received a vision in which he was given sacred seeds that were to be planted in a promised land to the west set out in search of the land. He apparently used a women's quarrel over meat as a pretext for breaking away from the rest of his people, and about four hundred followers loaded their packdogs and went with him. Tribal traditions say the people settled in Alberta but found the winters too harsh; they moved south until they came to the Great Salt Lake in Utah. Moving east away from the arid landscape, they came to a place they named Where There Is a Fire, probably a burning coal vein and perhaps in Wyoming, although other parts of the migration story suggest movement farther south before they headed back to the northern plains and settled in northeastern Wyoming and southeastern Montana. The migrations covered thousands of miles over many generations, but Joseph Medicine Crow insists that the Crow split from the Hidatsas was deliberate, quick, and clean, with no gradual transition from earth lodge to tipi. "Yes, it took about one hundred years of wandering through the wilderness over long, long distances," he says. "The original migrants all died along the way, but it was their great-great-grandchildren and their children who brought the sacred seeds to the great mountains of the west—the Beartooths, the Crazy Mountains, the Bighorns, the Wind River Mountains, the Absarokas, and even the Grand Tetons." This became the Crow homeland, a country, said the nineteenth-century Crow chief Arapooish, that the Great Spirit had put "in exactly the right place."[138]

Choctaw, Creek, and Chickasaw legends tell of their ancestors moving west to east across the Mississippi. Southeastern migration legends may conflate ancient movements with seventeenth-century demographic disruptions, but Choctaw and Chickasaw traditions tell that the people together followed a sacred pole carried by their leader that pointed them eastward over many generations across MishaSipohni (the Mississippi River); the Choctaws settled in new homelands, and the Chickasaws carried on north.[139] Chickasaw traditions recorded in the eighteenth century recalled that they were "only a family from a great rich nation towards the sun setting." After their fathers dreamed "that away towards the sun rising was land of life," they migrated east, crossed the Mississippi, and took up residence in western Tennessee and northern Mississippi between the upper Yazoo and Tennessee Rivers.[140] Choctaws remembered the West as the direction of death from which their ancestors fled in ancient times, the land of the dead where spirits unable to reach the afterworld remained forever. Forced removal back to the West in the 1830s held a special horror for Choctaws.[141]

Like later pioneers in the West, Indian peoples who migrated did not usually move into empty space but intruded on lands occupied by other peoples. Climatic changes created imbalances between population and resources; resultant food shortages in some areas generated influxes of population into other areas. New bow and arrow technology produced greater hunting efficiency, added stress on resources, and, as indicated by the presence of small projectile points lodged in human bones, introduced more lethal weapons with which to contest resources.[142] Competition for place, position, and resources produced high-casualty warfare in some parts of the Great Plains hundreds of years before European contact. Around 1325 at least 486 men, women, and children were killed when their fortified village at Crow Creek on the Missouri River in South Dakota was attacked and burned. Most of the victims were scalped and mutilated. Limited skeletal evidence from the site suggested that the villagers, who were most likely Arikaras, were malnourished and that the massacre occurred as part of a conflict over scarce resources in a period of climate stress.[143] The magnitude of the violence at Crow Creek is unusual, but evidence of warfare, scalping, and mutilation is not.

When people migrated into new territories they encountered not only other peoples but also new land and new animals. Cheyenne stories recalled how, when their ancestors were north of the Missouri River, they were confused and starving "because animals were withheld from them." Finally, Nonoma, the Wolf Man, and Esceheman, the Old Woman, keepers of animal spirits of the plains, took pity on the people, and proper relationships were established. In a world where animals allowed themselves to be hunted, the newcomers had to create ritual relationships with their new homeland and its animal inhabitants. Rituals that tied the humans to the animals and the land also tied them together as a people; ceremonies defined societies.[144]

The Indian peoples whom Lewis and Clark encountered in the West had not sprung up as fully formed and distinct "tribes." They had emerged into their identities as they pioneered the West. Some had moved from lower worlds into this one; others had migrated to new lands. Some had separated from their parent group; some had amalgamated with other people. By their stories, their speech, their subsistence, their movements, their ceremonies, people came to identify themselves as distinct from others, using designations meaning "I am of *The People*, or *The First People*, or *Our Own Folk*, or *The Real People*." The Americans who followed Lewis and Clark west in the nineteenth century called the first peoples by different names, often using names given by other Indians.[145] Americans claimed the role of pioneers for themselves.

Chapter 2

Singing Up a New World

In the Wichita creation story, Bright Shining Woman "was given an ear of corn, whose use she did not know, but this was revealed to her in her heart; that it was to be her food; that it was Mother-Corn; that it was to be the food of the people who should exist in the future, to be used generation after generation; that from Mother-Corn the people should be nursed." Bright Shining Woman gave the corn to the women and told them how to plant and give thanks for it. With Mother-Corn "they could live and it would strengthen the young ones," she said; "Mother-Corn was to be used as long as the world should last."[1]

Wichita, Arikara, and Pawnee stories all include references to Corn Mother and to some form of odyssey that takes the people out of darkness on the path to becoming human beings. Since corn cultivation did not become widespread on the central plains until about A.D. 1000, these stories likely recall not the creation of the world itself but the creation of a new world in which a new ideology revered corn as the staple of life and women as its cultivators were becoming economically empowered.[2]

In many cultures, corn was and is considered kin. In ancient stories, corn and people emerged together from the same preworld; corn could become human, and humans could transform into corn.[3] Nahua people who still grow corn in the central highlands of Mexico liken themselves to corn in that they sprout from the earth and return to the earth when they die. Working in the fields not only cultivates the crops but also maintains a healthy spiritual relationship with the earth, from which both corn and people come. "Corn is our blood," they say.[4] Navajo origin stories tell that when First Man was made, white corn in a perfect shape was formed with him; First Woman was formed with a perfect ear of yellow corn.[5] Pueblo peoples account for corn in their creation stories and revere corn as the mother of the people and the culture. Corn, concludes one anthropologist, "pervades every aspect of Pueblo life from birth to death and from past to future."[6] An ancestral clan introduced corn to the Zuni people, telling them that the ears came from the flesh of seven maidens. Each of the corn maidens represents a corn plant; yellow corn, the oldest, represents winter and the North; blue corn represents water and the West; red represents summer and the South; and white represents daylight and the East. During the winter solstice Zuni farmers who were heads of their households "danced the corn," placing six perfect ears of corn in a basket and singing to them so the corn would not feel neglected.[7]

Singing to corn was an integral part of indigenous agriculture as a way to bring the crop to maturity and to ensure its health and productivity: "There were songs when the corn was knee-high, songs when the tassels were formed, songs when the ears were formed, songs when they were ripe," wrote Pueblo anthropologist Alfonso Ortiz, echoing anthropologist Ruth Benedict.[8] Indian farmers nurtured corn with management, prayer, and song. In the process, they transformed their world.

Becoming Corn People

For virtually the entire span of human life on earth people lived as hunters and gatherers, harvesting wild plants and animals. Then, about ten thousand years ago, at various places around the world "the rules of human existence changed."[9] Within a relatively short period (about five thousand years), people began cultivating domesticated plants in Southeast and Southwest Asia, China, South America, Mesoamerica, the Andes, and the southeastern United States. The shift from gathering food to growing it ultimately entailed a changed relationship with the environment and altered the structures and organization of human societies. As people cleared lands, cultivated and stored foods, and adopted new technologies for farming, they became tied to the land in new ways and lived in more populous and sedentary communities, in villages, towns, and finally cities.[10] Corn literally made some Indian societies: "The great cultures, the enduring cultures, were all built on maize," said Alfonso Ortiz, speaking from the perspective of his Puebloan, corn-built culture.[11] The evolution of corn and of the societies that domesticated and developed it is seamlessly interwoven.[12]

Why did hunters and gatherers become farmers? What compelled people who for thousands of years had made their living by harvesting wild food with a relatively low expenditure of labor to turn to the labor-intensive cultivation of plants? Why did they do it when they did? What was the relationship between forces such as climatic stress or population pressure and human intention? The process likely occurred slowly, step by step: crop production at first supplemented and only gradually surpassed hunting and gathering as the principal means of subsistence as changes in climate rendered existing sources and strategies precarious and reinforced the value of producing and storing food surpluses. Corn may have been no better than some indigenous plants in terms of crop yield, reliability, and nutritional content, but it was easier to harvest and provided a more predictable source of food. Archaeologists have long debated the "chicken and egg" relationship between population growth and the origins of agriculture. Did limited resources restrict population growth until the development of agriculture removed natural restrictions? Or did growing populations tax available resources and provide the incentive for people to intensify food production, experiment with agriculture, and turn from mobility to sedentation as a means of reducing uncertainty?[13]

Corn did not produce instant and dramatic changes of lifestyle. Hunter-gatherers incorporated the use of cultigens with minimal changes to their environment, economy, society, or culture. In many areas corn served as a supplement to existing systems of plant husbandry. Scholars debate the pace of the transition from foragers to farmers, but increasing reliance on corn brought far-reaching change.[14]

Farming, as a more sedentary occupation, brought shorter birth spacing and, as a labor-intensive subsistence activity, provided both incentive and food for larger families. Planting, cultivating, harvesting, and storing corn provided the opportunity to create a margin of safety against hunger and to build a surplus for trade. Once corn production proved successful, communities devoted more time and energy to it. People often became less mobile, built more substantial residences near the fields where they spent more of their time, and developed more effective means of storage. Villages grew into towns. Food surpluses supported a growing population of nonfarmers, new kinds of leaders, and in some places increasing social stratification. Corn may also have increased conflict, as people defended fields and surpluses against enemies who sought to exploit the people's lands or raid their stores.[15]

Corn may also have changed peoples' sense of their place in the universe. Calvin Martin argues that hunter-gatherers lived in confidence that animals would, eventually, always give themselves up, that nature would provide. Farmers lived with uncertainty—crops might fail, cosmic forces might withhold the rains. Mobile hunter-gatherers did not have priests: individual hunters interacted with animal and plant beings and resorted to shamans when their own powers failed them. Shamans possessed special powers derived from their own connection and communication with spirit beings. Farming communities, on the other hand, created ceremonial spaces and buildings devoted to ritual. Priests monopolized ritual and invoked their sacred knowledge to mediate with and propitiate the forces whose power hung over the lives of crop-growing humans. Calendrical rituals associated with the cycle of clearing fields, planting, and harvesting became, and remain, crucial in Native farming communities. The adoption of agriculture, the attempt to stockpile supplies of grown food as insurance against future shortfalls, and the rearrangements of social order and timing required to do so represented a major shift in relations and understandings between humans and plant and animal life. The coming of the Neolithic, says Martin, "marks the onset of the dangerous process of denying will to individual plants and animals and repositioning their will in cosmic or meteorological forces. In practical terms, the scheduling of plant and animal florescence and reproduction were denied those beings and placed, instead, within the increasingly remote and esoteric realm of sky beings."[16]

The origins of corn or maize are enigmatic and controversial.[17] Its ancestor is widely believed to be teosinte, a small-cob grass that grew in Central America and still grows in parts of Mexico, Guatemala, and Honduras.[18] The earliest known corn was dated to approximately 5500 B.C. from the Tehuacán Valley in Mexico, where people developed small-scale agriculture between about 5200 and 3400 B.C. and practiced more intense crop cultivation over the next thousand years. But new dating methods, notably, accelerator mass spectroscopic analysis of the archaeologically recovered cultigens, has produced significantly more recent dates than those achieved by conventional radiocarbon dating methods: corn agriculture in Mesoamerica may not have developed before 3500 B.C.[19] Over time, corn spread north from Mexico, into the American Southwest, to the Midwest and the eastern woodlands, south to Guatemala, Peru, and Bolivia, and eventually into Colombia and Ecuador.

Crops developed in Southwest Asia's "Fertile Crescent" spread rapidly east and west across Eurasia, finding hospitable climates and growing conditions at similar latitudes. But the predominantly north-south axis of the American hemisphere meant that crops had to adapt to colder climates and shorter growing seasons as they edged north. It took Mexican corn, beans, and squash many centuries to reach the American Southwest and many more to spread into the northern plains and Northeast. Teosinte cannot survive north of twenty-seven degrees north latitude (that is, about four hundred miles south of El Paso) and is sensitive to drought and cold weather. The biological evolution into a plant that could adapt to new environments would have taken thousands of years.[20]

Climate and plant evolution contributed to the process, but corn's diffusion required human innovation. Domesticated corn does not disperse seed and reproduce without human care and cultivation. "The only reason we have corn today is that for thousands of years humans have selected seeds and planted them," says Jane Mt. Pleasant, an Iroquois agronomist who studies Native methods of cultivation and crop yields.[21] Farmers took the seeds of the plants that did best in their environments; developed new strains adapted to the drier soils, more arid climates, and shorter growing seasons of the Southwest; and experimented with different ways of hilling soil to protect the plants. Chapalote crossed with teosinte to produce a hybrid. Within a few hundred years, this hybrid interbred with a new species from Mexico, an eight-row flour corn called Harinoso de Ocho or Maíz de Ocho. From this pool of diverse corn types all future varieties of southwestern corn developed. In the eastern woodlands the innovators would likely have been women. By about A.D. 900 they had evolved a hardy eight-row corn, known as Northern Flint, from the ten- to twelve-row Chapalote, and the species spread through the northeastern woodlands. Northern Flint, together with the Southern Dent variety that entered the Southeast sometime later, formed the basis for all the modern varieties of hybrid corn grown around the world today.[22] Euro-American farmers did not make similar progress in plant breeding until they developed agricultural experiment stations in the late nineteenth century. In various parts of the world, indigenous farmers applying strategies and techniques based on knowledge of ecological conditions and processes (what today would be termed *agroecology*) have often succeeded in growing crops in locations that would appear incapable of cultivation by modern industrial agriculture.[23]

The first plants domesticated in South America and Mexico were squashes and gourds, and they were introduced to the North. Squash does not have as much nutritional value as corn, but like corn it can be dried and stored. Squash gourds can also be used as containers and water bottles.[24] Beans began to appear in the Southwest between 500 and

300 B.C. In addition to providing excellent protein themselves, beans contain lysine, an amino acid missing in corn and squash that aids the digestion of the protein in corn. Moreover, beans return nitrogen, which corn depletes, to the soil. Corn, beans, and squash provide a nutritious diet and, when planted together, minimize the depletion of nutrients. This trinity of crops—the "three sisters" of Native American agriculture—spread across much of North America. Corn cultivation became the staff of life in huge areas of the Native American West and exerted its influence deep into regions where it could not be grown.

More substantial residential architecture and ceramic storage containers began to appear as people stayed put to cultivate and harvest their crops. Ceramic vessels were more versatile and durable than baskets for storing and cooking and made it possible to cook corn as a gruel and weaning food. But they were also heavier and more fragile, ill suited to people following a mobile lifestyle. The changes did not occur suddenly or completely, however. Some peoples lived in small communities and led mobile lives as foragers who also cultivated corn. Societies did not necessarily abandon mobility when they adopted food production and pottery; in fact, they often employed sedentation and mobility simultaneously as complementary strategies.[25]

Adopting an agricultural way of life was not an unmixed blessing. It did not produce a decrease in labor, especially for women, who, in addition to planting, hoeing, harvesting, and grinding corn, gathered wild plants, prepared food, collected fuel and water, cared for children, made and washed clothing, wove baskets and mats, and began to make pottery. In communities where corn was the staple food, women worked at the grinding bins "at least three hours a day, in sickness and health, throughout life." But as settlement size increased, corn grinding became a group rather than an individual activity. Women spent more time in the company of women, a shift in work patterns that probably increased productivity but also had important social consequences and may have produced an increase in women's status.[26]

More people living in a single area for longer periods of time placed greater stress on the environment and, perhaps, on the people themselves. People who became farmers may have become less healthy than hunter-gatherers. A diet of corn provides little iron or calcium and could produce nutritional deficiencies. Osteoporosis, rare among hunters and gatherers, sometimes reached extreme conditions among corn eaters. More congested and sedentary living patterns may have rendered people more susceptible to bacteria and parasites. Infant mortality rates remained high; life expectancy remained low.[27] As evidenced by the acorn-rich societies of coastal California, people who lived in fertile areas did not necessarily adopt corn. Likewise, people who grew corn did not always remain wedded to it; Cheyenne Indians who grew corn on the Missouri River in North Dakota would abandon their fields and villages in the eighteenth century and move into the heart of the Great Plains grasslands to pursue a mobile life as equestrian buffalo hunters (see chapter 6).

Nevertheless, corn spread far and wide, producing a slow and quiet revolution in ancient North America. Indian farmers who adopted and adapted corn also adopted new ideologies and the religious rituals, ritual knowledge, and maize symbolism needed to propitiate and direct the forces that brought rain and fertility. Images, ideas, and influences followed kernels across cultural, tribal, and linguistic boundaries. After years of cultural adaptation to agriculture, nearly all the corn-growing peoples of the Americas gave corn a sacred role at the center of daily ritual, prayer, and worldviews. Corn became a religious and cultural icon, and corncobs appeared on ritually important figurines from Mexico to the Mississippi. By A.D. 600–900 Pueblo people used multicolored kernels in ceremonies and offered ears of corn, corn pollen, and cornmeal in prayer. They also offered ears of corn as gifts. In an area of the world characterized by an arid climate, unpredictable and limited rainfall, and short growing seasons, Pueblo people depended on prayer and ritual to bring rain and fertility. "Here corn is God!" declared a sixteenth-century Spanish priest.[28]

First Farmers and Town Builders in the Southwest

In the American Southwest, domesticated corn was the foundation of a cultural evolution spanning twenty-five centuries and a precondition for the development of towns and villages.[29] The Southwest is a region of mountains, mesas, canyons, and plains punctuated by low basins and characterized by an arid or semiarid climate and low and unpredictable rainfall. The deserts of southwestern Arizona and the plateau country of northeastern Arizona and northwestern New Mexico are the driest areas, the mountainous regions of central Arizona and west-central New Mexico are the wettest, although there are other localized areas of high precipitation, such as the San Francisco Peaks and Sangre de Cristos.

The Southwest lies in the rain shadow of the Coast Ranges and the Sierra Nevada and between two major sources of atmospheric moisture, the Pacific Ocean and the Gulf of Mexico, and experiences a precipitation pattern unique in the West. With local variations, in the summer rainfall from thunderstorms comes from the Gulf and the Pacific; in the winter precipitation comes mainly from large storms that sweep in from the Pacific. Spring and fall bring less rainfall and sometimes none at all.[30] Climate may have been more moist in past eras, but the region was not particularly conducive to agriculture, especially corn, a plant adapted to the humid tropics. Yet Indian farmers grew corn, irrigated deserts, and built towns in the Southwest.

Determining when corn agriculture was adopted in the Southwest is difficult. Corn was grown in other regions for thousands of years before it arrived in the Southwest, and archaeological evidence of the presence of corncobs or kernels may indicate that corn was being traded rather than farmed. Moreover, communities could grow small amounts of corn without altering their essential way of life. Fully fledged "maize-dependent complexes" evolved over time as southwestern people adapted Mexican varieties and developed agricultural practices suited to southwestern conditions.[31] Older estimates that corn first appeared in the Southwest between 3500 and 2000 B.C. have been revised in favor of much more conservative estimates—perhaps only a few hundred years B.C.[32] Recent redating using accelerator mass spectroscopic analysis techniques seems to indicate that the spread of corn into the Southwest was relatively more rapid than previously thought and that only a thousand to fourteen hundred years was needed for corn to spread from the highlands of Mexico to the San Juan Basin.[33]

The first corn was probably planted in gardens along with wild weeds and did not produce a high yield. As many as two thousand years passed between the initial use of domesticated corn and the first evidence, generally dated between fifteen hundred and a thousand years ago, that economic systems developed based primarily on growing corn. The ancient hunter-gatherers of the Southwest did not set out deliberately to become farmers. They augmented a diet based on hunting and gathering wild plant foods and continued to forage seasonally in different vegetation zones, generally occupying lowland areas in winter and spring, then moving to mountain areas during the summer and fall. Agriculture was just another system for procuring food. Cultivation of crops may in some cases have made for more efficient foraging tactics by allowing longer occupation of certain areas and more intensive utilization of natural resources.[34]

Once corn growing curtailed mobility and the need for wide-ranging foraging, southwestern peoples began to produce pottery. Clay pots began to appear by about A.D. 200, and "pottery had become ubiquitous throughout the Southwest by about A.D. 300."[35] Between A.D. 200 and 900 a gradual spread of sedentary villages occurred in the Southwest. These first farmers of the Southwest developed and spread techniques for building multistory clusters of contiguous rooms and separate ceremonial chambers, "a distinctively Southwestern Indian architectural creation" that the Spaniards recognized as *pueblos*—towns—when they arrived in the sixteenth century.[36]

As agriculture and more permanent settlement patterns spread throughout the Southwest, different cultural traditions developed: the Hohokam in southern Arizona, the Mogollon in the border region of Arizona–New Mexico and Chihuahua, and the Anasazi of the Colorado Plateau and present Four Corners region. The traditions have been defined according to architectural style, material culture, geographic location, and settlement pattern, but just how distinctive they were as social and political structures remains open to question.[37]

The Sonoran desert occupies most of south-central and southwestern Arizona, western Sonora, and most of the Baja California peninsula. It is an unlikely spot for farming. Summer temperatures regularly exceed one hundred degrees Fahrenheit, while annual rainfall rarely exceeds seven inches. Rainfall is heaviest during the summer monsoon season, when masses of warm, moist air from the Gulf of Mexico collide with hot, dry air rising from the desert mountain ranges to produce spectacular lightning thunderstorms. Pacific storms peter out to deliver rainfall in the winter. The rest of the year brings little rain. Yet for a thousand years and over an area of some twenty-five thousand square miles, Hohokam people lived in this demanding environment, centered on the rugged country of the lower Colorado River Valley and the Arizona Upland. They created the largest permanent irrigation systems in ancient North America to bring water to the desert and grow crops, and they built communities and developed regional exchange networks.[38]

Archaeological research on the Hohokam got off to a slow start. Anasazi ruins to the north were so impressive and summer fieldwork in the Sonora was so unattractive that most archaeologists devoted their efforts and attention elsewhere. But in the later twentieth century mil-

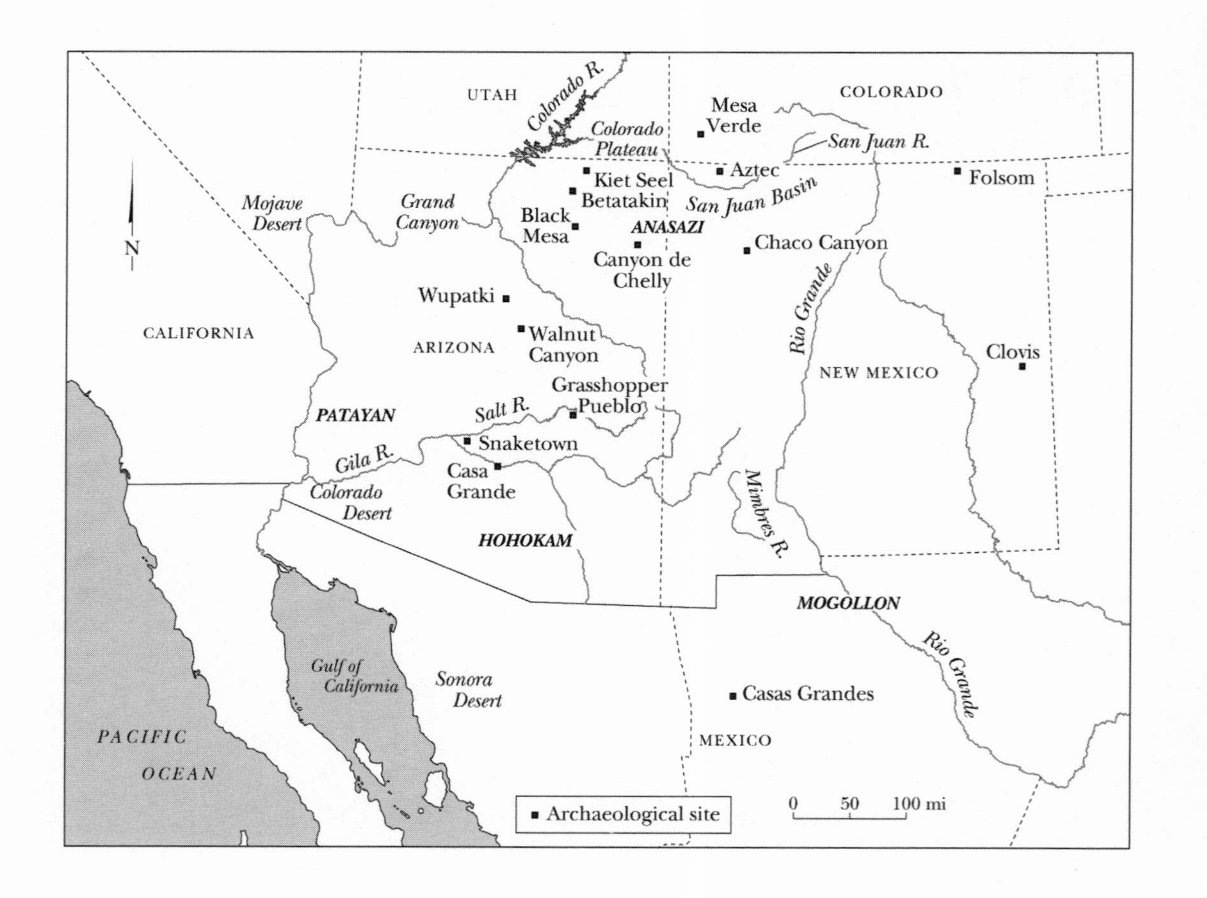

3. The Old Southwest, ca. 1000–1500

lions of Americans migrated to live air-conditioned lives in southern Arizona, generating a frenzy of construction and development projects in what was once the Hohokam heartland. Millions of dollars were spent on archaeological investigations at the sites slated for development. The largest construction project, the Central Arizona Project, was designed to distribute water to land once irrigated by the Hohokam and had the most impact on Hohokam sites. Ironically, the mass invasion of the Hohokam homeland that resulted in the urban sprawl of Tucson and Phoenix also generated a huge increase in knowledge about the Hohokam.[39]

The Hohokam became archaeologically recognizable about the time of Christ, although some scholars argue for several hundred years later. The idea that the Hohokam were immigrants from Mesoamerica and brought their irrigation technology with them has generally been superseded by evidence that they were descendants of indigenous hunting and gathering peoples of southern Arizona known to archaeologists as the Cochise tradition. The early Hohokam, living primarily within the Phoenix Basin, were distinguished by small villages composed of brush shelters built in shallow elongated pits, reddish brown coiled and grooved pottery (decorated after about A.D. 500), cremation burials, and agriculture. Around A.D. 800–1000 the Hohokam began to expand up the tributaries of the Salt and Gila Rivers, develop more sophisticated and more extensive irrigation systems, make more elaborate pottery, and build platform mounds and ball courts, probably indicating increased interaction with Mesoamerica.[40]

The Gila River, which rises in the mountains of western New Mexico, and its principal tributary, the Salt River, rising in the mountains of east-central Arizona, were the centers of Hohokam life and agriculture. Together draining an area of some 72,000 square miles, the rivers were fuller flowing a thousand years ago than their dried-up riverbeds would suggest today and produced rich marshlands at their juncture. Where the Salt, Gila, Agua Fria, Verde, and Santa Cruz Rivers came together, lush valleys formed, and ecological conditions were far more rich and diverse than today. Hohokam people grew corn, beans, and squash, perhaps getting two harvests a year, one by utilizing spring runoff, the other from the summer rains. They grew agave, tobacco, cotton, and probably also amaranths, chenopods, a little barley, and other native grasses. They gathered cholla, yucca, saguaro fruit, prickly pear, mesquite pods, and various fruits and seeds for consumption and storage. Archaeological pollen and faunal remains reveal forty to fifty species of domesticated and wild plants in the Hohokam diet. By one estimate the Sonoran desert contains more than 250 native plant species that Indians have used as food. The Hohokam may also have engaged in the horticulture of wild plants. Far from being a barren wasteland, the Hohokam homeland held bounty for a gathering economy: plants were plentiful, predictable, and storable, with diverse resources within relatively easy reach at different elevations and harvesttimes of different staple species spread over the year. The Hohokam also hunted rabbits, mule deer, and antelope.[41]

Hohokam people added to this diet with an impressive agricultural technology. At first, they watered crops by the natural action of floods and rainstorms. They practiced both floodwater farming and "dry" farming—capturing rain and runoff and guiding it to their fields—and stored water in reservoirs, wells, and catchment basins. Around 800 they developed more sophisticated irrigation. Initially, communities built simple canal systems with a few branch channels, but by the twelfth and thirteenth centuries the systems had grown and integrated to produce networks of canals with multiple distribution canals, each watering several settlements. The Hohokam created a network of plastered canals as much as ten feet deep and thirty feet wide, transported water hundreds of miles, and raised it as much as fifty feet above the river channel. They could now grow crops above the floodplains. In the Salt River Valley alone, they built fourteen major canal systems with 360 miles of main canals and 1,000 miles of lateral canals and distribution channels, the largest irrigation system in aboriginal North America. (The modern city of Phoenix employs a canal system virtually superimposed on the Hohokam system for diverting water from the Salt River.)[42] Some areas were laced with as many as forty canals per square mile. Hohokam society was clearly capable of coordinating a sizeable collective labor force.[43]

Freed from dependence on the unpredictable Gila River, Hohokam people were able to store crops and develop larger and more permanent communities. Population estimates for the Hohokam have varied widely, from twenty thousand to more than three hundred thousand, but most now agree that the Salt River Valley alone may have supported a population of almost fifty thousand.[44]

When anthropologist Frank Cushing came across the Hohokam site at Mesa Grande southeast of Phoenix in the late nineteenth century, he described it as the most extensive ancient site he had seen. "Before us, toward the north, east, and south, a long series of elevations which I at once recognized as house mounds, lay stretched out in seemingly endless succession." Mesa Grande is the largest Hohokam site; most settlements numbered hundreds rather than thousands, and dispersed settlements were more typical than towns.[45] Snaketown, also near present-day Phoenix, was occupied continuously for a thousand years, but earlier estimates of a population of up to two thousand have been replaced by more conservative estimates of five or six hundred inhabitants.[46]

Until relatively recently, Hohokam archaeology focused on sites and tended to compare everything to Snaketown. Growing attention to ball courts—large oval depressions, usually surrounded by earthen embankments—has revealed greater appreciation of Hohokam as a regional system. Ball games had sacred connotations in Native Mesoamerica and seem to have spread north to the Hohokam, who began constructing ball courts sometime after 775. Snaketown contained two ball courts, the larger of which could have accommodated five hundred people on its embankments. Archaeologists have identified more than 200 Hohokam ball courts at 163 sites. Even if, as archaeologist David Wilcox put it, "the methodology involved little more than connecting the dots," these sites suggest a regional network where people of different communities came together for ball court rituals, ceremonies, and trade. The proliferation of ball courts may have served to reinforce social and economic integration after a large stream flow in A.D. 888 and a disastrous flood in 899 caused populations to disperse over a larger area and make new small settlements in areas like the Tonto Basin that were more conducive to dry farming. The ball court system also helped to orchestrate long-distance exchanges. At its height the Hohokam exchange system may have had ties to Chaco Canyon in the north, to Mesoamerica, and to Kayenta Anasazi, Mimbres Mogollon, Yumans, and coastal Californian groups, as in historic times Pimas also went to the Pacific Coast.[47]

There was more flooding in the 1080s. Snaketown declined around 1100, and Hohokam settlements underwent a series of rapid changes after about 1200. No new ball courts were constructed after 1150, and the large ball courts were abandoned. But other forms of public architecture became important, notably, massive towers and platform mounds surrounded by large rectangular compound walls that may indicate the emergence of elite families who controlled ritual and the management of resources. At Casa Grande, near Phoenix, Hohokam people around 1300 constructed a massive castlelike structure with adobe walls five feet thick. The Casa Grande tower served as an astronomical observatory, and several similar towers have been identified.[48]

A major flood in 1358 destroyed most of the Hohokam canal networks. People who had struggled for centuries to water their lands finally abandoned them because of too much water.[49] By about 1400, the thousand-year presence of the Hohokam ended. The word Hohokam originates from a Pima, or Akimel O'odham, phrase meaning "all used up."[50] Earthquakes, drought, catastrophic floods, invading enemies, and internal conflicts have all been offered as explanations for their demise, but the Hohokam may simply have succeeded too well. Irrigation can make the desert bloom, but, as anthropologist Shepard Krech cautions, "it is a lethal blossom." Overirrigation may have produced waterlogging and salinization of the soil, ultimately destroying the crops it had allowed to flourish for hundreds of years. As the lands they had irrigated and cultivated were no longer able to sustain them, the Hohokam abandoned the towns they had built and moved away to other ecological zones, probably mingling with other peoples and becoming ancestors of the Akimel O'odham (Pimas) and Tohono O'odham (Papagos).[51] O'odham tradition recounts that as they came from the east and took over the Salt River Valley, they defeated the Hohokam, whom they called Sivanyi, in a pitched battle at Pueblo Grande, located in present-day Phoenix, and killed the Sivanyi leader, Yellow Buzzard.[52]

Northwest of the Hohokam, Payatan people occupied an equally forbidding homeland, a vast desert region stretching from Gila Bend to California and from Yuma northeast to the Grand Canyon. But whereas the Hohokam responded to the demands of their environment by building canals, becoming sedentary, and increasing their reliance on farming, the Payatan did not have large rivers irrigated with gravity-fed systems, and they responded with mobility, establishing temporary campsites as they moved seasonally across the desert landscape to hunt and gather specific sources of game and plant life in specific regions. They appear to have occupied summer camps along the Gila and Colorado Rivers for longer periods, planting, tending, and harvesting corn and other crops. They constructed larger villages on the shores of Lake Cahuila, which provided abundant sources of fish, waterfowl, and plant life. The largest Payatan villages are believed to have disappeared under the silt or been washed away by the raging floods that periodically carried vast amounts of snowmelt down the seventeen-hundred-mile Colorado River before it was tamed by the dam constructions of the twentieth century. As in the case of the Hohokam, early archaeologists were rarely tempted to excavate Payatan sites in the summer heat. Intaglios provide only a glimpse into the lives of the people who were probably the ancestors of modern-day Yuman peoples such as the Havasupais, Hualapais, Quechans, and Mojaves.[53]

Looking primarily at styles of pottery and architecture, archaeologists have identified two major cultural traditions as ancestral to the Pueblos of more recent history: the Mogollon of central Arizona and New Mexico and northern Mexico and the Anasazi of the Colorado Plateau. Ironically, neither of the names they use to identify these ancestors is Puebloan. Mogollon comes from the Mogollon Mountains, named for Juan Ignacio Flores Mogollón, Spanish governor of New Mexico from 1712 to 1715. Anasazi means "enemy ancestors" in Navajo, but after rancher-archaeologist Richard Wetherill used it in the 1880s for the ruins at Mesa Verde it became widely used in southwestern archaeology because it was far less cumbersome than the more technical composite term "Basketmaker-Pueblo."[54] The term "ancestral Pueblos" is now often preferred.

The people of the Mogollon tradition occupied an enormous area of rugged mountains and valleys stretching from the Arizona–New Mexico border south into Chihuahua and Sonora. Mogollon farmers developed deep planting and floodwater irrigation techniques suited to the lowland deserts and produced a type of Chapalote corn with larger ears and more rows of kernels.[55] They lived in settlements of loosely arranged pit houses and fashioned distinctive brown or reddish brown pottery by hand coiling, scraping, and polishing. The first Mogollon pottery and pit houses date to around A.D. 200. After about 1000 Mogollon people developed more compact villages composed of blocks of contiguous rectangular rooms centered around open plazas. The earliest Mogollon pots were plain brown ware and did not replace baskets, which were more serviceable to people on the move. But as Mogollon people became more sedentary they developed new ceramic art forms. The people who lived along the Mimbres River in New Mexico created a distinctive and now world famous ceramic style. Using long yucca-fiber brushes, they decorated their pottery with black paint on white, a color scheme they may have adopted from Anasazi peoples to the north. Later Mogollon architecture also reflected Anasazi influences, especially after the late thirteenth century, when refugees from drought in their Colorado Plateau homelands headed for the mountains of the Mogollon. Large apartment-style communities such as the 335-room Turkey Creek Pueblo, estimated to have been founded around 1240 in the Point of Pines region, and the 500-room Grasshopper Pueblo in western Arizona, with its 55-foot-long Great Kiva, reflected population aggregation as well as increased tensions. By the mid-1300s corn agriculture could no longer feed the growing population. Mogollon farmers began to leave the mountains of central Arizona and search for farmland elsewhere. By 1450 their villages were deserted. When the Spaniards marched through the area a century later they described it as a vast *despoblado*, a wasteland. In time, pressured by chain reactions and population shuffling on the southern plains, Western Apaches occupied what had once been the Mogollon mountain homeland and made it Apachería.[56]

Over the course of some twenty-five generations, Anasazi in the San Juan Basin shifted their economic emphasis: from hunters and gatherers who supplemented their diet by growing corn, beans, and squash, they developed into semisedentary village farmers who supplemented their diet by foraging.[57] Like the Mogollon, the way of life known as Anasazi emerged when people who practiced a mixed economy of hunting, gathering, and corn agriculture developed pottery. In most of Anasazi country—centered on the San Juan Basin but spreading over much of the Colorado Plateau and northern New Mexico—pottery began to appear around A.D. 300 and was widespread by 500. By the sixth century, the Anasazi were living in communities of shallow pit houses built of wattle and daub, but dramatic shifts in housing patterns occurred between 700 and 900.[58]

In some areas people began to live for part of the year in small structures constructed aboveground from chipped sandstone rock set in masonry. When adobe structures were combined to share adjoining walls, a new architectural form evolved. South-facing rooms became aligned around a plaza, usually with the rear facade toward the prevailing northerly winds or sheltered against a cliff. During winter days the adobe soaked up solar heat and radiated it into the rooms at night. Nestled under sandstone cliffs or located in valley bottoms and constructed "with only the available materials of earth, stone, and sunlight," writes anthropologist Peter Nabokov, the compact apartment-like town clusters of the Anasazi "integrated the most advanced inventory of building types, special-use rooms, construction methods, and road and water management systems in the continent." As new rooms and upper stories were added, families slept in the upper front rooms warmed by the passive solar-heating properties of adobe. Interior rooms in the rear were used for storage. Pit houses were retained for communal and ritual purposes, probably evolving into kivas.[59] The pit house-to-pueblo transition (what archaeologists call the PPT) did not mean a shift from "simple" to "complex" society, but it naturally entailed changes in sociopolitical organization.[60]

In the northeastern Arizona homeland of the Kayenta Anasazi, the sixteen-year Black Mesa Archaeological Project gathered data from thousands of surveyed and more than one hundred excavated sites. People inhabited northern Black Mesa for at least four thousand years and began growing corn by 300 to 200 B.C. The Anasazi inhabitants lived in dispersed small settlements, often on a seasonal basis. Even when population increased dramatically early in the eleventh century, the old patterns of dispersed settlement continued: villages increased in number, not in size. In the twelfth century, as elsewhere in the Southwest, population fell, construction ceased, and northern Black Mesa was depopulated by A.D. 1150.[61]

At Chaco Canyon in the San Juan Basin, Anasazi people constructed large towns, congregated in large communities, and left behind spectacular ruins. The first detailed records of Chaco were made by Lt. James Simpson, a surveyor with a U.S. military expedition into Navajo country in 1849. Simpson recorded eleven of the major ruins in the canyon, and Richard Kern, the expedition artist, made sketches of them.[62] In 1896 Richard Wetherill carried out excavations of the canyon and employed Navajo workers, a practice in southwestern archaeology that endured for fifty years. (Wetherill claimed he had the power to ward off evil spirits associated with working at the site, but Navajo workers more likely put more faith in Enemyway and Blessingway ceremonies for protection and cleansing.) In 1907 Chaco Canyon was included among the first group of sites accorded national monument status by President Theodore Roosevelt. The ruins at Chaco have been a source of perpetual fascination, discussion, and debate, but in recent years archaeologists have widened their focus, away from the sites themselves, to get a fuller understanding of Chaco as a far-reaching regional system.[63]

Chaco Canyon lies in a desert. Archaeologist Linda S. Cordell described it as "a small slash in the relatively featureless, barren, and dry San Juan Basin," a bleak landscape of some twenty-six thousand square miles.[64] Yet Anasazi people grew corn here and made it a center of exchange and ritual. Probably five thousand and perhaps as many as fifteen thousand people inhabited the area by 1100, though some archaeologists favor lower figures, pointing out that earlier estimates were based on the assumption that every room was a living space, whereas in fact many rooms were storage spaces. The size of the Chacoan pueblos does not necessarily indicate great populations.[65]

Between about 900 and 1150 the people of Chaco built a dozen towns, or "great houses," and scores of small settlements. They used at least two hundred thousand timbers in these construction projects, mostly from ponderosa pines, which they felled and trimmed in distant highlands and carried forty or fifty miles to the canyon. Tree-ring-dating techniques applied to the beams allow archaeologists to establish detailed chronologies of construction. An inventory and analysis of more than four thousand pieces of wood in Pueblo Bonito provided a record of how the wood had been procured, used, and reused over time. The dressed stone masonry of Chaco also reflects a high level of craftsmanship. By the estimate of one architect, more than one million dressed stones went into building Pueblo Bonito alone, "up to one million pounds of stone veneer to be quarried, carried, dressed, and put into place." Town building in Chaco Canyon required immense organization and expenditure of labor.[66]

D-shaped Pueblo Bonito was the largest great house in the canyon. Construction on Pueblo Bonito began in the ninth century. Dendrochronology (tree-ring dating) together with analyses of different masonry styles, ground plans, and methods of joining walls indicate several major phases, mainly in the eleventh century, with different portions built at different times during the next three hundred years.[67] Pueblo Bonito's crescent-shape design took full advantage of solar heating during the winter: during the course of the day each section of the pueblo would be heated, beginning on the western side, as the sun ran its course. Built above the floodplain, the pueblo was tucked beneath the mesa cliffs, protected from cold northern winds.[68] Once five stories high, Pueblo Bonito contained between six and eight hundred rooms and about forty kivas. Archaeologist Neil Judd wrote in the 1920s: "No other apartment house of comparable size was known in America or in the Old World until the Spanish Flats were erected in 1882 at 59th Street and Seventh Avenue, New York City." Judd probably overestimated the size of the resident population, which likely numbered hundreds rather than thousands, but his romantic image of an ancient desert metropolis caught public attention in the aftermath of World War I, when a disillusioned generation that included Mabel Dodge Luhan, John Collier, and D. H. Lawrence looked to the Indian Southwest for qualities lacking in their own society.[69] By any standards, Pueblo Bonito was an impressive structure, built by people without metal tools, wheels, and draft animals.

2. Aerial photograph of the ruins of Pueblo Bonito. (Courtesy, National Park Service, Chaco Culture National Historical Park. Chaco Archive neg. no. 25462.)

Chacoans also built dams, ditches, canals, and reservoirs to collect water and transport it to their fields. The water-controlling system was virtually continuous along the north side of the canyon, where the major pueblos and most of the population were located and where runoff from the large expanses of bedrock along the rim of the canyon provided water for collection and channeling. Chacoans not only controlled the flow of runoff water but may also have tried to slow the erosion of topsoil and farmland. Where water was the single most vital source of life, its management and engineering were crucial to survival.[70]

Chacoan people and communities were not confined to Chaco Canyon. By the early twelfth century at least seventy communities scattered over twenty-five thousand square miles of northwestern New Mexico, southern Colorado, and into Arizona were linked to Chaco through networks of exchange and ritual.[71] Roads were as much a feature of Chacoan civilization as canals were for Hohokam.[72] More than four hundred miles of straight roads radiated from Chaco Canyon. Most of the roads, many of which are still visible, were probably constructed between

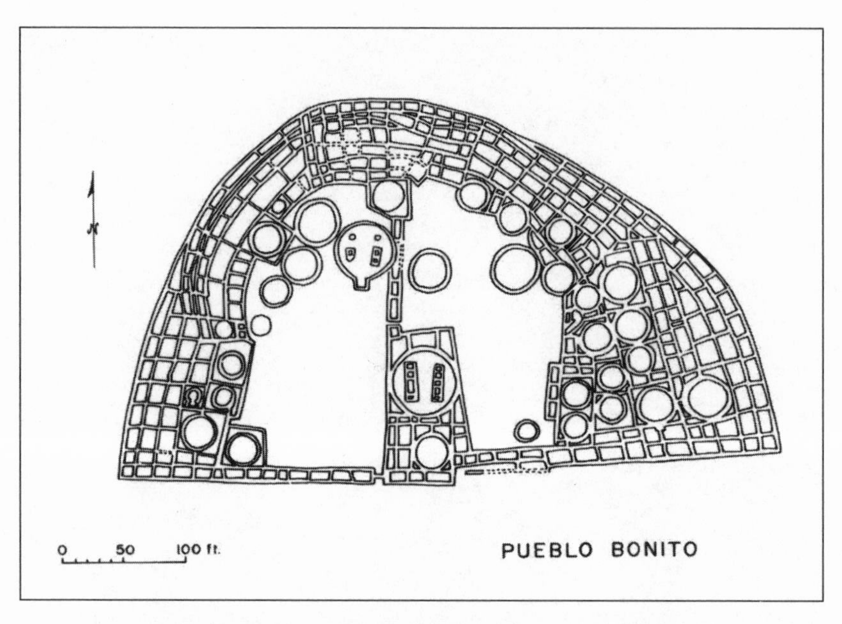

3. Ground plan of Pueblo Bonito. (Courtesy, National Park Service, Chaco Culture National Historical Park. Chaco Archive neg. no. 20809. By Jerry Livingston.)

1075 and 1140. They were not just desert paths but typically involved construction of roadbeds, curbs, bordering walls, ramps, and stairways. Some roads were thirty feet wide. Some extended more than sixty miles and connected several outlying sites to each other and to Chaco Canyon. Several major roads converged on an area dominated by Pueblo Bonito, Chetro Ketl, and Casa Rinconada, suggesting that Chaco was the nerve center of a network of sites throughout the San Juan Basin. How far the roads extended beyond remains unclear. Economic explanations alone do not fully explain the system, which includes roads of different widths, roads that ran parallel in places, and roads that terminated abruptly. Roads may have been started and not finished, although short segments of road pointing the proper direction and providing symbolic alignment possibly served the same purpose as completed highways. The roads may have had ceremonial purposes, served as highways for messengers, and symbolized the directions by which different clans originally came to Chaco. They probably provided a variety of social, religious, and economic links between Chaco and outlying communities. Building, maintaining, and using the roads served to integrate and unify, socially, politically, and symbolically, the various components of what scholars call the "Chaco system."[73]

The people of Chaco Canyon seem to have orchestrated the movement of resources via the road system. The roads may have brought food and goods from outlying districts to Chaco, where they were stored, redistributed, and mobilized by leaders for communal ceremonial events in conjunction with construction projects. Chacoans traded turquoise for seashells from the Gulf of California, copper bells from northern or western Mexico, exotic birds and feathers from Central America, and minerals and ores from the Rocky Mountains. Outlying communities may have provided the canyon with food, firewood, yucca fiber, nuts, seeds, herbs, and basket-making materials as well as ceramics, salt, cotton, and turquoise. The exact nature of the exchange system—what the people of the canyon provided in return—is not clear; it probably involved religious and ceremonial ties as well as economic exchange. People came together for formalized trade fairs. Chaco seems to have dominated the production and trade of finished turquoise in the region—more than fifty-six thousand pieces of turquoise have been recovered at Pueblo Bonito, and Neil Judd discovered a four-strand turquoise necklace that contained twenty-five hundred turquoise disks, each one of which had been painstakingly made by rubbing against sandstone and then drilled. But the nearest source of turquoise was the Cerrillos mines, almost a hundred miles east, near Santa Fe. Pottery came to Chaco from the Red Mesa Valley, forty-three miles to the south, from Chuska Canyon, thirty-seven miles to the west, and from the San Juan River Valley, forty-seven miles north. Many of the trade goods seem to have been consumed in Chaco Canyon rather than redistributed to other parts of the system, lending weight to the idea that the canyon was a political, economic, and ceremonial center, perhaps dominated by an elite who "hoarded" ritual knowledge.[74]

Little is known about the structure and functioning of Chacoan society and politics or the sources and implementation of elite power, allowing room for considerable speculation. Biological anthropologists Christy and Jacqueline Turner argued that evidence of cannibalism in the Chaco area after about A.D. 900 indicated that terror and human sacrifice were employed as instruments of social control. Pointing to Mexican connections and similarities, they even hypothesized that invading Toltec warriors had imposed their religious and political system on the Native peoples of the Chaco region.[75]

In a land of infrequent rain, Chaco priests watched the skies, tracking the seasonal course of the sun, following the rhythms of the sky, predicting and praying for rain. Several sites reveal evidence that Chacoans marked the summer solstice, observing the play of sunlight at sunrise and sunset, and used the interplay of light and shadow on petroglyphs to pinpoint the key astronomical demarcations of the seasons. Near the top of Fajada Butte in Chaco Canyon, where three slabs of fallen rock rest in a vertical position against the rock wall, Chacoans carved a spiral petroglyph onto the cliff wall; at midday on the summer solstice the sunlight that streams between the center and right-hand slab cuts like a dagger of light through the center of the spiral.[76]

Like later pioneers in the American West, the Anasazi experienced cycles of boom and bust that sometimes resulted in places being occupied and then abandoned. People came together to share resources and defenses but then dispersed as their numbers taxed the environment and their social mechanisms.[77] The Anasazi reached their greatest territorial extent and the Chaco system developed during a time of sufficient rainfall for corn growing, roughly 900–1100. But then, in David Stuart's words, "something went horribly wrong." Prayers for rain went unanswered, and drought gripped the region for several years. Tree rings show that drought struck the San Juan Basin in 1130 and persisted until about 1180. Water tables dropped throughout the Colorado Plateau during the twelfth century. Farmers who had extended their communities and fields to areas where soil and growing conditions were marginal for corn cultivation were hard hit. People abandoned some areas and retreated to a "shrinking core." At Chaco there may have been just too many people for the area to support during times of drought or even under normal arid conditions. The Chaco system had relied on regular surpluses and failed when drought-stricken resources diminished. Chaco's storehouses of corn became depleted. People moved away, and hundreds of sites were abandoned. No new Chacoan buildings were constructed after 1150. Instead, population increased in areas around Chaco Canyon as emigrants formed large aggregated settlements. Many larger Pueblo communities grew up as scores of smaller communities were abandoned. Cliff Palace, Spruce Tree House, and other cliff sites were constructed at Mesa Verde in southwestern Colorado. Antelope House and White House in Canyon de Chelly were begun before the drought but seem to have expanded to accommodate a growing population during the drought years. In what is now Navajo National Monument, Kiet Seel, the largest cliff dwelling in Arizona, and Betatakin were founded after 1250, flourished briefly, and were deserted by 1300.[78]

The northern San Juan region that includes Mesa Verde was occupied by Anasazi people from at least 500 to 1300. Surveys in Mesa Verde National Park have documented 4,372 archaeological sites. The central Mesa Verde region appears to have experienced significant depopulation sometime in the tenth century, but population peaked between 1150 and 1250—what archaeologists call the post-Chaco era. Dozens of multistory pueblos were built during this time. Most Anasazi inhabited mesa-top villages, but at Mesa Verde itself they built predominantly cliff dwellings. New rooms were added over time until more than two hundred rooms in a multitiered fortresslike cliff dwelling provided defense against enemies. South-facing cliff houses also acted as immense solar collectors in the winter, catching the sun as it passed low in the sky, and provided cool shade in the summer, when the sun passed high above the overhanging rock. Fields at Mesa Verde were on the mesa tops. Some Mesa Verdean people may have reoccupied Chaco Canyon: for about one hundred years after Chaco was abandoned, there seems to have been an influx of people who took over some Chacoan sites, built some of their own, and used Mesa Verde–style black-on-white pottery.[79]

Cliff Palace, the largest and best preserved of the Mesa Verde cliff dwellings, with 220 rooms and 23 kivas, was "discovered" by Richard Wetherill late in 1888. He and his brother-in-law were herding stray cattle into Cliff Canyon. Seeking shelter for the night, Wetherill happened to look up at the canyon wall, a scene re-created by a character in Willa Cather's novel *The Professor's House.* A thousand feet above him, perched in a cavern in the cliff, he saw "a little city of stone, asleep, . . . looking down into the canyon with the calmness of eternity. . . . I knew at once that I had come upon the city of some extinct civilization, hidden away in this inaccessible mesa for centuries, preserved in the dry air and almost perpetual sunlight like a fly in amber, guarded by the cliff and the river and the desert."[80]

Mesa Verde is impressive, but its fame may have obscured the importance of other sites. Nearby Montezuma Valley contained several large pueblos, one of which, known as Yellow Jacket, had about eighteen hundred rooms and probably housed about twenty-five hundred people, more than the whole population of Mesa Verde.[81] The largest northern San Juan Basin site was Aztec, located on the north side of the San Juan River close to the present border between New Mexico and Colorado. Aztec continued Chaco's architectural and perhaps its political traditions.

In comparison, suggests one archaeologist, Mesa Verde may in fact have been "a bit of a backwater."[82]

By 1300 the people who had built the massive stone structures of the Four Corners region had gone. Why they left their homes has never been clear. Many factors have been blamed, but their exact role and interaction remain a mystery. As people moved and adjusted to the long twelfth-century drought that contributed to the collapse of the Chacoan system, they confronted the coldest period since the late seventh century. A major drought occurred from 1276 to 1299, and the climate seems to have fluctuated irregularly between about 1250 and 1450. These climatic changes all affected peoples' ability to sustain agriculture in certain areas and prompted movement to others, for instance, from upland areas to lower elevations where farming was less risky in cold weather. Local migrations produced regional fluctuations in population and sometimes significant shifts in relations between communities. Nevertheless, exact correlations between weather and migration patterns remain elusive.[83]

Environmental stress generated new levels of competition and conflict. When the climate took a turn for the worse it reduced the carrying capacity of the land and intensified competition for access to limited resources in areas where previously favorable climate had increased the carrying capacity and generated population growth. Overhunting may have added to the crisis: farming peoples often obtained meat and protein by trading with hunting peoples, but they also hunted themselves and may have subjected local animal populations to stress, especially in times of drought. Despite the pervasive popular image of the Pueblo Southwest as a peaceful place, competition and conflict were recurrent features of life for two thousand years, and warfare appears to have increased in level and intensity after about 1250. People congregated in more defensive locations in canyon walls and on mesa tops and built more defensive structures like stone towers. Burned sites occur more frequently. At Castle Rock Pueblo in southwestern Colorado, the inhabitants appear to have died in a thirteenth-century surprise attack. New military technologies appear to have been adopted between 1200 and 1450: warriors began using the more lethal sinew-backed recurved bow; animal-hide shields replaced wicker shields. Rock art and kiva murals displayed more warriors and shields after 1300, suggesting increased conflict and reflecting an ideology and iconography of war. It is not clear whom the inhabitants of the Southwest were fighting. Even if Ute and Athapaskan intruders from the north arrived as early as the fourteenth century, before they obtained horses they would have posed little direct threat to fortified and populous Anasazi villages, although small hit-and-run raids on fields and settlements would have taken a toll. Factionalism within individual communities almost certainly occurred, and there may have been open conflict between different Anasazi communities. Some scholars suggest that population aggregation coupled with poor sanitary practices may have caused epidemic disease, but hard evidence is lacking. Other scholars see evidence of cannibalism, indicating starvation and increasing levels of both internal and external violence. Whatever the causes, increased warfare and social violence generated chain reactions in migration, settlement patterns, and social structure. The repercussions were still being played out when the Spaniards invaded the Southwest in the mid-sixteenth century and met Pueblos living in defensive walled towns.[84]

The ruins preserved in the dry climate of the Southwest create an illusion of sudden and catastrophic abandonment. They may be better understood as evidence of a common process of movement, rebuilding, and adjusting to change, even calamity. The perceived "great abandonments" were less dramatic than they appear to Euro-American eyes accustomed to seeing stability of settlement as an indicator of community health and survival. Indian people often employed both sedentation and mobility as separate but complementary strategies, with individuals and households moving every one or two generations while communities persisted in the same area. Leaving one area for another and remaking aggregate communities as people reassembled in new areas seems to have been a common pattern. There is little evidence of people fleeing their homes in blind panic and clear evidence of planned movements. People made choices based on the alternatives available; they knew where they were going and why, and their decisions to move involved both "push" and "pull" factors. Changing times and the drier conditions that prevailed in the late twelfth and thirteenth centuries did not propel people into a sudden mass exodus but prompted them first to pull away from the San Juan Basin and other marginal areas and congregate into larger settlements in the Mesa Verde region. Then, in the late thirteenth century, people moved toward more fertile areas like the Rio Grande Valley, the Tonto Basin and mountains of Arizona, the Hopi Mesas, or farther to the south and southwest. Contractions in Anasazi settlement in some areas produced expansion in others. The abandonment of first Chaco Canyon and then Mesa Verde marked shifts in the center of gravity of the ancient Pueblo world, not the end of that world.[85]

When Spaniards arrived in the Southwest, they speculated about the empty regions they saw, conjuring up mysteries about vanished civilizations. In reality, discontinuities in regional occupations may sometimes be better explained by people shifting from hunting and gathering to agriculture and back rather than by dramatic events such as drought, disease, environmental degradation, and nomadic raids.[86] Whereas archaeologists want to trace migrations with specific sites, places, and dates, writes Tessie Naranjo of Santa Clara, Pueblo people are more concerned with the general idea of movement: "The old people moved continuously—and that was the way it was." Seen this way, the mystery of disappearance may be understood as a normal, even essential part of life: "Explanations are not necessary—only stories which remind, acknowledge, and honor the power and force of movement. People have moved from place to place and joined and separated again throughout our past, and we have incorporated it into our songs, stories, and myths because we must continually remember that, without movement, there is no life."[87]

Pueblo origin stories and histories involved migration, whether from lower to upper worlds or from place to place. Zuni and Hopi traditions remember Chaco Canyon as a place where their ancestors lived, an important stopping point on the way to finding their center place. A map of Zuni origins and migrations includes Chaco Canyon as one of the northernmost places on their travels through the Southwest.[88]

Archaeologists have only relatively recently begun to examine the migrations from the Four Corners to the Rio Grande and elsewhere as an explanation of culture change in the Southwest.[89] Some scholars believe that new ceremonies drew people eastward to the Rio Grande. The kachina cult, or elements of it, may have originated in western Mexico, but eventually it spread throughout the entire Pueblo world, uniting peoples of different regions and languages in a common relation to the kachinas, ancestral beings who bring rain, harmony, and well-being. Elaborately costumed and masked kachina dancers representing the ancestors led communities in ceremonies and prayers for rain; kiva walls displayed murals of kachina figures and dancers. The kachinas seem to have appeared in the Pueblo world toward the end of the period of migrations, when new peoples were arriving in the Rio Grande Valley and the western Pueblo area from the San Juan. In a period of drought, farming peoples may well have placed increased belief in the spirits that brought rain. As more and more people adopted kachina ceremonies, they formed ceremonial relationships that cut across ties of kinship and language, promoted exchange, and generated a common Pueblo cultural identity.[90] Hopi tradition as recounted by Don Talayesva recalled a "golden age," with ample rain, good crops, and plenty to eat. "The Katcinas [*sic*] lived within or near the village, and whenever they danced or the people held their ceremonies, it always rained. Everybody was happy."[91]

According to one account, Pueblo people had a rather different explanation for the movement of peoples to the Rio Grande. They said that the Anasazi "kept a great black snake in the kiva, who had power over their life." They fed him deer, rabbits, antelope, bison, and birds, and he gave them corn, squash, berries, yucca, cactus, and all they needed to wear. Then one night he left them. They followed his tracks to the Rio Grande. Unable to live without the serpent who provided rain and fertility, they gathered up their things and moved to the river, "where they found another town already living. There they took up their lives again amidst the gods of that place."[92]

Many people who left the Four Corners area migrated south into territory occupied by other Anasazi and Mogollon peoples. Some founded new settlements; others amalgamated into existing communities. According to origin stories from Acoma, the people left White House (which may have been Chaco, Aztec, or in Canyon de Chelly) and moved south. When they reached a place called Ako (Acoma), they split: one group chose to stay there; the others continued south. The Zunis tell a similar story. It is possible that the groups who continued south went to Casas Grandes in northern Chihuahua.[93]

Casas Grandes seems to be key to understanding the workings of the southwestern Indian world in the thirteenth and fourteenth centuries. Also called Paquimé, and not to be confused with the Hohokam site at Casa Grande in Arizona, Casas Grandes was part of the larger Mogollon world for most of its history; it resembled Mogollon culture in its styles of artifacts and patterns of settlement, and the inhabitants of the area lived in small farming villages. But by the fourteenth century a major trade center had developed at Casas Grandes, and population congregated there. With more than two thousand rooms at its height, Casas Grandes was a major desert town, with large multistory adobe houses, public buildings, open plazas, earthen and stone mounds, ball courts, covered irrigation, and drainage systems. Recently designated a World Heritage Site by the United Nations, Casas Grandes was the largest "prehistoric settlement" in the American Southwest or the Mexican Northwest. Its immediate area of influence may have been quite small, but evidence from hundreds of sites indicates that between about 1200 and 1450 it was the center of a huge sphere of interaction, reaching over tens of thousands of square miles, with connections to Sonora, Texas, Arizona, and the emerging Pueblo cultures of New Mexico, demonstrated most clearly in shared religious motifs. It was a major trade center. Turquoise, copper, marine shells, and pottery were exchanged and distributed over long distances. Exotic birds and turkeys were bred and traded for their feathers—more than three hundred scarlet macaw skeletons were uncovered at the site in the twentieth century. For more than two hundred years, the Casas Grandes region formed a nexus between the American Southwest and Mesoamerica.[94]

Casas Grandes is 390 miles south of Chaco Canyon. The fact that it stands on the same meridian line as Chaco and Aztec to the north has provoked speculation that the three sites were intentionally aligned to symbolize their connection and continuity, with each site dominating for a time (Chaco, ca. 900–1125; Aztec, ca. 1110–1275; Casas Grandes, ca. 1250–1450) and that a ruling elite perpetuated itself over five centuries by moving the ceremonial city and integrating local populations into the political and prestige exchange economy. Chacoan influence spread over time as well as territory.[95] Around 1350, new trade routes running up the west coast of Mexico began to compete with Casas Grandes.[96] Casas Grandes was burned and abandoned in the 1400s. Nevertheless, the items and ideas that spread from Chihuahua helped the peoples living at Hopi in northeastern Arizona and on the central Rio Grande to transform their culture, alter traditional Anasazi patterns of settlement, and create the uniquely Puebloan world the Spanish saw in the sixteenth century.[97]

Groups from the north and other surrounding regions moved into Hopi country. In Hopi legend, this time may mark the emergence of the people into the Fourth World and the beginning of clan migrations across long distances and past abandoned pueblos before they finally settled in the present Hopi homeland and established their collective identity. At Homol'ovi, near Winslow, Arizona, four separate pueblos were occupied during the late thirteenth and fourteenth centuries.[98]

The newcomers arrived at a time when the inhabitants of the area were themselves responding to drought and declining resources. Their immigration prompted or perhaps accelerated significant changes in the pattern, structure, and size of Hopi settlements. In the twelfth century, settlements were generally dispersed along major drainages or along mesa edges near springs. But after about 1250 and increasingly during the "Great Drought" period of 1275–1300, populations aggregated into larger villages on the four mesas where the historic Hopi villages are located. Hopi settlements grew, sometimes severalfold. Hopi oral histories as recalled by Don Talayesva, born in 1890, recounted that when a new clan arrived at Oraibi and asked permission to settle in the village, the chief usually inquired whether they had a ceremony for producing rain. If they had, he would admit them to the village.[99]

Hopi stories suggest that corn existed before humans emerged on to the earth. Müy'ingwa, the "male maize spirit" or "father of the underworld," was said to be covered with grains of corn and had ears of corn for feet. Other stories referred to "corn maidens" as spirits. Hopis buried corn kernels or seeds with their deceased, symbolizing a link between death and fertility. In one Hopi story, the sacred directions and their colors represented the "chief" clouds and type of corn for which they were responsible, including yellow, blue, red, white, black, and speckled or sweet corn.[100]

The Hopis' ancestors became expert desert farmers and created a unique form of Chapalote corn now known as "Hopi corn." They planted several kernels in a hole to ensure that stalks would be produced and planted deep so that roots would have a chance to stabilize in desert soils.[101] As Don Talayesva recalled, Hopis learned long ago that successful farming required watching the skies and keeping track of the sun and the seasons: "Old Talasemptewa, who was almost blind, would sit out on the housetop of the special Sun Clan house and watch the sun's progress toward its summer home. He untied a knot in a string for each day. When the sun arose at certain mesa peaks, he passed the word around that it was time to plant sweet corn, ordinary corn, string beans, melons, squash, lima beans, and other seeds. On a certain date he would announce that it was too late for any more planting."[102]

By prayer and management, Hopi people cultivated corn crops out of the desert. When the Navajos arrived—at first in dribs and drabs and then every year at harvesttime—they called the Hopis "corn eaters."[103] When a Spanish expedition reached the Hopi town of Walpi in 1582, more than one thousand people came to meet them, carrying earthen jars of water "and with rabbits, cooked venison, tortillas, atole (corn flour gruel), and beans, cooked calabashes, and quantities of corn and pinole." Although there were many mouths to feed, "heaps of food were left over."[104]

Hopis today work in many different occupations, but corn remains central to their worldview and cosmology. Working in the fields, explains Hopi scholar Emory Sekaquaptewa, "symbolizes their emergence to humanity" and allows them to "reexperience the creation of their world." According to the Hopi creation story, they chose blue corn to symbolize their life once they emerged to a new level of humanity. Blue corn represents a life of hardship and humility because it requires more work and care than other strains but is also the strongest and most durable. The Hopis plant at least two dozen varieties, although mostly blue and white corn. Some varieties are adapted to drought conditions, some have short growing seasons, and some withstand strong winds. Planting corn at different elevations and at different times in the season ensures some harvest even if spring comes late or frost comes early. Hopi identity and existence as a people still rest on corn and its care.[105]

Like their contemporaries in medieval Europe, the first farmers and town builders of the Southwest lived short lives—life expectancy for the people of Chaco Canyon was about twenty-seven years.[106] But they lived there a very long time, building communities based on corn and water, moving away and merging into other peoples when circumstances demanded, and leaving impressive evidence of their presence and powerful reminders of their passing. By the time Spaniards arrived in the Southwest, Pueblo life centered on three main areas: the Rio Grande, Acoma/Zuni, and Hopi.[107] So-called abandoned places continued to play vital roles in Pueblo life and still do. "Pueblo people visit the old ruins to breathe in the strength of the place and 'those who have gone before,'" said a writer from Santa Clara.[108]

Mississippian Corn Chiefdoms

Farther east, people constructed corn-based societies that built mounds and townscapes so impressive that nineteenth-century archaeologists argued they must have been the work of a "pre-Indian civilization" driven out or destroyed by historic Indians.[109] Indian women in the river valleys of eastern North America began domesticating indigenous plants such as sunflower, squash, marsh elder, chenopod, sumpweed, and goosefoot between about 2000 and 1000 B.C., but it took perhaps a thousand years for domesticated crops to become a substantial food source. Over time they added several more seed crops, but hunting and gathering remained the mainstay. People in eastern Kentucky, Tennessee, and the Ozarks were growing domesticated small grains, oil seeds, squash, and other crops by about 1000 B.C. This "eastern agricultural complex" had spread north to the Ohio Valley and Illinois and as far west as Kansas by 200 B.C. to A.D. 200. Corn was introduced by A.D. 200, but it remained a minor crop for hundreds of years and only very gradually became the staple food of eastern farmers.[110]

Local domesticated plants may have contributed to the florescence of the Hopewellian culture in the Ohio region that emerged from that of the Adena about the time of Christ and flourished for some four centuries. Hopewellian people built more elaborate burial mounds and earthen architecture and developed greater ceremonial complexity. Two core areas, identified by high concentrations of Hopewell-style artifacts, existed in southern Ohio and around the Illinois and Mississippi River Valleys in Illinois. The people spread their culture through extensive exchange networks and obtained valuable raw materials from vast distances: grizzly bear teeth from the Rockies; obsidian for spear points and blades from Yellowstone; silver from Ontario; copper from the Great Lakes; mica and copper from the southern Appalachians; galena from the upper Mississippi; quartz from Arkansas; pottery, marine shells, turtle shells, and shark and alligator teeth from the Gulf of Mexico. Hopewellian craftsmen and artists fashioned the raw materials into tools and intricate ornaments and also made local imitations of items from afar. Many of the items were deposited with the dead in mortuary mounds; others were traded to other communities.

The Hopewellian way of life endured until around A.D. 400. Then, a thousand years before first European contacts, mound building decreased and changed in nature. Exchange networks collapsed. Some scholars have associated the Hopewellian decline with the spread and intensification of corn agriculture, arguing that long-distance exchange networks by individuals vying for personal prestige became less important than diversifying crops, developing food storage systems, and maintaining local ties.

Between about A.D. 500 and 800 corn agriculture spread throughout eastern North America. Then, over the next two hundred years, the climate became warmer and moister, and corn production and consumption increased greatly. In the northeastern United States and Great Lakes region sometime before A.D. 900, a variety of corn appeared that required only a short growing season and was drought and frost resistant. This hardy Northern Flint corn opened the Northeast to agriculture and sustained seven centuries of cultural development. Corn spread rapidly and widely toward the 120-day frost-free growing season limit of cultivation. Woodland peoples continued to practice long-established patterns of hunting, fishing, and foraging, but after about A.D. 1000 corn became the major field crop. A system of agriculture based on corn, beans, and squash, supplemented with a variety of cultivated plant foods, fish, and white-tailed deer, became the core of society and the economy throughout much of the eastern woodlands.[111]

In the Fort Ancient area of the Middle Ohio Valley, for example, the transition to corn agriculture that occurred around 1000 produced more villages and increased social organization within the villages. Stockaded Fort Ancient villages included space for daily domestic activities and space reserved for sacred activities such as solstice alignments. The famous Great Serpent Mound in Ohio, more than twelve hundred feet long, was built during the Fort Ancient culture.[112]

In the hands and the history of Mississippian societies, corn offered a new and powerful vehicle for change.[113] Beginning in the lower Mississippi Valley around A.D. 700, Mississippian cultures spread north toward the Great Lakes, east to Florida and the Carolinas, and west to the edge of the prairies. They reached their largest geographical extent between 1100 and 1300 and endured for as long as six centuries, up to and beyond European contact. Mississippian societies typically were agriculturally based settlements close to floodplains with relatively large populations and complex ceremonial and political structures. Powerful chiefs from elite families collected tribute, mobilized labor, and distributed food among their followers, waged war against neighboring chiefdoms, were buried with large quantities of exotic goods, and appear to have been worshiped. Mississippian towns contained temples, public buildings, and elite residences built atop earthen mounds around open plazas where ceremonies and ball games took place. Mississippian ceremonial art was characterized by common motifs: crosses, sun circles, forked eyes, hands and eyes, long-nosed gods, serpents, falcons, and female figurines as fertility symbolism reflecting the importance of corn agriculture. The reoccurrence of such themes and symbols in Mississippian sites indicates that a shared ceremonial complex and ideology stretched across the south from eastern locations like Etowah, Georgia, and Moundville, Alabama, as far west as related Caddoan mound-building cultures at Spiro, Oklahoma, and as far north as Aztalan in Wisconsin.[114]

About the time the Normans were invading England and Christendom was embarking on the first Crusades, Mississippian culture peaked near present-day St. Louis with the emergence of the largest town in pre-Columbian North America, a paramount chiefdom unlike anything seen before or since.[115] Where the Illinois and Missouri feed into the Mississippi, the rivers meander, forming swamps and oxbow lakes and creating a floodplain environment known as the American Bottom. Though only twenty-five miles long and a dozen miles across at its widest point, the American Bottom borders several ecological zones and was rich in game, plants, and aquatic resources.[116] Once field agriculture was established in its fertile soils, it supported for centuries probably the highest concentration of population in precontact America north of Mexico. The town was long gone when the French arrived in the seventeenth century, and the Mississippi Valley had experienced considerable shifting and mingling of peoples. The French named the site Cahokia after the Indians of the Illinois confederacy who were living there.[117]

People were living in small sedentary villages with scattered farmsteads at or near the site by the sixth century, and a thousand or more people lived there around A.D. 1000. Then things changed quite abruptly because of a phenomenon Timothy Pauketat chose to call a "Big Bang in the Bottom."[118] Between 900 and 1200, a global warming trend correlated with an influx of moist tropical air to bring increased summer rainfall into the plains and allowed the adoption of farming in regions farther west than had previously been possible. During what archaeologists call the Lohmann phase, the people living in the American Bottom adopted full-scale corn agriculture. Corn grew well during the hot humid summers on the fertile floodplains. The people of Cahokia relied on it as a crucial part of a diet that also included nuts, berries, sunflower, marsh elder, chenopod, squash, beans, many varieties of fish and waterfowl, as well as deer and small mammals.[119]

Population increased dramatically, settlement patterns were reorganized, people began to congregate in and around Cahokia in nucleated villages, a large town developed for the first time, and political power was consolidated. A marked increase in mound building and plaza construction transformed the landscape of the region. Newly formed elites may also have developed a new ideology and manipulated the symbols of belief, mediating between common people and cosmic forces. They appear to have maintained their positions through displays of power, ceremonies of world renewal, monumental architecture, control of food distribution, trade in prestige goods, mobilization of labor, and perhaps the use and threat of ritual violence. As Cahokia grew it pulled people from surrounding areas into its orbit; rival chiefdoms in the area appear to have gravitated toward Cahokia and been absorbed.[120]

Cahokia was a planned town and a sacred landscape, a place of mounds, plazas, and temples. "Downtown" Cahokia covered an area of five square miles. Over the years, Cahokia people built more than one hundred earthen mounds of various sizes and functions grouped around six open plazas. The remains of Cahokia's spectacular mounds can still be seen after five hundred years of erosion. The central mound—known as Monks Mound after Trappist monks who lived in the area in the nineteenth century and planted gardens on its terraces—was built in stages between 1050 and 1200 and comprised four terraces. Covering sixteen acres at its base, standing one hundred feet high, and containing twenty-two million cubic feet of earth, it is the largest ancient earthwork in North America. "What a stupendous pile of earth!" declared Henry Brackenridge, the first person to describe in detail Cahokia and other sites that Lewis and Clark had missed. He was "struck with a degree of astonishment, not unlike that which is experienced in contemplating the Egyptian pyramids." Later writers have drawn similar comparisons.[121] Monks Mound supported a temple and faced south toward the sun. Four plazas surrounded it, one at each of the cardinal directions. A wooden palisade encircled the great mound and its great plaza. Other mounds and plazas lay outside the wall, as did an exact circle of sacred red cedar posts that archaeologists christened the "American Woodhenge" and that was probably used during the twelfth century as a calendrical device to determine the exact timing for the performance of ceremonies.[122] Other town sites, each with their own mounds, plazas, and wattle-and-daub houses, lay scattered outside Cahokia.

Like Chaco, Cahokia offers glimpses into a world we have lost and leaves us with more questions than answers. Burial practices provide some of the most compelling evidence of the hierarchical nature of Cahokian society. Excavations at Cahokia's Mound 72, a seven-foot-high burial mound, revealed high-status individuals interred with thousands of marine shells; elaborate displays of goods; artifacts fashioned from nonlocal materials such as copper, mica, and chert; and slaves and young women to accompany them. One man was laid out on a platform of twenty thousand shell beads arranged in the form of a bird; another grave contained fifty young women; many skeletons displayed evidence of ritual mutilation and sacrifice. After each elite burial, another layer of

4. Cahokia Mounds, ca. 1150, by Lloyd K. Townshend. (Courtesy, Cahokia Mounds State Historic Site)

earth was added to the mound. Ordinary folk were buried in both mound centers and outlying locations and were accompanied by common objects or by nothing at all.[123]

Conventional wisdom interprets the presence of numerous large mounds to indicate large populations controlled and organized by a chiefly elite, but conventional wisdom sometimes rests on assertion and assumption rather than hard evidence. Large mounds and accumulations of fancy goods do not necessarily mean a heavily populated, economically specialized, and politically centralized society. Spiritual motivation rather than a controlled labor force may explain Native American mounds.[124] The ethnohistory of the Southeast indicates the existence of some kind of hierarchy, but much of what we think we know about Cahokia may be little more than our best guess.

Archaeologists debate, sometimes vehemently, about whether Cahokia was a chiefdom or a state; the extent to which Cahokian society was hierarchical and politically centralized; how power was projected; the role of ritual violence, sacred ceremonies, and trade as measures of social and political control; the nature and extent of Cahokia's influence on surrounding communities and distant peoples; the purposes and meanings of exotic goods excavated from Cahokian burial mounds; what distinguished Cahokia from other Mississippian societies; whether labor was specialized; and the exact role of the American Bottom environment in Cahokia's rise and decline.[125] Some see it as a complex chiefdom—a kinship-based society in which leaders inherited their positions and maintained them through control of knowledge, displays of wealth and power, and personal qualities and charisma. Others see it as a state—a society characterized by distinct social classes; a bureaucracy; a market economy; coercive power; and the control of religion, resources, and territorial expansion—or at least an incipient state. Cahokia never quite became a state, says Thomas Emerson, but "it sure as hell is a different kind of chiefdom."[126]

As do scholars of ancient North America everywhere, scholars of Cahokia disagree about numbers. It was the largest settlement north of the Rio Grande until it was surpassed by New York City and Philadelphia at the end of the eighteenth century. But population estimates vary widely: was Cahokia an urban center with high-density occupation, or was it an aggregation of monumental architecture and ritual spaces, which do not necessarily denote a large residential populace? At its height, Cahokia and its surrounding area may have supported a population somewhere between ten and thirty thousand—probably about the size of medieval London. Cahokia itself may have had fewer than ten thousand inhabitants; larger estimates likely embrace the whole population of the American Bottom.[127]

Rich agriculture and riverine transportation tied Cahokia to long-distance interregional exchange routes reaching into a vast hinterland. Most of the goods traveling by river in the heart of the continent passed its way. Cahokians exchanged items and ideas with communities as far north as Red Wing and Lake Pepin in Minnesota, with Aztalan in Wisconsin, as well as in Iowa and at the junction of the Ohio and Mississippi Rivers. Much exchange probably took the form of reciprocal gift giving among elites rather than marketplace transactions. Shells from the Atlantic, copper from Lake Superior, obsidian from the Rocky Mountains, and mica from the southern Appalachians all made their way to Cahokia.[128] For three hundred years Cahokia loomed large as a political, economic, and ceremonial center in the heart of the continent.[129]

In the fourteenth century, Cahokia went into decline. Consistent with just about every other aspect of Cahokia's history, scholars disagree about the rate and causes of the decline.[130] It may have come from within, a product of political instability and increasing social discord. Most likely, growing population depleted the surpluses necessary to support it and degraded the agricultural lands in the floodplain during a period of climatic change and shorter growing seasons as the "Little Ice Age" began to take hold. As in the Southwest, agricultural success as well as crop failure may have contributed to the collapse. Archaeological evidence also suggests increasing pressure from enemies.[131] Cahokia's population dispersed into smaller communities or migrated to other regions of the Midwest. There may have been a general pattern of movement out of the central Mississippi and lower Ohio River Valleys in the late fifteenth and early sixteenth centuries and a reshuffling of peoples. By 1500 groups speaking a variety of Siouan, Algonkian, Muskogean, and Caddoan languages likely inhabited the Mississippi Valley.[132] The decline and abandonment of the once-thriving metropolis no doubt reverberated throughout the middle of North America, and its legacies and stories had diffused among many peoples long before Europeans arrived in the area.

Europeans saw traces of the Mississippian societies that had gone before in the Natchez chiefdom of the lower Mississippi Valley. Despite the devastation wrought by European diseases, the Natchez were still a flourishing sun-worshiping theocracy when French explorer Antoine Le

Page Du Pratz spent time among them in the early eighteenth century. The Natchez chief, the Great Sun, lived on the main temple mound and had the power of life and death over his followers; below him was a class of nobles, then a class of honored men, and finally the commoners. When the Great Sun's younger brother, the Tattooed Serpent, died, his two wives, his servant, his pipe bearer, and several old women who offered their lives were ritually strangled. Du Pratz caught a glimpse of the Mississippian mound-building cultures that had been built on corn and endured for centuries.[133] But it was a last look—the French virtually annihilated the Natchez in 1731.

Corn Towns on the Prairies

In the early 1930s, Oklahoma was associated with dust bowl poverty rather than get-rich-quick schemes and opportunities for great wealth. But some people hit pay dirt there. Relic hunters excavating earthworks at Spiro in eastern Oklahoma literally mined burial mounds for their treasures and at one point even attempted to dynamite them. Craig Mound, the largest of the earthworks, yielded a mass of beads, pipes, pendants, pots, copper plaques, marine shell gorgets, and other ceremonial art that found a ready market among private dealers and museums. Newspapers at that time described it as a "King Tut Tomb in the Arkansas Valley." Public repulsion at the vandalism of the relic hunters and a sudden awakening to the pre-Columbian artistry contained in the mounds prompted the Oklahoma legislature in 1935 to pass an antiquities act, one of the earliest state statutes to attempt to reduce looting. The artifacts that survived the plunder, especially the fragments of shell cups and gorgets that were scattered across the country in museums and private collections, revealed that Spiro had been a major Mississippian political, ceremonial, and trade center.

Dit-the, or Spiro, lay at the western edge of the Mississippian world. Located on the Arkansas River between the Ozark Highlands and the Ouachita Mountains where the woodlands taper off and merge into the vast plains, it shared the iconography and ideology of the southeastern ceremonial complex and engaged in exchange networks that fanned west across the plains. High-ranking chiefs demonstrated and reinforced their power through rituals, distribution of food, exchange of prestige items, and sumptuous mound burials. Like Cahokia, Spiro was a town of temples and ritual spaces, a center for the conduct of seasonal ceremonies and the rituals that accompanied planting, harvesting, and death. Occupied from about A.D. 800, Spiro lacked the fortifications of other large Mississippian civic-ceremonial centers. Like many of those centers, it was abandoned by about 1450, possibly as a result of climatic change that reduced reliance on sedentary farming and increased mobile buffalo hunting, thereby undermining the ranked social structures and exchange networks that had sustained the elites.[134]

Spiro's abandonment is often taken as evidence that its inhabitants moved away and that other people who became the Caddos of historic times took over. Seen from a Caddo perspective, the continuities are much stronger. Caddos originated in the lower Mississippi Valley and spread west along the river systems. The Caddoan tradition of the Arkansas River Valley thus represented the most western reach of the southeastern ceremonial complex but emerged relatively independent of Mississippian developments in the southeast and displayed considerable diversity. Caddoan societies shared corn agriculture, ranked systems of social authority, civic-ceremonial centers, and mortuary rituals with their Mississippian neighbors, but they maintained their own sociopolitical systems and economic patterns that tied them to the plains.[135]

Caddo tradition says that long ago the people lived underground in darkness. Then they began moving westward and came out of the ground into a world of light. To help them in their new world, the women carried corn and pumpkin seeds; the men, pipes and flints. Sometime between 700 and 800, they settled the area between the Arkansas River and the middle reaches of the Red, Sabine, Angelina, and Neches Rivers and adopted corn agriculture. Corn and pumpkins were the primary crops (they grew two crops of corn each year), later combined with beans and squash.[136] (Peoples living on the eastern edges of the plains began to cultivate corn and beans in fertile valley bottoms as warmer and wetter climatic conditions between about 700 and 1100 brought warm Pacific air to the plains and fostered westward expansion of the tall-grass prairie.)[137] Population grew. A new political and social system developed based on rank and status in which chiefs wielded both political and religious authority. Ceremonies brought good crops, and mounds bolstered the authority of priest-chiefs. Elite individuals were buried with exotic goods from other regions, and the Caddos participated in far-reaching exchange networks.[138]

As Caddo culture flourished two groups of Caddo societies developed separated by the Ouachita Mountains, one to the north along the

Two faces of Spiro. *(Fig. 5)* Stone pipe effigy representing a woman grinding corn from Spiro Mound, Oklahoma, ca. 1200. (Museum of the American Indian, Heye Foundation, New York. Courtesy, Werner Forman/Art Resource, New York.)

(Fig. 6) Red stone pipe bowl representing a warrior killing an enemy from Spiro Mound. (Courtesy, National Museum of the American Indian, Smithsonian Institution, neg. no. T214088. Photo by David Heald.)

Arkansas River in western Arkansas and eastern Oklahoma, the other in the mountains and south along the Red River in what is now the common border region of Louisiana, Texas, Oklahoma, and Arkansas.[139] Large towns of thatched houses built around a ceremonial plaza and burial and temple mounds, as at Spiro, were often surrounded by smaller villages scattered along rivers and streams. The central town and temple mound and the outlying rural hamlets together formed a single community. The priest-chief in the town with the temple mound provided political leadership and religious ceremonies; satellite villages provided warriors, workers, and food and goods for the central town. Temple mound towns remained as ceremonial centers after the people dispersed into scattered settlements. Early Europeans identified these communities as "tribes," but they were really small chiefdoms. On occasion, a priest-chief might increase his power and territory and bring several communities together as a single chiefdom under his leadership. The Hasinai chiefdom or confederacy embraced ten such communities of subchiefdoms by the time Europeans encountered it in the seventeenth century.[140]

Individuals inherited their positions in Caddo society according to how close their genealogy placed them to the chief. Priest-chiefs, or *xinesí*, wielded great authority as heads of a lineage considered to be descended from the sun. The sun was essential to the agriculture on which Caddo society depended, and the *xinesí* performed the rituals that brought bountiful crops. The priest-chiefs controlled resources and their distribution, made decisions of peace and war, and seem to have commanded the labor and loyalty of their people. When they died, they were buried in the temples or in burial mounds, surrounded by lavish grave goods. But the *xinesí* did not rule alone with absolute power. They consulted with other high-ranking men and sought consensus; they led by example rather than by coercion; and their authority depended upon their generosity—by redistributing wealth, tributes, and food among their people, they created obligations and built loyalty.[141] The *xinesí* ruled a large multicommunity chiefdom. Below the *xinesí*, the *caddí* governed a single community. The *caddí* held office by heredity and for life; they designated the time for planting and deployed the labor, presided over the temple, and handled daily affairs with the advice and assistance of a council of high-ranking elders. *Canahas*, principal men and elders from the outlying villages, represented their communities. Lesser functionaries occupied other ranks and fulfilled other duties.[142]

Divided by rank and status, Caddo society was bound by clan and kinship and by shared subsistence practices. Men broke the soil, but women planted the crops. Elder women controlled the dome-shaped lodges that housed members of several related families and also controlled the fields. When Caddos went on foot to the prairies in the fall, the men hunted buffalo and the women dressed the meat and hides, though deer hunting was more important in prehorse days.[143]

Located where the southeastern woodlands met the western prairies and producing bountiful crops, the Caddos were well placed to participate in exchange networks. Key trails fanning as far afield as Florida and Casas Grandes, Cahokia and the Rio Grande pueblos passed through

Caddo country, linking the Caddos to distant Indian worlds and positioning them at the crossroads of trade. The Caddos probably exchanged corn, beans, and squash to the Wichitas and other Plains people for buffalo meat. They traded salt, which they obtained from saline springs near the Red and Ouachita Rivers, to southeastern Indians. They earned a reputation as bow makers and traded bows and the bois d'arc, or Osage orange wood, from which they made them. As evidenced by excavations at Spiro, the trade networks furnished the Caddos with many exotic, status-enhancing ceremonial goods: seashells from the Florida Gulf Coast, copper from the Great Lakes, mica and marble from the Appalachians, galena and flint from the Ozarks, and ceramics.

Caddo chiefs controlled the trade, redistributing some of the imported goods and further bolstering the theocratic chiefdoms they headed. The chiefs acquired the goods needed to perform the religious rituals that brought forth the crops that fed the people and fueled the trade that brought the goods.[144] The exchange networks also spread ideas and influences. At the westernmost edge of the Mississippian culture tradition, the Caddos appear to have helped spread the ceremonial complex that dominated the Southeast between 1250 and 1450. Goods displaying characteristic ceremonial complex motifs have been unearthed at Caddo sites, and Caddo items and southeastern items have been found together at northern and southern plains sites.[145]

Over the course of more than five hundred years, the Caddos developed powerful political chiefdoms, organized complex ranked societies, erected ceremonial centers and temple mounds, and participated in long-distance exchange networks. At their height they may have numbered more than two hundred thousand people.[146] The people who emerged from underground with corn seeds in their hands had built an impressive civilization.

Then, around 1350, they experienced a series of crises. Decreased rainfall on the central plains and prairies made corn production more precarious. Caddo fields could no longer sustain the large concentrations of population and the hierarchical social system that had developed. Chiefs whose power rested on their demonstrated ability to intercede with the gods and ensure good crops lost prestige. The Caddos stopped building earthen temples and burial mounds. Burial practices became less elaborate, and the Caddos began to bury their dead individually rather than holding mass burials. Chiefdoms and hierarchical societies survived, but the great chiefdom at Spiro broke apart. Many of its inhabitants dispersed into smaller villages; others moved south to join Caddos living along the Red River and in east Texas.[147]

The Caddos had to adjust to the new conditions. Oral tradition indicates that the people turned their attention to the west.[148] During the first half of the fifteenth century, they supplemented their trade connections to the east and southeast with more extensive trade with Wichitas who lived in semisedentary villages along the upper Brazos, upper Red, and upper Canadian Rivers. The Wichitas had already established trade with the Pueblo peoples, exchanging buffalo meat for corn: as climate change pushed the buffalo farther east, where the grass was more lush, the Pueblos found it more difficult to get the meat they wanted to supplement their corn diet, while the Wichitas, who had access to the herds, needed more corn in trade to supplement shortages caused by the drought. The Caddos began to tap into this trade system by carrying pottery, salt, and bois d'arc to the Wichitas and getting from the Wichitas items they had in turn obtained from the Pueblos. The Red River was a natural avenue to the Rio Grande villages, and as trade gathered momentum, the Caddos began to trade more directly with the Pueblos.[149]

But direct Caddo-Pueblo exchange was barely established before the arrival of Athapaskan peoples onto the southern plains disrupted it. Incoming Athapaskan hunter-gatherers formed exchange alliances with Pueblo farmers in the Pecos Valley and Galisteo Basin, squeezing out the Wichitas and Caddos as the major suppliers of buffalo meat to the Pueblos. Caddo connections with the Pueblos did not evaporate entirely (Francisco Vásquez de Coronado found a couple of Caddoan speakers at Pecos in 1541), but the Caddos had to look elsewhere and make new trade connections. They made them with the Jumanos and Coahuiltecans to the south. No sooner had they adjusted to the Athapaskan intrusion than other people on the move—Spaniards from Hernando de Soto's expedition in the east and from Coronado's expedition in the west—stumbled into their world.[150] Coronado met Teyas and Apaches in the Texas Panhandle. Sixty years later, Juan de Oñate met Apaches but no Teyas. In years to come, escalating European competition and shifting Native balances of power placed the Caddos and their neighbors in a cauldron of conflict and upheaval.

Hunters and horticulturalists living in small communities scattered along the tributaries of the Republican River in present-day western Nebraska and Kansas were growing corn by 1000, the earliest people to have attempted cultivation of domestic crops west of the one hundredth meridian. At the beginning of the thirteenth century a huge drought struck the Great Plains, and people abandoned their earth lodges and moved east. But horticulturalists had reestablished themselves on the Loup River by the fifteenth century as the climate improved.[151]

Pawnee people established a balance between hunting and planting corn. They built their earth lodges, planted their crops, and spent about half the year in the valleys of the Loup, Republican, and Platte Rivers. In winter and summer they moved west to hunt buffalo. Through their ceremonies they annually renewed and maintained the earth, and their seasonal cycles of planting and hunting followed elaborate rituals. In Pawnee cosmology the stars served as intermediaries between *tirawahat* (heaven) and earth. The stars gave the Pawnees medicine bundles that governed the ceremonial cycle of rituals necessary to ensure successful hunts and harvests. Pawnees grew at least four varieties of sacred corn. White or Mother Corn, the most sacred, represented a star in the southwestern sky (the evening star); black corn represented a star in the northeast; yellow corn, a star in the northwest; and red corn, a star in the southeast. Four ancient Skidi Pawnee villages are said to have had four bundles known as the Four Directions bundles, and the villages were arranged so as to represent on earth the position of the stars in the heavens from which the bundles had come: the southwestern village had the white corn bundle; the northeastern village the black corn bundle, and so on. Four large posts in the Pawnee earth lodges represented the four stars and their colors, and corn of each color was used in rites performed at the foot of each post. Pawnee priests observed the positions of the stars to learn exactly when to plant, when to hunt, and when to begin the ceremonies that ensured the continuation of the whole cycle. Sacred corn kernels were kept in the sky bundles and ritually planted each season. One of the plants became Young Corn Mother, who would watch over the people and ensure a good harvest. Only by obtaining this life-giving contact through ceremony could the Pawnees be certain that corn would grow and buffalo be hunted. When Quaker missionaries in the nineteenth century attempted to persuade the Pawnees to give up hunting and concentrate on farming, their arguments made no sense: buffalo meat was vital to the ceremonies pledged to the medicine bundles to bring good crops.[152]

Pawnee women produced those crops using digging sticks, rakes made from antlers, and hoes made of trimmed and sharpened buffalo scapulas with wooden handles. Prior to planting the corn seeds, Pawnee men helped to clear the fields. The women first soaked the kernels and, when they were ready for planting, dug small holes and placed six or seven kernels in each corn hill. As elsewhere in America, corn, squash, and beans were planted in the same fields. In time, Pawnee women grew seven varieties of pumpkins and squash, eight varieties of beans, and at least thirteen varieties of corn. Sacred corn was grown in a separate consecrated field to prevent it from being contaminated by common corn.[153] Women tended and watched their corn "as a mother cherishes her children," wrote ethnobotanist Melvin Gilmore, looking back from the 1920s. Anthropologist Gene Weltfish said that the young corn plant was carried through a series of ritual steps, symbolizing a girl's birth, infancy, and growth to first motherhood. "The corn would then mature and become Mother of the people."[154]

A semisedentary horticultural way of life, in which people grew corn in the river valleys and hunted buffalo on the plains, was also introduced by about 1000 into the northern plains.[155] On the Great Bend of the Missouri River, Arikaras, Mandans, and Hidatsas transformed corn to fit their environment and built communities based on corn. Corn growing constituted a reenactment of ancestors' stories and a reaffirmation of their identity. In the Arikara creation story Mother Corn led her people into the Missouri Valley and turned herself into corn so the people would have seed to plant.[156] By the eighteenth century, Lakota winter counts used the symbol of an ear of corn to depict both Arikara and Pawnee enemies.[157]

The Mandans were really "corn people living down underground," say tribal traditions, but many hundreds of years ago the Mandan "corn people" emerged onto the earth's surface somewhere near the Missouri River. After the people reached the upper world, their chief, Good Fur Robe, located and laid out their first village with the houses in rows to represent a field of corn and allotted fields among the families and seeds to the women.[158] Mandans and Hidatsas entrusted rituals for ensuring good crops to the corn priest and to the women of the Goose society. The corn priest distributed the sacred seed and sang and drummed for the Goose society. Goose society women made ceremonial offerings when geese and other water birds began migrating south in the fall. The geese took the spirits of the corn and other crops with them to the Old Woman Who Never Dies, who lived during the winter in a large earth lodge on an island near the mouth of the Mississippi River. Not until the geese returned in the spring, as messengers from the Old Woman Who Never Dies, did the women of the Goose society begin preplanting feasts and fertility songs. Some women were believed to have corn spirits in their body and had special powers, notably, the ability to pull ears of corn out of their throats.[159] Like the Pueblos and Pawnees, Mandan and Hidatsa women sang up their corn plants, because the corn needed to be cared for like a child.[160]

Huge cornfields tended and harvested by Mandan, Hidatsa, and Arikara women provided an agricultural surplus that became the basis for tribal prosperity and trade with hunters from the plains. Trader Alexander Henry noted that Hidatsa women not only grew the corn, they also negotiated the terms of its exchange.[161] Spanish, French-Canadian, and British traders, followed by Lewis and Clark, remarked on the cornucopia that attracted dozens of Plains tribes to the earth lodge villages of the Mandans, Hidatsas, and Arikaras. The men of the Lewis and Clark expedition consumed several hundred bushels of corn during their winter at the Mandan villages in 1804–5.[162]

Corn at Contact

By the time Europeans penetrated Indian America, corn had spread to the limits of its growing season. When Frenchman Jacques Cartier visited the Iroquoian town of Hochelaga (modern Montreal) in 1536, he found it inhabited by several thousand people and surrounded by extensive fields of corn. The Hochelagans brought the Frenchmen fish and loaves of corn bread and threw so much of it into their boats "that it seemed to rain bread."[163] Gabriel Sagard, a Récollet missionary who visited the Hurons north of Lake Ontario in the 1620s, said that Huron women using wooden hoes grew enough corn each year so that they had a two- or three-year surplus to guard against crop failure and enough left over to trade to other tribes. Huron cornfields were kept so clear of weeds that they looked like roads, but they were so huge that Sagard, traveling from village to village, lost his way in the cornfields more often than in the prairies and forests. Jesuit Jean de Brébeuf said the Hurons prepared corn in more than twenty different ways.[164] Nicolas de La Salle reported corn "*everywhere*" throughout the Great Lakes region in the early 1680s.[165] Nicolas Perrot, who lived among them in the late seventeenth century, reported that the Great Lakes Indians' favorite food was corn, kidney beans, and squash. Without them the Indians thought they were going hungry, no matter how much meat and fish they might have, "Indian corn being to them what bread is to Frenchmen."[166]

But corn was not everything. The hunting and farming ways of life that Indian peoples pioneered in the West did not develop in isolation. In large swaths of the country they interacted and were mutually dependent: hunters supplemented their meat diets with the carbohydrates the farmers produced; farmers needed meat, protein, and buffalo robes. Corn was an important source of food not only to the people who grew it but to hunting peoples who traded with them. Spaniards saw Plains hunters travel on foot to trade buffalo meat and robes for corn at Taos, Pecos, and Picuris pueblos on the eastern and northern frontiers of Pueblo country. They also saw them trading other Indians as slaves. Spaniards supplemented Pueblo agriculture; they introduced wheat, barley, cabbage, onions, lettuce, radishes, cantaloupes, and watermelons from their Iberian homelands, and Oñate brought north crops that were native to Mexico: chilies, tomatoes, Mexican varieties of beans, and cultivated tobacco. He also brought new types of corn previously unknown to Pueblo farmers: a variety called Cristolina de Chihuahua, characterized by a long, large cob, is believed to have cross-pollinated with native corns, producing a hybrid that greatly increased crop yields. Almost two centuries later, despite the disruptions to the Native economy unleashed by Spanish colonialism, the governor of New Mexico wrote: "Agriculture comes so natural to these Indians that their pueblos are the storehouses of all kinds of grain (especially corn). Thither come the Spanish citizens to make purchases."[167]

Indians who had mastered corn production were quick to adopt new crops and fruits from the Old World even before they had met Europeans. When the French reached the Arkansas River in the 1680s they found Quapaw women growing corn, pumpkins, melons, sunflowers, beans, as well as peaches and plums; Spaniards in 1690 saw Teyas fields planted with corn, beans, pumpkins, and watermelons.[168] Food became one of the most important components in the development of frontier exchange economies.[169]

Invading European armies relied on fields and stores of Indian corn to supply them and targeted those same food supplies as the most effective way of inflicting damage on Indian communities. Spanish armies reeled from Indian village to village—from corn supply to corn supply—as they wandered across the South.[170] Coronado and Oñate's conquistadors depended on Pueblo corn. French armies burned Iroquois crops in the eighteenth century; a French campaign against the Foxes in 1728 cut down corn "of so great a quantity that one could not believe it without seeing it."[171] The British razed Cherokee cornfields in 1760. Gen. John Sullivan's troops burned thousands of bushels of corn and cut down orchards during their march through Iroquois country in 1779; "the Quantity of Corn in the towns is far beyond what any body has imagined," reported one of the army's physicians. Gen. Anthony Wayne's victory at Fallen Timbers in 1794 allowed him to destroy the Indian cornfields on the Auglaize and Maumee Rivers in northwestern Ohio; Wayne called the area "the grand emporium of the hostile Indians of the West" and said he had never seen "such immense fields of corn, in any part of America, from Canada to Florida."[172]

Long before Europeans arrived in North America, corn had made its way from Mexico into the Indian West and spread north and east into the woodlands. Indians were growing some seven hundred species of corn. For thousands of years most of Indian America pulsed with the quiet rhythm of planting, cultivating, and harvesting corn. Countless generations of women sang up the stalks and ground the kernels into flour by scraping large manos on heavy metates with deep troughs or by pounding pestles into mortars. Peoples who did not grow corn traded for it. Invaders stole it and destroyed it. It fed Indians and pioneers and shaped the history of North America over hundreds of years. Eventually, in final irony, the U.S. government ignored that history and insisted that Indian people give up their old ways of life and become farmers.

Part 2

Invaders South and North, 1500–1730

Chapter 3

Sons of the Sun and People of the Earth

People lived short and sometimes violent lives. Most of them died in the same place they were born. They communicated by the spoken word, observed natural phenomena for meanings and omens, and embodied "every event, every action . . . in expressive and solemn forms, which raised them to the dignity of a ritual." The description refers not to precontact Indian America—although it fits—but to late medieval Europe.[1] But in the fifteenth century, wrote the Scottish historian William Robertson in his 1777 *History of America*, "Providence decreed that men were to pass the limits within which they had been so long confined, and open themselves to a more ample field wherein to display their talents, their enterprise and courage." Richard Haklyut likened the migrations of Europeans to the swarming of bees and saw the colonies as a place where "superfluous peoples" could create the kind of lives denied them in Europe. The expansion of Europe meant the invasion of America and the eventual destruction of much of the world that Indian peoples had created by 1500. It also meant the creation of new worlds for Indians and Europeans alike, of new societies unlike anything that had existed previously in Europe or America.[2]

Spain led late medieval Europe's assault on Indian America. In the sixteenth century Spaniards hammered at the southern portals of the Native American West, pushed deep into the continent, and left searing impressions in many Indian communities. In their journals, chronicles, reports, and cartography, the Spaniards left glimpses of an Indian world that at this distance we can perhaps only imagine.[3] In those writings, as José Rabasa points out, they also began the process of producing colonial knowledge and imposing colonial rule: writing, "as the memory of subordination, as the record of theft, as the erasure of culture, as the process of territorialization, and as the imposition of regimes of law," created and perpetuated power structures.[4]

Muslim power had limited Spain's expansion and influenced its development throughout the Middle Ages. The marriage of Ferdinand, king of Aragon, to Isabel, queen of Castile and León, provided a unity that Spain had formerly lacked, and in January 1492, their armies took possession of Granada, the last Moorish stronghold on the Iberian peninsula. Ferdinand and Isabel's grandson, Charles I of Spain, completed the unification of the peninsula—with the exception of Portugal, which was added in 1580. The once-embattled and divided Spanish enjoyed a century of power and empire building.

Seven centuries of warfare to drive out the "infidels" left an indelible mark on the Christian warrior culture of Spain. After Christopher Columbus hit land in October 1492, Spaniards soon looked across the ocean for new empires to build; young noblemen looked to America for infidels to fight. As the "God-appointed scourge of Islam," Spaniards employed the language of the *reconquista* to describe their conquests of Indian lands; the conquistadors were the heirs of El Cid, the legendary knight who had fought the Moors in the eleventh century.

Spanish law required Spanish conquistadors to read to the Indians they encountered the *requerimiento,* a document worked out by theologians in 1513 at the request of the king of Spain. Indian people understood neither its language nor its concepts. The *requerimiento* required them to acknowledge the Church as supreme over the world, the pope as high priest, and the king and queen of Spain as lords of their lands. If they did so, the Spaniards would receive them in love and charity, leave them in possession of their lands and free from servitude, and not compel them to become Christians. But if they refused, the *requerimiento* continued, "we shall forcibly enter into your country and shall make war against you in all ways and manners that we can, and shall subject you to the yoke and obedience of the Church and of their Highnesses; we shall take you and your wives and your children, and shall make slaves of them, and as such shall sell and dispose of them as their Highnesses may command; and we shall take away your goods, and shall do all the harm and damage that we can, as to vassals who do not obey, and refuse to receive their lord." Furthermore, the blame for these deaths would lie with the Indians, not with the Spaniards, who had given the Indians fair warning.[5] Derived from the Muslim *jihad* and incorporating an Islamic-inspired summons to submit to a superior religion, the *requerimiento* was, in historian Patricia Seed's words, a "ritualized protocol for declaring war against indigenous peoples."[6]

Armed with a papal mandate to extend Christianity to the new lands and a royal mandate to reduce Native peoples to submission, Spaniards, more than any other colonizing power, aspired to rival Rome as "lords of all the world."[7] The empire they built was enormous. As Herbert Bolton pointed out more than eighty years ago, the colonies Spain established in North America were the "tail of the dog"; the real Spanish American empire lay between the Rio Grande and Buenos Aires. While France and England established tiny and sometimes abortive settlements on the East Coast of North America, Spaniards set up governments, cities, churches, and schools in South America. The universities of Lima and Mexico were founded in 1551, eighty-five years before Harvard. Potosí, in what is now Bolivia, was the richest mining center in the world and had a population of 120,000 in 1581. In New Spain, the frontier moved north, not west. Viewed from Madrid, Lima, or Mexico City, the colonies and outposts Spain established in what is now the American West were the northern military and missionary frontiers of a great South American empire.[8]

Indian peoples from Florida to California, from Peru to the Great Plains felt the impact of Spanish power and purpose. Spanish soldiers, priests, and colonists brought huge changes to the Indians' world. They also became a part of that world. They lived with Indians, exploited them, tried to convert them, fought them, and made allies with them against common enemies. Like many other Spaniards, when Capt. Hernando de Alarcón met Indians on the Colorado, "I gave them to understand that I came from the sun, at which they were very amazed."[9] Indian people had ample opportunity to question whether Spaniards were sons of the sun or of less divine parentage.

First Sons

In the late fall of 1528, Indians in east Texas came upon a group of bearded and bedraggled men who had washed up on the Gulf Coast. The Indians, probably Karankawas, were astonished and brought their women and children to look at the strangers, who were so thin they looked "like the figure of death itself." The Indians took pity on them (wept for them, the chronicle said), fed them roots and fish, and gave them shelter in their village. Then "half the natives died from a disease of the bowels."[10] The strange men were Spanish soldiers, would-be conquistadors and survivors of an ill-fated expedition that had landed first in Florida. It was the first of many encounters between Indians and Spaniards in the American West.

After Spanish soldiers and diseases devastated Native populations in Cuba and Hispaniola and toppled Native empires in Mexico and Peru, they pushed north. Motivated by tales of fabulous lands and riches and pursuing mythical goals, the northern expeditions were doomed to failure. Instead of winning epic victories, they became desperate struggles for survival; in place of heroic stories of conquest, they produced what one scholar has termed a "narrative discourse of failure."[11] In 1513 Juan Ponce de León skirted the coast of Florida. In 1521 he died there from wounds sustained in a battle with local Indians. Other Spaniards explored the Florida coastline, some of them looking for slaves. Lucas Vásquez de Ayllón attempted to establish a colony in 1526, but disease, hunger, and Indian resistance defeated his efforts.

The next year, King Charles I dispatched Álvar Núñez Cabeza de Vaca as royal treasurer and chief constable to accompany the expedition of Pánfilo de Narváez to Florida. Narváez, a veteran of campaigns in the Greater Antilles and Mexico, assembled six hundred followers and five ships, but desertions and a hurricane thinned their numbers before he reached Florida. Landing in Tampa Bay on the west coast, Narváez claimed Florida in the name of his king, then marched inland with his troops while his ships sailed up the coast with the supplies. At the Indian town of Apalachee in northern Florida, the men fled as the Spaniards approached, possibly on the assumption that warriors would not make war on women and children. They soon returned, first to ask for their families and peace and then to harass the invaders with guerrilla-style warfare.[12] Narváez marched west to the coast, but there was no sign of the ships, and his men began to die from hunger and sickness. In desperation the survivors built five makeshift boats or barges and set sail for New Spain. In November they were washed up on an island off the coast of Texas. Narváez and most of his followers returned to sea and were never seen again. Cabeza de Vaca and a few others survived, thanks to the Karankawa Indians.

The Spaniards stayed six and a half years on the Gulf of Mexico.[13] The Indians provided food and shelter; in return, the Spaniards practiced healing, which usually consisted of uttering prayers and making the sign of the cross. They traveled between the island and the mainland in search of food, often being held as slaves or captives by different bands. Most of the Spaniards died, but for Cabeza de Vaca, who had previously fought and killed Indians apparently without qualm, the Karankawas and Coahuiltecans became a lifeline.[14]

Eventually, Cabeza de Vaca and three companions—Alonso del Castillo Maldonado, Andrés Dorantes, and his Moorish slave, Estevanico—escaped to the mainland and began a long meandering trek across the West. At the Pecos River they ignored the advice of Indian guides to take a trail running southwestward, a route that would have saved them a thousand miles of hard travel through desert country. Instead they headed south across the Rio Grande, then turned northwest and headed for the Pacific Coast, which they believed to be much closer than it was. Finally, they turned south toward Mexico City. They traveled "through so many types of people and such diverse languages that memory is insufficient to be able to recount them," wrote Cabeza de Vaca.[15] On the "vast and beautiful" southern plains, they saw huge herds of buffalo. Cabeza de Vaca estimated the buffalo ranged over more than four hundred leagues and described them as about the same size as cattle in Spain but thought the meat was finer and fatter. All along the route, Indians fed on buffalo meat. They made blankets, moccasins, and shields from buffalo hides, and "they supply the land with a great quantity of hides."[16] The "people of the cows" whom Cabeza de Vaca described may have been Jumanos, since he was in their heartland, the junction of the Río Conchos and Rio Grande known as La Junta de los Ríos. Forty-seven years later, Antonio de Espejo claimed that the Jumanos remembered a black man and three white men passing through their country.[17]

Cabeza de Vaca began to practice surgery, and the Spaniards' reputation as healers preceded them in their travels. Indians treated them well and gave them food, skins, and other gifts.[18] Indians greeted and guided them, came from surrounding regions to see them, and said that "truly [they] were children of the sun." A group of Indians apparently invented the term to deceive another group, and the Spaniards took advantage of it.[19] At the town of Corazones in Sonora, the people gave them five emerald (perhaps a particularly green shade of turquoise) arrowheads and six hundred deer hearts.[20] It is not entirely clear how Cabeza de Vaca and his companions managed to become faith healers, and their claims have been disputed. They appear to have learned Native American practices of blowing, sucking, and laying on of hands and used plants, medicines, and stones believed to have special healing properties. In addition, their Christian prayers and Catholic rituals may have conveyed an impression of spirituality and power—the sign of the cross could have different meanings in different cultures. Cabeza de Vaca became a "Christian shaman." Haniel Long suggested that, by being stripped naked, spiritually as well as physically, Cabeza de Vaca found in Indian country the secret of tapping that reservoir of healing power that lies within us all but usually remains untapped. He was, says Long, "thrust into a world where nothing, if done for another, seems impossible." By the end of his journey Cabeza de Vaca recognized, in Long's words, that "the power of maintaining life in others lives within each of us, and from each of us does it recede when unused." The idea may seem far-fetched, but not apparently to modern-day Hopis, who believe that the power of healing lies in everyone.[21]

Adapting to Indian ways in order to survive gave Cabeza de Vaca a new appreciation of the Indians' humanity. Unable to assume an epic role as a conquistador, in his narrative he instead portrayed himself as an evangelist.[22] He advocated that Spanish conquest should proceed with justice, not as a campaign of destruction and looting but as a mission to bring Indians to salvation, living as settled Christians under Spanish rule. But the very moment of liberation from his years in Indian country starkly illustrated that humane conquest was a dream. In Sonora the Spaniards met an Indian wearing around his neck the buckle of a sword belt with an iron horseshoe sewn to it.[23] After they crossed the Río Yaqui, they saw more signs of Christians—and evidence of slave raids.

In 1500 Ferdinand and Isabel had issued a royal decree condemning Columbus's taking of Indian slaves in the Caribbean and outlawing the enslavement of Indians. But exceptions allowed Spaniards to enslave Indians who were guilty of cannibalism, idolatry, or sodomy or who were taken in a "just war" after refusing to heed the warnings of the *requerimiento*. Indian slavery quickly became fundamental to New Spain's economy, and Cabeza de Vaca encountered its vicious fingers reaching north. While Cabeza de Vaca and his companions were wandering the Southwest, Nuño Beltrán de Guzmán had conquered much of northwestern Mexico, looting and burning his way up the west coast and enslaving people by the thousands.[24] Nuño de Guzmán was recalled for his atrocities, but in 1533 Diego de Guzmán, his lieutenant and relative, led an expedition to the Río Yaqui, the farthest north the Spaniards had reached. The inhabitants fled for safety to the sierras, and the effects were still visible when Cabeza de Vaca and his companions arrived in the area three years later: "It was a thing that gave us great sorrow, seeing the land very fertile and very beautiful and very full of waterways and rivers, and seeing the places deserted and burned and the people so emaciated and sick, all of them having fled and in hiding." Not having sown any crops, they were reduced to eating roots

7. Nuño de Guzmán's conquest of northwestern Mexico as depicted by Guzmán's Tlaxcalan allies. (Courtesy, William L. Clements Library, University of Michigan)

and bark. They had little to give the four travelers, "being so displaced from their natural homeland that it seemed that they wished to die." They said Christians had burned their villages and carried off half the men and all the women and boys.[25]

The first Spaniards Cabeza de Vaca and his companions encountered were slave hunters. The Indians could not believe the four wanderers were Christians like the slavers. Cabeza de Vaca overheard the Indians saying that "we [Cabeza de Vaca and his companions] came from where the sun rose, and they [the slavers] from where it set; and that we cured the sick, and that they killed those who were well; and that we came naked and barefoot, and they went about dressed and on horses and with lances; and that we did not covet anything but rather, everything they gave us we later returned and remained with nothing, and that the others had no other objective but to steal everything they found."[26]

For western historian Bernard DeVoto, writing fifty years ago, Cabeza de Vaca "walked naked out of a miracle," and his story stood as both prelude and allegory for what would come later. "We ever held it certain that going toward the sunset we would find what we desired," wrote Cabeza de Vaca; "in four centuries no one ever said it more fully," wrote DeVoto.[27] Cabeza de Vaca's odyssey also fueled dreams in his own day. In Mexico City he and his companions told stories of emerald arrowheads and wealthy Indian nations in the north at a time when stories of Francisco Pizarro's conquests of the Inca Empire were fresh in people's minds. Cabeza de Vaca himself took a buffalo robe to the king's court, clear evidence of a new world to the north. Like other Spanish explorers and conquistadors, Cabeza de Vaca contributed to the culture of conquest with narratives that were designed and written with the anticipation that allegorical meanings would be drawn from the events they described.[28] But Cabeza de Vaca's example, experience, and influence could not prevail. When he and his fellow wanderers were first reunited with their countrymen, they attempted to communicate with them by ritual gift giving as they had learned in their travels through Indian country. But their offer of buffalo robes was not well received by Spaniards who thought in terms of tribute, not gift exchange.[29] Cabeza de Vaca advocated peaceful subjugation and evangelization of Native people, but even in his own administration as governor of the province of Río de la Plata from 1540 to 1545 he failed to curtail his countrymen's vicious exploitation of Indians. The Spaniards sent him back to Spain in chains.[30] Slaving and killing, not healing and humanity, became the marks of Spanish conquest. The children of the sun were a murderous brood.

In 1539 Hernando de Soto invaded what is now the southeastern United States. For four years, De Soto's army of more than six hundred men blundered and plundered their way through Florida, Georgia, Alabama, North and South Carolina, Tennessee, Mississippi, Louisiana, Arkansas, and Texas, searching for riches to match those won by Hernán Cortés in Mexico and Pizarro in Peru. They killed, kidnapped, raped, and enslaved hundreds of people and sent shock waves through Indian country.

Born in poverty in southeastern Spain a few years after Columbus's first voyage to America, Hernando de Soto came to the "new world" as a teenager and won his spurs in the bloody conquest of Panama between 1517 and 1523. He participated in the invasion of Nicaragua in 1523–

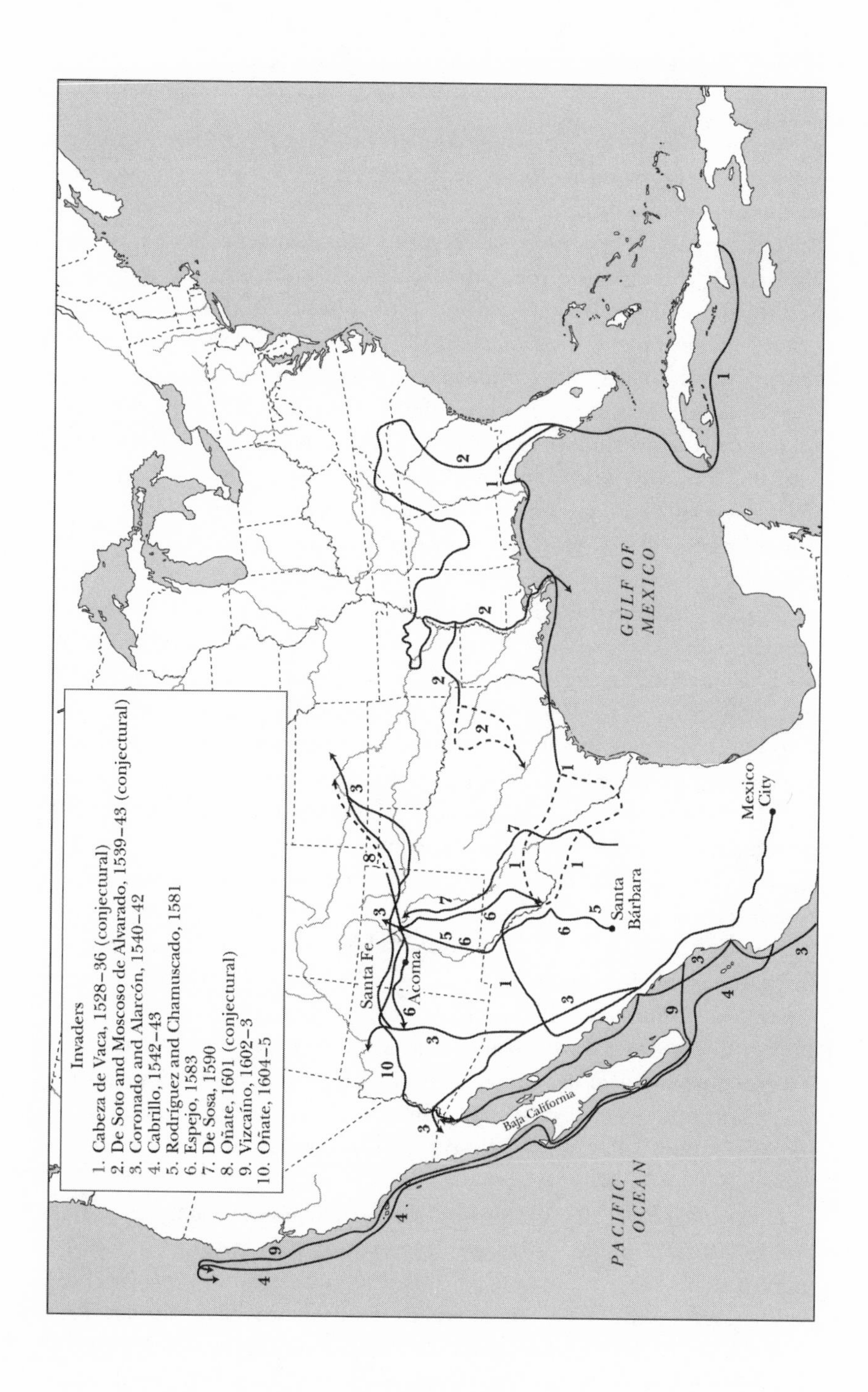

4. Spanish invasions

27 and was one of Pizarro's captains in the conquest of Peru in 1531–35, where, according to the chroniclers, he rode his charger so close to the face of the Inca emperor, Atahualpa, that the breath from the horse's nostrils moved the tassels hanging from the emperor's headgear. He earned a reputation for ruthless courage and returned to Spain a wealthy man. Appointed governor of Cuba, he secured official approval to undertake the conquest of *La Florida*, by which Spaniards meant the entire region now known as the southeastern United States.

Soon after De Soto's expedition landed at Tampa Bay in May 1539, on a foray inland the Spaniards came upon Juan Ortiz, who had been with the Narváez expedition and had been held captive by the Indians for ten years. Ortiz joined his countrymen as an interpreter. Pushing north, the Spaniards passed the following winter in Apalachee country near present-day Tallahassee, then headed on through Georgia and the Carolinas. At Cofitachequi in South Carolina, a young noblewoman and relative of the queen who ruled the town told the Spaniards she could not provide food because diseases had struck two years earlier. Instead, she allowed them to plunder freshwater pearls from a temple. Passing through Tennessee and into Alabama, the conquistadors encountered the giant cacique, or chief, Tascaluza, who fought them in a bloody day-long battle at the palisaded town of Mabila in October 1540. Hundreds of Indians died when their town became an inferno. According to the most reliable estimate, the Spaniards suffered 22 dead and 148 wounded but sustained a total of 688 wounds.[31]

Moving through the Moundville chiefdom along the Black Warrior River, the Spaniards suffered cold and hunger as they made their way across the Tombigbee River to the village of Chicaza in Mississippi, where they spent a hard winter. Increasing tensions with the Chicazas led to sporadic assaults, which took a further toll on Spanish morale and resources. In April 1541 they continued their march northwest into the Mississippi Valley, where, desperate for corn, they stormed into the province of Quizquiz.

On the banks of the Mississippi the Spaniards spent almost a month building four piraguas, or barges, large enough to transport horses and men. Indians from the chiefdom of Aquijo or Aqixo on the west bank paddled across the river, sometimes in fleets of canoes, to threaten and harass the invaders, but the actual crossing in May went unopposed. Spanish parties explored northward up the river, but the great city of Cahokia no longer existed, and they found few signs of wealth or food in that direction. De Soto's men spent two years west of the Mississippi, driven by the search for corn as much as for gold and searching for routes home as much as for paths to golden cities.[32]

When the Spaniards invaded the province of Casqui, the cacique sent gifts and came out to meet them as they approached his village, saying he wanted peace and, according to one chronicler, knowing "we were men from heaven." De Soto posed as a "son of the sun." He set up camp on the outskirts of the village and had a large cross erected on a temple mound. The ceremony apparently was followed by a rainstorm, which impressed the assembled Indians. De Soto then moved northeast up the Mississippi Valley, invaded, and spent a month in the chiefdom of Pacaha. Pacaha and Casqui were evidently rivals, and De Soto become caught up in local politics as their leaders vied for his support. Turning west, the conquistadors meandered through Arkansas, alternately negotiating and fighting with the Indians of the area. In the densely populated Arkansas River Valley, they met people who lived in wattle-and-daub houses; built flat-top mounds, though they did not use them as temples; made pottery; and, as the prestige goods recovered from Spiro mound testify, engaged in far-reaching trade. They hunted buffalo, but, most importantly from the viewpoint of the invaders, they cultivated extensive fields of corn.[33]

The army reached Tula, near present-day Fort Smith, in the fall of 1541. The Tulas differed from the Mississippian societies the Spaniards had been dealing with for months and seem to have been more closely culturally affiliated with peoples farther west. They lived in dispersed settlements, grew corn and hunted buffalo, and practiced cranial deformation and facial tattooing.[34] Tula warriors mounted fierce resistance, and, unlike many of the Indians the conquistadors had encountered previously, they were not afraid of lancers and horses. Tulas apparently hunted buffalo with lances as well as bows and arrows, and they used their lances against cavalry as they did to kill buffalo. After the Spaniards took possession of the town, the cacique and his entourage met them with a ritualized display of weeping—a formal greeting practice among Caddo peoples, as French visitors later described—and gave them gifts of buffalo hides.[35] By this time De Soto had lost 250 men and about 150 horses. There was little prospect of great populations or great wealth to the north or west. He decided to head back toward the southeast, march to the sea, and build boats that would take him and his men to Cuba or Mexico.[36]

The Spaniards passed the winter in the densely populated chiefdom of Utiangue, which stretched along the Arkansas River Valley from the region of present-day Little Rock to the mouth of the river. They obtained plenty of corn and beans from the Indians but suffered miserably from the cold. Interpreter Juan Ortiz died that winter. In March, with snow still flying, they continued down the Arkansas toward the Mississippi. De Soto was sick, and by now, in George Sabo's words, his persona as the "son of the sun" "had been rejected by everyone but himself." The Spaniards continually violated the Indians' expectations of reciprocity, and the Indians viewed them as "merely common human enemies."[37] Where the Arkansas meets the Mississippi, De Soto ordered his final slaughter: his lancers and foot soldiers killed more than one hundred people at the town of Anlico. On May 21, 1542, after drawing up his will, De Soto died of fever. His followers paddled his body to the middle of the Mississippi and sank it to prevent the Indians from finding it.

With Luis de Moscoso de Alvarado as leader, the bedraggled remnants of the once-formidable army tried to reach Mexico. Lacking ships and charts to sail the Mississippi and fearful of Indian power downriver, they resolved to go overland. For six months they wandered through southwestern Arkansas and east Texas, trying to stay alive and find their way to Mexico.[38] They were in the country of corn-growing Caddo peoples. The Indians of the chiefdom of Naguatex at first resisted their approach, but most kept at a safe distance while the Spaniards rested near the principal town in the Great Bend of the Red River, south of Fulton, Arkansas. The town consisted of dozens of farmsteads stretching along both sides of the river, a community rich in corn. The Spaniards stayed almost a month, consumed large quantities of corn, burned more, and forced Indian bearers to carry still more when they left; but when they headed back through Naguatex in the fall they found the houses they had burned had been rebuilt and were full of corn. The cacique of Naguatex provided the Spaniards with guides, probably to get them out of his territory. The guides led the invaders west and may have deliberately misled them—at least the Spaniards thought so; they hanged the guides and perhaps threw one of them to their dogs.[39]

When the Spaniards tried to cross the Red River they found it in flood, even though it was August, and were delayed for a week. Moscoso de Alvarado's motley army trudged into east Texas. Frustrated in their efforts to make headway to the west and with the countryside seeming to grow poorer the deeper they traveled into it, they turned and headed back to the Mississippi, harassed by Indians as they went. At one point,

Indian guides told them they were leading them to where there were other "Christians like us," but the reports of other Christians may have been month-old sightings of the Spaniards themselves: they were now retracing their steps.[40] They spent the winter of 1542–43 building boats and pillaging corn. In June they set sail down the Mississippi. Fending off Indian attacks from the banks and from canoes, they made it to the Gulf of Mexico. The survivors reached Spanish settlements in Veracruz in September 1543 and traveled on to Mexico City. After four years and four months and almost four thousand miles in Indian country, the conquistadors had found no great riches. Almost half of them had died in the attempt.

In the words of De Soto scholar Charles Hudson, the expedition constituted "an unimaginable calamity" for the Indian chiefdoms of the Southeast. It precipitated a long decline and marked "the beginning of the end of the world they had built for themselves."[41] Spanish terror tactics, firearms, and war dogs left a trail of devastation from Florida to Texas, and the human landscape of the South changed forever. The invaders entered a world full of Indians, passed through densely settled regions, and dealt with caciques carried on litters by their subjects. When Europeans returned to the interior regions of the Southeast in the next century, the great chiefdoms were gone, many of the towns had disappeared, and the people they met were fewer in number, less wealthy, and more scattered. Twenty years later, when Tristán de Luna led another Spanish expedition through the region, his men almost starved in places where De Soto's men had found well-fed communities. The Indians told the Spaniards their country had been powerful and prosperous until strangers looking like them had invaded it.[42]

Most of the powerful and populous chiefdoms that had dotted the Southeast in 1540 disappeared in the wake of the De Soto expedition. Scholars debate about how much of the massive depopulation and the collapse of the Mississippian societies was directly attributable to the *entrada*. It is likely that the Spaniards and their pigs and horses carried new diseases to the Indians of the Southeast, but the evidence is inconclusive. Drought and other factors took their toll. Indian populations in Arkansas declined in the century and a half following the expedition, but a disastrous drought between 1549 and 1577 and later disruptions from European diseases may have been the primary culprits. Whatever the combination of factors, Indian populations plummeted after De Soto's men passed through the region.[43]

Indian people tried to deal with the strangers by established methods of diplomacy, ritual, and gift giving, fled from their approach, harassed them with hit-and-run guerrilla tactics, and fought desperate pitched battles. The invasion doubtless disrupted balances of power among chiefdoms. The descendants of those chiefdoms rebuilt smaller communities and regrouped; later Europeans encountered villages and "tribes" of Creeks, Choctaws, Chickasaws, and others. In some cases the transition from chiefdom to tribe may already have been under way when the Spaniards passed through, and it was not complete when the first French explorers arrived at the beginning of the eighteenth century.[44] The Natchez in Mississippi preserved some of their ancient ways but also absorbed refugees from other, broken societies. When French explorers penetrated Arkansas 150 years after De Soto, they found Caddo and Quapaw villages nestled in river valleys along the region's peripheries, but the central portion of the territory was vacant. In the intervening period, Caddos had stopped building and burying their dead in elaborate mounds. Some areas, such as the Arkansas River Basin in Oklahoma where De Soto's men had encountered many flourishing communities, were abandoned. Many communities clustered together in several places and coalesced into new societies. By the eighteenth century, they emerged as regional confederacies dealing with Frenchmen to the east and a new generation of Spaniards to the west.[45]

Mexico Invades New Mexico

Pueblo peoples told and continue to tell stories of creation, emergence, and migration that brought the people from lower worlds into the present world. In the mid- to late 1500s, the Pueblos encountered other people who entered their world from the south, brought different stories, viewed the landscape in different ways, and threatened to sever the bonds that tied the Pueblos to their world and gave them their identity.

After Cabeza de Vaca and his companions arrived in Mexico City with tales of northern wonders, many Spaniards thought they were on the brink of locating the Seven Cities of Cíbola. Founded, legend had it, by seven bishops who fled from the Muslims in the twelfth century, the seven cities had not turned up in the West Indies; they must be somewhere in the vast mainland of North America.[46] The Spanish invasion of the North proceeded along several corridors. The first, established in the 1530s, reached up the west coast of Mexico from Nueva Galicia. A decade later a second, central corridor developed as the Spanish moved from one silver strike to another through Nueva Vizcaya (present-day Chihuahua and Durango) along the eastern edge of the Sierra Madre. Later routes would develop from Nuevo León into Texas in the northeast and into the Californias in the west.[47]

Antonio de Mendoza, viceroy of New Spain, dispatched a reconnaissance party northward in 1539. Franciscan friar Marcos de Niza set out toward the Zuni pueblos with Estevanico, whom he had purchased from Dorantes so that the Moor could act as guide. Estevanico forged ahead to the Zuni pueblo of Hawikuh, accompanied by some Christianized Pimas and some Tlaxcalan Indians from Mexico. He sent back messengers with a large cross, urging Marcos to hurry along to what he called Cíbola, the first of the fabled seven cities. Marcos followed in the Moor's footsteps, passing fertile valleys, meeting friendly people bedecked in turquoise, and hearing wondrous accounts of the towns to be found in the north. But then two bloodstained Indians appeared with news of Estevanico's death. Apparently, the Moor had been too aggressive in his demands for turquoise and women, although anthropologist Edmund Ladd, a member of the Zuni tribe, drawing on oral tradition, suggests that Estevanico may have been regarded as a spy for approaching Spanish forces and killed for that reason. Long-distance traders who brought macaw feathers, bells, and seashells from the south would also have brought news of Spanish slave raids: "They had seen with their own eyes whole villages wiped out by big grey-white dogs that ate the people and by men on great animals using fire sticks that could blow a hole right through you." They told how "the native people whom the white men captured were strung like rabbits on a rabbit stick and herded away to the mines to live and die in work." Estevanico, as a harbinger of Spanish conquest and ensuing chaos in the Pueblo world, apparently later gave rise to the black kachina known as Chakewaina, or Monster kachina.[48]

Marcos beat a hasty retreat but claimed to have stood on a hill within sight of Cíbola, a fine-looking pueblo, he said, "larger than the city of Mexico."[49] Rumors flew. Mendoza quickly organized another expedition, commanded by Francisco Vásquez de Coronado. According to Pedro de Castañeda Nájera, who wrote a chronicle of the expedition twenty years after it returned to Mexico, "there emanated so many tales of great wonders that in a few days there were recruited more than three hundred Spaniards and some eight hundred Indians of New Spain."[50] Coronado's force was a late medieval European army, with armor, lances, and crossbows. It was also a multiethnic invasion force composed of people from the Old World and the New. In addition to Castilian, Portuguese, Italian, and French soldiers, there were five Franciscans, Iberian-African servants and slaves, a German bugler, and a wandering Scot named Thomas Blake, rendered in the records as Tomás Blaque. Tlaxcalans, Mexicas, Tarascans, and other Native people of New Spain comprised the majority of the army, and some estimates suggest they numbered close to thirteen hundred.[51] (They had a fearsome reputation as warriors—Hernán Cortés's Tlaxcalan allies had perpetrated a slaughter of the Aztec inhabitants of Tenochtitlán that had shocked even the bloodstained conquistadors.)[52] The invasion of the northern frontier was carried out mainly by criollos (Spaniards born in America), mestizos, and allied Indians recruited to serve both as a labor force and as examples of acculturation for northern Indians. José Rabasa argues that "the culture of conquest that informed the push north beginning in the 1540s was as much the invention of Indians and mestizos from central Mexico as of Spaniards."[53] Fifteen hundred horses and mules and herds of sheep and cattle followed the army. Two ships commanded by Capt. Hernando de Alarcón were to accompany the expedition by sea. They sailed north from Acapulco up the Gulf of California, then headed up the Colorado River in small boats as far as the junction with the Gila River, where they were compelled to turn back as Coronado went inland.

When the soldiers came within sight of Cíbola, they found Hawikuh, a multistory mud and adobe town, not a glistening citadel. "The curses that some hurled at Fray Marcos were such that God forbid they may befall him," wrote Castañeda. Two hundred Zuni warriors placed themselves between the Spaniards and the town and scattered a line of sacred corn, symbolically closing the road. The Spaniards either ignored or misunderstood the gesture. According to Edmund Ladd, Coronado's arrival on July 7, 1540, probably interrupted the eight-day cycle of summer solstice ceremonies. The first skirmish occurred when the Spaniards intercepted a group of Zuni pilgrims traveling to or from the sacred lake Ko:thluwala:wa at the junction of the Zuni and Little Colorado Rivers. The smokes Coronado's men thought were signal fires were in fact part of a ceremony of the fire god Shu'la:witsi. When Coronado reached Hawikuh, the bow priests spread cornmeal across his path to indicate that the Spaniards should proceed no farther until the ceremonies were completed. Coronado had no idea what was going on. With a cry of "Santiago," the Spanish cavalry spurred across the line. The Zunis fought desperately, coming "almost to the heels of our horses to fire their arrows."

Coronado himself was knocked unconscious by stones hurled from the terraces of the pueblo. But the Spaniards soon seized Hawikuh. It was a disappointment. "Everything is the opposite of what [Marcos] related," said Coronado. "The Seven Cities are seven little villages." But the Zunis did have plenty of corn and efficient techniques for grinding it. "One of these Indian women here will grind as much as four of the Mexicans do," wrote Coronado, and he reckoned they made "the best tortillas I have ever seen anywhere." The hungry army threw open Hawikuh's storehouses and found "a sufficient supply of maize to relieve our needs."[54]

Three days after the town fell, three Indians came with turquoises and "some poor blankets" to make peace. Coronado greeted them with kind words and told them the purpose of his coming, that "they and all others in this province should become Christians and should accept the true God as their Lord and his Majesty as their king and earthly master." The Indians returned to their houses, packed up their belongings and families, and took off for the hills. Other Indians said that "it was foretold them more than fifty years ago that a people such as we are would come, and from the direction we have come, and that the whole country would be conquered." Indian women kept themselves hidden, standard practice when Spaniards arrived on the scene.[55]

Coronado's troops occupied Hawikuh until November. The commander sensed that the Indians refused "to tell me the truth in everything" because they thought he would soon have to leave. "As far as I can judge, it does not appear to me that there is any hope of getting gold or silver," he wrote glumly, but "if there is any, we shall get our share of it."[56]

From Hawikuh, Coronado sent his lieutenant Pedro de Tovar with seventeen horsemen and a detachment of foot soldiers to Tusayán, Hopi country in Arizona, which the Zunis described as "composed of seven pueblos of the same quality as their own" but with whom they were not on good terms. Juan de Padilla, a Franciscan friar "who had been a warrior in his youth," went with them. The Hopis apparently "had heard that Cíbola had been captured by very fierce men who rode animals that ate people." At the village of Kawaiokuh, the men came out to meet the Spaniards with bows, shields, and wooden clubs. They formed ranks and drew lines that they insisted the Spaniards must not cross. Speaking through an interpreter from Zuni, the Spaniards gave the Hopis "due warning." Some of the soldiers made motions to cross the line, and a Hopi warrior struck a horse with a club. Frustrated by the time being wasted in talking, Padilla said to Tovar, "Indeed, I do not know what we have come here for." When the soldiers heard this, they yelled "Santiago" and surged forward. They ran down many Indians, and others fled to the town. Immediately, the villagers came out with presents and asked for peace.[57] According to novelist and anthropologist Frank Waters, Hopis had long anticipated the prophesied return of their "lost white brother," Pahána, and Tovar was the first white man they had seen. Hopi tradition recounts that the Spaniards were conducted to Oraibi, fed, and met by the clan chiefs, but Spanish violence and curt behavior demonstrated that "Tovar was not the true Pahána." Finding no gold, the Spaniards soon departed.[58]

Spanish troops combed the area. Coronado sent García López de Cárdenas with a dozen men to the Colorado River. This time the Hopis offered no resistance when Spaniards came to their villages, and they supplied guides who led García López de Cárdenas and his men to the Grand Canyon; they were the first Europeans to see the great chasm. Castañeda listed a total of sixty-six pueblos and estimated a population of twenty thousand men.[59]

But there was no gold.

A month after Coronado took Hawikuh, a group of men arrived from Cicuye (Pecos). They said they had "learned that strange people, bold men who punished those who resisted them and gave good treatment to those who submitted, had come to make their acquaintance and be their friends." The Spaniards called the leader of the delegation Bigotes on account of his long moustache. The delegates said that if the strangers wished to travel east, they would guide them to the Rio Grande and to Pecos and even beyond to the land of the buffalo, which Bigotes described for them and showed displayed in a tattoo worn by one of his men. Coronado accepted the offer and dispatched Capt. Hernando Alvarado, Fray Juan de Padilla, and twenty men to go east with the Pecos emissaries.[60]

En route, Alvarado's men passed the towering pueblo at Acoma. Acoma warriors descended from their fortress ready to fight, but they accepted peace ("by approaching the horses, taking their sweat, and anointing themselves with it, making crosses with the fingers of their hands") and gave the Spaniards food and deerskins. What Alvarado saw as a sign of the cross was a traditional and common sign of welcome: seeing the soldiers were tired and their horses sweating and overridden, the Acomas crossed the second finger of each hand to indicate "our meeting" and crossed hands on each other to indicate "we are friends and will not harm each other." Later, as Coronado's army passed the rock,

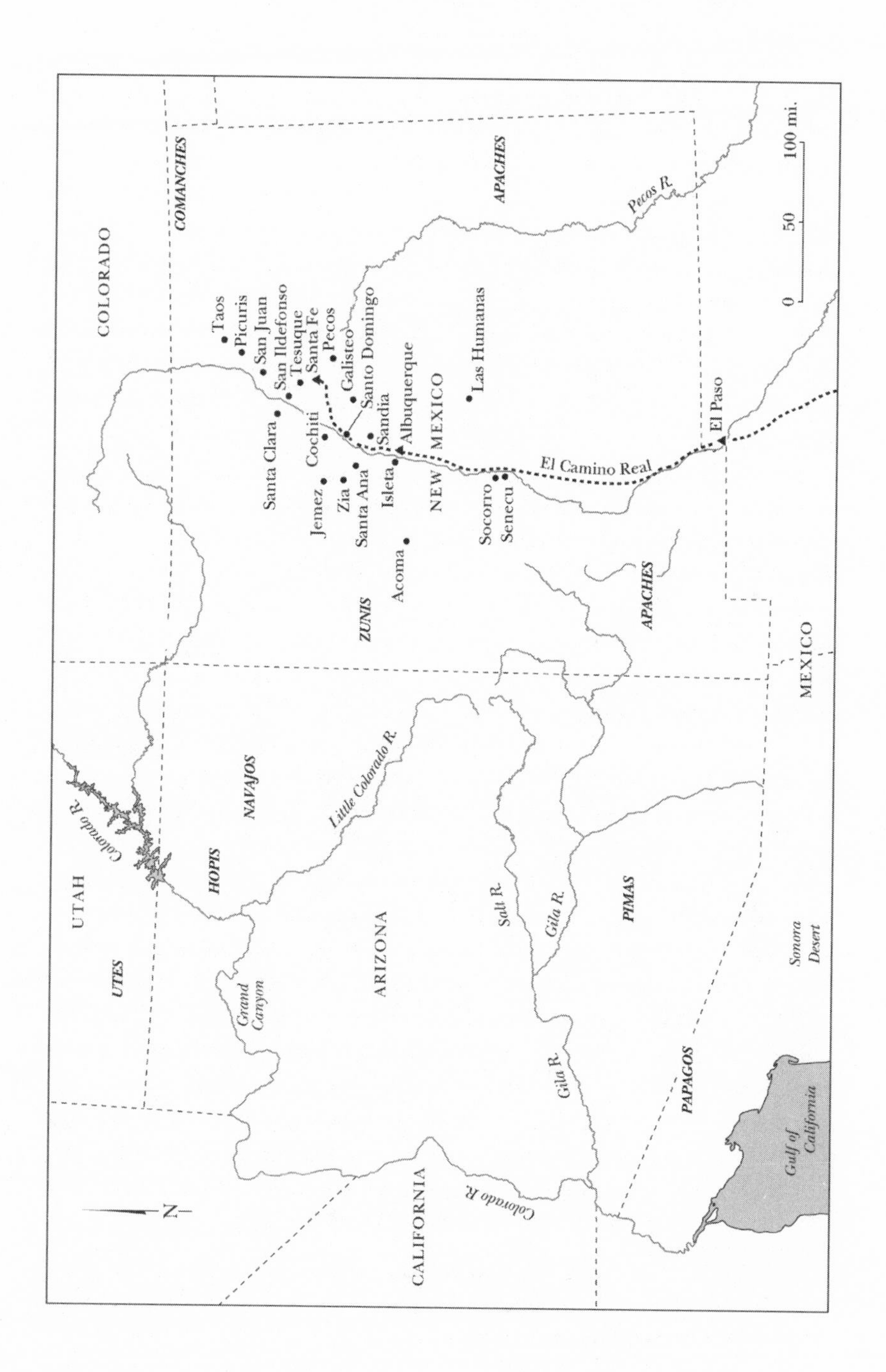

5. The Pueblo world, ca. 1680

some Spanish soldiers climbed up the narrow hand-hewn staircase to see the pueblo. They found it hard going and had to hand their weapons to one another as they clambered up the stairs. "The natives, on the contrary, go up and down so freely that they carry loads of provisions, and the women carry water, and they do not seem to touch the walls with their hands."[61]

When Alvarado reached Pecos, the people greeted the Spaniards with music from drums and bone whistles and gave them clothing and turquoise. The Spaniards recognized the functional architecture of the square pueblo, surrounded by a low stone wall and perched on a rock in the center of a vast plaza. "The houses are all alike, four stories high. One can walk on the roofs over the whole pueblo, there being no streets to prevent this." There were no doors on the ground floor, and the inhabitants used moveable ladders to climb to corridors, which also served as streets, on the inner side of the pueblos. Those houses that faced the open country sat back to back with those on the patio, and in time of war the inhabitants entered them through the interior ones. "The people of this town pride themselves that no one has been able to subjugate them, while they dominate the pueblos they wish." Such glimpses, notes Peter Nabokov, "are all that Spanish sources yield of late-period Pueblo architecture, whose built forms had undergone six centuries of change and decline."[62]

Located on a mesa overlooking the Pecos River, Pecos was the gateway from the Pueblo world to the Great Plains. It was not unusual to find Plains Indians there. Alvarado took as interpreter and guide an Indian slave from the central plains, probably a Pawnee or Wichita. The Spaniards called him El Turco (the Turk) "because he looked like one."[63] He said there were large towns and great riches in his native land of Quivira and promised to lead them there. After a reconnaissance to the plains, Alvarado proceeded to Tiguex (Albuquerque) pueblo, where General Cárdenas was preparing winter quarters, and rendezvoused with Coronado, who "rejoiced greatly" at the Turk's news. The Turk's tales grew more fantastic with each telling. He claimed that

> in his land there was a river, flowing through plains, which was two leagues wide, with fish as large as horses and a great number of very large canoes with sails, carrying more than twenty oarsmen on each side. The nobles, he said, traveled in the stern, seated under canopies, and at the prow there was a large golden eagle. He stated further that the lord of that land took his siesta under a large tree from which hung numerous golden jingle bells, and

> he was pleased as they played in the wind. He added that the common table service of all was generally of wrought silver, and that the pitchers, dishes, and bowls were made of gold.

The Turk may have had in mind mound towns on the Mississippi, but he certainly embellished his description. He told his tales with conviction and played his audience: "When they showed him jewels made of tin, he smelled them and said it was not gold, that he knew gold and silver very well, and that he cared little for other metals." According to one Spaniard, "all of us believed him." The Turk "expressed himself so well that it seemed as if what he was saying was true and that he had seen it. Later it looked as if the devil had spoken through him."[64] With images of great civilizations and great wealth beckoning them out onto the Great Plains, the Spaniards settled down for an impatient winter at Tiguex.

The southern Tewa Pueblos in the region soon regretted the Spanish presence. Spanish demands for corn, blankets, and women sparked hostilities. One soldier "ravished or attempted to ravish" a woman while the husband held his horse outside. The Indian complained to Coronado and identified the soldier, but the crime went unpunished. Violence broke out. The pueblo of Arenal, which was probably located on the east side of the Rio Grande not far from Sandia pueblo, rose in rebellion.[65] Spanish cavalry, together with Indian allies from Mexico, quickly quelled the uprising, and the Indians made peace. General Cárdenas, however, claimed to know nothing of the peace and adhered to his orders to take no prisoners. He ordered stakes driven into the ground at which to burn the Indians. Seeing the fate in store for them, the Indians fought desperately to escape. Spanish infantry drove them off, and Spanish cavalry rode them down. Castañeda said there were two hundred prisoners; other sources suggest the figure was probably closer to eighty. At any rate, "none escaped alive except a few who had remained concealed in the pueblo and who fled that night." Cárdenas was later tried in Spain for his crimes against Indians and died in prison.[66] At the pueblo of Moho, the Indians resisted the Spaniards in a siege that lasted fifty days. As their water ran low, they gave up one hundred of their women and children. Rather than surrender, they abandoned their pueblo, whereupon they "were overcome and pacified."[67] After a vicious war, the Tiwas retreated to impregnable locations atop distant mesas. They resisted Spanish inducements to return, and the "twelve pueblos of Tiguex were never resettled as long as the army remained in that region."[68]

Other Pueblos adopted the strategy of waving the Spaniards north, hoping they would get lost in the vast plains. As the ice thawed on the Rio Grande, Coronado led his army from Tiguex to Pecos in preparation for the venture to Quivira. Fourteen days' travel into the plains, near the present border of New Mexico and Texas, they met buffalo-hunting Querechos, Athapaskan-speaking people living in the Canadian River drainage and the upper part of the Llano Estacado, ancestors of the Apaches and Navajos.[69] They came out of their tents to scrutinize the strangers. According to Castañeda, they were "so skillful in the use of signs that it seemed as if they spoke" and "made everything so clear that an interpreter was not necessary." The Querechos told of a huge river and "gave lavish reports of settlements, all east of our present location."[70] Coronado's men pushed on.

The limitless Llano Estacado engulfed them and left them struggling for words to describe the power of the landscape. "Traveling in these plains is like traveling at sea," wrote one. "The land is so level that the men got lost when they draw half a league away," said another. It was "as if we were surrounded by the sea. Here the guides lost their bearings because there is nowhere a stone, hill, tree, bush, or anything of the sort," wrote Coronado. "The land is the shape of a ball," said Castañeda, "for wherever a man stands he is surrounded by the sky at the distance of a crossbow shot." Diego López and an advance party of ten men traveled twenty leagues looking for settlements but saw "nothing but cattle and sky."[71] Environmental historian Dan Flores, who has spent much of his adult life living there, describes the Staked Plain:

> It sprawls across a whopping five degrees of latitude (from 31 to 36 degrees north) and three and a half degrees of longitude (101 to 1041/2 degrees west). It is roughly 300 miles north-south by 150 miles east-west, a bit shy of 50,000 square miles altogether. Atop Luciano Mesa on its northward rim it is almost 6,000 feet above the sea, but less than 2,500 feet where the Concho River drains off its southeastern edge. That's a surface slope of only about 20 feet per mile, slight enough to be imperceptible to the eye.[72]

No wonder the Spaniards who tried to cross the Llano Estacado in the sixteenth century felt totally at sea. The violent weather of west Texas added to their discomfort and disorientation: Coronado had the priests hold a special mass to give thanks for their survival after a spring hailstorm pounded the army with great stones.[73]

Buffalo were everywhere. Indians traveled across the plains, hunting them and using dogs as pack animals. Tanned buffalo skins provided tipis, clothes, moccasins, and ropes. From the sinews the Indians made thread to tie their clothes and tipis. From the bones they shaped tools and weapons. Bladders functioned as jugs and drinking containers. Dung served instead of firewood, "since there is no other fuel in that land." The Indians' diet consisted almost wholly of buffalo meat, which they ate "slightly roasted and heated over the dung." In the winter they traveled to the nearest pueblos to trade their prepared hides.[74]

After thirty-seven days, the army reached the country of people they called Teyas. Teyas occupied the central and southern regions of the Llano Estacado when the Spaniards arrived, but their bands also ranged west into Arizona and New Mexico. Their identity and linguistic affiliation are less certain than those of their Athapaskan-speaking Querecho neighbors. They are often identified as Caddos, but many authors have suggested that they were the people later identified as Jumanos. The Teyas Coronado met may have been a band of Eastern Apaches, Jumanos, Wichitas, or Plains Caddos.[75]

Castañeda called the Staked Plain "a densely populated country," but it was not what the Spaniards were looking for, and the expedition was running short of provisions. Coronado realized the Turk had deceived them. He also realized that his expedition was too large to be supported logistically on the plains. He sent the rest of his command back to Tiguex and with a party of thirty chosen men pressed on in search of Quivira. The Turk went along in chains. They traveled for forty-eight days, living off buffalo meat cooked over fires of buffalo dung. When they reached Quivira, they found only the grass-hut villages of Wichita Indians in Kansas. Coronado spent more than three weeks in the area. He reported twenty-five villages and a great diversity of languages, "since the people in each town speak their own." The people grew corn and lived well.[76]

But there was no gold.

Coronado demanded why the Turk "had lied to them and guided them so perversely." The Indian replied that the people of Pecos had asked him to take the Spaniards out onto the plains and lead them astray. "Thus, through lack of provisions, their horses would die and they themselves would become so feeble that, upon their return, the people of Cicuye could kill them easily and so obtain revenge for what the Spaniards had done to them." Coronado had the Turk garroted.[77] Then a fall from his horse left Coronado with severe head injuries. Meanwhile, the Mixtón War, which had broken out in western Mexico, and uprisings in Sonora prompted a return. With "nothing in Quivira to induce them to return to that land," the would-be conquistadors turned wearily back to Mexico. "As nothing in this world depends on the plans of men but on the will of Almighty God, it was his design that our desires should not be fulfilled," reflected Castañeda.[78] In the spring of 1542, the dispirited army began the long trek back to New Spain, dragging Coronado on a litter between two mules. Back in Mexico City, he was charged with mismanaging the expedition and stood trial before the royal Audiencia.

Sailing up the west coast of California in 1542, Juan Rodríguez Cabrillo landed at a harbor he called San Miguel (now San Diego). Local Ipai or Kumeyaay Indians told him that in the interior "men like us were traveling about, bearded, clothed and armed . . . killing many native Indians."[79] It was a pretty apt summary of Coronado's expedition. The great silver strikes in Zacatecas diverted Spanish attention southward, and not for almost another forty years, when Spanish mines and settlements pushed north into Chihuahua, did another Spanish expedition penetrate the Pueblo world. But word of Coronado's expedition spread, memories of it lingered, and it had lasting effects in many ways. At least one member of the expedition, Juan de Troyano, brought home a Pueblo girl and married her.[80]

In 1542–43, Spain passed a series of "New Laws" designed to curb and control abuses of Indians in the Americas. They had limited effects, and in 1573 the crown introduced a second series of reforms. The new rules forbade "conquests" and established regulations for peaceful colonization and missionization of Native peoples. New ventures had to obtain a specific license from the king, and missionary initiatives were to receive preference over civilian colonization projects.[81] In fact, mining and missionizing went hand in hand as Spaniards continued to penetrate northward. In 1567 about thirty Spanish families colonized Santa Bárbara on the Río Conchos in southern Chihuahua. At first they were surrounded by the local Concho Indians, but sometime after 1579 large numbers of Tlaxcalan Indians moved in. Santa Bárbara became a mining center, and in the 1580s expeditions from there began raiding north for slaves to work the mines.[82]

In 1581 Capt. Francisco Sánchez Chamuscado and Fray Agustín Rodríguez, with two other missionaries, nineteen Indians, and seven soldiers, set out from Santa Bárbara to convert the Pueblos to Christianity and to find new mines. They doubtless encountered Jumanos as they made their way down the Conchos to La Junta. From La Junta the expedition made its way north along the Rio Grande. Chamuscado named the region San Felipe de Nuevo México; the name was soon shortened to Nuevo México.[83] The Spaniards tried to win over the Indians with gifts and impress them with their firearms, which, they thought, showed the Indians they were "children of the sun." The Indians reciprocated with corn, beans, calabashes, cotton blankets, and tanned buffalo skins, although Spanish requests for food produced some tense moments. As the Spaniards pushed up the Rio Grande they saw many pueblos on good, level land and houses clustered around well-planned plazas and streets. They counted sixty-one pueblos and recorded the number of houses and stories in the pueblos. The population may have exceeded 130,000 people.[84]

Traveling past Acoma, the Chamuscado party explored Zuni country. They were impressed by what they saw. "The valley is the best that has been discovered, since all of it is cultivated and not a grain of corn is lost," wrote chronicler Hernán Gallegos. "All of the houses are of stone, which is indeed amazing," he continued. "There is not a house of two or three stories that does not have eight rooms or more, which surprised us more than anything else, together with the fact that the houses are whitewashed and painted inside and out."[85]

One of the missionaries who attempted to make his own way back to Santa Bárbara was killed by Indians. Fray Rodríguez and the other missionary decided to remain in Tiguex country when the expedition returned home, but the Indians killed them both soon after the Spaniards left. Chamuscado himself became ill on the return journey. Following medical practice of the time, he was bled. Lacking lancets, his men used a horseshoe nail "as soldiers do in time of need." Chamuscado did not make it home.[86]

A relief party, led by Antonio de Espejo, set out in 1582 to look for the now-dead missionaries and for new mines. Espejo assured the Pueblos that he came in peace, and the Indians overcame their initial fears. The inhabitants of each town came out to meet the Spaniards, led them to their pueblos, and gave them "turkeys, corn, beans, and tortillas, with other kinds of bread, which they make more skillfully than the Mexican people," wrote Espejo.[87] The Pueblos had ample resources upon which to draw: fields planted with corn, beans, calabashes, and tobacco and crops either seasonal, dependent on rainfall, or "irrigated by means of good ditches." Espejo recorded many aspects of Pueblo life: houses of three and four stories; women grinding corn on large stones; clothing made from cotton blankets, buffalo hides, and dressed chamois skins; women, their hair neatly arranged in two whorls over their ears, wearing cotton skirts, often embroidered with colored thread, and over the shoulders a blanket like that worn by the Mexican Indians; and everyone wearing shoes or boots with soles of buffalo hide and uppers of dressed deerskin.

Espejo estimated that Acoma held more than six thousand people. "Acoma is built on top of a lofty rock, more than fifty estados high," he wrote, "and out of the rock itself the natives have hewn stairs by which they ascend and descend to and from the pueblo. It is a veritable stronghold, with water cisterns at the top and quantities of provisions stored in the pueblo." Acoma's fields were located two leagues from the pueblo near the San Jose River and were irrigated by streams diverted from a marsh near the river. The Acomas gave Espejo's men blankets and chamois skins, leather belts made from strips of buffalo hide, and supplies of corn and turkeys.[88]

But Spanish abuses and demands for food and turquoise quickly turned hospitality to hostility. The conquistadors retaliated with brutality: at a pueblo called Puaray Espejo had thirty Indians burned alive when the villagers refused to feed his troops. At Zuni the people told the Spaniards there was gold in a region of lakes sixty days' travel away and that Coronado had traveled only twelve days before turning back. In Hopi country, forewarned of hostility, Espejo's men took 150 Indians with them, but the Hopis greeted them with gifts of corn and cotton blankets.[89]

Espejo recommended the Rio Grande Valley as a favorable site for colonization, but, not surprisingly, the Pueblos resisted the next Spanish *entrada* from the south. When Gaspar Castaño de Sosa led a party of colonists to Pecos late in December 1590, the residents took up defensive positions on the terraces of the pueblo. The Spaniards first offered gifts, then a demonstration of their firepower before taking the town by storm. The inhabitants disappeared through a labyrinth of underground passages, leaving stores of corn, beans, and flour to the Spaniards. The pueblo held "such an abundant supply of corn that everyone marveled. . . . [E]ach house had two or three rooms full of it, all of excellent quality." All along the Rio Grande, Castaño de Sosa and his men saw fields of corn and other vegetables irrigated by canals that "would be incredible to anyone who had not seen them with his own eyes."[90] Castaño de Sosa's expedition was illegal, as he had not obtained a contract from the viceroy for the colonization expedition. He was arrested and returned to Mexico in chains.

8. Pictograph of Spaniards on horseback in Cañon del Muerto, Arizona. (Courtesy, Arizona State Museum, University of Arizona. Photo by Helga Teiwes.)

About three years after Castaño de Sosa's expedition, Antonio Gutiérrez de Humaña and Francisco Leyva de Bonilla launched another unauthorized expedition. Leaving Santa Bárbara with a small party, they followed in the tracks of Chamuscado and Espejo down the Río Conchos and up the Rio Grande. They spent about a year at San Ildefonso pueblo, presumably searching for mines, and then set out in search of Quivira. Somewhere in central Kansas Humaña killed Leyva in a quarrel. Plains Indians killed the rest, except for one Native servant named Jusepe who escaped, was captured by Apaches, and escaped back to Pecos a year later.[91]

The Colonization and Missionization of New Mexico

In 1998 plans to construct a Cuarto Centenario memorial in honor of New Mexico's first governor, Juan de Oñate, sparked heated debate between the state's Native American and Hispanic citizens. In Espanola, someone took an electric saw to a twelve-foot-high bronze statue of Oñate on horseback and severed his right foot "on behalf of our brothers and sisters of Acoma Pueblo," according to a statement issued to the media.[92] The founding father of New Mexico left a bitter legacy.

Oñate and his nephews, Juan and Vicente de Zaldívar, who figured prominently in the conquest and colonization of New Mexico, were members of two intricately related families who ranked high in the silver aristocracy of northern New Spain.[93] The Oñate family had grown wealthy from silver mining, ranches, and *encomiendas*, grants of Indian tribute and labor in return for defending Indians and instructing them in the Christian faith. The son of Cristóbal de Oñate, Juan de Oñate as a youth had accompanied his father on campaigns against the Chichimecas. By the time he was in his twenties he was organizing and leading his own campaigns against them. He married a woman who was a granddaughter of Cortés and a great-granddaughter of Moctezuma. In 1592 Oñate was appointed *alcalde mayor*, or chief civil officer, of the new Spanish settlement of San Luis Potosí, some two hundred miles northwest of Mexico City, but he had his eyes set on leading the expedition to establish the Spanish colonization of New Mexico on a firmer footing.[94]

Finally, in 1598 he marched north to Pueblo country with 129 soldiers, colonists, and their families, 10 priests, and numerous Indian servants. By one estimate, the expedition comprised a total of 560 people, about one fifth of them women. Most came from Mexico, Spain, and Portugal, although three soldiers were listed as being from Belgium, Italy, and Greece. Eighty wagons and carts, pulled by oxen and mules, creaked under the weight of baggage, tools, supplies of maize, wheat, wine, oil, and sugar, mining and blacksmithing equipment, medical supplies, powder and lead, and eighty thousand glass beads for trade with the Indians. Thousands of sheep and goats and hundreds of horses and cattle accompanied the column, which was said to have stretched for two miles.[95] With Sgt. Maj. Vicente de Zaldívar and Indian guides scouting the way, the expedition lurched north from the Río Conchos across the Chihuahuan desert, pioneering the wagon route that later became the Camino Real linking New Mexico to New Spain.[96] The colonists reached San Juan pueblo in the summer of 1598. Coronado's expedition had been a military foray, bent on exploration; this one was bent on colonization and had come to stay.[97]

Like every Spanish expedition, Oñate's people arrived hungry and in need of Pueblo food. Spanish-Pueblo relations followed a now familiar pattern. Oñate sent men ahead with eighty pack animals to fetch corn. "They brought back the animals, all loaded, although it was against the wishes of the natives and to their great grief," wrote one member of the expedition. "As we had run short of food so far back, when we reached the said pueblos, we had to support ourselves by taking as much as we could from each one. Because of this and other annoyances, the Indians fear us so much that, on seeing us approach from afar, they flee to the mountains with their women and children, abandoning their homes, and so we take whatever we wish from them."[98]

At the time Oñate arrived in the Rio Grande region, there were about eighty-one occupied pueblos, although he also found deserted pueblos all along the Rio Grande Valley.[99] He held public ceremonies and informed the leaders of various Pueblo communities that they were now subjects of Philip II of Spain, who wished to save their souls and "maintain them in . . . peace and justice and defend them against their enemies." Although the chiefs reportedly agreed "with spontaneous signs of pleasure and accord" to become vassals of a distant monarch, Oñate emphasized that if they failed to obey they would be punished "as transgressors of the orders of their king and natural master."[100] Oñate took over the Tewa pueblo at Yunque (*yúngé*, "mockingbird place") just across the Rio Grande from San Juan pueblo and renamed it San Gabriel as the first Spanish colonial capital in New Mexico.[101] He divided the province into six districts under Spanish administration and assigned each one to a priest. The colonists had come in search of wealth and were not inclined to labor in the fields to feed the infant colony. They endured a hard winter. Oñate rewarded his colonists with *encomiendas*. Each Pueblo household was required to provide corn and cotton blankets. The tribute was insufficient to support the Spaniards and had a ruinous effect on the Pueblos, for whom the concept of taxation was totally alien.[102]

As usual, Acoma impressed the Spaniards. (Fray Alonso de Benavides, prone to exaggeration, said it was "the most amazing in strength and location that could be found in the whole world.")[103] Many soldiers and Indians attended Oñate's ceremony of obedience at Acoma, and an Indian named Tomás served as interpreter.[104] But initially amicable relations broke down in bloodshed and retribution.

Oñate appointed Juan de Zaldívar to lead an expedition to Zuni. Running low on supplies, Zaldívar sent a patrol to meet with Acoma guides and request food, firewood, and water. The Acomas gave some of these items, but the Spaniards were not satisfied, and an officer seized some of the Acoma religious leaders. When Zaldívar arrived at Acoma, he ordered the release of the priests, but the Acomas refused to provide any more assistance. According to Indians who testified later, the Spaniards then stole a turkey or killed or wounded an Indian. Inferences from oral history indicate that the soldiers may have attacked some of the women in their homes. Whatever the cause, the Acomas turned on the intruders, killed Zaldívar and ten soldiers, and tossed their bodies off the cliffs.[105] The other members of the party survived by jumping down the rocks.

Oñate promptly dispatched a retaliatory expedition to make an example of the rebels. "Unless this pueblo was punished and destroyed for the treachery and outrage committed, there would be no safe place anywhere in New Mexico, nor could it be colonized," testified one Spanish officer. Oñate agreed: "The greatest force we possess at present to defend our friends and ourselves is the prestige of the Spanish nation, by fear of which the Indians have been kept in check," he wrote.[106] Persuaded that war against Acoma was justified, Oñate appointed Vicente de Zaldívar, younger brother of Juan de Zaldívar, to lead the expedition. Oñate instructed Zaldívar to offer terms for surrender: the Acomas should deliver up those responsible for the killings, abandon their stronghold, and move down the valley where the ministers of the holy gospel could better teach them. But when the seventy-two Spanish soldiers reached Acoma in late January, the people were prepared for battle. Three times the interpreter offered them the Spanish terms, but the Indians hurled insults, rocks, and javelins and called them "Castilian whoremongers."[107]

The battle began in midafternoon and raged all day. Feigning an assault at one side of the mesa, Zaldívar and his men scaled both the northern and southern mesas, hauled up two pieces of artillery, and turned the cannons on the inhabitants. Rather than fall into Spanish hands, said the soldiers, Indians "ran from house to house and killed each other without sparing their children, however small, or their wives." Capt. Luis Gasco de Velasco, the treasurer of the expedition who became an outspoken critic of Oñate, said that the Acomas surrendered and gave the Spaniards blankets and food but that Zaldívar ordered the Indians thrown from the cliffs. An estimated eight hundred Acomas died; five hundred women and children and eighty men were taken captive. Many escaped through the labyrinth of tunnels and passages between the houses.[108] According to Alonso Sánchez, treasurer of New Mexico, the Indians asserted, "without being asked, that in the heat of the battle they had seen someone on a white horse, dressed in white, a red emblem on his breast, and spear in his hand." The Spaniards believed that "without special aid from our God it would have been impossible to gain such a victory."[109]

In Spanish eyes, Acoma had to be dealt with according to Spanish law, since the Indians had broken their sworn oath of obedience to the king. The prisoners were taken to Santo Domingo, where Oñate filed formal charges on February 9. A defense attorney was appointed, and testimony was heard from both sides. On February 12 Oñate pronounced sentence. Males over age twenty-five (two dozen of them) were sentenced to twenty-five years in slavery and were to have their right foot amputated. Males between twelve and twenty-five and women between twelve and twenty were sentenced to twenty years of servitude. Children under twelve Oñate declared "free and innocent of the grave offense for which I punish their parents." He handed the girls over to the missionaries to be distributed in monasteries or other places where they might "attain the knowledge of God and the salvation of their souls." Boys were placed under Zaldívar to achieve the same goal. Two Hopis, visitors to Acoma at the time of the assault, had their right hands amputated and were sent home as living examples of the punishment meted out to those who resisted Spanish power. Such "theater of terror" was familiar to Spaniards and Moors but new and shocking to Pueblos. "All this," claimed Oñate, "left the land pacified and intimidated."[110]

Word of Oñate's sentences spread to other pueblos, and examples of Spanish power were visited on other peoples. In 1600–1601, Tompiro Indians, apparently unimpressed by the example the Spanish had set at Acoma, rose in rebellion. Vicente de Zaldívar took charge of its suppression. After a three-day battle, he burned the three Jumano Tompiro pueblos, killed eight to nine hundred people, and took four hundred prisoners.[111]

Spanish demands on Indian communities continued, but they were not enough to sustain the colonization effort in a harsh and unfamiliar land where the year was said to be "eight months of winter and four of hell."[112] Oñate and those who remained loyal to him tried to portray a colony that was becoming self-supporting, surrounded by happy Indians who willingly gave up food and eagerly accepted conversion.[113] But the viceroy ordered an investigation into conditions in New Mexico, and reports of starvation among the colonists and brutality toward the Indians continued to filter back to Mexico City.

The system of levying tribute in food and blankets left the Indians cold, hungry, and fearful. "The feelings of the natives against supplying it cannot be exaggerated," wrote Gasco de Velasco to the viceroy in March 1601. "They weep and cry out as if they and all their descendants were being killed." Sometimes the Spaniards seized blankets by force, "even when it is snowing, leaving the poor Indian women stark naked, holding their babes to their breasts." But in the end, he added, "necessity has compelled us to do this to keep from starving to death."[114] In three years, according to witnesses, Oñate's colonists depleted a six-year supply of corn stored up by Rio Grande Pueblos.[115] Franciscan priests reported that Spaniards abused Indian women: "I know for certain that the soldiers have violated them often along the roads," said one. Many people fled to the mountains and resisted conversion, "for they said that if we who are Christians caused so much harm and violence, why should they become Christian." The Indians "think that we are all evil and that the king who sent us here is ineffective and a tyrant."[116]

Many colonists concluded that their continued presence in New Mexico would only bring ruin to the Indians and themselves. In 1601, while Oñate led a reconnaissance of the Great Plains, three quarters of his colony's population pulled out and returned south to Santa Bárbara on the Conchos.[117] Lieutenant Governor Francisco de Sosa Peñalosa and twenty-five soldiers with their families and servants remained. Oñate continued to explore, searching the lower Colorado River for precious metals and a route to the Gulf of California, but in June 1606 the king ordered Oñate recalled to Mexico City. In 1614 the viceregal court found him guilty of a number of charges, including undue severity in the suppression of the Acoma rebellion. Oñate spent most of the remainder of his life trying to clear his name and restore his honor.

After the failure of Oñate's colonizing efforts, Viceroy Montesclaros ordered the colonization of New Mexico abandoned. But Franciscans still saw potential in the area: thousands of people, settled farmers living in towns, represented a field of souls the Church could not ignore. Missionaries claimed that thousands of converts had been made, so the colony could not be abandoned. In 1608 Philip III authorized the Franciscans to remain in New Mexico, and in 1609 Pedro de Peralta was appointed governor. By that time no more than two hundred Spanish colonists remained in the province, huddled around San Gabriel. Peralta arrived with a dozen soldiers and eight Franciscan missionaries and promptly moved the administrative capital to Santa Fe. The new villa was laid out in Spanish form around a plaza, with government buildings, a church, and homes for its citizens, but it was mostly built by Indian labor. A religious capital was set up in the pueblo of Santo Domingo, twenty-five miles to the southwest, symbolizing the separation of secular and religious authority, a separation that was formalized by viceregal decree in 1621. The Spanish did not intend to abandon their new Mexico, but it was now to be a royal mission province rather than a profit-making colony.[118]

Spain moved toward taking control of the resources, labor, and souls of the Native people and began to impose a Spanish political structure on the Pueblo world. In the next twenty years, the Spaniards built churches and set up Native secular and church officers in all the pueblos. At the town level, Spanish officials appointed an Indian governor or lieutenant governor, an *alguacil* (sheriff), and councilmen responsible for maintaining law and order, punishing offenders, and implementing Spanish policies. They selected those individuals most likely to comply with Spanish purposes and presented them with canes of office. Missionaries appointed *fiscales*, guardians of the mission church, who were responsible for maintaining the church, arranging burials and festivals, and disciplining those the friars thought had violated Church teachings. Coupled with the assault on Native beliefs, rituals, and languages, these programs drew the Pueblos into the Spanish Empire. But some Pueblos simply accepted the new town governments alongside their existing village government; they kept the new officials separate in name and function from their other leaders and used them as intermediaries in dealing with the Spanish invaders.[119]

As part of Oñate's program of colonization, thirty-five *encomiendas* were awarded to soldiers who had participated in the occupation of New Mexico. The *encomenderos* participated in governing the colony and were entitled to tribute from the Indians living on the land in the form of labor, crops, and cotton cloth. They were also required to draw on the Indians they held in *encomienda* to provide manpower for the defense of the colony when needed and to furnish weapons and horses. By law, *encomenderos* were not supposed to live amidst their Indian subjects, but the law was widely ignored, and there was persistent friction between Indians and Spaniards and between settlers and missionaries.[120]

Like the secular wing controlled by Oñate and succeeding governors, the Church exploited Pueblo people and produce for its own ends. Once they accepted baptism, Indians were expected to work in the Church's fields. Most Pueblos may have accepted baptism reluctantly, but there were practical reasons for doing so. Spanish seizures of their food stores disrupted relations with surrounding hunting tribes. Hunger and the threat of Apache and Navajo raids jeopardized Pueblo survival. Baptism gave access to mission food and Spanish military protection.[121]

Franciscan priests assumed the lead in bringing Spanish civilization to the Pueblos. As in the rest of New Spain, the priests' goal was to "reduce" Indians from their "barbarous" state, settle them into communities centered on mission churches, and instruct them in the Christian faith and "civilized" ways. The missionaries compelled the Indians to build churches, form congregations, attend services, and receive the sacraments. They forbade dancing and ceremonies and confiscated and destroyed religious objects such as kachina masks and prayer sticks. They demanded that people change their attitudes toward sex: what Pueblo men and women regarded as natural, life-affirming, and perhaps even sacred acts uniting male and female, celibate missionaries saw as "sins of the flesh." Pueblo women traditionally enjoyed considerable influence as a result of their control of the household, their production of corn, and their fertility. The patriarchal Catholic Church sought to terminate women's fertility societies and to undermine female influence in Pueblo communities.[122]

In 1625 Fray Alonso de Benavides arrived in New Mexico as the new custodian. He intensified the missionary agenda in the province and, as commissary of the Holy Office of the Inquisition, introduced that office and its powers into New Mexico. His dream was to found a Franciscan province in New Mexico with diocesan powers and, says one historian, "himself as first bishop."[123] To that end, when he left New Mexico he wrote a lengthy official report in 1630, revised in 1634. His *Memorial* was likely the first comprehensive account of the colony the king of Spain received, but it was a public relations pitch. Benavides described Spanish conversions in glowing terms and provided wildly inflated numbers. In a land "teeming with people," more than five hundred thousand souls had converted to Christianity. After centuries in which the devil had reigned without opposition, God had sent the light of heaven to the Pueblos of the Rio Grande through the sons of Saint Francis. "All the Indians are now converted, baptized, and very well ministered to, with thirty-three convents and churches in the principal pueblos and more than one hundred and fifty churches throughout the other pueblos," he wrote. Where "scarcely thirty years earlier all was idolatry and worship of the devil, without any vestige of civilization, today they all worship our true God and Lord." The country was "dotted with churches, convents, and crosses along the roads," and the people lived "like perfect Christians." But instances of Pueblo resistance penetrated even Benavides's dream world. In 1627 an old Pueblo shaman confronted the friar as he was preaching in the Piros region. "You Christians are crazy," declared the old man. "You desire and pretend that this pueblo shall also be crazy. . . . You go through the streets in groups, flagellating yourselves, and it is not well that the people of this pueblo should commit such madness as spilling their own blood by scourging themselves."[124]

For centuries, Pueblo people had survived by their prayers, relying on their rituals to provide them with food and water in a harsh land. Now the religion that had sustained them was under assault. Pueblo people resisted the friars in many and sometimes subtle ways, as illustrated by events at Pecos. Fray Pedro de Ortega reached Pecos in 1620. He was a young man, he had come to stay, and he was determined to save souls. He launched an all-out assault on Pecos religion. Two thousand inhabitants of Pecos stood and watched as Ortega smashed their "idols." Between 1621 and 1625 Pecos laborers built the church. Whereas Pueblo architecture depended on horizontal layers, Christian churches emphasized height to express the glory of God. The church at Pecos was, in historian John Kessell's words, architecturally unique and transitional: "a sixteenth-century Mexican fortress-church in the medieval tradition, rendered in adobe in the baroque age at the ends of the earth." For almost sixty years Pecos people attended mass, but in 1680 they burned and demolished the monumental church. In the twentieth century, archaeologists working at the site of the abandoned pueblo unearthed a stone figure that, like many other objects, had been "reverently reassembled" and laid in a specially prepared hiding place. "At Pecos, as in central Mexico," notes Kessell, "idols hid beneath altars, or beneath the earth of the plaza, and the people knew."[125]

The Spaniards established a mission at Zuni in 1629, but the people killed their resident priest three years later. At Taos the people killed their missionary and burned the mission in 1639. Franciscan missionaries began to arrive in Hopi communities in northern Arizona in 1628–29, backed by soldiers. Hopis built churches under Franciscan direction at Awatovi, the easternmost village, at Shungopovi below present-day Second Mesa, and at Oraibi, the westernmost village. Some Hopis accepted Christianity, but they referred to the church at Oraibi, even in the twentieth century, as the "slave church," and when the rains stopped Hopi priests conducted forbidden ceremonies in secret to end the drought.[126]

Wherever Catholic missionaries trod, religious interactions produced defiance as well as conversion, rebellions as well as syncretism, "idols behind altars," and different forms of Catholicism among different people.[127] Many Indians kept Spanish missionaries at arm's length; some fled to surrounding mesas or joined Pueblos more distant from Spanish control. Others adjusted to the Spanish presence and adopted some of the outward forms of Catholicism but took their own religion underground in their kivas. Missionaries were unable to stamp out traditional beliefs and rituals even among Pueblos who participated in Catholic services. According to Ramón Gutiérrez, most Pueblos allied themselves to the Christians to get food and protection, not to embrace an alien religion. "Thus whether the Puebloans offered feathers and corn meal to the cross as they had to their prayer-sticks, honored the Christ child on Christmas as they had the Twin War Gods during the winter solstice, or flogged themselves on Good Friday as they had called the rain goods, the meanings attached to these acts were fundamentally rooted in Pueblo concepts."[128] Franciscan friars did not supplant village priests and medicine men. "Kivas and village plazas, not churches and mission compounds, remained the focus of village life," wrote Pueblo anthropologist Alfonso Ortiz. "The Christian faith was, if accepted to any degree, regarded as a supplement, not an alternative, to a religion that had served the Pueblos and their ancestors well."[129]

Some Pueblo religious leaders acquired positions in the Church's organization as *fiscales* and often played a pivotal role in the daily struggle between Spanish priests intent on eradicating heathen beliefs and customs and Pueblo people equally intent on protecting traditional values and practices. They negotiated a middle way between outright resistance and total acceptance, publicly practicing Christianity while covertly preserving old ways. Pueblo culture, strong at the core, absorbed change on its edges.[130] But in 1680, after decades of accommodation, the Pueblos would rid themselves of their troublesome priests.

Pueblos and Spaniards in a Wider Indian World

The Pueblo peoples along the Rio Grande bore the brunt of Spanish invasion, missionization, and colonization north of Mexico. Sedentary farming communities nestled along the Rio Grande Valley seemed well suited for conversion into communities of Christian peasant farmers tilling their fields within the sound of mission bells. But as Spaniards intruded into the Pueblo world they were also establishing missions, mines, ranches, and presidios among Indian peoples in other regions on the northern frontiers of New Spain, and their invasions of Pueblo country and beyond brought them into contact with Athapaskan peoples who had migrated southward and now surrounded the Pueblos. And Spanish reconnaissance expeditions onto the Great Plains allowed the Europeans to see pieces of a very different Indian world even as they introduced changes to it.

The discovery of silver at Zacatecas in 1546 brought a rush of Spaniards. From there, miners and missionaries moved out into Indian country. Soldiers and missionaries moved slowly up the west coast, establishing presidios and missions as they moved from tribe to tribe.[131] While Franciscan missionaries trudged north along the Camino Real to spread the word of God among the Pueblos, Jesuits labored among the Native peoples of Sinaloa, Sonora, Nueva Vizcaya, and Arizona. Members of the Society of Jesus, founded in 1539–40, served as soldiers of Christ in China, Japan, India, as well as America and became an international organization that exerted its influence in the courts of Europe. Between 1591, when they began missionary work in northwestern Mexico, and 1767, when they were expelled from the Americas, the Jesuits built up an extensive bureaucracy and considerable power. Franciscans and Dominicans often competed with them for royal support and Native converts, and secular authorities often viewed their power and their zeal with suspicion and resentment. But, like their brothers in New France, Jesuit missionaries in New Spain went deep into Indian country, where they witnessed and generated far-reaching changes. They saw their mission as a battle between themselves, aided by God, and the devil and his Indian shamans. In this struggle they fought for the souls of deluded Indian "children," prisoners of Satan who could, with God's grace flowing through His missionaries, be saved and transformed from heathen savages into Christians.[132]

The Jesuits went into Indian communities, risked—some said sought—martyrdom, learned Native languages and customs, tried to eradicate what they regarded as idolatry, and took on Native spiritual leaders. They struggled to avoid the snares set for them by the devil, and they saw his hand at work all around them in the heathenish practices of the people they had vowed to save. They endeavored to learn Native ways but only to change them. They viewed what they learned through a lens of intolerance. When Indian people addressed animals and snakes as "grandfather," for example, the Jesuits did not dispute that the animals spoke to the Indians, but they attributed the phenomenon to the devil; "he has not forgotten how successful he was in assuming this same shape to cause the downfall of our first mother," wrote Andrés Pérez de Ribas, one of the first two Jesuit missionaries to the Yaquis in 1617.[133]

God worked in mysterious ways, but it all made sense to Pérez de Ribas. God placed the richest silver mines among the fiercest and most numerous Indian populations—the Chichimecas, Zacatecas, and Tepehuans—in order to preserve the silver "for the defense of the Catholic Faith and Church" and to allow the Jesuits to spread the gospel "among peoples who[m] His clemency did not scorn." As the Spaniards opened up the mines and extracted the ore, they also harvested a treasure of souls.[134]

Pérez de Ribas understood that Spanish missionary efforts made headway in the turmoil of a disease environment. God brought epidemic diseases, which undermined the influence of Native shamans who had neither predicted nor prevented the disaster and could not cure its victims and which delivered thousands of souls for baptism that might otherwise have gone to Satan. The epidemic of smallpox and measles that hit Sinaloa in 1593, for example, "carried heaps of Indians to their death," but, wrote Pérez de Ribas, it gave the Jesuits an opportunity to demonstrate their self-sacrifice and their care for the suffering people. They tended the sick, heard confessions, baptized, anointed, and helped bury the dead. The scenes were horrible to behold, but almost all the dead received the Holy Sacraments. Pérez de Ribas could only conclude that "God had ordained this illness, which provided so many souls with eternal bliss and salvation."[135] By 1600 the Jesuits had baptized thousands of people in Sinaloa.[136]

By the time the Spaniards pushed into what is now the southwestern United States, epidemics of Old World diseases were widespread in northwestern Mexico. Smallpox, measles, influenza, and other infectious diseases raced unchecked through Indian communities, producing demographic collapse, economic disruption, social and political restructuring, and shifts in settlement patterns. The ravages of disease may even have contributed to some of the abandonments in the Southwest normally assumed to have occurred before Europeans invaded America. Conquistadors, mines, and missions all helped spread the epidemics northward, afflicting Native populations in Arizona and New Mexico by the mid-seventeenth century if not before.

God also favored Spanish arms in battle against the Indians so that they could be "reduced" and remade into Christians. Nowhere was this more evident than in the Spanish war against the Yaquis of Sonora. The Yaquis had resisted Diego de Guzmán's slaving expedition in 1533. Numbering some thirty thousand people distributed among eighty *rancherías*, they were powerful, bellicose, and resistant to Christianity. In 1610 they defeated Capt. Diego Martínez de Hurdaide, the military commander of the west coast region, repulsing his force of two thousand Indians and forty Spanish soldiers. Hurdaide then assembled the largest army that had ever been raised in northwestern Mexico and marched back to Yaqui country with four thousand Indians and fifty Spanish cavalry. This time the Yaquis routed his army. Then, suddenly, they asked for peace. Victory, asserted Pérez de Ribas, was "due more to the hand of God than to weapons," and "the devil came out quite badly." More likely, the Yaquis adopted a pragmatic approach that included pursuing alliance rather than continual conflict with the newcomers.[137]

In 1617 Pérez de Ribas and Italian Jesuit Tomás Basilio, escorted by two Yaqui leaders and without Spanish escort, entered Yaqui county. Thousands of Yaquis carrying small wooden crosses in their hands welcomed them, and the missionaries passed under arches made of cane that had been erected for them. On the first day they baptized two hundred people; in six months they had baptized four thousand. In the early 1620s the Yaquis were persuaded to move from their scattered *rancherías* into eight larger towns clustered around newly built churches. There were never more than half a dozen Jesuit priests in Yaqui country, but "almost the entire nation was instructed and baptized." Whatever their motivation, by taking the initiative and establishing the terms on which Spaniards and Christianity entered their country, the Yaquis laid the basis for a collaborative relationship that endured for nearly a century and a quarter. They also established the foundations for an enduring and distinctly Yaqui Catholicism, in which people attended the services of the Roman Catholic Church and participated in its rituals but practiced the bulk of their religion "in the Yaqui church, the Yaqui plaza, and the Yaqui household."[138]

The lands of the Seri Indians in central coastal Sonora and on Tiburón Island in the Gulf of California held no riches and offered few incentives for Spanish colonization. Seris did not practice agriculture and did not live in settled villages. Instead, they traveled across the desert and sea in search of food, moving from camp to camp. They lacked all the markers of civilization Europeans employed: "They live like cattle, without God, without law, without faith, without Princes, and without houses," Jesuit missionary Adam Gilg reported in 1692.[139] As godless nomads, in the eyes of Gilg and his Jesuit colleagues, they cried out to be saved. The

Jesuits entered Seri country in 1679 and had established two missions before 1700. Although the Spanish made no sustained efforts to colonize Seri territory, they embarked on a campaign to transform the Seris from wandering heathens into settled Christians. Some Seris came into the missions and settled down to plant corn, but most resisted and raided the missions. After seventy years of struggling to transform Seri society and culture, the Jesuits admitted failure and abandoned the missions.[140]

The Spaniards knew there was a vast Indian world beyond the reach of the missions. Expeditions from Coronado to Oñate had reported sightings of nomadic hunter-gatherers in the open territory surrounding the various pueblos and noted that they both raided and traded with the Pueblos. Sixteenth-century Spanish chronicles provide the first documentation of the long-distance exchange systems that had developed between peoples on the plains and Pueblos along the Rio Grande. Where the southern plains met the Pueblo world, peoples from two different ecological zones regularly met and traded. Hunters and gatherers from the southern high plains brought hides, meat, and fat down to the Rio Grande Valley, where, below seven thousand feet, the Pueblos grew an abundance of corn and also produced ceramics and cotton blankets. Pecos, sitting at the eastern edge of the Pueblo world, was capable of producing enough surplus corn to trade with Plains groups each year and also set aside an insurance against lean years. As the climate became drier between the thirteenth and sixteenth centuries, decreasing rainfall rendered Plains peoples' horticulture increasingly precarious, and they became more specialized in their economic orientation. Plains and Pueblo peoples thus relied on their neighbors to provide a buffer against periodic scarcities and local shortfalls in crop yields or hunting.

Exchange also occurred in times of plenty. Plains buffalo hunters required the carbohydrates produced by the Pueblos; Pueblos needed the meat protein provided by the buffalo hunters. Archaeological research reveals evidence of material goods being traded and new technologies being adopted long before Europeans arrived. Pottery from the Rio Grande was being carried onto the southern plains by the fifteenth century, and buffalo hunters began manufacturing Pueblo-style cooking and storage containers. But the artifacts on the ground tell less about the exchange of ideas, the conversations that took place via translation and sign language, and the personal interactions that accompanied the barter as mutually beneficial trading relations developed into networks of interdependence. Plains Indians probably married into Pueblo communities, but relations were not always amicable. Plains Indians also on occasion raided Pueblos, acquiring Pueblo foodstuffs by force while perhaps simultaneously discouraging Pueblos from doing their own hunting on the plains.[141]

The trade-based relationships that developed between Pueblo farmers and Plains hunters also altered the relations of both groups with Caddo hunter-farmers along the Red and Arkansas Rivers as Athapaskans replaced Caddos as the primary trade partners of the Pueblos. The exchange systems that functioned between Pueblos villagers, southern plains nomads, and Wichita-Caddo farmers and hunters continued, but the arrivals of new peoples—Athapaskans from the north and Spaniards from the south—disrupted old systems and produced new ones. Athapaskan peoples who pushed into the southern plains replaced the Antelope Creek people in the exchange system with the Pueblos. The establishment of Spanish silver-mining settlements in Nueva Vizcaya in the mid- to late 1500s led to a new east-west network in which the Plains Jumanos operated as middlemen, holding annual trade fairs with Caddos in central Texas.[142]

Coronado's expedition recorded the first documentary reference to the Athapaskans as "Querechos." In 1582 Espejo encountered a group of Querechos, or "mountain dwellers," living near Mount Taylor and cultivating patches of corn. These people, who were probably Navajos, also came down to the pueblos, "mingling and trading with them, bringing them salt, game (such as deer, rabbits, and hares), dressed chamois skins, and other goods in exchange for cotton blankets and various articles accepted in payment."[143] The Navajos emerged fully into "recorded history" in the 1620s when the Spaniards began to distinguish them from the Apaches. Fray Gerónimo de Zárate Salmerón, who went to Jemez pueblo as a missionary in 1622, reported in 1626 that the Jemez referred to people living north of them between the Chama and San Juan Rivers as "Apaches del Navajo" or "Apache Indians of Nabajú." The term seems to have derived from a compound Tewa word, indicating that these Apaches had cultivated field in arroyos or *cañadas* and describing what they did rather than a specific place. In 1630 Fray Alonso de Benavides distinguished these Apaches from others who lived farther away and lived by hunting. The Apaches of Navajo, he said, were "great workers," for Navajo signified "big planted fields."[144]

In 1598 Vicente de Zaldívar set out to explore the buffalo plains east of Pecos. At the Canadian River he met large numbers of Vaquero or Plains Apaches coming back from trading at Picuris and Taos, where they exchanged meat, hides, tallow, suet, and salt for cotton, blankets, pottery, maize, and turquoise. The Plains Apaches set up a village of fifty tipis "made of tanned hides, very bright red and white in color," that impressed Zaldívar by their size and light weight. They used shaggy dogs to transport their tipi poles, tipi covers, and packs of meat and corn. "They drive great trains of them," said Zaldívar. "It is a sight to see them traveling, the ends of the poles dragging on the ground, nearly all of them snarling in their encounters." Buffalo were numerous on the plains—Zaldívar estimated he had seen one hundred thousand. Apaches hunted them with short and powerful Turkish-style bows and flint arrows, killing them "at the first shot with the greatest skill" from ambushes in brush blinds made at their watering places. "There are numerous Indians in those lands," wrote Zaldívar. "They live in rancherías, in the aforesaid tents made of hides. They always follow the cattle, and they are as well sheltered in their pavilions as they could be in any house." The Apaches apparently hoped the Spaniards would assist them against the Jumanos or Xumanos, "which is the name they give to a nation of Indians who are striped like the Chichimecos."[145] But the Apaches kept the Spaniards at arm's length: Oñate described them as "a people that has not yet publicly rendered obedience to his majesty, as I had the other provinces do."[146]

Trade between Plains Apaches and Pecos developed in the sixteenth century, soon after the Apaches adapted to life on the plains. The volume of trade picked up in the second half of the century, as evidenced by the increasing numbers of flint knives, bone scrapers, and other Plains artifacts excavated by archaeologists at Pecos. After 1598 grains, fruits, livestock, metal weapons, guns, and other items introduced by the Spaniards were added to the trade.[147] The Pueblo-Apache trade was fully established by 1601. When Francisco de Valverde investigated conditions in New Mexico, he found the Pueblos traded "only with the buffalo-hunting Vaquero Indians, who bring them dried meat, fat, and dressed skins for clothing themselves. They give them maize in trade and cotton blankets painted in various colors, which the Vaqueros do not have."[148] Each year around harvesttime in the late summer and fall hundreds of Apaches traveled to the Pueblos and set up their white tents. "Overnight," as John Kessell pictures the scene at Pecos, "the open grassy valley that spread out to the east and southeast . . . was transformed into an Apache rendezvous with clusters of conical skin tipis, running children, yapping dogs, and the smoke of a hundred fires."[149] In addition to meat and buffalo robes, the Apaches sometimes brought captives, Quivirans taken from Caddo neighbors farther east.[150]

When Oñate set out onto the plains in 1601 he found *rancherías* of Apaches dotted across the grasslands and following the buffalo herds. The Apaches welcomed him in peace "by raising their hands to the sun" and impressed him as "masters of the plains." Several Apaches were living among the Escanajaques, who have been variously identified as Plains Apaches (called Cantis or Kantsi by the Caddos), as a northern group of Tonkawas, as Kansas or Osages, as Iscanis, and as a subdivision of the Wichitas. Oñate's men were able to communicate with them via a Mexican Indian who had lived for a year with the Plains Apaches.[151] The Spaniards came to a Wichita "great settlement" of more than twelve hundred grass huts on the banks of the Arkansas River. The houses "were all round, made of forked wooden poles joined together by sticks and on the outside covered with straw." Most of them were "two spears high" and capable of holding eight or ten people. The town was surrounded by cornfields and gardens.[152] Reports spoke of other, larger towns farther along, but the Escanajaques were enemies of the Wichitas at the time and turned hostile when the Spaniards refused to allow them to rob the inhabitants.[153]

Plains Apaches seem to have preferred to trade with Pueblos rather than fight them.[154] Nevertheless, the Spaniards saw evidence of conflict as well as commerce. Spanish soldiers passed the ruins of abandoned towns and *despoblados*, regions empty of population. Some of the pueblos Coronado saw were no longer there when Oñate went through. Pressure from Athapaskan migrations no doubt pushed weaker groups to congregate with stronger neighbors. Warfare between different pueblos may also have accounted for some of the depopulation.[155] The Spaniards, however, heard mostly about raiders from the plains. "All that we could find out about it," wrote Castañeda, referring to some abandoned pueblos seen by Coronado's men, "was that some sixteen years before some people called Teyas had come in large numbers to that land and had destroyed those pueblos." The Teyas also besieged Pecos, but it proved too strong for them, and they made peace and left. They now came to trade each winter and camped outside the pueblo, but the Pecos did not entirely trust them. An oral tradition recorded by Adolph Bandelier at Santo Domingo pueblo in the 1880s describes an attack and siege of Pecos by the warriors from a tribe called the Kiraush, a tradition that accords well with archaeological evidence for warfare at Pecos around 1515 and with Castañeda's account.[156] If these Teyas were Caddos, their attack on Pecos

9. Tom Lovell, *Pecos Pueblo around 1500.* (Courtesy, Abell-Hanger Foundation and the Permian Basin Petroleum Museum, Library and Hall of Fame of Midland, Texas, where this painting is on display)

may be explained as a response to the developing Athapaskan-Pueblo trade that threatened their economic role: the semisedentary Caddo farmers and hunters had previously been the people who supplied plains products to the Pueblos.[157]

The Native American Southwest was undergoing dramatic change when European eyes saw it for the first time and as the Spaniards endeavored to incorporate its populations into their empire. The Spaniards arrived in the wake of climatic change, migrations, and shifts in population and power. They also introduced powerful forces of change themselves. Diseases spread north along ancient trade routes and through Spanish colonization corridors. By the first decade of the seventeenth century, Apaches and Navajos were acquiring horses and becoming far more mobile and efficient warriors and hunters. Spanish tribute demands eroded the surpluses that the Pueblos had formerly traded with the nomads. Mounted Apaches who could not obtain corn in trade were well equipped to take it by force. In such circumstances, Spanish promises of protection had added appeal for the Pueblos and may have stimulated conversion. Spaniards regularly conducted raids against Apaches and Navajos to secure slaves and encouraged Pueblos to do likewise. Meanwhile, Hispanic New Mexicans began to participate in intertribal trade fairs and to build on Plains-Pueblo precedents in trading with Plains Indians, foreshadowing the Comanchero trade of later years.[158]

Change was part of life in the Southwest, and all the people living there by the early seventeenth century—Pueblos, Apaches, Navajos, Spaniards—had experienced and contributed to it. But the cost of the changes the Spaniards insisted upon proved too high for Indians to accept or for Spaniards to enforce. Even before the death of Philip II in 1598, Spanish power had passed high tide, and it continued to wane in the next century. Draining overseas commitments, wars against England and France and in the Netherlands and Italy, destructive economic policies, and the waging of a relentless rearguard struggle against the Protestant Reformation all contributed to the crisis and the bankruptcy of the monarchy. So did Indian slaves, whom the Spanish worked to death in their American gold and silver mines, although they could never know it. The huge quantities of gold and silver the Indians mined and the Spanish galleons shipped across the Atlantic helped to fuel inflation in Europe. By 1600 prices in Spain were four times what they had been in 1500.[159] Distracted by troubles in Europe and spread thin across the globe, the Spanish lacked the manpower and resources to keep the Indians of New Spain completely under their heel. In everyday acts of resistance and in recurrent rebellions, Indian peoples constantly tested Spanish rule.

Chapter 4

Rebellions and Reconquests

In 1680, in an unprecedented act of united resistance, the Pueblo Indians of New Mexico rose up in sudden and synchronized fury, turned on their Spanish oppressors, and in six weeks drove them from the Pueblo homelands for a dozen years. From an Anglo-American perspective this Pueblo Revolt, as it is generally called, seems like an isolated and unique event: nothing else quite like it occurred within the country that became the United States. But to limit consideration of the revolt to events that occurred north of a border that did not exist at the time impedes understanding the event in its full context and consequences. Seen from Mexico City in the late seventeenth century, Indian rebellions against the mission system were a recurrent feature of life on the northern frontiers of New Spain. This one generated an "epidemic" of rebellions by Pueblos, Conchos, Tarahumaras, Mansos, Sanos, Pimas, Opatas, and Apaches that challenged the Spanish colonial order in New Mexico, Nueva Vizcaya, and Sonora. It was part of a "Great Northern Rebellion."[1] Seen from Native American communities, the revolt was a dramatic bid for independence in an ongoing process of resisting foreign domination by responses that ranged from partial accommodation to open rebellion.[2]

The Pueblo War of Independence

Pueblo historian Joe S. Sando calls the Pueblo Revolt "the first American revolution."[3] As with that other American revolution, scholars debate its causes; analyze the impact of economic, social, and religious factors; assess the role of individual leaders; and account for the timing and success of the revolt.[4] The revolt was unique in its size and success, but it occurred in a context of rebellion and resistance that was long established and widespread. Everywhere in Spain's American empire, Native people fought against conquest, colonialism, and Catholicism, sometimes in full-blown wars of rebellion, sometimes in small everyday acts designed to keep Spaniards and their ways at arm's length. Spanish invasion, colonization, and missionization produced divisions within Indian communities but also sparked wars of united resistance. The wars frequently involved movements of cultural revitalization, in which shamans invoked a vision of the past and inspired their followers with the promise of a future free of Spanish domination. Spaniards, especially the missionaries, saw such revolts as the devil's handiwork, carried out by his agents, the Indian "sorcerers."[5]

Cortés's conquest of the Aztec Empire did not end Native resistance in Mexico. In western Mexico the Mixtón War of 1540–41 was followed by recurrent conflicts with various Native groups throughout the rest of the century. Discovery of the fabulous silver mines of Zacatecas in 1546 provoked America's first mining rush. The Chichimeca Indians resisted and fought the Spaniards from 1550 to 1590 in what was probably the longest and most costly continuous conflict between Indians and Europeans. The Spanish crown lacked the financial resources to sustain a full-scale war against the Chichimecas; consequently, Spanish captains often raised forces at their own expense and recouped their expenditures by selling war captives as slaves. In the course of the war Spain developed military techniques that would become standard strategies when fighting Indians farther north: presidios served as buffers against attack and housed "flying companies" of light troops to counter Indian raids. After the war, Jesuit missionaries began work among the Chichimecas. According to Father Andrés Pérez de Ribas, only the introduction of the gospel finally brought peace to this fierce people.[6]

In Sinaloa in 1600–1601 the "fierce and warlike" Zuaque nation, which Pérez de Ribas said "prided itself as a killer of Spaniards," rebelled. The Spanish quelled the rebellion and hanged forty-two prisoners.[7] From 1601 to 1603 the Acaxees in the Sierre Madre of northwestern Durango revolted, destroying the Spanish mines and missions.[8] In 1610 their southern neighbors and enemies, the Xiximes, rebelled. The Tehuecos in Sinaloa followed suit the next year.[9] In November 1616 the Tepehuan Indians in Nueva Vizcaya coordinated a nativist rebellion that reverberated among other tribes and across the whole northwestern frontier of New Spain. They killed eight missionaries and about two hundred Spaniards, mostly people in the mining towns along the eastern slopes of the Sierra Madre. The Spaniards seized and executed seventy-five of the principal leaders, but it took them two years to quash the revolt, hunting the Indians down in canyon strongholds. Perhaps one thousand Tepehuans died, many of them in mass executions. According to Pérez de Ribas, it cost the Spaniards eight hundred thousand pesos to suppress the rebellion.[10] In 1640 Tobosos in southern Chihuahua revolted. Their eastern neighbors, the Tarahumaras, rebelled in 1648, 1650, and 1652, as did the Conchos and other groups in eastern Nueva Vizcaya. Gabriel Tepórame, who led the second and third Tarahumara revolts, was executed in 1652. The Spaniards regained control, but their advance into northern Tarahumara country was slowed for twenty years.[11]

Nuevo León, which comprised parts of what is today northeastern Mexico and south Texas, experienced Indian "uprisings" in the 1660s. According to Juan Bautista Chapa, "the Indians of the north began to make trouble everywhere." The Spanish retaliated with raids against the Cacaxtle Indians, who lived along the lower Rio Grande and in south Texas; Fernando de Azcué's expedition in 1665 killed one hundred Indians while "an old Indian woman played the flute to give the Cacaxtle courage." The Indians stole livestock, burned houses, and killed Spaniards. According to Fray Francisco de Ribera, they made their victims say "Jesus" before they dispatched them. In Ribera's opinion, the Spaniards had "lived incautiously" with the Indians and been far too lenient with them. The rebels had to be subdued, otherwise "all this has served for nothing more than to have many Spaniards die far from their homelands at the hands of these Indians for whom they have worked." Indians from the north continued to raid Nuevo León during the later 1660s. The San Antonio Valley was depopulated after an Indian called Cualiteguache, who had been "reared among Christian Spaniards," led a "great uprising" of six hundred Indians, killed the priest, and drove the livestock from the ranches.[12]

In New Mexico for more than eighty years Pueblo peoples had endured Spanish persecution of their religious rituals and priests, Spanish demands for corn and labor, and Spanish abuses of their women. Far removed from Mexico City and few in number, Spanish colonists endured their harsh northern environment in part by learning from and learning to live with the Indian inhabitants. Through influence and intermarriage, Pueblo people eroded the cultural barriers that separated Indians and Spaniards in New Mexico and drove a cultural wedge between the Spanish colonists of New Mexico and the mother colony in the south.[13] But in the late seventeenth century New Mexico was plagued by disease, famine, and escalating conflict. Continued coexistence and accommodation threatened to destroy the Pueblos. Survival seemed to demand reasserting old ways and casting off imposed orders. Pueblos did both. In doing so they set the northern frontier of New Spain ablaze and remade the Spanish colonial order.

Like New England Algonkians who entered John Eliot's mission towns and Hurons who accepted baptism from Jesuit fathers, many Indians who embraced Christianity on New Spain's northern frontiers did so at a time when their communities were reeling under the hammer blows of disease.[14] In 1638 the commissary general of the Franciscan order reported that smallpox and other diseases had been raging for several years, cutting the Pueblo population from sixty thousand to forty thousand.[15] In an epidemic around 1640 some three thousand Pueblos perished. At Pecos the population in the 1620s stood at about two thousand; by 1641 it had dropped to fewer than twelve hundred. "Mary of the Angels," notes historian John Kessell, "just let them die."[16]

The mission program was losing momentum by midcentury. The more distant Pueblos—Acoma, Zuni, Hopi, Taos, Jemez, and Picuris—continued to resist, and there were signs of resistance from medicine men and war captains at Isleta, Cochiti, Alameda, and San Felipe.[17] Many people from Taos fled to the plains and built a new village at an Apache settlement in western Kansas named El Cuartelejo, where they remained for twenty years.[18] Another revolt at Jemez ended with the hanging of twenty-nine Indians. In 1650 the Tiwas, Keres, Jemez, and some Apaches planned a revolt, but word reached the Spaniards. Three years later, Jemez, two Tiguex towns, and some Keres towns rebelled in conjunction with Apache groups. Many Indians were arrested, nine leaders from Isleta, Alameda, San Felipe, Cochiti, and Jemez were hanged, and many others were sold as slaves. Several years later, Taos circulated two deerskins calling for a revolt. The Hopis refused to accept them, and plans were postponed, but, said one Pueblo many years later after the Spaniards were expelled, "they always kept in their hearts the desire to carry it out, so as to live as they are living today."[19] As their misfortunes increased, many Pueblos blamed Spanish assaults on their ceremonies, which brought rain and kept the world in balance.

Years of drought and famine aggravated Pueblo relations with Plains nomads. There was no continuous Pueblo-Athapaskan enmity. Faraón Apaches traveled to Pecos to trade, Jicarillas came to Taos, Plains Apaches dealt with Picuris, Salinero Apaches traded at Zuni, and Navajos traded at

Jemez. Enjoying a lucrative position as suppliers of buffalo hides, Apaches traded with Pueblos and with Spaniards. Different groups of Apaches frequently colluded with the Pueblos against the Spaniards, and some Pueblos escaped Spanish oppression by joining Navajos and other "heathen" bands, with whom, wrote one Spanish priest, "they enjoy greater happiness . . . since they live according to their whims, and in complete freedom."[20] But the Spanish disrupted trade relations, alienated Apaches, and fueled hostilities between Pueblos and Athapaskans. In 1635 Governor Luis de Rosas began slave raids against Apaches. Christian Indians at Pecos were horrified: the attack would disrupt trade relations and invite retaliation on them. In January 1664 Governor Diego Dionisio de Peñalosa prohibited nomadic Indians from entering pueblos, ostensibly to end hostilities but in reality to ensure Spaniards a middleman role in the trade; the Indians simply evaded the intent of Peñalosa's order by conducting their exchange out on the plains. Apaches continued to trade hides, meat, and Quivira captives at Pecos as late as 1670; as John Kessell observed, they "preferred to be the middle men in the slave traffic rather than the object of it." Nevertheless, drought and tribute demands ate up food surpluses that Pueblos had previously traded to Plains nomads. Apaches who had once come to trade now increasingly came to raid Pueblo granaries and livestock.[21]

Apaches suffered so severely from famine in 1658 that the next year they came to the pueblos to sell slaves and perhaps even their own children for food. Franciscans purchased many of the children in order to convert them.[22] Famine stalked the land again between 1667 and 1672 and became so severe that Spaniards and Indians alike were reduced to eating hides and leather straps. In 1671 a great pestilence killed people and cattle. Apache raids intensified.[23] In the years preceding the revolt, according to Fray Silvestre Vélez de Escalante, who wrote a concise history of New Mexico, the Apaches destroyed seven pueblos. Southern Tompiros abandoned their villages between 1661 and 1671 and merged with other groups.[24]

Small contingents of Spanish soldiers were no match for mounted Apaches. Nevertheless, successive Spanish governors attempted to punish them. In the 1650s Governor Juan de Samaniego y Xaca took the field in retaliation for a Navajo raid on Jemez; he surprised the Navajos during a ceremony, killed several of them, took more than two hundred prisoners, and liberated the captives they had taken from Jemez. When Governor Bernardo López de Mendizábal took office in 1659 he vowed to lay waste to Apache crops and dispatched Juan Domínguez on campaign to the Rio Grande, where he hit the Apaches hard.[25] By the end of the decade, most Apaches were hostile to the Spaniards and were raiding pueblos under Spanish control. "The whole land is at war with the widespread heathen nation of the Apache Indians, who kill all the Christian Indians they can find," wrote Fray Juan Bernal in 1669. "No road is safe; everyone travels at risk of his life, for the heathen traverse them all, being courageous and brave, and they hurl themselves at danger like people who know no God nor that there is any hell."[26] In a pattern repeated elsewhere on the northern frontier, Apaches became "specialists in violence" in resisting Spanish expansion.[27]

In 1675 and twice in 1678 Juan Domínguez, now a veteran, led campaigns into Navajo country. In the second campaign of 1678 he fended off an ambush, burned villages, destroyed more than twenty-five hundred *fanegas* (about thirty-seven hundred bushels) of corn, captured women and children, and carried off plunder. The Navajos responded a month later with an attack on Acoma. Navajo-Spanish hostilities were ingrained by the time of the revolt, and Navajos offered a ready refuge for Pueblo peoples fleeing Spanish oppression and retribution.[28]

The combined effects of disease, drought, famine, and warfare scythed Pueblo populations. Many smaller settlements were abandoned, "and rooms that had once filled with laughter, music, and the sounds of corn being ground fell silent."[29] Conservative estimates place the Pueblo population at perhaps 60,000 in 1540; others go as high as 220,000 in 1500 and 100,000 in the late sixteenth century. By 1680 the Pueblos numbered 17,000. Fifty of the eighty-one pueblos occupied in 1598 had been abandoned by 1680, with the greatest loss during the disease years 1636–41.[30] Clearly, the new religion was no more effective than the old in protecting the Pueblos against new disasters.

With their world catastrophically out of balance, Pueblo people turned again to ancient dances, ceremonies, and prayers to restore harmony.[31] But they could no longer practice their traditional religion without incurring punishment from watchful missionaries. In 1655 Fray Salvador de Guerra caught a Hopi named Juan Cuna in "an act of idolatry." The priest whipped him until he was "bathed in blood," then drenched him in burning turpentine.[32] Friars tried to suppress the resurgence of Pueblo ceremonialism; Pueblos resisted. "To give up their religion would have been like giving up life itself," writes Pueblo historian Joe Sando.[33] Pueblo women expressed veiled resistance to religious persecution in the pottery they made, manipulating symbols such as cross motifs to convey their own meanings. In the designs they painted and even the processes they used, Pueblo women reflected the persistence and revitalization of Pueblo values in the face of Spanish oppression.[34]

Whatever hold the Franciscans had over the Pueblos, their authority eroded in bickering with Spanish civil authorities. Because New Mexico was a mission province, the Church expected the civil authorities to promote and protect the work of the missions; colonial administrators had different ideas. Each side accused the other of exerting undue influence. Governors accused friars of abusing their positions, whipping Indians who refused to attend mass and raping Indian girls even as they insisted that Indians follow strict new codes of sexual behavior. Franciscans accused state officials of heresy and immorality. Between 1610 and 1650 relations deteriorated almost to the point of civil war. By the early 1660s the Inquisition was playing an increasingly prominent role. Things came to a head during the governorship of López de Mendizábal, who took office in 1659. López believed the governor to be overall head of the province; the missionaries believed that they were responsible for its spiritual affairs. López butted heads with the missionaries on issues of policy. He set restrictions on Pueblo mission labor and conducted investigations into misconduct by Spanish priests. Dismissing kachina dances as merely "Indian foolishness," he allowed the ceremonies to be performed publicly. The Franciscans regarded kachina dances as idolatry; in refusing to root them out López was failing to carry out his duty and undermining their work. In 1661 the Franciscan custodian proclaimed an absolute prohibition on all kachina dances and "idolatrous materials." Missionaries raided kivas, from which they seized sixteen hundred kachina masks, prayer sticks, and religious effigies and consigned them to a bonfire. Personality conflicts aggravated philosophical differences. The Inquisition investigated charges against López, and in 1662 he was arrested and returned in shackles to Mexico to stand trial. He died in prison two years later. López's successor, Diego Dionisio de Peñalosa, was also arrested and tried by the Holy Inquisition. He was accused of immorality, mistreating Indians, and ridiculing religion and the missionaries. Ruined and banished from New Spain, Peñalosa returned to Europe, where he offered his services to the French crown.[35]

But even as the missionaries demonstrated their power over the secular authorities, their influence among the Indians was crumbling. Catholic rituals failed to bring rain or stop disease. During the initial years of conquest, the friars' vow of chastity may have impressed the Indians as a sign of their spiritual power, but, in Ramón Gutiérrez's words, "as time passed and isolation increased, the flesh became weak." Spanish soldiers could not protect the Pueblos against Apache raiders; Spanish priests could not protect them against drought and pestilence; Pueblo husbands and fathers could not protect their wives and daughters against the priests.[36]

In 1673 Tewa Indians publicly performed traditional dances and ceremonies prohibited by the Spanish government. When Governor Juan Francisco Treviño arrived in the province two years later, he launched a campaign of intimidation. Forty-seven medicine men were arrested and admitted under torture that they practiced witchcraft. Treviño ordered three medicine men hanged and the others to be flogged and sold into slavery. Among those whipped was a medicine man from San Juan named Popé. Another committed suicide. Infuriated by Treviño's actions, seventy Tewas marched to Santa Fe and threatened to kill the governor and the settlers if the medicine men were not released. Treviño released his captives. Spaniards were forced to reassess earlier views of Pueblos as docile peasants living quiet Christian lives. "They have been found to be so pleased with liberty of conscience and so attached to the belief in the worship of Satan that up to the present not a *sign* has been visible of their ever having been Christians," lamented Fray Francisco de Ayeta in December 1681; "most of them have never forsaken idolatry, and they appear to be Christians more by force than to be Indians who are reduced to the Holy Faith," added Sgt. Maj. Luis de Quintana.[37] Pushed to extremes, the Pueblos would defend their religion.

In the confrontation at Santa Fe the Pueblos had won an opening skirmish and gained the initiative. Ever since Oñate's time Spaniards had played upon Pueblo religious and political disunity and exploited divisions between clans and moieties. The crises of the 1670s demonstrated the need for united action that transcended local rivalries. More Pueblo people listened to leaders who urged taking drastic steps to expel the Spaniards and "cleanse the Pueblo homeland."[38] A synchronized revolt by the combined forces of the Pueblos would provide the strength needed to overthrow the Spanish rule.

The first move to open conflict came in the north, from Tewa and northern Tiwa leaders. Spaniards credited Popé with masterminding the revolt, but, as in most Pueblo endeavors, representatives from each village would have helped plan and execute it. Of all the leaders of the revolt,

Popé appears to have been the only one from the Christianized Pueblos who was known only by his Native name. The name may have been Po-'png(pumpkin or squash mountain), but the late Alfonso Ortiz, himself from San Juan, suggested that it more likely meant "ripe cultigens," indicating that the bearer was a priest in the Summer moiety.[39] Popé may have inspired the organization of the revolt, but the idea of a rebellion was nothing new. Many Pueblos had been waiting for an opportunity to throw off Spanish domination, and many leaders played important roles: Luis Tupatú, governor of Picuris and "an Indian respected among all the nations"; El Jaca of Taos; Alonso Catiti from Santo Domingo; Luis Cuniju from Jemez; Antonio Bolsas of Tanos; Cristóbal Yope of San Lázaro; and Antonio Malacate of Keres.[40]

According to one twentieth-century Franciscan scholar, the leaders of the revolt were primarily mixed-bloods, who were "more active and restless by nature" than the peaceful Pueblos. In this controversial interpretation, Domingo Naranjo, a part-African Indian who posed as a representative of the god Pohé-Yemo, was the driving personality.[41] Governor Antonio de Otermín also blamed "the confident coyotes, mestizos, and mulattoes, all of whom are skillful horsemen and know how to manage harquebuses and lances," for inciting the Pueblos "to disobedience and boldness." The evidence for mixed-blood leadership is shaky, but the revolt does seem to have embraced Indians, African-Americans, and black Indians in the kind of common alliance that Spanish colonial policy, like that of the English colonies in the Southeast, was designed to prevent. Native Americans and *castas* (mixed-bloods) shared marginal status in Spanish New Mexico as well as a common interest in ridding themselves of Spanish oppression. "By joining Pueblo rebels," suggests one scholar of Indian-African interaction and intermarriage in colonial New Mexico, "castas constructed a group identity as 'not Spanish,' which meant they would no longer acquiesce, at least for the revolt years, to Spanish domination over Puebloans and castas alike."[42] As their population grew, more mestizo people occupied positions as *alcaldes, fiscales,* and village leaders. Positioned to serve as brokers between Pueblos and Spaniards, many of them became part of a network working for revolt.[43]

In many meetings, often held on festival days to avoid attracting attention, chiefs and medicine men in the northern pueblos formulated plans for revolution. Only the leaders were entrusted with details of the plot until a short while before the outbreak. Popé realized that many people were sympathetic to the Spaniards and missionaries. Fearing that his son-in-law Nicolas Bua, governor of San Juan pueblo, was planning to inform the Spaniards of the plans, Popé had him killed.[44] To evade Spanish punishment, Popé then left San Juan for Taos, where the inhabitants let him hide in one of their kivas. Here Popé experienced a vision in which three Pueblo spirits instructed him with the knowledge to execute the revolt. Popé's vision propelled his rise to prominence in the eyes of the Pueblos. According to Alfonso Ortiz, he was "invoking sacred culture heroes as his ultimate rationale and guides for the rebellion he was planning." Recalling the three kachinas to challenge the Christian Trinity of the Father, Son, and Holy Ghost may also have helped win over Christianized Pueblos.[45] Popé was instructed to send a cord of maguey fibers to each Pueblo with knots for each day indicating the countdown to the revolt.

The Pueblos planned to strike in unison at a time when the Spaniards would be low on supplies, just before the arrival of the Spanish supply caravan from the south. They would cut off the Spanish capital at Santa Fe and overwhelm the outlying areas. Fewer than three thousand Spanish people lived in New Mexico, mainly along the Rio Grande between Isleta and Taos. For the first time, the united strength of the Pueblos would be turned against them.[46] As historian David Weber notes, it required careful planning to coordinate "an offensive involving some 17,000 Pueblos living in more than two dozen independent towns spread out over several hundred miles and further separated by at least six different languages and countless dialects, many of them mutually unintelligible."[47]

On August 9, 1680, runners carrying strings with two knots went from pueblo to pueblo, "under penalty of death if they revealed the secret." The caciques of Tanos, San Marcos, and La Cienega opposed the rebellion and warned the Spaniards. Two of the runners were arrested and taken to Santa Fe for interrogation under torture. They revealed the date of the revolt and were promptly hanged in the center of town. New messengers went out carrying a chord with a single knot.[48]

The next morning, a Sunday, the storm struck. According to Governor Otermín, "the entire uprising occurred in one day and at the same hour." Only a miracle prevented everyone from being killed.[49] As it was, the viceroy of New Spain reported to the king seven months later that the Indians "fell upon all the pueblos and farms at the same time with such vigor and cruelty" that they killed 19 priests and 2 lay brothers and more than 380 Spaniards, "not sparing the defenselessness of the women and children." They burned the churches, "seizing the images of the saints and profaning the holy vessels with such shocking desecrations and insolences that it is indecent to mention them."[50]

The Hopi term for the Spanish priests was *tota'tsi*, "dictator, demanding person."[51] At Oraibi, where Spanish priests had extracted Hopi labor, desecrated Hopi religion, denigrated Hopi culture, and abused Hopi women, the men met in the kiva to discuss what they should do. The Badger clan volunteered to kill the priest. Dressed in kachina masks and costumes, they attacked the church, killed the soldiers and the priest, and threw the priest's body off the mesa. Other Hopi villages followed suit. Four priests died at Hopi that day, including Fray José de Trujillo at Shungopovi, "a brilliant student of Scripture and intensely spiritual man" who had several times expressed a wish for martyrdom. The Hopis dismantled the "slave churches," taking them down "stone by stone," and built new kivas. At Oraibi they scattered the rubble of the church to the four directions.[52]

The rebel Indians laid siege to Santa Fe for nine days and cut off the town's water supply. According to Governor Otermín, more than twenty-five hundred Indians surrounded the villa, entrenching themselves in its houses and at the entrances of streets. They had plenty of harquebuses and ammunition and kept the Spaniards pinned down. Almost all of the soldiers at the post were wounded. Rather than die from starvation and thirst, Otermín fought his way through the Pueblo cordon, inflicting heavy casualties and taking forty-seven prisoners. Wounded in the face and chest, Otermín interrogated the prisoners and then had them executed for treason. The Spaniards made for Isleta, which had not revolted. Then Otermín led about one thousand Spanish soldiers, "their families and servants[,] . . . Mexican natives, and all classes of people" in retreat south to El Paso, which was then located on the other side of the Rio Grande at present-day Ciudad Juárez in Chihuahua.[53] The Pueblos watched from the mesas but did not attempt to stop them. They apparently said, "We have killed as many Spaniards as they have killed of our number, and we care not if they leave, as we will then live at ease."[54] The revolutionaries plundered Spanish houses and made a bonfire of government and Church records in the square at Santa Fe.

The revolutionary leaders demanded that the people remove crucifixes and rosaries from their necks, cease speaking Spanish, and grow only native crops. Some people plunged into rivers and scrubbed themselves and their clothing, believing that this would cleanse them of "the condition created by the Holy sacrament." Popé and his lieutenants traveled throughout the province ordering everyone to return to the old ways: "This was the better life and the one they desired, because the God of the Spaniards was worth nothing and theirs was very strong, the Spaniard's God being rotten wood." Revolutionaries desecrated churches—some were converted into barns—and smashed Catholic images and objects. At Sandia, retreating Spaniards found the altar, sculptures, and chalices smeared with excrement and the arms of a life-size statue of Saint Francis hacked off with an axe. The Indians, said Otermín, were "demon blinded."[55] The Pueblos had turned the tables in the contest of cultures; they had learned well from the Spanish "the functions of iconoclasm in political spectacle."[56]

The Pueblos were not totally united behind the revolution. Pecos appears to have been divided. Southern Tiwas were less committed than were northern groups. The southernmost Pueblos, the Piros and Tompiros, refused to join the rebellion, and many of them accompanied the Spanish refugees to El Paso. In 1681 Otermín attempted to retake the province. Using Isleta as a temporary headquarters, he dispatched *maestro de campo* Juan Domínguez de Mendoza and sixty men northward to the pueblos of Alameda, Puaray, Sandia, and Cochiti. At Cochiti, said Mendoza in later years, the assembled chiefs were eagerly receiving peace when news came that Otermín was burning Alameda, Puaray, and Sandia. Altogether, the Spaniards burned eight pueblos and sacked three villages, all of them in the south among the peoples who had been least involved in the revolt.[57] "The year 1681 is burned into [the people of Sandia's] historic memory," notes Joe Sando. They seem to have migrated to Hopi country, and Sandia lay abandoned until the 1740s, when it was resettled by refugees from various pueblos and Hopi.[58] Otermín also burned Isleta and carried 385 captives downriver, where they were resettled near El Paso between the "loyal" communities at Socorro del Sur and Senecú del Sur, which had been formed by the Piro and Tiwa people who had accompanied the retreating Spaniards in 1680. In their new homes, it was hoped, the people from Isleta would take up the life of Christian peasant farmers.[59]

Elsewhere, Pueblo resistance remained strong. Otermín was able to do little more than interrogate captured Indians as to their motives "for rebelling, forsaking the law of God and obedience to his Majesty, and committing such grave and atrocious crimes." Indians said that "the uprising had been deliberated upon for a long time." Some blamed Popé or the devil or said they did. Others cited continued Spanish oppression and said they were "tired of the work they had to do for the Spaniards . . . and, that being weary, they rebelled." They told Mendoza "they had risen because they had not received justice." Eighty-year-old Pedro Naranjo declared that "the resentment which all the Indians have in their hearts has been so strong, from the time this kingdom was discovered, because the religious and the Spaniards took away their idols and forbade their sorceries and idolatries." He had "heard this resentment spoken of since he was of an age to understand."[60] When Otermín asked, "Tell me, who was the leader of the revolt?" one Towa man replied, "His name is Payastiabo, and he lives up that way." Payastiabo—in Tewa, P'ose yemu—is Pohé-yemu, the deity whom Pueblos address when making prayers. From the European point of view, Popé was the leader of the Pueblo Revolt of 1680; from the Pueblo perspective, Pueblo gods led the successful rebellion.[61] As they had during the Tepehuan revolt in 1616–20, Spanish missionaries represented the Pueblo war as the work of the devil rather than as a millenarian movement triggered by the effects of European diseases and Spanish colonialism.[62]

For the first time since Oñate came in 1598, the Rio Grande was empty of Spaniards. Pueblos did not have to give up corn, blankets, or labor in tribute. They could practice their ceremonies in the open and teach their children the old ways without fear of punishment. Their women were free from abuse.[63] Pueblos breathed in the freedom they had won.

An Epidemic of Rebellions

Hearing the "lamentable news" from the north, Spanish officials feared they stood to lose Nueva Vizcaya, Sonora, and other provinces if the Indian nations followed "the example of the rebel Indians of New Mexico."[64] They had good reason to be afraid. The crises that spurred the Pueblo peoples to desperate acts in 1680 also took a toll on other Indian peoples living on New Spain's northwestern frontier. As in New Mexico, Spaniards encroached on Indian land, exploited Indian labor, and disrupted Native patterns of food production and exchange. As in the north, Spanish missionaries—Jesuits and Dominicans as well as Franciscans—were at work trying to save Indian souls; rearrange Native social, political, and economic structures; and resettle seminomadic peoples into peasant farming communities. Like the Pueblos, Indian peoples in these regions suffered from Old World diseases and escalating raids by newly mounted Apaches. Major silver strikes brought a steady intrusion of population and ensnared Indian people in the brutal mining economy of northern New Spain. Like their northern neighbors, Native peoples in northwestern Mexico adjusted to the power of the Spanish state by incorporating things they wanted, enduring things they could not avoid, and resisting through negotiation, flight, and revolt.[65] As in New Mexico, different elements of Spanish colonial society came into conflict as Jesuit missionaries, soldiers, and settlers clashed over Indian land and labor.[66] Wars like the Pueblo Revolt were nothing new in the mountain and desert regions of northern Mexico.

The Pueblo Revolt inspired other Indian peoples, especially bands of seminomadic Athapaskans, to challenge the Spaniards. Following the withdrawal of Spanish colonists and Indian refugees from New Mexico, many Apaches shifted their attention southward and began raiding in the El Paso and Casas Grandes areas, further weakening Spanish defenses and sending repercussions through intertribal relations in the surrounding regions.[67] But, though the Pueblo victory undoubtedly inspired Indian resistance south of New Mexico, other causes also fueled revolt.

In northeastern Sonora, several Opata leaders conspired to rebel in 1681 and rid their homeland of Spanish miners, ranchers, and missionaries as the Pueblos had done. But word of their plans leaked out, and the Spaniards moved quickly to snuff out the revolt. They arrested leaders in most of the Opata communities and rounded up dozens of suspects for interrogation. Fifteen Opatas were condemned to death, four were sentenced to hard labor for up to ten years, and others were whipped and tortured. Under interrogation, the Opatas pointed to abuses at the hands of Spanish soldiers and missionaries and excessive demands for labor in Spanish mines as root causes of their resentment. They blamed drought and famine on Spanish livestock, which "dried up all the springs and ruined the land."[68]

The executions of that summer did nothing to remove Opata discontent. There were more rumors of rebellion in the fall, and again the Spaniards rounded up suspects and extracted confessions. Opatas fled to the mountains until Lieutenant Governor Francisco Cuervo y Valdés offered them pardon if they returned to their villages, obeyed their priests, and tended to their fields.[69] The fragile peace survived. By 1688 there were twenty-two missions in Opata country with ten thousand Indians reported to be living around them. Spanish men married Opata women, many Opatas learned to speak Spanish, and Spaniards employed Opata warriors in campaigns against other tribes. As Spanish settlement

6. The provinces and peoples of northern New Spain

from the south and Apache raids from the northeast increased, Spanish-Opata ties grew into an alliance that lasted for more than a hundred years. Opata people took new opportunities as laborers and direct producers in the colonial economy and exchanged their labor and military service in return for recognition of their collective claim to land.[70]

Nueva Vizcaya had been in turmoil through the 1670s, with a mere one hundred troops to defend the entire province.[71] Indians were reported wandering the province, committing murders and robberies. The influx of more than three thousand New Mexican refugees placed the community of El Paso under tremendous pressure and strained relations with the neighboring Suma and Manso Indians, who were rumored to be on the brink of revolt throughout 1680–81. Indians in Nueva Vizcaya rebelled in 1683. Work in the mines and plantations ground to a virtual halt, and the province was temporarily cut off from the rest of New Spain. The Chisos, Julimes, and other nations, generally referred to as Conchos, occupied the road from El Parral to Sonora and Salinas, depriving the mines of supplies of salt, "without which silver, which is the most abundant mineral, cannot be extracted with mercury."[72] Mansos, Janos, and Sumas continued to talk of rebellion. In May 1684 they killed a priest in present-day Janos, precipitating a general exodus from the missions.[73] With limited manpower and resources, Governor of New Mexico Domingo Jironza Petriz de Cruzate attempted to stem their flight and then gathered his troops and Indian allies for punitive expeditions in the field. In June and July his forces dislodged some two thousand Indians from a defensive position on a *peñol* (freestanding rock) near Casas Grandes and burned a Manso *ranchería.* But the Indians retreated to a new position, held off the Spanish assault, and raided livestock and grain stores.

Reinforced by Indian allies from Sonora—who now included Opatas—and by settlers, the Spanish launched punishing new offensives in the fall. New Mexican officer Roque Madrid led soldiers from the El Paso presidio in an attack on a Suma sierra stronghold at the end of September. "I have never seen such a battle in all my life," he reported. "The fighting was the most savage ever seen, and I did all the damage I could to them. We killed more than forty and wounded many more."[74] Capt. Francisco Ramírez de Salazar led four campaigns against the Mansos and Sumas. "We fought up and down on the mountain sierra, in the canyons, and among the rocks," he reported of one battle. "We lost our horses, saddles, blankets, and many other things. There were so many enemies and the mountain was so rugged that we had to fight on foot." During another all-day battle "we killed many of them," but, "as always, these Indians find their strength in the mountains, and they fled to all parts. It was impossible to pursue them, although we all wished to vanquish them." Finally, in December Ramírez caught the enemy on the flatlands. He had only twelve soldiers, eight lancers, and more than one hundred Indian allies, and he estimated the enemy force at more than two thousand. But "His divine majesty gave us a miracle, for we attacked with such ferocity and killed so many of them that they threw themselves, screaming, in front of the horses, begging for peace."[75] As Indian resistance broke down, "the usual mass executions of Indian ringleaders ensued."[76]

Some two thousand rebel Indians made peace at Ojo Caliente in December 1684. In mid-1685 many Sumas, Conchos, and Mansos agreed to return to live under Spanish rule. Others fought on, along with the Janos, Jocomes, Tobosos, Chisos, and Apache bands from the Gila and Siete Ríos region. Many settlers fled south, and any hopes of a Spanish reconquest of New Mexico were postponed. Confronted with so many rebellions—reports spoke of "more than 100 nations"—in desert and mountain terrain where Indians held the advantages and Spanish cavalry were ineffective, Spaniards had to adopt new tactics. Recognizing their inability to subdue Indian enemies by offensive war, they erected a series of new presidios to keep the enemy out of Spanish-held territory.[77]

The 1684–85 revolt never really ended. In 1686 Sumas, Mansos, Janos, Jocomes, and their allies stepped up their raids and carried the war west to Sonora. In 1688 Capt. Juan Fernández de la Fuente, an experienced Indian fighter, led campaigns from his presidio at Casas Grandes. In August he inflicted a crushing defeat on the Janos, Jocomes, and Sumas, killing two hundred men and capturing their women and children. The war dragged on.[78]

Then the Lower Pimas in Sonora revolted. These people had met Cabeza de Vaca, had served as allies of the Spanish in their war against the Yaquis, and had accepted Spanish missions.[79] One Indian blamed the uprising on "Spaniards who took away their land and populated it with horses and cattle" so that "the Indians could no longer cultivate their land."[80] But soldiers from Sinaloa seem to have sparked off the war when they raided a peaceful Pima village at Mototicachi in 1688, killing fifty people and carrying off more than 125 women and children as slaves, "as if they were the prisoners of a just war." The governor of Nueva Vizcaya, Juan Isidro de Pardiñas, ordered an inquiry ("Both Christians and gentiles must be spared the horrors of such excesses," he declared), but the damage was done. The Pimas retaliated and forced abandonment of "the best mines" in Sonora. Spanish campaigns went out under standing orders "to find any means of pacifying and reducing the Pimas." Fernández destroyed Pima crops and villages. Many Pimas surrendered, but the war continued to spread. "We must remember the example of New Mexico, where the enemy is more obstinate and rebellious than ever and is waging a long war," warned Governor Pardiñas, who feared the consequences if "the many nations should join together." He kept up constant war against the Pimas to force them "to crave peace."[81]

In 1689 uprisings broke out among Indians in Nuevo León, and the missions at San Bernardino and San Antonio were abandoned. Spanish expeditions, said Juan Bautista Chapa, "bore little fruit, because these natives are very astute and are seldom found on the plains where we could capture them." Some of the "guiltiest" were caught and hanged, but the land "remained in a worse state than before."[82]

In the spring of 1690 Tarahumaras and Conchos rose in revolt. In January 1691 soldiers and officials in Sonora petitioned for a presidio and garrison to help fend off Indian attacks: "Each day the rebels are making new conversions," they said. "Many nations that were at peace before are now declared as enemies." Spanish forces were inadequate to stem raids by Pimas, Sobaipuris, Sumas, Jocomes, Janos, Seris, Conchos, and Apaches. Spanish campaigns against the Tarahumaras relied heavily on Indian allies, some of whom had only recently been at war against the Spanish.[83]

In 1693 the viceregal visitor, Joseph Francisco Marín, surveyed conditions in Nueva Vizcaya. He reported that the Tepehuan Indians had been at peace for years and that both the Tepehuans and Tarahumaras were now "highly Hispanicized" and applied themselves to raising cattle and farming. He was equally optimistic that there was no fear of uprising in Sinaloa, where the inhabitants lived as peaceful Christian peasants.[84] Marín provided an extensive list of the Indian nations inhabiting the northwestern frontiers of New Spain, many of whom he described as "more peaceful than warlike." But like Pardiñas, he feared the prospect of many nations waging a united war. The Spaniards were hard-pressed to contain the lightning guerrilla warfare of these peoples; if they ever let loose their combined strength, Spanish defenses would be unable to withstand them. The best Spanish strategy, Marín advocated, was to sow seeds of discord among the nations, maintain the presidios at full strength, and send out squads of presidial soldiers and Indian auxiliaries to search out enemy Indians in their homes and *rancherías* and "to punish them all at once and to destroy them."[85] The presidio at Janos was critical: it confronted the Apaches as well as the various "rebellious nations," constantly rendered aid to Sonora, and protected the Camino Real lifeline.[86]

In 1695 the Upper Pimas revolted. The Spanish mining frontier had pushed north to the borders of Upper Pima country by the mid-seventeenth century, but not until 1687 did the mission frontier reach Pimería Alta, the name applied to the northern region of Sonora and the southern part of Arizona that was home to the Ootam or Pima people. It came in the person of Father Eusebio Kino. Described by his successor as "merciful to others, but cruel to himself," Kino was an energetic, ascetic, and far-ranging Italian Jesuit. Over the course of twenty-five years he traveled thousands of miles by foot and on horseback, sometimes alone and sometimes with other missionary companions. By the mid-1690s Kino was in contact with Ootam groups; he also traveled to the Yuma Indians on the Colorado River and into California. He preached to the Pimas in their own language, "dispatched Christian messages and talks in all directions," and founded two dozen missions. In addition to his missionary zeal, Kino was an explorer, cartographer, writer, and cattle rancher, introducing livestock, grains, and fruits to the missions he founded.[87]

Kino was a remarkable priest and a remarkable presence, but, like the Pueblos in New Mexico, Pimas found themselves pressured and pestered to supply labor, attend religious services, give up traditional marriages practices, and adopt Christian-style monogamy. The Jesuits even employed Opatas—traditional enemies of the Pimas—as overseers. The usual combination of abuses on the Spanish missionary, mining, and military frontier drove the Pimas to rebellion.[88] In the spring of 1695 they killed two Spanish priests and some Opata overseers.[89] Still haunted by memories of the Pueblo Revolt, the Spanish retaliated with brutal punishments, but the reprisals only fanned the flames of revolt. Kino managed to bring Pima headmen to Tupo to negotiate a peace agreement, but presidial soldiers and their Seri allies massacred many of the unarmed Pimas.[90]

A real war erupted. Gen. Juan Fernández de la Fuente, who was assembling his forces for a campaign against Apache strongholds, rapidly diverted them to the western deserts, and the governor of Nueva Vizcaya ordered a massive response.[91] Fernández found his forces inadequate to the task of quelling the Pimas while at the same time punishing those Janos, Jocomes, Mansos, Chinarras, and Apaches who remained united in opposition and clung to the rugged sierra where they lived. "From the mountain peaks they are able to do whatever they wish," he complained.[92] The Spanish mustered Indian allies to assist presidial troops in searching out and destroying Pima *rancherías.* Juan Fernández kept a daily journal of his four-month campaign—a campaign he would much rather have waged against the Apaches—and of the brutal warfare required to quell the rebellion.[93]

The Spaniards sent Indian couriers with crosses to offer the Pimas a choice: peace and pardon if they handed over the leaders of the rebellion and returned to their pueblos or "a war of fire and blood . . . putting to the sword both adults and children, regardless of sex or age," if they refused or delayed.[94] Many Pimas fought on, but eventually, under the pressure of Spanish sorties and the Spanish ultimatum, most came in and accepted Spanish terms. While military officers interrogated Indians about why they had rebelled, Kino and his missionaries began the work of restoring the Indians to their Christian duties. By the end of August, when Spanish troops returned to the pueblo of Tupo, the site of the massacre, the Indians had erected crosses and arches along the road. They came out to greet the Spaniards, said they were happy to live in peace, and blamed the devil for inciting them to revolt. "We . . . left them all rejoicing," Fernández wrote in his journal.[95]

There were few other occasions for rejoicing. With the Pimas quelled, Fernández turned his attention back to campaigning against Sumas, Mansos, Janos, Chinarras, and Apaches in the Gila River Valley and Chiricahua Mountains. The Indians played cat and mouse with Spanish patrols in the woods and mountains, and the soldiers suffered illness and thirst. The Spaniards withdrew from the field and returned to their presidios, knowing it was a war they could not win and that the Indians would gather to exact vengeance as soon as they left. "Experience has shown," Fernández complained, "that every winter when the tribes feel that the Spanish cavalry has become exhausted, they come to the frontiers of Sonora and Casas Grandes. From there they operate freely since the severe weather and the rough territory prevent us from going to war with them."[96]

In 1696 an Opata leader called Pablo Quilme or Quihue attempted to organize a revolt. He asserted that the Spaniards were his people's worst enemies, worse even than the Apaches. In particular, he protested

Spanish seizure of Indians for forced labor and of children for servants. The movement was suppressed before it gathered momentum; ten leaders were hanged, and Quilme was killed. The Opatas did not challenge Spanish colonial rule again until 1820.[97] Also in 1696 the Upper Tarahumaras revolted again. The brutal war dragged on for two years. Whole bands of Tarahumaras chose to die in battle rather than surrender, and the Spaniards stuck the severed heads of Tarahumara leaders on posts along roadsides. By the time the Spanish put down this final rebellion, their conquest of the Tarahumaras had taken almost one hundred years. The Tarahumaras turned from outright rebellion to more subtle forms of resistance.[98]

Much of New Spain's northwestern frontier remained in the throes of conflict through the 1690s. Indians rose up in violent fury against their Spanish oppressors, raided Spaniards and their Indian allies, and drove off horses and livestock. Spanish forces sought out and destroyed Indian *rancherías*, but no sooner did they snuff out rebellion in one area than it broke out in another. Truces were patched together, but peace proved fragile and temporary. Many Indians made peace under duress and resumed raiding once Spanish forces moved on to do battle elsewhere. The late seventeenth century saw the most dramatic epidemic of rebellions against Spanish rule but by no means the end of them. Indian peoples who had resisted the expansion of the colonial frontier continued to resist the imposition of colonial rule. The raids that Spaniards characterized as rebellions never really stopped in the provinces south of New Mexico. Apache raiders swept down from the north, and Hispanic and Native inhabitants lived in a state of almost constant war. Indian wars of resistance would erupt throughout the eighteenth century. In the early nineteenth century the tradition of venting expression in outbursts of rural collective violence, in the words of one historian, "rocked and eventually helped topple the colonial regime."[99]

The new governor of New Mexico, Diego de Vargas Zapata Luján Ponce de León, had prepared campaigns against the rebels in the south and against Apaches but insisted that it was more important to subdue New Mexico, "the origin of all of the rest of the revolutions."[100] As long as the Pueblos remained independent, their example served as a beacon for the southern peoples in their wars. The "freedom fever" that seeped south from New Mexico must be quashed.[101]

The Reconquest of New Mexico

As Fray Juan de Jesús was being humiliated at Jemez in 1680 (he was forced to ride naked on a pig's back through the town and then was beaten to death), he is reputed to have said, "Do with me as you wish, for this joy of yours will not last more than ten years, after which you will consume each other in wars." [102] Within the decade, the unity that the Pueblos had brought to bear so effectively in August 1680 was gone. Spanish forces returned to restore the rule of king and Christ, by diplomacy and persuasion if possible, by fire and sword if necessary.

The Spanish reconquest of New Mexico often seems little more than an inevitable aftermath to the briefly successful Pueblo Revolt: Popé abuses his power, the fragile Pueblo unity disintegrates, and Diego de Vargas easily and efficiently restores Spanish dominion. But reconquest involved more than raising the banner of the king before repentant Indians gathered in pueblo plazas. The Pueblo Revolt initiated sixteen years of Pueblo-Spanish warfare, and restoring crown rule involved a series of bloody campaigns carried out amid revived inter-Pueblo conflict. Thanks to the documents compiled, translated, and edited by historian John Kessell and his colleagues in the Vargas project, a much fuller picture of this tumultuous period in New Mexico's history is now available. Vargas drew on his own ambition and energy rather than on an overtaxed treasury in Mexico City to carry out the reconquest. He appears to have spent as much time penning reports to bring his achievements to the attention of his superiors and his king as he did in the saddle. He was, in Kessell's words, both "heroic conqueror and strutting peacock." As a result, the documentation for the reconquest is rich and detailed if a tad lopsided. [103]

Divisions among the Pueblos surfaced soon after the expulsion of the Spaniards. Many Pueblos were reluctant to follow the commands of their revolutionary leaders to discard the European goods and tools that had made their lives easier. Others balked at abandoning spouses they had married as Christians. Popé began to act like the Spanish tyrants he had expelled, threatening to punish those who broke his rules and demanding that his followers bow before him. But while Popé reveled in displaying power, his real power faded away. He had promised peace and prosperity, but Apaches continued to raid Pueblo communities, and droughts continued to shrivel Pueblo crops. Disillusioned followers pulled away from Popé. Civil war erupted at some pueblos between his supporters and opponents, and caciques, medicine men, and warriors competed for position. Some people voted with their feet and moved to new locations or joined other pueblos. Hungry Pueblos began to prey on the granaries of neighboring communities. The Keres of Zia, Santa Ana, San Felipe, Cochiti, and Santo Domingo joined forces with Jemez, Taos, and Pecos against the Tewas, Tanos, and Picuris. The Tewas and Tanos deposed Popé and replaced him with Luis Tupatú. Popé was reelected in 1688 but died soon after, and Tupatú was chosen as leader again. The Keres leader, Alonso Catiti, died, and the Keres alliance unraveled, with each Keres pueblo acting independently. Acoma split: some moved away from the rock, and the two remaining groups fought each other. Zunis fought Hopis. Apaches were at peace with some Pueblos but waged war against the Jemez, Taos, Picuris, and Tewas. Utes raided everyone, especially the Taos, Tewas, and Jemez.[104] Abandonment and resettlement of villages was nothing new in the Pueblo world, but the breakup, movement, and restoration of communities that occurred after 1680 reoriented that world.[105]

Meanwhile, the Spaniards were not idle. In 1681 they established a presidio at El Paso to protect the refugee population. Franciscans who had been expelled from their missions in the north began to build mission communities near La Junta de los Ríos.[106] In 1688 Pedro Reneros de Posada "invaded New Mexico, reached the pueblo of Zia, captured some horses and some sheep and returned to El Paso, having," noted Escalante, "accomplished nothing else."[107] Governor Jironza, who had launched punitive campaigns against the Apaches, Janos, Mansos, and Sumas, made a bloody *entrada* into New Mexico in 1689. At Zia the inhabitants fought with "desperate courage"; when the Spaniards set fire to the pueblo, many of them burned alive on the tops of their houses rather than surrender. More than six hundred men, women, and children died. Four old men who were taken alive were promptly shot in the plaza. The survivors fled west to Jemez. "It is not proven that in this expedition anything else was accomplished," commented Escalante. Jironza laid plans for another invasion in 1690 but was compelled to divert his energies to quelling revolt around El Paso.[108]

The Spaniards apparently acquired an important ally this time. War captain Bartolomé de Ojeda fought against them in defense of Zia. Badly wounded, he surrendered and asked for a Franciscan friar to hear his confession. He was taken to El Paso for questioning and began to serve as an informant and intermediary. Vargas stood as godparent at the baptism of his children.[109] In 1691 or 1692 a group of men from Jemez, Zia, Santa Ana, San Felipe, and Pecos, together with some Tanos, went to El Paso to parlay with the Spaniards and, according to tribal history, invited the Spaniards to return.[110]

In August 1692 Diego de Vargas embarked on a campaign of "Armed Reconnaissance and Ritual Repossession."[111] With fifty soldiers and their officers, ten armed citizens, one hundred Pueblos from the El Paso region, three Franciscan friars, wagons, a small cannon, a mortar, and livestock, Vargas set out to restore the kingdom of New Mexico "even if all the power of the world opposes it." If the Indians resisted he vowed to "destroy them by force of arms, saving only the little boys and girls."[112] He found Cochiti and Santo Domingo abandoned. At San Felipe the inhabitants fled, but one rode back and said in Castilian that the people wanted peace with the Spaniards so that the soldiers would help the people against the Tewas and Tanos, who were making war on them.[113] Vargas spread the word that he had come not "to kill them, rob them, and carry off their women and children, but to pardon them so they might again become Christians." He employed a Tewa chief, Domingo ("I saw he had a heart that could be reduced," he said), as an intermediary to carry his message to the rebels. Domingo assured him sadly that he had already been preaching the virtues of peace to his people, "reminding them of what had happened at Zia Pueblo."[114]

In September Vargas entered Santa Fe. The Indians were defiant and frightened at first but gradually came out to the plaza and asked for peace, "which I gave them all, with all my love." Vargas had the royal standard raised three times and, speaking through an interpreter, assured the Indians they would be pardoned and returned to the holy faith and the king's protection: "They were his vassals, and in his royal name, I was returning to revalidate and reclaim his possession not only of this kingdom, provinces, and all the land, but also of them." He pardoned the Indians, the friars absolved them, and mass was held in Santa Fe for the first time in a dozen years.[115]

Luis Tupatú, don Luis of the Picuris, "governor of all the pueblos of the Tewas and Tanos," sent word that he wanted peace and would come and see Vargas, but he feared for his safety. Vargas guaranteed him safe-conduct, and the chief and a retinue of followers came down from the mountains around Santa Fe. The meeting between the two governors was conducted with formality on both sides. On his forehead Tupatú wore a palm-straw or yucca-fiber band that looked like a diadem, woven like a cordon with a heart-shaped shell in the middle above his head. He held a small silver image of Christ in his hands and wore a rosary Vargas had sent him around his neck. Vargas greeted him "kindly with warm words and chocolate," which they drank together. When Tupatú departed at nightfall, he gave Vargas animal skins as a symbol of peace; Vargas gave him one of his saddle horses. "The last thing I told him was that I was going to leave him as governor and he would have to report to me and see that the Indians were good Christians."[116]

Next morning, Tupatú returned with leaders from the Tewas, Tanos, and Picuris to discuss peace terms. Vargas gave him a public audience and breakfast with the missionary fathers, while "a great crowd of people" gathered around the tent. Vargas insisted that the fathers had to absolve the Indians of their apostasy before he could pardon them. Tupatú knelt and received absolution. Vargas also insisted on visiting the various pueblos, taking the friars with him. Men who had separated from wives they had married as Christians would be returned to live with their wives and would give up other women. Children born since the revolt would be baptized as Christians. "The reverend fathers would do this with all their love, because that was what I had brought them for," said Vargas. Those pueblos and people who did not comply with his instructions he "would destroy once and for all." Tupatú pointed out that it would be difficult to gather all the people who had fled to the mountains and mesas. Now that Santa Fe had surrendered, he suggested, perhaps Vargas could return to El Paso and come back within a year, by which time Tupatú would have reassembled the people, and they would be ready to render their obedience. Vargas refused to be gotten rid of so easily: he would wait for the Indians to come down to their pueblos. Tupatú and his brother Lorenzo each offered to assist Vargas in making war against Taos, Pecos, and other pueblos who were friendly to their enemies, the Faraón Apaches. With repeated assurances that he "should not be judged by fear of his proven treachery," Tupatú left before sunset.[117]

The fathers baptized 122 children who had been born since the revolt. Indian leaders who had defied Vargas from the fortress now asked him to be godfather to their children: "Their mothers brought them to me so that I might carry them in my arms, as I did, to receive the water of holy baptism." By standing as godparent, or *compadre,* Vargas brought Indians into the special and reciprocal relationship that existed in Spanish Catholic society among parent, godparent, and godchild while at the same time performing a social function that would have been familiar to Indian people. Priests, officers, soldiers, and interpreters with Vargas also acted as godfathers.[118]

During the next four months, Vargas visited a dozen pueblos. In each one he ritually pardoned the inhabitants and raised the royal banner, while the friars gave absolution and baptized children. The Indians were suspicious, afraid the Spaniards intended retribution and would take their women and children. In some cases they were ready to fight, but by boldness and patience, by exploiting Pueblo disunity, and by offering pardon and salvation as the alternative to certain destruction, Vargas prevailed in securing ritual submissions.

He traveled as far west as Zuni and the Hopi villages. At Awatovi on Antelope Mesa, where the Hopis had stoned their priest to death and destroyed the mission church, he threatened the inhabitants with total destruction. Having secured the gateway to the province of Tusayan, he then traveled, accompanied by the Awatovi chief, to Walpi, Shungopovi, and Mishongnovi. He secured submission by intimidation everywhere except at Oraibi.[119]

By mid-December 1692 Vargas was back in El Paso: "No one has had the boldness to do what I have done up to now through divine will," he boasted.[120] Not content to have his deeds reach royal attention through normal channels, Vargas dictated an "endless memorial" to the king, recounting in dramatic detail how he had restored New Mexico at his own expense, something his predecessors, despite great cost to the royal treasury, had failed to achieve. New Mexico contained twenty-three pueblos, he told his king. "I leave them not only conquered for your royal crown, but also subjugated to evangelical law, having baptized 2,214 people of all ages male and female. I have freed and taken away 76 captives and successfully rescued the holy vessels, divine images, and book. . . . Those barbarians have again recognized our holy faith and left their apostasy."[121]

But even Vargas realized that his bloodless conquest would prove illusory without stronger Spanish power and a permanent presence that included women as well as men. Five hundred families must be settled in New Mexico and supported with a presidio and one hundred soldiers: "To do otherwise would be to risk losing everything," he wrote at the end of his campaign report, " . . . like casting a grain of salt into the sea." In the fall of 1693 he departed El Paso with a column of several hundred colonists, mostly New Mexican refugees of the 1680 revolt and their families, and toiled north to Santa Fe.[122]

Pecos, Santa Ana, Zia, and San Felipe received him and adhered to the agreements they had made in 1692, but other Pueblos were watchful and defiant.[123] Santa Fe was again in Indian hands, and the Indians refused to vacate the town. Weakened by hunger and hard travel in bad weather, the colonists set up winter camp outside the walls. Indians hurled insults and stones from the ramparts, shouting that reinforcements were on the way and the colonists would all be killed. Juan de Ye, governor of Pecos and a man the Spaniards believed to be trustworthy, warned them that the Tewas, Tanos, and Picuris, joined by Apaches, were plotting to attack them.[124] Negotiations broke down, and Vargas resorted to war without quarter. Aided by allies from Pecos, Zia, Santa Ana, and San Felipe, the Spaniards stormed Santa Fe and took it after a two-day battle. Vargas rounded up seventy of the young men and charged them as traitors to the king and enemies of God. A priest gave them absolution, and Vargas "ordered them shot at once." He distributed four hundred women and children as servants among his colonists.[125]

The mass execution was intended to deter further resistance. Instead, New Mexico became a war zone, and Vargas battled to translate his ritual conquest of the previous year into harsh reality. Many Pueblos continued to resist from mesa-top fortresses and mountain refuges, raiding Spanish herds as well as striking at the "loyal" pueblos. Vargas tried to induce them to return to the king's protection, but it required a nine-month war of attrition to repossess most of the pueblos and restore the missionaries.[126]

In January 1694 Bartolomé de Ojeda, Vargas's staunch Keres ally, sent word from Zia that the Indians assembled at Jemez and Cochiti mesa wanted to make war. "Everyone has revolted," he warned. Fearing a league between the Keres rebels, the Tewas, and the Apaches, the pueblos of Zia, Santa Ana, and San Felipe asked for Spanish protection.[127] Vargas resorted to patrolling the rebels' pueblos and assaulting their strongholds.[128] In March he laid siege to the Tewa Indians gathered on San Ildefonso Mesa overlooking the Rio Grande Valley but was unsuccessful and returned to Santa Fe.[129] In April, while a group of rebel Indians ran off horses and cattle from Santa Fe, Vargas attacked the Mesa of La Cieneguilla of Cochiti (now known as Horn Mesa), which he described as "straight up, with rocks everywhere." Bartolomé de Ojeda knew the approaches and led forty men up a cattle path, catching the rebels in the rear, while the Spaniards attacked up two other approaches. They seized the mesa and captured 13 warriors, 342 noncombatants, and 900 sheep and goats. As soon as the priests absolved them, Vargas had the warriors shot.[130] In May he attempted another raid on San Ildefonso.[131] In early July he marched against Taos. The inhabitants fled to the mountains, and the soldiers emptied the abandoned pueblo of its remaining stores of corn. As they withdrew, smoke signals went up from the mountain ranges, and Indians harassed them.[132]

In late July Vargas launched a predawn raid on the fortified *peñol* of the Jemez (Mesa de Guadalupe, or San Diego Mesa). He employed the same tactics that had worked at La Cieneguilla: while the main Spanish force attacked, Indian allies led another squadron up a trail at the rear of the *peñol*. At least eighty-four Jemez people died. Seven threw themselves from the cliff. Four men and one woman were burned to death; two Indians were executed, including an Apache who assisted the rebels. The Spaniards took 361 noncombatants prisoner and seized sheep and goats. Given the obstacles they had to overcome, said Vargas, it was "a victory more than miraculous." The Spaniards later captured and interrogated a Keres chief from Santo Domingo who had injured his leg jumping from the *peñol* during the battle. He told them that the people who escaped had scattered: some to Taos, some to Cochiti, others to join the Navajos. His own people had abandoned their pueblo at Santo Domingo and fled to the mountains.[133]

Vargas returned to San Ildefonso Mesa at the beginning of September. After a three-day siege, the Indians surrendered, and Vargas pardoned them on condition they return to their pueblos.[134] At the end of the month he entered Jemez. In a pattern repeated at other pueblos, he assigned a missionary and handed out canes of office to those men chosen to serve as governor, lieutenant governor, *alcalde*, *alguacil*, captain, war captains, and *fiscales*. He installed Bartolomé de Ojeda as governor of Santa Ana. By the end of the year only Picuris, Taos, Acoma, Zuni, and Hopi remained unconquered.[135]

But still there was no peace. As redeveloper of New Mexico, Vargas "play[ed] god," says historian John Kessell, "rearranging people and their lives." He had dispossessed the Tanos and Tewas living at Santa Fe to make room for his colonists. Now, in the spring of 1695, he established a villa for new colonists at Santa Cruz, three hours' ride north of Santa Fe. The colonists were discontented. There was hunger and disease in the winter of 1695–96. Fifty-two of the one hundred soldiers allocated to defend the colony had died, and Vargas had fewer than half of the five hundred families he wanted.[136] Tanos talked openly in their own language about revenge. By the spring, rumors were flying. Indian men and women "moved by compassion" warned their missionaries of impending revolt. The missionaries requested armed guards, and the colonists pleaded for protection.[137]

On June 4, 1696, Pueblo Indians killed twenty-one Spaniards and five missionaries. They burned and desecrated churches, abandoned their pueblos, and went up to the mesas and mountain ranges. At San Ildefonso the priest, along with some Spanish men, women, and children, died of suffocation when the Indians set fire to the convent where they had taken refuge. At San Cristóbal Indians killed the two missionaries, stripped them, and left them lying face up on the ground in the form of a cross. According to Fray Francisco de Vargas, an Indian woman who was there said that some of the women "put their arms around them and wept over them," lamenting the priests' deaths and "the hardships which they expected to undergo in the mountains with their children." Some of the men felt the same way, but their leaders silenced them, preferring "to die in rebellion and apostasy rather than to yield or subject themselves to the yoke of the church."[138] At Cochiti, according to one account, the people wanted to kill the priest because he had had sexual relations with a married woman. He fled on foot for San Felipe at four in the morning, disguised in women's clothes. He dashed off a short letter warning Governor Vargas: "Keep your saddle in close view and your hat on your head."[139]

Dispossessed Tanos, along with Tewas, Picuris, Taos, Tiwas, Jemez, and Keres from Santo Domingo and Cochiti, took up arms. Indian prisoners later said they rebelled because of rumors that Vargas planned to kill all the adult males, perhaps a reference to rash threats made to try and quell growing discontent. For many medicine men and war chiefs, this was "the last stand" in their fight to throw off the Spanish yoke.[140] Bartolomé de Ojeda warned Vargas that tribes were gathering at Acoma. Indian prisoners under interrogation confirmed that Hopis, Zunis, Apaches, Navajos, and Utes were expected to join them. Ojeda's pueblo at Zia, which had been burned by the Spaniards in 1689, now feared assault by Indian enemies.[141] Allied leaders furnished warriors to prove their loyalty to Spain. A Pueblo revolt became a Pueblo civil war.

Given the rapidity with which rebellions had spread after the 1680 revolt, Spain was determined to quash this one promptly. Vargas dragged himself from his sickbed, where he had almost died of typhus, and reacted swiftly. Sensitive to charges that the revolt could have been prevented had he heeded warnings and petitions from the friars, he set out to get the job done. He summoned the governors and war captains of the various pueblos and told them he was still strong enough to attack them and that the people had better live in peace and hand over the "rabble-rousers." He assembled his presidial soldiers and militia and one hundred warriors from Pecos and launched search-and-destroy missions against the rebels: "I would seek them out on the mesas and in the cañadas, mountain ranges, canyons, and hills, wherever they might be," he declared.[142]

As before, his strategy was to offer pardon if the rebels would hand over their ringleaders, war without quarter if they refused; as in 1694 he campaigned by handing out alternately chocolate and death sentences. Vargas's justice was swift and severe. For example, when Lorenzo, a Tano Indian who lived at San Cristóbal, was captured, he denied participating in the revolt and claimed he was ill when the Indians killed their priests. Vargas ordered that he be given absolution, then had him hanged "from one of the tallest pines."[143] Executions by hanging and firing squad marked Vargas's progress through Pueblo country.

Afflicted by dissension and drought, the rebels could not repeat the successes of 1680. In July Vargas launched a dawn raid on the Cochiti rebels, filtering through a canyon in the sierra. The Indians fled, leaving six men dead, thirty-one women and children as prisoners, and much booty. Vargas sent an old woman with a cross drawn on a piece of paper to try and bring back the people with assurances that they would be spared.[144] Miguel de Lara, with sixteen men-at-arms and Indian allies, won a short but bloody battle over the Jemez rebels.[145] Before the month was over, Vargas attacked the Tewas' stronghold in the funnel canyons of the sierra. Lucas Naranjo, a mixed-blood chief whom Vargas had installed as war captain at Santa Clara in 1694 and who was now "the prime mover of this uprising," waited in ambush with his men. There was an exchange of fire, and a bullet hit Naranjo in his Adam's apple and exited through the nape of his neck. A soldier cut off his head. By the time the head was delivered to Vargas, a pistol shot through the right temple had caused the brains to spill out: "It gave me great pleasure to see the said rebel apostate dog in that condition," wrote the governor. He gave one of Naranjo's hands to his Pecos allies. The Spaniards estimated they had killed ten Indians in the battle. "From the streams of blood on the boulders, we could see how many were yet to die."[146] Again, Vargas sent old women with crosses drawn on paper, promising that if the people came down from the mountains and worked in their cornfields, he would pardon and defend them, but that if they refused, "I would return and kill all of them."[147]

In mid-August Vargas laid siege to Acoma for three days, but, lacking the forces to carry out an assault on the heavily fortified *peñol* and fearing Apaches were close at hand, he withdrew, burning the Indians' fields.[148] Later that month, Roque Madrid, Vargas's lieutenant general of cavalry, captured Miguel Saxete, governor of San Juan. (Saxete blamed Juan Griego for inciting the revolt; Griego blamed the deceased Naranjo.) The friars pleaded for Saxete's life, and Vargas dispatched him to Picuris to talk with the governor, his brother Antonio.[149] Felipe Chistoe of Pecos produced grisly testimony of his loyalty, hanging four rebel leaders and sending Vargas the head of a fifth, an action that brought his already-fractured community to the brink of disintegration.[150]

In September Vargas marched to Taos. The town was empty, and the few Indians in the fields fled as the Spaniards approached, sending smoke signals to warn their people. Vargas dislodged them from their canyon refuge, capturing stores of clothing, hides, and corn. When Governor Francisco Pacheco and his people yielded, Vargas let them return in peace to their pueblo but ordered them to bring him the head of anyone who "went to them with evil talk."[151]

Early in October Vargas turned on Picuris. He found the pueblo abandoned; the inhabitants, accompanied by a number of Tewas, Tanos, and Apaches, had fled eastward toward the buffalo plains. Vargas went in pursuit and caught up with them. He captured eighty men, women, and children. Antonio, the governor, was wounded. The women prisoners blamed him for inciting rebellion, and Vargas had him shot. He erected a cross to mark the site of his victory and took the prisoners to Santa Fe to be distributed as hostages. Others escaped, only to be captured by Cuartelejo Apaches in western Kansas.[152]

With winter approaching, the weather turned cold. Vargas lost hundreds of horses, and his exhausted men nourished themselves with "melted snow, roasted maize, and the meat of the dead horses."[153] Under steady pressure from Spanish patrols with Indian allies, Pueblo people straggled down from the mountains and surrendered. Some of the rebel leaders were executed. Hundreds of people fled west and were taken in by Hopis and Navajos, although the extent of the Pueblo refugee influx into Navajo country has recently been questioned.[154] By November the war was over.

In July 1697 Rodríguez Cubero arrived in Santa Fe to take over as governor. Diego de Vargas was arrested and compelled to answer complaints that he had mishandled the 1696 revolt, endangered the settlers, and exploited his office for financial gain. In 1704, back as governor of New Mexico after two years of litigation in Mexico City, he took sick and died while leading an expedition against the Faraón Apaches in the Sandia Mountains.[155]

After the Reconquest

By 1698 the great revolts were over. Spain had weathered the storms of Indian rebellion, and the Pueblo war of independence had sputtered out in a series of brutal little campaigns. Pueblos remained divided on whether and how to resist Spanish colonialism. Spain was back in control of Sonora and New Mexico, and most of the rebel tribes of Nueva Vizcaya had been defeated. The Spaniards responded to the rebellions with an expanded presidio system supplemented with flying companies of mounted troops to provide rapid response to Indian raids. But Indian resistance had also demonstrated that the Spanish empire in the north depended on negotiated peace as much as on military force.[156]

In present-day Arizona many refugees who fled Spanish reconquest of the Rio Grande stayed put, anti-Spanish sentiment remained strong, and resistance continued long after the reconquest of New Mexico. The Hopis took a harder line than most of the Rio Grande Pueblos. In the 1690s they moved the villages of Walpi, Shungopovi, and Mishongnovi from the bases to the tops of their respective mesas, anticipating that they would provide sanctuary to refugees from New Mexico and have to fend off Spanish reprisals. The Hopis retained useful items of Spanish origin such as wool, new crops, and domesticated animals but rejected other Spanish influences. Hopi potters who had incorporated Spanish design motifs in their ceramics now totally rejected them.[157] Tewa people who had fled west during the reconquest and established the village of Hano, or Tewa, the easternmost of the Hopi villages on First Mesa, around 1700 also held on to their own language and ways in a Hopi world. According to Hopi-Tewa elder Albert Yava, they were the only refugee community who stayed among the Hopis "without losing our own culture and our own traditions."[158]

After Awatovi submitted to Vargas, the church was rebuilt, and a Spanish priest returned in 1700. The restoration of Catholicism posed a renewed threat to Hopi ceremonialism and outraged some of the Hopi communities to the west, who conspired to attack the village. According to Hopi accounts, during a time of tension between Awatovi and Oraibi and leadership rivalry within Awatovi, an Awatovi chief named Ta'palo requested assistance from other Hopis to restore traditional ways and extinguish Christianity. "My children over in Awatovi are out of control," he said. "The elders are nothing to them. They are ravishing the women and girls. Our shrines and ceremonies are in shambles. They don't mean anything. These Spaniards, nothing but sorcerers and witches, are hoping to settle here for good." In late 1700 or early 1701 Francisco de Espeleta, the headman of Oraibi who before 1680 had been baptized and learned to read, raised one hundred warriors from Oraibi, Mishongnovi, and Walpi to destroy Awatovi and root out the evil influence of the Christians. It was a forceful message of Hopi cultural independence and community restoration.[159]

Hopi oral tradition recounts what followed: "Just as the sky turned the colors of the yellow dawn, Ta'palo rose to his feet on the kiva roof. He waved his blanket in the air, whereupon the attackers climbed to the top of the mesa and began the assault. There were many of them, so many in fact that they filled the village of Awatovi. They exactly followed the orders they had received. Running from kiva to kiva, they found that the men were inside. Immediately, they pulled out the ladders, depriving those inside of any chance to escape." The warriors brought finely shredded bark and greasewood kindling, which they lit and hurled into the kivas, throwing stacks of wood down onto the flames and firing arrows at the men inside. "Now the raiders stormed into all the houses. Wherever they came across a man, no matter whether young or old, they killed him. Some they simply grabbed and cast into the kiva. Not a single man or boy did they spare." Pulverizing bundles of dry chili that were hanging on the walls, the attackers scattered the powder into the kivas on top of the flames and then closed up the hatches so the smoke could not escape. "There was crying, screaming, and coughing. After awhile the roof beams caught fire. As they flamed up they began to collapse, one after the other. Finally, the screams died down and it became still. Eventually, the roofs caved in on the dead, burying them. Then there was just silence."[160] The raiders rounded up the surviving women and children for distribution in other Hopi villages and leveled Awatovi to the ground so that none of the survivors would ever think of returning there. Some Hopis fleeing the destruction of Awatovi are said to have taken up residence with Navajos living in Canyon de Chelly.[161]

Spanish soldiers in Hopi country fared as poorly as Spanish missionaries. In July 1701 Governor Rodríguez Cubero led an expedition from

Santa Fe to avenge the destruction of Awatovi. But when the Hopis withdrew to their mesa-top strongholds and prepared for siege, he abandoned the campaign. (Burial records show that two Zuni men died fighting on the side of the Spaniards.)[162] Subsequent campaigns fared little better. In 1716 New Mexico governor Felix Martínez led an expedition into Hopi country to bring back the people who had fled west rather than accept Spanish reconquest and imposition of Catholicism in the Rio Grande pueblos. More than one hundred Jemez refugees and some Tewas and Santo Domingans returned with him, but the Tanos who had settled on First Mesa near the Hopi village of Walpi remained defiant. Martínez burned their crops at the foot of the mesa, but they refused to return.[163]

The Hopis remained independent of Spanish control. They chose what they wanted from the Spaniards and incorporated foreign ideas and things by imbuing them with their own values, a strategy of cultural preservation that Hartman Lomawaima calls "Hopification." Passive resistance, cautious diplomacy, and selective borrowing and synthesizing proved effective in thwarting Spanish efforts to convert and change the Hopis.[164] The neighboring Zunis also found ways to preserve their culture from Spanish inroads. On the eve of Spanish invasion, the Zunis occupied six large villages. Several times between 1540 and 1680 they abandoned their villages and took refuge on the stronghold mesa of Dowa Yallame. After 1680, fearing reprisals, they established a year-round village on the mesa and stayed there for sixteen years. When they finally came down, they consolidated into a single village at Halona:we. Zuni population declined as the Hispanic presence increased, but Frank Hamilton Cushing described Zuni culture during this time as like "a drop of oil in water, surrounded and touched at every point, yet in no place penetrated or changed inwardly by the flood of alien belief that descended on it."[165]

Pueblo refugees, or at least increasing Pueblo contacts, alliances, and exchanges, added new elements to the fabric of Navajo life. Navajos integrated livestock into their everyday lives and their identity. Sheep changed the lives of Navajo women, who owned the herds and, with the help of their children, did the herding, shearing, and butchering. As the sheep herds increased in size, they demanded new pastures. Pueblos also brought sheep-herding and wool-making techniques they had learned from the Spanish, and their own customs and ceremonies found their way into Navajo culture. The acquisition of horses meanwhile allowed Navajos to extend their range. They expanded westward into lands once occupied by Anasazi, settling their matrilocal extended families in sheltered canyons and moving with the seasonal needs of their livestock.[166]

Warfare between Navajos and Spaniards in the early eighteenth century may have represented a continuation of the Pueblo war of independence by the Navajos and the Pueblo refugees who lived among them.[167] The Vargas documents contain recurrent references to Navajos assisting Pueblo resistance fighters. Vargas's successor, Francisco Cuervo y Valdés, waged vigorous war against the Navajos during his two years in office, dispatching contingents of Hispanic soldiers with Pueblo allies. The Navajos' success in adapting to their new lifestyle actually made them more vulnerable to assault. Their herds of horses and sheep, combined with their increased agricultural activity and accumulations of cotton and wool textiles, limited their mobility. They built defensible communities on mesas away from their fields, but their herds, and the women and children who tended them, remained exposed to raiders. Navajos suffered severely from slaving forays by Spaniards and Indians, which fueled and perhaps prolonged Navajo hostilities. The first captives specifically identified as Navajos appeared in New Mexican baptismal records in 1705. In the summer of that year, Roque Madrid's hardened Spanish troops and Pueblo Indians battled thirst and heat in a relentless campaign through Navajo country, attacking settlements and destroying corn. On one occasion they overtook two women, one a Christian from Jemez, the other Navajo. "I immediately separated them, putting them to the torture so that they would tell me where they were from, what they were doing there, or where their camps were," Madrid wrote matter-of-factly in his journal. On another occasion "I found the Indians about to kill an old woman and stopped them. She then fervently requested the water of baptism. She was baptized, and then they killed her." Other campaigns followed a similar pattern: Roque Madrid invaded Navajo country via the Chama Valley in 1714, killed about thirty Navajos, and seized two hundred *fanegas* of corn and more than one hundred sheep. Navajo leaders sued for peace. By 1720 the Navajos had made peace with New Mexico, and Navajo trade in textiles, baskets, hides, and captives developed into a significant part of the Spanish and Pueblo economy of New Mexico.[168]

Navajos needed peace with Spain as Ute and Comanche raids from the north intensified in the eighteenth century. Many Navajos retreated higher onto mesa tops, where they built stone houses and towers as defenses. The *pueblitos* at Old Fort Ruin and Three Corn Ruin in the San Rafael Canyon both appear to have been built and abandoned in the eighteenth century; Navajo tradition that may refer to Three Corn Ruin suggests it was abandoned after a Ute attack.[169] Apaches, Navajos, Utes, and Comanches now posed a greater threat to the Pueblos than did Spaniards. Spanish records cite many instances of Pueblo-Pueblo conflict in the seventeenth century, but by the early eighteenth century references to Pueblo warfare deal almost exclusively with Athapaskans; growing threats from Apaches and Navajos pushed Pueblos to unite against the common enemy. Pueblo warriors regularly accompanied Hispanic soldiers on expeditions into Apache and Navajo country. Likewise, Opatas and Pimas who had battled Spaniards in the late seventeenth century served alongside them in their wars against Apaches in the eighteenth century.[170]

In New Mexico the desire for freedom did not die. Sitting in Madrid around 1703, Juan de Villagutierre y Sotomayor, *relator*, or narrator, of the Council of the Indies, wrote of the Pueblos: "Rarely does one see them traveling, one or two by themselves, even though the journey might be a long one, when they are not singing all the way about the happy or sad events of war and peace and other things that happened to their elders which they enjoyed when they were free, from which it is clear that their desire to return to their former freedom is ever present."[171] Fray Francisco de Vargas doubted that the rebellious Pueblos would ever fully submit to the holy faith and suspected they wanted "peace with the Spaniards only for their trade and commerce and not to observe our holy laws."[172] He was probably close to the mark. The Pueblos were divided and devastated by the Spanish reconquest, but they "outlived the trauma." They compromised, made concessions, and agreed to accept Catholicism, but they remained Pueblo.[173]

Pueblos had tried to regain their independence by war and had failed. They had to find ways to preserve their world within a Spanish colonial world. Indians began to return to their pueblos; churches were rebuilt. About one hundred refugees from Cochiti, Santo Domingo, Jemez, and Cieneguilla had fled to Acoma during the reconquest in 1692; five years later, some of them established a new community at Laguna and made peace with Spain in 1698.[174] The Spaniards attempted to bring back Pueblos who had fled the Rio Grande and taken refuge on the plains to the east or in the high desert country to the west. Pueblos and Hispanos began to reconstruct patterns of coexistence that had unraveled in 1680. Both remembered the bloodshed of the war years, learned from that "momentous shared event," and rebuilt their lives, communities, and

10. Hide painting depicting an attack by mounted Spanish militia and Mexican Indian allies against Plains Indians, ca. 1693–1719, painted ca. 1720–29. (Courtesy, Museum of New Mexico, neg. no. 149797) The Indian attackers may be Opatas, Pimas, or Tarascans; the defenders most likely Apaches. The women and children who watch from the palisaded mesa top may be the primary object of the attack—slave raids on Apache *rancherías* were common. On the scene as slave raid, see Brooks, *Captives and Cousins*, 133.

colonies in ways that "ensured the cultural diversity of New Mexico."[175] The Pueblos had thrown off the Spanish yoke for a time, but they never completely reversed the cultural transformations generated by Spanish contacts. They continued to grow Spanish crops, herd Spanish livestock, and make woolen clothing. As David Weber notes, Pueblos were just as selective in rejecting aspects of Hispanic culture as they had been in accepting them.[176] Accommodation and careful coexistence offered Pueblos a path of survival and a role in the remaking of New Mexico.

About three thousand Spaniards lived in New Mexico in 1680. The Spanish-speaking population increased steadily after the 1696 Revolt. In 1697 it was estimated at fifteen hundred; in 1752 there were thirty-four hundred Spaniards and mixed-bloods in the colony. Twenty-five years later the population had almost doubled, and it doubled again between 1776 and 1789. By 1790 the total population of New Mexico reached more than thirty thousand people. Indian populations, meanwhile, continued to decline.[177] But, like the Pueblos, Spaniards remembered the lessons of the wars of independence and adopted more pragmatic approaches. Missionaries found ways to compromise and turned a blind eye to certain Native "superstitions" as they shifted "from crusading intolerance to pragmatic accommodation."[178] The Pueblo Revolt broke the hold of the missionaries on New Mexico. In the eighteenth century the governors strengthened their influence on the colony.

Vargas had assured Pueblo leaders that the *encomienda* would not be reestablished; instead, the colonists would adhere to the "Laws of the Indies" that protected lands that were farmed, irrigated, and inhabited by Native people and prohibited compulsory Christianization and forced labor. In 1697 the *fiscal* and viceroy categorically denied a petition by the settlers of Santa Cruz to use forced Indian labor. They recognized that "the abuse of repartimiento Indians" had constituted a major cause of the revolts. Indians must be required to do no more than contract to work for the person who pays them best, they instructed; forced labor was "the road to ruin" for both Indians and Spaniards.[179] In the eighteenth century the colonial government of New Mexico made grants of land from the royal domain to Indian pueblos as well as to families and communities of settlers and imposed guidelines for settlement patterns. The laws protecting Indian lands and water were vague and not consistently applied. Nevertheless, advocates were available to mediate social conflict, and disputes led to court rather than to revolt.[180] Spanish laws and legal institutions that were rooted in medieval European tradition underwent significant modification by the eighteenth century, providing the basis for a new political and social order in northern New Spain.[181]

The society that developed in New Mexico was a mixture of Hispanic and Indian cultures. The invaders brought their own cultural baggage, which, though it retained a distinct Spanish character, already showed the influence of Native peoples and the environment in Mexico. Some of it proved useless in New Mexico; some of it underwent additional modification. When Oñate established the first European colony in 1598 he had hoped to keep Indian and Spanish peoples separate, but changes cut both ways. The colonists lived in an Indian world, surrounded and vastly outnumbered by Indian people. Indian influences and Indian ways inevitably seeped into the culture of the new Mexico the Spaniards were trying to build. The colonists were fifteen hundred miles and six months' travel from Mexico City. Heavily laden mission supply caravans left Mexico City in midsummer, creaked along the Camino Real (averaging ten miles a day), and tried to reach New Mexico in the late fall or early winter, but they came irregularly, usually every two to four years. Oñate and his companions brought carts and wagons carrying the clothes they were accustomed to wearing in Mexico. The men had velvet suits with high collars and lace cuffs, satin caps, and richly embossed and stitched leather shoes from Cordova in Spain. The women brought decorated silk dresses, brightly colored slippers, and embroidered shawls imported from Manila. But the Spaniards had little opportunity to wear such fine clothes along the Rio Grande, and before long they were wearing clothes made of *gamuza* (chamois) or buckskin. Buckskin remained the standard clothing of New Mexicans, Indian or Hispanic, until cheap American cloth reached the New Mexican market in large quantities after the opening of the Santa Fe Trail in 1821.[182]

Unlike Oñate's colonists, most of the *pobladores,* or pioneers, who came to New Mexico in the late seventeenth and early eighteenth centuries did not expect to get rich quick. They knew New Mexico was a tough place to settle, and they came prepared to work hard and to feed, clothe, and sustain themselves. The majority of the people who settled in New Mexico and developed its distinctive society were not aristocrats, government officials, or missionaries but *paisanos,* ordinary country folk who, like the Pueblos, farmed and lived in villages. Even after Santa Cruz was established in 1695 and Albuquerque was founded in 1706, most Spanish-speaking people lived in frontier communities dispersed along the Rio Grande, clusters of families who worked the land and raised livestock in small ranches. Isolated from sources of Spanish support, they were forced to be self-sufficient and to improvise. They adapted Spanish customs and practices to New Mexican conditions and developed their own rural folk society, folk culture, folk art, and folk religion. They lived in adobe-style houses, ate Indian as well as Mexican food, used pottery made by Indian women, wore cloth woven by Indian women, and did paintings on buffalo hides. With no doctors or medical facilities of their own, they incorporated Indian herbs and remedies into their folk medicine, and, according to some reports, wives of unfaithful settler-soldiers resorted to Indian servants for love potions to help win back their husbands' affections. Often, colonists and Indians lived in mixed communities.[183] Some people of Hispanic descent adapted to the Plains environment to such an extent that they became *ciboleros*, far-ranging buffalo hunters and traders who added a Hispanic dimension to the trade that had existed for centuries between the plains and the pueblos.[184]

Indians rejected some things but embraced others. Spanish colonists brought new foods—wheat, cabbages, lettuce, chilies from Mexico, onions, radishes, peas, chickpeas, new varieties of corn, and melons, which may have arrived with Coronado—and peach, plum, apricot, and cherry trees. They introduced chickens, which competed with the Indians' domesticated turkeys. They brought horses, donkeys, cattle, pigs, and *churros*, a breed of Spanish sheep well adapted to semiarid conditions. Spanish cattle ranching spread north with the mining frontier and eventually extended from Texas to California.[185] Spanish missions pioneered sheep raising in the Southwest. Flocks of thousands of sheep produced coarse wool and, in time, resulted in overgrazing and arroyo cutting. Wool supplemented and in some cases replaced cotton, and Pueblos learned new techniques of weaving. Sheep spread to the Navajos and by the eighteenth century had produced a change in direction "from an incipient agricultural society to a herding one."[186] Indians readily adopted Spanish tools and, when they could get them, Spanish weapons. Spanish words and phrases seeped easily into Indian usage. Indian peoples used Spanish words for new concepts such as God, godparents, the Virgin Mary, saint, Christmas and Easter, Sunday, mass, and various ritual terms. They used Spanish terms of measuring time and distance and Spanish names for the many new things introduced by Spanish invasion: as anthropologist Edward H. Spicer said, "Work, governor, town, horse, cow, housecat, knife, and others had become parts of the vocabularies of Indian languages from Tarahumara to Tiwa." [187] Adjustments to Spanish invasion manifested themselves in numerous ways: Pueblo potters stopped using mineral-based paints after Spaniards commandeered the lead mines; instead, they began applying the vegetable paints that became a distinctive feature of Pueblo pottery.[188]

The population of New Mexico was ethnically mixed from the start. The term "Spaniard" applied to Castilians, Andalusians, Catalans, Basques, and other people from the Iberian peninsula as well as their mestizo or criollo descendants in America. Spanish expeditions included foreigners from other European countries, Indians from Mexico, and some African slaves. Santa Fe in the 1600s contained an entire barrio of several hundred Tlaxcala Indians whom Oñate had brought from central Mexico.[189] The invaders were also relatively small in number, and most "married out." As the population of New Mexico grew, it also grew more mixed. Ethnic lines blurred, and people of mixed ancestry often occupied positions in New Mexican government and society.[190]

Native peoples had raided each other for captives long before Europeans arrived, but as Indians began to participate in the Spanish slave trade, the taking and exchange of captives expanded in scope and assumed new meaning. Indian slaves became part of the cycle of raiding and trading by which horses, people, and corn changed hands. Many captives were destined for service in Spanish households and silver mines. They became an important part of the economy of New Mexico and ultimately part of the human landscape. Spanish priests condemned the practice of slavery, but Spanish mines and ranches provided an insatiable demand. Spaniards also had a duty to buy captives. In 1681 the Spanish colonial legal code obligated Christians to ransom captive Indians from other Indians. The code was reinforced after 1694, when a group of Navajos rode into Santa Fe with Pawnee children to sell. When the Spaniards refused to ransom the captives the Navajos beheaded them on the spot. After this incident the crown authorized paying captive ransoms from the royal treasury.[191] Many captives remained in servitude in New Mexico and added a new component to the colony's population. Apache, Navajo, Ute, Jumano, Caddo, and Pawnee slaves and their offspring, known as *genízaros*, worked as domestic servants, laborers, herders, and muleteers. Some learned trades and became blacksmiths, silversmiths, masons, and weavers. Many seem to have been assimilated into Hispanic households, but as a group they remained on the lowest rungs of New Mexican society. *Genízaros* frequently served as auxiliaries and allies against Apaches and other plains raiders.[192]

Over time, the Spaniards produced multiple categories by which to identify ethnicity and status. The child of a Spanish father and a black woman was a mulatto; the child of a Spanish father and an Indian woman was a mestizo; the offspring of a mestizo father and a Spanish mother was a *castizo*; a *lobo* was a person of black and Indian heritage; a *coyote* had mestizo and Indian as well as Spanish and Indian ancestry; and so on. *Genízaro* originally referred to Indians who had been ransomed as captives and raised in Hispanic households but came to be applied more liberally. By the eighteenth century, caste-conscious Spaniards, for whom personal honor was key to social status, placed themselves at the top of a social pyramid, with Spanish freeholders below them, Pueblo Indians below them, and*genízaros* at the bottom.[193]

But the very proliferation of categories demonstrated the failure of Oñate's plans to keep the Spanish apart as a separate people. A Pueblo prisoner interrogated in 1681 was asked if the Pueblos thought the Spaniards would return and what the Pueblo reaction was likely to be. He replied that some said the Pueblos would fight to the death if the Spaniards returned, but "others said that in the end they must come and gain the kingdom because they were sons of the land and had grown up with the natives."[194] The sons of the sun had become sons of the land.

New Mexico was no gem in the Spanish imperial crown; "this miserable kingdom is the most remote edge of the Christian realm in this New World and is devoid of all human resources," wrote acting governor Juan Paéz Hurtado in 1707.[195] As it had before the Pueblo Revolt, the colony drained Spanish coffers far more than it contributed. But it assumed increasing strategic value in the eighteenth century as a buffer against European and Indian enemies. New Mexico and Texas were both propped up economically and maintained at great expense as barriers to guard more wealthy provinces against threats from the north.

By 1700 the Spanish frontier stopped at a line between the outposts at Janos and Fronteras, just south of the present border between the United States and Mexico. Ranches and mining communities in the area had been abandoned. Farther west, Father Kino crossed the southwestern Arizona desert, reached the Gila River, and made contact with Yumans from the Colorado River, but Pima resistance had also slowed the pace of advance. A strip of territory almost 250 miles wide—roughly from Casas Grandes to Zuni—now separated the Sonora-Chihuahua part of the frontier from New Mexico. As Apache bands under pressures from the east (see chapter 6) extended their raids westward they increasingly dominated the region until an "Apache corridor" separated Spanish New Mexico from the rest of New Spain.[196]

On the northeastern frontier, Spaniards and Indians began to hear rumors and reports of a new kind of men appearing on the southern plains. Indians from the Rio Grande told Governor Pardiñas in 1688 that "some foreign people are in that territory . . . and are trying to thrust themselves upon the natives." An Indian from the Cíbolo nation said he had seen some men "clothed and with harquebuses" arrive at a *ranchería* between the Rio Grande and the Nueces River. "They called these men Moors because they brought coats or breastplates of steel, and helmets on their heads. They visited these Indians there many times and gave them axes, knives, beads, copper kettles, and sometimes clothing, and made gifts to the women of ribbons and other little things, and for this reason they had warm friendship for them." The strangers were survivors from La Salle's ill-fated Texas colony, some of whom had made their way west to Texas and begun trading with the Indians. The Spaniards dispatched scouting parties to gather accurate information and made preparations to defend their provinces against the perceived French threat.[197]

French missions and trading posts in the Mississippi Valley curtailed English expansion westward, but they also provided bases for forays against northern New Spain. In 1691 the Spanish established Texas (from the Hasinai word for "friends," *ta'-sha*) as a frontier province designed to protect the silver-mining provinces of northern and central Mexico.[198] They attempted to build a series of missions and presidios there as a buffer against French penetration and colonization. Fray Damian Massanet established a mission among the Hasinais, but epidemics in 1691 and 1692 strained relations. Situated on key exchange routes, Caddos were vulnerable to epidemics traveling from Spaniards in New Mexico and from French on the Mississippi. In 1691 about three thousand Hasinais died in a plague, reported Spanish priest Francisco Casañas. The Hasinais blamed Spanish priests for the outbreak. Hasinais also resented Spanish soldiers' abuses of their women and Spanish priests' attempts to undermine their religion. In 1693 they forced Massanet and the Spaniards out of Caddo country. The next year the viceroy of Mexico ordered the province of Texas to be abandoned.[199]

Frenchmen continued to be sighted on the southern plains. In the fall of 1695 Plains Apaches trading at Picuris brought word that "a great number of Frenchmen came toward the Buffalo Plains, driving the Apaches to this vicinity because of the many attacks they make against them." Vargas dispatched Roque Madrid to interrogate the Apaches and gain information about these fair-haired men. It turned out the Apaches had not seen them for themselves, they had only heard reports. However, it was, as Vargas wrote to Conde de Galvé, "a matter of great concern."[200] The tentacles of French exploration and empire building had reached across the Great Lakes, down the Mississippi, and out onto the southern plains. The great revolts that engulfed New Mexico, Nueva Vizcaya, and Sonora between 1680 and 1696 had brought a halt to Spanish expansion in the north. Now, with peace restored, Spain had to confront growing incursions from Apaches pushed against their frontiers by Comanches and from Frenchmen in Texas and Louisiana who seemed intent on reaching Mexican silver mines and building Indian alliances on Spanish frontiers.[201]

Early in 1700, news reached Santa Fe that Frenchmen had destroyed a village of Jumanos on the eastern plains.[202] Knowing that French traders and emissaries were active in Pawnee country, New Mexican officials dispatched a series of expeditions into the territory northeast of New Mexico and made renewed efforts to secure Texas as a buffer. In 1706–7, as part of Cuervo y Valdéz's plans to protect and unite the Pueblos against the Apaches and Navajos, Juan de Ulibarrí led a force of Spanish soldiers and Pueblo allies to El Cuartelejo in western Kansas to retrieve Picuris Indians who had been living there since 1696. Their chief, Lorenzo, had requested assistance in returning home. Ulibarrí's expedition consisted of twenty-eight presidial soldiers, a dozen settlers, and one hundred Pueblo Indians. José Naranjo from Santa Clara acted as chief scout. Also in the expedition was Jean L'Archevêque, a Frenchman who had been an accomplice in the murder of La Salle, had lived among the Indians, and had made his way to Spanish New Mexico, where he settled after his marriage. The expedition traveled through Jicarilla Apache country and into eastern Colorado. The various Apache bands received them well, and Ulibarrí "liberated" sixty-two Picuris, including Lorenzo and Juan Tupatú, son of Luis Tupatú. The Apaches asked Ulibarrí to accompany them on a campaign against the Pawnees seven days' journey away and told him of tribes beyond who had guns. The Apaches sold Pawnee captives in New Mexico, but Pawnees also captured Apache women and children to sell in the east. Utes and Comanches also raided Apachería. Ulibarrí met Apaches who had attacked an Indian village to the east where they said they had killed and scalped a European and a white woman who was with him. Among their plunder was a "red-lined cap," traditional headgear of a French voyageur. In 1708 voyageurs were reported to have ascended three or four hundred leagues up the Missouri as well as to the foothills of the Rocky Mountains.[203]

The Spaniards feared that the French instigated intertribal conflicts that jeopardized Spanish alliances with the Indians. In 1714, guided by José Naranjo, Governor Juan Paéz Hurtado led an expedition of more than two hundred men onto the plains to try and quell the conflicts but failed to learn more specific information about French activities.[204]

In 1716 the French moved up the Red River and established a garrison post near the Caddo village of Natchitoches. Spain responded with another round of missionary efforts in Texas. In 1718 the governor of Texas, Martín de Alarcón, established the mission San Antonio de Valero (the future Alamo) to serve the many bands of Coahuiltecans and other

Indians in the area who had been displaced by Spanish and Apache conflicts. A second mission, San José, was built in 1720, and three other missions were established nearby in 1731. Together with a presidio and settlement, the five Franciscan missions formed the core of the Spanish community of San Antonio de Béxar, which became the capital of Texas in 1773. Within the mission walls, neophytes lived a highly structured life of work and worship, but the missionaries never fully succeeded in breaking down the Indians' traditional ways of life and complained that there were not enough soldiers to make the Indians toe the line. Coahuiltecans entered the missions primarily to escape being caught in the escalating conflicts between Apaches and Comanches. On the Gulf Coast Karankawas incorporated missions into their seasonal migrations between coast and prairie as an additional source of food.[205]

In 1719, as Antonio Valverde y Cosío, governor of New Mexico, was leading an expedition of sixty soldiers and two hundred Pueblos against the Utes and Comanches, they met a wounded "Paloma" Apache from northeast of El Cuartelejo. This Plains Apache told them that French, Pawnees, and Jumanos had attacked his people from ambush while they were planting corn and that the French had built two pueblos: "In them they live together with the said Pawnees and Jumanos Indians, to whom they have given long guns which they taught them to shoot." It seemed clear, reported Valverde, that "the design of the enemy is to advance little by little into the interior."[206]

Spanish concerns about French activities became acute when France and England declared war on Spain in January 1719.[207] The French caught the Spanish off guard. In May they captured Pensacola; in June the French commander at Natchitoches and six soldiers "captured" the Spanish mission San Miguel de los Adaes, nearby on the Sabine River, from a lay brother and a single soldier. The Spaniards pulled back to the border of Tejas country on the Trinity River.[208] A soldier passing through New Mexico brought a wild report of six thousand French soldiers just seventy leagues from Santa Fe.[209] In 1720 the marqués de San Miguel de Aguayo led an expedition from Coahuila that in the next eighteen months established four new presidios, most notably at Los Adaes, with a one-hundred-man garrison. Los Adaes served as the capital of Spanish Texas from 1729 until it was closed in 1773.[210] Also in 1720 Viceroy Valero ordered Valverde to establish a presidio to block possible French advances.[211]

In June Valverde dispatched his lieutenant, Pedro de Villasur, from

11. Detail of a hide painting depicting the battle at the Spanish camp. Although difficult to identify here, Villasur, distinguished by the braid on his uniform, lies at the right center, below the fallen horse; L'Archevêque is in the cluster of soldiers. José Naranjo also died. (Courtesy, Museum of New Mexico, neg. no. 158345)

Santa Fe to Pawnee country. Villasur's force consisted of forty-five Spaniards, sixty Pueblos, a priest, and a Pawnee captive. Naranjo led the way as scout. Jean L'Archevêque went along as the French-speaking interpreter. En route, in present-day Colorado, a group of Jicarilla Apaches joined the expedition. Pushing northeast, Villasur reached the Platte River in mid-August. When they encountered Pawnees, Villasur had L'Archevêque write a note in French for them to take to their village. The Pawnees returned with illegible writing on old paper and a linen flag. But the attempt at negotiation failed. When Villasur made camp in long grass, the Pawnees began to circle it. Early next morning a volley of musket fire ripped through the camp, followed by a shower of arrows. Villasur, Naranjo, and L'Archevêque fell dead. More than two thirds of the Spanish force were killed or wounded. The Jicarillas made their escape, but only half a dozen of the others survived the massacre, reaching Santa Fe twenty-two days later. Half the garrison of Santa Fe died in the battle. A series of investigations into the disaster blamed Valverde for sending out an inexperienced officer, and he was removed from office.[212]

After the Villasur disaster, Spain was unable to carry out plans for defense against French advances and Apache, Ute, and Comanche raids. The initiative in reaching across the plains passed firmly to the French. Spaniards investigated reports of illegal French trading from Louisiana into New Mexico but could do little to stop it.[213] In 1724 Brig. Gen. Pedro de Rivera y Villalón began a tour of inspection of the military establishments throughout northern New Spain that lasted three years and covered seven thousand miles. He visited more than one hundred presidios and missions on the northern frontier. His report, later adopted as the *Reglamento* of 1729, recommended reorganizing presidial defenses and trimming expenses. It set the tone for Spanish frontier policy for the rest of the century.[214] Distracted by developments in Europe and constantly responding to Indian revolts elsewhere, Spain could spare few men and little money for the northern frontiers. Meanwhile, new Native powers, often attracted and propelled by forces the Spaniards themselves had unleashed, rendered the Spanish hold even more precarious and the lives of Hispanic settlers even more perilous.

Chapter 5

Calumet and Fleur-de-lys

When Makataimeshekiakiak was an old man he related his autobiography as the celebrated Sauk chief Black Hawk. He began by telling how his great grandfather, Na-nà-ma-kee, or Thunder, met a Frenchman. At that time, Sauk tradition said, the people lived on the St. Lawrence River. Na-nà-ma-kee dreamed for four years that he would meet a white man. Finally, the Great Spirit directed him to take his two brothers and travel east to a place where he would meet the white man. When the Sauks arrived, the man, who may have been Samuel de Champlain, took Na-nà-ma-kee by the hand and welcomed him into his tent. "He told him that he was the son of the King of France—that he had been dreaming for four years—that the Great Spirit had directed him to come here, where he should meet a nation of people who had never yet seen a white man—that they should be his children, and he should be their father." Although the king had laughed at him and warned him he would find only an uninhabited land of lakes and mountains, the Frenchman had insisted on fitting out an expedition and "had now landed on the very day that the Great Spirit had told him, in his dreams, that he should meet his children." He gave Na-nà-ma-kee a medal, which he hung around his neck, and then "Na-nà-ma-kee informed him of *his* dreaming."[1]

The notion that Indians and Frenchmen shared a special affinity has a long history. While Indian peoples were resisting Spanish conquistadors in the South, Indians in the Great Lakes and the Mississippi Valley were smoking the calumet with French explorers. While English colonists invaded Indian lands and put bounties on Indian scalps, French traders exchanged merchandise for furs, married into Indian societies, and fathered Indian children. Frenchmen gave gifts, they carefully cultivated relationships with Indian leaders, and they learned how to do business in Indian country. Indian relationships with the Frenchmen who emerged from Na-nà-ma-kee's dreams were far-reaching and long-lasting, but they were rarely smooth, often strained, and sometimes broke apart completely. Even at its best, the relationship was part of a colonial project in which France endeavored to build an empire in the West on Indian resources.

New Men in Birchbark Canoes

Writing in the 1630s, Jesuit Paul Le Jeune noted that migration from France was an annual phenomenon. "For, although the Soil of our country is very fertile, the French women . . . are still more so; and thence it happens that our ancient Gauls, in want of land, went to seek it in different parts of Europe." Since Frenchmen continued to leave the home country "to make their fortunes among Strangers," asked Le Jeune, "would it not be better to empty Old France into New, by means of Colonies which could be sent there, than to people Foreign countries[?]"[2] Migration to New France never reached the magnitude that Le Jeune envisaged, and land in Canada was not the magnet for colonists that it was farther south. Nevertheless, seventeenth-century French explorers, traders, and priests followed the waterways of North America in search of passages to China, beaver pelts, and souls to save. They paddled from the Gulf of the St. Lawrence River, up the Ottawa River, across the Great Lakes, through the Illinois country, and down the Mississippi to Louisiana and the Gulf of Mexico. Rivers feeding into the Mississippi provided routes to the West. By the end of the century, Frenchmen had made contact with Indian peoples from the northern Great Lakes to the Gulf of Mexico and from the Atlantic to the Great Plains.

As Frenchmen pushed west, the reports and journals they penned brought many Indians into written history. The histories Indians preserved often gave a very different slant on things. Anishinabe history as passed down across the generations and committed to writing by Anishinabe authors in the nineteenth century places Anishinabe people center stage in the Great Lakes world before 1800, with Frenchmen and their actions very much peripheral to Indian-Indian relations. Pierre-Esprit Radisson portrayed French traders around Lake Superior as "caesars" and "demigods" in Indian country; Anishinabe histories depicted them as hapless individuals dependent for survival on Indian kindness.[3]

Indians on the east coast of Canada recalled floating islands approaching their shores as they met French fishermen and explorers for the first time.[4] In 1535, while Cabeza de Vaca was wandering and healing his way across the Southwest, French mariner Jacques Cartier sailed up the St. Lawrence and called it the "Great River of Canada." At Chaleur Bay, Mi'kmaq Indians held up beaver pelts on sticks, indicating their eagerness to trade and their prior experience in trading with Europeans. At Hochelaga (present-day Montreal), Indians took Cartier up a mountain (which he called Mont Royal) and pointed out where the Ottawa River entered the St. Lawrence and the land that stretched beyond, "a green tapestry sewn with silver thread." Far to the west were seas of fresh water, they told him; the largest and most distant "on the rim of the world." It was the first time the French heard of the Great Lakes and their first sight of the river route that would take them west.[5]

Cartier saw crops and orchards covering the banks of the St. Lawrence. Seventy years later, when Samuel de Champlain traveled the same route, villages were abandoned, and the river banks were overgrown. Most likely, epidemic diseases and intertribal warfare generated by competition for European trade had depopulated the valley. At the site of the Indian village of Stadacona, Champlain founded Quebec City in 1608 and set France on the path to an empire built on the fur trade. Indians played crucial roles in establishing the patterns and terms of that empire. Champlain began a policy of sending young men into Indian villages to learn Native ways of living and speaking. He made alliances with local tribes to gain access to fur territories farther west; they made alliances with the French to obtain European trade goods, which they funneled along trade routes that stretched to Lake Superior.[6] When the French made alliances with the Montagnais, Algonkins, and other tribes of the St. Lawrence Valley they laid the basis for trading connections with Ottawas, Hurons, and other peoples in the heart of the continent.

Beavers, according to Jesuit Pierre de Charlevoix, were "one of the greatest wonders in nature." But to Frenchmen they were more valuable dead than alive: their pelts constituted "the principal article in the commerce of New France."[7] Traders paid the best prices for beaver pelts that had become greased and supple from being worn next to the skin. Indians "could not understand why these men came so far to search for their worn-out beaver robes," said Sieur Bacqueville de La Potherie, but "they admired all the wares brought to them by the French."[8] Frenchmen offered their metal goods and their religion in the hope of winning Indian allies, customers, and converts. Indians offered beaver pelts, qualified allegiance, and limited access to their souls.

Writing in 1728, Virginian William Byrd lamented that the English "hardly know anything of the Appalachian Mountains, that are no where above 250 miles from the sea." The French, on the other hand, "who are later comers, have rang'd from Quebec Southward as far as the Mouth of the Mississippi." Byrd blamed the discrepancy on the fact that Englishmen insisted on traveling on horseback, whereas the French "have performed it all on foot." But Byrd was wrong on two counts: the French were in North America before the English, and they penetrated Indian country not on foot but by birchbark canoe.[9] They followed Indian guides, paddled Indian canoes, and traveled Indian routes.

The birchbark canoe was the French key to the heart of the continent. Using materials readily available in north country forests, Indian craftsmen expertly constructed canoes by stitching and sealing overlapping sheets of bark around a frame of bent cedar ribs. Canoes were light, flexible, and maneuverable; they were also durable and easily mended. Sulpician missionary René de Bréhant de Galinée, who traveled west by birchbark canoe, said it was essential for traveling the rapids-strewn rivers above Montreal. There was "no conveyance either better or swifter; . . . nothing here more beautiful and convenient," although he had to admit that a passenger was "not a finger's breadth, but the thickness of five or six sheets of paper, from death." Another account described the birchbark canoe as "a species of vehicle the most spiritual, but at the same time the most perilous that can be imagined." Paddling the treacherous rapids of the upper country required great skill that could only be acquired by long practice. Claude Le Beau, who traveled with Huron paddlers, called canoes "the masterpiece" of Indian art, "fragile machines" capable of carrying immense loads at great speed. Modern tools accelerated the rate at which birchbark canoes could be built; they did not enhance the canoes' performance. "The materials were simple. But the structure was not," writes John McPhee. "An adroit technology had come down with the tribes from immemorial time."[10]

In McPhee's estimation, it is possible "to go almost anywhere" in Canada by canoe. Canada is one quarter water; its rivers, lakes, and streams contain one sixth of the world's fresh water. Between the Atlantic and the Pacific, on the routes used by fur traders, the longest portage was no more than a dozen miles.[11] Champlain reckoned that by using canoes as the Indians did, it would be possible "to see all there is, good and bad, in a year or two."[12] Indians could draw maps tracing waterways deep into the interior of the continent. Jean Talon, intendant of New France from

1665 to 1672, saw the possibilities for creating a vast river empire: "This country," he wrote, "is laid out in such a way that by means of the St. Lawrence one can go everywhere inland, thanks to the lakes which lead to its source in the West and to the rivers that flow into it along its shores, opening the way to the North and South." Talon sent out adventurers to keep journals, make written reports on their return, and take ritual possession of the lands they explored by erecting the king's arms. Finance minister Jean-Baptiste Colbert and Louis XIV feared that overextension might jeopardize New France, but in Talon's vision of empire, the French would travel the rivers to the west, claim the region before the English could, and find the route to the China Sea.[13]

The St. Lawrence–Great Lakes waterway drew the French west. The expansiveness of the Great Lakes and the concentration of tribes around their waters opened up other channels of communication, and Indian people came there from vast distances to trade.[14] Father Charles Albanel noted that it was not uncommon for Indians "to be extremely cautious in granting strangers a passage, by way of their rivers, to distant Nations. The rivers," he explained, "are to them what fields are to the French, their sole source of subsistence—whether in the form of fish and game, or in that of traffic."[15] Great Lakes Indians pursued seasonal economies: hunting, fishing, collecting maple sugar, and harvesting wild rice. Their world was centered on water and connected by canoes.

French missionaries entered Indian country by canoe and expected to share in the daily canoe culture of the people they lived among. "Never make them wait for you in embarking," wrote Father Jean de Brébeuf in his instructions for Jesuits heading to Huron country. "Try and eat at daybreak unless you can take your meal with you in the canoe"; "be prompt in embarking and disembarking; and tuck up your gowns so that they will not get wet, and so that you will not carry either water or sand into the canoe"; "be careful not to annoy anyone in the canoe with your hat"; "do not begin to paddle unless you are inclined to continue paddling. Take from the start the place in the canoe that you wish to keep." In addition to the discomforts and dangers of canoe travel, the missionaries had literally to pull their weight at portages: "We carried our canoes thirty five times, and dragged them at least fifty," complained Brébeuf of his second journey from the St. Lawrence to Huronia.[16] Brébeuf's advice on canoe etiquette and endurance was well taken. Father Claude-Jean Allouez, traveling by canoe with two Indians to Nipissing country, paddled eighteen leagues in one day, "from daybreak until after sunset, without respite and without landing," and, having reached Lake Nipigon, "spent six days in paddling from island to island." Pierre de Charlevoix complained loudly and at length about the dangers, discomforts, and disagreeable companions one had to endure during a canoe voyage.[17]

The French first used Algonkin and Huron canoes, which measured between thirteen and sixteen feet in length. But as the fur trade grew they built larger craft, eventually producing canoes more than thirty feet long and capable of carrying up to five tons of cargo. Farther south they used pirogues, or dugouts.[18] Canoe travel not only enabled Frenchmen to travel farther into Indian America than did their English rivals, but, as Gordon Sayre suggests, it also influenced how they wrote about their explorations. Frenchmen encountered and came to know the landscape as "a waterscape, a lacy network of rivers and lakes connected by portages." Even the beaver, the most sought after resource, inhabited the rivers and lakes rather than the forests in between. French maps traced rivers and lakes like a road map through Indian country against a blank background of forested tribal territory.[19]

When Jesuit missionary Father Jacques Marquette and Canadian fur trader Louis Joliet set out from Michilimackinac in 1673 to find the mouth of the Mississippi, they depended on Indian food (corn and smoked meat) and on Indian canoes and knowledge to get them where they were going. It was a voyage "the duration of which we could not foresee." Joliet could speak half a dozen Indian languages and systematically gathered information from Indians who knew the country toward which he was heading. Marquette recorded in his journal: "We even traced out from their reports a Map of the whole of that New Country; on it we indicated the rivers which we were to navigate, the names of the peoples and of the places through which we were to pass, the Course of the great River, and the direction we were to follow when we reached it."[20] On his return Marquette made a short portage from the Illinois River to Lake Michigan. He recognized that digging a relatively short canal at the place the Indians called Checagou would link the two great watersheds of North America, the St. Lawrence River system, which drains the Great Lakes into the Atlantic 1,880 miles to the northeast, and the Mississippi, which flows into the Gulf of Mexico 1,500 miles to the south. The canal, built a century and a half later, made Chicago "the fulcrum of the major east-west and north-south transportation axes serving the interior of the continent."[21]

For Jesuit missionaries, the canoe journey into Indian country also marked a spiritual passage from a place where the light of Christianity shone to a "heart of darkness" where Satan reigned.[22] It was up to them to dispel the darkness.

Pelts, Plagues, and Priests

The land the French called Huronia stretched twenty miles north to south and thirty-five miles across between Lake Simcoe and Georgian Bay in present-day Ontario. Its inhabitants knew their homeland as Wendake and themselves as Wendat. Four tribes—the Arendarhonon, Attignawantan, Attigneenongnahac, and Tahontaenrat—constituted the Wendat confederacy, between twenty and thirty thousand people living in a score of villages.[23] Living at the northern limit of southern Ontario's rich farmland, they occupied a prime trading location between two ecological zones, with hunter-gatherers to their north and sedentary farmers in their territory and to the south.[24] Most of their villages were built near areas of sandy, well-drained soil suitable for growing corn and located near streams. Two hundred miles of trails linked their villages and branched out to other tribes, and interconnecting canoe routes via river and lake gave easy access to vast areas of the north.[25] Wendat women grew a surplus of corn that Wendat men exchanged for animal skins, meat, and fish from tribes in the north. Their corn was so important to northern hunters that Jesuits called Huronia "the granary of most of the Algonquians."[26] In trade with other Iroquoian-speakers to the south, they obtained tobacco and other items those tribes had obtained from tribes to the south of them: raccoon-skin robes, wampum, exotic shells, and gourds. Exchanges through reciprocal gift giving reinforced and extended the network of social relations within the confederacy.[27]

Wendat people had obtained European trade goods via Indian middlemen before they came into contact with Europeans,[28] but they were receptive to French efforts to open direct trade. In 1609 Wendat and Algonkin warriors showed up in Quebec and asked Champlain for support in a raid against their enemies, the Iroquois (the Mohawks, Oneidas, Onondagas, Cayugas, and Senecas), in present-day upstate New York. Champlain was eager to establish commercial relations and agreed. With two companions he accompanied the Indians to the lake he named for himself and gunned down several Mohawk chiefs in a battle on the shore. The Wendats called the French Agnonha, the Iron People; the French called the Wendats Hurons, from the French word *hure*, meaning "boar" and signifying "savage" in the colloquial French of the period.[29] The Wendat people entered written history with a derogatory name assigned by European allies; their homeland, the object of much French attention, became Huronia. For Frenchmen looking west, Huronia was a gateway to rivers, furs, and distant Indian worlds.

In 1610, to symbolize and strengthen the alliance, Champlain arranged for a young Huron man named Savignon to accompany him to France. Savignon met Louis XIII but evidently was not impressed by the poverty and punishments he witnessed in French society. Two years later, Champlain dispatched a young man named Étienne Brulé to live among the Hurons, learn the language, and strengthen trade connections. Brulé later "went Indian." He may have been the first European to see Lakes Erie and Superior.[30] In 1615, to cement the alliance, Champlain traveled to Huronia. He made treaties of friendship with village headmen, noted the fertility of the land, and got himself into another battle against the Iroquois, who were increasingly threatened by the growing alliance between their old enemies and the newcomers. A Huron chief named Atironta reciprocated by visiting Quebec with Champlain the next year. Despite opposition from Montagnais and Algonkins, Hurons began traveling to the St. Lawrence to trade directly with the French.[31]

As in their dealings with other peoples, Hurons gave and expected gifts as proof of friendship. They despised French traders who haggled over the price of individual pelts, behavior they regarded as contrary to the reciprocal spirit of alliance.[32] Some French traders lived among the Hurons and married Huron wives, but the bulk of the trade was carried out by Hurons traveling to the French. They delivered vast quantities of beaver pelts. As beavers became depleted in Huronia (Paul Le Jeune said the Hurons had exterminated their own beavers by 1635), the Hurons turned to their Algonkian trading partners in the north, exchanging corn and beans for pelts, which they then carried to the French. As the northern hunting peoples spent more time trapping for the fur trade and less time hunting and fishing for subsistence, they in turn became increasingly dependent on the Hurons for corn. Ottawas, who were far-ranging traders themselves but seem not to have had direct contact with the French before 1650, met Hurons returning from the St. Lawrence each summer and exchanged furs, shell beads, pigments, and possibly copper from Lake Superior for the manufactured goods the Hurons carried. By trading corn to northern partners for furs and then trading furs to the French for manufactured goods, the Hurons managed to maintain a trade economy and a middleman position until the Iroquois reduced the network to a shambles in midcentury.[33] In 1642 the French founded Montreal at the junction of the St. Lawrence and the Ottawa, the river that led west to the Huron country, the Great Lakes, and beyond.

In the French vision of empire, Huronia was a potential center of Catholicism as well as commerce. Récollet missionaries Joseph LeCaron and Gabriel Théodat de Sagard lived there during the winter of 1623–24. The Hurons welcomed them with their customary hospitality. Sagard wrote: "If they were Christians these would be families among whom God would take pleasure to dwell." But the Récollets insisted that Indians who accepted Christianity should give up their Indian ways and live like French Catholics. Hurons showed little interest in Récollet preaching or in becoming Christians.[34]

Their world was changing around them, however. In 1628, after a four-year conflict, the Mohawks defeated the Mahicans on the Hudson River, securing direct access to Dutch trading posts and injecting new power into Iroquois dealings with their neighbors.[35] Quebec fell to the English in 1629, and Champlain returned to France. The losses were restored by a peace settlement in Europe, and Champlain was back in 1633. He and his agents dreamed of finding a great river to the west that would lead to China and the riches of the Orient, but their immediate goal was the Great Lakes. In 1634 Champlain sent Jean Nicollet west as an ambassador to the "People of the Sea." Nicollet was an experienced trader. Like Brulé, he had lived with Indians as a young man and learned their language. Accompanied by Huron guides, he was the first European to see Lake Michigan. When he reached Green Bay, he dressed in a Chinese robe of damask embroidered with flowers and birds and fired pistols in salute to the People of the Sea, whom he supposed to be Chinese but who turned out to be Ho-Chunk, or Winnebagos. From Green Bay, Nicollet journeyed to the Fox River in Wisconsin. He heard of but did not meet the Sioux.[36]

The annual Huron trade convoys that traveled down to Quebec had averaged 200 traders in 60 canoes, with each canoe carrying about 200 pounds of furs. In July 1633, the year Champlain returned, 500 Hurons arrived in 150 canoes. Champlain told them that if they wanted to maintain their trading alliance with the French they would have to accept Jesuit missionaries in their villages.[37] The Hurons had no intention of giving up their own religion, and tolerating the black-robed priests probably seemed a small price to pay for preserving French trade. In the French eyes, however, the Jesuits were forerunners in establishing a foothold in the West. Accompanying Champlain on his return from France was Father Jean de Brébeuf, who led the Jesuit mission to Huronia. Brébeuf had already spent three years in Huronia, where he had lived in the village of Toanché and learned the language, but he had baptized only one person.[38] Now he was returning to continue his life's work. He set out again for Huronia in 1634 and, with the exception of three years in Quebec, spent the rest of his life there.

The Jesuits worked diligently among the northern tribes. They learned the Native languages and customs. They did not steal Indian land or chase Indian women. They traveled by canoe and snowshoe, shared Indian lodges and food, displayed impressive shamanistic powers, and dedicated their lives to their calling. The personal danger, deprivation, and discomfort they endured paled in comparison with the goals of their work and "the joy that one feels when he has baptized a Savage who dies soon afterwards, and flies directly to Heaven to become an Angel."[39] Jesuits were far less insistent than the Récollets that Indians must cease being Indians before they could become Christians. They tried to reach Hurons on their own cultural terms, and, though they rarely overcame their own cultural prejudices, many missionaries tried to make sense of the Huron way of life.[40] They followed the customs of the country, preached the gospel using Huron metaphors, and attended Huron councils. Brébeuf presented the Hurons with a wampum belt, telling them it would "smooth the difficulties of the road to Paradise."[41] Jesuits participated in sharing rituals and were impressed by Huron hospitality: "I do not know if anything similar in this regard, is to be found anywhere," Brébeuf wrote.[42]

Nevertheless, the Jesuits were out to save the world. When they built small bark chapels and erected wooden crosses in Indian villages they not only proclaimed God's presence but also symbolically opened Indian country to the gospel and reinscribed the spiritual landscape.[43] At places like Sainte Marie, their headquarters on the Wye River, they tried to recreate islands of European culture.[44] They tried to congregate Indian people into settled Christian communities and supplanted Huron place-names with French ones: Taenhatentaron was changed to Saint Ignace, Gahouedoe to Saint Joseph, and so on. Throughout New France, many Indians accepted the Catholic faith, settled in French mission villages, attended mass, and wore crucifixes. Women in particular seem to have found in Catholicism new roles and a means to enhance their status, and some became devout Catholics.[45]

But missionary-Indian encounters were complex, ongoing interactions that involved negotiation, adjustment, and mutual exchange. Indian peoples resisted, accommodated, incorporated, reinterpreted, and reshaped Christianity, sometimes utilizing its symbols and tapping its power even as they rejected its doctrine and withstood its assaults. Missionaries could not control how Indian peoples interpreted their teachings, how they understood the Virgin Mary, or how they appropriated Christian symbols for their own purposes. Indians, not missionaries, decided what role and shape Christianity would assume in their cultures. Missionaries commonly searched for points of similarity between Native religions and their own, made concessions to indigenous cultural practices, and even participated, willingly or not, in the transformation of Christianity into an Indian religion.[46]

Hurons held the missionaries at arm's length. They tolerated the black robes because they wanted French trade, but Brébeuf's mission struggled in its early years: "Their ears were deaf to my prayers and my remonstrances," he wrote.[47] Missionaries often mistook the Native etiquette of noncontradiction for acceptance of their preaching: "You must know that we have a 'yes' that means 'no,' " a Huron told Father Claude Dablon.[48]

The Hurons resented the missionaries' intrusion into their rituals and ceremonies. The Jesuits criticized Huron sexual practices (premarital intercourse was regarded as normal), gender relations (women enjoyed considerable influence and sexual freedom), child rearing (children were allowed great freedom and were not disciplined by physical punishment), and festivals (particularly the Feast of the Dead, in which the bones of deceased friends and relatives were disinterred, adorned, and reburied in a single grave, a reminder that the living should live in solidarity and friendship), and they refused to participate in Huron healing ceremonies.[49] The Jesuits won few converts. Some expressed a desire to go to heaven only when Jesuits told them their deceased relatives had gone there. "For my part, I have no desire to go to heaven," announced another. "I have no acquaintances there, and the French who are there would not care to give me anything to eat."[50]

The Hurons fended off Jesuit attempts to change them: "We have our own ways of doing things, and you yours," said one sachem.[51] "Their usual reply is *oniondechouten*, 'Such is the custom of our country,"' Brébeuf complained. "We have fought this excuse and have taken it from their mouths, but not yet from their hearts." Father François Le Mercier complained that newly baptized Christians gave "nothing but fine words" and then returned to their old customs and beliefs.[52] After three years of "unremitting toil," the Jesuits counted only one hundred Huron converts, mostly sick infants and old people who had died soon after baptism. Warriors scorned their efforts, and medicine men opposed their work.[53]

But the missionaries brought their message of salvation at a time when the Hurons saw their world falling apart. The water highway that carried Frenchmen and Indian traders between Quebec and Huronia also communicated disease. The Hurons' location and participation in trade networks guaranteed that European germs as well as European goods entered their villages, and diseases undoubtedly took a far heavier toll in crowded Huron longhouses than in the dispersed hunting camps of northern Algonkian hunters.[54] An unidentified disease broke out in 1634. It began with a violent fever, "was followed by a sort of measles or smallpox, different however, from that common in France," accompanied in some cases by blindness, and terminated with diarrhea. Huron traders may have brought it home from Three Rivers; almost all of the returning canoe party were afflicted.[55] Influenza hit Huronia in 1636. Drought struck, and shamans tried in vain to bring rain: "Dreaming, fasting, dancing, were all to no purpose."[56] Another epidemic occurred in 1637. At the village of Ihonatiria, Father Mercier hoped that baptizing thirty or forty little children before the disease carried them off had secured their eternal happiness.[57]

Smallpox struck in 1639–40, when Hurons returning from Quebec met infected Algonkins en route. Father Jerôme Lalement saw God's hand at work: Hurons had refused to listen to their missionaries; "it therefore pleased God to pull their ears through a certain kind of pestilence." Lalement watched as "the disease spread from house to house, from town to town, and eventually affected the entire country." In anguish at the loss of loved ones, people turned in rage against the Jesuits. They saw that "where we baptized most people, that was in fact where the most died." Some said the black robes "had a secret understanding with the disease," since the missionaries remained healthy even though they breathed the same infected air as everyone else. Many Hurons feared they were sorcerers, and some wanted to kill them. "They accuse us," wrote Le Jeune, "of intending nothing else than the destruction and ruin of the world, since we will not deliver them from their troubles, nor permit them to provide themselves with the ordinary remedies employed in their country from all time against their misfortunes." But to have killed the

Jesuits would have jeopardized their trading alliance with the French. Instead, some Hurons turned to the Jesuit fathers in desperation.[58]

By 1640 the Huron population was about half what it had been in 1634.[59] Scholars disagree as to whether epidemics played a major role in spreading Christianity by undermining the people's belief in the power of their traditional religions.[60] Huron shamans had failed to forewarn or protect the people from the catastrophe; the Jesuit shamans who were unaffected by the disease were clearly men of considerable power—perhaps they had some answers, perhaps their baptisms offered some protection. In 1639 the missionaries reported three hundred baptisms.[61] More than one thousand Hurons received baptism during the 1640 smallpox epidemic, but by the spring only a few professed to be Christians. Baptisms averaged around 100 a year until 1643, 150 a year thereafter. In 1646, after years of missionary endeavor, only about five hundred Hurons considered themselves Christians.[62]

Many of those who accepted baptism saw it as a curative ritual rather than a path to heaven. "You would say, to hear them talk, that their sole aim in becoming Christians was to live long,—they, or at least their children," complained Lalement.[63] And there were other, more pragmatic incentives. The Hurons became increasingly dependent on French manufactured goods and French military assistance. Indians who became Christians were theoretically French citizens and thereby entitled to trade discounts. The Compagnie des Cents Associés, which had the monopoly of trade, applied a double standard of pricing to Indians: Christians paid less than pagans. Moreover, only Christian Indians were permitted to buy guns, a practice that placed Hurons at a disadvantage with their Iroquois enemies, whose Dutch and English traders made no such distinctions: by 1648, the Iroquois had four times as many firearms as the Hurons. Meanwhile, divisions between Christians and non-Christians undermined Huron unity. The Jesuit cultural and spiritual assault weakened the confederacy; Iroquois assault destroyed it.[64]

Killing Fields and Middle Grounds

When Champlain opened fire on the Iroquois in 1609, he introduced a deadly new element into Indian warfare. In the hands of skillful archers, bows and arrows often provided more rapid and accurate fire than seventeenth-century muskets, which were heavy, unreliable, and inaccurate and required constant maintenance. But guns had greater psychological impact, and Indian warriors quickly adopted guerrilla tactics that allowed them to employ the new weapons with deadly effect.[65] Guns were acquired from Europeans, and Europeans usually wanted beaver pelts in exchange. Competition for trade and furs became intense, while guns and metal weapons made intertribal conflict more lethal. Although the Mohawks gained access to Dutch trading posts on the Hudson River, the Iroquois lacked the beaver pelts—the purchasing power—of the tribes to their north. As they depleted beavers in their own country, Iroquois hunters began to encroach on the territories of other tribes and raid other people for the furs they had harvested; the Iroquois also fought for traditional goals—honor, revenge, and captives. In the so-called Beaver Wars from the 1630s to the 1650s, the Iroquois raided as far afield as the Great Lakes, the Carolinas, New England, and Quebec.[66]

Until the late 1640s the eastern tribes of the Iroquois confederacy—the Mohawks and Oneidas—tended to focus their attacks on the Ottawa and St. Lawrence River Valleys. The Senecas and other western tribes attacked Huronia, and Hurons avenged their dead with attacks on Iroquois country. But Iroquois raids on the Hurons increased in severity as the decade wore on.[67] Sometime around 1646 the Senecas enlisted the support of the Mohawks, who had the most guns, for a massive assault. They attacked Huronia and then turned on the Nipissings and Ottawas, who would have been their major trading partners had they been seeking only to capture the Huron trade. By dispersing the Hurons and their neighbors, Seneca hunting and raiding parties could penetrate northern fur-bearing territories from which they had previously been barred.[68]

The Iroquois were fighting for survival to offset their economic disadvantages and population losses in a world rendered perilous by European weapons and diseases.[69] By the early 1640s European diseases had cut their population in half, to about ten thousand, and the death toll continued to mount. Iroquois warriors traditionally went to war to quicken the dead, often by taking captives for torture or adoption. Now, with hundreds of deaths to avenge, the mourning war complex obligated war parties to range far and wide in search of captives. Nicolas Perrot, a *coureur de bois* (woods runner), interpreter, and agent who lived among the Indians for more than thirty years, said that the Iroquois "carried away many families from among their enemies, and spared the lives of the children, who became, when grown, so many warriors in their service."[70] "So far as I can divine," wrote Jesuit Isaac Jogues, "it is the design of the Iroquois to capture all the Hurons, if it is possible; to put the chiefs and a great part of the nation to death, and with the rest form one nation and one country."[71] The Hurons would have understood. Sagard noted that Hurons tortured male captives to death but usually spared women and children, "saving or keeping them for themselves or to make presents of them to others, who have previously lost some of their own in war and make much of the substitutes, just as if they were actually their own children."[72]

Warriors from all five Iroquois nations united to dismantle the Huron confederacy village by village. In 1648 a force of several hundred Iroquois destroyed Teanaostaiaé, one of the largest and best-fortified Huron towns, killing or capturing an estimated seven hundred people and spreading terror.[73] Throughout the summer and the following winter, thousands of Hurons sought food and shelter at Sainte Marie.[74] In the spring of 1649 one thousand Iroquois warriors attacked Taenhatentaron (Saint Ignace) and Saint Louis. They destroyed the mission villages and tortured to death Fathers Brébeuf and Gabriel Lalemant.[75] Iroquois war parties roamed Huronia. Starvation plagued the granary of the North.[76]

Baptisms increased dramatically as the Iroquois storm overwhelmed the Hurons: nearly thirteen hundred people between 1646 and 1647, seventeen hundred between 1648 and 1649, eighteen hundred in 1649. "By the summer of 1648," reckons Bruce Trigger, "about one Huron in five was a Christian and as the crisis deepened, this figure rose to almost one in two." At Sainte Marie famine and plague added to the woes of war: "All are miserably perishing together," wrote missionary Paul Ragueneau. He found solace in believing the calamity was good for their souls: "Never before has faith gone more deeply into hearts, or the name of Christian been more glorious, than in the midst of the disasters to a stricken people." Ragueneau claimed that three thousand Hurons were baptized in 1649. They may have hoped to join deceased relatives in heaven.[77]

The Hurons fled their fields and villages, "the people of each scattering where they could." The missions lay in ruins: "In a single day, and almost in a moment, we saw consumed our work of nearly ten years," wrote Ragueneau. "We, the Shepherds, followed our fleeing flock."[78] Some Hurons took refuge at Gadehoe, or Christian Island, off the western tip of the Penetanguishene Peninsula, where they endured a famine winter of horrors: skeletal mothers watched their children die; people were reduced to eating human flesh.[79] Many refugees were adopted into Iroquois communities; some took shelter among other tribes. Some

Hurons fled to Quebec and eventually resettled at the mission village of Lorette near Quebec.[80] Hurons who fled to the Tionnantatés (the Petun, or "tobacco," Hurons), Neutral, and Erie peoples found only temporary refuge. Famine and the Iroquois followed hard on their heels. The Iroquois had defeated the Tionnantatés by 1650, the Neutrals by 1651, the Eries by 1657.[81] They extended their campaigns from the St. Lawrence to the Mississippi and adopted so many captives to replace their mounting losses that by the 1660s Jesuit observers reckoned more than one thousand baptized Hurons were living among the Iroquois, and two thirds of the inhabitants of some villages were Iroquois by adoption, not by birth.[82]

Those Hurons who had joined the Tionnantatés moved with them to Michilimackinac Island in the summer of 1650, but Iroquois pressure compelled them to move again, first to Green Bay and then to the head of the Black River in Wisconsin. By 1661 they had moved to Chequamegon Bay on the southwestern shore of Lake Superior, where they settled near a group of Ottawa refugees. There they were safe from the Iroquois but not from hunger or the Sioux. The winter was severe, and the Indians suffered terribly from starvation, eating their dogs, bark from trees, entrails from earlier kills, anything they could to survive: "We became the very image of death," wrote Pierre-Esprit Radisson, who was there. Five hundred died. When war broke out between the Sioux and the Hurons and Ottawas, the latter tribes abandoned their fields and villages and moved back to the north of Lake Huron by 1671. After 1701 the Tionnontatés-Hurons resettled near the trading post of Fort Pontchartrain on the Detroit River, where, in time, they assumed a new collective identity as Wyandots.[83]

By the second half of the seventeenth century the Great Lakes region had become a war zone. The Iroquois not only crushed France's Huron allies but, said Bacqueville de La Potherie, they "regarded the French as a people who were not acquainted with their mode of warfare and were incapable of vanquishing them, not knowing [how to make] their way through the forests of the country."[84] Epidemics and Iroquois wars combined to produce a diaspora. The shores of Lake Huron and the eastern shore of Lake Michigan were deserted; a huge area between the Ohio River and the northern Great Lakes lay empty—what Richard White calls the "Iroquois shatter zone." The center of Indian population shifted to Wisconsin, where Huron and Algonkian fugitives crowded into Winnebago and Menominee territory. Between the western Great Lakes and the Mississippi, Hurons, Petuns, Winnebagos, Menominees, Ottawas,

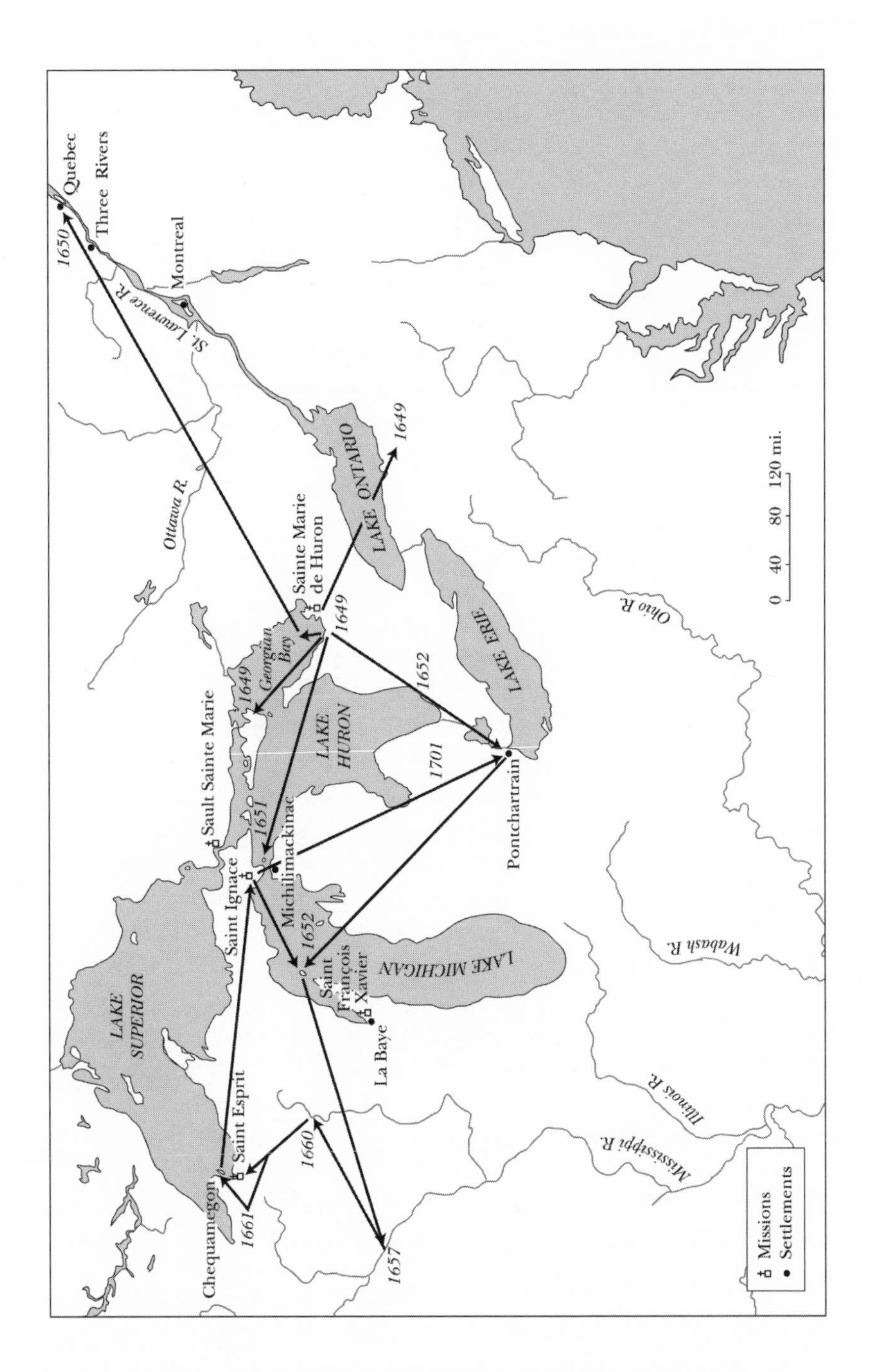

7. The Huron diaspora. (Adapted from Helen Hornbeck Tanner, ed., *Atlas of Great Lakes Indian History* [Norman: University of Oklahoma Press, 1987].)

Potawatomis, Sauks, Foxes, Miamis, Illinois, Kickapoos, and others mingled and mixed; remnants of different tribes huddled together in hastily assembled refugee villages, attempting to match Iroquois firepower with numbers. Iroquois war parties pursued them, traveling hundreds of miles to strike. Overcrowding depleted agricultural and hunting resources, and famine rendered villages ever more vulnerable to epidemic. Jesuit, Récollet, and Sulpician missionaries searched for souls amid the chaos.[85]

The Lakes peoples fought back. In 1662 Ojibwe, Ottawa, and Nipissing warriors inflicted a major defeat on the Iroquois at the southeastern tip of Lake Superior. But as they tried to escape the Iroquois in the east, they ran into the Sioux, whom some Jesuits characterized as the "Iroquois of the West." The Ilimouec or Alimouek (Illinois) had been pushed out of their homelands: "They used to be a populous nation, divided into ten large Villages," said Father Claude-Jean Allouez in the late 1660s, "but now they are reduced to two, continual wars with the Nadouessi [Sioux] on the one side and the Iroquois on the other having well-nigh exterminated them." The Sioux drove Huron and Ottawa refugees back east to Michilimackinac in 1670. Two years later they defeated a large war party of Hurons, Ottawas, Foxes, and Potawatomis and "slew them in great numbers," said Nicolas Perrot. Other refugees held them in fear. "The Nadouessious and the Iroquois are eating us," a Miami chief told Allouez. "Take pity on us. We are often ill, our children are dying, we are hungry."[86] The Miamis also told Allouez they had taken refuge west of a great river called "Messi-Sipi," six days' journey away.[87]

With the old fur trade system in ruins, the French had to build new exchange networks. Frenchmen in search of furs now had to go west themselves rather than wait for Huron middlemen to come to them. *Coureurs de bois* began to push west. Indian women who married French trappers incorporated them into their kin-based societies, developed new economic roles for themselves, and laid the base for enduring Franco-Indian communities in the western Great Lakes region.[88] Ottawas took over from the Hurons as key players in the French fur trade. In 1654 the Iroquois agreed to a peace, and the trade route to the St. Lawrence was safe for a time. That year more than one hundred Indian traders loaded with beaver pelts paddled down the Ottawa River. Most of them were Ottawas, making their first trip to the St. Lawrence, guided by several Hurons who had fled from the Iroquois assault. Médard Chovart, sieur de Groseilliers, and another Frenchman, who remains anonymous, accompanied the Ottawas back to the Great Lakes.[89] In 1656 they returned to Three Rivers with fifty fur-laden canoes and more than two hundred Ottawas as well as traders from other western tribes. But war resumed, and the Iroquois restored their blockade of the Ottawa–St. Lawrence route.

Groseilliers and his brother-in-law Pierre-Esprit Radisson, who had been captured and adopted by Mohawks as a boy, made several fur-hunting voyages with Indian canoe parties, pushing as far west as the Mississippi and Lake Superior. Radisson wrote an account of his voyages in English, published in 1669, to recommend himself for employment by the English, who were organizing the Hudson's Bay Company (chartered by Charles II in 1670). His chronologically garbled narrative contains much fabrication but provides glimpses of the upheaval the midcentury wars had caused in the western Great Lakes. Traveling with displaced Hurons and Ottawas, Radisson and Groseilliers tried in the spring of 1660 to enlist paddlers to canoe down the Ottawa River. Few were willing to run the Iroquois blockade. "Would you bring us to be killed?" they asked. "The Iroquois are everywhere about the river and undoubtedly will destroy us if we go down, and afterwards our wives and those that stayed behind."[90] Nevertheless, according to one account, so many fur-laden canoes of the "Far Nations" accompanied Radisson and Groseilliers down the Ottawa River and on to Montreal that year that they "did almost cover ye whole river."[91]

Ottawas dominated the restored French fur trade network for the next quarter century and played an increasing role in French plans for exploration, commerce, and missionization.[92] The French recognized that their location astride the great canoe route between the St. Lawrence and the Great Lakes gave them a lucrative role as middlemen. The name Odawa (Odawak, plural) comes from *adawe* (to trade), and the French applied it as a generic term to any Indians from the West who traveled east to trade: "The Outaouacs claim that the great river [i.e., the Ottawa] belongs to them, and that no nation can launch a boat on it without their consent," said Allouez, who spent a quarter of a century among the western tribes. "Therefore all who go to trade with the French, although of widely different nations, bear the general name of Outaouacs, under whose auspices they make the journey."[93]

Many Ottawas moved across the lakes to seek refuge from Iroquois attacks and occupied the western shores of Lake Superior. Chequamegon Bay became an Ottawa trade center, "a resort for all the tribes of the Northwest" and the first of the "rallying points" where the French and the Far Nations joined in alliance and stood firm against the Iroquois. The

12. *Noble Indien de la Nation Ottawa*, late seventeenth century. (Courtesy, National Archives of Canada, C-070664)

French chose it as the site for a Great Lakes mission. Allouez, following Nicollet's route to Green Bay, established the mission of Saint Esprit there in 1665 to service more than fifty villages, "which comprise diverse peoples." By the time he arrived, the Ottawa village had grown into a great multitribal community: "They number eight hundred men bearing arms but are gathered together from seven different nations, living in peace, mingled one with another." Allouez had the opportunity to address Potawatomis, Illinois, Sauks, Foxes, Ojibwes, Crees, and others. Many of the displaced Algonkians relied on the Ottawas for trade goods, and Allouez promised them the French would clear the highways of river pirates and make commerce safe. He also "preached Jesus Christ to all these nations."[94]

But Chequamegon proved not to be a safe haven. Conflict with the Sioux to the west and a temporary peace with the Iroquois in the east sent some Indian groups back to Lake Huron and to new "Outaouac missions" at the intersections of the upper Great Lakes. In 1668 the French established a trade center and mission at the Ojibwe village of Bawating at Sault Sainte Marie, a strategic and commercial site at the foot of the long rapids by which the waters of Lake Superior discharge into Lakes Huron and Michigan. Indians from a score of different tribes came there in the summer to fish for the prized Great Lakes whitefish. Ottawas used it as a base for canoe traffic. Bernard DeVoto called the Sault "a hub of the Indian world and one of the prime centers of North American geography." When the Hurons and Ottawas from Chequamegon Bay moved back to Michilimackinac, Marquette followed them and in 1670 founded the mission of Saint Ignatius at the Straits of Michilimackinac, at the junction of Lake Michigan and Lake Huron, with an Ottawa village on one side and a Huron village on the other. Corn and whitefish were plentiful in the area. Again, Ottawas managed a far-ranging canoe traffic and even sold birchbark canoes to the French. Mackinac Island became "the general meeting place for all of the French traders," a launching site for canoe expeditions to the tribes beyond, and, in French imaginations, an access point to waterways leading to a "Western Sea [that] can only be the Japan Sea."[95]

The Jesuits had great expectations of their Ottawa missions: "More than three hundred baptisms conferred in one year; more than twenty-five Nations illuminated by the light of the Gospel; many sick persons restored to health in a very extraordinary manner; Churches erected and Crosses planted in the midst of idolatry; the Faith borne far to the North and the South," announced *The Jesuit Relations* of 1671–72.[96] Missionaries translated prayers into Huron and Ottawa. But when Henri Joutel visited Michilimackinac in 1688 he was not impressed, "those People being downright Libertines, and there are very often none but a few Women in their Churches."[97]

Indian peoples also congregated at the Bay of the Puans, or Green Bay, on the northwestern shore of Lake Michigan. The area was fertile, supporting large fields of corn, with abundant game, fish, and fowl. By 1660 Potawatomis, Sauks, Menominees, and other peoples had joined the Puans, or Winnebagos, who lived there. Missionaries and traders followed the Indians. In December 1669 Allouez established Saint François Xavier mission there. The missionaries were attracted by the fact that it was "the great—and the only—thoroughfare for all the surrounding Nations, who maintain a constant intercourse, either in visiting or trading." They hoped their chapel would give them access to many nations and thousands of souls. Eight French traders who were wintering there attended the first mass. But this area too had been devastated by war. The Winnebagos had been "reduced to nothing from their very flourishing and populous state in the past by the Ilinois [*sic*]," and the Menominees had been "almost exterminated by the wars." Six hundred Indians from four nations lived in a nearby village, the resident Winnebagos joined by Potawatomis, Sauks, and Foxes from the southern Great Lakes. At its peak population concentration, the intertribal community around Green Bay may have numbered ten thousand people.[98] In 1676 seven or eight families of Ioways ("aiaoua or nadoessi mascouteins") arrived at Green Bay from "12 days' journey beyond the great River Mississippi," carrying buffalo robes and red calumets. The Ioways may have been previously contacted by Ottawas who had traveled west in their attempts to escape the Iroquois.[99]

The Jesuits accounted Saint François Xavier "the center of all the missions" among the many Indian nations of the area. "Here is a great Field for Gospel workers," they said. Jesuit fathers traveled from village to village, working this field tirelessly. But ten years after the mission was established Father Louis André counted "more than 500 christians on the whole bay." An Indian chief, disputing Jesuit arguments, provided an explanation: "We care very little whether it be the devil or God who gives us food." Most continued to seek guidance in dreams rather than or as well as in prayers and Bibles. Even among the Menominees, whom André accounted the most receptive to Christianity, warriors still "blackened themselves and fasted in order to dream of the Nadouessi, their enemy."[100]

Christianity offered hope to some Indian people, and they built new communities around the missions. For others, it was barely relevant.

By 1680 the Ottawas had been French allies for almost thirty years. They ranged far and wide to obtain beaver pelts from other people to the west; from Crees, Assiniboines, and Sioux to the north; from Sauks, Foxes, Potawatomis, Winnebagos, Menominees, Mascoutens, Miamis, and Illinois to the south. In this way they supplied "two-thirds of the Beaver that is sent to France." [101] But in 1680 the Iroquois launched a new round of assaults in the West. They struck the Illinois, a loose but formidable Algonkian confederacy that included the Kaskaskia, Cahokia, Tamaroa, Peoria, Michigamea, and perhaps a dozen other tribes. Archaeologists report evidence of human occupation at Kaskaskia dating back to A.D. 800. By 1667 the Illinois were traveling to the French mission and post at Chequamegon to trade, and the Jesuits established a mission among the Illinois in 1675. [102] Allouez described Kaskaskia as "formerly composed of but one nation, that of the Kachkachkia," and Marquette reported seventy-four cabins there in 1673. But by 1677 it had become a refugee center, with people from eight tribes living there. "One cannot well satisfy himself as to the number of people who compose that village," said Allouez, and he counted cabins instead of heads, finding 351, which might have translated into six or seven thousand residents. [103] The Great Village, as the French called it, also served as the political, economic, and religious center of the Illinois confederacy, where the tribes gathered to reaffirm their ties in planting and harvesting, feasting, rituals, and lacrosse games. But the Iroquois attacked the Illinois, defeated the Tamaroa division of the confederacy, and attacked the Great Village, killing or capturing hundreds of people. [104] The Illinois and Ottawas appealed to the French for help.

Fearing loss of the beaver trade with the Ottawas and more distant tribes, the French recognized they had to stop the Iroquois. [105] They knew they could not do so without Indian allies. Trader-agents like Nicolas Perrot, Henri de Tonti, Daniel Greysolon Duluth, and Pierre-Charles Le Sueur worked among the tribes to create a united front against the Iroquois. Nicolas de La Salle built a wooden fort on a rock on the bank of the Illinois River (later known as Starved Rock). Illinois who had been driven off by the Iroquois returned, and Miamis, Kickapoos, Shawnees, as well as some Abenakis and Mahicans from New England gravitated to him: "M. De La Salle caused the Illinois to make an alliance with the Miamis, the Shawnoes, and the Mascoutins, for defence against the

Iroquois." French sources and later historians credit the French with erecting and maintaining the anti-Iroquois coalition, but it is debatable whether Algonkian peoples who had their own long-standing and far-reaching alliances needed a Frenchman to unite them against a common threat.[106]

The French more likely nurtured and mediated the alliance and worked to keep the allied tribes bound to France in the face of growing competition from English trade goods and amid recurrent feelings of distrust. It was a demanding and often frustrating task. Even the experienced Nicolas Perrot struggled to understand an Indian's mind: "He speaks in one way and thinks in another. If his friend's interest accord with his own, he is ready to render him a service; if not, he always takes the path by which he can most easily attain his own ends."[107] In other words, Indians pursued Indian, not French, agendas. They may in fact have brought the French into their existing alliances as new members. Like Crows, Pawnees, Arikaras, and Shoshones who fought alongside the United States against the Sioux in the nineteenth century, they were not pawns; they used non-Native allies in their own struggles and for their own purposes.[108]

Keeping the Franco-Indian alliance intact amid the centrifugal pressures of cultural misunderstandings, conflicting interests, and shifting bases of power required constant attention, a willingness to compromise, endless negotiation, and skillful diplomacy on the part of all participants. French imperial politics and Algonkian village politics merged as each group adjusted to the cultural expectations of the other with a common interest in maintaining peace and trade. French leaders and Indian chiefs negotiated what Richard White termed a "middle ground" of coexistence. Employing the kinship language of forest diplomacy, the French claimed to be "fathers" to the Indians, and Indians often addressed them as such; but fulfilling that role meant giving gifts, not giving orders, observing rituals, not expecting obedience, and bestowing protection, not invoking paternal authority. The French channeled trade goods into Indian villages via selected chiefs, recognizing the traditional chiefly role of redistributing goods among their people while at the same time reinforcing the influence of their client chiefs. The people whom French traders and missionaries met or followed west of the Great Lakes had to construct new lives and new relationships in the West. They employed old and proven forms in dealing with the new peoples, French and Indian, whom they encountered, turning strangers and potential enemies into friends and real or symbolic kinsfolk through gift exchange, intermarriage, and the calumet ceremony. Some chiefs developed new roles as "alliance chiefs," working to maintain the alliance that was also the source of their power. Mediating disputes and preserving peace was not an easy task, but, in a world where an altercation between individuals could lead to a spiral of blood feud and clan vengeance, it was essential: the alternative might well be a bloodbath.[109]

When the French followed the tide of Indian population movement west, they entered a new world of chaos and conflict, but they also entered a world where the metaphors and mechanisms were available to bring cooperation and coexistence. For Indian people, peace meant more than a lack of conflict or ending hostilities; it was a state of being that "required a positive assumption of moral duties."[110] Calumets, their stems decorated with different-colored feathers to indicate peace, war, or other purposes, were crucial in maintaining order and doing business. The calumet ceremony, in which Indians danced and smoked the pipe when strangers arrived, was a prerequisite for negotiation and an essential foundation for good relations. "There is nothing more mysterious or respected among them" than the calumet, wrote Marquette. "It seems to be the God of peace and of war, the Arbiter of life and of death." Indians carried calumets as passports guaranteeing safe passage through other tribes' territory. They also used them "to put an end to Their disputes, to strengthen Their alliances, and to speak to Strangers."[111] The calumet ceremony transformed strangers into kin, enemies into friends. Perrot, who lived among the tribes of the Great Lakes at the height of the turmoil, described its power: "The calumet halts the warriors belonging to the tribe of those who have sung it, and arrests the vengeance which they could lawfully take for their tribesmen who have been slain. The calumet also compels the suspension of hostilities and secures the reception of deputies from hostile tribes who undertake to visit those whose people have been recently slain by theirs. It is, in one word, the calumet which has authority to confirm everything, and which renders solemn oaths binding."[112] With the calumet, humans could achieve peace and understanding even in the volatile Midwest in the late seventeenth century; without the calumet, chaos reigned unchecked.

The French may have contributed to the spread of the calumet through Indian America. The repercussions of their intrusion and presence certainly contributed to the need for its healing ceremony. By the second half of the seventeenth century, ritually smoking a pipe was an essential prelude to negotiations and trading relationships from the St. Lawrence River to the mouth of the Mississippi and out onto the western prairies.[113] Frenchmen would have to learn how to use Native mechanisms to achieve cooperation; they would have to replace war with dance as the reality and metaphor for conducting relations with other peoples.[114]

In time, the French constructed a network of alliances with Indian tribes from the mouth of the St. Lawrence to the mouth of the Mississippi. Intermarriage, adoption, and new roles as godparents produced networks of both indigenous and Catholic kinship in Indian villages and fur trade communities on the western Great Lakes.[115] When missionaries built chapels among the western tribes, fur traders established trading posts; small garrisons of soldiers arrived to protect the missionaries and control traders. "In this fashion," wrote Canadian historian William Eccles, "French authority was extended over the interior of the continent. By these means the writ of the King of France ran for thousands of miles in the far reaches of the North American wilderness." [116] But it was a fragile base on which to construct an empire. When, for example, Iroquois attacks and English trading terms prompted the Ottawas to falter in their allegiance, Louis de Buade, comte de Frontenac, fired off a message reminding them of their obligations: "I have given you your country; I have driven the horrors of war from it," he stormed. "You had no home before that. You were wandering about and exposed to the Iroquois tempests." Their French father would punish the Iroquois and could also punish ungrateful children. Nevertheless, Ottawas visiting Montreal were promised the lower trade rates they demanded.[117]

New trade rivalries complicated old enmities. Intertribal relationships were constantly shifting and often volatile. New kinship relations within and between crowded communities produced increased loyalties and complicated local disputes. French reports from the West in 1696–97 indicated that "affairs were in great confusion throughout all those countries, and the different Nations allied to us seemed disposed to wage war among themselves." The diplomatic situation west of the Great Lakes sometimes resembled that of Europe in 1914 on the eve of the First World War: the French feared that "these Upper Nations will be drawn into a general war by the alliances existing between almost all of them."[118]

But the alliance the Indians and the French built stopped the Iroquois storm. Armed and organized with French assistance, warriors from the refugee settlements carried the war home to the Iroquois. [119] French armies invaded Iroquoia from the east, and warriors from western tribes rendezvoused with the marquis de Denonville's invasion of Seneca country in 1687.[120] About the same time, the Ojibwes and their neighbors appear to have shifted from defense to offense. Traditional histories from several tribes tell of victories over the Iroquois, including a defeat of the Senecas in a canoe battle on Lake Erie. Mississauga, Ottawa, Ojibwe, and Huron warriors drove the Iroquois from Ontario, and the Mississaugas took over northern lakeshore village sites of the Iroquois. By 1700, Ojibwe and Ottawa traditions assert, the Iroquois had been soundly beaten. Northern warriors even raided deep into Iroquoia.[121] The Miamis, who thirty years earlier had complained the Iroquois were devouring them, also began to turn the tables: "They trouble the Iroquois greatly," said Antoine de Lamothe Cadillac, "and are always plucking his hair or feathers."[122]

By 1700 the Iroquois could no longer sustain the war effort in the West. "The Far Indians have now again killed many of our people," they told the English.[123] Recurrent warfare and epidemic disease produced losses of such magnitude that traditional practices of adopting war captives could no longer offset them. Caught up in the growing conflict between England and France, Iroquois leaders saw a bleak future if they continued along the paths they had been traveling. They decided on a new course of action and secured through diplomacy some of what they had been unable to win in war. In a long round of negotiations beginning in 1697 and culminating in the Great Peace of Montreal in 1701, they made peace with the western tribes and agreed to remain neutral in the contests between France and England. The new policy allowed the Iroquois to play the French and the English against each other rather than be caught in their crossfire and gave them access to hunting grounds now shared with Great Lakes nations. In the summer of 1701 a great cavalcade of representatives from the Hurons, Ottawas, Ojibwes, Potawatomis, Sauks, Foxes, Winnebagos, Menominees, Kickapoos, Mascoutens, Miamis, Illinois, Nipissings, and others made the long canoe voyage down the Ottawa River to Montreal, where they joined their eastern allies in ratifying the peace with the Iroquois. Thirteen hundred representatives from almost forty Native nations, from Acadia to the edges of the Great Plains and from James Bay to southern Illinois, spent three weeks in negotiation and ceremony. Then their leaders fixed their marks to a great peace accord, one of the most significant diplomatic events in early American history. The Iroquois wars were over, and the western tribes were relieved of the threat that had plagued them for more than half a century.[124]

The reverberations of the Algonkian-Huron diaspora and the Franco-Algonkian-Huron alliance were felt far to the west. Once displaced Algonkians obtained guns from the French, they in turn attacked Quapaws, Poncas, Omahas, and other Dhegihan Siouans who had taken up residence beyond the Mississippi and pushed them westward farther into the prairie-plains region. Sometime in the seventeenth century, probably between 1650 and 1674, the Omahas and Poncas split, the latter abandoning horticulture and taking up the life of buffalo hunters. As Siouan-speaking peoples ventured west to hunt buffalo, they clashed with Caddo peoples. Algonkians raided sedentary farming peoples to their west for slaves, selling them to the French and British in exchange for manufactured goods.[125]

The Sioux probably saw guns for the first time in the hands of Huron refugees in the early 1650s.[126] Nicolas Perrot said the displaced tribes who crowded into their territory from the east regarded the Sioux living at the west end of Lake Superior as easy prey because they lacked iron weapons.[127] Nevertheless, the Sioux were a formidable force, with perhaps as many as thirty-eight thousand people living in the upper Mississippi watershed. The French called them "Nadouessiou," derived from the Algonkian term for enemy, but they referred to themselves as Dakotas, Nakotas, or Lakotas, meaning "allies." The western Sioux tribes—the Yanktons, Yanktonais, and Tetons or Lakotas—still lived between the upper Mississippi and Red River Valleys but already were edging west, a movement that would take the Lakotas out onto the Great Plains. The Assiniboines had broken off from their Yankton relatives sometime before 1640, when they were first mentioned in *The Jesuit Relations.* The eastern Sioux—the Mdewakantons, Wahpetons, Wahpekutes, and Sissetons, collectively known as the Dakotas—remained behind in the upper Mississippi Valley. When Jesuits reached Sault Sainte Marie in 1641, the Indians assembled there told them the Sioux and other nations to the west "have never known Europeans and have never heard of God." The Sioux practiced a mobile subsistence economy, moving between woodlands, lakes, and prairies; fishing; harvesting wild rice, berries, nuts, and roots; tapping sugar maples; hunting buffalo; and trading for corn with neighbors on the Missouri and Wisconsin Rivers.[128]

As the western Great Lakes region became an asylum for displaced peoples, the Sioux fought against Fox, Potawatomi, Ottawa, Mascouten, Kickapoo, Miami, and Huron immigrants along a conflict zone that stretched from Lake Superior to the Illinois River. Algonkians and Hurons tried to prevent guns from reaching the Sioux, and the Sioux worked hard to break the Algonkian grip on trade with the French.[129]

Pierre-Esprit Radisson provided perhaps the first written account of the Sioux, whom he met in 1660 and called the "nation of the Beef." Weeping tears of welcome, eight Sioux ambassadors presented gifts of food and smoked with the Frenchmen red stone calumets decorated with feathers, "pipes of peace and of the wars, that they pull out very seldom—when there is occasion for heaven and earth." The French showed them iron arrow points and weapons, threw gunpowder on the fire to impress them that "we were the devils of the earth," and feasted with them for a week in their encampment.[130] Shortly after, Indians from eighteen different nations gathered at a rendezvous with the Frenchmen. Thirty Sioux warriors arrived, the advance guard of a larger party. "They were all proper men, and dressed with paint," said Radisson, but they had "nothing but bows and arrows," and their arrow points were made from stag horn. The next day, the rest of the Sioux "arrived with an incredible pomp." The men, their hair greased and standing in tufts, wore paint and feathers, copper and turquoise jewelry, leggings embroidered with quill work, moose hides and deerskins, and white painted robes of beaver skins. The elders approached, wearing heavy buffalo robes and holding their medicine pouches, "in which all the world is enclosed." The women unfolded bundles made of tipi skins and had the lodges up in less than half an hour. The Sioux made speeches, gave gifts of beaver skins, and promised to be faithful allies to the French. They came looking for trade to help them defend themselves against the "Christinos," or Crees, saying that "the true means to get the victory was to have a thunder. (They meant a gun, calling it miniskoick.)"[131] The Crees, said Radisson, were "a wandering nation, and containeth a vast country" and "the best huntsmen of all America."[132] Crees too wanted French trade, and the French were more interested in promoting peace with and between the two tribes than in arming the Sioux to defeat the Crees. Father Allouez in 1665–66 reported that the Sioux had a reputation as a "warlike nation," feared by all their neighbors, but that they had no muskets and used only bows and arrows and clubs.[133]

Though "everyone" in New France believed that it would be impossible to open trade with the Sioux because they lived eight hundred leagues from the French settlements and were "at war generally with all sorts of tribes," Daniel Greysolon Duluth resolved to do so. In September 1678 he set out with seven companions "to attempt the exploration of the

Nadouecioux and the Assenipoualaks [Assiniboines,] who were unknown to us, and to cause them to make peace with all the nations around Lake Superior who dwell in the dominion of our invincible monarch." By July 1679 he had set up the king's standard in the village of Issati near Lake Mille Lacs, "where never Frenchman had been." In the fall he brought Assiniboines and other nations together at a rendezvous at the western tip of Lake Superior to begin the process of making peace between them and their Sioux enemies. The next summer he secured the release of a Récollet missionary, Father Louis Hennepin, who had been captured by the Sioux. Duluth's peace mission to the Sioux, Cree, Assiniboine, and Ojibwe peoples living west and north of Lake Superior in part aimed to prevent Indians from gravitating to Hudson Bay, where the English began operations in 1670. He also hoped to find passage to the Western Sea.[134]

Pierre-Charles Le Sueur accompanied Nicolas Perrot in his travels to Sioux country and was present when Perrot "took possession" of the upper Mississippi country in May 1689.[135] He built a post at Chequamegon Bay in 1692 and endeavored to open a northern trade route to the Sioux, among whom he was said to possess "great influences." In 1695 he took a Sioux chief, Tioscate, to Montreal along with a delegation of other Sioux and Ojibwes and a cargo of beaver pelts. Tioscate, "the first of his nation to have seen Canada," died in Montreal.[136] Most Mdewakanton warriors had guns by 1700, but most Sioux were moving west; only Mdewakanton and Sisseton bands remained in the woodlands. They headed west, argues historian Gary Anderson, not because the Ojibwes drove them out (that was just Ojibwe bragging) but because better commercial advantages beckoned on the Mississippi River and animal populations were being depleted in the woodlands.[137] Wisconsin became less contested ground.

Tioscate had asked the governor for more traders, but his request went unheeded. In 1696 the French government decided to place a temporary check on its expensive program of exploration and closed its trading operations in the West. French markets were glutted with furs, and ministers feared overextending their fragile empire. French officials were also growing concerned about the effect of Indian country on French colonial society, as exemplified by the *coureurs de bois.* The French established their first colonies expecting that colonists and Indians would mingle and create a single people; Indians who became Christians "should be supposed and held to be French nationals, and as such might come to live in France whenever they wished," and children of mixed marriages would be regarded as French citizens.[138] The idea, of course, was that Indians would become "Frenchified." The *coureurs de bois* suggested instead that Frenchmen were becoming Indianized, a worrying development for empire builders. Some two hundred *coureurs de bois* were living in Indian country by the end of the century. Most of these men were the sons of indentured servants and the underclass, and they seem to have taken to the freedom and egalitarian society they found. Missionaries deplored the fact that they lived with and like Indians, wearing Indian clothes, sleeping with Indian women, and acquiring Indian "vices"; officials worried about their trading activities and the impact of their independence on colonial French society. "The great evil of the *coureurs de bois* is known to my lord," wrote the marquis de Denonville, governor-general of Canada in 1688, "but not to its true extent; it depopulates the country of good men, renders them unmanageable, impossible to discipline, debauched. It makes of them, and their families, nobles wearing the sword and lace, all gentlemen and ladies. They will no longer consider working on the land, and that combined with the fact that the settlements are scattered results in the children of this country being raised like Indians and as undisciplined as them." [139] Despite warnings that it would drive Indian customers into the arms of English traders, the government in 1696 banned fur traders from the western Great Lakes, ceased granting trading licenses, and abandoned its western posts. Officials assured western Indians that they would receive better treatment by bringing their pelts to the trade fairs in Montreal than by dealing with unscrupulous traders in the woods. [140] The ban remained in effect for two decades, but French traders did not disappear from the western Great Lakes. In a world where kinship ties mattered more than nationality and where trading followed Indian practices more than French proclamations, many of them stayed and carried on their trade, illegally and out of official view, in the villages of their Indian wives. [141]

The Mississippi and Beyond

The Mississippi River meanders almost twenty-five hundred miles from its source at Lake Itasca in Minnesota to the Gulf of Mexico. Fed by the Missouri, the Ohio, the Arkansas, the Red, and many other substantial rivers, it draws snowmelt from both the Bighorn Mountains and the Alleghenies over an area greater than the subcontinent of India. Even before they had seen it, the Mississippi commanded French attention as the key to empire in the West, although at first they believed it flowed west into the Gulf of California and offered passage to the Orient. Realizing that the Mississippi flowed south not west hardly diminished its importance. Having descended it with La Salle, Henri de Tonti speculated the Mississippi River Valley "might produce every year peltries to the amount of 2,000 crowns, and abundance of lead and timber for ships. Commerce in silk might be established there, and a port to harbor ships and form a base for the Gulf of Mexico. Pearls will be found, and even if wheat could not be had below, the upper river would furnish it, and one could furnish the [West Indian sugar] islands with what they need, such as lumber, vegetables, grain, and salt beef."[142] One hundred thirty years later, Thomas Jefferson shared Tonti's appreciation of the significance of the Mississippi: whoever controlled its mouth controlled America's destiny. "There is on the globe," said the third president, referring to New Orleans, "one single spot, the possessor of which is our natural and habitual enemy."[143]

The French operated on the assumption that "discovery" of a great river conveyed inceptive title to all the territory drained by that river. That title could be confirmed by subsequent occupation. More than any other European nation, France sought Native consent to justify its own political authority. Instead of reading documents to bemused Native audiences, as the Spaniards did with the *requerimiento*, Frenchmen choreographed rituals of political possession and interpreted Indian participation to indicate acceptance of French colonial governance.[144] In June 1671 at Sault Sainte Marie, amid music and pageantry and with four Jesuit fathers in attendance, Simon François Daumont, sieur de St. Lusson, subdelegate of the intendant of New France, announced to representatives from fourteen Indian nations that the king of France, Louis XIV, was taking possession of the Mississippi Valley, "the territories from Montreal as far as the South Sea, covering the utmost extent and range possible." A cross and the French flag were raised to shouts of "Vive le roi!" The assembled Indians were informed that from this moment they were "dependent on his Majesty, subject to be controlled by his laws and to follow his customs," and under his royal protection. Nicolas Perrot interpreted the commission so that the Indians could "tell and communicate it to their neighbors who are said to be very numerous, inhabiting even to the sea coast." Whether or not Perrot succeeded in conveying these strange concepts to fourteen different nations, with these words France laid claim to "a territory of unknown extent, the key to the richest valley in the world."[145]

Canadian historian William Eccles, an expatriate Yorkshireman who apparently never lost his Yorkshire bluntness, dismissed the whole thing as a charade. The French claims "had about as much substance as the claim of the kings of England to the crown of France." In reality, they were made simply to exclude the English. The Indians had no real knowledge of what was going on and were probably nonplussed. "The notion that these strangers could somehow claim to have taken possession of their lands would have seemed utterly ridiculous to them; they might as well have laid claim to the air," said Eccles. As for their now being under the protection of a king thousands of miles away, "that too would have appeared nonsensical, since it was obviously the French who required the protection of the Indians in that part of the world." Eccles was right; French outposts in Indian country were generally only symbols of empire, puny trading posts that operated on Indian sufferance. A more likely version of the episode was related by Ojibwe historian William Warren, a descendant of one of St. Lusson's companions, who recorded the account preserved by the descendants of Ke-che-ne-zuh of the Crane clan, who represented the Ojibwes at the ceremony. The collective memory of Warren's mother's people was that St. Lusson had requested free passage through the Indians' country to trade in their villages. "He asked that the fires of the French and the Ojibwey nations be made one, and everlasting" and "promised the protection of the great French nation against all their enemies." Ojibwes apparently had no recollection of having ceded their lands to France. [146] Most likely, the French did not believe they had acquired actual title to the territory they claimed but rather the right to establish posts and missions and conduct trade; the Indians did not give up either land or sovereignty and probably thought they were simply incorporating new people into their existing exchange systems.[147]

Having claimed the Mississippi River Valley, the French had to find out what the river was, locate its source and its mouth, and establish their hold on it before English and Spanish rivals got there.[148] Doing so required that they establish relations with the Indian peoples who lived on its banks, from Minnesota to the Gulf of Mexico. Contact with those peoples would open communications with other tribes farther west.[149] Frenchmen looked north as well as south in their search for a route to the West. Duluth explored the portage routes from Lake Superior to the headwaters of the Mississippi. Both Duluth and Jacques de Noyon, who canoed up the Kaministiquia River, perhaps as far as Lake of the Woods, heard reports of a great body of water to the west, which they took to be the much-sought Western Ocean but which was in fact Lake Winnipeg. If Noyon reached Lake of the Woods in 1688–89, he was farther west than any Frenchman before him. The first European to reach Lake Winnipeg, however, was Henry Kelsay, "a very active Lad, delighting much in Indian Company," whom the Hudson's Bay Company sent west with a party of Crees and instructions to invite distant tribes down to the bay to trade. "Traveling always with Indians," Kelsay in 1690–91 went beyond Lake Winnipeg via the Saskatchewan River and spent the winter on the plains of western Canada, where he encountered Assiniboines and probably Atsinas or Gros Ventres, who cited fear of the Crees and inexperience in canoes as reasons for not making the long journey to trade at Hudson Bay.[150] Cadillac believed that the Minnesota, or Saint Peter's, River that ran through Sioux country was "as large and fine as the Mississippi," which it joined, and that by following it for a thousand leagues one might locate the route to the Western Sea. He suspected that the Mississippi itself rose near "the great lake of the Assiniboine [Lake Winnipeg], from which spring an endless number of rivers" and which the Indians called the "grandfather of all the lakes." The Assiniboines apparently reported that "after traversing the lakes and rivers for 100 days towards the setting sun, you come to the salt sea, beyond which, they say, there is no more land. If this be true," said Cadillac, "it can only be the western sea."[151]

Frenchmen who traveled down the Mississippi found it took them south, not west. In May 1673 Jacques Marquette and Louis Joliet set out from Saint Ignace mission at Michilimackinac with five men in canoes to follow the great river to its outlet. Traveling west to Green Bay and then up the Fox River, they met Menominees who warned them of great dangers if they proceeded down the Mississippi as well as Mascoutens, Kickapoos, and Miamis who had been pushed out of their homelands by the Iroquois. Miami guides led them overland to the Wisconsin River. From there they headed down the Mississippi.[152]

Following the Mississippi for more than sixty leagues, they arrived in June at villages of the Peorias, members of the Illinois confederacy. Peorias were farmers and buffalo hunters. The town of the great chief consisted of three hundred large houses and, Marquette and Joliet agreed, held about eight thousand people. They welcomed the French with the calumet, offering the pipe to the sun. "I was reassured when I observed these Ceremonies," wrote Marquette, "for I judged thereby that they were our allies." The Illinois gave him a calumet to "serve as a safeguard among all the Nations through whom I had to pass during my voyage."[153] Illinois warriors bought guns from France's Indian allies and employed them in slave raids against enemies to the south and west who had no European trade connections and no metal weapons. After renewed Iroquois assaults in 1680 drove the Illinois back across the Mississippi, many took refuge among the Osages, whom they had previously raided for slaves.[154]

Marquette and Joliet's calm passage downriver was transformed into a torrent where the Missouri entered the main channel of the Mississippi in full flood. Marquette called the Missouri "Pekitanouï." He noted there were many Indian villages along its banks and hoped it might be the route to the Vermilion, or California, Sea, since the direction the Mississippi was flowing indicated it would discharge into the Gulf of Mexico.[155] As they passed the mouth of the Ohio, Marquette's party found "the people called Chaouanons in so great numbers that in one district there are as many as 23 villages, and 15 in another, quite near one another." The Shawnees appeared to be "not at all warlike" and unable to defend themselves against Iroquois war parties, who carried off Shawnee captives "like flocks of sheep."[156]

The expedition reached the mouth of the Arkansas River. Quapaw Indians told them they were only ten days from the sea, but, realizing that the Mississippi was carrying them toward the Spaniards, Joliet and Marquette paddled back upriver.[157] Although they did not visit all the tribes, they produced a map showing the locations of the villages of the Osages, Pawnees, Missouris, Kansas, Otos, and others west of the Mississippi.[158] Marquette returned to the Illinois in 1675 to begin the mission he had promised. He preached to fifteen hundred men at Kaskaskia but fell ill and died as he was returning along the eastern shore of Lake Michigan.[159]

The Marquette-Joliet expedition confirmed that the Mississippi flowed into the Gulf of Mexico and that a practicable waterway existed between Canada and the South. Not only was a French empire possible in the West, but it could be strategically designed to halt English expansion westward. Pursuing the imperial vision of Jean Talon and of Frontenac, governor of New France from 1672 to 1682 (and again from 1689 to 1698), René-Robert Cavelier, sieur de La Salle, endeavored to secure the Mississippi River Valley for France.

The Iroquois had told La Salle of a great river system in the West that he believed must flow into the Gulf of California and open a passage to China.[160] Already well traveled in the Ohio and Great Lakes country, La Salle planned to establish a line of posts that would link the St.

Lawrence, the Great Lakes, and the Mississippi in a huge arc of commerce and give France an economic base that would dominate the heart of the continent.[161] In 1678, with support from Frontenac, he secured royal permission to explore the western part of New France: "There is nothing closer to our heart than the discovery of that country, where it appears a way may be found to penetrate as far as Mexico." La Salle was prohibited from trading with the Ottawas and other Indians who brought furs to Montreal but was given a monopoly of the trade in buffalo hides. He was to undertake the voyage at his own expense but was granted the right to establish trading posts and to trade with the Indians in the Mississippi Valley, something that scholars have interpreted as an attempt by Frontenac and La Salle to create a fur-trading monopoly for themselves under the guise of exploration for the crown.[162] Between 1679 and 1681 La Salle was busy in the Great Lakes region.[163] In 1681–82 he set out in canoes, following the route of Joliet and Marquette down the Mississippi. La Salle's party included his lieutenant, Henri de Tonti (a metal-fisted Italian who had lost a hand in the wars in Sicily); twenty-one other Frenchmen; eighteen Mahican, Abenaki, and Sokoki Indian men (displaced by escalating warfare from their New England lands); ten Indian women; and three children. Passing the mouth of the Arkansas River, where Joliet and Marquette had turned back, La Salle began to encounter Indian peoples Frenchmen had never seen before—Taensas, Chickasaws, and Natchez—but who retained memories of De Soto's invasion 140 years earlier.[164]

Frenchmen who ventured into Arkansas in the late seventeenth century saw a very different world from the one De Soto's conquistadors had blundered into. In 1541 thousands of Indian people lived in mound villages surrounded by vast fields of corn. But drought, disease, and migration drastically reduced the area's human population. The Casqui, Pacacha, Colingua, Utiangue, Quigualtam, and Lacane people who had lived there had disappeared by the time the French arrived. The large and thriving ceremonial centers were gone: in 1686 Henri de Tonti constructed Arkansas Post—the first European trading post in Arkansas—at the base of an abandoned sixteenth-century Mississippian ceremonial mound. Most of central Arkansas was empty of people, which made it a region rich in animals and a hunter's paradise. The only survivors of the rich Mississippian civilizations of De Soto's time were the Cadodacho Caddos living on the big bend of the Red River and the Cahinnio Caddos in the upper Ouachita River Valley. Dhegihan emigrants had pushed in from the East: Osages lived north of the Ozark plateau, Quapaws near the mouth of the Arkansas and White Rivers.[165] Michigameas, members of the Illinois confederacy, had moved south into Arkansas and functioned for a time as intermediaries between the French and the Quapaws.[166]

After the Quapaws descended the Mississippi, eventually settling on the Arkansas River, they became known as Ugaxpa, "drifted downstream," to their Dhegihan Siouan relatives. When the French met them in the 1670s and 1680s, the Quapaws were still adjusting to the new country. They occupied four villages near the confluence of the Arkansas and the Mississippi; lived in multifamily, bark-covered longhouses surrounding an open ceremonial plaza, with extensive cornfields close by; and hunted buffalo and deer. They were also incorporating European imports that had spread into the interior of the continent: French visitors noted watermelons, peach trees, and domesticated fowl in their villages. The French called them Arkansas, but eventually they became known as Quapaws, a name derived from the village of Kappa.[167]

When La Salle's party entered Kappa in the spring of 1682, the Indians greeted them with a calumet dance, a feast, and an exchange of gifts. La Salle ceremonially took possession of the land for the king of France with the "consent" of the assembled Quapaws. La Salle's party visited two other Quapaw villages and passed through Quapaw country again on their return upriver. Nicolas de La Salle described the Quapaws as "good folk who are willing to do anything for the French."[168] The calumet ceremony served to create the bonds of friendship that were necessary for the French to secure safe passage, establish trade, and form alliances. Among Siouan-speaking peoples like the Quapaws, however, the calumet ceremony was a deeply spiritual ritual of adoption between communities that made "sacred kinship." Before the Quapaws could deal with the French they had to perform the calumet ceremony as a way of establishing ritual ties with the newcomers and according them a position and status within their social system. The French accepted the calumet, although they did not understand its full significance or the need for regular renewal of the relationships it established, just as Quapaws did not understand the full range of meanings Frenchmen attached to the cross they offered them. La Salle's men were being made into Quapaws.[169]

In April 1682 La Salle sighted the sea and raised a cross and the arms of France, claiming the region—Louisiana—for Louis XIV. With appropriate chants, musket volleys, and theater of possession, a handful of Frenchmen proclaimed that the territory stretching from the Alleghenies to the Rocky Mountains and from the Gulf of Mexico to the headwaters of the Missouri belonged to the French crown. As usual, the French assumed that Indian peoples who had made alliances with the king of France would consent to become his subjects. The ceremony included declarations that the Sioux at the headwaters of the Mississippi, the Shawnees around the mouth of the Ohio, and the Illinois, Quapaws, Natchez, Chickasaws, and other allied tribes all apparently consented to the crown taking possession of their lands, their rivers, their resources, and even themselves.[170]

The colonial government in Quebec refused to support La Salle's plan to erect a string of forts from the Illinois River to the mouth of the Mississippi. La Salle returned to France late in 1683, where he proposed leading an expedition to the Mississippi via the Gulf of Mexico and establishing a post there as a base from which to extend Christianity, conquer Nueva Vizcaya, and unlock the natural wealth in the heart of the continent. The French government and exiled former Spanish governor of New Mexico Diego Dionisio de Peñalosa had hatched a plan to seize the territories of Gran Quivira and Teguay, which, said Peñalosa, were rich in silver and located on the eastern frontier of New Mexico.[171] In April 1684 La Salle was granted a royal commission to establish and govern the projected colony. His duties included confirming the Indians' allegiance to the crown, leading them to the true faith, and maintaining intertribal peace.[172]

In 1684 La Salle and some 280 colonists set sail. Dissension and ill fortune plagued the expedition. They missed the mouth of the Mississippi and landed four hundred miles to the west on the coast of Texas at Matagorda Bay.[173] They built a settlement there and named it Fort Saint Louis. Disease, desertion, and hunger all took a toll. In the winter of 1685–86 La Salle made a number of forays, accompanied by a Shawnee guide named Nika, and may even have gotten as far west as the Rio Grande. In 1686 he tried and failed to find the Mississippi, traveling deep into Caddo land. The next year he tried again with seventeen companions, including Henri Joutel, who wrote a journal of the expedition, and an eleven-year-old boy named Pierre Talon, whom he took along to learn the Caddo language. But mutiny and violent quarrels erupted. La Salle was murdered somewhere near the Brazos River; five others died. The survivors split; some stayed with the Hasinai Caddos. Half a dozen others, including Joutel, La Salle's brother l'Abbé Jean Cavelier, and Father Anastius Douay pressed on.[174]

La Salle's men were the first Europeans to pass through Caddo country since the members of the De Soto–Moscoso expedition spent three months in 1542 wandering through the Naguatex chiefdom in east Texas and Louisiana. Since then, the Caddos had suffered devastating diseases, and although the intensity of the epidemics no doubt varied from region to region, the Caddo population had plummeted from as many as two hundred thousand to as few as ten thousand. (Within the next century it would drop by a further 80 percent.) The name Caddo derives from a French abbreviation of Kadohadacho, "real chief," and came to be applied collectively to people regarded as members of a single tribe. But when the French arrived the Caddos actually consisted of about twenty-five communities in several geographic clusters, gathered, or gathering, in three loose confederacies. The western or southern Caddos of the Hasinai confederacy (whom the French called Cenis and the Spanish called Tejas) occupied between nine and twelve communities in the Neches and Agelina River Valley region of east Texas. The Cadodacho confederacy and the Natchitoches confederacy (which appears to have fully formed in response to French contact) were located on the Red River to the north and east in what are now the border regions of present-day Texas, Oklahoma, Arkansas, and Louisiana. Despite falling population, the re-formed Caddo communities were still powerful theocratic chiefdoms and a major power between the Mississippi and the Rio Grande. Father Douay described one Hasinai village as "one of the largest and most populous I have seen in America," with hamlets of ten or twelve beehive-shaped cabins, some sixty feet in diameter and housing eight or ten families, stretched over "at least twenty leagues."[175]

The Caddos were under increasing pressure from mounted Apache raiders, and Hasinai people moving from more exposed country to the north and northwest found a measure of protection in the dense woodlands along the Neches and Angelina Rivers. But the Hasinais themselves already had horses and some Spanish goods. Trade routes that spanned huge distances passed through Caddo territory, and Indians shuttled in and out of Caddo villages. Caddos exchanged corn, hides, salt, pottery, baskets, and bois d'arc bows. The Hasinais occupied a gateway position for much of east Texas, the Red River Valley, and the Gulf Coast region. When Father Douay and La Salle's party visited the Hasinais in 1686 they saw "many things which undoubtedly came from the Spaniards, such as dollars, and other pieces of money, silver spoons, lace of every kind, clothes and horses." They even saw a papal bull exempting Spaniards in Mexico from fasting during the summer. Hasinai elites—the *xinesí* and

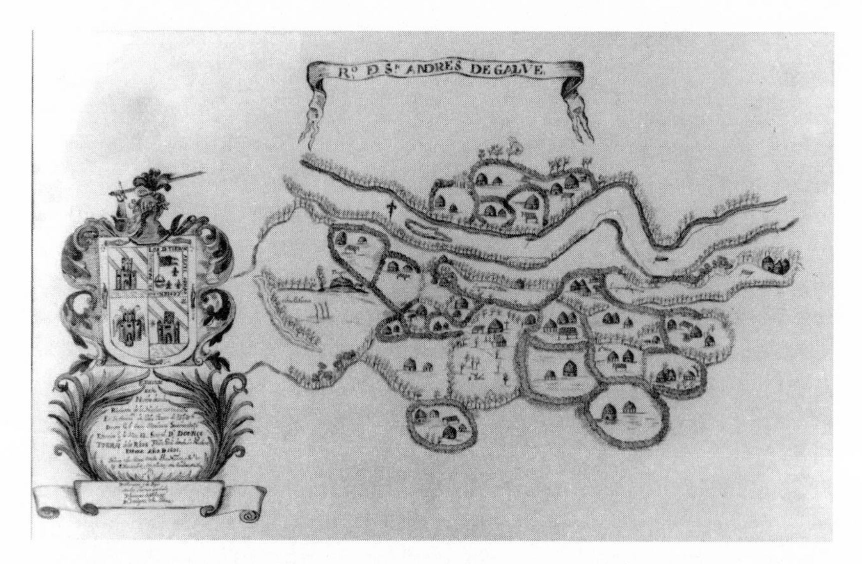

13. Téran map of 1691. Drawing of a Caddo settlement on the Great Bend of the Red River by an anonymous member of the Domingo Téran de los Ríos expedition in 1691. (Bryan Map Collection, CN 00920, Center for American History, University of Texas at Austin)

caddí—appear to have controlled the channels and distribution of trade and used prestige goods to reinforce their status. The Caddos got the Spanish goods from Jumano middlemen who ranged between the Rio Grande and east Texas, between Pueblo and Plains trading fairs.[176]

The French and Spanish each recognized the position and power of the Caddos and courted their allegiance.[177] The Caddos seem to have been receptive to newcomers. They were accustomed to making friendship pacts with neighboring peoples as a way of buffering their tribal borderlands.[178] Now they extended their exchange relationships to incorporate Europeans, who promised merchandise and military assistance. But they did so on their own terms. They welcomed deserters from La Salle's company and through marriage and ritual transformed them into kin, into Caddos. In the spring of 1687, when Joutel was sleeping among the Cenis or Hasinais, he "became aware of a naked man with a bow and some arrows in his hand who came to sit near me without speaking to me." The man turned out to be a French sailor named Ruter or Rutel who had deserted La Salle and had been living with the Indians. He and another sailor, Jacques Grollet, had adapted Indian ways; they were naked and tattooed, had taken several wives, and had fought with the Caddos against their enemies.[179] The Caddos no doubt saw in the French

14. George Catlin, *Village of the Pawnee Picts at the Base of the Rocky Mountains, Western Texas,* 1852. Catlin's picture shows the kind of lodges the Wichitas (Pawnee Picts) and their Caddo neighbors inhabited. (From the Collection of the Gilcrease Museum, Tulsa, accession no. 0176.2124)

a potential source of trade and military assistance, but first they had to incorporate the newcomers into their kinship system and establish formal alliances. Kinship meant creating bonds of reciprocal obligation and trust and could be created through gifts, adoption, marriage, or ritual.[180] The Caddos greeted Joutel and his companions with elaborate ceremonies and offered them food, lodging, and women, an act of kinship-forming gift giving that Europeans regularly misinterpreted as lewdness.[181] As the Quapaws had done with La Salle, the Caddos smoked the calumet as a prerequisite for further dealings. But, as descendants of the Mississippian societies of old, they retained a much more hierarchical character than did egalitarian Siouan peoples like the Quapaws. The Quapaw calumet ceremony established relationships between groups; the Caddo calumet ceremony appears to have established relationships between elite individuals within each group as a prerequisite to those individuals acting on behalf of their respective community in its dealings with the other.[182]

Hungry and lost, Joutel and his companions wanted the Indians to feed them and speed them on their way. But the Caddos and Quapaws would not deliver what the Frenchmen wanted without making them go through the protocols of concluding a trade alliance in return for military assistance. When Joutel's party reached the Arkansas River in July 1687, the Quapaws of the village of Osotouy received them with their usual hospitality. But when Joutel requested a guide the Indians asked the Frenchmen to go to war with them and use their guns against their enemies. They offered the Frenchmen lodging and women. "From this point," notes Gordon Sayre, "departed a dialectic of competing promises." Joutel promised axes and knives in return for a guide who would lead them to the Mississippi or the nearest French post. The Indians responded with warnings that the neighboring nations were hostile. Joutel raised his offer. Finally, in return for a few knives, an Indian agreed to serve as guide and led them to the frontier of the next tribe, "where the guide turned back and the cycle began all over again." Sayre regards the whole business as a sham, but for Quapaws the exchange of gifts, assurances, and even sexual partners established obligations and bonds that turned strangers into allies who could be helped on their way. In this manner, the beleaguered Frenchmen passed through the four Quapaw communities, from Osotouy, to Tourima, to Tongigua, to Kappa.[183] Like their countrymen in the western Great Lakes, Joutel's Frenchmen were adrift in a world in which one did business on Indian terms. Joutel's party finally reached Arkansas Post, which Henri de Tonti had built in Quapaw country the year before.

While the members of the La Salle expedition were seeing evidence of Spanish contact among the Indians they encountered, Indians were telling the Spaniards about Frenchmen on the southern plains. It did not take the news long to travel once Frenchmen entered Caddo country. Jumano traders told the French about Spaniards in New Mexico and told the Spaniards about the Frenchmen they saw in the Hasinai villages.

The French intruders threatened to drive a wedge between Spanish settlements in Florida and Mexico. The Council of the Indies in 1686 declared prompt action "to pluck out the thorn that has been thrust into the heart of America." Spanish expeditions set out by land and sea to find La Salle and his settlement, but by the time they found the colony, the threat was over. They saw evidence of shipwrecks and heard reports from Indians. Gen. Alonso de León, veteran of wars against the Indians in northwestern Mexico, led a small detachment of soldiers northeast across the Rio Grande in 1687 and found a Frenchman living with the Coahuiltecan Indians. Jean Géry, who had deserted La Salle, was tattooed like an Indian and "seated on buffalo robes, as if they were a throne." The Spaniards interrogated him and then sent him to Mexico City, where he "occasioned more than a little excitement." Then, in 1689, papers that had passed from Hasinai to Jumano to Cíbolo and finally to Spanish hands reached officials in New Mexico. The papers contained a parchment painting of a ship on the margins of which was a message from two of La Salle's men who were living among the Hasinais: Jacques Grollet and Jean L'Archevêque, an accomplice to the assassination. "I do not know what sort of people you are," wrote L'Archevêque. "We are French[;] we are among the savages[;] we would like much to be Among the Christians such as we are[.] . . . we are sorely grieved to be among beasts like these who believe neither in God nor in anything. Gentlemen, if you are willing to take us away, you have only to send a message. . . . we will deliver ourselves up to you." De León found the ruins of Fort Saint Louis and liberated the two Frenchmen. Grollet and L'Archevêque were "naked except for an antelope's skin, with their faces, breasts, and arms painted like the Indians." They were given clothes, interrogated, and sent first to Mexico and then to Spain. (L'Archevêque would later join Villasur's expedition. Tattooed like a Caddo, the exiled Frenchman died fighting with Spaniards and Pueblos against the Pawnees in the battle at the Platte.) They told de León that smallpox had killed more than one hundred people at Fort Saint Louis and that Indians had killed the rest. The Spanish found graphic evidence of the massacre—the body of a woman riddled with arrows, books scattered around on the ground. "These are the judgments of God that we cannot fathom," wrote Juan Bautista Chapa, who accompanied the de León expedition. He suspected it might also be God's punishment for France's violation of the papal mandate of 1494, which gave Spain right of discovery in the New World.[184]

De León also rescued a handful of survivors, mainly children named Talon. Their father had been "lost in the woods." Pierre Talon had been living among the Hasinais for three years since La Salle took him there to learn the language. He said they had treated him kindly and tattooed him as if he had been one of their own children. He had witnessed the murders that occurred at Fort Saint Louis. His sister and three brothers had been present when Karankawa Indians destroyed the fort around Christmas 1688 and gave the only eye-witness account of the massacre. The Karankawas killed their mother, but the children were adopted, treated well, and raised as Indians. They bore Karankawa tattoos for the rest of their lives. The children were taken as servants into the household of the Spanish viceroy, the conde de Galvé, but only when Pierre and his brother Jean-Baptiste returned to France were they questioned as to the fate of La Salle's colony and their experiences among the Indians.[185]

The Talon brothers were interrogated in preparation for Iberville's first voyage to the Gulf of Mexico in 1699. Pierre Le Moyne, sieur d'Iberville, a soldier of fortune who had made a reputation fighting the English, was dispatched to locate the mouth of the Mississippi, "select a good site that can be defended with a few men, and block entry to the river by other nations." He built and garrisoned Fort Maurepas on Biloxi Bay, the first of a series of French posts around Mobile Bay and the mouth of the Mississippi. The province of Louisiana was founded. Iberville made two more voyages to the gulf, in 1699–1700 and 1701–2, convinced that France needed a strong presence there to block English expansion from the Carolinas. He relied heavily on family talent to do so: his brother, Jean Baptiste Le Moyne, sieur de Bienville, became governor of Louisiana; cousin Louis Juchereau de St. Denis carried French trade and diplomacy to the Louisiana-Texas border; cousin by marriage Pierre-Charles Le Sueur pushed to the headwaters of the Mississippi.[186]

French explorers were back in Caddo villages within a year of the founding of Louisiana. Iberville planned to make the trade in beaver and buffalo skins a major part of the colony's economy. He requested Jesuit missionaries for the tribes and sent young men to live in Indian communities. By gathering Indian tribes at strategic locations he hoped to develop French trade and block British expansion.[187] With his brother Bienville and Father Douay, survivor of La Salle's enterprise, Iberville attempted to explore higher upriver and to learn more about the Indians and their contacts with the Spanish and English. He cultivated relations with the Natchez, Taensas, Biloxis, Bayougoulas, Houmas, Chitimachas, and other tribes, giving them gifts and "making them understand that with this calumet I was uniting them to the French and that we were from now on one." He spent a lot of time sitting and smoking ceremonially, something, he admitted in his journal, he found very unpleasant, "as I have never been a smoker."[188] In the spring of 1700 Bienville, who developed a facility in Indian languages, journeyed west with twenty-two Canadians, half a dozen Taensas, and a Wichita guide toward the Red River. They slogged through rain and swamps ("Never in our lives have our men and I been so tired"), smoked the calumet with the Natchitoches, obtained corn and boats from the Yatasi, but were forced to give up the trek before reaching the Cadodachos. Bienville heard plenty of reports about Spaniards and Indian contacts with them.[189]

Henri de Tonti and a party of *habitans,* or French settlers, from the Illinois country descended the Mississippi and linked up with Iberville. In 1702 Iberville dispatched him on an embassy to the Choctaws and Chickasaws, among whom the French feared growing English influence. Tonti was the first documented European to visit the Choctaws, and he initiated a French-Choctaw alliance.[190] He appears to have died in Mobile in 1704. Jesuit priests also established a couple of small mission outposts on the lower Mississippi.

Disease followed the newcomers. In 1698–99 smallpox devastated the Quapaws. The residents of Kappa and Tongigua combined to establish a single village on the western bank of the river. Father Buffon Saint Cosme, who visited it less than a month after the epidemic had run its course, saw "nothing but graves." All the children had died and "a great many women." No more than one hundred men were left, and "we were deeply afflicted at finding this nation of the Acansças, formerly so numerous, entirely destroyed by war and by disease."[191] Tunicas and Indians around Biloxi Bay died in great numbers, and the epidemic may have raged throughout the entire lower Mississippi Valley. One village of between 200 and 250 men still had the smallpox when Iberville visited in the spring of 1699. The disease "had killed one-fourth of the people." A year later, an epidemic that produced diarrhea killed more than half the people in one Houma village. "The women bewail their dead night and day," wrote a French priest who saw the village in mourning.[192] The ravages of disease continued to affect both the size and location of the Indian population in the lower Mississippi Valley: estimated at more than sixty-six thousand in 1700, it was reduced by more than two thirds in the next half century.[193]

Iberville planned to gain access to the mineral resources at the northern reaches of the Mississippi and to exclude British traders from Sioux country. Pierre-Charles Le Sueur, who had traveled the country around the headwaters of the Mississippi, had obtained a license in France to open the copper mines that were supposed to exist on the Blue Earth River in Minnesota. His plans were delayed when he was captured by the English, but he made it back to America with Iberville. He now headed back up the Mississippi with nineteen men. They passed through Quapaw and Illinois country, where the Indians greeted them with the customary calumet ceremony, and on up to the Sioux, whom Le Sueur hoped to use as workers in his copper mines. The Frenchmen built a small post and spent the winter there, but what Le Sueur thought was copper ore turned out to be clay. He returned down the Mississippi and sailed back to France with Iberville in 1702.[194]

By the turn of the century, Jesuit missionaries had pushed west from Quebec to the western Great Lakes and were active at key points along the Mississippi. The West beckoned them: "There remains unknown to Europeans, up to the present time, an immense portion of Canada, beyond the Mississippi river, situated beneath a milder sky, well-inhabited, and abounding in animal and vegetable life; the whole, deprived of true life and of salvation. This region calls to the generous soldiers of Christ."[195] The French also felt more secular callings. They hoped to open trade routes to the mining areas of northern New Spain and to establish a base for a French invasion of Mexico should events in Europe warrant it. They began to feel their way toward Spanish territory through Indian country. As the French and Spanish frontiers clashed in their world, the Caddos and Wichitas attempted to draw the Europeans into kinship relations, giving gifts of skins, horses, and wives and expecting gifts of guns and manufactured goods in return. French traders did better than Spanish officials and missionaries in maintaining the obligations of kinship.[196] In 1713 Governor Cadillac dispatched Canadian officer Louis Juchereau de St. Denis to the Rio Grande. Traveling through Caddo country with Pierre and Robert Talon as interpreters and guides and hoping to establish trade with the Spanish, St. Denis's party arrived at the presidio of San Juan Bautista del Río Grande in the fall of 1714. St. Denis was sent to Mexico City for interrogation, but he married the granddaughter of presidio commander Capt. Diego Ramón and accepted service under the Spanish crown. In 1716 he accompanied his new relative Domingo Ramón on an expedition to Texas to establish missions and a presidio but was arrested for trafficking in contraband and spent six months in a Mexican jail. He returned to Natchitoches in 1720 and served as post commander until his death in 1744. Fluent in Caddoan and "possessing a firm grasp of fictive kinship," St. Denis established French relations on a solid footing with the Wichitas and Caddos.[197]

The French founded New Orleans in 1718. The government transferred all rights of commerce within the colony to financial speculator John Law's newly founded Company of the West, renamed the Company of the Indies in 1719. Between 1717 and 1720 more than eighteen hundred people were shipped to Louisiana, including Germans and Swiss as well as men and women from the streets of France. They settled along the Mississippi and the Gulf Coast and lived by farming, herding, hunting, gathering, fishing, and trading. They interacted with the local Houma, Tunica, Chitimacha, and Acolapissa Indians as well as with African slaves. Famine and fever struck in 1719–21. Corruption and inefficiency plagued the colony, and colonial authorities had little control over illicit trapping and trade networks that developed between Europeans, Indians, and African slaves.[198]

In 1719 Claude Charles Du Tisné, one of Bienville's officers and an experienced Indian negotiator, left Kaskaskia and traveled up the Missouri on behalf of the Company of the Indies. He was the first European on record to visit the Osages, who traded him some horses they had stolen from the Pawnees but who tried to dissuade him from carrying on to meet the Pawnees himself. Du Tisné persisted, planted a French flag in a Pawnee village, and traded with them, obtaining a mule with a Spanish brand; but the Pawnees refused to let him proceed to the Padoucas, who were probably Plains Apaches. Du Tisné later recommended uniting the Pawnees and Padoucas to give the French access to Spanish territory.[199]

While the governor of Texas, Martín de Alarcón, headed west in 1718, Jean-Baptiste Bénard de La Harpe headed east from Louisiana. He traveled up the Red River to open trade relations with the Indians along the route and with the Spaniards in New Mexico, to ascertain the sources of the Red and Arkansas Rivers, and to lay French claim to the territory.[200] La Harpe smoked the calumet with various tribes of the Natchez and Caddo confederacies, many of whom were suffering from raids by Chickasaws and other enemies. He dispensed gifts liberally, his generosity rendered the more urgent by the proximity of the Spaniards in Texas, and established a post among the Nasoni group of Caddos. As he proceeded along his route, he and Alarcón exchanged letters in a formal sparring of territorial claims. The Spaniard warned the Frenchman to quit Spanish territory; the Frenchman countered that all land drained by rivers that emptied into the Mississippi belonged to France by right of La Salle's discovery in 1684. The Spaniards' protests and efforts to draw the Caddos into their orbit were not enough to break the French connection initiated by La Salle's men, reinforced by St. Denis, Bienville, and La Harpe, and solidified by French merchandise and marriages. Decimated by new diseases, harried by mounted raiders to their south and west, and with Indians to their north and east toting guns, the scattered groups of the Caddo confederacy became increasingly dependent on French allies and French trade. Even Caddos who lived near the Spanish in Texas continued to deal with the French on the Red River.[201]

In December 1721 La Harpe left New Orleans on a second expedition, traveling through Texas. The Spanish believed he was "inciting the Indians against Spain" and had him arrested.[202] The French meanwhile tried to occupy the lower Missouri, which they believed led to Santa Fe. Southward-moving Comanches blocked French efforts to reach New Mexico, just as they blocked Spanish advances to the northeast. The Spaniards recognized the utility of the Comanche barrier to French and English expansion, but the French tried to breach it. Étienne Véniard, sieur de Bourgmont, who had lived several years among the Missouris and had an Indian wife, was appointed commandant of the Missouri, with instructions to establish a post on the river and form an alliance with the Padoucas.[203] He left Paris in June 1722 and in November 1723 established Fort Orléans at the site of the Missouri village. The Osages welcomed him, recognizing that he represented a new source of firearms. The next spring Bourgmont and eight Frenchmen, accompanied by sixty-four Osages and one hundred Missouris, set out to establish peace with the Padoucas. Bourgmont traveled farther west than the French had been before. He assembled delegates from the Osages, Ioways, Otos, Pawnees, and Kansas and, despite ill health, pushed on to the Padoucas. On behalf of the king, "who is chief of all Indian nations," he gave them French merchandise and presented a French flag to the "head chief" and urged him to keep it white. The Padoucas agreed to make peace with the various tribes and to share the trade with them. They promised to trade with the French and, if they wished, to take them to trade with the Spanish, twelve days' travel away. "They come to visit every spring," said the chief, "but they are not like you who give us a quantity of merchandise such as we have never seen before." The Spaniards traded only a few horses, knives, and inferior axes; they did not trade in guns, powder, lead, kettles, and blankets like the French, "our true friends." The Padoucas invited the Frenchmen to a feast of buffalo meat, "gave them a thousand caresses[,] and offered them their daughters." The chief smoked with Bourgmont and pledged his undying friendship. Grabbing a handful of dirt, he announced: "Now I regard the Spaniards as I do this dirt."[204] The next year, Bourgmont returned to France with a delegation that included an Osage chief, an Oto, an Illinois, and a Missouri chief and girl. In Paris the visitors were decked out in dress coats and plumed hats

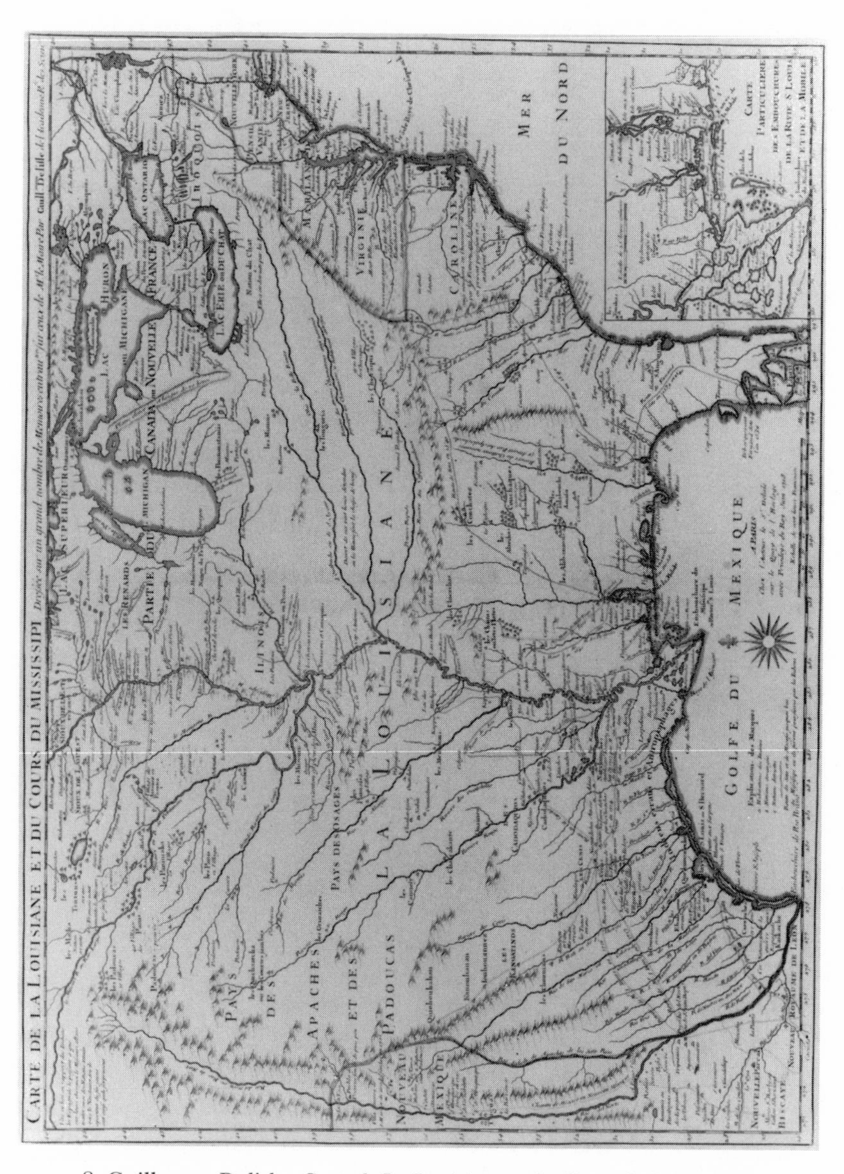

8. Guillaume Delisle, *Carte de La Louisiane et du Cours du Mississippi*, 1718. (CN 04405, Center for American History, University of Texas at Austin) The first detailed map of the Gulf region and the Mississippi, Delisle's map shows Texas and Albuquerque; the routes taken by De Soto, Moscoso, Tonty, and Denis; and the location of the "Padoucas" and other Native peoples. It also shows two trade routes between the Mississippi Valley and Carolina: one connects English with Chickasaws and other Indians across the Mississippi; the other shows a French route.

and presented to the king, who gave them medallions, swords, and other gifts.[205]

In 1739 Pierre and Paul Mallet and eight companions traveled from Illinois country up the Platte River. (The French name for the river was a translation of the Omaha and Oto terms for "flat river," *nibtháçka* or *nibráska.*)[206] Passing through Comanche country, they reached Santa Fe, guided part of the way by an Arikara slave they picked up. They spent nine months in confinement in Santa Fe, which they described as inhabited by some eight hundred Spanish and mestizo families, with a number of Indian villages nearby. The garrison consisted of only eighty soldiers, "a bad gang and poorly armed." One Frenchman married a Spanish woman and remained (two years later he was executed for "inciting" Indians to rebellion), but the rest of the party returned safely via the Arkansas River. The Mallets demonstrated that French trade with New Mexico was possible, but Spain responded by applying a new hard-line policy against intruders. (Not until 1821, after the Mexican Revolution, was William Becknell able to initiate regular trade with Santa Fe.)[207] In 1741 André Fabry de La Bruyère, a clerk or notary in the navy who had apparently had some experience in previous French explorations in Louisiana, volunteered to lead an expedition to follow up on the Mallets' discovery. The Mallets themselves accompanied the expedition. From New Orleans, Fabry's party traveled to the Forks of the Arkansas and into the Canadian and met an Osage war party en route to attack Mentos (Wichitas), but they failed to reach Santa Fe.[208]

Frenchmen in the North, meanwhile, continued to search for the Western Sea. After the Treaty of Utrecht in 1713 excluded France from the northwest fur trade at Hudson Bay, the French tried to expand their trade northwest of Lake Superior. Pierre Gaultier de Varennes, sieur de La Vérendrye, a veteran of wars against Britain in both Europe and North America, was appointed commandant of the Nipigon trading post, north of Lake Superior, in 1726. He built up the French fur trade in the area and gathered information and backing for a voyage to find a route from Winnipeg to the Pacific. With three sons, a nephew, and a party of soldiers and voyageurs, he set out in 1731, establishing posts along the way, one on Rainy Lake in 1731, another on Lake of the Woods in 1732, and Fort Maurepas on Lake Winnipeg in 1734. These and later posts around Lake Manitoba and Lake Winnipegosis were known collectively as Posts of the Western Sea and competed with the English posts at Hudson Bay for the trade of the region. La Vérendrye had to interrupt his efforts with several trips to Montreal to try and obtain official backing, but in 1738 he visited the Mandan villages and left two Frenchmen there to learn the language and gather information. Four years later, he sent two of his sons to explore southwest beyond the Mandan villages. They met Indians who spoke Spanish, but they turned back at the Black Hills.

Ambivalent Allies

In the seventeenth century, Indians in the West encountered Frenchmen who arrived by water searching for furs, souls, passages to China, a New World empire, or some kind of freedom. But the French lacked real power in Indian country. France adhered to a policy of confining European settlement to the St. Lawrence Valley. French presence in the West, as Cornelius Jaenen described it, "was *minoritaire* demographically, culturally and politically." The best they could do was develop and sustain a relationship of mutual dependency with the Indian nations who called the shots there.[209]

Indians smoked the calumet with Frenchmen, slept with them, transformed them into kin, fought with them, competed for their trade, and contracted their diseases. The ambiguities and complexities of the relations between the people of the fleur-de-lys and the people of the calumet are reflected in Osage traditions of their first meeting with Europeans in the late seventeenth century. Two Frenchmen came paddling upriver to the Osage villages accompanied by two Ni-Sho-Dse, warriors of the Smoky Water People (Missouris). The history of the event, said Osage tribal historian John Joseph Mathews, became "garbled in tribal memory," but the Little Ones (as the Osages referred to themselves) remembered they had never seen or smelled anything like these strange *coureurs de bois.* They called them I'n-Shta-Heh, Heavy Eyebrows, a name with no dignity, and their odor "became a tribal memory." The people thought they must represent a tribe of little importance. "In the village they flashed their eyes everywhere and let them rest for long moments on the women and girls. There were grease swipes from their fingers on their buckskin leggings. They were like camp dogs who wag their tails and slaver when there is fresh meat to be trimmed, and the same cajoling expectancy was in their laughs. They stood long to look at the buffalo robes, piled and waiting to be tanned." The Frenchmen returned downriver, and the Osages chuckled at their strange ways.[210] But other *coureurs de bois* came. They worried the Osages when they whistled, "since only ghosts whistled," but they lived with them, learned their language, married their women, ate their food, and brought an energetic, freedom-loving spirit and sense of humor that, Mathews said, the Osages appreciated. (William Warren said pretty much the same for the Ojibwes.)[211] Frenchmen also brought steel axes and guns. The Little Ones and the Heavy Eyebrows needed each other and became longtime allies. But it was a tumultuous relationship: "There would be many a buckskin shirt handed down decorated with the scalps of *I'n-Shta-Heh.*"[212]

Franco-Indian alliances, painstakingly constructed in the seventeenth century, would hold for much of the eighteenth century as long as interests intersected. Franco-Indian families and communities emerged, but there would be bother and bloodshed.

Part 3

Winning and Losing in the West, 1700–1800

Chapter 6

The Coming of the Centaurs

The extinction of horses in North America thirteen thousand years ago "left the continent horseless for the first time in 45 million years." Horses continued to evolve in Eurasia, and when the Spaniards invaded America they brought with them Iberian Arab horses, the products of that continued evolution. Once those horses reached the West and were reunited with the open plains and grasslands, Dan Flores imagines, they experienced a "joyous homecoming" and "went kicking, galloping, and whinnying their way back in."[1]

Many authorities on the role of the horse in Indian life have argued that its overall effect was to enable people to do the same things more easily and to follow essentially the same way of life they had before.[2] Certainly, there were many changes long before horses arrived, there was much continuity amid the changes they brought, and many of those changes were in degree rather than direction. But not since the spread of corn had the West seen such a powerful force of change. Indians acquired horses as other forces of change—European goods, guns, and germs—rendered their world increasingly volatile. Guns penetrated the plains from the Northeast and East as horses spread from the Southwest. Indian peoples competed for them as they did for horses. Possession of guns, like possession of horses, could determine a group's success and even survival in a world of escalating conflict, although the impact of guns was curtailed by their generally small numbers and their limited accuracy when used by or against men on horseback.[3] But, like corn, horses changed how many people lived their lives, saw their world, and organized their societies. Pedestrians became equestrians. When corn came, some Indian peoples gave up a mobile hunting life and adopted a sedentary farming existence; when horses came, some people gave up a sedentary farming existence and adopted a mobile hunting life.

Horses across the West

Hernán Cortés brought the first horses to mainland America in 1519. By midcentury there were tens of thousands of horses in Mexico.[4] In 1581 Francisco Sánchez Chamuscado's Rio Grande expedition left a horse with the Caguate or Otomoaco Indians, "who talked to it as if it were a person." But, contrary to popular legend, it is unlikely that the horse herds of the West grew from Spanish strays.[5] As the Spanish mining frontier pushed north, Indians in Nueva Vizcaya and Nuevo León rustled livestock, and Indians throughout most of northern Mexico had horses by 1600. There were herds of wild horses in Chihuahua by the 1620s. Indian traders and raiders took some horses into Texas and New Mexico, and Spanish colonization efforts brought more: some 350 horses, mares, colts, and mules, besides thousands of sheep, goats, and cattle, accompanied Juan de Oñate to New Mexico in 1598. Oñate took seven hundred horses with him when he went in search of Quivira in 1601. The Spaniards not only introduced the livestock that Indian people incorporated into their economies and societies, they also developed the techniques of what eventually became the western ranching industry, working large herds from horseback. (French and English herders east of the Mississippi were rarely mounted.) In 1621 Spanish authorities in New Mexico permitted *encomenderos* to mount Indian converts as herders and teamsters, in contrast to the usual policy of prohibiting Indians from riding. Some of the first cowboys in the American West, therefore, were Indians—the beginning of a tradition that has continued for almost four hundred years.[6] Rebels "liberated" hundreds of horses during the Pueblo Revolt. By 1680 Indians in all of Texas and New Mexico had horses, as did many Native people in Arizona. Apache, Ute, and Jumano traders diffused horses to other peoples to the north and east.[7]

Traders who had for centuries traveled on foot with packs of dogs now traveled farther and faster on horseback. Across huge areas of the West, horses themselves quickly became the most important item of trade. In time, a web of trade routes funneled horses out of the Southwest, north through the Rockies, and north and east across the Great Plains.[8] Many of the people who participated in this funneling were themselves moving and reshaping their societies in response to the presence of horses. Apaches may have obtained some of their first horses from Pueblos, but Plains Apaches soon were bringing horses to trade at Pueblo fairs. Jumanos, operating as middlemen between New

Mexico and Texas, transported horses to the Hasinais and their Caddo neighbors. Henri de Tonti noted that the "Cadodaquis possess about thirty horses, which they call *cavalis.*" The Indians protected their horses' breasts with a leather covering, "a proof that they are not very far from the Spaniards," although leather horse armor may also indicate that the Caddos had been in contact and conflict with Plains Apaches, who had modified Spanish armor to suit their own needs and traditions. The Caddos most likely obtained their mounts from Jumano middlemen rather than directly from the Spanish. In 1687 La Salle's brother l'Abbé Jean Cavelier and Father Anastius Douay met Caddos who had horses and spoke Spanish. Tonti traded four horses, two of which bore Spanish brands, from the Natchez, who, he said, took advantage of occasional wars with the Spaniards to drive off horses. Spanish livestock, left behind when the Texas missions were abandoned in 1693, added to the Hasinai herds.[9]

La Salle in 1682 heard that Gattackas (Kiowa Apaches) and Manrhoats (Kiowas) had plenty of horses, probably stolen from Mexico, and were trading them to Panas (Wichitas or Pawnees).[10] If the identification is correct, some Kiowas were raiding and trading far to the south at a time when most Kiowas were still living near the Black Hills. Osage historian John Joseph Mathews said "there is no tribal memory" and little or nothing in oral traditions about when his people first acquired horses, but he felt sure that if their Pawnee enemies and Missouri relatives had them by 1682, Osages must have had them too. They would have stolen them from the Pawnees or traded them from the Missouris and Kiowas.[11] Kiowas and Kiowa Apaches also traded horses to Caddos, Ioways, and Otos. Poncas acquired mounts by theft or by "smoking" for them, as horses passed along lower and middle Missouri trade networks via the calumet ceremony.[12] Claude Charles Du Tisné found Wichitas in Oklahoma mounted in 1719, with "saddles and bridles similar to those of the Spaniards." He counted three hundred horses at two Wichita villages and bought two horses and a mule bearing a Spanish brand. Kansa Indians traded horses to Étienne Véniard, sieur de Bourgmont in 1724.[13] Mississippi Choctaws acquired horses by 1690 and used them in deer-hunting expeditions, deerskin trading, and warfare.[14]

Farther west, the Comanches and Utes traded horses to the Shoshones. The Shoshones traded them to the Crows and to the Salish and Nez Perces in the Plateau region, who traded them to the Blackfeet, as did the Arapahos. The Blackfeet and Gros Ventres traded them to the Assiniboines. Hudson's Bay Company traders saw horses with brands that were probably Spanish in Cree-Assiniboine country in the 1750s.[15] The Crows, Kiowas, Arapahos, Cheyennes, and others drove herds of horses to the villages of the Mandans, Hidatsas, and Arikaras, who sometimes traveled to the Black Hills to trade for them. Lakotas obtained horses at the Arikara villages and traded them to their eastern Yankton, Yanktonai, and Dakota relatives. Some people took more direct routes, traveling to Santa Fe and other trade centers to buy or steal horses themselves.

Popular myth would have Indians swinging easily onto their first horses and riding off bareback to a new life of unrestrained mobility, but of course it was not that simple. People had to acquire or develop the appropriate knowledge, skills, understanding, and rituals for dealing with horses. When they acquired horses, many Indians also took over elements of a Spanish horse culture that had evolved over thousands of years.[16] They had to arrange their movements, adjust the size of their encampments, and limit the length of time they stayed in one place to ensure that their horses had sufficient pasture and water. Winter demanded they expend considerable energy and labor to provide their herds with adequate forage and fresh water. They gave horses access to the bark of cottonwood trees in the stream valleys where they camped, and women gathered cottonwood as supplemental winter forage on the plains.[17]

Herds had to be increased and improved by selective breeding; they had to be protected from adverse weather, animal predators, and enemy raiders. Horses had to be broken, trained, roped, picketed, hobbled, fed, watered, groomed, sung to. They had to be treated for sore feet, saddle sores, colic and distemper, broken bones, chills. Stallions had to be gelded, mares and colts cared for. War ponies and buffalo-hunting ponies received special care and training, and a close relationship was fostered between horse and rider. Horses brought additions to material culture: saddles, saddle blankets, bridles, rawhide ropes, stirrups, quirts, parfleche bags, larger travois, and larger tipis.[18] Moving camp entailed loading belongings onto horse-pulled travois and driving herds of horses.

Horses indicated wealth and status, denoted rank among the Blackfeet, and constituted the principal form of property even among the Lakotas, who believed "the only prestige attached to property was in giving it away."[19] They were essential to young men courting as the gift price for a bride. They featured prominently in Plains Indian pictographic art, and pictographic prayers for horses dating from the earliest periods of horse

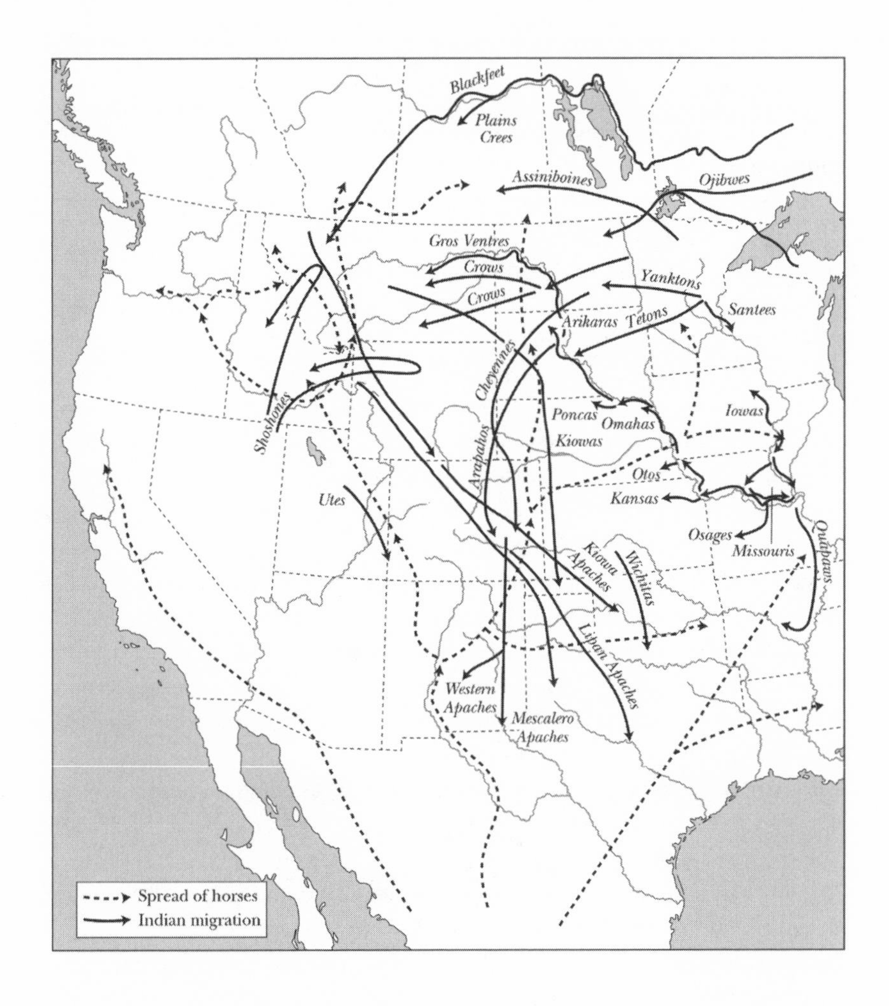

9. Horse diffusion and population movements on the Great Plains. Tribal movements c. 1500–1800 adapted from Helen H. Tanner, ed., *The Settling of North America: The Atlas of the Great Migrations into North America from the Ice Age to the Present* [New York: Macmillan, 1995]).

diffusion have been found at several rock art sites in the northern plains and eastern Rockies.[20]

Plains Indians acquired horses in the middle of the period of climatic change known as the Little Ice Age (ca. 1550–1850). After three centuries of dry, warm weather had cut buffalo numbers on the plains and driven out many human residents, moist conditions returned. As buffalo populations recovered, their human hunters returned from the mountains to the west and the prairies to the east. But now, increasingly, they hunted from horseback. Horses and buffalo became the economic and cultural base of the societies that developed.[21]

Indians retained some hunting techniques from prehorse days, such as the surround, impounding, and buffalo jump drives. Hudson's Bay Company trader Matthew Cocking in 1772 and North West Company trader Duncan McGillivray in the 1790s both reported Blackfeet in the Saskatchewan country using buffalo pounds.[22] Buffalo jump and kill sites at Hell's Half Acre, near Casper, Wyoming, and Head Smashed In, southern Alberta, continued to be used after hunters had horses. But mounted hunters could develop far more efficient techniques for harvesting herds. Buffalo running became the preferred method of hunting. Buffalo-hunting horses were carefully selected and long-winded. Trained to respond to thigh and knee pressure and to swerve away from their quarry after the release of an arrow, they left their riders free to operate short and powerful bows. Hunters knew where to strike to make the most efficient kill: an arrow projected at the side of the buffalo, just behind the last rib and about a third of the way down from the backbone to the belly, had only to pierce the hide and a thin layer of muscle before penetrating the intestinal cavity and possibly the liver and the diaphragm. The Padoucas, said Bourgmont, "choose the fattest ones and shoot arrows into them which penetrate a foot into the animals' bellies" and "kill like that all they want."[23] Plains scholar John C. Ewers reckoned that two Blackfeet riders "could kill enough buffalo to provide over a ton of meat in a matter of minutes on a single chase." When hunting was good there was plenty of meat for everyone. Mounted hunters could follow the herds more closely and had access to supplies of fresh meat on the hoof during most of the year. Horses also allowed bands to transport dried meat to their winter camps for sustenance during the hard months and to exchange greater quantities of meat and hides at farming villages on the edges of the plains.[24]

Women's status seems to have declined in the individualistic, male-dominated herding and equestrian hunting culture that developed, especially as it became linked to the European hide trade. In prehorse days, communal hunts involved collective effort and collective ownership. Now men's arrows, shot from horseback, marked the kill as property; women butchered it. In the late summer and fall they dried the surplus meat, pounded and packed it in buffalo paunches, and poured in melted fat to make pemmican or cut it in strips and stored it in parfleche bags. A good hunter could kill enough buffalo to keep several women busy with meat and hides and could now feed more people than had been possible in prehorse days. At a time when male losses were increasing in the escalating horseback warfare, successful hunters sometimes took several wives. Horses relieved women of many of the burdens of transportation and may have allowed them more time to develop art and craft skills with which they embellished the new paraphernalia, but camps now moved over greater distances, lodges increased in size, and there were more material possessions to pack and load.[25] But prosperity, mobility, and reduced fear of hunger appear to have masked or lessened the impact of such changes. Pretty Shield, a Crow Indian woman who related her life story in the early twentieth century, said her grandmothers recalled how in the old days they used to travel on foot and load packs onto dogs and that old women who were worn out had to be left behind to die. "All this was changed by the horse," Pretty Shield said. "Even the old people could ride. Ahh, I came into a happy world. There was always fat meat, glad singing, and much dancing in our villages. Our people's hearts were then as light as breath-feathers."[26]

Using horses instead of only dogs for transportation allowed people to move heavier loads, go farther, and travel faster. By John Ewers's calculations, "animal for animal the horse was eight times as efficient as the dog as a burden bearer": packing two hundred pounds on its back or pulling three hundred pounds on a travois, a horse could transport four times as much weight as a heavily burdened dog and travel twice the distance in a day. But horses did not immediately terminate the use of dogs as animals of burden. Jean-Baptiste Bénard de La Harpe, on the Red River from 1718 to 1720, noted that Lipan Apaches with horses still transported tipis by dog; Bourgmont in 1724 watched a village of eleven hundred Kansas move their baggage on the backs of three hundred dogs and on the backs of their women. In 1738 Pierre Gaultier de Varennes, sieur de La Vérendrye, noted the same thing among Assiniboines in the Red River region of Manitoba who had no horses; seventy years later the

Assiniboines had horses but still used dogs for transportation, preserving their mounts for buffalo hunting. The Assiniboines were often accounted to be poor in horses, but people with plenty of horses used dogs as well as horses for carrying baggage, especially during cold and snowy conditions, to reduce the strain on their horses. Fur trader Peter Pond saw the Sioux on the upper Mississippi doing so on the eve of the American Revolution; traders reported tribes on the Saskatchewan River doing it in the 1770s and 1790s. The Blackfeet may have retained dog travois for light transportation as much as a century after they obtained horses, although Matthew Cocking remarked that horses gave Blackfeet women a great advantage over women of other northern tribes "who are either carrying or hauling on Sledges every day of the year."[27]

Buffalo provided more than meat. "The buffalo alone, besides its flesh, which takes first place among healthful and savory meats, supplies them liberally with whatever they desire in the way of conveniences," wrote Athanase de Mézières, traveling the southern plains in the 1770s.

> The brains they use so often to soften skins; the horns for spoons and drinking vessels; the shoulder bones to dig and clear off the land; the tendons for thread and for bow-strings; the hoof, as glue for arrows; from the mane they make ropes and girths; from the wool, garters, belts, and various ornaments. The skin furnishes harness, lassos, shields, tents, shirts, leggins, shoes, and blankets for protection against the cold—truly valuable treasures, easily acquired, quietly possessed, and lightly missed, which liberally supply an infinite number of people, whom we consider poverty-stricken, with an excess of those necessities which perpetuate our struggles, anxieties, and discords.[28]

Ewers listed some ninety nonfood uses of the buffalo in Blackfeet material culture and the respective parts of the animal they came from. Robes, shirts, leggings, mittens, lodge covers, bedcovers, belts, shields, saddlebags, parfleche bags, bridles, halters, saddle straps, and picket ropes were made from the skin; cups, spoons, ladles, and powder flasks were fashioned from horn; thread, bow backs, and bow strings were made from twisted sinew; fat provided a medium for mixing paint and polish; paunches became water buckets; dung provided fuel; and the boiled phallus made glue.[29] Buffalo meat and hides could also be exchanged for other things: Plains Indians were "commercial hunters," trading buffalo parts to farming villages on the Rio Grande and the Missouri and Arkansas Rivers.[30]

The buffalo seemed inexhaustible. The chief of the Archithinues told trader Anthony Henday, "They never wanted food, as they followed the Buffalo and killed them with the Bows and Arrows." (The name Archithinue appears to have referred to various groups living beyond the Hudson Bay trading network and included but was not limited to the Blackfeet.) Henday saw Indians kill buffalo for their tongues and leave the meat for the wolves.[31] Matthew Cocking described the northwestern plains as a "plentiful Country of provisions, for when the present stock is expended, an Indian need only mount his Horse, taking his Gun or Bow, & in a short time return with his Horse loaded with meat, supplying his neighbors also." Equestrian hunters in prime buffalo country enjoyed an independence from European commodities that traders remarked upon with regular frustration.[32]

As had hunters in prehorse days, equestrian buffalo-hunting people developed close and reciprocal relations with the animals that sustained their lives. The Cheyenne language contained twenty-seven words for buffalo, depending upon the animals' age, sex, and condition.[33] The story of the coming of White Buffalo Calf Woman conveys the importance of buffalo in Lakota cosmology. During a time of famine, two hunters encountered a beautiful woman who told them she had been sent by the buffalo people with a message. One of the men lusted after her and was destroyed; the other returned to his village with the news.[34] The next day White Buffalo Calf Woman appeared with a pipe as a gift from the buffalo tribe. She taught the Lakotas their duties and then smoked the pipe with them. Lakotas developed rituals, prayers, songs, and ceremonies for buffalo hunting. Buffalos, like humans, originated in the earth and were relatives. The buffalo "was the embodiment of sacrifice that others might live." It gave its body to feed the people, and the people regarded it as a strong and cooperative being that conveyed gifts of healing, hunting, and leadership. Buffalo appeared in more visions among Plains Indians than any other of the "below powers."[35] Killing a white buffalo was a sacred act that merited record in winter counts as the most significant event of the year.[36]

The interaction of Indians, horses, buffalo, and grasslands created new ecological situations that required new sociocultural arrangements linked to the annual cycle of the buffalo. Mounted hunters mirrored the actions of their mobile food supply; bands fluctuated in number and size in response to the movements of the herds. During winter months they dispersed into small bands, which also permitted their horse herds to find good pasturage. In the summer they came together in larger groups for ceremony, for communal hunts, to renew relationships, and to reaffirm their oneness as a people. In the great camp circles that formed in the summer months sun dances were performed and police societies functioned. Kinship ties and an ethic of communal cooperation countered the social decentralization and fragmentation occasioned when the herds dispersed.[37]

Horses changed situations between tribes as well as within tribes and in doing so produced significant changes in the tribal map of the West.[38] People moved onto and across the plains, jostled for position, formed new alliances, competed for resources, and vied to acquire or defend prime locations in exchange networks. Horses shifted the balance of power away from sedentary and semisedentary farming communities and in favor of mobile hunting groups. Horses were commodities of exchange as well as instruments for war and hunting; stealing horses was an act of production as well as a path to status. Raiding for horses became both a cause of war and a way of war. Organizing for new levels of warfare brought more centralized political structures and stronger patterns of leadership.[39]

People who centered their lives and visions on horses transformed themselves. In historian Elliott West's view, horses inspired people "to redeem their existence." Newly mobile communities were capable of exploiting the rich resources of their environment in new ways and to new levels. Horses brought to the Great Plains "a vast expansion of power made possible by tapping energy that had always been locked beyond reach. Suddenly people could use grass, the most prolific storeplace of the sun's gift, to hunt, move, and fight with a vigor unimaginable before." The new solar economy beckoned peoples to the plains: "Invaders swept in, seized the possibility, and revised the country and themselves."[40] In N. Scott Momaday's retelling of tribal history, the Kiowas remade themselves as a people when they moved south and east onto the open plains and acquired horses: "Their ancient nomadic spirit was suddenly free of the ground." They did not quite become centaurs (men and horses remained separate creatures), but, as Momaday remembered from his own first horse, "there were moments when there was practically no telling us apart."[41]

All Change on the Southern Plains

When Spaniards ventured onto the Great Plains in the sixteenth century, they saw Indians who hunted buffalo, lived in skin tipis, and traveled great distances to trade with other Indians. These basic patterns of life continued long after horses became part of the southern plains landscape, but pressures increased and participants changed. In the late sixteenth century the Jumanos and allied peoples dominated the Native exchange system that operated between Rio Grande trade fairs in the West and Caddo and Wichita villages in the East. The Apaches took over in the late seventeenth century. In the eighteenth century the Comanches pushed the Apaches off the plains, took over their hunting territories, and made themselves the dominant power on the southern plains. The movements of horse-riding and horse-raiding Apaches, Utes, and Comanches generated chain reactions and population shifts across the Southwest.[42]

The Jumanos lived in the southern plains of west Texas and eastern New Mexico. After about 1100 Jumanos were farming in the central Rio Grande Valley, but they also made buffalo hunts into the plains. By the time the Spaniards penetrated the area they were active—and most visible in the records—as long-distance traders. Jumano caravans carried buffalo hides, bows and arrows, corn, salt, turquoise, and livestock between Indian villages as far apart as the Caddos in Louisiana and the Pueblos in New Mexico, and the Jumanos held intertribal trade fairs. A cluster of Jumano villages at La Junta de los Ríos, at the confluence of the Rio Grande and its tributary, the Río Conchos, formed a meeting ground and a gateway at the intersection of routes linking Mexico, New Mexico, the southern plains, and the gulf plains. Jumano bands often incorporated refugees from other areas, including former mission Indians from northern Mexico. The Jumanos became a people of diverse ethnic and linguistic origins related through trade and marriage, and they traded so extensively that the Spaniards applied the name loosely and broadly to various groups of Indians. Historians, anthropologists, and linguists disagree about their precise identity. The Jumanos appear in the historical records in glimpses in Texas, New Mexico, Nueva Vizcaya, and Coahuila, sometimes as settled farmers, sometimes as buffalo-hunting nomads. They obtained many horses through their ties to the Spanish, built their herds on the rich grasslands of their heartland, and earned a reputation as horse traders. One of the towns of the Tompiro Pueblos was called Humanas, "because," said Fray Alonso de Benavides, "this nation often comes there to trade and barter." Shuttling back and forth across the southern plains, the Jumanos carried news as well as goods: Jumanos met Frenchmen from La Salle's expedition in the Hasinai villages, told the Spanish about La Salle's settlement, and guided them to it.[43]

A noted Jumano chief named Juan Sabeata, apparently an apostate from a northern Mexican mission, seems to have led annual caravans to exchange Spanish goods at the Hasinai villages. In 1682 Sabeata led a Jumano delegation to El Paso, where the Spanish had taken refuge after the Pueblo Revolt. He listed three dozen "tribes" who were allied to the Jumanos. He asked for missionaries, promising ten thousand souls among the Jumanos and Julimes. He also, and this was no doubt his real purpose, asked the Spanish for protection against the Apaches. An influential culture broker, Sabeata spent the best part of a decade working back and forth between Spanish and French newcomers on the southern plains, trying to bolster Jumano fortunes that were being buffeted by Apache pressures. The world the Jumanos had built was on the verge of collapse.[44]

The collapse came quickly. Periods of severe drought occurred in the early eighteenth century, cutting into the buffalo herds in south Texas that Cabeza de Vaca had seen in such numbers. Epidemics of disease, probably carried along well-traveled trade routes, spread through the Conchos River Valley of northern Mexico into Texas and New Mexico: smallpox in the 1670s, 1687–88, and 1706; malaria and dysentery in 1717–18. Many small tribes whom the Jumanos counted in their alliance were obliterated. Trading partners were devastated: the Hasinais still numbered ten or eleven thousand in 1690 but were cut to two thousand by 1720. The Jumanos found themselves without a network of allies and trading partners. Sometime after 1693, when the Spanish briefly abandoned Texas, Jumano caravans from La Junta stopped making their annual treks across the plains, and the Jumano exchange network may have collapsed entirely in the smallpox epidemic of 1706. Jumanos returned to a more sedentary life as farmers around La Junta, where the population by 1715 was about one tenth of what it had been in 1580. Many of the dozens of Texas tribes mentioned in early Spanish records disappeared from written history; references to Jumanos became very sparse. People from shattered tribes joined other groups, and some Jumanos joined other displaced peoples at what became known as Ranchería Grande. Some refugees took up residence in Spanish missions, where Indian populations continued to dwindle as disease, confinement, infanticide, and Apache raids took their toll. Many Jumanos threw in their lot with the Apaches.[45]

Apaches and Jumanos may have been in contention since before the Spaniards arrived, and early Spanish records report instances where the Jumanos seemed to be more than holding their own.[46] But the Apaches seized the opportunity presented by Spanish horses and Jumano troubles to establish their dominance in the Jumano heartland. Pushing south, they took over Jumano hunting territories and the disintegrating Jumano trade networks. Apaches saw their first horses when Spaniards rode out onto the Great Plains in the sixteenth century. The Apaches—called Querechos and Vaqueros by the Spanish—were already buffalo hunters, but they traveled on foot and transported their goods by dogs. The Spaniards were unclear about who these people were and about the relationships between the different groups. Apaches and Navajos emerged more clearly into recorded history in the seventeenth century.

They came into view riding horses. Stories about how they had obtained horses became woven into mythology and memory. Tribal legends regarded them as a gift from the gods rather than a by-product of European invasion. Like other Indian people, Navajos and Apaches at first traveled over the earth with their possessions on their backs or on teams of pack dogs. Then Europeans appeared "riding this animal which belonged to the gods." The Indians were puzzled as to why the gods had given this gift to the white man and not to them. Their culture heroes had not chosen wisely, selecting other things instead of horses. But once the gods put horses on the earth, the people tracked them down with ceremony and song. Raids for horses became sacred missions that could only succeed if the proper songs were song, special language spoken, taboos observed, and rituals performed. Navajos and Apaches boasted of the magical powers they employed in raiding for horses; their enemies agreed. Horses became central to their way of life, "the things by which men lived."[47]

Apaches acquired horses early in the seventeenth century. They got some from the Pueblos in the first decade; in the 1630s they began to retaliate against Spanish slave raids by driving off Spanish horse herds.[48] Some Spaniards reported that they lived solely by hunting, but most Apaches now followed a seminomadic lifestyle and pursued an economy that revolved around corn, buffalo, and horses. Horses gave the Apaches the mobility to exploit different resources, to relocate in times of drought, to trade and raid over great distances in order to get corn, goods, and more horses. Their population seems to have grown, and by the 1650s they were expanding their domain. Apaches on horseback traveled more easily to Pueblo trade fairs. When Spanish tribute demands disrupted the fairs, Apaches on horseback raided Pueblo fields and storehouses.

When the Spaniards returned to New Mexico in the 1690s, the Apaches welcomed their herds of horses and the renewal of the trade fairs. They developed an effective style of mounted warfare: they protected their horses with leather armor modified from the Spanish style, wielded lances tipped with metal saber blades, and used short bows for effective firepower from horseback. By the beginning of the eighteenth century, Plains Apache *rancherías* were located in river valleys throughout eastern New Mexico, Colorado, western Nebraska, Kansas, Oklahoma, and Texas. Apache raiders ranged far and wide virtually at will.[49]

While the Jicarilla Apaches remained in the north, along the Arkansas and Canadian River Valleys, southern Apaches—variously identified by the Spanish as Faraóns, Natagés, Mescaleros, Pelones, and Lipans—pushed into the southern plains of Texas, replacing the Jumanos as the dominant power in the area and forcing the Wichitas east along the Red River.[50] Adapting to the environment they found there, they developed a pattern of seasonal mobility that integrated village farming in the river valleys with buffalo hunting on the plains. Lipan and Mescalero Apaches took over the old Jumano exchange economy and revived trade routes that other peoples had pioneered. Non-Apache peoples continued to operate within the Apache exchange network, and the Apaches continued the Jumano practice of extending alliances through trade and marriage. In a pattern that would become common in shifting Native demographics on the southern plains, the Apache takeover involved incorporating other peoples into a larger and emerging Apache identity.[51]

Apaches adopted captives, but, having been targeted themselves, they knew well the Spanish market for slaves. They took captives from other tribes and traded them for horses to the Spanish, who sent them south to work in the silver mines of northern Mexico.[52] In 1694 Vargas met with a Plains Apache chief, drank chocolate with him, and pumped him for information as to whether there was any silver in his land and, if so, how far away it was. The Apache held up his fingers to show it was twenty-five to thirty days from his *ranchería* to Quivira, Wichita country. "The Indians of his ranchería knew it well, inasmuch as they went to make war on them to bring away many young men they had to sell for horses."[53] After the Spanish reestablished themselves in New Mexico, settlers from Santa Fe resumed trade with the Jicarilla Apaches and visited their country to buy captives with horses.[54] The Apaches then raided east for more captives.

Even as the Apaches wrested control of the southern plains from the Jumanos, other Indians to the north, especially the Comanches, were beginning to edge in and contest their victory. By the early eighteenth century, northern Apaches, the Jicarillas, were practicing horticulture. Like the Navajos, they found it made them more vulnerable to fast-moving mounted raiders. Faraón Apaches raided northern Apache neighbors as well as Spaniards and Pueblos. Drought added to the Jicarillas' woes. As early as 1706 Spanish officials were reporting the collapse of Apache power in the northeast, and in 1719 they reported the Jicarillas were in full retreat. In 1715 thirty Jicarilla Apaches joined Juan Paéz Hurtado's Spanish-Pueblo force on a futile month-long campaign against the Faraóns. In 1719 Chief Carlana of the Sierra Blanca and Jicarilla Apaches told Governor Antonio Valverde y Cosío that half his people had retreated deeper into Apache country to seek refuge from Comanche and Ute attacks, and he and his warriors joined Valverde's expedition against the Utes and Comanches. Four years later Carlana went to Santa Fe to ask Governor Juan Domingo de Bustamente for protection. He and his people agreed that, in return for a presidio with fifty soldiers, they would accept missionaries, settle down, and become vassals of Spain. But the presidio was never built, Comanches took over the region, and the Jicarillas dispersed. By the 1730s the Jicarillas had virtually abandoned the plains, moving west toward Taos and Pecos and returning only for occasional buffalo hunts. Other northern Apaches followed suit.[55] Some Apaches headed for San Antonio, where they could trade and find shelter and protection at the mission and presidio. Lipan Apaches who moved east and south came into conflict with Spanish settlements in Texas and Coahuila.[56]

As the Comanches expanded onto the southern plains and pushed the Plains Apaches against the Spaniards, more and more Apache women and children were taken captive. New Mexican records between 1700 and 1750 list more baptisms under the general category "Apache" than any other group: 47 in the 1700s, 26 in the 1710s, 97 in the 1720s, 136 in the 1730s, a peak of 313 in the 1740s, and 166 in the 1750s. The records do not say how many of these people were taken captive by the Spaniards themselves and how many were captured by Comanches who then sold them in New Mexico.[57] At the same time, as reported in a Spanish document of 1716, the Pawnees of Nebraska were trading large numbers of Apache captives to the French.[58]

Various Apache bands regrouped as they were edged off the plains, and some old identities broke down as bands merged. Long-standing enmities mattered less as Apache people battled Comanches in the north and

Spaniards in the south.[59] Tribal identifications, never particularly precise in colonial records, became even more hazy as different groups of people moved in, moved out, and mingled in territories formerly associated with a single tribe. A powerful nation of mounted Indians called Padoucas held sway over the plains from Nebraska to Texas during the seventeenth and eighteenth centuries. The term Padouca, commonly applied to Plains Apaches by their eastern neighbors and the French, remained in use after the mid-eighteenth century, by which time the Apaches had left the plains. By then the name probably referred to Kiowa Apaches, the only Athapaskan-speaking people left on the high plains, or to Comanches who had taken over areas formerly inhabited by Apaches. According to tribal historian John Joseph Mathews, the Osages fought the A-Pa-Tsi (Apaches) until 1700 and then fought the Pa-Do'-n-Ka (Comanches).[60]

Apache pressure on Spanish mines, settlements, and herds increased as the Apaches themselves came under increasing pressure. Pushed southwestward from the plains into the Basin and Range environment, they remade Apachería by basing it on an economy of horseback raiding. They resorted to foraging rather than horticulture, and bands became smaller. Deprived of access to buffalo grounds, they came to rely more on horse meat, replenishing their herds with Spanish livestock. Cut off from trade to the Pueblos, they extended their raids south into Sonora, Nueva Vizcaya, and Coahuila as well as raiding in Texas and New Mexico. By the 1730s Apache onslaughts closed many Sonora mines. The Spaniards identified the Apaches as their major threat, encouraged other tribes to attack them, and continued to buy Apache captives. A "mutually predatory relationship" developed in which Apaches raided Spaniards for food and Spaniards raided Apaches for workers to produce the food.[61]

The Spanish colonial empire found its northern frontiers, like its southern frontiers, confined by a raiding economy in which Indians rode "Old World animals to drive off Old World animals."[62] Apaches, as Juan Bautista de Anza the Elder (who died fighting them) realized, made a distinction between warfare, in which the primary object was to kill as many of the enemy as possible in revenge for the death of kinsmen, and raiding, the purpose of which was to run off livestock and "to elude, not engage, their enemies."[63] Spaniards were unable to control the Apaches but launched regular campaigns of retaliation against them. Warfare with Apaches and enslavement of Apache and Navajo captives became "unquestioned facts of life" on the northern frontier.[64]

Horses probably reached the Great Basin in the early 1600s. Southern

Paiutes living in arid territory in southern Utah, southeastern Nevada, the Mojave Desert, and part of Arizona north of the Grand Canyon seem to have seen the new animals as competitors for sparse grass foods rather than as a new form of transportation. For a long time, Southern Paiutes ate horses rather than rode them. But neighbors to the north lived in environments much richer in grasslands and were better placed to exploit the new opportnities.[65] Prior to acquiring horses, Ute family bands followed a mobile hunting and gathering cycle that enabled them to wrest a living from a harsh environment, but Southern Ute tradition recalls acquiring horses from Spaniards "probably around 1640."[66] Utes took to horses and transformed their economy, their social organization, and their relations with surrounding peoples. Mounted, Utes could travel out onto the plains to hunt buffalo. They formed large hunting parties to bring meat and hides for whole villages as bands began to live in larger camps than had previously been feasible. Mounted, they could escape, or rally more quickly, when enemies from the plains threatened or when mounted Apaches and Navajos raided their country for captives. Leaders attained and exercised unprecedented authority in organizing the people for hunting and war. "Suddenly," concluded Elizabeth John, "the scale of Ute life had exploded: their subsistence, warfare, and social life. But everything hinged upon plenty of horses."[67]

At first, when the Utes were short of meat and hides to trade and horses were difficult to obtain, some Utes seem to have even bartered children for horses. But by 1700 they had plenty of hides, plenty of meat, and enough horses that they could trade them to their Comanche relatives who were coming down from the north. With Comanches as allies, the Utes were able to step up their raids on the Apaches, Navajos, and Pueblos. In the second half of the century, mobile and militarized bands of Utes riding horses and wielding new weapons preyed on weaker Southern Paiute and Shoshonean peoples in the Great Basin. They carried captive women and children to the New Mexican trade fairs and bartered them for more horses, weapons, and food. Spanish ears caught little distinction between related languages, and Spanish records often identified Paiute captives as "Utes," adding to the impression that the Utes were selling their own children.[68]

By the early sixteenth century, groups of Shoshonean speakers were filtering through the passes in the Front Range of the Rocky Mountains and onto the Great Plains. Some moved north; others took a more southerly route. The Utes called them "Kumantsi" or "Komantcia." They met Spaniards early in the eighteenth century when they accompanied Utes to the trade fair in Taos. The newcomers called themselves "Numu" (Numunu, plural), but the Spaniards called them by their Ute name, and they entered written history as Comanches.[69]

The Comanche leader Mopechucope, or Old Owl, told Sam Houston in 1844 that central and west Texas was "Comanche land and ever has been." But old Yamparika Comanches told the interpreter at their agency in the 1880s that they "came from the Rocky Mountains, north of the head-waters of the Arkansas River, about one hundred and fifty or two hundred years ago, which country they inhabited with the Shoshones." The idea that they came from the Northwest was generally accepted by all or most Comanches, said the interpreter. Shoshones in the north said that the Comanches "left them and went south in search of game and ponies."[70]

They found both. The Comanche word for horse was *puc* (*puuku; puki*, "one's personal horse"), but a rich equestrian vocabulary included seventeen different terms just to describe horses on the basis of color.[71] Formerly generalist hunter-gatherers, Comanches restructured their economy around horses and buffalo. In time, they transformed themselves into pastoralists, herding livestock as well as hunting buffalo. They became so specialized as horse and buffalo people that they lost much of their old plant lore, with a consequent decline in status for their women. Freed from fear of starvation, they seem to have abandoned old mechanisms of keeping their population in line with available resources by infanticide and polyandry; instead, they adopted captive children and polygyny to help expand their population. In the view of environmental historian Dan Flores, Comanches "exploited the available thermodynamic energy streaming from their sun god more totally and directly than anyone else ever had." In doing so, they "were digging themselves into a narrow ecological groove, but so long as the herds lasted it was a potent groove indeed. And the herds were enormous." At its height, the Comanche domain embraced 240,000 square miles of southern plains territory that supported 7 or 8 million buffalo and 2 million wild mustangs. Comanches, in Mézières's words, became "skillful in the management of the horse, to the raising of which they devote themselves."[72]

The southern plains are vast, but the Comanches immediately clashed with the Apaches in competition over natural resources, trade routes, and markets. Both groups needed the same river valleys. Apaches used them for their mixed hunting and farming economy; Comanches needed them to feed, water, and shelter their growing horse herds. The Comanches also tried to oust the Apaches from their role as traders with the Spanish and Pueblos in New Mexico, just as the Apaches had ousted the Jumanos.[73]

Comanche-Apache conflicts continued into the nineteenth century, but all-out war lasted only a few decades. The Apaches' way of life as semisedentary farmers and hunters made their villages vulnerable to Comanche cavalry and guerrilla warfare. Comanche raiders struck Apache *rancherías* in the streambeds of southwestern Nebraska and western Kansas, knowing where to find them during the spring and summer agricultural cycles. Apaches told a Spanish officer in 1723 how a large Comanche war party had swept down on them "in their rancherías in such a manner that they could not make use of weapons for their defense. They launched themselves with such daring and resolution that they killed many men, carrying off their women and children as captives." The Apaches found it difficult to retaliate. The Comanches restricted Apache buffalo hunting on the plains and disrupted Apache trade in hides and captives to Taos, Pecos, and Picuris. In addition, the Comanches began to get French guns but blocked French traders from reaching westward along the Arkansas and Red Rivers. The Apaches would have to turn to the Spaniards for guns, but Spanish policy prohibited selling firearms to Indians.[74]

The Comanches pushed the Jicarilla Apaches from the frontiers of northeastern New Mexico and swept to the upper Red River early in the 1720s. Apache tradition remembered a nine-day battle, after which the defeated Lipan Apaches fled the region.[75] Most Apache bands abandoned the plains and fled west toward the Sangre de Cristo Mountains. By the early 1730s the Comanches had taken over most of the major river valleys of the southwestern plains as well as the trade with New Mexico. By 1740 they had driven the Apaches south of the Canadian River. In the 1750s they took over the Texas plains. Comanche population rose as dramatically as Apache population fell.[76] The southern plains, where Spaniards had seen Apaches on foot in 1540, had become the Comanchería.

A Spanish map, dated 1778, shows clusters of Comanche tipis and includes a legend explaining the Comanches' presence on the southern plains and their transformation into horse people:

> The Comanche nation some years ago appeared first to the Yutes. They said they left the northern border, breaking through several nations and the said

> Yutes took them to trade with the Spaniards, bringing a multitude of dogs loaded with their hides and tents. They acquired horses and weapons of iron, and they have had so much practice in the management of horses and arms, that they excel all other tribes in agility and skill, making themselves lords and masters of all the buffalo country, wresting it from the Apache Nation, who were the most extensive known in America, destroying many Nations of them and those which remain have been pushed to the frontiers of the Provinces of Our King.[77]

Spanish records portrayed Comanche movement onto the southern plains as characterized by war and disruption, but the reverberations of Spanish colonialism surely contributed to the upheaval. The Comanches made a place for themselves in the ecological and human landscape of the southern plains by ritual and alliance as well as conflict and built a hegemony that was economic as much as military.[78] They solidified their position by securing a key middleman role in the trade networks that crisscrossed the southern plains and, to a large extent, determined success or failure in the volatile new world. Comanches regularly turned up at Pueblo trade fairs, where, in return for tanned skins, buffalo hides, and captives, they obtained corn, cloth, and Spanish goods. Comanches traded at Taos in preference to Pecos, which had been the central fair in the days when the Apaches controlled the trade. In the east, trading sometimes with the French in Louisiana but mainly via Wichitas (the Taovayas, Tawakonis, Iscanis, and Wichitas proper), the Comanches exchanged horses, mules, and slaves for guns and metalware, corn, beans, squash, and fruit, which they needed to compensate for carbohydrate deficiency in their diet of meat. The reciprocal benefits of the exchange allowed the Comanches to extend their trade networks, but the Wichitas remained central to the operation of the system: they exported Comanche horses, mules, and products of the hunt; they imported horticultural produce and tobacco; and they in turn acted as middlemen between the Comanches and the French. The Comanches took over a far-reaching exchange network, rebuilt it around the huge surpluses of horses and buffalo hides they produced, and positioned themselves as the mobile axis of a trade network that spanned several environmental zones and passed a great variety of trade items through the hands of many different peoples. Comanche trade with the Wichitas and through them to the French continued even after Osages pushed the Wichitas to the Red River in the late 1750s. Intra-Comanche exchanges funneled livestock and manufactured goods from band to band.[79]

Spain never quite seemed to know what to do about the Comanche trade. The crown prohibited selling guns to Indians, which meant that the Comanches turned to the French for firearms and often raided rather than traded in New Mexico—on occasion Comanches even sold guns to Spaniards![80] Spanish colonial authorities tried to regulate Comanche trade at the Pueblo fairs but did little to curtail it. They dared not retaliate against Comanche raids with a strict ban on trade for fear of losing the Comanches to the French. Spanish-Comanche relations in New Mexico alternated between trade and warfare until the 1770s.[81] The situation was further complicated by the fact that frontier communities distant from the centers of Spanish authority formed their own trading partnerships with specific bands.

Comanches raided and traded extensively for captives. Fray Miguel de Menchero in 1744 described a new *genízaro* settlement composed of people from various nations who had been taken captive by the "Comanche Apaches," who were so far-ranging, "so bellicose and so brave," that they dominated all the tribes of the interior country. "They sell people of all these nations to the Spaniards of the kingdom, by whom they are held in servitude, the adults being instructed by the fathers and the children baptized."[82] Comanches also took captives, especially women and children, as a way of strengthening their population. Taking captive women as additional wives enhanced the status and wealth of Comanche men, since wives tanned the buffalo hides their husbands exchanged at the trade fairs. Comanches kidnapped Apaches, Utes, Pueblos, Pawnees, Wichitas, Caddos, *genízaros*, and Hispanos and absorbed them into their communities as Comanches. Comanche villages often rang with the sound of many languages. Like the Iroquois in the seventeenth-century Northeast, the Comanches in the eighteenth-century Southwest appear to have been one of America's true melting pots.[83]

As the Comanches moved, absorbed other peoples, and restructured themselves in response to new situations and opportunities, Spanish colonial officials struggled to deal with a people who were evolving into a new nation.[84] Adopting the "take-me-to-your-leader" approach common to colonizing powers, they sought to identify chiefs by handing out silver-headed canes of office, medals, and other symbols of authority and tried to centralize their dealings. But Comanche band structure was loose, individualism fiercely guarded, and leadership relatively limited. A Comanche chief typically exerted authority only within his own band and sometimes led only so long as his followers followed: "Some obey him, others do not," summed up one observer.[85] As Comanches built a new way of life around the horse they tended to gather in larger bands, but bands remained fluid and flexible, and Comanche *rancherías* were widely dispersed to allow their large herds adequate pasture and water. "They have no fixed habitation, neither do they plant crops, but live in perpetual motion, never stopping in a place except while it abounds in cattle [buffalo]," wrote Mézières. "This obliges them to divide themselves into an infinite number of little bands for the purpose of seeking better pastures for their horses, and cattle for their own food. This explains why they separate from their chiefs, following out their individual whims, and doing damage which the others can neither prevent nor remedy when it comes to their notice."[86]

While most Comanches were building a trade network in the north and east, some migrated southeast to Texas in the 1740s and 1750s. The Comanches gradually split into two main branches. In the northwest, the Yamparikas (root eaters), Jupes (timber people), and some Kotsotekas (buffalo eaters) lived in the region from the upper Canadian to the Arkansas River and were often labeled Northern or Western Comanches. Those Kotsotekas and other groups who moved south first and lived around the middle Red River Valley formed a southern or eastern branch, often referred to collectively as the Cuchantica or Cuchaneo Comanches and known later as the Penatekas, Kwahadis, and Hois. Comanche populations and band structures fluctuated as they consolidated their hold on the southern plains, to the confusion of Spanish colonists.[87]

As the Comanches spread south, other tribes who sought access to Spanish herds had to find a way past them or else raid the Comanches for the horses they had obtained from the Spaniards. The Comanches recouped their losses by almost continual raids on Spanish ranches.[88] They also raided pueblos: between 1744 and 1749 Comanches killed 150 people at Pecos alone.[89] But raiding was part of the Comanche production system, along with hunting, herding, and trading, and was controlled. They aimed to exploit Spanish and Pueblo communities as a source of livestock, not to destroy them.[90]

In 1749 Tomás Vélez Cachupín became governor of New Mexico. He inherited an embattled colony, "completely exposed to attacks by all the barbarous tribes that surround the province," and lacked adequate military resources to deal with the equestrian raiders. He took measures to resettle towns north and northwest of Santa Fe that had been abandoned as a result of Ute and Comanche raids. He also worked to secure peace with the Utes and Comanches, in part to make them a buffer against the growing French threat from the east.[91] He permitted Comanches trading privileges at the Pueblo trade fairs so long as they refrained from raiding, and he punished Comanche raids with swift retaliatory actions. In November 1751 he personally led a force of Hispanic soldiers and Pueblo allies in pursuit of a Comanche war party that had attacked the pueblo of Galisteo. The Spaniards caught up with the Comanches at a water hole and pinned them down with gunfire through the night. Ninety-six of the 145 Comanches died; the survivors straggled in to surrender the next morning. Vélez Cachupín's considerate treatment of his prisoners, who included six women and three children, won him a reputation for mercy as well as hard fighting.[92]

Vélez Cachupín secured a respite from Comanche pressure as long as he was in office to manage the peace. Writing to his successor in 1754, he urged him to cultivate Indian alliances. "The condition of this government and its circumstances, due to its organization and the diversity of the nations which surround it, must be ruled more with the skillful measures and policies of peace than those which provoke incidents of war," he wrote. The Comanches, Utes, and Apaches constituted formidable foes, and "the small forces which this province has would be crushed by tribes of their size if they conspired against it." There was not an Indian nation in the region "in which a kind word does not have more effect than the execution of the sword," he maintained, having tried both approaches. The Comanches in particular demanded tactful handling. "Sit down with them and command tobacco for them so that they may smoke as is their custom," he advised as the best way to receive visiting Comanche chiefs. "Show them every mark of friendship, without employing threats," he advocated. "I have done so and have been able to win the love they profess for me." Lest his successor underestimate the need to master Indian diplomacy, Vélez Cachupín reminded him that Spain lacked the forces to resist Comanche attacks and that the French were competing for Comanche allegiance: "If this tribe should change its idea and declare war, your grace may fear the complete ruin of this government."[93]

Vélez Cachupín worked hard to cultivate relations with Comanche chiefs and to keep the peace intact. The Comanches turned their attention to Texas. After hard-pressed Apaches in Texas made a treaty with the Spanish in 1749, Spain established a mission and presidio on the San Saba River for the Lipan Apaches in 1757. But in 1758 a large war party, estimated at more than one thousand Comanche and

Norteño warriors, destroyed the mission, killing two missionaries and half a dozen soldiers. (The Norteños, "nations of the North," included the Wichitas, Tonkawas, Tawakonis, Xaranames, Kichais, and Taovayas. The Spanish sometimes counted Caddos and Comanches as Norteños as well, although Comanche power and actions generally demanded separate attention. The San Saba war party seems to have included Caddos, Wichitas, Bidais, Yojuanes, and Tonkawas as well as Comanches.) It was the first major Comanche attack on the Spaniards in Texas but by no means the last. A retaliatory expedition of six hundred soldiers, militia, and Lipan allies, led by Col. Diego Ortiz Parrilla, floundered in an ineffective attack on a Taovaya village on the Red River the next year. Unable to subdue the Comanches, Spanish Indian policy in Texas vacillated between war and appeasement.[94]

And the peace in New Mexico did not last. When Bishop Pedro Tamarón visited the province in 1760, he found Galisteo pueblo "in a bad way" as a result of Comanche raids. Even as some Comanche bands traded at Taos, others would attack more distant pueblos. Those who were at peace and trading would say to the governor, "Don't be too trusting. Remember, there are rogues among us, just as there are among you. Hang any of them you catch."[95] That summer, hostilities erupted at Taos. Comanches attacked the fort there, killed all the men, and carried off fifty-six captives, mostly Spanish children. The new governor, Manuel del Portillos y Urrisola, demanded the return of the captives, and when a village of Comanches arrived in December he seized their chiefs, surrounded their camp, and opened fire with muskets and cannons. He killed more than three hundred Comanches and took more than four hundred captives. When Vélez Cachupín returned as governor in 1762, he found the Comanches on the brink of all-out war. He quickly dispatched six Comanche women captives as emissaries, inviting the Comanches to come to Santa Fe for peace talks. A Comanche delegation arrived a month later, armed with guns, powder, and shot obtained from the French. Vélez Cachupín reestablished peace and sent them away well fed and loaded with presents and bundles of tobacco, "so that, in the councils of their chiefs, principal men, and elders, they might smoke and consider well their resolution in regard to my purposes."[96] But it was a shaky peace.

It unraveled after Pedro Fermín de Mendinueta took over as governor of New Mexico in 1767. Mendinueta waged open warfare against the Comanches and enlisted Pueblo, Ute, and Apache warriors to assist him.[97]

The Comanches retaliated. In August 1774 Mendinueta pursued a war party of one hundred Comanches who had swept down on Pecos and defeated them on the upper Red River. In September Carlos Fernández and six hundred Hispanic soldiers and Pueblo allies surprised a Comanche village, cannonaded the camp, and pinned down the inhabitants in a wooded enclosure for two hours. An estimated 250 men, women, and children were killed; "shot and shell has no respect for sex or age," Mendinueta noted in his report. He took more than one hundred captives.[98]

The war was taking its toll on both sides, but for the most part the Comanches held the initiative and continued their raids without respite. Their war parties slipped easily through the rugged country of high sierras and rocky hills and attacked settlements in New Mexico "from all sides." The Spaniards lacked the defenses to hold them or the men and horses to mount effective pursuits.[99] The transfer of Louisiana from France to Spain and the movement of Indians onto the plains after the Seven Years' War disrupted the supplies of firearms Comanches had obtained via their Wichita allies and brought mounting competition from the Osages and Pawnees. The Comanches adjusted to the new situation by trading for Anglo-American guns instead.[100]

By 1770, according to Athanase de Mézières, the Comanches were scattered from the Missouri River to the frontier presidios of New Spain. They were "a people so numerous and so haughty that when asked their number, they make no difficulty in comparing it to that of the stars." Their skills as horsemen were unequaled, and they never asked for or granted truces. Their huge territory provided abundant pasturage for their horses and vast herds of buffalo, which furnished them with clothing, food, and shelter. In Mézières's opinion, they possessed almost "all of the conveniences of the earth." They despised Indian peoples who were dependent on European trade, calling them "slaves of the Europeans."[101]

The Comanches were lords of the southern plains, and they owed it all to horses. They had built a way of life around horses and buffalo, trading and raiding, and they had grown in numbers, from seven or eight thousand in 1690 to as many as twenty thousand less than a century later.[102] But the world they had built on horseback was coming under increasing pressure, some of it self-inflicted. Comanche population (kept high by incorporating other people) and Comanche horse herds (estimated at two or three mounts per person and growing) competed with buffalo for grass and water in riverine habitats. The buffalo herds—the Comanche

15. Lino Sanchez y Tapia (?–1838), *Comanches du Texas Occidental.* (From the Collection of the Gilcrease Museum, Tulsa, accession no. 4016.336)

larder—appear to have been declining on the southern plains by the end of the eighteenth century.[103]

Shifting Balances of Power in the Northwest

While some groups pushed south along the front range of the Rockies and entered recorded history as the Comanches, others moved north, so that by 1700 a continuous band of Shoshone-Comanche speakers stretched from southern Alberta to southern Colorado along the eastern slope of the Rockies. According to a story recorded by nineteenth-century traveler George Ruxton, Shoshone tradition explained their split from the Comanches as the result of a dispute between two hunters.[104]

During the eighteenth century the people later known as Shoshones were usually called Snakes by their Comanche cousins as well as by Blackfeet, Gros Ventres, and others.[105] The term Snake was widely used, referring sometimes to Shoshones and Comanches together, sometimes to Shoshones, Bannocks, and Paiutes, sometimes to any tribes living on the eastern slope of the central Rockies, and perhaps also to the Kiowas when they lived in the Black Hills. The use of the snake movement in sign language may have referred to the old Shoshone practice of weaving grass lodges, or it may simply have indicated "enemy," since many western peoples metaphorically termed strangers and adversaries "snakes."[106] Migration onto the plains gave Shoshones access to new sources of power and prosperity, but their transition to the horse and buffalo culture was neither sudden nor complete. Plains Shoshones came to be distinguished from their relatives west of the Rockies by location, subsistence, and cultural adaptation, but Shoshone band organization was flexible, and the same family might be called "fish eaters" when they lived in the West and "buffalo eaters" when they joined an eastern band. Eastern Shoshones were also sometimes differentiated between "buffalo eaters" and "mountain sheep eaters." Kiowa tradition remembers Shoshones living in grass lodges when Kiowas first met them on the plains. Shoshone elders interviewed on the Wind River reservation in Wyoming in the early twentieth century "remembered the grass lodges of their early childhood, with willow frames walled with grass," and recalled a life "when they had no horses, when small game took the place of buffalo and the people lacked the skin-covered tepees of more recent times."[107]

More and more Shoshones filtered through South Pass onto the buffalo-rich plains of Wyoming and Montana. Documentary evidence and archaeological finds—distinctive, flat-bottomed Shoshonean pottery in the Laramie Basin, a probable Shoshonean kill site in the same area, petroglyphs of possible Shoshonean origin in the Wind River Valley and the southern Big Horn Basin, a bundle burial in southern Wyoming, tools, campsites, and lodge remains—all indicate that Shoshone people were on the northwestern plains in significant numbers by the eighteenth century. By the 1730s they seem to have occupied a range from the Saskatchewan to the Platte.[108]

Shoshones in southern Idaho probably obtained horses by about 1700. Tradition says they got them from their Comanche relatives, although Utes in western Colorado may also have supplied them with mounts. Comanches and Utes moved horses west of the Continental Divide; Shoshones then funneled them throughout the Northwest, supplying directly or indirectly the Cayuses, Yakimas, Walla Wallas, Palouses, Nez Perces, Flatheads, Coeur d'Alenes, Pend d'Oreilles, Spokanes, Kalispels, and other Columbia Plateau peoples as well as Crows.[109] The Kalispels were located along the Pend Oreille River, an east-west trade route that offered the best route through the mountains toward the Columbia River. They connected with other exchange systems, trading with Colvilles at Kettle Falls and at the Spokane trade center near the major salmon fishery at Spokane Falls. The introduction of horses into the Plateau increased people's seasonal mobility between fishing grounds, buffalo-hunting grounds, and areas in which to gather berries, plants, roots, and camas bulbs. It also expanded the range, volume, and level of activity along the Columbia trade network.[110]

Increased buffalo hunting required collective organization and greater mobility and generated changes in Shoshone society. Chieftainship developed to a new level as leaders emerged to coordinate the hunts, maintain order, and organize military responses. Nevertheless, Lewis and Clark noted that each Shoshone was "his own sovereign master" and followed his own mind; the authority of the chief was no more than "mere admonition supported by the influence which . . . his own exemplary conduct may have acquired him in the minds of the individuals who compose the band."[111]

Early possession of horses and a strategic location that allowed continued access to southern horse traders gave the Shoshones a distinct edge over unmounted neighbors. Indian raiders identified as Snakes ranged from the Saskatchewan to the Missouri and even clashed with

Plains Apache bands in western Nebraska and northeastern Colorado, although these raiders may well have been Comanches or Kiowas.[112]

In the winter of 1787–88, a Cree Indian named Saukamappee, or Young Man, who was living among the Blackfeet gave fur trader David Thompson, who was living in his tipi, an account of how his adopted people first encountered horses sometime around 1730.[113] Thompson, a Welshman working for the North West Company, described Saukamappee as "an old man of at least 75 to 80 years of age, . . . his face slightly marked with the smallpox." In the battles of old, said Saukamappee, Shoshones and Piegans had lined up in ranks behind large rawhide shields, fired arrows at each other, and sustained and inflicted few casualties. But Shoshone cavalry brought a new kind of warfare to the northwestern plains. Piegans long remembered their first encounter with horses: "The Snake Indians and their allies had *Misstutin* (Big Dogs, that is Horses), on which they rode, swift as the Deer, on which they dashed at the Peeagans, and with their stone *Pukamoggan* knocked them on the head, and they thus lost several of their best men."[114] Petroglyphs at Verdigris Coulee, along the Milk River in southern Alberta, record a very similar encounter, probably from the same era. The scenes depict pedestrian and mounted warriors in combat; both still carry large shields, and some of the horses wear leather armor, which was used only briefly on the northwestern plains.[115]

When La Vérendrye's sons ventured onto the northern plains in 1743 Indian informants told them the "Gens de Serpents" had destroyed seventeen Indian camps in the Black Hills a couple of years earlier, killing all the men and old women and carrying off the young women as slaves to sell for horses and merchandise. Infected by their Indian guides' fear, the French explorers turned and headed for home without seeing more than a rumor of the dreaded "Snakes." As historian George E. Hyde commented, the account conveys "the impression of a group of Frenchmen moving about, lost in a great smoke cloud through which the dim shapes of Indian bands move, ghostlike." But thirty years later Hudson's Bay Company trader Matthew Cocking found that fear of enemies identified as "Snake Indians" was still widespread among the tribes on the far northern plains.[116]

However, the ascendancy of the Gens de Serpents was already in decline before Cocking heard of their prowess. It was only a matter of time before neighbors adopted horses into their own cultures and arsenals. Shoshone horse herds soon attracted enemy raiders. Cayuse traditions recalled that, sometime before 1750, a war party of Cayuses and Umatillas was encamped on a tributary of the Snake River when it encountered Shoshone warriors riding what appeared to be elk or deer. The Cayuse chief, Ococtuin, hastened to make a truce with the Shoshones. The Cayuses returned with a pair of Spanish mounts, which provided seed for their own herds. The Cayuses quickly adapted their lives to horses. They pushed east to the foothills of the Blue Mountains. In summer they crossed the mountains to the Grande Ronde or moved to Walla Walla Valley, where they shared lush pastures with their Nez Perce allies. They participated as middlemen in trade rendezvous, exchanging dried salmon, shells, and sometimes slaves they had obtained at The Dalles. They also began raiding Shoshone horse herds and raided west of the Cascade Mountains, ranging as far as northern California for slaves.[117] Flathead and Crow raiders also targeted Shoshone horse herds.

Learning that the Cayuses had obtained horses from the Shoshones, the Nez Perces sent a party south to trade for ponies. Nez Perce tradition says that they bought their first horse, a white mare in foal, from the Shoshones. Before anyone tried to ride her they sat around for days watching her every move, learning her habits. The mare and her colt became the basis for the Nez Perce herds. By midcentury the Nez Perces were mounted, and their horse herds flourished in the green and sheltered valleys of their homeland. Nez Perces practiced selective breeding and built some of the biggest horse herds on the continent. By the time they discovered Lewis and Clark in September 1805, the Nez Perces owned "immence numbers" of horses, some of which were "pided [pied] with large spots of white irregularly scattered and intermixed with the black brown bey or some other dark colour"—the Appaloosas for which they became famous. In the old days, small groups of Nez Perces had ventured on foot across the Bitterroot Mountains to hunt buffalo on the plains and visit Flatheads in the Bitterroot Valley; now whole villages packed their horses and traveled the Lolo Trail and other passes over the mountains. Sometimes Cayuses, Umatillas, and Walla Wallas accompanied them. They carried with them dried fish, salmon oil, berries and roots, camas and huckleberry cakes, horn bows, mountain grass hemp, and shells they had acquired at The Dalles in trade with Columbia River peoples. East of the Bitterroots they traded with Flatheads and Shoshones for buffalo products, beadwork, feather work, and stone pipes that intertribal traders had brought west across the plains. They also, along with their Salish and

Sahaptian allies, found themselves clashing increasingly with mounted war parties of Blackfeet.[118]

In order to ensure continued supplies of horses, mules, and European metal goods from the south, the Shoshones bartered war captives, tapping into the Spanish-Indian slave trade that had developed in the Southwest. The Shoshones themselves often fell victim to Ute slave raids, and they now extended the slave-raiding frontier to the northern plains, ranging far and wide in search of captives. Archaeological finds of Shoshonean and Crow pottery together in the same campsites have been interpreted as evidence that one group was stealing women from the other or trading them. Shoshone slave raids reaffirmed the Shoshones' position as *the* enemy for the surrounding tribes. Shoshones raided for captives, which they exchanged for horses and goods in the south; their victims raided the Shoshones for vengeance and for horses.[119]

The Shoshones quickly lost their equestrian advantage to the Blackfeet—the Piegans, Bloods, and Siksikas. Blackfeet oral history attributes acquisition of horses to a chief named Shaved Head who "found them among the mountain Indians about 1725 and brought the first animals to the Blackfeet people." The Blackfeet probably had acquired horses by the second quarter of the eighteenth century. Blackfeet religion and cosmology interpreted cycles of history that included preglacial time, and a longer tribal memory may have recalled the horse of ancient days, but the Blackfeet who encountered the Shoshone cavalry in Saukamappee's account evidently had not seen horses before.[120] Whether it was a meeting or a reunion, Blackfeet took to horses rapidly. By the time Anthony Henday met them in 1754, they had "plenty of fine horses of all Colours, and are very Dexterous in Rideing, & managing ye Same." Fur trader Alexander Henry reported that "some of the Blackfeet own 40 to 60 horses. But the Piegans have by far the greatest numbers; I heard of one man who had 300."[121]

Blackfeet males embraced the equestrian warrior-hunter culture wholeheartedly: "War, women, horses and buffalo are all their delights," said Henry, "and all these they have at their command." They emerged as the most formidable power on the northern plains. War, said Henry, was their "principal occupation," and horse stealing, said trader Edward Umfreville, was "their principal inducement in going to war." One group of Piegans traveled all the way to the Southwest to steal Spanish horses and mules.[122] The herds of the Shoshones and their neighbors presented prime targets nearer to home.

The Piegans, said trader David Thompson, "were always the frontier tribe" and bore the brunt of the Shoshones' attacks. Saukamappee related how, unable to compete with Shoshone horsepower, the Piegans enlisted help from the Crees and Assiniboines, who sent ten warriors armed with muskets. In a battle that probably occurred in the late 1730s they gunned down some fifty Shoshone warriors and put the startled survivors to flight.[123] The Shoshone threat seems to have pushed the Blackfeet into a loose alliance with Gros Ventres, Sarcees, Crees, and Assiniboines. This northern coalition regularly contested the northwestern plains with the Shoshones, Flatheads, Kutenais, and Crows throughout the rest of the century.[124]

The Blackfeet and their allies enjoyed increasing access to supplies of guns, ammunition, and metal weapons at the same time as they closed the gap on the Shoshones in terms of horse power.[125] European trade goods began to filter west soon after the Hudson's Bay Company was chartered in 1670 and York Factory was built on the bay's western shore in 1684. Despite changing hands several times as Britain and France contested the area, York Factory emerged as the most important source of European merchandise for the peoples of western interior Canada. Indian trappers, traders, and middlemen around the bay brought in pelts and then returned inland with British goods, which they traded to hunting bands for more pelts.[126]

Prior to 1670 Crees and Assiniboines had been part of the Ottawa-French trading system, but with the development of Hudson Bay trade they acquired guns and began operating as middlemen in the evolving British networks. French traders began to infiltrate the interior, and in 1734 La Vérendrye established Fort Maurepas at the southern end of Lake Winnipeg to trade with the Crees and Assiniboines. La Vérendrye's son, Louis-Joseph, reached the Saskatchewan River in 1739, and two years later another son, Pierre, built the first fort (Fort Bourbon) at the mouth of the river. The French built another post at the junction of the North and South Saskatchewan Rivers in 1753. These small outposts diverted some trade away from Hudson Bay and funneled merchandise deep into Indian country. Crees and Assiniboines traded at the new posts rather than make the long trek to the bay, but they maintained trade connections with both the British and the French. They peddled guns and steel weapons from the traders and carried them to the Blackfeet and their allies. It is widely believed that the Crees moved west under the impetus of the fur trade, although the evidence for such a move may well have been overstated, and the notion that gun-toting Crees immediately clashed with the Blackfeet is erroneous. The loose alliance between Crees and Blackfeet that developed around 1730 persisted throughout most of the century. Crees wanted access to horses, and trade with Blackfeet to their west provided it; Blackfeet wanted access to military hardware via the Crees. The Crees made the Blackfeet pay well: in 1766 Crees were paying fourteen beavers per gun and selling them to the Blackfeet for fifty beavers; a hatchet costing one beaver sold for six beavers. Nevertheless, the trade tipped the balance in the Blackfeet power struggle with the Shoshones.[127]

The Hudson's Bay Company tried to counter French presence in the vast territory of the interior by sending employees to winter there and establish trade relations with the people who lived "on the back of this Land."[128] In June 1754 Anthony Henday set out from York Factory. Accompanied by two Indian guides, Connawapa and Attickosish, and an Indian "bedfellow," Henday traveled 114 days into the country of the Archithinue Indians in an effort to "bring such foreign Indians Down to trade." Henday met a two-hundred-lodge band of Archithinues, smoked with their leader, and gave them presents. They gave him a variety of excuses for not being able to come to the Hudson Bay posts the following summer—they followed the buffalo, they could not canoe. Most Blackfeet preferred to pay Cree and Assiniboine prices rather than make an arduous journey to trade for the same goods at the bay posts.[129]

After the fall of New France, traders from Montreal continued to challenge the Hudson's Bay Company in the West. Canadian peddlers began operating on the Saskatchewan. The Hudson's Bay Company realized it must follow suit or lose out to its aggressive new competitors. The company established inland posts, initiating a period of intense competition. In 1772 Matthew Cocking traveled to the northwestern plains to induce the Blackfeet to trade at York Factory, but the Blackfeet were not interested. "It surprises me to perceive what a warm side the Natives hath to the French Canadians," wrote Cocking.[130] In 1774 the company sent explorer Samuel Hearne to build its first post on the Saskatchewan. Other, smaller companies and free-lance operators joined the contest for Indian furs. In 1779 the first North West Company was formed, successor companies being formed and re-formed in later years. As Montreal and Hudson Bay traders opened direct trade with Indian producers at interior posts, Western Crees and Assiniboines lost their lucrative middleman role. But the new situation also offered new niches in the trade network.

The Assiniboines and Crees, who may have moved southwest of Lake Winnipeg into the grasslands of Manitoba and Saskatchewan, began supplying the trading posts with buffalo meat.[131] As the North West Company extended its operations into western Canada, Iroquois from Kahnawake and other villages in the St. Lawrence Valley began to sign on as canoemen and trappers. By the end of the century Iroquois participation in the western fur trade was established and growing.[132]

Competition between rival fur-trading companies became cutthroat. In the winter of 1794–95 five different competitors worked against one another at the mouth of the Winnipeg River. Indian customers played off rival traders, pushing them to pay higher prices and extend more credit. Europeans appointed more "trade chiefs" and gave more presents. Violence, animal slaughter, and alcohol consumption all increased dramatically.[133] The North West–Hudson's Bay Company competition continued until 1821, when the companies merged, and the new Hudson's Bay Company monopolized the trade.

Armed and mounted, the Blackfeet led the offensive against the Shoshones, pushing them south and west off the northern plains. Smallpox slowed the Blackfeet assault in the 1780s, but the famed Piegan war chief Kutenai Appe led 250 warriors against the Shoshones in 1787. That same year, Saukamappee told David Thompson that all the lands held by the Blackfeet tribes were formerly held by the Kutenais, Flatheads, and Shoshones but that those peoples had now been "driven across the mountains." [134] The Blackfeet kept up the pressure. [135] Shoshones relinquished their hold on the plains of southern Alberta and northern Montana and retreated into the Rocky Mountain ranges of Wyoming and Idaho, where Lewis and Clark met them. The Shoshones still "abounded" in horses, and they continued to travel south and trade with the Spaniards (Lewis and Clark saw Spanish trade goods, Spanish dollars, and mounts with Spanish brands), but they could not get guns. [136] The Blackfeet prevented Canadian traders from peddling firearms to the western tribes, and Spanish policy forbade selling guns to Indians, so the Shoshones' southern trading partners had few firearms to spare. Shoshone tradition recalled that, before Lewis and Clark entered their territory, "we knew nothing about guns except their effects."[137] Shoshones still wore leather armor at the time of Lewis and Clark's visit, but it offered little protection against guns. [138] Piegans raided Shoshone horse herds with impunity, called the Shoshones old women, and boasted they could kill them with sticks and stones.[139]

Lewis and Clark obtained information that led them to believe a great Snake nation occupied the plains, but their information was out of date.[140] Cut off from the gun trade and pressed by the Blackfeet, the Shoshones and their neighbors welcomed the Americans and their promise of trade. Jealously guarding the control over the gun trade they had established, the Blackfeet not surprisingly reacted with hostility when Lewis and Clark explained that the Americans intended to unite and arm the western tribes. Hostilities with the Blackfeet continued during the years of the American Rocky Mountain fur trade.[141]

Corn Power to Horse Power on the Upper Missouri

When corn spread to the upper Missouri, the Mandans, Hidatsas, and Arikaras, like other peoples who lived on the banks of the river, had surrounded their villages with cornfields. They hunted buffalo on the plains, and they ate well. Their villages lay where hunters and farmers met, and they grew prosperous and powerful. When horses began to arrive from the Southwest and European metal goods and guns filtered in from the Northeast, the Mandans and their neighbors continued to do well, trading horses and manufactured goods as well as corn and meat. La Vérendrye, who accompanied an Assiniboine trading party to the Mandan villages in 1738, described the Mandans as "very industrious." They sowed "quantities of corn, beans, peas, oats, and other grains," which they traded to neighboring tribes, who came to the villages to get them. "They are sharp traders," he said, "and clear the Assiniboine out of everything they have in the way of guns, powder, ball, kettles, axes, knives and awls."[142] Village women produced surpluses of corn, beans, squash, and tobacco, "not only sufficient to supply their own wants," noted trader John McDonnell in the 1790s, "but also to sell and give away to all strangers that enter their villages."[143]

Horses were just beginning to arrive in the area northeast of the Black Hills when La Vérendrye was on the upper Missouri. The Assiniboines with whom he traveled had no horses, and he made no mention of the Mandans having any, but three years later his son returned from those villages with two horses. In 1792 French trader Jacques d'Église saw horses with Mexican saddles and bridles there, and in 1796, according to Jean-Baptiste Truteau, Assiniboines were obtaining horses as well as corn and tobacco in their exchanges at the Mandan and Hidatsa villages.[144] Arikaras seem to have owned horses at the time of La Vérendrye's visit to the Mandans, as did tribes living southwest toward the Black Hills.[145] Pierre-Antoine Tabeau, a French trader from St. Louis who was at the Arikara villages in 1803–4, was told that the Arikaras used to transport corn, tobacco, and European goods "to the foot of the Black Hills," where they participated in a trading fair with Kiowas, Kiowa Apaches, Cheyennes, Arapahos, and Comanches and exchanged their goods for dressed deerskins, shirts of antelope skin decorated with porcupine quills, moccasins, and dried meat. Increasingly, Arikaras were able to offer guns in trade, for which the Plains tribes gave horses, "the most important article of trade with the Ricaras." The Indians told Tabeau they got their horses by trade or raid from Spaniards at "San Antonio or Santa Fe."[146] Lewis and Clark noted that Kiowas and Kiowa Apaches raised "a great number of horses," which they traded to the Missouri village tribes for European goods.[147]

By the mid-eighteenth century, the Mandans, Hidatsas, and Arikaras had made their villages into a great trading rendezvous. Originally a market where corn, beans, and squash were exchanged for meat and hides, the farming villages on the upper Missouri developed into an exchange center for European goods and Plains produce as well and for guns and horses in particular. The villages were well positioned to take advantage of the convergence of the northeast-moving horse frontier and the southwest-moving gun frontier. From the Northeast they obtained manufactured goods, either direct from French and British traders or via Cree and Assiniboine middlemen; from the West they received horses and the products of the plains; from the Southwest came more horses plus goods of Spanish and Pueblo origin. Assiniboines, Crees, Ojibwes, Crows, Blackfeet, Flatheads, Nez Perces, Shoshones, Cheyennes, Arapahos, Kiowas, Kiowa Apaches, Pawnees, Poncas, and various Sioux bands all visited the upper Missouri villages, either regularly or intermittently. The visitors passed on what they obtained to more distant neighbors, often at vastly inflated rates. In this way the Mandan-Hidatsa-Arikara trade center interconnected with other exchange centers—the Wichita, Caddo, and Pawnee on the prairies to the south; the Comanche network on the southwestern plains; the Pueblos on the Rio Grande; the Columbia River networks beyond the Rocky Mountains; and, via British traders and Montreal, the fur houses and markets of Europe.[148] As historian James Ronda points out, these trade networks bound the West together in "a great circle of hands." Every conceivable item passed through them: corn from Arikara fields, squash from Mandan gardens, fancy clothing made by Cheyenne women, dried salmon from Columbia River fishing peoples, bear grass baskets from Pacific Coast Chinooks. Lewis and Clark's men saw Spanish horse gear in upper Missouri villages, British teapots on the Columbia, and war hatchets they themselves had made at Fort Mandan in the hands of Indians in Idaho: the hatchets had traveled west faster than they had![149]

But even as earth lodge villages on the upper Missouri buzzed with the activity of visiting trading bands and the babel of a dozen different languages, the future was slipping away from them. The horses, guns, and trade networks that enhanced their power and prosperity also, in time, unraveled the world they had built around their earth lodge villages. Horses, guns, and epidemics empowered enemies to challenge the once-formidable villages. Friends and neighbors moved out onto the plains and took up a horse and buffalo way of life, but sedentary farming people with huge cornfields lacked sufficient pasturage to amass large herds. Earth lodge villages that had been palisaded for safety became death traps when European diseases ran along trade routes that formerly brought prosperity. The exchange network that centered on the villages of the Mandans, Hidatsas, and Arikaras held up as long as the three tribes did, that is, until their mass destruction in the 1837 smallpox epidemic. But long before that their earth lodge villages ceased to be a safe haven, and other peoples embraced a future that revolved around riding horses and hunting buffalo on the plains, not cultivating corn on the banks of the Missouri.[150]

The Crow Indians had split off from their Hidatsa relatives and moved out onto the plains even before horses reached the area. When they finally arrived in northern Wyoming and southern Montana, they were still pedestrians. Around 1725 or 1730 a war party that had been to the Green River in Wyoming brought back the first horse the Crows had seen. One man who stood too close to the animal received a swift kick in the belly, earning a nickname for himself and eventually a name for his band, the Kicked in the Bellies. About the same time a party of Mountain Crows who had traveled as far as the Great Salt Lake brought back several horses. In another story, Crows got their first horses from the Nez Perces. On their way home, a Crow man saw horses in a dream, and when he went looking for them he found several emerging from a lake. Crow war parties were soon heading south and west to bring back more. By the time La Vérendrye met a band of Crows in 1743, they had enough horses that they were able to provide the explorers with fresh mounts.[151]

The Crows began a regular commerce, traveling across the Rockies to trade for horses with the Flatheads, Nez Perces, and Shoshones and then driving the herds east to the villages of their Hidatsa relatives, where they exchanged them for corn, tobacco, and European goods. They built up a lucrative trade and guarded it jealously.[152]

By trading, raiding, and breeding, the Crows rapidly built up their herds. A man who acquired many horses and who displayed generosity in giving them away achieved status in society.[153] The Crows earned a reputation as skilled horse people. North West Company trader François-Antoine Larocque said they were excellent riders; trained from infancy, they could guide their horses without a bridle or hang on one side of their ponies, invisible to their enemies. "Everybody rides," he wrote. "Men, Women & Children. The females ride astride as the men do. A Child that is too young to keep his saddle is tied to it, and a small whip is tied to his wrist—he whips away and gallops or trots the whole day if occasion requires."[154] According to tribal historian Joseph Medicine Crow, other tribes used the travois to transport their equipment and people, but "the Crows all rode, from tiny tots to old people, and used packhorses. In this way they could travel fast over any kind of terrain."[155]

A Crow community on the move was a colorful equestrian cavalcade, and Crows missed no opportunity to display their wealth in horses and their skills on horseback. North West Company trader Charles Mckenzie was present when a band of three hundred lodges with two thousand horses arrived at the Hidatsa villages in June 1805. The Crows "presented the handsomest appearance that one could imagine—all on horseback. Children of small size were lashed to the Saddles, and those above the age of six could manage a horse—the women had wooden saddles—most of the men had none." They halted on rising ground behind the village and formed a circle: "[W]hen the Chief addressed them, they then descended full speed—rode through the Village, exhibiting their dexterity in horsemanship in a thousand shapes—I was astonished to see their agility and address:—and I could believe they were the best riders in the world."[156]

Crows attributed spiritual powers to horses. They regarded them as emissaries of the "Great Power." Like other animals, they were capable of conveying sacred gift powers to human supplicants, to whom they appeared in a dream or vision or during a fasting experience. Men with good horse medicine would generally own many horses, would often be successful horse raiders, and would sing special songs about horses in ceremonies and dances.[157]

As horses became an integral part of Crow life, so too did war. Warriors raided for horses and fought for status; tribes clashed over hunting grounds and resources. Crow horse raiders, who expected to return home mounted, are said to have *walked* as far as the middle course of the Missouri River and across the Continental Divide to steal horses.[158] Young men sought visions that would bring them success in battle against their enemies, joined warrior societies that encouraged and sustained their martial spirit, and participated in elaborate rituals in preparation for war and horse stealing. Crow warriors boasted they were invincible on horseback but confessed that, dismounted, they were no match for their enemies.[159] In time, as neighboring tribes coveted their rich hunting grounds and horse herds, the Crows lived increasingly in a state of siege, fighting a desperate struggle to hold onto their homeland.[160] They survived and, despite the U.S. government's program of slaughtering their horse herds in the 1920s, they remained a horse culture, as evidenced by the equestrian parades held every August at Crow Fair. As Joseph Medicine Crow said, "Thanks to Columbus for bringing the horse back to America!"[161]

The Kiowas, who were neighbors of the Crows for much of the eighteenth century, surely agreed. Kiowa traditions tell that the people lived in "a region of great cold and deep snows in or beyond the mountains at the extreme sources of the Yellowstone and the Missouri" in western Montana. Life there was hard, and, after a hunting quarrel between two chiefs, some of the people began to migrate in the late seventeenth century. From the headwaters of the Yellowstone they traveled east to the Black Hills, where they befriended the Crows.[162] At this time the Kiowas had no horses but used only dogs and the travois. But as they moved out onto the plains, they acquired horses. "The great adventure of the Kiowas was a going forth into the heart of the continent," wrote Kiowa author N. Scott Momaday. Pushed out of the Black Hills by the Sioux and Cheyennes, they moved south through Wyoming along the front range of the Rockies and toward the Wichita Mountains in Oklahoma. By the time they reached the southern plains they had been transformed. "In the course of that long migration they had come of age as a people," said Momaday. They became allied with the Comanches sometime around 1790, and together they dominated the southern plains. Kiowas ranged across western Oklahoma, northern Texas, northeastern New Mexico, southeastern Colorado, and southwestern Kansas, traded with Pueblos in New Mexico, and raided deep into Mexico as well as against other Indian tribes. They lived in small, independent bands and came together each summer in the Sun Dance, the central ceremony of the tribe, during which they reaffirmed their unity, renewed relationships, and hunted buffalo, the foundation of the Kiowa economy and culture.[163]

Oral tradition as related by John Stands in Timber in the twentieth century recalled that the ancestors of the Cheyennes originally lived by hunting, fishing, and gathering "in another country, where great waters were all around them"—the western Great Lakes. When Cheyennes first appeared in historical documents in the seventeenth century they were living in Minnesota, between the Mississippi and Mille Lacs. Their name derived from the Dakota Chaiena, or "red speakers," referring to people who spoke a language the Dakotas could not understand but who were not enemies. George Bent, son of William Bent and a Cheyenne mother, said, "Our people call themselves Tsis tsis tas, meaning 'People alike' or simply 'our people,' but by the whites we have always been termed 'Cheyennes,' from a Sioux word, Shai ena, which means 'people speaking a strange tongue.'"[164]

Around the time of the Pueblo Revolt, as Comanches began moving toward the southern plains, Cheyennes began to move from their homes on the Mississippi toward the Minnesota River, where they lived in sedentary farming villages. They then moved to the James River in eastern North Dakota. From the 1720s one portion of the Cheyennes, perhaps nine hundred people, occupied a palisaded village of about seventy earth lodges at the Biesterfeldt site on the Sheyenne River in southeastern North Dakota. They grew corn but also conducted occasional buffalo hunts and had some horses. Sometime before 1790, while most of the community was away on a hunt, an Ojibwe war party destroyed the village. Describing what appears to have been the same attack, an Ojibwe chief named Sheshepaskut told trader David Thompson that they "put every one to death, except three Women." According to Dakota tradition, however, refugee Cheyennes from this village fled to another village at the mouth of Porcupine Creek near the present border between North and South Dakota.[165] They and other Cheyenne bands then moved west again and built villages on the Missouri and the Grand River in South Dakota. They were poised to migrate onto the high plains and, like the Kiowas, remake themselves as a people.[166]

In Cheyenne tradition, the prophet Sweet Medicine had visited the Black Hills and returned with four sacred arrows, two to bring success in hunting, two to destroy their enemies. Sweet Medicine had also foretold the coming of an animal with a shaggy neck and a tail trailing almost to the ground that would transform the people's lives: "This animal will carry you on its back and help you in many ways," he said. "Those far hills that seem only a blue vision in the distance take many days to reach now; but with this animal you can get there in a short time, so fear him not." When the first Cheyenne saw horses, sometime in the early eighteenth century, "he thought of the prophecy of Sweet Medicine, that there would be animals with round hoofs and shaggy manes and tails, and men could ride on their backs into the Blue Vision. He went back to the village and told the old Indians, and they remembered."[167] Another tradition tells that when Cheyennes first saw traders bring horses to their villages they asked Maheo, the All Being, for horses of their own. Maheo replied that the Cheyennes could have horses. They could even go and take them from the Comanches. "But remember this," he warned:

> If you have horses everything will be changed for you forever. You will have to move around a lot to find pasture for your horses. You will have to give up gardening and live by hunting and gathering, like the Comanches. And you will have to come out of your earth lodge houses and live in tents. I will tell your women how to make them, and how to decorate them. And there will be other changes. You will have to have fights with other tribes, who will want your pasture land or the places where you hunt. You will have to have real soldiers, who can protect the people. Think before you decide.[168]

The Cheyennes made their choice. In the words of trader Pierre-Antoine Tabeau, "They abandoned agriculture and their hearths and became a nomadic people."[169] Heading out onto the plains and "putting the whole society on horseback" was a momentous decision and not likely one embraced by all Cheyennes at one time.[170] As the prophecies foretold, they changed so much that "they became a people apart from those who had lived before," writes historian Elliott West. "Their world's center had shifted; its horizons lay on a new pivot. They were now the Tsistsistas, the Called Out People."[171]

For many years, the Cheyennes lived near a people called the Suhtais, but the Suhtais were a distinct group, speaking their own dialect, and remained so until the 1830s, when they joined the Cheyennes permanently. John Stands in Timber recalled that the Cheyennes joined with the Suhtai people "sometime during their travels" from the east. George Bent said they met while still on the plains north of the Missouri.[172] Tsistsistas, Suhtais, and Arapahos would often camp together, and Arapahos (often referred to in the records as Caninanbiches) traveled with the Cheyennes to trade at the Missouri villages. The Arapahos appear to have moved onto the plains just ahead of the Cheyennes but may not have separated from the Gros Ventres until the end of the century.[173]

Like American settlers who came later, notes Elliott West, the Cheyennes were "drawn westward by alluring opportunities." In their case the opportunities were horses, vast buffalo herds, and the chance to become middlemen in the huge trade system they had seen operating at the Missouri villages. "Now the Cheyennes have ceased to till the ground," wrote Tabeau, "they roam over the prairies west of the Missouri on this side of the Black Hills, from which side they come regularly at the beginning of August to visit their old and faithful allies, the Ricaras." They shuttled back and forth between farming villages on the Missouri River and hunting camps deep in the plains and functioned as middlemen in a huge and intricate exchange network that transmitted European commodities across the plains. Out on the plains, horses were a medium of exchange for guns and other European manufactured goods, a fact that further impelled the Cheyennes toward an equestrian life.[174] After 1800 they swung south to the central plains.

But they were moving into a world where other people already lived and where other newcomers too were remaking themselves around horses and buffalo. Their new homes were zones of conflict long before Americans arrived. They gained great freedom and mobility, but they grew dependent—on buffalo, on horses, on trade. "By becoming people of the horse," writes West, "the Cheyennes were stepping into an ecological arrangement, a relationship among land, climate, and resources that was more complex and precarious than they could have guessed."[175] Like tragic heroes in some ancient Greek myth, the Cheyennes would pay dearly for having their wishes come true.

Like the Cheyennes, Sioux people also moved west to take advantage of new opportunities. The initial stages of the move seem to have occurred as part of the displacement of Great Lakes peoples under Iroquois pressure in the seventeenth century. By the 1680s, when the French opened direct trade with the Sioux, western groups—Lakotas, Yanktons, and Yanktonais—had already moved to the prairie regions of southern and western Minnesota, where they gave up agriculture and took up buffalo hunting in the warmer seasons of the year, retreating into the forests during the winter and trading their pelts at the French posts in the spring. But they did not yet have horses.[176]

The Sioux migration was often attributed to pressure from Crees and Ojibwes armed with guns, but the Sioux were pulled not pushed onto the plains. Eastern Sioux groups absorbed the pressure from the Ojibwes and said their western kinsfolk moved west for better hunting.[177] Nevertheless, as Yanktons and Lakotas moved west, they fought a rearguard action against Ojibwes, Crees, and Assiniboines. La Vérendrye said they had been "carrying on war from time immemorial . . . continually forming war parties to invade one another's territory," although smallpox among the Crees in 1737 put a temporary hold on hostilities. Alexander Henry explained that the Sioux and Ojibwes waged "perpetual war" over the hunting territory that existed between them; Jonathan Carver said their wars "had continued without interruption for more than forty winters."[178] The Sioux group nearest to the Crees in the seventeenth century were a division of the Yanktonais who later became a separate tribe, the Assiniboines. They found themselves in a difficult position as neutrals, became allied to the Crees, and by the end of the century were fighting with them against the Sioux and other enemies.[179]

Lakota winter counts refer to horses stolen from other tribes as early as the first decade of the eighteenth century.[180] Jonathan Carver made no mention of horses among the Dakotas on the upper Mississippi in 1768 and indicated that the horse frontier was still some distance to the west, but western Sioux had horses long before that, and fur trader Peter Pond saw "a Grate Number of Horses" among the Yanktons in 1775.[181] A Cheyenne tradition claimed that they provided the Sioux with their first horses. The Sioux, they said, followed them as they moved west of the Missouri and out toward the Black Hills, but they had no horses and carried their possessions on dog travois: "The Cheyennes took pity on them and occasionally gave them a horse." Sioux also got horses indirectly from Cheyennes via trade with the Arikaras.[182]

But in the eighteenth century the Lakotas had little trouble getting guns, which reached them from their eastern relatives, who traded directly with the British on the Saint Peter's River. As the Sioux moved west they pushed aside Ioways and Otos, clashed with Omahas, and by midcentury came up against the fortified earth lodge villages of the Arikaras, Mandans, and Hidatsas. A winter count kept by the Oglala family of American Horse recorded that Standing Bear led the first party of Oglalas to the Black Hills in 1775 or 1776.[183] Most Lakotas were still east of the Missouri at this time, where they occupied a large swath of buffalo country in North and South Dakota, and they subjected the Arikaras in particular to increasingly hostile pressure. Archaeological excavations at the Larson site, an Arikara village occupied between 1750 and 1785, revealed the remains of seventy-one bodies, male and female, ranging in age from four to almost fifty, scalped and mutilated. Musket balls and arrowheads among the skeletons and evidence of fire suggest that the attackers breached the wooden palisades, killed the people who had fled to their homes for refuge, and burned the village.[184] Arikara tradition said that around the mid-eighteenth century they had one thousand lodges, each housing about twenty people, and could field four thousand warriors. Disease and enemy raids reduced them to three hundred lodges by the time of the American Revolution. By 1800 they were down to 150 lodges in three weak villages and practically at the mercy of the Sioux.[185]

By the time Lewis and Clark arrived on the upper Missouri, the Sioux had broken the dominance of the Mandans, Hidatsas, and Arikaras and reduced the balance of power on the river to a shambles. The farming peoples were a shadow of their former strength. Scottish trader John McDonnell said the Sioux were "the most powerful nation in all the interior country." Cheyenne traditions recalled early peaceful encounters with the Sioux, but Lewis and Clark met Cheyennes at the Arikara villages who said they were at war with no nation "except the Sieoux with whome they have ever since their remembrance been on a difencive war."[186] After a tense confrontation with Brulé Sioux during the expedition's ascent of the Missouri, Lewis and Clark pronounced them the "pirates of the Missouri." They predicted that the citizens of the United States would never be able to fully exploit the advantages offered by the Missouri until "these people are reduced to order, by coercive measures." Zebulon Pike in 1806 pronounced the Sioux "the most warlike and independent nation of Indians within the boundaries of the United States."[187]

During the course of the eighteenth century, Arapahos, Gros Ventres, Assiniboines, Blackfeet, Comanches, Kiowas, Cheyennes, and Lakotas all embraced the new technology of the horse and staked out their places on the Great Plains. The future, it seemed, belonged to those peoples who remade themselves on horseback and built new lives on the buffalo-rich grasslands. The people who underwent the transformation abandoned their "ecological safety nets" in order to specialize in year-round buffalo hunting, which provided more food than did a diversified hunting, gathering, and farming economy. What they lost in diversity they made up for by increased trade with those peoples who had not abandoned the old ways and, increasingly, with newcomers who offered

16. Mandan robe thought to have been collected by Lewis and Clark and to depict a battle with the Sioux around 1797. (Courtesy, Peabody Museum of Archaeology and Ethnology, Harvard University. Photo by Hillel Burger, N27515.)

new goods. Any lingering attachments to farming ways of life evaporated in the wake of devastating smallpox epidemics that turned earth lodge villages into graveyards and shifted the balance of power to nomadic buffalo hunters.[188]

But the gods give no gifts without exacting a price. Horses, like corn, were not an unmixed blessing. They brought increasing competition between humans and took their toll on the environment. On the southern plains increasing numbers of equestrian hunters employing more effective hunting techniques and building larger horse herds began to put stress on the great buffalo herds. Despite an ethos that required restraint and respect in hunting, the Indians' annual harvest of buffalo began to exceed the herds' natural increase in periods when the toll taken by wolves, fire, habitat degradation, and drought was high. Buffalo populations were falling even before American soldiers, hunters, and ranchers began to destroy the herds in the second half of the nineteenth century.[189] The world that the horse Indians built and that they assumed would last forever would last no longer than that of the ranchers and farmers who replaced them.

Chapter 7

People In Between and People on the Edge

At the beginning of the eighteenth century most people living in the American West had never laid eyes on a European. The West was Indian country, and Europeans were a rarity. But the tentacles of European empires began to reach deep into the Indian West. European presences and pretensions marked out zones of contest, and European influences generated significant changes in people's lives. Many frontiers—equestrian, epidemiological, technological, ecological, cultural, tribal, and imperial—clashed, intersected, and fused in both the trans-Appalachian and the trans-Mississippi West. Tribal homelands, centers of the universe for those who lived there, were transformed into contested borderlands "in between" rival empires. Indian nations and communities conducted relations with Europeans and with other Indian peoples who surrounded and intruded on their homelands. With access to Spanish horses and French guns, peoples like the Osages and Comanches were hardly victims caught between powerful empires. They dominated the worlds they inhabited, exploited foreigners who tentatively impinged on their domains, and preserved their independence and their lands. Viewed this way, Indians were not "people in between"; Europeans were "people on the edge." Few Indian peoples escaped the repercussions of European competition for trade, empire, and allies, but many shaped the terms of the contests.[1]

Spain, France, and Britain waged recurrent conflicts in eighteenth-century North America, occasionally battling it out in Indian territory and always sending reverberations through Indian country. As horses spread from the Southwest, guns and powder from French and British traders in the Northeast and East flowed onto the plains. Slave raiders and traders also reached deep into the plains. Until the 1780s Spanish prohibitions on trading guns to Indians limited the number of firearms trickling north but did little to stop the arms race on the plains, where Indians sometimes outgunned Spaniards and sometimes became gun dealers themselves. Where people were located, or positioned themselves, on the shifting horse and gun frontiers greatly affected their chances for survival and success.[2]

Struggles for hegemony in the West were often decided by events in the East; on the high seas, where naval power could sustain or sever supply routes that fueled fur trade connections and Indian alliances; on European battlefields; and at treaty tables in European capitals, where huge swaths of territory changed hands without reference to Native inhabitants. Indians not only felt the repercussions of imperial competition, they also participated as allies and enemies of the contesting empires. They fought for their own reasons as their own interests and goals intersected with or jarred against those of the European powers, they participated in colonial systems when they chose to or when they had no choice, and they resisted amalgamation when they had the option or the power to do so. European power bases lay far distant from American frontiers; real power on the frontiers often lay with the Indian nations "in between." Imperial contests were played out at the village level, where European traders and agents solicited and sustained Indian support and rival chiefs and factions supported one power or the other, or one power *then* the other, or pursued a precarious neutrality. And, always, Indians understood that other people's empires rested on Native lands and resources.

The Bloody Edges of Empire

In 1700 Charles II of Spain died without an heir, plunging Europe into the War of the Spanish Succession. The next year Iroquois delegates made peace with the "Far Nations," the French in Montreal, and the English in Albany and officially opted out of involvement in imperial conflicts, a strategy that enabled them to rebuild their strength during the next fifty to sixty years.[3] Meanwhile, England and France glowered at each other across Iroquoia and the Ohio Valley and competed for the Indian fur trade. Farther west, Spain, France, and England angled for position and influence in Indian country. In Louisiana and the Southwest, France and Spain nervously listened for reports of each other's activities and rumors of each other's intentions. Like blind men feeling an elephant, they groped toward each other across the plains. Indian guides led expeditions west from Louisiana and Illinois and east from New Mexico along ancient trails that had served as routes for generations of traders and explorers.[4] French and Spanish officials both feared the intrusion of English commerce and colonists. Traders and "explorers" from competing European nations showed up in Indian villages, eager to establish exchange with Indian people and alert for news of "other men like us." On occasion, Indians knew before Europeans that European nations were at war.[5]

Europeans courted Indians as customers in trade, as partners in diplomacy, and as allies in war. Indians courted Europeans for the same reasons. Europeans fomented, aggravated, and exploited Indian rivalries and sucked Indian people into dependence on European markets. Indians played the field created by European competition to bolster their diplomatic, economic, and military positions. Indian allies accompanied European expeditions, pointing the way, striking old enemies, and getting embroiled in new disputes. Indian groups shifted location to take advantage of new opportunities or to escape enemies empowered by horses or firearms. The tangle of conflicting, overlapping, and shifting alliances unleashed forces that spread violence and destruction far beyond the edges of empire.

The tentacles of empire often reached first for slaves. European colonization of America generated a massive trade in slaves that reached deep into Africa and transported thousands of African people in chains across the Atlantic. It also generated a trade in slaves that reached deep into America and hauled hundreds of Indian people to silver mines in northeastern Mexico, to New France, and via Charles Town, South Carolina, to the Caribbean. As European goods and African slaves flowed into America, animal skins and Indian slaves flowed out. [6] After the settlement of Charles Town in 1670, English colonists initiated trade with southeastern Indians that extended by way of the Tennessee River to the Chickasaws and reached to the Mississippi. Armed with British guns, Chickasaw warriors traveled down the Mississippi to raid Choctaws and across it to raid Caddos, selling their captives to the British for more guns: "No imployment pleases the Chickasaws so well as slave Catching," observed Carolina trader Thomas Nairne. In just ten years, Iberville reminded the Chickasaws in 1702, they had taken more than five hundred Choctaw captives and killed another eighteen hundred but had lost eight hundred men themselves in wars waged "so that the English can get slaves." English traders reached the Quapaw villages before the end of the seventeenth century, and Quapaw warriors crossed the Mississippi and raided the Yazoo Valley for slaves to trade for British goods and guns.

Slave raids had a major impact on population decline and dislocation in the lower Mississippi Valley.[7]

Indians with French weapons made slave raids on tribes west of the Missouri. "Panis" became a generic term for Indian slave in French colonial discourse, referring to Wichitas and other enslaved people as well as Pawnees.[8] In 1682 Michigamea Indians presented La Salle with "two Panis slaves," a boy and a woman. The boy, probably a Wichita, had been taken captive by Panimahas, possibly Skidi Pawnees, and passed along an Indian slave network first to the Osages and then to the Missouris before the latter gave him to the Michigameas.[9] At the Montreal peace conference in 1701 a Potawatomi chief named Onanguicé presented Governor-General Louis Hector de Callière with "a small slave" to atone for the death of a Frenchman at Potawatomi hands: "Here is a little flesh that we offer you," he said. "We took it in a country where the People go on horse."[10] Illinois Indians appear to have raided across the Mississippi for captives before the French arrived, but by the first decade of the eighteenth century the French were actively encouraging their raids and selling the captives to the English. In 1715 one hundred *coureurs de bois* left Michilimackinac for Tamaroa or Cahokia to join others already active in an illegal trade: on the Missouri River they bought slaves captured by Indians in the West and then sold them to the English in Carolina.[11] Farther north, Crees and Assiniboines took captives in their wars against the Sioux (in one attack on a Sioux camp in 1741 the raiders netted a column of captives that stretched for 250 yards) and sold them in Michilimackinac and elsewhere to French traders, who in turn sold them at high profits in Canada.[12] Purchasing Indian slaves or accepting them as gifts allowed the French to cement alliances with the Indians who provided the slaves as well as to obtain and exploit captive human labor.[13]

The labor demands of the Spanish mining frontier prompted Indians to raid Indians and sell them into slavery in return for Spanish horses and merchandise.[14] Apaches, Comanches, and other mounted Indians from the plains and Southwest raided the Pawnees for slaves to sell to the Spaniards. People identified as Pawnees appear in the baptismal and burial records of pueblos and towns in northern New Mexico by the early 1700s.[15] At the same time, the Pawnees appear to have raided the Apaches for captives to trade to the French.[16] Indians who trafficked in slaves knew they would find a ready market. New Mexican parish records list the baptisms of nearly eight hundred Apache women and children—victims of slave raids—between 1700 and 1760.[17]

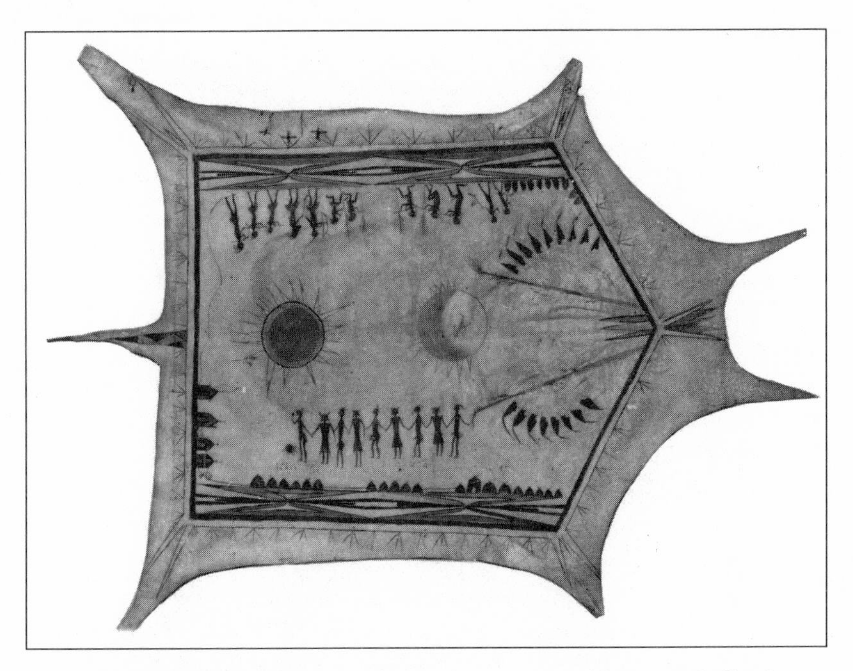

17. Quapaw "Three Villages" buffalo robe, ca. 1750. (Courtesy, Collection Musée de l'Homme, Paris) The painted hide features two feathered calumets near the apex of the borders, representations of the sun and moon, four Indian villages, and a French village and fort. Above the three villages grouped together are written "Ackansas" (the French and Illinois name for the Quapaws) and the names of the three Quapaw villages: Osotoy, Towima, and Kappa. The action depicts a battle between the Quapaws and another tribe (probably the Chickasaws) and a scalp dance to celebrate the victory. A line runs from the Quapaw villages through the French fort to the battle site, probably indicating that the Quapaws traveled via Arkansas Post (Arnold, *Rumble of a Distant Drum*, 63–76.)

Guns and horses became keys to power, and human slaves became the currency with which to purchase them. When Cadodacho Indians from the Red River fired their muskets to welcome Governor of Texas Martín Alarcón's party in 1718, the Spaniards noted the Indians had more guns than they did. Fray Francisco Céliz, who accompanied the expedition, had no doubts about where the Indians got their firepower. Two Frenchmen living among the Cadodachos "are the ones through whose hands the French acquire slaves and other things of that land from the Indians," he wrote. "Since the Indians are so interested in muskets, powder, bullets, and clothing, which they exchange for young slaves, wars are maintained and even brought about among the Indians themselves, causing many tribes to be destroyed who would otherwise be converted to Christianity. There is sufficient proof of this."[18]

In the second half of the century Utes conducted a deadly cycle of raiding and trading between the Great Basin and New Mexico, carrying hundreds of women and children into captivity and extending the slave-catching net of the Spanish Empire far to the west. Utes and Spaniards alike relied on captives from the Great Basin, and the slave trade bound them in alliance.[19] The Utes' captives took their place in New Mexican colonial society as *genízaro* servants and laborers. The *genízaro* inhabitants of Abiquiu on the Chama River maintained dealings with the Utes, even though Ute raids twice compelled them to abandon the village. When Hispanic settlers abandoned it after a devastating Ute-Comanche raid in 1747, Governor Tomás Vélez Cachupín awarded a community land grant to thirty-four *genízaro* families to build their own pueblo and to serve as a buffer zone. Abiquiu functioned as an intermediary between Spaniards and Utes and conducted its own trade relations with Utes, who sometimes brought captive children there. By Ned Blackhawk's calculations, Abiquiu over time became home to as many as one thousand unidentified Indian captives.[20]

Europeans wrestled unsuccessfully with their dilemmas over the Indian slave trade. Colonial governments frowned on it and sometimes banned it, but they more often turned a blind eye to it or actively encouraged it. Trafficking in slaves not only provided the colonies with labor but also fomented and perpetuated divisions between the tribes.[21] In French Illinois Indian slaves comprised 10 percent of the population by 1754, and even in Louisiana, where African slaves obviated the need for Indian labor, Indian slavery was well established by the time Spain took possession in the 1760s.[22] Fray Pedro Serrano in 1761 denounced Spanish complicity in purchasing captives from Comanches and other Plains Indians at the Pueblo fairs and in the ritualized public rapes that, he claimed, often accompanied the transaction: "It is the truth that when these barbarians bring a certain number of Indian women to sell, among them many young maidens and girls, before delivering them to the Christians who buy them, if they are ten years old or over, they deflower and corrupt them in the sight of innumerable assemblies of barbarians and Catholics."[23] The "going rate" for an "Indian girl twelve to twenty years old" was "two good horses and some trifles."[24]

Not to purchase captives, however, might, as Navajos had demonstrated in 1694, ensure their deaths. Spanish authorities, soldiers, and individuals ransomed both Spanish and Indian captives from *indios bárbaros.* Seized in violence and traded as commodities, captives sometimes bridged cultural barriers. Captive women and children often assumed a new place and identity through adoption and marriage. Returning captives to their home communities could lubricate diplomatic relations. Captives and returned captives served as intermediaries and interpreters and forged kinship ties that transcended ethnic boundaries. Rescuing and ransoming captives was a common practice and part of the overall Hispanic-Indian trade on the northern frontiers. As happened elsewhere in North America when Europeans were abducted by Indians, some captives preferred to remain with their Indian captors, and some of those who returned faced traumatic readjustment.[25] Sometimes Indians bought Spanish captives from other Indians and turned a sizable profit by ransoming them in San Antonio for horses, mules, or merchandise.[26]

Empire building sometimes depended on negotiation and coexistence rather than force and coercion. The French built an empire in the West based on a network of carefully cultivated Indian alliances and earned a reputation for good dealings with Indian peoples. Frenchmen usually had little choice but to pursue good relations with the people whose world they entered and whose power could permit or prevent France's great goal of linking the settlements in Canada, Illinois, and Louisiana. As rival European powers pushed into the heart of the continent, the French in Louisiana relied heavily on allies like the Quapaws to assist them in wars against other tribes and pose a barrier to English expansion.[27] Nevertheless, generosity gave way to genocide when French imperial goals were threatened.

The once-formidable Natchez had been decimated by European disease but coexisted and traded with the French after the newcomers built a military outpost at Fort Rosalie in their territory in 1716. But Natchez complained of French arrogance, and, according to French naval officer Jean-Bernard Bossu, who traveled through the region more than a quarter century later, the commander of Fort Rosalie "insulted and infuriated the very people he should have been handling gently." When the officer demanded that the Natchez vacate one of their villages and cede the land, Natchez elders conferred in council and concluded unanimously to destroy the French. In Bossu's account one of the elders echoed the sentiments that the Natchez noble Stung Serpent had expressed to Antoine Le Page Du Pratz in 1723. "Before the French came to our lands," said the elder, "we were men, we were happy with what we had, we walked boldly upon all our paths, because then we were our own masters. But today we tread gropingly, fearing thorns. We walk like the slaves we will soon be, since they already treat us as though we were."[28]

In November 1729 Natchez warriors attacked Fort Rosalie and slaughtered the garrison. A bloody war ensued in which the French employed Choctaw allies and African slaves. "It is important to destroy that nation as soon as the affairs of the colony permit it," asserted Étienne Boucher de Périer, who had replaced Jean Baptiste Lemoyne, sieur de Bienville, as governor of Louisiana. "We do not need armies to destroy them; we need only parties of thirty or fifty, either by themselves or at the head of the Indians who are bound to us."[29] By the end of 1731, according to one report, the combined effects of disease and French assaults had reduced the Natchez to "about one hundred fighting men, about thirty old men capable of nothing, and few women."[30] Many of the survivors took refuge with the Chickasaws.

The Chickasaws said they had ten thousand warriors when they came from the West, but chronic warfare reduced their numbers: the French in 1731 estimated they had about three thousand people, including six hundred warriors, and two or three hundred Natchez refugees.[31] Harboring France's enemies and allied to British traders from Charles Town, the Chickasaws threatened French efforts to link their Illinois and Louisiana settlements. The French attacked them with all the strength they could muster. They encouraged Choctaws and Quapaws to lift Chickasaw scalps and paid for them "at the accustomed rate and in the accustomed manner." The Chickasaws repulsed the French and their Choctaw allies and gravitated closer to the English, who gladly supplied them with guns and ammunition to help thwart French ambitions on the Mississippi.[32] The Chickasaws survived in a cauldron of conflict and earned a formidable reputation among Indians and French alike as a people who lived "at war with all nations."[33]

The Choctaws were the major power in the region when the French arrived on the Gulf Coast. Separated from the Chickasaws with whom, both tribal traditions agree, they had migrated from the West, the Choctaws may have numbered as many as twenty or thirty thousand people living in forty or fifty autonomous towns.[34] Heirs of the Mississippian societies that flourished before Spanish invasion, they may have emerged as a people in the wake of epidemics and other upheavals triggered by European contact.[35] Bienville described the Louisiana region in 1726 as "formerly the most densely populated with Indians." But wars and diseases had destroyed many nations, and most of those who survived were feeble remnants. Only the Choctaws, he wrote, "can give us any ideas of what the Indians formerly were."[36] Choctaws saw in the French an opportunity to counter attacks by Creeks from the East and Chickasaws from the North, both of whom raided them for slaves, which they sold for guns to the British. The French seized the opportunity to win Choctaw allegiance and armed them with guns to fend off the slavers. France and Britain competed for the lucrative Choctaw deerskin trade; Choctaw deerskins were shipped by the thousands to France and England, and European goods flowed into Choctaw country. Europeans found it frustrating to deal with a nation "composed of fifty-one villages and consequently fifty-one chiefs" but made things worse by meddling in Choctaw politics; they appointed their own medal chiefs, funneled guns and other merchandise through them, and fostered the conditions that enabled an ambitious warrior like Red Shoe to rise to power until a French-paid assassin ended his career. The Choctaws played off French and English rivals and preserved their political independence even as they grew economically dependent on European goods. Divisions within the nation facilitated the Choctaws' strategy: different factions sided with different powers, French and English traders and agents were active in different Choctaw villages, and rival Choctaw chiefs gave professions of loyalty to rival European kings. The British and French resented having to play by the Choctaws' rules, but they had no choice: "As long as there is a single Choctaw Indian in the colony he will always be a cause of considerable expense for the King because of all the devious devices that are put into practice to hold this nation in equilibrium, which makes it necessary for us to treat it with consideration," complained one French official. It was a dangerous game, and the Choctaw nation turned on itself in open civil war in 1748–50, but the Choctaws survived the British-French contest for empire.[37]

French ambitions in the North met resistance from the Mesquakies, the Red Earth People, who lived along the Wolf and Fox Rivers in Wisconsin. The Mesquakies were called Outagami, People of the Opposite Shore, by their Ojibwe neighbors and enemies. Mesquakie traditional history recalls that when Frenchmen asked the first Mesquakies they met who they were, the Mesquakies named their war chief clan, the Fox. The French erroneously assigned the clan name to the whole tribe, calling them Renards, or Foxes.[38] Early French reports described them as people "of a very gentle disposition."[39] But relations deteriorated rapidly. After the Ojibwes pushed them from Michigan into Wisconsin up against the

Sioux early in the seventeenth century, the Foxes lay at the western edge of the French trade orbit. They stood between the French and potential new markets among the Sioux and other peoples on the upper Mississippi. They resisted French efforts to control the fur trade and undermine their role as middlemen. Their warriors frequently killed traders and carried the calumet of war west to the Otos and Ioways and east to the Iroquois. Their war chiefs exerted increasing influence, and the Kiyagamohag warrior society consistently defended their lands against intrusion. By 1700 war had become a normal state of affairs for the Foxes, but their insistence on keeping the French out of the Minnesota and Des Moines trade routes made them the target of warfare of a kind they had never experienced before.[40]

They "are a cunning and malignant tribe," wrote Antoine de Lamothe Cadillac. "They are settled on a very fine river in a country that is very good in every way. This tribe is becoming powerful, and for that reason it grows constantly more insolent. I think that if we had not had the war with the Iroquois on our hands, we should have taken steps to humble this tribe, for they have attacked and robbed Frenchmen many times."[41] French efforts to "humble" the tribe lasted more than thirty years.

In 1701 Cadillac established a new fort at Detroit and invited Ottawas, Hurons, Miamis, Potawatomis, and Ojibwes to resettle in eastern Michigan with the promise of good trade terms. Within a few years nearly six thousand Indians had settled in the area, and Cadillac boasted of his new settlement as the "Paris of America."[42] In 1710 he invited the Sauks, Foxes, Mascoutens, and Kickapoos to relocate. Two Fox villages accepted the invitation and moved back into their Michigan homelands. But Cadillac's plans to build a trade center backfired. Relocating villages produced volatile intertribal relations, and Cadillac was reassigned to a new post in Louisiana. His successors viewed the Foxes as troublemakers openly receptive to British trade. Tensions escalated, killings occurred, and by 1712 there was open war between the Foxes and Mascoutens and the French, Ottawas, and Potawatomis. The Foxes and Mascoutens attacked Detroit; the French and their allies laid siege to the fortified Fox and Mascouten village. Despite the Fox chief Pemoussa's defiant boast that they were immortal, the Foxes suffered heavily. Forced to make a desperate nighttime escape during a thunderstorm, they were cut to pieces the next day where the Detroit River joins Lake Saint Clair. The war spread west, and Foxes from Wisconsin continued to battle the French and their Indian allies until 1716.[43]

Between 1719 and 1726 the Foxes were at war with the Illinois confederacy and, by extension, hostile to the Illinois's French allies. All hands seemed to be against them. As the French expanded their trade connections on the upper Mississippi, they sought water routes through Fox country. Fearing the Foxes were intriguing with the Sioux in the West and the pro-English Iroquois in the East, the French moved to isolate and destroy them.[44] First, the French built a post among the Sioux—Fort Beauharnois on Lake Pepin.[45] Then in 1727 Governor Charles de La Boische de Beauharnois declared war on the Foxes. A French army invaded Fox country in the summer of 1728 but succeeded only in burning corn and cabins.[46]

French efforts "to destroy this audacious and rebellious tribe" culminated in the summer of 1730.[47] French trader-agents spent the preceding winter trying to foment trouble between the Foxes and their Sac, Kickapoo, and Mascouten allies. Isolated politically and militarily, a band of about 950 Fox people fled their villages on the Illinois River and headed southeast in a bid to find refuge among the Senecas. Pursued by the French and their allies, they erected a palisaded fort in a grove of trees next to a small river in northeastern Illinois. As the Foxes dug in for a siege, French agents sang the war song in Indian villages, and French power converged on the site. Robert de St. Ange brought French regulars, Creole traders, and four hundred Illinois warriors from Fort Chartres; Nicolas-Antoine Coulon de Villiers arrived from Fort Saint Joseph with three hundred Miamis, Potawatomis, and Sauks; trader Simon Réaume brought four hundred Weas and Piankeshaws. Hopelessly outnumbered, running short of food, and exposed to the August heat, the Foxes offered to surrender. They dropped more than three hundred children over the palisades in an effort to touch the hearts of the Indians in the besieging force, "calling out to them that since they hungered after their own flesh that all they had to do was eat of it and quench their thirst with the blood of their close relatives, although they were innocent of the offenses that their fathers had committed." The besieging Indians received the children "with open arms," and the Sauks provided safe refuge for them, but the French ended further communications by keeping up a continuous fire on the fort. The Foxes offered to surrender to the tribes in return for their lives and brought their children to parlay with the French in an effort to elicit mercy, but the French commanders refused to grant quarter. On September 1 another French force arrived with two hundred Miami, Potawatomi, and Huron allies and a proclamation from Governor

Beauharnois prohibiting any surrender. The French were determined to exterminate the Foxes.

A week later, after an eighteen-day siege and in a grim repetition of the disaster at Fort Detroit eighteen years before, the Foxes attempted a desperate breakout under cover of darkness during a violent thunderstorm. The cries of their children alerted French sentries, and the French and their Indian allies easily caught up with them the next day. Three hundred Fox men and boys formed a thin line in the hope of buying time for the women and children to escape, but the twelve-hundred-strong French and Indian army quickly cut them down and then pursued the hungry and exhausted women and children as they fled across the prairie. Two hundred Fox warriors and three hundred women and children died in the slaughter. Captured warriors were tortured and burned at the stake. Perhaps fifty warriors escaped. In December 1731 Christian Iroquois and Hurons attacked the surviving Foxes in their village. By 1732 the Fox population had been reduced to approximately fifty men and adolescent boys and ninety women and children.

Some Foxes found refuge among the Sauks around Green Bay, but Beauharnois wanted them rounded up, taken to Montreal, and divided among the mission villages. Otherwise, he ordered, "kill Them without thinking of making a single Prisoner, so as not to leave one of the race alive in the upper Country."[48] But when the French arrived with Menominee, Ottawa, and Ojibwe allies to seize the Fox refugees, Sauks and Foxes joined forces and fought them off. Confronted with the prospect of unraveling Indian alliances and escalating opposition, Beauharnois finally granted the Foxes pardon in 1738 and ordered them to be consolidated with the Sauks in one village at Green Bay. Though some Sauks and Foxes remained around Green Bay or on the Fox River, most had moved to the lower Rock River by 1750.[49] During the later years of the eighteenth century, more Foxes formed settlements in northeastern Iowa, where lead mined by Fox women became an important trade commodity, especially after Julien Dubuque married into the tribe in the 1780s and promoted its commercial development.[50]

The French relished the fruits of genocide: "This will give peace to the colony and will increase its commerce through possession of the lands that they occupied, where our Indians dared not hunt for fear of these fearsome enemies." With the Fox barrier removed, "communications will soon be open for the Mississippi as well as for the Sioux settlements."[51]

But events in Europe affected Indian and European fortunes in the

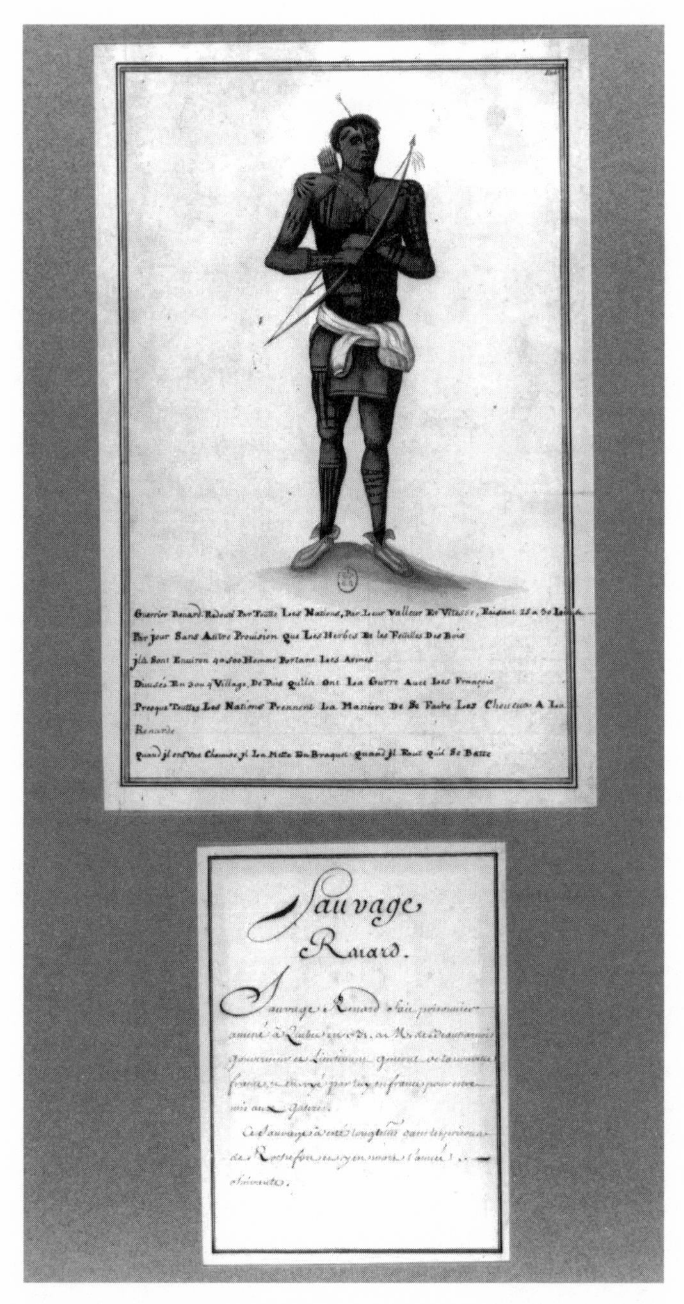

18. Watercolor painted in Quebec around 1730 of a Fox warrior who had been captured by Miamis and given to Governor Beauharnois. The governor sent him to France, where he died in prison in 1732. (Courtesy, Cliché Bibliothèque Nationale de France, Paris)

West. British naval superiority during the War of the Austrian Succession (King George's War, 1744–48) severely curtailed the trade goods available to the French, and few French traders went into Indian country during the war years. Supply lines reopened as the war came to an end. About the same time, the Comanches and Wichitas forged an alliance that allowed French traders to push farther west and gave Comanches access to French guns via their Wichita friends. Sales of guns to the Comanches intensified Comanche pressure on the Apaches, which generated increased Apache raiding for horses, weapons, and food in Texas and New Mexico.

Early in 1748 Comanches visiting Taos reported that thirty-three Frenchmen had arrived at their village twenty leagues away to trade flintlock muskets for mules. The specter of Frenchmen "insinuating themselves" into Comanchería and arming the "numerous and warlike" Comanches alarmed Spaniards already conscious of their vulnerability. Vélez Cachupín interrogated three Frenchmen who traveled to Taos with Comanches for the annual trade fair in the spring of 1749, and several French traders pushed their way through to Santa Fe between 1749 and 1752.[52]

Pierre Mallet, now a widower, his wife having died in childbirth, returned to New Mexico with another expedition in the summer of 1751, traveling from Natchitoches with Governor-General Pierre Rigaud de Vaudreuil's proposal for opening trade between Louisiana and New Mexico. But a band of Comanches roughed them up, helped themselves to their merchandise, and took all of their papers and letters. When the party reached Pecos, the Spanish arrested them and sent them to El Paso and then to Mexico City for interrogation. From there they were shipped to Spain and disappeared from the records.[53] In 1752 Jean Chapuis and Louis Feulli led a trading expedition from the Illinois country to the lower Platte River, on to the Kansa villages, and then to New Mexico, planning to establish a trade route that incorporated both Spaniards and Indians, with Comanches and "Panis" supplying horses for the trek across the plains.[54]

Spanish-Comanche relations during the first half of the eighteenth century consisted mainly of conflict punctuated by occasional truces and Comanche visits to trade fairs at Taos and Pecos. In this era Spain wanted to settle nomadic Indians near missions and transform them into farmers; France wanted to trade with them. French traders distributed presents, opened trade connections, built alliances with the Comanches, and demonstrated a better understanding of the essential role that giving and receiving gifts played in establishing, strengthening, and maintaining good relations.[55] By the mid-1750s, according to Vélez Cachupín's investigations, the French-Comanche trade was well established. Frenchmen exchanged guns, metal weapons, and cloth for Comanche hides, horses, mules, and war captives. The trade not only strengthened French ties with the most powerful Indian nation in the region but also gave the French traders "practical knowledge of the land adjacent to our settlements which they freely travel by permission of the Comanches." By such means, it seemed, France intended to take over the area, cut off Spanish expansion by way of New Mexico, and acquire domination of the continent. Vélez Cachupín urged subsequent governors of New Mexico "to maintain the friendship and commerce of the Comanche tribe, diverting as much of it as possible from the French, because the Comanche tribe is the only one that could impede access to that terrain and be the ruin of New Mexico, due to its strength, use of firearms, and skill at waging war on foot or on horseback."[56] The Comanches were the prize in a diplomatic and economic tug of war across the southern plains, a contest they were quite capable of exploiting to their own advantage.

Other tribes did not fare so well. The convergence of the Spanish and French frontiers, combined with drought, disease, and warfare, hit the Caddos and Wichitas hard in the first half of the eighteenth century. Jean-Baptiste Bénard de La Harpe negotiated with Wichita band chiefs in 1719, and the Wichitas came to depend on French guns and ammunition to hold their own against mounted raiders from their southwest, from Chickasaws armed with British guns, and from the powerful Osages who operated as middlemen between French traders on the lower Missouri and tribes on the plains and who often resorted to war to maintain their control of trade and their "prairie hegemony." To escape growing pressures from the North and East, Tawakoni Wichitas retreated south, first to the Red River and then to the Sabine River, and requested French protection. La Harpe and Claude Charles Du Tisné had found more than a dozen Wichita villages in the Arkansas Valley in 1719. By 1750 there were only two or three villages, located near the head of navigation for access to French traders and on the edges of the plains for access to buffalo hunting. Around 1750 the Wichitas made peace with the Pawnees and then mediated peace between the Pawnees and Comanches. Early the next year warriors from the three tribes attacked an Osage village. The Osages requested help from the French, but it was not forthcoming.[57]

Spanish Texas remained a vast defensive borderland in which Indians predominated. Even after epidemics that had torn through the region in the previous century, eighteenth-century Spanish expeditions recorded the names of about 140 Indian tribes and bands.[58] Spaniards felt powerless to halt the incursions of French traders and Indian raiders. French trade goods from Louisiana lured Indians away from Spanish missions. Increasingly bold raids by Lipan Apaches, pushed south by the Comanches, revealed the defensive inadequacies of Spanish presidios.[59] By midcentury, every Caddo town was reported to have a French trader living in it. "The French have all the Indians of this province devoted to them," complained Governor Jacinto de Barrios y Jáuregui, "due to the presents which they make them of powder, vermilion, muskets, beads, and other things valued by the Indians." Every Cadodacho, Nacogdoche, Nabedeche, and Teyas Indian seemed to be wearing a "mirror, belt of fringes, epaulets, and breech clout—all French goods." In addition, the French regarded the Indians "so highly that civilized persons marry the Indian women without incurring blame, for the French find their greatest glory in that which is profitable to them." Governor Barrios was engaged in an unequal tug-of-war for Indian allegiance: "The Spaniards offer fair words; the French fair words and presents." Even when Spaniards did supply merchandise, they could not match French prices, and the Indians "do not want our muskets or cloth, since the latter lacks the white edges which so pleases their vanity, the [French powder] is of a quicker action, and the beads are of a better color and of different shapes." In 1754 Barrio demanded that the French withdraw from Texas.[60]

By the middle of the eighteenth century the French had asserted their hold on the Mississippi, and French voyageurs, *coureurs de bois*, traders, and explorers had penetrated the trans-Mississippi West as far as the Rocky Mountains. French trade was seeping through to New Mexico, and French traders were active on the upper Missouri. But the French were spread thin. Only at Fort Detroit, Kaskaskia, and Cahokia in the Illinois country and on the lower Mississippi were they able to establish small agricultural settlements. Elsewhere, French presence consisted of small fur trade posts—a few log buildings surrounded by a palisade. In such circumstances the most important task for French commanders in the West was usually not to wage war on Indians but to prevent or negotiate an end to intertribal wars that jeopardized French presence and purposes.[61] For the most part, Frenchmen lived in the West at Indian sufferance or as individuals married into Indian communities.[62]

Even so, their presence was alarming to the Spaniards, who could do lit-

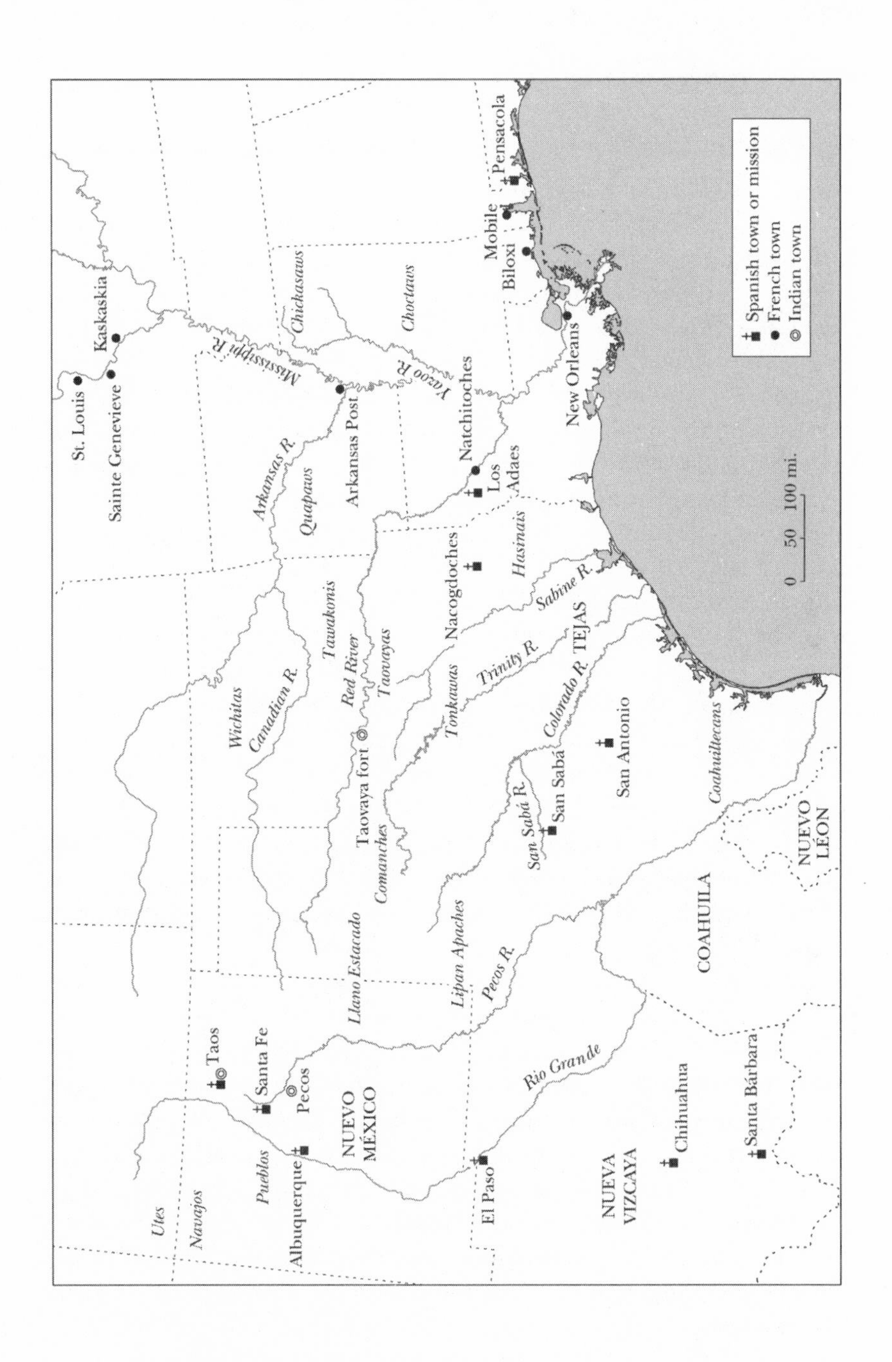

10. Spanish-French-Indian frontiers in the mid–eighteenth century. (Adapted from Weber, *The Spanish Frontier in North America.*)

tle about it. In Europe continued crises and foreign embroilments sapped Spanish energies and drained the royal treasury. In the Americas Spain struggled with recurrent revolts among the Indian peoples it claimed to rule. In Andean Peru and Bolivia alone Native peoples rose up in violent defiance of colonial authorities more than one hundred times between 1720 and 1790.[63] Pericúes and Guaicuro Indians in lower California revolted in 1734.[64] In Sonora, Yaquis and Mayos revolted in 1740–41; Guaymas in 1706 and 1750; Upanguaymas in 1750; southern Ootams in 1724–25, 1737, 1740, 1750, 1763, and 1768–71; Seris in 1706, 1724, 1730, 1740–41, 1749–52, 1758, 1763, 1766, and 1768–72; Upper Pimas in 1740, 1751–52, and throughout the 1760s; and Papagos in 1751–52 and the 1760s. Between the 1740s and the 1760s, with the exception of the Opatas and Eudeves, every group missionized by the Jesuits took up arms against the Spanish Empire. At the same time, Apaches launched mounting raids, and other Indian peoples pressed in from the North. "Seldom," wrote Jack D. Forbes, "have invaders enjoyed a conquest less!"[65]

Increasing competition between Jesuits and Spanish settlers over Indian land and labor, combined with drought, flood, and famine, pushed Yaquis to revolt against Spanish rule in 1740. They sent petitions to the viceregal court in Mexico City demanding that certain missionaries be removed, that non-Indians be expelled from their villages, that compulsory labor at the missions be ended, and that they be free to bear arms and to work and sell their produce outside the missions. The rebellion spread to include Mayos, Lower Pimas, and "just about every indigenous nation" in northwestern Mexico until the number of insurgents may have reached as high as fourteen thousand. Estimates of one thousand Spanish and three thousand Yaqui deaths appear to be gross exaggerations, but the revolt was a devastating jolt to Spanish colonial rule and contributed to the erosion of Jesuit power.[66] On the coast Spanish-Seri relations deteriorated until, in the late 1740s, the Jesuits abandoned the Seri missions. Having failed to transform Seri society and culture, the Spanish attempted to destroy the Seris as a people and to deport them by sea. The effort required the greatest mobilization of military force in the history of colonial Sonora and resulted in two decades of bloody and draining guerrilla warfare.[67]

In 1751 the Upper Pimas revolted. Their leader, Luis Oacpicagigua of Sáric, spoke Spanish and had fought with the Spanish against the Seris. More than one thousand Pima warriors attacked Spanish mining communities, missions, and ranches. The Spaniards defeated the Pimas, inflicting "great destruction without any loss on our part." But the Seri and Pima revolts threatened the very survival of Spanish Sonora at a time of escalating Apache raids and effectively killed Jesuit hopes of extending their mission operations farther northward. The Jesuit missions had still not recovered from the revolts when the king ordered them expelled from New Spain in 1767.[68]

Stretched thin, the Spanish were hard-pressed to contain Osages, Comanches, Utes, and Apaches on their northern frontiers. New Spain had neither the manpower nor the resources to keep its eastern frontiers closed to French intrusion. Spanish officials issued plenty of protests, but French withdrawal from the West would be determined not by Spanish decree but by events taking place in the Ohio Valley.

The Ohio Valley and a World War in Indian Country

The Ohio River runs almost one thousand miles from the Appalachians to the Mississippi and drains an area of more than two thousand square miles. By the middle of the eighteenth century the French, the British, and the Iroquois all claimed it. France needed it to connect its settlements in Canada and the Illinois country and based its claim on La Salle's so-called discovery. The French feared British expansion into the Ohio country would threaten their position in the West; Britons living in seaboard capitals or poring over maps in London feared the French were building a huge arc of empire that threatened to strangle the British colonies.[69] The British cited colonial charters that granted them land west as far as the Pacific and reaffirmed their claims to the land by claiming the Iroquois as subjects. The Iroquois claimed the Ohio country by right of conquest in the seventeenth century and designated local headmen ("half kings") to represent their interests in the region. The confederacy claimed to act as spokesmen for western Indians in dealing with the British. The British were happy to have them do so. The crown tried to leverage control over western tribes via its Iroquois "subjects" and claimed sovereignty over the territories the Iroquois had "conquered." As Francis Jennings put it, "Frenchmen knew what nonsense this was and refused, literally, to give ground." France likewise tried to maintain good relations with the Iroquois. The Iroquois made the most of the situation by playing British, French, and rival English colonies against each other.[70]

The peoples who lived in the Ohio country, meanwhile, endeavored to preserve their lands, cultures, and communities against outside pressures and pretensions. The region that had been largely depopulated by the Iroquois wars a century earlier became a rich hunting territory, a common and contested ground, and home to both indigenous and migrant groups. Shawnees, displaced to the Southeast by war in the last half of the seventeenth century, returned and resettled in the Ohio Valley in the first half of the eighteenth century. Delawares joined them, pushed across the Appalachians by English pressure. Senecas and some "French Mohawks" who splintered off from the Iroquois confederacy moved into the country south of Lake Erie. Wyandots, descendants of Wendat or Huron people who had fled south after the destruction of Huronia, inhabited the west end of the lake. Miamis were attracted from the West by trade with the British to the east. Mascoutens and Kickapoos moved in from the Illinois country. Migrant peoples remade the Ohio country as an Indian refuge, a crossroads of trade and cultures. It was a world of multiethnic villages outside the French alliance and beyond the authority of the Iroquois confederacy.[71]

But the homelands they constructed were the focus of imperial ambitions. Britain and France each believed that whoever won the Ohio country would win the continent. The Forks of the Ohio, where the Ohio, Allegheny, and Monongahela Rivers meet, was the gateway to the West. Britain and France each had to assert its power there through Indian allies and through trade. Indian migrants to the area came with existing ties to outsiders: to relatives who remained in the East, to Pennsylvania, to Virginia, to the Iroquois, to the French, and, in some cases, to all of them. Village and imperial politics became inseparable, and the region became a kaleidoscope of quarrels between European powers, English colonies, private traders, various tribes, and factions within tribes.[72] Ohio Indians played off the French, the British, and the Iroquois; on occasion, they flew French and British flags simultaneously over their lodges.[73] Strategists in Paris, London, and Onondaga all had their eyes on the Ohio country.

At the Treaty of Lancaster, Pennsylvania, in 1744, Onondaga spokesman Canasatego ceded land between the Susquehanna River and the Allegheny Mountains as well as remaining Iroquois claims to land within the boundaries of Virginia and Maryland. He did not realize (and apparently was not told) that Virginia's colonial charter placed its western boundary at the Pacific Ocean. In the colonists' eyes the Iroquois had relinquished their claims to the Ohio country, and it was open for trade and settlement.[74] As far as the British were concerned, the Iroquois had

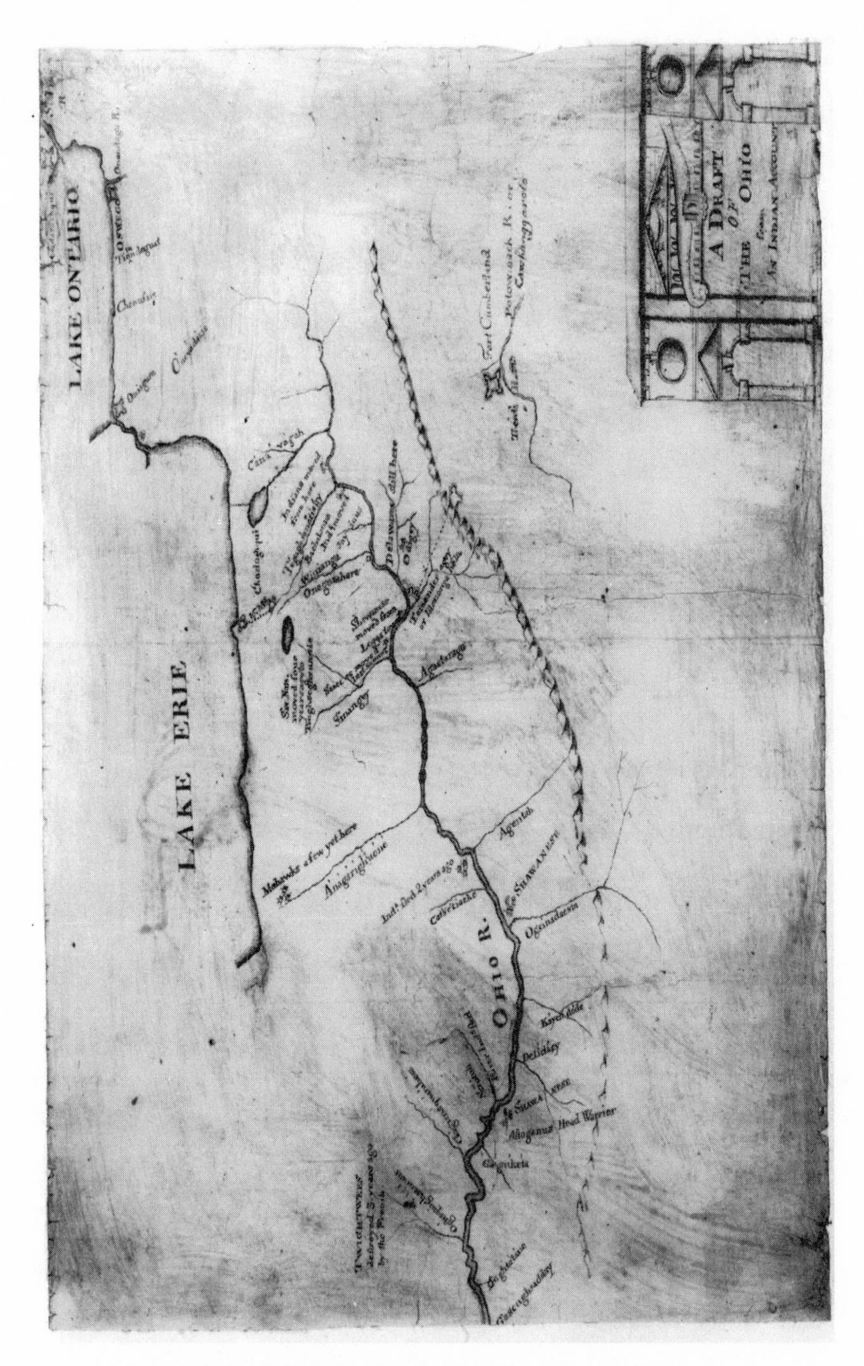

11. A draft of the Ohio from an Indian account. (Courtesy, William L. Clements Library, University of Michigan)

been removed from the contest and would serve primarily as the conduit through which to exert influence over the tribes living there.

British activities in the area alarmed the French. British manufactures generally beat French in quality and price, and they filtered into the Ohio country at a rate the French could not match. Indian people often gravitated to British traders. The tribes of the Miami confederacy, "a very considerable Nation . . . of vast importance to the French on the Lakes," occupied territory in the borderland between French and British claims and had virtually dictated the terms of their relationship with the French. But they began trading with the British in the 1730s and sought to forge an alliance with Pennsylvania. The English, who knew them as Twightwees, were eager to cultivate the connection, as the Miami confederacy's twenty towns and one thousand warriors made them "the most powerful People to the Westward of the English Settlements." A British-Miami alliance would interrupt French communications with French forts on the Mississippi and open intercourse between Pennsylvania and the great river.[75]

In 1747 the chief of the Piankeshaw band of Miamis, Memeskia, known to the French as LaDemoiselle and to the British as Old Briton, moved his village of four hundred families from the Wabash River in what is now northern Indiana to Pickawillany on the Miami River in Ohio and entered into alliance with Pennsylvania. Pickawillany became a major trade center and a target for retaliation by the French, who could not allow increasing Indian independence and British influence to threaten the connections between Canada and Louisiana. In 1749 Pierre-Joseph Céleron led an expedition down the Ohio to try and stem the tide of "seductions" to British trade goods. Along the way he buried lead plates proclaiming French possession of the region, but when he reached Pickawillany, he failed to convince, coerce, or threaten Memeskia into moving his people back to the Wabash. Instead, Memeskia strengthened his ties with the British, and other bands gravitated to Pickawillany's trade orbit. A group of Miamis told the English in 1751 that "their Nation was mostly for the English & hated the French," that despite French efforts to stop them "125 Canoes of their Nation were gone to trade with the Philadelphians," and that "they were come to suck our Milk [rum], which was always good." Further French bribes and threats proved ineffective, and French officials feared that their western Indian alliance might collapse under the weight of British trade goods. In 1752 a war party of 250 Ottawas and Ojibwes, led by Charles Langlade, son of an Ottawa woman and a French trader, launched a surprise attack on Pickawillany. They captured the Miami women and children and several British traders, killed Memeskia, and ritually ate him "before our Faces." The survivors of Memeskia's bid for independence "now look[ed] upon ourselves as lost People" and returned west to French influence, while Pennsylvanians scurried back across the mountains.[76]

The Ohio Company of Virginia planned to sell lands at the confluence of the Allegheny and Monongahela Rivers to settlers. Between September 1750 and March 1752 the company dispatched Christopher Gist on two journeys "to the Westward of the great Mountains" to survey lands as far down as the falls of the Ohio. Gist's instructions were to note the mountain passes, the width and depth of the rivers, the quality of the soil, as well as "what Nations of Indians inhabit there, their Strength & Numbers, who they trade with, & in what Com'odities they deal." He found plenty of rich land: "It wants Nothing but Cultivation to make it a most delightfull Country," he reported. [77] But he was surveying Indian land. Early in his first journey, Indians "began to enquire my Business, and because I did not readily inform them, they began to suspect me, and said, I was come to settle the Indian's Land, and they knew I should never go Home again safe." Gist did make it home, but on his return journey an Indian who spoke good English confronted him, saying that the Delaware chiefs King Beaver (Tamaqua) and Oppamylucah "desired to know where the Indian's Land lay, for that the French claimed all the Land on one Side the River Ohio & the English on the other Side." Gist remembered that Oppamylucah had asked him the same question on the journey out; "I was at a Loss to answer him as I now also was."[78]

At the Treaty of Logstown in June 1752, the half king, Tanaghrisson, and the Mingoes confirmed to Virginia what had been granted at Lancaster eight years before: all the lands of that colony to the "Sun setting." The commissioners assured the Indians that the king wanted their lands only so that "we might live together as one people, and keep them from the French who wou'd be bad neighbors." The Iroquois initially refused to accede to Virginia's version of the Lancaster treaty, maintaining they had ceded land only to the Alleghenies, but private conversations with Tanaghrisson—what Francis Jennings described as the "boys in the back room"—did the trick, and they consented to British settlements "on the southern or eastern Parts of the River Ohio."[79]

As Pennsylvanian and Virginian trade reached west, France responded by abandoning the tried-and-tested politics of the middle ground and attempting to control the Ohio country by force. A haven from conflict was about to become a battlefield.[80] In 1753 Capt. Paul Marin de La Malgue led a force of Canadian troops and Indians from the missions on the St. Lawrence River into the Ohio country and began building a string of four forts stretching from Lake Erie to the Forks of the Ohio. Late that year, Governor Robert Dinwiddie of Virginia dispatched twenty-one-year-old Maj. George Washington to Fort Le Boeuf to demand that the French withdraw. The French responded that "it was their absolute Design to take Possession of the Ohio, and by G—— they would do it."[81] In 1754 the French began building star-shaped Fort Duquesne at the Forks of the Ohio. Washington was sent again with a small force of soldiers and Indian warriors under Tanaghrisson to eject the French. They surprised a party of French soldiers, there was a skirmish, and Tanaghrisson and his warriors killed the French officer Joseph Coloun de Villiers de Jumonville and ten French soldiers. Washington erected a stockade, named Fort Necessity, at Great Meadows just west of the Alleghenies but was compelled to surrender to a superior French and Indian force. The Virginian troops were permitted to evacuate the fort with their arms and colors, but Washington signed capitulation terms that accepted responsibility for Jumonville's murder, and he resigned his commission when he returned home.[82] In Francis Jennings's blunt opinion, "the brawling at the forks of the Ohio was not the cause of the Seven Years' War; rather it served as an excuse for powerful Englishmen who wanted to fight France."[83] That may be true, but Britain and France were both being pulled into war by a tangled web of connections, alliances, rivalries, and loyalties that defied official efforts to establish, maintain, and clarify imperial boundaries.[84]

As indicated by their names in the colonies (King William's War, Queen Anne's War, King George's War), previous imperial conflicts had begun in Europe and spread to North America. But the Seven Years' War (1756–63) actually began in scattered fighting around the Forks of the Ohio and spread to the world. It has been called the very first world war, and with good reason: it involved British and French, Americans and Canadians, American Indians, Prussians, Austrians, Russians, Spaniards, and East Indian moguls; it was fought in North America, the Caribbean Islands, West Africa, India, and Continental Europe as well as on the oceans. "So long as the world has stood there has not been such a War," Moravian ambassador Christian Frederick Post said to the Ohio Delawares.[85] Winning the war required global strategies and unprecedented levels of spending and taxation. By the time it was over Britain laid claim to an empire greater than that of imperial Rome.

The global conflict inevitably reverberated through Indian country, placing tribes on a war footing and adding to the tumults already battering their world. The war was debated in Onondaga and Kuskusky as well as in Paris and London. Europeans bestowed commissions and support on war chiefs, undermining traditional systems of shared power and consensus politics. Wampum belts and speeches reached villages far to the west, summoning warriors to come to the aid of their French or English father, warning chiefs not to trust French or English emissaries who would lead them to destruction, and promising good or hard times in the event of a French or English victory. Indians traveled hundreds of miles to fight alongside and against European regulars and colonial militia, and they clashed with other Indians. European and colonial armies trudged through Indian country, built and besieged forts there, fought battles there, and sometimes destroyed Indian villages. Indian and European methods of fighting mingled and sometimes became indistinguishable.[86] As war disrupted normal economic patterns, Indian communities became increasingly dependent on British or French allies to provide them with food, clothing, and trade, which rendered the end of the war all the more catastrophic: when allies deserted, supplies dried up. Much of the territory that changed hands at the conclusion of the war was Indian land. Indian communities from New France to New Mexico felt the reverberations of the conflict.

Indians who participated directly in the war fought mainly with the French, sometimes with the British, sometimes with one then the other. Council-fire rhetoric to the contrary, they did so not out of love for the French or the British but in a consistent effort to keep their country independent of either. Tanaghrisson told the French:

> Fathers, Both you and the English are white, we live in a Country between; therefore the Land belongs to neither one nor t'other: But the Great Being above allow'd it to be a Place of Residence for us; so Fathers, I desire you to withdraw, as I have done our Brothers the English; for I will keep you at Arms length: I lay this down as a Trial for both, to see which will have the greatest Regard to it, and that Side we will stand by, and make equal Sharers with us. Our Brothers the English have heard this, and I now come to tell it to you, for I am not afraid to discharge you off this Land.[87]

The "country between" was Indian land, off limits to English and French alike except for purposes of trade. Many of the Indian people inhabiting the Ohio Valley had already lost homelands; they were not about to let it happen again without a fight. They adhered consistently to Tanaghrisson's position and attempted to "hold the scales & direct the Ballance" between competing French and English power, a strategy that explains apparent shifts in conduct during the conflicts that followed as they backed the ally most likely to help them secure their goal.[88] New York's Indian secretary, Peter Wraxall, recognized that Indians saw the British-French struggle as "a point of selfish Ambition in us both . . . and are apprehensive that which ever Nation gains their Point will become their Masters not their deliverers." Dr. Samuel Johnson, safe in London, said much the same thing but, being Samuel Johnson, put it a tad more bluntly: "The American dispute between the French and us is therefore only the quarrel of two robbers for the spoils of a passenger. . . . [E]ach is endeavoring the destruction of the other with the help of the Indians, whose interest is that both should be destroyed."[89] Capt. Pierre Pouchot, the French commander at Fort Niagara, explained that the contending powers ignored the Indians' rights as "the natural owners of the country," but "the natives find it very strange that others should fight for a country where the author of life has, in their view, created them, where they have always lived & of which the bones of their ancestors have had possession from the beginning of time. They are unwilling to recognize any foreigner as their master, just as they have none among themselves."[90] For Indians this war, like so many others, was a war over Indian lands and who would claim them. Indians wanted to see neither European power victorious if the victors intended to stay.

French influence among the tribes soared after Washington's surrender. The British, argued Indian agent Daniel Claus, would have to show the Indians that "they can do more by Strength, than the French with their idle stories."[91] In the spring of 1755 Southern Indian Superintendent Edmund Atkin presented a report to the Board of Trade warning that if the British colonies did not establish a uniform and regulated method of dealing with the Indians, they risked losing the friendship of the few friends they had.[92] By the end of the year his predictions had virtually come true. Gen. Edward Braddock made another attempt against Fort Duquesne at the head of more than two thousand troops, the largest army that had ever been assembled in North America. Braddock ignored Indian advice and refused to give assurances that Indian lands would be protected under a British regime. Instead, he told the Delaware war chief Shingas, not a man to be snubbed, that "no Savage shou'd inherit the Land." Shingas retorted that "if they might not have Liberty To Live on the Land they wou'd not Fight for it." Only the half king, Scarouady, and a handful of Mingo warriors stayed with Braddock. Some Shawnees, Delawares, Mingoes, and Miamis from the Ohio Valley went over to the French, joining Ottawas, Potawatomis, and Ojibwes from the Great Lakes and even Osages and Otos from beyond the Mississippi. Others stood by and watched Braddock blunder into disaster.[93]

When Braddock's men crossed the Monongahela after hacking a road through the wilderness, they felt the worst was behind them. Fort Duquesne seemed ripe for the picking. But the French dispatched a unit composed primarily of Indians from the Great Lakes. The two forces crashed into one another, and in the ensuing confusion the Indians went for cover and fired from behind trees on British soldiers, who stood in ranks and attempted to fire in volleys. Braddock had several horses killed under him, and he took a bullet through the lungs; George Washington, his aide, escaped unharmed. Another aide, Capt. Robert Orme, who was wounded in the action, described "a very irregular & confused attack" and spreading panic: "All was anarchy, no order, no discipline." Orme and Washington blamed the regular troops and commended the courage of the officers who "got themselves murder'd by distinguishing themselves in leading their men on."[94] The army suffered almost one thousand casualties. Ohio Valley Indians who had hesitated now joined the French, in part "to shew the Six Nations that they are no longer Women, by which they mean no longer under their Subjection." They even threatened to attack any of the Six Nations who took up the hatchet against the French. Sir William Johnson urged the Iroquois to reassert their influence over their western "allies and dependents" but with little effect.[95] The Iroquois assured Onontio (their term for the French governor of Canada) that they would remain neutral. Only the Mohawks stuck with the British. As news of Braddock's defeat and Indian attacks spread along the frontiers, swarms of backcountry settlers—"Men, Women & Children, most of them barefoot"—streamed east for safety.[96]

Unlike Braddock, Canadian-born Governor-General Vaudreuil appreciated his Indian allies. Following the example of his governor father, who had dispatched war parties against the New England frontier, Vaudreuil saw Indian guerrilla warfare and mounting offensives in the Ohio Valley as New France's best defense and best chance of victory. The marquis de Montcalm, who arrived in North America to take command of the French forces in 1756, preferred to defend the St. Lawrence Valley and fight pitched battles.[97] But regular troops were in short supply in New France, and Montcalm had little choice but to use Canadian militia and Indian allies. Indians, said Montcalm's aide de camp, Louis Antoine de Bougainville, were "a necessary evil."[98]

Bougainville knew the realities and the complex inner workings of an alliance that demanded constant attention, careful management, and frequent compromise. He denounced Indians as unreliable scouts, exhausting diplomats, and bloodthirsty warriors who made endless demands on limited supplies of French merchandise, alcohol, and patience. "One is a slave to Indians in this country," he complained. French officers could not plan and execute strategy without consulting Indian leaders, while French soldiers were in danger of being corrupted "by the example of the Indians and Canadians, breathing an air permeated with independence." But the French had no choice: "In the midst of the woods of America one can no more do without them than without cavalry in open country." A short, plump, asthmatic scholar-soldier who later gained fame for circumnavigating the world, Bougainville mastered the protocols of council fire diplomacy, sang the war song with Indian warriors, and was adopted by Nipissings and Kahnawake Mohawks. "In this sort of warfare it is necessary to adjust to their ways," he wrote.[99]

In the early years of the war, France's Indian allies came primarily from mission communities in eastern Canada, the Seven Nations along the St. Lawrence River, and others. More than eight hundred Iroquois, Hurons, Algonkins, Nipissings, Abenakis, Penobscots, and Maliseets accompanied Montcalm's army. The French regarded them as their most reliable allies.[100] While Eastern Delawares and other Indians along the Susquehanna Valley tried to remain neutral, Western Delawares, Shawnees, and others in the Ohio country sided with France as the best hope of preserving their lands from English invasion. In addition, by the summer of 1757 hundreds of "Indians of the Far West" had joined the army, drawn to the French by ties of trade, alliance, and kinship and by the promise of war honors. Almost one thousand Ottawas, Menominees, Ojibwes, Mississaugas, Potawatomis, Winnebagos, Sauks, Foxes, and even ten Ioways aligned themselves with Montcalm's regulars and militia. Bougainville described the western Indians as "naked save for a breechclout, and painted in black, red and blue, etc. Their heads are shaved and feathers ornament them. In their lengthened ear[lobes] are rings of brass wire.

They have beaver skins for covering, and carry lances, arrows and quivers made of buffalo skin."[101]

The French and Indian forces racked up some impressive victories. In 1756 they captured Fort Oswego, which gave France control of Lake Ontario and upset the balance in Iroquoia that had formerly been maintained between a French fort (Niagara) in Seneca country and a British fort (Oswego) in Oneida country. Indian raiders kept frontier settlements in Pennsylvania, Maryland, and Virginia in constant alarm. The British struck back. Col. John Armstrong and three hundred Pennsylvania troops destroyed the Delaware town at Upper Kittaning on the Allegheny River in 1756, killing the Delaware chief Captain Jacobs, burning cornfields, and recovering some English prisoners. Pennsylvania and Virginia offered bounties for Indian scalps.[102] Virginia called on the Cherokees and Catawbas for help. The Cherokees took up the war axe and used it "with good Success."[103]

In 1757 the British garrison at Fort William Henry on Lake George surrendered to Montcalm's army. But Montcalm's victory turned into a disaster for everyone. His Indian allies attacked the surrendered garrison, grabbing scalps and captives. The slaughter—made famous by the book and movie versions of James Fenimore Cooper's *The Last of the Mohicans*—stained Montcalm's honor: "All Europe will oblige us to justify ourselves," wrote Bougainville.[104] It stiffened Anglo-American resolve and jeopardized the safety of Frenchmen who subsequently fell into British hands. By accepting the British surrender without consulting his Indian allies, Montcalm alienated warriors who had traveled hundreds of miles to secure scalps, plunder, captives, and war honors—and who then proceeded to collect what they had come so far to get. The massacre, according to historian Ian Steele, was "the price of mixing irregular and regular war."[105]

Among those who fell victim to the tomahawk in the fort's hospital were smallpox patients. Disease always walked hand in hand with war. Indian men who joined French and English colonial armies found themselves in communities of thousands of people, larger than most of the colonial cities and with even fewer facilities for hygiene and sanitation. Veterans of disease-ridden encampments often carried sickness with them when they returned from war zones. An epidemic of smallpox had spread among the peoples of the Ohio River and Great Lakes in 1752, but during the Seven Years' War more people than ever before were on the move in the interior of North America, creating ideal conditions for the spread of the disease. Western warriors contracted smallpox from the sick and wounded at Fort William Henry or caught it from Seven Nations allies and then carried it home to their families. "The smallpox has made great ravages again among the Indians of the Far West," wrote Bougainville in December 1757. Indian participation in the war fluctuated with the ravages of smallpox. Disenchanted with their French father and racked with disease in their own villages, Indians would never again turn out in such numbers to fight alongside the French.[106]

Smallpox ravaged the Great Lakes region. The Potawatomis were especially hard hit.[107] Andrew J. Blackbird, a Michigan Ottawa writing in the late nineteenth century, related a story from tribal oral tradition that offered an explanation for an epidemic that erupted after the warriors returned from Montcalm's army. According to the story, a group of Ottawas visiting Montreal bought a series of tin boxes, stacked one inside the other. When they got home they opened the boxes and found "mouldy particles" in the last one. A "terrible sickness" ensued, killing entire families. "The whole coast of Arbre Croche, . . . a continuous village some fifteen or sixteen miles long[,] . . . was entirely depopulated and laid waste." It is possible that the Indians had obtained a container of smallpox matter collected for inoculation and contracted a much more severe case of the disease than would have been expected among European patients. Blackbird's story blamed the British for selling the box to the Indians, although the British did not take Montreal until 1760. "Montreal" in the story may simply indicate toward Montreal.[108] For most Anishinabe people, distant from the main theaters of conflict, smallpox loomed much larger in their consciousness than did the Seven Years' War.[109]

The British, meanwhile, began to mount a joint national and colonial war effort that carried them from the dark days of defeat to stunning victories all around the globe. William Pitt took over as prime minister after a period of ministerial instability and pursued the war with new vigor and new strategies. His plan, simply, was to reduce France from an imperial power to a Continental power by stripping it of its colonies, especially in North America. He increased the subsidies that enabled German allies to keep French and Austrian armies bogged down in European bloodbaths. In North America he mended fences with colonial assemblies who had been alienated by previous British commanders, while British agents tried to neutralize France's Indian allies.

Despite Gen. James Abercromby's disastrous attack on Fort Ticonderoga in 1758, the British war effort gathered momentum. In July that same year British regulars and New England militia (many of whom were

Indians) captured Louisburg overlooking the mouth of the St. Lawrence River. In August Col. John Bradstreet captured Fort Frontenac on Lake Ontario. French supply lines to the West were severed. French-Indian relations began to unravel. Teedyuscung and the Eastern Delawares made peace with Pennsylvania. Teedyuscung distanced himself from the French, blaming them for the English and Delawares that "lye dead on the Fronteers among the Bushes."[110]

Ohio Indians too proved receptive to British overtures, and the British offered to negotiate with them directly, without Iroquois mediators. Moravian missionary Christian Frederick Post made two trips to the Ohio country in 1758 as an ambassador from Pennsylvania, the second in the company of a Delaware chief named Pisquetomen.[111] "Why don't you & the French fight in the old country and on the sea?" the Delawares asked Post. "Why do you come to fight on our land? This makes everybody believe you want only to take & settle the Land." Traders had told them that the English and French had "contrived the war, to waste the Indians between you," that they intended "to kill all the Indians and then divide the land among themselves."[112] Why would the English "wonder at our joining with the French in this present war? Why can't you get sober and once think Impartially?" an Ohio Delaware named Ackowanothio asked Pennsylvania's negotiator, Conrad Weiser. Despite all the abuses the Indians had suffered at English hands, "were we but sure that you will not take our Lands on the Ohio, or the West side of Allegeny Hills from us; we can drive away the French when we please."[113] Peace required assurances that Indian lands would be protected.

Now the British provided the assurances that Braddock had withheld. At the Treaty of Easton in the fall of 1758 Conrad Weiser and Sir William Johnson's deputy, George Croghan, effectively neutralized France's Indian allies.[114] They restored some lands between the Susquehanna River and the Alleghenies, guaranteed that no intrusions would be made west of the mountains without Native consent to the crown, and promised to establish fair and regulated trade. Reassured that the region would be safe from English possession once the war was over and seeing the way the war was going, Ohio Indians made peace. Pisquetomen's brother, Tamaqua, who emerged as a key mediator in dealings with the British, carried news of the treaty west to the Ohio.[115] The peace cleared the way for Gen. John Forbes to advance unopposed toward Fort Duquesne. The French could not contest the Forks of the Ohio without Indian support. In November they blew up the fort and retreated. "I do not mention the Beautiful river," wrote Montcalm. "Nothing can be done for it now." Forbes's army took possession of "the finest and most fertile Country of America" and laid open "to all His Majesty's Subjects a Vein of treasure, which, if rightly managed, may prove richer than the Mines of *Mexico, the Trade with the numerous Nations of Western Indians*," wrote an anonymous correspondent in the army.[116]

Indians had other ideas. They wanted the destruction of Fort Duquesne to mark the end of European occupation, not just a change in the occupying nation. Three days after Fort Duquesne fell, Tamaqua (Beaver) advised Forbes: "Brother, I would tell you, in a most soft, loving and friendly manner, to go back over the mountains and stay there." Another was more blunt: if the British settled west of the mountains, he warned, "all the nations would be against them. . . . It would be a great war, and never come to peace again."[117] Broken in health, the dying Forbes advised Jeffery Amherst, the new commander in North America, that preserving the West depended on preserving the Indians' allegiance. But that required assuring the Indians that their lands were safe, even though the road that Forbes had cut to Fort Duquesne opened the Ohio country to British settlement. Indians would have preferred "there were neither French nor English at the Beautiful river." They were "heartily tired of the war." By the spring of 1759 the French troops who remained at posts in the Ohio Valley were so poorly supplied that the Indians complained, "'Tis not the French who are fighting, 'tis we."[118]

Then in July 1759 the British captured Fort Niagara. The French commander of the fort, Pierre Pouchot, described the passage via Niagara as "the most frequented of the American continent" because the tongue of land linked three Great Lakes and functioned as a trading center that brought Indians "from all parts of the continent." William Johnson predicted that if the British could control Lake Ontario and destroy Fort Niagara, they could secure the western Indians through trade and "shake the whole French Indian Interest to the Center & disconcert if not totally subvert their whole System of Indian Trade & Power upon this Continent." Bougainville agreed: Niagara was the key to the West, and if Britain ever got a real navy on Lake Ontario, it "would chase us out of the Far West."[119] After discussion with the Iroquois and other Indians who accompanied the British army, the local Senecas deserted the French: what use was a French fort on Seneca land if the French could not deliver trade goods?[120] The loss of Fort Niagara severed supply routes between Montreal and other posts on the Great Lakes and dealt another blow to the French position in Indian country: Charles Power, an English captive who lived six years with the Wyandots, said it convinced the Indians that the English could beat the French.[121] With the defection of its Indian allies, France could no longer hold the West; with the loss of Fort Niagara, it could no longer supply the West. The Franco-Indian alliance came apart so rapidly that Ohio Indians became alarmed: they did not want French troops and forts on their land, but a complete French defeat left no counterweight to British power in the region.[122]

In September 1759 Gen. James Wolfe turned a stalled siege at Quebec into a dramatic victory. Wolfe died in the battle; so did Montcalm.[123] In November Adm. Edward Hawke destroyed the French Atlantic fleet in a storm-tossed melee at Quiberon Bay, and Britain won command of the seas. The British Isles were free from the threat of French invasion; beleaguered French forces in Canada could expect no reinforcements; France's Indian alliance in the West would wither from lack of supplies; and France's remaining overseas empire could be picked apart. "Our bells are worn threadbare with ringing for victories," crowed Horace Walpole.[124]

As the French war effort collapsed, Indians pursued new diplomatic initiatives. In August 1760 Ottawas, Miamis, Wyandots, Potawatomis, Shawnees, Delawares, and Iroquois gathered at Fort Pitt and listened to promises that Britain would provide trade and would not deprive them of their lands if they behaved as "faithful allies." The western Indians pledged to hold fast the chain of friendship. In December George Croghan informed a group of Ottawas "who had an English flag" that the British had captured Montreal and were about to take possession of Detroit, Michilimackinac, and other western posts. He "assured them by a Belt of Wampum that all Nations of Indians should enjoy a free Trade with their brethren the English and be protected in peaceable possession of their hunting Country as long as they adhered to His Majesty's Interest." The Ottawas said they were happy to exchange French fathers for English brothers who were better able to supply them. Gen. Jeffery Amherst reiterated promises of trade and peace the next year.[125]

In November 1762 Britain, France, and Spain signed preliminary peace terms. The Peace of Paris was finalized the following February. Outraged by British concessions elsewhere, out of office, and in failing health, William Pitt returned to the House of Commons and delivered a three-hour speech denouncing the treaty as a betrayal of all he had worked for; London crowds rioted in the streets, even stoning the king's coach. But

British gains were enormous. In North America France handed over all its territory east of the Mississippi except New Orleans and guaranteed British subjects unrestricted navigation of the river.[126] Unfortunately, the Peace of Paris brought little peace to North America. Britain's victory and attempts to regulate its newly acquired empire in the West generated protests, resistance movements, and, ultimately, wars of independence in both Indian country and the American colonies.

War against Empire

Even as western Indians sought accommodation with the British and the king's men assured them they had no designs on Indian land, British-Indian relations were unraveling. The Cherokees had been trading partners with South Carolina for more than thirty years and had even sent warriors to support Forbes's campaign against Fort Duquesne.[127] But Virginians killed some of the Cherokees on their way home, and Cherokee chiefs were unable to restrain their warriors in the face of constant encroachment on their hunting territories. The Cherokees went to war in 1760, but smallpox struck, and Lt. Col. James Grant's army of Highland regulars, South Carolina militia, and Indian allies burned all fifteen of the Middle Towns, destroying the crops Cherokees needed for winter food. Attakullakulla, the chief aptly known as Little Carpenter for his diplomatic ability to fashion agreements, sued for peace and blamed the French for "stirring us up to war against our Brothers the English."[128] The "Western Indians" refused to join the Cherokees in their war, and some offered to assist the British.[129] But they would soon change their tune.

French commanders in Indian country announced that the war was over and that French and English hearts were now one, but the peace terms reinforced rather than removed growing anxieties among western Indians.[130] They were stunned to learn that France had handed over their lands to Britain without even consulting them: they were undefeated, and the French had no right to give up their country to anyone.[131] Fort Pitt, which the British built between 1759 and 1761 and named after their prime minister, was a far more formidable fortress than Fort Duquesne had been. Standing at the very junction of the Allegheny and Monongahela Rivers, the pentagon-shaped fortress with bastions projecting from each point was an imposing symbol of imperial presence that boded ill for Indian independence.[132] The British army built or reoccupied a dozen more forts between 1758 and 1762. British assurances that they had no designs on Indian lands rang hollow in Indian ears.

The Indians resented the presence of the garrisons and what they represented, but the main threat to Indian lands came not from the redcoats but from colonists they could not control.[133] British victory seemed to remove the "French and Indian menace" that Anglo-Americans had long regarded as their only barrier to settlement in the West. Crowds of settlers headed west into the Ohio country, southwest down the Shenandoah Valley into the Carolina backcountry, and northward up the Connecticut River.[134] The Ohio Company, dormant since 1754, resumed its activities. Col. Henry Bouquet frustrated their efforts: after assuming command of Fort Pitt, he refused offers to become a partner in the company and instead issued a proclamation in October 1761 prohibiting settlements west of the Alleghenies and protecting Indian lands in accordance with the Treaty of Easton.[135] But British armed force in the West was a very thin red line. Most of the western posts were garrisoned by a handful of soldiers, isolated from supply and support, and often dependent on Indian hunters for provisions. Even when the army tried to eject squatters, its efforts were inadequate to the task. Many of the intruders carried a culture of Indian hating developed during the war.[136] The clash of French and British imperial ambitions gave way to a clash of British imperial and American colonial ambitions.

Indians resented the new British presence and power. In 1761 an Ojibwe chief named Minavavana, also known as the Grand Sauteur, met trader Alexander Henry at Michilimackinac and, speaking through interpreters, gave him a piece of his mind. Staring the trader in the eye, he flatly rejected British pretensions to Indian lands on the basis of having defeated the French: "Englishman, although you have conquered the French, you have not conquered us! We are not your slaves. These lakes, these woods and mountains were left to us by our ancestors. They are our inheritance and we will part with them to none." The Indians had lost many young men in the war against the English, and the spirits of the slain warriors had to be satisfied. The spirits of the dead could "be satisfied in either of two ways; the first is by spilling the blood of the nation by which they fell; the other by covering the bodies of the dead, and thus allaying the resentment of their relatives. This is done by making presents." But, Minavavana admonished, "your king has never sent us any presents, nor entered into any treaty with us, wherefore he and we are still at war; and

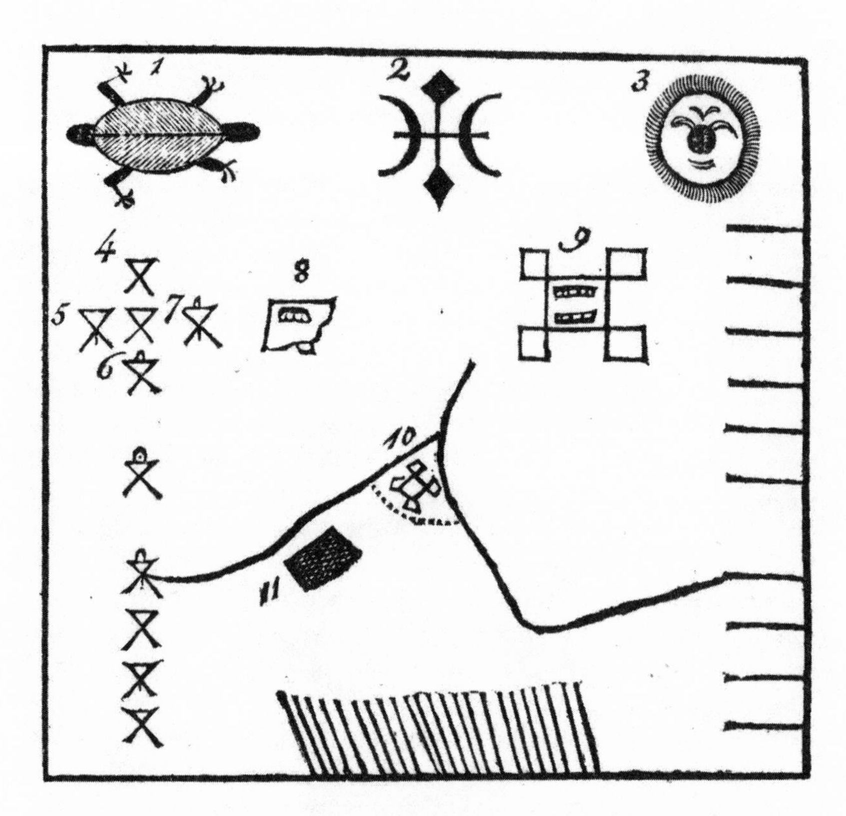

12. Map depicting British occupation of Ohio Indian country. Drawn on sugar maple bark by a Delaware named Wingenund, the drawing shows clan symbols, enemies killed and captured, and British forts. Fort Pitt is 10. (Courtesy, Newberry Library, Chicago)

until he does these things we must consider that we have no other father, nor friend among the white men than the King of France."[137]

The Indians expected the British to lubricate their diplomacy with gifts, as the French had, but Britain, on the brink of financial ruin at the end of the most expensive war it had ever fought, cut back on expensive gift giving. Jeffery Amherst exacerbated the Indians' worst fears. Arrogant and ignorant of Indian ways, Amherst viewed an empire as something to be governed, not negotiated and cultivated by giving gifts to Indians. He demanded the return of prisoners, many of whom had been adopted and were now, in Indian eyes, Indians. His soldiers and his forts threatened Indian lands, and British traders entered Indian village for profit, not for exchange between allies. Dispensing with gifts would make trade more cost-effective. In 1761 Amherst prohibited all gift giving at the western posts and placed limits on the amounts of powder and lead that Indians could obtain in trade. Capt. Donald Campbell at Fort Detroit feared the consequences of such policies among the Indians at the outposts, "as our small Garrisons are at their Mercy," and tried to keep the news secret. Sir William Johnson warned that too much economy would alienate the Indians and compromise the safety of British outposts but found "it is not in my power to Convince the General thereof." By insisting on retrenchment, Amherst radically altered British-Indian relations and placed British soldiers, settlers, and traders in Indian country in a precarious position.[138] By sending in troops and withholding gifts, he sent Indians a clear message, reinforced by the language of British officers, that Britain intended to "reduce" them to submission and take over their land.[139]

Indians were not inclined to accept Englishmen in the place of the French who had been ousted from their lands. Famine and disease stalked the trans-Appalachian West at the end of the Seven Years' War. Sick and hungry Indians blamed the parsimonious trespassers.[140] Senecas began circulating war belts calling for multitribal resistance as early as 1761, and the western Seneca chief Guyasuta advocated a plan of united Indian action. Seneca warriors told William Johnson that they had taken charge of affairs out of the hands of their sachems, "a parcell of Old People who say much, but who mean and act very little."[141] Among the Delawares, men like Tamaqua who counseled moderation were being drowned out by new militant voices. A prophet named Neolin gave spiritual force to Indian discontent, preaching that they could redeem themselves as Indians only by casting off alien influences and returning to traditional ways. An Ottawa war chief named Pontiac turned anti-British sentiment into direct action. At Fort Detroit in April 1763 he urged delegates from the Three Fires Confederacy—the Ottawas, Potawatomis, and Ojibwes—to pick up Delaware war belts and expel the British.[142]

The war is commonly associated with Pontiac, although he lacked the overarching authority to orchestrate and organize the Indian war effort. It has been variously interpreted as a conspiracy, a rebellion, a revolt, an uprising, a war of defense, and, most recently, a conflict about speech and status as well as land.[143] Normally considered an aftermath to the Seven Years' War, it also marked a continuation of that war in its western theater, where Indian fighters who had not been defeated refused to accept the conditions of peace that Britain imposed and France accepted. It was also a war of independence in which, a dozen years before the American colonists, Indian peoples in the trans-Appalachian West resisted the British Empire and compelled the British to think seriously about the place of Indians in that empire.[144]

Like the Pueblo Revolt, Pontiac's War was initially successful, was wrongly attributed to a single leader, and has received considerable attention as a unique event that demands explanation. But like the Pueblo conflict, it is hardly unique when seen in a broader context of widespread and ongoing Indian resistance to domination from outside. Indian warriors in the eighteenth century did not just line up on one side or another in European contests for empire; they also, from the Ohio Valley to the Gulf of California and from the Great Lakes to the southern cone of South America, fought their own wars against empires to defend their lands, resources, and ways of life. Some waged everyday resistance against the demands of colonial systems. Some, like the Apaches, Comanches, Utes, and Navajos, resisted Spanish incursions and pushed back Spanish frontiers by constant raids even as they extended the impacts of Spanish colonialism to other peoples. Others waged massive wars of resistance. The enormous attention paid to later successful wars of independence by American colonists against the British Empire and by Latin American peoples against the Spanish Empire obscures earlier wars of independence waged by Indian nations throughout the West and throughout the Americas.[145]

British officials then and Anglo-American historians since saw Pontiac's War as a French-inspired conspiracy. British conduct certainly generated nostalgia for the French, rumors of an imminent return of the French king's forces to North America filtered through Indian country and into the history books, and some French residents lent a hand to undermining British control. But the war was fought for Indian, not French, reasons. French people continued to live in Great Lakes and Illinois Indian country as they had for years, but it was the Indians who tried to persuade the French to join them, not vice-versa. Indians went to war hoping to wake up the French king, who must surely have fallen asleep.[146]

In May 1763 Pontiac's warriors tried to take Detroit by surprise. The British foiled the attempt, forcing a siege that lasted six months.[147] The Indian alliance took the British posts at Sandusky, Saint Joseph, and Miami in May. In June Ottawas and Ojibwes captured Michilimackinac by staging a lacrosse game in front of the fort, pursuing the ball inside, and then turning on the garrison. The forts at Le Boeuf, Venango, and Presque Isle followed.[148] Before the Senecas killed the commander at Fort Venango they made him write down a list of their grievances: they cited lack of trade and high prices and the presence of the British fort on their lands, which "induced them to believe they intended to possess all their country."[149] In July Indians besieging Detroit ambushed troops from the garrison at the Battle of Bloody Run. At its height the war zone encompassed a vast area between the Great Lakes, the Appalachians, and the Mississippi. Five hundred British soldiers and some two thousand settlers died. Britain's hard-won empire west of the Appalachians was all but swept away: only Forts Pitt, Detroit, and Niagara remained "of all that had been purchased with so much blood and treasure."[150] Delaware and Shawnee chiefs made sure the commander at Fort Pitt understood the causes of the conflict: "You marched your armies into our country, and built forts here, though we told you, again and again, that we wished you to move," Turtle's Heart told Capt. Simeon Ecuyer. "My Brothers, this land is ours, and not yours."[151]

Amherst responded by employing whatever measures were necessary to "extirpate" the Indians: "I wish to hear of no prisoners," he told Col. Henry Bouquet.[152] Whether or not he ordered the use of germ warfare, Amherst certainly favored it. Delawares who came to negotiate at Fort Pitt in the spring of 1763 were given blankets from the smallpox hospital, and smallpox ravaged Indian villages that summer.[153] Bouquet and an army of five hundred men fought off an Indian attack at Bushy Run and relieved Fort Pitt in August.[154] William Johnson worked through the Iroquois to prevent the war from spreading, to split the Indian confederacy, and to pit the Iroquois against the western tribes.[155] But Seneca warriors cut to pieces a British supply train and two companies of infantry at Devil's Hole on the Niagara portage in September.[156] "The Measures you had taken for putting an End to the Indian War, have not yet produced the desired Effects," the king informed Amherst.[157]

Pontiac's War hastened British plans to implement a boundary line between Indian lands and colonial settlements so peace could be preserved once the Indians had been "reduced to due Submission." The royal proclamation of October 1763 established the Appalachian Mountains as the boundary and prohibited private purchases of Indian lands; only the crown's representatives acting in formal council with Indian nations could negotiate such transfers, and only licensed traders would be permitted to operate in Indian country. By such measures the government sought to prevent "all just Cause of Discontent, and Uneasiness" among the Indians in the future.[158] In the meantime, the army waged total war against them.[159] At the same time, eruptions of race hatred such as the Paxton Boys' massacre of Conestoga Indians in Pennsylvania in the winter of 1763–64 did little to convince Indians that peace was possible with the British. As Gen. Thomas Gage noted, there was little point negotiating peace with any Indian nations so long as the frontier people were disposed to "killing every defenceless Indian they met with."[160]

Disease, shortage of supplies, and the separate agendas of individual tribes undermined the Indian war effort. Shawnees sent word in June 1764 that they were ready for peace, although they blamed the British for the war. The Indians had warned the redcoats not to take possession of Detroit, but the first thing they did was build a fort there: "That was one Chief Reason for entering into a War against you, as we had sufficient reason to think you intended taking our country from Us." Six Nations delegates said much the same thing.[161] William Johnson made peace with the Senecas—in his view the key to securing peace—and summoned the western tribes to a conference at Niagara in July 1764, but many Ohio Indians kept fighting.[162]

Two British armies invaded Ohio in 1764, carrying the war "into the heart of [the Indians'] own country."[163] John Bradstreet marched south from Fort Niagara in the summer and offered the tribes preliminary, and unauthorized, peace terms. Bradstreet's superiors thought he had been duped by Shawnees and Delawares who negotiated only to ward off his assault: "They have been treating with us on one side, and cutting our Throats on the other," said General Gage.[164] Ignoring Bradstreet's phony peace, Bouquet marched west from Fort Pitt that fall with fifteen hundred men and dictated peace terms to the Delawares, Shawnees, and Mingoes. The French could no longer assist them, he said; the other tribes had made peace, and the Six Nations had joined the British. "We now surround you, having gained possession of all the waters of the Ohio, the Mississippi, the Miamis, and the lakes. . . . It is therefore in our power totally to extirpate you from being a people." As the price of peace, Bouquet demanded that within twelve days the Indians hand over "all the prisoners in your possession, without any exception; Englishmen, Frenchmen, women and children; whether adopted in your tribe, married, or living amongst you under any denomination and pretence whatsoever, together with all negroes." Guyasuta urged the tribes to comply.[165] In November the Indians delivered two hundred captives, and the Shawnees promised to bring in one hundred more in the spring. The Indians displayed the "utmost reluctance" in parting with their captives, and many of the prisoners shed tears at their liberation.[166]

Britain was anxious to take control of the Illinois country and believed that peace with Pontiac could secure it.[167] But Pontiac remained aloof, rejecting all wampum belts sent by Amherst: "We want none of them," he said, according to an anonymous French source. "Tell your general to withdraw all of his people promptly from our lands. We do not intend to allow any of them to set foot there. The cession by Onontio of which you haughtily speak to us arouses two very different responses in our hearts: laughter at the mad pretension of your master, and tears at the misfortunes of our father."[168] Bradstreet sent Capt. Thomas Morris and an Oneida named Thomas King to carry news of the peace he had made in Ohio, but their embassy proved futile. Pontiac asked Morris "whether I was come to tell lies, like the rest of my countrymen," and asserted that Onontio was not crushed "but had got upon his legs again." When Morris pointed out that the king of France had ceded the Indians' lands to the king of England, a Miami chief "started up and spoke very loud . . . and laughed." Morris's interpreter whispered in his ear that he was lucky the Miami treated his news with contempt rather than anger and suggested that he sit down and shut up. Morris was lucky to escape with his life.[169] As Bernard DeVoto aptly noted many years ago, the western tribes "refused to see themselves otherwise than as sovereign peoples who owned the West and who tolerated the white man there only on a commercial basis."[170] The West was Indian country, no matter what the Peace of Paris said.

But the peace process was gathering momentum. In May 1765 western Indians met with George Croghan at Fort Pitt to reach terms of peace.

Shawnees delivered captives to Bouquet as promised. "Father," they said, "here is your Flesh and Blood." It was the first time Shawnees had addressed the British as "fathers," a term they previously reserved for the French. The occasion signaled a new era of Shawnee accommodation with the British, although Shawnee and British understandings of what constituted a father's role and obligations varied widely. Two months later the Shawnees ratified their treaty and made a final treaty with William Johnson, as did Mingo and Delaware delegates who had dealt with Bouquet.[171] That summer Croghan journeyed to the Illinois and Wabash, met Pontiac, and reached terms of peace that offered restoration of trade and a measure of protection. Croghan described Pontiac as "a shrewd sensible Indian of few words, & commands more respect amongst those Nations than any Indian I ever saw could do amongst his own Tribe." Lt. Alexander Fraser, who accompanied him, was equally impressed: "He is the most sensible man among all the Nations and the most humane Indian I ever saw," he wrote. Pontiac accompanied Croghan back to Detroit to make a final peace and sent the peace pipe to William Johnson as a sign that he had taken the king of England for his father. "The War," said Pontiac, "is all over." At Oswego in July 1766 Pontiac took Sir William by the hand, the western delegates and the Six Nations exchanged war belts, and Pontiac's War was formally concluded.[172] Three years later, Pontiac was dead, assassinated by a Peoria Indian. According to Zebulon Pike in 1806, who misidentified Pontiac as a Sauk chief, the murder sparked a war of revenge that resulted in the "almost entire destruction" of the Cahokias, Kaskaskias, Peorias, and Illinois; but Pike was misinformed.[173]

The Indians did not win the war, but they achieved some victories. Britain continued to regard them as under imperial dominion but modified Amherst's vision of empire to fit the realities of the Indian West. By war and diplomacy, western Indians inserted themselves as equal partners in the Covenant Chain alliance system between Britain and the Six Nations, a status symbolized by the fact that the final conference took place at Oswego, not at Onondaga. The British recognized that peace in the West required extending royal protection to Indian country, fulfilling promises to protect Indian land, and regulating the activities of traders.[174] In its Plan for the Future Management of Indian Affairs, drawn up in 1764, the Board of Trade recommended establishing two superintendencies, restoring the practice of gift giving, and regulating trade.[175] The army tried to enforce the proclamation line as a clear boundary to Indian lands and ejected settlers who had trespassed beyond the Appalachians.[176] Financing the new imperial program required new fiscal measures, and attempts to tax the American colonists unleashed a new round of conflict within the empire the crown had just secured.[177] The British were to prove no more successful in building stable relations with non-Native peoples in the American colonies than they had been with Native peoples in the American West.[178]

To Anglo-American settlers and speculators, it seemed that the French-Indian barrier in the West had been replaced by a British-Indian barrier. Colonists who had fought and bled in the Seven Years' War were not about to be deprived of the fruits of victory by a distant British government. Land speculators would not watch their investments in Indian country slip away. Writing in 1767 to Capt. William Crawford, George Washington said, "I can never look upon that Proclamation in any other light (but this I may say between ourselves) than as a temporary expedient to quiet the Minds of the Indians & [one that] must fall of course in a few years especially when those Indians are consenting to our Occupying the Lands. [A]ny Person therefore who neglects the present opportunity of hunting out good Lands & in some Measure Marking & distinguishing them for their own (in order to keep others from settling them) will never regain it."[179] The British government could not control its subjects. Indian chiefs could not control young warriors angered by the invasion of their lands.[180] (Crawford became Washington's close friend and coagent in land speculation. Fifteen years later Delaware warriors exacting ritual vengeance for murdered kinsfolk tortured him to death, a martyr to the cause of converting Indian lands into American real estate.)

Pressures from land speculators induced the British to bulge the proclamation line westward. At the Treaty of Fort Stanwix in New York in 1768, Sir William Johnson negotiated a huge cession of land south of the Ohio from the Iroquois. Johnson satisfied a variety of interests, including his own, but he ignored the Ohio Indians and exceeded his instructions from the home government. The Iroquois ceded lands they did not control to the British, who could not control them. They essentially diverted pressure from Iroquoia by ceding the Kentucky hunting grounds of the Shawnees. Johnson's management of the treaty "created new Ground of Disgust" among the Indians whose lands were ceded.[181] The influence of the Six Nations plummeted among the western tribes. Shawnees, already emerging as a leading force in Ohio Indian resistance, began to circulate war belts in opposition to the cession.

The Fort Stanwix treaty made the Ohio River the dividing line between

Indian and white land. The British government recognized that a boundary line was essential for preserving peace, but, Gage warned, "if means are not fallen upon to protect the Indians in their Persons and Propertys, it matters little where the Boundarys are fixed." The hunters, traders, and settlers who crowded onto Indian lands were, in Gage's words, "too Numerous, too Lawless and Licentious ever to be restrained." Britain could not keep its subjects off Indian lands on the western rim of the empire.[182]

In 1771 the British abandoned the western posts. Indian peoples who had opposed the presence of British garrisons in their homelands now confronted unchecked invasions by settlers and land developers.[183] In 1773 Daniel Boone led a party of settlers through the Cumberland Gap into Kentucky, although Shawnees and Cherokees turned them back, and Boone's sixteen-year-old son died in the conflict.[184] Kentucky drove a huge wedge into the heart of Indian country—and the blood flowed. Settlers and speculators streamed into the area, confident that the land had been purchased; Shawnees killed them as they trespassed on Shawnee land, cut Shawnee forests, and killed Shawnee game. By 1774 there may have been fifty thousand whites west of the Appalachians.[185] Virginians and Shawnees went to war that year—Lord Dunmore's War—and fought a day-long battle at Point Pleasant. When the smoke cleared and the peace talks were over, the Shawnees had lost Kentucky. In the spring of 1775 Boone led another group of settlers into Kentucky and established Boonesborough. But the war for the Ohio country was not over. Shawnees would occupy the front line of defense against Anglo-American expansion for another twenty years.

Reverberations in the West

The impacts of world war reverberated south and west of Hudson Bay, where British and French traders vied for Indian beaver trade; up the Missouri River, which Britain, France, and Spain each saw as their avenue to the Western Sea; and onto the western prairies and plains. British naval blockades severed supply lines from France to Montreal, and British victories in the western theater cut off traders in the interior. As the French began to abandon their western posts, their Indian customers were compelled to look to the Hudson's Bay Company to supply their needs. After the collapse of the French Empire in North America in 1763, Montreal-based traders challenged the century-old monopoly of the Hudson's Bay Company by pushing west into Indian country rather than waiting for Indian traders to bring pelts into the posts around the bay. The Hudson's Bay Company had no choice but to follow suit and in 1774 expanded its operations inland.[186]

The effects of the Seven Years' War and the peace that ended it also reverberated the length of the Mississippi Valley. Though distant from the main zones of the conflict, Chickasaws suffered heavily: "We are daily cut off by our Enemies the French and their Indians who seems to be resolved to drive us from this Land," they told the governor of South Carolina in 1756. "We have had no less than four Armies against us this Winter and have lost 20 of our Warriours and many of our Wives and Children carried alive, our Towns sett on Fire in the Night and burnt down, many of our Houses &c. Destroyed." They were determined never to give up their lands and never to forsake the English, but they needed guns and ammunition "to enable us to outlive our Enemies." [187] Not entirely victims, Chickasaws preyed on French trade upriver from New Orleans. In November 1763 the English governor of Mobile and the French governor of New Orleans met in council with the Choctaws to convey the terms of peace and explain that the Choctaws would now be under British, not French, jurisdiction and would receive all their trade from the English. [188] Choctaws who had become accustomed to being courted by French, British, and Spanish emissaries during the war had to adjust their tactics.

West of the Mississippi, the war interrupted the flow of French trade to Indian allies. Wichitas began to retreat from the Arkansas to the Red River, where they would be at a safer distance from the Osages and have access to trade from Natchitoches rather than from New Orleans. When they rebuilt their homes they moved their houses closer together and encircled them with palisades. Their move to the Red River helped push out the Lipan Apaches. [189] The Norteños who destroyed the Spanish mission to the Lipan Apaches at San Sabá in Texas in 1758 were armed with French guns, and some wore French clothing. The Norteños who repulsed Col. Diego Ortiz Parrilla's assault on their village the next year flew a French flag. Spaniards attributed both the "massacre" at San Sabá and Ortiz Parrilla's defeat to French muskets and machinations. [190] As Norteños kept up the pressure on the Lipans, the Lipans turned to raiding Spanish herds and settlements.[191]

For most of the war, France and Spain kept a watchful eye on one another over vast stretches of the southern plains, while Indians raided and traded across the intervening zones of competition. But in 1762 Charles III of Spain joined France in the war against Britain in a futile effort to avert total British victory in North America and promptly lost Florida for his troubles. In November 1762, at the secret Treaty of Fontainebleau, France ceded Louisiana west of the Mississippi to Spain, partly as compensation but primarily to keep it out of British hands. The cession added a huge chunk of territory to Spain's already burdensome empire. The Mississippi River was now the boundary between Britain and Spain in North America. British traders replaced French traders as the major threat in Spanish minds, although French traders continued to live and operate in Spanish territory. When news of the peace settlement reached Indian country, the French and Spanish both had some explaining to do, and many Indian peoples had to rethink their positions and strategies. Now that French Louisiana and Spanish Texas were colonies of the same crown, French and Spanish officials began telling Indians that they were now one people. In 1765 Spain formally took possession of upper Louisiana and dispatched Antonio de Ulloa to New Orleans with one hundred troops as first governor and captain general of the province. Ulloa built new posts and settlements along the Mississippi as defenses against British threats and cultivated relations with Indians in the Illinois country, inviting them to meet with him in council and offering gifts and inducements to relocate.

Indian peoples were already crossing the Mississippi to escape the ravages and results of the war. When the British took over Fort Chartres and introduced new trade regulations, French and Indian inhabitants alike abandoned their homes and property and moved west. Communities like Kaskaskia, Cahokia, and Chartres became depopulated. New towns across the river at St. Louis and Sainte Genevieve emerged as major fur-trading centers as French merchants refocused their attention from the North to the West, channeling pelts to New Orleans instead of Montreal. *Coureurs de bois* who had formerly operated in the Illinois country now traded with Indian peoples up the Missouri River, although on occasion they still traded east of the Mississippi in defiance of British authority.[192] Many Indian customers and relatives went west with French traders or maintained ties with them by crossing the Mississippi to trade. After the British occupied Illinois country in 1765, most of the Illinois Indians moved west of the Mississippi, although they seem to have shifted residence easily from one bank to the other.[193] Kickapoos had hunted in the West and even lived in present-day Iowa during the late 1720s; in 1765 a band of seventy-five families led by Serena moved to Spanish Louisiana and settled on the Missouri River near St. Louis.[194] Acadian refugees, expelled by the British, also added to the influx of French immigrants into Spanish Louisiana.

Imperial politics did not always or immediately alter existing social realities. At the grassroots level there was plenty of business as usual between the same people. The royal proclamation of 1763 presumed to keep Europeans out of the West, but some Indian communities had been incorporating Frenchmen for a century. The kinship networks Indian women had created with French men resisted British penetration and continued to dominate the western Great Lakes fur trade. Hundreds of French traders still arrived at Michilimackinac each summer to exchange pelts: more than 85 percent of Michilimackinac traders in 1767 were French. British trade goods flowed freely into Indian country, but many of the personnel conveying those goods were French.[195] British observers looking across the Mississippi saw "a Strange Mixture of French and Spanish Government . . . so that there is no knowing to whom the Country belongs."[196] Indian people who lived there probably had no doubts about the answer to that question, but the new Spanish regime was diverse. French inhabitants had protested the Spanish takeover in 1765, and Governor Alejandro O'Reilly with two thousand troops quelled a rebellion in 1769. In their newly acquired territories, both Britain and Spain relied on locally influential individuals and families with established connections in Indian communities. That often meant Frenchmen with Indian wives. As Jay Gitlin points out, empires were more able than nations to accommodate peoples of different cultures, and North American frontiers were multinational social landscapes. Imperial policies often came to be implemented by people whose identities and loyalties transcended national and ethnic lines and who were well positioned to pursue personal agendas. St. Louis was not founded until the end of the French regime and grew up under Spanish dominion, but it still had a distinctly French character when the United States acquired it.[197]

Charles III responded to the new map of North America by appointing José de Gálvez *visitador* (visitor general) of New Spain in 1765 with instructions to reorganize the entire administrative system and institute fiscal reforms. Gálvez went further and attempted to expand military authority and centralize control over the northern provinces. In 1766 the marquis de Rubí was assigned to inspect the presidios on the northern frontier from Texas to Sonora and to report on the imperial adjustments and financial reductions necessary after the shift of international boundaries. In two years Rubí visited almost two dozen posts and traveled more than seventy-six hundred miles. Nicolás de Lafora, an engineer who kept a diary of the tour, saw a precarious Spanish presence and predominant Indian power. Comanches and Apaches raided at will. Epidemic disease between 1762 and 1766 had devastated the Karankawas, hit the Lipan Apaches, and cut the mission population around San Antonio in half, but Texas was still a world full of Indians.[198] The Spanish population was limited to the missions and presidios of San Antonio, La Bahía, Orcoquizac, and Los Adaes. The northern tribes traded with the French and supplied the Comanches and other tribes with guns and goods. The Indians had little respect for the Spanish: "We are admitted only as friends, but without any authority." The king's forces, sighed Lafora, "are in the shameful position of supplicants." Spanish troops were ineffective in dealing with the hit-and-run warfare of the Apaches, who were "amazing in their conduct, vigilance, speed, order, and endurance." Like other colonial and American commanders, Lafora argued that "the only method of terrorizing, subjecting, or even annihilating these Indians . . . is a continuous offensive war in their own territory."[199]

Rubí recommended reorganizing defenses to reflect realities, with a line of fifteen presidios from the Gulf of Mexico to the Gulf of California to meet the Indian threat. Only the presidios at La Bahía and San Antonio would be retained in Texas.[200] Rubí identified the Apaches as the major enemy and urged a war of extermination against them.[201] His recommendations were largely implemented in the New Regulations for Presidios issued by royal order in 1772. The new policy did result in a new offensive against the Apaches, but Spain lacked the military capacity to sustain such warfare against enemies whose fighting techniques were uniquely adapted to the northern frontier environment. Frontier defense depended on Hispanic and mestizo soldier-settlers who garrisoned the presidios and on Indian allies. Local realities and lack of resources limited implementation of grand imperial plans.[202]

The transfer of Louisiana greatly increased the range of Spanish contacts with Indian peoples, from the Gulf of Mexico to Canada. Spain had to try and keep on good terms with these "new tribes," some of whom had been allies, some enemies of the French, and, at the same time, keep them hostile to the English, who were intruding on the west bank of the Mississippi and up the Missouri. The new situation demanded new Indian policies. Instead of relying on a system of missions and presidios as they had on the northern provinces of New Spain, Governor Antonio de Ulloa and his successor, Alejandro O'Reilly, followed the French system of cultivating Indian relations through the fur trade and gift giving. They left operation of the system largely in the hands of French agents, licensed French traders to go freely among the tribes of Louisiana and Texas, and continued to operate out of the French trading centers at St. Louis, Arkansas Post, and Natchitoches. The Spaniards had to learn to manage Indian relations as the French had done, and the Indians pushed the Spaniards to be the kind of allies the French had been. Individual officers, agents, and chiefs had to build new relationships on the edges of empires.[203]

An Irish-born governor, Alejandro O'Reilly, enlisted Paris-born Athanase de Mézières to serve as lieutenant governor of upper Louisiana. Mézières was a former Indian trader and officer at Natchitoches. His first wife, who died in 1748, had been one of Louis Juchereau de St. Denis's daughters. His orders were to get the Indians to accept the Spanish takeover, keep out the English, arrest renegade French hunters, and make allies of the Norteños. A major component of Mézières's peace plan involved inducing Norteños to settle closer to Spanish settlements in order to consolidate the frontier from Louisiana to New Mexico and act as a buffer against the British and their Indian allies. He called on other well-placed Natchitoches French traders to exert their influence among the Norteños. In the spring of 1770 he appointed as a medal chief the Cadodacho leader Tinhioüen, "a man of talent and of great authority in all of the neighboring bands." In the fall he traveled to the Cadodacho village on the Red River and, with Tinhioüen's aid, began forging peace. "There are now no Frenchmen in these lands," the Frenchman told the Indians. "We are all Spaniards." He traveled to the upper Brazos River and the Red River, making treaties with the Kichais, Tawakonis, Iscanis, Cahinnios, Taovayas, Tonkawas, and Wichitas. He reminded the Wichitas of their precarious position: caught between the Osages, Comanches, Apaches, and Spaniards, they were "in the midst of four fires, which, raising their horrible flames, would reduce them to ashes as easily as the voracious fire consumes the dry grass of the meadows" if they did not make peace. The Wichitas saw his point and maintained an uneasy alliance with Spain, although they had to make up for shortages of guns by trading horses and mules to illegal French traders from the Arkansas River who got guns and ammunition from the British.[204]

Mézières persuaded some groups to relocate nearer to the Spanish settlements and form a cordon with other nations. In 1772 some six hundred Panimahas (Skidi Pawnees) and their families settled near the Wichitas on the Red River, where they remained for six years.[205] He hoped to induce the Comanches to give up their nomadic hunting way of life and form settlements that would extend the cordon to New Mexico, but the Comanches were not impressed, and so it was hoped the cordon allies would aid in their "reduction."[206]

Mézières's Norteño diplomacy constituted only one piece of Spanish Indian policy. As the baron de Ripperdá explained to the viceroy in 1772, Spain needed "not only to keep those nations quiet, subjugate the Comancha [*sic*], castigate the Apache, and cause them to love us through continual intercourse, but also to prevent the invasions which are to be expected from the nations protected by the English and in time of war from the English themselves."[207] It was a tall order and one beyond Spanish resources. Spain could not keep Britain out of the West. In 1768 seventeen loads of British guns reached the Comanches via Jumano traders. In 1772 Taovayas on the upper Red River had British guns, and British traders in Texas boasted they could trade wherever they pleased.[208] The Spaniards were not able to subjugate the Comanches, castigate the Apaches, or control the Osages.

The Osages, who had been dealing with French traders since the end of the seventeenth century, now learned that Spaniards claimed their land. But Spain soon discovered that Osages recognized only one power: Osage power. The Osages had moved west as part of the Dhegihan migration that also carried Quapaws, Poncas, Omahas, and Kansas from the Ohio Valley to new homes beyond the Mississippi.[209] By 1673, when Father Marquette first recorded their name on his map, the Osages were living on the prairies between the Missouri and Arkansas Rivers. They inhabited large villages in the spring and fall, dispersed to hunt buffalo on the plains in the summer, and wintered near the forests. They could raise more than a thousand warriors: observers regularly estimated that the "Big" Osages on the upper Osage River could muster seven or eight hundred warriors; the "Little" Osages on the Missouri two to three hundred.[210] Their warriors had a fierce reputation. When La Harpe traveled the Red River in 1718–20, his Indian guides feared running into the Osages. They had good reason to be concerned. When a war party of twenty Osages appeared, they made peaceful gestures to the Frenchmen but made it clear they intended to scalp the guides. Only a combination of threats and gifts persuaded them to think better of it.[211] The French realized they had better cultivate Osage allegiance, and an Osage chief accompanied Bourgmont's delegation to Paris in 1725. The Osages would spend the rest of the century dealing with European powers on their own terms, exploiting their geographic, economic, and numerical advantages at the expense of other Indian peoples, and maintaining their position in a world of shifting international contests and territorial boundaries.

Osages had horses by 1690. They traded them from Kansas and Kiowas and stole them from Pawnees, Padoucas, and Plains Apaches. Well positioned to trade with the French, they were among the first tribes on the lower Missouri to obtain firearms (*wa-ho-to'n-the,* "it causes things to cry out"). By the mid-eighteenth century they possessed so many that gun parts far outnumber stone projectile points in the archaeological remains at Osage village sites from that period.[212] The Osages prevented French traders from dealing directly with the tribes to their south and west—the Wichitas, Pawnees, Plains Apaches, and Texas Caddos—who were unable to obtain guns from the Spanish. When Du Tisné visited two Wichita villages in 1719 he saw only half a dozen guns there, and the Wichitas were eager to trade for more, but the Osages opposed his visits to both the Wichitas and the Comanches.[213] The Osages operated as middlemen, dealing with the French at their posts and controlling what trade went out onto the prairies.

The Osages maintained peace and trade with the French in the East to secure guns; in the West they turned their guns on Wichitas, Pawnees, and Caddos; raided them for horses, pelts, and captives; and hunted their buffalo grounds with impunity. Osage warriors now more often rode out against their enemies wearing yellow face paint, "since yellow was the mark of the captive." They used captive straps ceremonially cut from the hind leg of a buffalo hide and carried in the treated heart sac of the buffalo to lead the captives east, where the French would pay for them with muskets, knives, and hatchets. The Osages plundered and killed French traders they found trespassing on their land or breaching their blockade, but the French needed to keep on good terms with them as the key to the Missouri River highway.[214] But though often waged for economic reasons, Osage warfare remained hedged with ritual activities; an Osage war party was "as much a religious ceremony as it was a military operation."[215]

Some French traders evaded the Osage blockade and reached Wichita villages on the Red River and Pawnee villages on the Platte and Republican Rivers. After the Comanches made peace with the Wichitas and Pawnees in the late 1740s they had access to guns, and the Comanche-

Wichita-Pawnee alliance launched counterattacks on the Osages in the early 1750s. But supply shortages during the Seven Years' War curtailed the activities of French traders on the plains. The Osages tightened their hold on what French trade remained, supplemented it with increasing British trade, and expanded their raids. They forced the Wichitas to abandon their last village on the Arkansas. Mobile Comanche hunting groups escaped most of the Osage attacks and directed their energies farther west; the Osages preferred to fight people who posed a more direct threat to their territory in the East. The headwaters of the Cimarron, Canadian, and Washita Rivers became a neutral zone between the Osages and Comanches, leaving the Osages to dominate the prairie-plains between the Arkansas and Red Rivers.[216]

When Spain took over Louisiana, it attempted to ensure that only licensed traders operated in Indian country and placed restrictions on trading guns to Indians. Governor O'Reilly also outlawed trading for Indian slaves and trading for livestock, most of which was probably stolen from Spanish herds in Texas and New Mexico. The Osages had no intention of observing bans that threatened to undermine the hegemony they had built up. They turned to French traders operating out of what was now British Canada and British traders operating out of the Ohio Valley and the Illinois country. Spanish commanders demanded that the Osages give up the British flags they had erected in their villages. The Osages made sure the British knew they were being courted by the Spaniards and continued to trade with them.[217] But British occupation of Canada and the Illinois country gave other tribes access to the British weapons trade. Sauks, Foxes, Kickapoos, Potawatomis, Shawnees, Delawares, and other peoples, many of whom were shifting west as a result of the war, looked to the rich Osage hunting grounds in the Ozarks and Ouachitas and began to raid Osage villages for horses and slaves. The Osages in turn increased their raids on the Caddos and Wichitas to their southwest, stealing livestock, slaves, and pelts to trade for weapons to defend themselves. In Spanish eyes the Osages kept the region in turmoil.[218]

Many Osages gravitated south to the Arkansas River Valley, where, during the later part of the century, a third Osage band developed, independent of those on the Osage and Missouri Rivers. According to Mézières, in the spring of 1770 Osages had been hostile to the other Indians of the region "from time immemorial," but since "malefactors" infested the Arkansas River and "incited them with powder, balls, fusils, and other munitions" they had increased their raids in his district, stealing women, children, horses, and mules and turning the whole area into a "pitiful theater of outrageous robberies and bloody encounters." Osage attacks pushed many Indians into Texas, where they in turn raided Spanish settlements and livestock.[219] The Osages dominated the Arkansas River. They threatened, robbed, and sometimes killed European traders they caught there. They also dominated the fur trade of St. Louis and Spanish Illinois.[220] The Spaniards regarded them as fickle and treacherous, which simply indicates that Osages pursued Osage, not Spanish, interests. As they had in the past, Osages manipulated European rivalries to protect their own power and independence, securing guns for themselves while denying them to rival tribes. Spanish officials patched together short-lived truces with Osage bands but despaired of achieving a lasting peace. "There is no other remedy than their extermination," wrote Luis de Unzaga y Amezaga, governor of Louisiana, in 1772, "but we are not in a position to apply it because [we] lack people and supplies, and lastly because of the expense."[221]

Spain turned to other Indian nations to help keep the Osages in check and to act as a buffer zone for Spanish settlements in Texas. Mézières enlisted the Caddos and Quapaws. The Osage nation had "made itself justly execrable to us and to all the tribes of this region," he said, and the Quapaws and Caddos were eager for an opportunity "to avenge the common injury." He hoped to launch an attack on the Osage villages, but the campaign did not materialize.[222]

Trade embargos were no more effective. In 1773 Lieutenant Governor Pedro Joseph Piernas suspended all trade with the Little Osages and Missouris in retaliation for the murder of three French traders. British traders from Illinois immediately seized the opportunity and hurried up the Missouri to capture the trade of the Osages and Missouris, and Piernas had to launch an expedition to expel them.[223] The Osages had many options available to them; the Spaniards had their hands full dealing with Seris and Yaquis, Apaches and Comanches. Osages, not Spaniards, called the shots on the prairies between the Missouri and the Arkansas.

Yet they had built their dominance in a volatile world. Like other Indian peoples who effectively played the geopolitical field, the Osages too felt the impact of social changes, heightened tensions between elder chiefs and younger warriors, and increasing distance between the divisions of the tribe.[224] Like European powers who successively laid claim to their territory, the Osages found that dominance was fleeting. When empires collided in Indian country, even winners paid dearly.

Chapter 8

The Killing Years

Twenty years after France transferred its North American empire east of the Mississippi to Britain and Louisiana west of the Mississippi to Spain, at another Peace of Paris Britain transferred to the United States all its territorial claims south of the Great Lakes, north of Florida, and east of the Mississippi. Spain transferred Louisiana back to France. Twenty years after that France sold Louisiana to the United States. Though peacefully transferred on paper in Paris, Indian territories in the West were often scenes of turmoil and sometimes veritable killing fields: the impact of the American Revolution reverberated across the Mississippi; Spain stepped up its efforts to hold in check Indian nations on its northern frontiers; Indian peoples on the Pacific Coast were pulled firmly into the orbit of European contact; and a massive smallpox pandemic turned large areas of the West into a graveyard. Meanwhile, the new United States looked west to build an empire of its own.

A Revolution Pushes West

Indian leaders understood that the war for American independence was also a war about Indian land. In Indian country it became both a civil war and a world war, and for many Indian peoples it was one phase of a twenty-year war that continued at least until the Treaty of Greenville in 1795.[1] Before it was over, a whole generation had grown up knowing little but war. In the West, Indian peoples felt the repercussions of a conflict that ultimately brought a new nation to their homelands and plunged them into their own wars for independence.

At first most Indians tried to avoid becoming entangled in what looked to them like an English civil war. But Britons, Americans, and eventually Spaniards courted the support of tribes far distant from eastern battlefields, and British and Spanish agents sent flags, medals, and presents into Indian villages on the Mississippi and Missouri.[2] Neutrality became increasingly precarious, even impossible, and many tribes split over what course of action to pursue. Fernando de Leyba told the governor of Louisiana, Bernardo de Gálvez, in the summer of 1778 that the war was "causing a great number of Indian tribes to go from one side to the other without knowing which side to take."[3]

The Iroquois confederacy fractured as Oneidas and Tuscaroras sided with the Americans, while most Mohawks, Senecas, Onondagas, and Cayugas supported Britain. American armies marched through Iroquois country, destroying towns, fields, and food supplies. Refugees fled to British posts for relief from cold and starvation, and several thousand Indian people huddled in miserable shelters around Fort Niagara.[4]

Henry Hamilton, the British commander at Fort Detroit, and George Morgan, the American Indian agent at Fort Pitt, competed for Indian support in the Ohio country. Wyandots led by Half King and groups of disaffected warriors joined the British, but most leaders tried to remain neutral. White Eyes led the Delawares into signing a treaty of alliance with the United States in 1778, but after he was murdered by American militia, many warriors followed Hopocan, or Captain Pipe, and sided with the British. In 1780 American troops burned the Delaware capital at Coshocton. Those Delawares who lived in separate villages under the guidance of Moravian missionaries also paid dearly for their neutrality: in 1782 American militia marched to the town of Gnadenhütten, rounded up the inhabitants, and bludgeoned to death ninety-six men, women, and children.[5]

The Shawnees occupied a crucial yet precarious position between the frontiers of Virginia and Kentucky and the British and their Indian allies closer to Detroit. Shawnee chiefs told the Virginians in July 1775, "We are often inclined to believe there is no resting place for us and that your Intentions were [*sic*] to deprive us entirely of our whole Country."[6] At first most Shawnees endeavored to remain neutral. As American encroachments persisted, Shawnee warriors began traveling to Detroit to accept Hamilton's war belt. Chief Cornstalk tried to preserve his people's fragile neutrality, but he was unable to restrain his "foolish Young Men." When Cornstalk was killed by Americans in 1777, most Shawnees made common cause with the redcoats. Thomas Jefferson wanted to see the Shawnees exterminated or driven from their lands and advocated turning other tribes against them.[7] The Shawnees were once again on the front lines in the struggle for the Ohio country: "We have always been the frontier," they told the British.[8]

Shawnees raided American settlements in Kentucky; American troops burned Shawnee crops and villages. In 1779 Kentuckians under Col. John Bowman attacked the principal town of Chillicothe on the Little Miami River. The Shawnee chief Black Fish received a mortal wound. In 1780 the Shawnees burned Chillicothe themselves rather than let it fall to George Rogers Clark and fought a full-scale battle at Piqua on the Mad River. Clark turned his artillery on the village council house, in which many of the people had taken refuge, and his men spent two days burning cornfields and plundering Shawnee graves for burial goods and scalps. Shawnee refugees filtered into Detroit, seeking food and shelter from the British. Clark returned to Shawnee country in the fall of 1782. According to Daniel Boone, who accompanied the expedition, Clark burned five villages, "entirely destroyed their corn and other fruits, and spread desolation through their country."[9] Shawnee warriors also carried the war to the Americans, participated in the rout of Boone's Kentuckians at Blue Licks, and assisted in the defeat of William Crawford's expedition in 1782. Then, just as it seemed the Shawnees were winning their war, British officers and agents began urging the chiefs to restrain their warriors and tried to sell them the Peace of Paris as the path to a new era of peace. But the struggle that terminated in 1783 for redcoats and patriots did not end for the Shawnees.

British agents recruited Indian warriors from the western Great Lakes to fight in eastern campaigns.[10] The Mdewakanton Santee chief Wabasha apparently visited Quebec in 1776 and was given a general's commission in 1778.[11] Winnebagos turned out for the British in 1779, although they feared enemy tribes would attack their villages in their absence.[12] As they had been at the beginning of the Seven Years' War, Miami Indians were pulled by the appeals of the contending parties, and the Miami council at Kekionga struggled to maintain a united front against American expansion. Wabash Indians and some Great Lakes tribes swung to the crown when Henry Hamilton arrived in the region. But in the summer of 1778 George Rogers Clark captured French settlements in southern Illinois on the Mississippi and at Vincennes in Indiana. In February 1779 he took Vincennes again and captured Hamilton. Clark's triumphs proved short-lived, but they produced some shifts in tribal allegiances. After France joined the war, a Franco-Indian force destroyed Kekionga in 1780. The duel for Indian allegiance waged between Clark and the British continued.[13] Potawatomis near Detroit consistently supported Britain, but other Potawatomi bands in Illinois and Wisconsin shifted allegiance during the course of the war.[14] Wabash and Illinois Kickapoos lent support to Clark, but as the flood of American settlers increased, Kickapoos and Potawatomis both turned back to the British and resisted American expansion.[15]

Sauk and Fox Indians on the upper Mississippi were counted British allies, but they also tried to maintain relations with the Americans and with the Spaniards at St. Louis.[16] Sauk and Fox warriors joined one thousand British and Indians—mainly Sioux under Wabasha and Ojibwes—who attacked St. Louis in May 1780, but the attack failed and dealt a blow to British prestige among western tribes. A Spanish-American expedition burned the village at Saukenuk on Rock River in retaliation, and many Sauk and Fox people switched allegiance to Spain. The new Spanish lieutenant governor, Francisco Cruzat, worked vigorously to secure Indian allies as the best defense for St. Louis. A force of Spanish volunteers and Indian allies captured the British post at Fort Saint Joseph by surprise in February 1781 and held it for a day. Tribal leaders surrendered their British flags and medals, and Cruzat replaced them with Spanish ones.[17] A young Kaskaskia chief, Jean Baptiste de Coigne, enlisted "under the flag of his fourth allegiance." Having dealt with first France and then Britain before the conflict, he now shifted allegiance first to Spain and then to Virginia. In de Coigne's view Virginians, French, and Spaniards were "all as one."[18]

In the South relentless American land hunger pushed the Cherokees into war. At Sycamore Shoals in 1775, for instance, Richard Henderson and the Transylvania Company, which had hired Daniel Boone to make surveys west of the Cumberland Mountains, bought almost twenty million acres of Cherokee land between the Kentucky and Cumberland Rivers.[19] Despite the illegality of the purchase, Boone and other squatters pushed through the Cumberland Gap into Kentucky. For almost two decades, Kentucky would be "dark and bloody ground" as Indians and invaders battled over it.[20] When the Revolution broke out, Dragging Canoe and angry Cherokee warriors accepted a war belt from northern delegates, while the older chiefs who had sold the lands watched in silent dejection. Barely had the Cherokees launched their attacks on the backcountry settlements than expeditions from Virginia and North and South Carolina invaded their country, burning their towns and crops. The older chiefs regained the initiative and sued for peace. Many younger warriors followed the lead of Dragging Canoe, seceding to form new communities on the Chickamauga River in Tennessee, which became the core of Cherokee resistance until 1795. American armies marching through Cherokee country did not always distinguish between Cherokee friends and Cherokee foes, and by the end of the Revolution the Cherokee nation was on its knees.[21]

On the lower Mississippi, as Britain and Spain courted their allegiance, Choctaws employed the play-off system they had used to good effect in the past as a way of maintaining independence and securing trade goods. Once again the nation split into factions. The majority supported Britain, but the Six Towns district, closest to New Orleans, favored Spain, and Choctaws from opposing districts came into conflict.[22] Before British agents could set about securing the Choctaws as allies against the Americans, they had first to mediate an end to their conflict with the Creeks that they themselves had fomented several years earlier when British Indian policy had aimed at keeping Indian tribes divided against themselves rather than united against the Americans. This and the Cherokees' experience gave the Creeks ample reason to drag their feet, although most eventually supported Britain.[23] The Chickasaws generally supported the British as they continued their own struggle for independence against all comers.[24]

The Revolution dislocated thousands of Indian people. Families fled the horrors of war; villages relocated to escape American assault. Communities splintered and reassembled, sometimes amalgamating with other communities. Refugees flooded into Niagara, Detroit, and St. Louis; Iroquois from New York relocated to new homes on the Grand River in Ontario. By the war's end, Indians in Ohio were crowded into the northwestern reaches of their territory, where they created multitribal, multivillage communities.[25] The end of the Revolution opened the way for a renewed invasion of Indian lands by backcountry settlers, who ignored federal attempts to regulate the frontier. George Washington warned that their "rage" for Indian lands would "inevitably produce a war with the western tribes."[26] American soldiers, impressed by the cornucopia they had destroyed in Indian fields and villages during the war, were eager to seize fertile Indian lands once the war was over. A delegation of 260 Iroquois, Shawnee, Cherokee, Chickasaw, Choctaw, and "Loup" Indians visiting St. Louis in the summer of 1784 told Lieutenant Governor Cruzat that the Revolution was "the greatest blow that could have been dealt us, unless it had been our total destruction." The Americans had swarmed "like a plague of locusts" into the Ohio Valley, driving the Indians from their lands and treating them as their cruelest enemies, "so that today hunger and the impetuous torrent of war which they impose upon us with other terrible calamities, have brought our villages to a struggle with death."[27]

The new United States claimed Indian lands as far west as the Mississippi by right of conquest. American commissioners, often with troops at their backs, demanded lands from the Iroquois at Fort Stanwix in 1784; from the Delawares, Wyandots, and their neighbors at Fort McIntosh in 1785; and from the Shawnees at Fort Finney in 1786. The Treaties of Hopewell, with the Cherokees (1785) and the Choctaws and Chickasaws (1786), confirmed tribal boundaries but did little to preserve them.[28] Captain Johnny of the Shawnees told the Americans, "You are drawing so close to us that we can almost hear the noise of your axes felling our Trees and settling our Country" and warned that if settlers crossed the Ohio, "we shall take up a Rod and whip them back to your side."[29] In 1765 Shawnees had arrived at Fort Pitt beating drums and singing the song of peace to reach an accommodation with the British. In 1786 Shawnees arrived at Fort Finney beating drums and singing the song of peace, hoping to reach an accommodation with the Americans. But the Americans exacted a much higher price: tribal lands east of the Great Miami River. Shawnee leaders complained that their people barely had enough land on which to live and grow corn: "This is not the way to make a good or lasting Peace [,] to take our Chiefs Prisoners and come with Soldiers at your Backs," they warned.[30] Months later, Kentucky militia invaded Shawnee country, burned several villages, killed some women and children, and hatcheted to death Chief Moluntha under his American flag as he clutched a copy of the treaty.

Some Shawnee families migrated west, but others moved south to join Cherokee and Creek warriors in their fight. Meanwhile, Mingoes, Senecas, and Cherokees joined Shawnee communities to continue the war effort. With Shawnees at its core, a confederacy of northwestern tribes emerged that rejected treaties signed by individual tribes and refused to accept American settlement west of the Ohio River. Delegates from the Iroquois, Hurons, Delawares, Shawnees, Ottawas, Ojibwes, Potawatomis, Miamis, and Wabash River tribes assembled in council at the mouth of the Detroit River in December 1786. They sent a message to Congress, assuring the Americans of their desire for peace yet insisting that any cession of lands "should be made in the most public manner, and by the united voice of the confederacy; holding all partial treaties as void and of no effect."[31] Led by the Shawnee war chief Blue Jacket, Mohawk

Joseph Brant, Little Turtle of the Miamis, and Buckongahelas of the Delawares, the confederacy prepared to resist American expansion by force if necessary.[32]

As Indian leaders tried to ensure that the united nations rather than the individual tribes dealt with the United States, Congress tried to ensure that the United States rather than the individual states dealt with the Indians. The Northwest Ordinance of 1787 proclaimed that the United States would observe the "utmost good faith" in its dealings with Indian people; their lands would not be invaded or taken from them except in "just and lawful wars authorized by Congress." But the ordinance also laid out a blueprint for national expansion onto Indian lands. Following the vision of westward expansion outlined in Thomas Jefferson's Plan of Government for the Western Territory four years earlier, which had divided the trans-Appalachian West into sixteen states, the ordinance divided the Northwest Territory into districts. After passing through territorial status with their own territorial governments and reaching a population of sixty thousand inhabitants, the districts would become states, "on an equal footing with the original States, in all respects whatever." By assuring western settlers that their territorial or colonial status was temporary and that they would become equal participants in the process of empire building, the Northwest Ordinance, notes historian Eric Hinderaker, "reinvented empire in a way that solved some of the most vexing problems British policymakers had earlier faced" at the same time that it demonstrated Congress's commitment to western expansion.[33] Ohio, Indiana, Illinois, Michigan, and Wisconsin eventually entered the union as states from the Northwest Territory, and most states west of the Mississippi entered after passing through the territorial stage as stipulated by the ordinance.

In an effort to regulate conditions on the frontier and reaffirm that conduct of Indian affairs rested with the federal government, not the states, Congress passed the Indian Trade and Intercourse Act in 1790: only licensed traders were permitted to operate in Indian country, and no transfers of Indian land were valid without congressional approval. But, like the British after 1763, the U.S. government failed to control its own citizens on distant frontiers. Individual states, jealous of their rights and resentful of any attempts by the federal government to interfere in their affairs, frequently made treaties that never received congressional approval. Squatters and land speculators paid little or no attention to the laws. Indians who resisted these intrusions were subjected to "just and lawful wars."

But Indian power remained formidable in much of the western territory that the United States claimed as its own. In 1790 the warriors of the northwestern confederacy, ably led by Little Turtle and Blue Jacket, defeated Gen. Josiah Harmar's invading army of fifteen hundred men. A year later Little Turtle routed Gen. Arthur St. Clair's army, inflicting over nine hundred casualties, with some six hundred dead. Indian victories made a mockery of American claims to their lands by rights of conquest.

Joseph Brant and the Iroquois were ready to reach a compromise with the United States, but western warriors who had just defeated two American armies were in no mood to give up the Ohio River as the boundary to their country: "Look back and view the lands from whence we have been driven," they told Congress. "We can retreat no further."[34] By the time Gen. Anthony Wayne led his new American army into Indian country in 1794 the confederacy was no longer united. At the Battle of Fallen Timbers in northwestern Ohio, a reduced Indian force confronted Wayne's troops in a tangle of trees felled by a tornado but were driven from the field by the American cannon, cavalry, and bayonets. The British commander at nearby Fort Miami closed his gates on the Indians—preoccupied with developments in revolutionary France, Britain had no desire to be pulled into another American war. Wayne proceeded to destroy the extensive cornfields on the Auglaize and Maumee Rivers. By 1795 the war for Ohio was lost; the old chiefs sought accommodation with the Americans. At the Treaty of Greenville, more than a thousand Indian delegates accepted Wayne's terms and ceded to the United States two thirds of present-day Ohio and part of Indiana.[35]

Defeat, loss of land, and continued disruption of traditional ways generated further upheaval and despair in Indian communities in the Old Northwest. But Shawnees once again found themselves the frontier of resistance to American expansion in the first decade of the nineteenth century, when the Shawnee Prophet preached moral and religious reform, and Tecumseh led a pan-Indian defense of remaining tribal lands.[36]

Indian peoples in the Old Southwest also felt American power closing in on them. Chickasaws on the Mississippi River, for example, had responded to American threats of invasion during the Revolution by offering to meet them halfway and threatening to cut off their heads. By the end of the war they were sending very different signals and peace messages to Congress. Shut off from British trade and embroiled in hostilities with other tribes, Chickasaw headmen looked to both Spain and the United States. Spanish and American agents in turn competed for

Chickasaw allegiance and the right to build a trading post at Chickasaw Bluffs, present-day Memphis. Delegates from six villages attended the Mobile Congress in 1784, placing themselves under Spanish protection and promising to trade exclusively with Spanish-licensed traders. Two years later Chickasaws promised the Americans the same trade monopoly at the Treaty of Hopewell.[37] By 1795 Spain was pulling out of the region. At the Treaty of San Lorenzo, Spain relinquished the Yazoo strip, opened the Mississippi to free American navigation, and agreed to withdraw all garrisons from territory north of the thirty-first parallel. The Chickasaws confronted shrinking foreign policy options as the United States emerged as the major power in the postwar lower Mississippi Valley. A Chickasaw chief named Ugulayacabe (Wolf's Friend) demanded to know how Spain could abandon his people to the Americans "like the smaller animals to the jaws of the Tiger and the bear. . . . We perceive in them the cunning of the Rattle snake who caresses the Squirrel he intends to devour."[38] Chickasaws and Choctaws hunted more often west of the Mississippi, clashed with tribes in the Arkansas region, and stole livestock as far west as Natchitoches.[39]

Hundreds of other Indians drifted west of the Mississippi to seek refuge in Spanish-claimed territory. Most crossed where the Ohio meets the Mississippi near the future site of New Madrid. Spanish authorities encouraged their relocation to help provide a buffer against American expansion and against more powerful tribes like the Osages. Shawnee traditions say they began to cross the Mississippi as early as 1763, but during the Revolution hundreds of Shawnees, led by Yellow Hawk and Black Stump, left their Ohio homelands and migrated to Missouri. More migrated across the Mississippi after the war. They settled near Cape Girardeau under the auspices of the Spanish government, and Spain tried to enlist them against the Osages.[40] A group of Miami Indians requested permission to settle on the west bank of the Mississippi in 1788.

Many Indians moved to the Arkansas country. Emigrant Cherokees established a new community on the Saint Francis River in 1782; other Cherokees followed, mainly Chickamaugas, who continued their raids on American settlements from Spanish Louisiana.[41] Abenaki Indians—or at least people the Spaniards called Abenaki—turned up in Arkansas after the Revolution. Most of them settled on the Saint Francis River. The Spanish feared that the immigrants would deplete the region of game and ally themselves with the Osages. Spanish authorities urged the Abenakis to fight the Osages as a way of proving their loyalty. In fact, the

Abenakis came into recurrent conflict with the Osages as they encroached on their lands. For immigrant tribes, as for other peoples in the Arkansas-Missouri region, the Osages posed a formidable threat.[42] Positioned close to Arkansas Post, Quapaws mediated the influx of refugees and tried to incorporate Cherokee and other newcomers in the same way as, a century before, they had incorporated French newcomers.[43] But displaced peoples from the East constituted, in the words of one Spanish report, "an indirect step against the tranquility of the Interior Provinces of New Spain." As they edged into Osage and Pawnee hunting territories, they pushed those tribes into Comanche ranges, increasing Comanche pressure on the Apaches and the northern frontier of New Spain.[44]

When France sold Louisiana to the United States, some five hundred families of emigrant Delawares, Shawnees, Miamis, Chickasaws, Cherokees, and Peorias were living along the Saint Francis River in the neighborhood of New Madrid, Cape Girardeau, and the surrounding region. When Lewis and Clark headed west, they came upon Indians who had moved west ahead of them to escape American settlement: Kickapoos from Illinois, some of whom would eventually migrate as far as northern Mexico; Shawnees at Cape Girardeau; and Delawares, including a chief William Clark remembered seeing at the Treaty of Greenville eighteen years before and five hundred miles to the east.[45] But Indians who migrated west to escape American expansion only succeeded in buying themselves time. As a Spanish official in Sonora warned in 1783, "A new and independent power has now arisen on our continent. Its people are active, industrious, and aggressive."[46]

War and Some Peace in the Provincias Internas

As *visitador* in America, José de Gálvez had prepared plans for reorganizing the government of New Spain. Back in Spain, as minister of the Indies, he was able to put his plans into effect. In 1776 the Council of the Indies created the Provincias Internas (Interior Provinces). The entire northern region of New Spain—Nueva Vizcaya, Coahuila, Sonora, Sinaloa, Texas, New Mexico, and the Californias—was separated from the jurisdiction of the viceroy in Mexico City and placed as an independent frontier command under a new military government directly responsible to the king. Despite the reforms initiated by the Bourbon monarchy, missionary endeavors into new regions, and increased military efforts, Spanish presence on the rim of Christendom remained precarious, and

Spanish power attenuated the farther it reached into a world dominated by still-powerful Indian nations—Spanish Texas in 1778 consisted of the villa of San Antonio, two presidios, and seven missions surrounded by scores of Indian groups.[47] In South America Indian revolution rocked Spanish colonial rule—in 1780 indigenous resistance in the Andean highlands of southern Peru and Bolivia culminated in the massive revolt led by Tupac Amaru and a civil war that in two years claimed one hundred thousand lives out of a population of approximately 1.2 million.[48]

Between 1771 and 1776 Indian raiders on the northern frontiers had killed hundreds of Spanish subjects as well as carrying off captives and livestock and destroying property.[49] The diversion of attention and resources to the Revolution limited the effectiveness of Spain's plans to try and subdue the *indios bárbaros* as well as to finally "extinguish" the Seris, with whom hostilities continued through the Revolutionary era.[50] French-born Teodoro de Croix, appointed commander general of the Provincias Internas, saw "the constant ravages of the hostile Indians" as his greatest challenge. Holding a series of war councils with his commanders, he formulated new policies for dealing with the escalating Comanche and Apache raids and with other nations to the northeast.[51] Adopting a policy first proposed by the marquis de Rubí in 1768, Spain would now pursue peace with Comanches in order to wage war more effectively against Apaches.[52] In place of the piecemeal defensive strategies of the past, Spanish commanders now initiated campaigns designed to divide and conquer: "The vanquishment of the heathen consists in obliging them to destroy one another," wrote Viceroy Bernardo de Gálvez (nephew of José de Gálvez) in his instructions in 1786.[53]

Spain continued to try and enlist the Norteños, the "nations of the North," in Texas as barriers against British incursions and as allies against Apache and Osage enemies. It was a demanding task in a region rendered tumultuous by the repercussions of imperial conflict and the migrations of Indian peoples jostling for position and trade. Spanish-Norteño diplomacy was complicated and time-consuming. Shared interests in curtailing Apache or Osage raids did not guarantee smooth relations or united action. In 1778, for example, Athanase de Mézières undertook an arduous expedition from San Antonio de Béxar to revisit the nations of the upper Trinity, Brazos, and Red Rivers and repair relations after years of neglect.[54] A recent epidemic (which carried off Mézières's wife, a son, and a daughter in one week) had swept through the area, causing demographic and political disruption.[55] In 1779 Mézières found that the

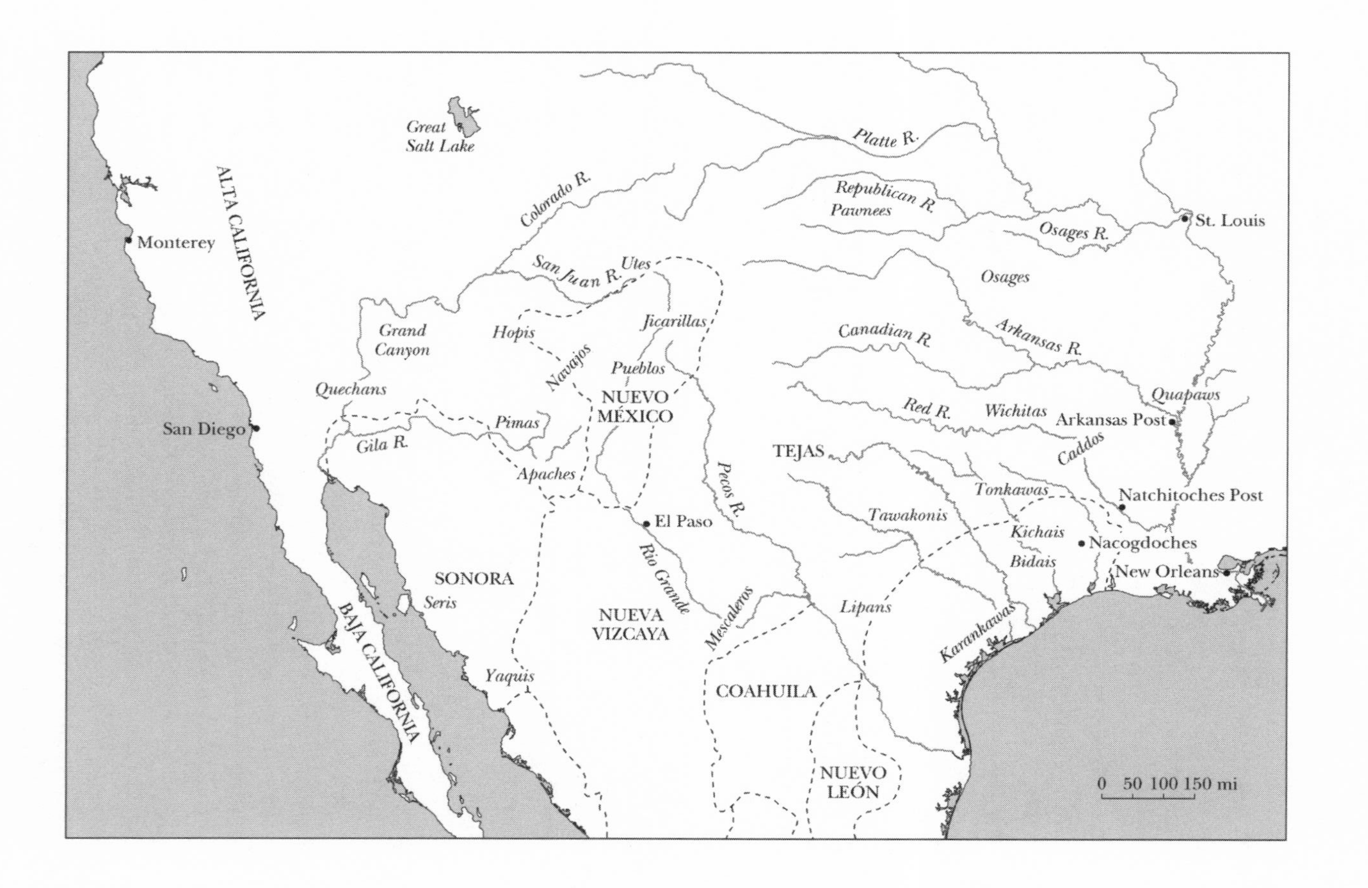

13. The Provincias Internas

epidemic had killed all but 150 men among the Tonkawas, including all their old leaders. Their new head chief was an adopted Apache captive called Tosche, whom the Spaniards knew as El Mocho, a powerful orator and a "lover of disturbances" who had participated in the attack on the San Sabá mission in 1758. Mézières had orders to get rid of him. He arranged for three Tonkawas to travel with El Mocho to Natchitoches and kill the chief en route. But the would-be assassins fell victim to the epidemic, and Mézières had no choice but to cultivate relations with El Mocho. Not until 1784 did Spain succeed in having El Mocho assassinated.[56]

The fluid and fragile nature of Native leadership was a shaky foundation on which to build imperial policies, and the Spaniards had to adjust their expectations as to what leaders could accomplish. "No chief exerts himself to have a following; he knows that when there is no pay there is no obligation," wrote Mézières of the Tonkawas. A leader attracted followers by the example he set and the devotion he won. Volunteers were free to withdraw without censure. Mézières paused "to wonder at a liberty which keeps in harmony peoples seemingly irrational, but would cause the fall of those who flatter themselves that they are more prudent and wise!"[57]

International competition as well as village politics worked against Spanish efforts to implement multitribal alliances. Spanish policy prohibited selling guns to Indians on the frontiers, but French traders in Louisiana and British traders from east of the Mississippi channeled so many firearms into Indian hands that Spanish soldiers sometimes were in danger of being outgunned. Norteños had so many firearms that "they trade them to the citizens of San Antonio de Bejar for any trifle whatever" as well as to Comanches and Apaches, who became skilled in their use. Lipan Apaches learned to manufacture their own gunpowder.[58]

In the country between the Missouri and Arkansas Rivers, the Osages, "the most numerous of the nations of the Missouri," continued to thwart Spanish attempts to subdue them.[59] They drove out and sometimes killed European hunters who trespassed in the Arkansas Valley and the Ozarks, ignored Spanish trade restrictions, and traded at will with British traders operating out of the Illinois country and Canada. By the time of the Revolution they dominated the fur trade of St. Louis and Spanish Illinois, bringing hundreds of deerskins from their vast hunting territory. Osage warriors ranged against other tribes, carrying off pelts, horses, and slaves. The Spaniards repeatedly tried to apply economic sanctions and frequently advocated open war. But trade embargoes only produced more raids, and the Osages practiced effective brinkmanship: when Spain threatened war, Osage headmen opened negotiations, blaming depredations on individuals they could not control.[60]

Mézières planned to create an alliance of Comanches, Wichitas, and Caddos as a barrier to protect Spanish Texas against Osage raids and proposed a campaign to end "their rapine, assassination, and outlandish barbarity." He would arm the allies while at the same time cutting off the Osages from trade at Arkansas Post and St. Louis. With thirteen hundred Indian auxiliaries from a dozen tribes, he would strike the Osage villages at harvesttime, capture their horses and fields, cut off their water, and then ignite their lodges with a hail of fire arrows. His Indian allies would slaughter the Osages as they fled from their burning homes.[61] But Spain's entry in 1779 into what was becoming a global struggle against the British Empire ruled out any likelihood that additional resources would be directed to the Provincias Internas. The campaign never materialized, and Mézières died before his embassies to the Norteños bore fruit and before the trade he had promised could be extended to the tribes.[62] Osages continued to kill hunters who trespassed on the Arkansas River, to raid almost at will, and to treat Spanish pretensions with disdain.[63]

The Osages also resisted encroachments by eastern emigrant tribes. By the 1780s they were fighting off competition from Potawatomis, Kickapoos, Sauks, Foxes, Ioways, and other tribes to their northeast; from Shawnees, Delawares, Miamis, and others pushed west by American expansion; and from Choctaws, Chickasaws, and Cherokees who crossed the Mississippi to hunt and raid in the Ozarks.[64] The Osages dominated and sometimes attacked the Quapaws but tolerated their presence on the Arkansas River as a buffer against the Chickasaws and Choctaws. Caught between the Osages and encroaching tribes from the Southeast, the Quapaws relied on the Spanish at Arkansas Post. They reluctantly served in Spanish campaigns against the Osages and requested guns from the Spanish to defend themselves against the Osages.[65] Osages and Pawnees clashed over the buffalo grounds along the Arkansas and Smoky Hill Rivers, and the Osages maintained an alliance with the Kansas to their north to help keep the Pawnees out of the region.[66]

Pressured from the north and east, the Osages began traveling south and west onto the plains more often during the late eighteenth century. A band (under the leadership of Big Foot, Big Track, or Makes Tracks Far Away) moved south to the Three Forks region of the Arkansas Valley to trade at Arkansas Post, began to emerge as an incipient third division of the tribe, and challenged the traditional leadership. Clermont and Lafond, two prominent Big Osage chiefs, tried in vain to stem the southward movement, as did the Spanish.[67] Southern Osages hunted buffalo, stole horses, and fought with Plains tribes.

The Osages pushed the Wichitas and Caddos south and west. "The Osages are continually killing us and stealing our horses, as well as those of other nations," complained a Taovaya chief named Qui Te Sain to Gálvez in November 1780. The Taovayas lacked guns and ammunition with which to defend themselves against well-armed Osages. Employed as a barrier, Caddos suffered terribly from Osage attacks; some claimed they dared not go out hunting lest they run into Osage war parties, and they beseeched the Spanish to supply them with guns.[68] The Cadodacho chief Tinhioüen repeatedly demanded a Spanish war against the Osages and became so incensed by Spain's failure to do more than apply economic sanctions that he struck a Spanish commandant in the face.[69] In the winter and spring of 1785–86, Osages attacked the Grand Caddo town and drove the Taovayas and Wichitas from their villages on the Red River. The Wichitas fled for a time to the Pedernales River, 250 miles to the south. Some joined Tawakoni relatives on the Brazos. The Wichitas were pushed completely onto the plains. Governor Esteban Miró supplied the Caddos with guns and ammunition and encouraged other tribes to fight against the Osages. He prepared for war but, fearful of British traders and American expansion, backed away from open conflict, preferring to threaten, conciliate, and cut off trade. Subsequent planned campaigns proved equally ineffective.[70]

Spain had little choice but to dance to the tune the Osages called: "The Osages are the worst two tribes that we have on the Missouri," Manuel Pérez, lieutenant governor of St. Louis, told Miró in 1790, "and at the same time the strongest, the more so if they unite. For this reason it is necessary to temporize with them to some extent, handle them as tactfully as possible in order to restrain their excesses, as the few forces in the country do not permit anything else."[71] Even when Spain declared war on the Osages in 1793 little changed. An Osage war party made a demonstration of power at Sainte Genevieve, but otherwise, wrote Osage historian John Joseph Mathews, "there is little in the tribal memory . . . to indicate that they did much more than ride over the land in black and orange bluff-paint singing their war songs." Since their main purpose was to prevent Spanish merchants in St. Louis and Sainte Genevieve from sending guns and goods to enemy tribes upriver, this probably constituted victory.[72] When Louis XVI was guillotined the same year, Spain declared war against the Revolution in France and abandoned its phony war against the Osages. Tact and trade, not war, was the way to deal with the Osages.

Baron Francisco Luis Hector Carondelet, governor of Louisiana, granted monopoly of the Osage trade to French trader Auguste Chouteau and his younger half-brother Pierre, who spent much time living with the Big Osages. The Chouteaus named their trading post near the forks of the Osage River Fort Carondelet, and the monopoly was renewed twice until 1802, when it was granted to a Spanish trader, Manuel Lisa. In exchange, the brothers tried to mediate peace between Spain and the Osages.[73] A delegation of six Osages accompanied Auguste Chouteau to New Orleans in 1794 to meet with Carondelet, but Chickasaws attacked them on the way home and killed three of the delegates. Spain tried to preserve its own peace with the Osages as well as peace between the Osages and other, smaller tribes who requested Spanish protection. But peace with the Osages was never total and always fragile, and they lived with every tribe's hand turned against them. "The Osages," declared a Chickasaw chief in 1793, "are at war with all men, white and red, steal the horses, and kill all the white men they find."[74]

In 1804 U.S. officials took charge of upper Louisiana, and the third foreign power in forty years laid claim to the region. But when Auguste or Pierre Chouteau sent a letter to the Osages on the Arkansas River, informing them that a new government had taken possession of the country, a chief named Cashesegra (Makes Tracks Far Away or Big Track) "threw the talking paper into the fire."[75] Real power between the Missouri and Red Rivers continued to rest with the Osages. "The truth is," wrote Thomas Jefferson, "they are the great nation South of the Missouri, their possession extending from thence to the Red River, as the Sioux are great North of that river. With these two powerful nations we must stand well, because in their quarter we are miserably weak."[76] When Thomas Freeman and Peter Custis set out up the Red River in 1806 on a voyage of exploration designed as the southwestern complement to Lewis and Clark's northwestern explorations, a Caddo chief named Dehahuit warned them they were likely to run into trouble with the Osages. He promised to "dance for a month" if the Americans killed any Osages.[77] The Osages continued as the dominant power in the region until they succumbed to American treaty making and the massive influx of eastern Indians during the first part of the nineteenth century.

In Texas and New Mexico, despite New Mexico governor Mendinueta's

19. Saint-Mémin, *Cashunghia, an Osage Warrior,* pencil, charcoal on paper, 1806. Cashesegra, sometimes called Big Foot, Big Track, or Makes Tracks Far Away, was a prominent Osage chief at the time the Louisiana Purchase transferred his homeland to the United States. (© Collection of the New-York Historical Society. Accession number 1860.90, neg. no. 1109.)

campaigns in the mid-1770s, the "numerous and warlike Comanche nation" remained Spain's most formidable opponent. In his report to Croix in 1777 Lt. Col. Hugo O'Conor described the Comanches as "natives and lords of the wide land that is enclosed by the cordilleras of New Mexico and the abundant Missouri River" and (paraphrasing Mézières seven years earlier) "a multitude so large and haughty that they consider themselves equal in number to the stars." They were armed and on the move, "spreading as a mob from the remotest part of the north to the most southerly country."[78] Raiding was as much a part of the Comanche economy as trading, and their attacks on New Mexico persisted: some continued raiding Pecos, Picuris, and Galisteo, while others went to Taos to trade. Under the combined impacts of Comanche raids and a severe drought that hit the plains in the mid-1770s, settlers retreated from the northern regions of New Mexico, and the province was on the defensive.[79]

But these were hard times for Comanches too. During the drought rivers ran dry, grass shriveled, and horses died. Comanches considered peace with New Mexico as a way of reviving trade to replenish their herds.[80] At the same time, Spain finally began to suppress the Franco-Comanche trade out of Louisiana and to redirect Louisiana's commercial ties northward. Migrant Indians continued to infiltrate the plains, producing chain reactions that pushed Comanches into conflict with Kiowas and Plains Apaches. British traders, who had been operating on the Red River in the early 1770s, became scarce on the southern plains after Spain entered the Revolutionary War and the Peace of Paris restricted the British to Canada. After dominating trade on the southern plains for more than thirty years, the Comanches faced an uncertain future and some hard decisions.[81] After smallpox wreaked havoc among them in the early 1780s,[82] they were inclined to consider the peace that Governor Juan Bautista de Anza offered them in the middle of the decade.

Appointed governor of New Mexico in 1779, Anza was a "Creole frontiersman," a veteran of campaigns in Sonora who had also forged a colonizing trail to San Francisco.[83] His father and grandfather had both died fighting Apaches. Anza was determined to defeat the Comanches as the best route to a lasting peace with them. He gathered a force of six hundred soldiers, settlers, and Pueblos, augmented it with two hundred Utes and Jicarillas who had old scores to settle, and marched into Comanchería in pursuit of Cuerno Verde (Green Horn), a Western Comanche war chief whom he described as the "scourge of the kingdom." Near present-day Pueblo in southern Colorado, he attacked Cuerno Verde's village while most of the men were away, scattered the inhabitants, captured fifty women and children, and rounded up five hundred horses. Though most of the Utes took off for home, Anza ambushed Cuerno Verde's returning warriors at the foot of Greenhorn Mountain. Surrounded and outnumbered a dozen to one, Cuerno Verde led fifty warriors in a defiant charge. When the smoke cleared, Cuerno Verde lay dead, along with his eldest son, four of his war chiefs, and eleven others, including a medicine man who had declared Cuerno Verde immortal.[84]

When Anza resumed his campaigns after the Revolutionary War, he insisted that no peace could be made unless all Comanches agreed. In 1785 Governor Domingo Cabello of Texas sent Francisco Xavier Chaves and Pedro Vial as peace emissaries to the Eastern Comanches. Chaves had been captured as a child by the Comanches and had lived first with them and then with the Taovayas; Vial, a French trader and blacksmith, had lived among the Taovayas. The emissaries brought a Comanche delegation to San Antonio, where they stayed three weeks and made peace with Cabello. "From now on the war is over between us and our brothers, the Spaniards; you will not see our footprints around San Antonio to rob you or do you harm," announced the Comanche chief Iron Shirt, who stipulated only one condition—that the Comanches be free to continue fighting their old enemies, the Lipan Apaches.[85] Four hundred Western Comanches from the Cuchanec, Yupe (People of the Timber), Yupine, and Yamparica (Root-Eater) bands came to Taos the same year seeking peace. They chose as their spokesman a Cuchanec chief, Ecueracapa, whom the Spanish regarded as their most distinguished leader "as much by his skill and valor in war as by his adroitness and intelligence in political matters." Alarmed by the prospect of peace between their Spanish allies and their Comanche enemies, the Utes dispatched two chiefs to Santa Fe first to protest against the proposed treaty and then to ensure that they would be included in it. A Western Comanche chief named Toroblanco (White Bull) insisted on continuing hostilities, but members of the peace faction assassinated him. Ecueracapa made peace initiatives through Pecos intermediaries. In 1786, while Americans made peace with Shawnees at Fort Finney, Anza met with Utes and Comanches at Pecos and ratified the peace at Taos. Spanish officials strengthened the peace by arranging for regular Comanche trade at Taos and Pecos, attentively cultivating good relations with the Comanches, and presenting gifts to Ecueracapa, whom Anza proposed designating "principal chief."[86]

Viceroy Bernardo de Gálvez in 1786 laid out his Indian policy: "swift and vigorous war with the Indians who declared it, peace with those who solicited it, and an attempt to win allies among the warlike nations by spreading the use of Spanish foods, drinks, weapons, and customs among them." As did his contemporary, U.S. Secretary of War Henry Knox, Gálvez recognized that peace and trade were more effective and economical than war in dealing with Indians: "We shall benefit by satisfying their desires," he wrote. "It will cost us less than what is now spent in considerable and useless reinforcements of troops. The Indians cannot live without our aid." [87] The Comanche peace was a coup for Anza and brought relief and benefits to Spanish New Mexico. The new system of alliances with Comanches and expanded commercial networks brought a generation of economic, demographic, and cultural growth throughout northern New Mexico. Northern regions that had been rendered uninhabitable were now resettled. In 1791 the governor said that because of the peace that reigned, ranching was expanding, and "all forms of livestock were multiplying infinitely."[88] The peace removed the Comanche barrier that, the Spaniards believed, blocked them from opening another branch of the Camino Real, connecting Santa Fe and San Antonio.[89]

The Comanches also agreed to join Spain in waging war against the Apaches. As Mézières had acknowledged in recommending such measures eight years earlier, "a proposal to repair to hands which have shed our blood, in order that they may shed the blood of other enemies, seems strange." But the Comanches were constantly at war with the Apaches, he reasoned, and employing them on campaigns would be the best way to guarantee their allegiance.[90] In compliance with the provisions of the treaty, Ecueracapa and other Western Comanche leaders assisted the beleaguered Spaniards in their "eternal war" against the Apaches.[91]

The Comanches also did well by the peace. They gained free trade access to Santa Fe and the pueblos. The gun trade was legalized. Some six thousand Comanches visited Pecos in the summer of 1786, and nine trade fairs were held at Taos, Pecos, and Picuris in 1787 alone. The Comanches were able to revive their trade network, which had been on the verge of collapse, and they once again enjoyed access to markets from east Texas to New Mexico, from Pawnee and Wichita villages in the north to San Antonio in the south. Comanche dominance of southern plains exchange networks was confirmed, and, as historian Gary Anderson points out, the Spanish understood that the commercial alliance was more important for the peace it ensured than for the profits it offered: "Given the terrible consequences of war with the Comanches," Spaniards always made sure their customers "left town in good humor."[92] Western Comanches made peace with the Kiowas and Plains Apaches after 1790 and were again operating a major trading network centered on the upper Arkansas, upper Canadian, Red, and Brazos Rivers. The 1786 peace is often credited with opening the southern plains to buffalo hunters (*ciboleros*) and traders from New Mexico—Hispanos, Pueblos and *genízaros* who became known as Comancheros. Traders from New Mexico had been trekking out onto the plains to deal with Indian buffalo hunters for years, but that trade was now official policy, and Spanish authorities tried to regulate the commerce and control illegal traders whose practices might jeopardize the peace. Hispanic traders traveling to the plains began to supplant the traditional prominence of Pueblo fairs in the exchange.[93] When American traders began to penetrate the southern plains by the turn of the century, they took their places alongside Comancheros, Kiowas, Plains Apaches, Cheyennes, Arapahos, Pawnees, and Shoshones, all of whom frequented the Comanche trading camps.[94] But the Comanches always had to fight to hold the high plains. In 1793 Ecueracapa died from wounds sustained in battle against the Pawnees, who threatened the northern reaches of Comanchería.[95]

The Comanche peace held, but Spanish conflicts with Apaches continued with little respite. Different bands of Apaches raided Spanish settlements in Texas, struck south into Nueva Vizcaya, and threatened Spanish commercial and mining operations in Sonora, a region already rendered turbulent by ethnic mixing, population movements, intertribal strife, and frequent rebellion.[96] Beginning in the 1770s, Spain intensified its "pacification" campaigns against the Apaches. Spaniards supported Norteño attacks on Lipan Apaches in Texas, attempted to turn Apaches against Apaches, and increased search-and-destroy campaigns against their *rancherías*. In the fall of 1775, in a series of fifteen encounters, Hugo O'Conor and his troops killed 130 people and gathered substantial captives, horses, mules, and plunder during a campaign into Apachería. He was back in the field in the fall of 1776. Spain paid bounties on pairs of Apache ears and resurrected an earlier policy of deporting Apache prisoners, sending them south in chain gangs to Mexico City, where they were distributed as servants in Spanish households. When some Apaches escaped and made the long trek back home, the Spaniards began sending them to Havana, thinking their island prison would contain them. But again some Apaches escaped, raiding Cuban settlements and taking refuge in the hills in the interior of the island, where some of their descendants live today.[97]

Apache fighting techniques stretched Spanish military capacities to the limit. To counter Apache attacks the Spanish frontier army numbered about three thousand men, poorly armed and equipped, poorly paid, and scattered across a vast territory, while Spanish policies vacillated, sometimes making peace overtures to some bands of Apaches while waging all-out war on others.[98] Hugo O'Conor had a dozen years of experience on the northern frontier. In a report to his successor, Teodoro de Croix, written in 1777, O'Conor outlined the measures Spain needed to take to defend its colonies. Well mounted and armed with guns they obtained from Indians near Louisiana, the Apaches waged a hit-and-run style of guerrilla warfare the Spaniards could not match. To meet the Apache threat, O'Conor explained, Spain needed to synchronize patrols from its presidios and launch large-scale offensive campaigns. Croix created companies of light troops for warfare against the Apaches.[99] Expeditions from Sonora, Nueva Vizcaya, and southern New Mexico invaded Apachería. Juan de Ugalde, governor of Coahuila, joined with the Mescalero Apaches against the Lipans in 1779 and then campaigned against the Mescaleros in 1781 and 1782, but the Spaniards suffered heavier casualties than the Apaches, and Croix removed Ugalde from his position.[100] Anza secured peace with the Navajos in 1786.[101] Spain now distinguished Navajos as separate from Apaches, against whom Gálvez that same year ordered war "without intermission in all of the provinces and at all times." Only with their submission or "total extermination" could the Provincias Internas be happy.[102]

Some bands of Chiricahuas in Sonora and some Mimbreño Apaches sued for peace in 1786–87, but Jacobo Ugarte, the commandant general of the Provincias Internas, carried on the war against Western Apaches from 1788 to 1790. Consistent with Gálvez's instructions, Ugarte's strategy was to create divisions among the Apaches, forming alliances with every band that sued for peace and turning them against bands who remained hostile.[103] In the fall of 1788 a force from Sonora consisting of presidial soldiers, recruits, and Opata and Pima allies struck Apaches on the headwaters of the Gila River, killing 54 people and carrying off 125 women and children into slavery.[104] Reinstated as commandant general of the eastern provinces, Ugalde launched a three-hundred-day campaign against the Lipans and Mescaleros in August 1789. In January 1790 his troops, aided by Comanche and Norteño allies, defeated a large body of Apaches at the Arroyo de la Soledad west of San Antonio. They killed thirty men, twenty-eight women, and one child and captured thirty women and children and eight hundred horses. Ugalde pressed the

Apaches hard in the following months, and Ugarte managed to hammer out a fragile truce with the Mescaleros.[105] The intensified assaults drove many Apaches to seek peace and settle around the presidios in *establecimientos de paz*: 450 Apaches lived around Janos by 1792, and for several years some Mescalero and Warm Springs Apaches settled at Sabinal, an experimental farming community established on the Rio Grande by Governor of New Mexico Fernando de la Concha. In all, Spain established eight reserves for Apaches in Sonora, Nueva Vizcaya, and New Mexico with a total population of approximately two thousand people in 1793.[106]

Elsewhere, the cycle of raid and counterraid continued. Comanches and Apaches waged war with what one Spanish officer described as a hatred "as old as the nations themselves." Well-armed Apaches continued to strike settlements in lightning raids, running off livestock and escaping back into Apachería. In Nueva Vizcaya they struck south to within twenty miles of the city of Durango. "They scale nearly inaccessible mountains, they cross arid deserts in order to exhaust their pursuers, and they employ endless stratagems to elude the attacks of their victims," wrote one officer.[107] The Apaches kept Spain's northern frontier on the defensive with hit-and-run raids, defeated Spanish pacification campaigns, and refused inducements to settle down. Confining the Apaches remained the major challenge confronting the Provincias Internas at the end of the century.

As usual, these campaigns pitted Indian against Indian as well as against mixed-blood presidial soldiers and militia. *Genízaros*, said Juan Agustín de Morfí, made "fine soldiers, very warlike, and most formidable against our enemies," even though they lived landless and in poverty among the Spaniards and sometimes had to go to war on foot and without guns.[108] Spain continued to rely heavily on the services of Pueblo, Pima, and Opata allies as auxiliaries. Sonora formed an all-O'odham regiment to fight the Apaches. Opata warriors earned Spanish praise for their bravery and "their great knowledge of the land, sierras, and watering places where the Western Apaches live." One officer rated them as crucial in campaigns against the Apaches as the Tlaxcalans had been in the conquest of the Aztecs. Military service likely provided Opata men with opportunities for economic and social advancement—wages and status—that were unavailable in their disrupted communities.[109]

Spain continued to edge through Pimería Alta and to implement the policy of *congregación*—resettling dispersed populations into compact communities. But Spanish missionaries made little headway in Arizona. In a report on Indian and mission affairs penned in 1773, Governor

Mendinueta noted the prodigious efforts made by Spanish governors and missionaries to "reduce" the pagan Indians. Two missions that had been established among the Navajos twenty years earlier had failed within a few days when the Navajos withdrew to the mountains, leaving the missionaries with no one to preach to. The Navajos' "natural wild disposition," wrote Mendinueta, left no hope of attracting them back "to the tranquil magnificence of our Catholic religion."[110]

The neighboring Hopis were more insulated from Spanish crusading than were Rio Grande Pueblos and better able to keep Spanish priests at arm's length. Spaniards who made the long trek to the Hopis' mesa-top villages had to pass through Zuni country, and the Hopis usually received advance warning of their coming. Hopi leaders presented a united front against Spanish missionaries and on occasion even debated with and denounced the priests in public confrontations. Franciscan Silvestre Vélez de Escalante met a cold reception in 1775 and lamented that the Hopi religion in 1775 was "the same as before they heard about the Gospel." When Fray Francisco Garcés visited Oraibi, the Hopis would not listen to him or sell him any corn. The next day Garcés climbed onto his mule, and a crowd of villagers escorted him out of their country. As Frank Waters noted, "It was July 4, 1776, and the Hopis were declaring their own independence."[111]

When Escalante returned to Hopi country with Francisco Atanasio Domínguez in November 1776, a large group of Hopis barred their way at Oraibi, "and one of them told us in Navajo not to enter the pueblo." At Shungopovi at the southern tip of Second Mesa, councilmen from several villages assembled. The friars communicated with them using a mixture of sign language and Navajo. When the friars began to preach, the Hopis at first maintained they could not understand them. When the missionaries pressed them, they made it clear that "they wanted to be our friends but not Christians." The councilmen from the villages on First Mesa met in the kiva before they spoke with the friars: they were interested in Spanish military assistance but not in the Spanish religion. The frustrated Franciscans said military assistance "against all infidels who should war against them" would be available, but only if they accepted Christianity. If they refused "to submit to the Christian religion," they were doomed to eternal damnation. The Hopis countered with one argument after another and flatly refused to give up the ways of their ancestors. The Franciscans withdrew "quite crestfallen" in the face of such "obstinacy." The "rebellious province of Moqui" (Hopi) was "pagan and governed by no other laws than its ancient customs," said Fray Juan Agustín de Morfí; Hopi priests were "inexorable in their purpose of remaining heathen, preserving these customs, and remaining in their desolated pueblos," said Teodoro de Croix. Sometimes the Hopis simply told the Spaniards what they wanted to hear, waited for them to leave, then went about their lives as before. Hopis, not Spaniards, decided which, if any, parts of Hispanic culture they would accept.[112]

Drought in Hopi country from 1777 to 1779 gave the Spaniards a chance to revive their efforts with offers of help. In 1780 Governor Anza himself brought a supply train of provisions, offered to relocate Hopi refugees in settlements on the Rio Grande, and stood ready to negotiate peace with their Navajo and Ute enemies. But even in crisis Hopis had little interest in talking religion.[113]

Hopi independence stood in the way of Spain's efforts to establish an overland route from Sonora to Alta California. In 1771 Fray Francisco Garcés and an Indian from Baja California named Sebastián Taraval pioneered an overland trail between Santa Fe and California, traveling eight hundred miles through desert country around the Colorado and Gila Rivers. Garcés was the first European to enter the Great Basin, dispelling the myth that a great inland sea existed in that region. In 1774 Garcés and Taraval accompanied Juan Bautista de Anza, who was then commander of the presidio at Tubac, on a thirty-four-man expedition across desert and mountains to Monterey and back, a distance of more than three thousand miles. The next year Anza led 240 soldiers and colonists, mainly poor families recruited from Sonora and Sinaloa, over the route and founded San Francisco in 1776. The presidio and pueblo of San Agustín del Tucson was established on the site of a Pima-Sobaipuris Indian village to protect the new overland route.[114] Meanwhile, Garcés looked for a more northern route that would avoid the Colorado Desert. As he traveled he brought the word of his God to the Quechans and Papagos: "I asked them if they wished with all their heart to be Christians and to admit the padres to their land, and they replied very cheerfully, 'Yes,'" he wrote. Fray Pedro Font said that Garcés was so suited to communicating with and walking among Indians that he seemed like an Indian himself.[115]

In 1776 the Franciscans Escalante and Domínguez led a small expedition, with three Ute guides, to find a northern route from Santa Fe to Monterey that would avoid Hopi and Apache country. They traveled with horses and mules through southwestern Colorado to the area of present-day Provo, Utah, where they heard about but did not see the Great Salt

Lake. Southern Paiutes ("Payuchis") showed them well-maintained trails leading to the Hopis and the Chemehuevis that presumably served as exchange routes. Lack of provisions and the oncoming winter forced the explorers to turn southeast across Arizona and back to Santa Fe. They failed in their goal of reaching the Pacific but trekked across fifteen hundred miles of rugged country in the Rocky Mountains, eastern Great Basin, and Colorado Plateau, most of it never before seen by Europeans, and they provided the first detailed written account of the extent of Navajo country. En route they preached the gospel to Ute and Paiute people "as well as the interpreter could manage it." In their wake, traders from Santa Fe reached deeper into Southern Paiute country, and part of the Escalante and Domínguez route later became the eastern section of the Old Spanish Trail.[116]

Spanish use of the "Yuma route" pioneered by Anza required they be on good terms with the Quechans at the junction of the Gila and Colorado Rivers, and that, the Spaniards believed, required missions among the Indians. The Quechan chief, Salvador Palma, "who is the great man among the Indians," cultivated good relations with Anza and received teachings from the Spanish fathers. He was baptized in Mexico City during a visit there with Anza, requested missions for his people, and promised to forge a multitribal coalition to assist Spain in its wars against the Apaches.[117] In 1777 Charles III ordered that Spanish soldiers and missionaries be sent to Quechan country.

But Spanish missions and settlements brought conflict rather than allegiance, and the Quechans closed the gateway to California. By this time the Quechans numbered about three thousand people and were obtaining horses via the humans-for-horses trade network that furnished slave labor for the Sonora mines. The demand for slaves produced increased warfare in the region, and two opposing multitribal coalitions emerged. The Quechans, Mohaves, Yavapais, Chemehuevis, and groups of Upper Pimas and Papagos raided back and forth with the Maricopas and Gila Pimas. Each coalition sought alliances with other tribes and with the Spaniards. Palma hoped a Spanish alliance would bolster his own position and assure his people a steady supply of horses, weapons, and other goods. But the Spaniards overestimated the extent of Palma's authority, and his brother Ygnacio Palma emerged as a rival contender in opposition to the Spaniards. As Spaniards interfered in Quechan affairs, drained food supplies, and failed to provide the quantities of trade goods the Quechans had expected, Ygnacio Palma's anti-Spanish position hardened, and even

Salvador Palma began to distance himself from his former allies. Tensions exploded in July 1781. The Quechans destroyed two Spanish missions at the junction of the Gila and Colorado Rivers, killed 105 Spanish men (including Garcés), women, and children, and took 76 captives. Spain launched a series of punitive campaigns against the Quechans and Mohaves. Gila Pimas, Maricopas, Kohounas, and Halchidomas accompanied Spanish expeditions, burning Quechan villages. The Quechans and their allies retaliated. Spain suspended military operations against the Quechans in 1784, but the intertribal warfare continued for almost fifty years, by which time the Kohounas and Halchidomas had disappeared as separate tribes. The Quechan revolt brought Spanish plans for the development of Alta California to a standstill.[118]

Meanwhile, Spain pushed on to the upper Missouri River, believed at the time to be the passage to the Western Sea, in a race against British advances from the East and Russian activities on the Northwest Coast. British traders from Canada continued to trade deep into the West even after the Revolution. The organization of the British companies, the experience of British and Canadian traders, and the price and quality of British goods all gave them an advantage over Spanish competitors. When peace with the Comanches in 1786 opened the way to the upper Missouri, Spanish officials and traders recognized it was vital to establish a presence there and wrest the Indian trade from the British. Exploring the Missouri, they believed, would also give access to "neighboring Asia, whence, by a different route, it is probable that the Russians are approaching."(!) Some officials dreamed of establishing a line of forts from St. Louis to the Pacific as the best means of protecting Spanish possessions against Russian and British advances.[119]

In 1792 Baron Carondelet opened the trade of the Illinois country to all Spanish subjects. When St. Louis merchants complained about such unrestricted freedom, he responded with a set of regulations that excluded foreigners and divided the upper Missouri by lot among the St. Louis merchants. The Company of Explorers of the Upper Missouri, a group of merchants generally known as the Missouri Company, was formed with a monopoly of trade to the Indians upriver from the Poncas. Jean-Baptiste Truteau was chosen to head the first expedition to the Mandan villages, where he was to build a fort. In instructions that heralded those issued to Lewis and Clark by Thomas Jefferson ten years later, Truteau was ordered to make note of all rivers entering the Missouri, to record information about all the Indian nations, to learn what he could about the Shoshones and the distance to the Rocky Mountains, and to wean the Indians away from trading with the British.[120]

Truteau left St. Louis in June 1794. The Indians upriver were anxious for trade but had plenty of options in British and French-Canadian traders. A teacher by profession, Truteau struggled to make headway as a trader in a world of intertribal politics and international competition. "The policy of the savages of this river is to prevent communication between us and the nations of the Upper Missouri, depriving them of munitions of war and other help that they would receive from us if we made our way there easily," he wrote as he approached Omaha country. The powerful Omaha chief, Blackbird, impressed him as "the most shrewd, the most deceitful and the greatest rascal of all the nations who inhabit the Missouri." The Indians blocked his way and demanded tribute. Sioux Indians insulted and stole from him. But he made it to the Arikara villages, where he stayed perhaps eighteen months, trading and gathering information about the country and peoples to the west.[121]

Other Spanish expeditions headed upriver. French trader Jacques d'Église led one, Scotsman James (Santiago) McKay another. Both had visited the Mandans before. McKay, who had worked for the North West Company, sent his Welsh lieutenant, John (Juan) Evans, to the Arikaras and Mandans with instructions again not unlike those furnished to Lewis and Clark. Evans had come to America in 1792 in search of a tribe of pale-skinned Indians reputed to be descended from an exiled eleventh-century Welsh chieftain named Madoc. Like Hugo O'Conor, McKay and Evans were men from the Celtic borderlands of Britain who wound up in the service of Spain. McKay urged the Spanish government to take prompt actions to counter English "intrigue" among the tribes of the Missouri "unless we desire to see ourselves exposed to abandon this magnificent country which must some day be a great resource to the prosperity and glory of the state." But Spanish exploration reached no farther north than the Mandans.[122] Clamorgan, Loisel and Company took over from the Missouri Company and sent more agents and merchandise upriver to the Mandan villages. But British traders were tightening their hold on the trade of the Missouri and pushing beyond to the Platte.[123] Lewis and Clark followed the route of the Spanish expeditions out of St. Louis and up the Missouri to the Mandan villages and did what Truteau had hoped to do: establish contact with the Shoshones, reach the Rockies, and search for a passage to the Western Sea.

Spain went to war with France in 1793, further reducing the resources and attention available for the Provincias Internas. Two years later, Spain signed the Treaty of San Lorenzo, making concessions to the United States. American pressures increased on Indian peoples in the territories Spain relinquished, and those peoples intruded on the territories of Indian peoples still under Spanish-claimed jurisdiction. A disastrous new war with England that broke out in 1796 and the threat of revolution within the Spanish Empire left few resources for maintaining alliances with the Comanches and Norteños. In the secret Treaty of San Ildefonso, Spain returned Louisiana to France in 1800. Three years later Napoleon Bonaparte, his dreams of a revived French Empire in the West crushed by slave revolts and disease in Haiti, sold it to the United States. Charles Dehault de Lassus, lieutenant governor of Louisiana, added a terse note to his list of trade licenses for 1804: "The Devil may take it all."[124] Indian peoples who had "slowly and painfully worked out their accommodations with the Spaniards" now faced "a people of very different law and custom and cast of mind."[125]

The World Rushed In

The era that brought Revolution on the East Coast also brought revolutionary changes to the West Coast. Indians in California entered Franciscan missions, and Indians on the north Pacific paddled their cedar canoes out to multimasted trading ships from the other side of the globe. In a generation or two European seafarers penetrated and dispelled the "fog of geographic ignorance" that had previously shielded the Northwest Coast from outsiders. It was, says historian Carlos Schwantes, "the world's last temperate zone coastline to yield its secrets to Euro-Americans."[126] Those secrets included Pacific sea otter skins, which Lewis and Clark described as "the most delicious fur in the world." Seventy years before the California gold rush, a rush for this soft gold brought the outside world to coastal regions farther north.[127] Indians wearing cloaks of sea otter skins stood in the prows of canoes holding aloft otter pelts as they approached trading ships. Coastal Indians became involved in a trade network that connected them to Europe, Hawaii, and China, became the focus of interest in European capitals, and witnessed the clash of competing imperial ambitions on the shores of their homelands. When Lewis and Clark descended the Columbia River to the Pacific, they met Indians who wore sailors' jackets and pants, drove hard bargains, and knew how to curse in English.[128] These people were accomplished traders, used to dealing with Russian, Spanish, British, and American ships and accustomed to stores of metal and manufactured goods. They showed little respect to the members of the Lewis and Clark expedition, who were a shabby-looking bunch with little to trade but promises.

Although hard evidence of precontact contagion is lacking, exchange networks that reached into Sonora, Baja California, and the Southwest make it unlikely that Indian peoples in Alta California had escaped epidemic diseases.[129] Spanish missions were begun in Baja California in 1697, but Indians in Alta California did not feel the full impact of European contact until 1769. José de Gálvez promoted the colonization and missionization of Alta California to ward off Russian threats from Alaska. After the king of Spain ordered the Jesuits out of his territories in 1767, Spanish missions in Baja California were transferred to the Franciscan order. Gaspar de Portolá led exploration parties to Alta California and "discovered" San Francisco Bay. The Indians at San Diego initially refused to come near them, "plainly shewing signs of fear of the strangers."[130] Franciscan Junípero Serra established the first Catholic mission at San Diego in 1769. Other missions and presidios followed: San Carlos Borromeo de Carmelo (1770), San Antonio de Padua (1771), San Gabriel (1771), San Luis Obispo de Tolosa (1772), San Juan Capistrano (1775), San Francisco (1776), San Buenaventura (1782), Santa Bárbara (1786).[131] The pueblo of Los Angeles was founded in 1781. By 1804 the Franciscans had established nineteen missions and congregated the bulk of the Indians of coastal California—some twenty thousand people—into new communities. Chumash and Kumeyaay people seem to have been pushed into missions by food shortages at a time when drought destroyed traditional plant foods, El Niño climate change disrupted fisheries, and Spanish sheep and cattle consumed the acorns that had comprised the staple diet for centuries.[132]

Missionaries labored to save Indian souls but brought misery to Indian lives. Friars segregated unmarried men and women into separate dormitories at night to enforce Catholic moral codes, imposed strict labor regimens, and resorted to whipping, branding, and solitary confinement to keep Indians on the path to "civilization and salvation." Visiting Spaniards saw the California missions promoting God's work and compared the "happy lot" of mission Indians with the "misery of savage life."[133] But foreign visitors saw apathy and defeat. "I have never seen one laugh," wrote one observer of the Indians at the Dolores mission in San Francisco. "They look as though they were interested in nothing." "A deep melancholy always clouds their faces, and their eyes are constantly fixed upon the ground," said another. Jean François de La Pérouse, who stopped off in California in 1786 during his ill-fated voyage around the world, likened the mission at Carmel to a West Indian slave plantation. "The men and women are collected by the sound of a bell; a missionary leads them to work, to the church, and to all their exercises." He saw men and women in stocks and in irons. When George Vancouver visited the mission at Santa Clara in November 1792 he saw little evidence that the Indians had benefited "or added one single ray of comfort to their own wretched condition" from the labor and dedication of the priests. "All the operations and functions both of body and mind, appeared to be carried on with a mechanical, lifeless, careless indifference," wrote Vancouver, who attributed the Indians' apathy to natural indolence rather than to the numbing effects of mission life.[134]

Missionaries pictured their neophytes as docile and submissive, themselves as benevolent fathers. But many Indians saw the missionaries as thieves, witches, and sexually aggressive. Noting that they were men without women, many Indians believed these self-described sons of the sun to be, as Junípero Serra observed, "sons of the mules on which they rode."[135] The mission system was backed by force and violence. Whipping, a particularly heinous punishment in Kumeyaay culture, was employed frequently to keep neophytes in line. Priests tried to alter Native patterns of sexuality and marriage and ostensibly enforced strict moral codes, but they also sometimes abused Indian women. Spanish soldiers often committed rape and evidently regarded sexual violence as "appropriate masculine behavior in the conquest of the native female population." Mission Indians were usually powerless to resist—but not always. Many ran away. Others turned to violence. Kumeyaay warriors attacked the settlement at San Diego in 1769. About eight hundred Indians from a number of villages attacked the mission in 1775, an outbreak sparked at least in part by Spanish abuses of Indian women.[136]

The rise in populations at the missions between 1769 and the end of the century stemmed from congregating converts in one place and masked a broader demographic collapse. Mission Indians died in epidemics of measles in 1769 and smallpox in 1781–82. Social controls and social disruption produced psychological trauma. Abortions, miscarriages, and deaths in childbirth reduced fertility rates among women. Poor diet, overcrowding, and unsanitary conditions produced appalling infant mortality rates, often with nine out of ten children dying before the age of eight.[137] The treatment accorded Indian people in the California missions prompted outrage and controversy when Junípero Serra, founder of the California mission system, was considered for canonization in the late twentieth century.[138]

Wreckage from Asian boats may have drifted to the Northwest Coast as early as seventeen hundred years ago. Oral tradition among Clatsops and Tillamooks recalls what may have been the wreck of a Spanish galleon on the Oregon coast in the fifteenth or sixteenth century.[139] But the peoples of the Pacific Northwest Coast had little direct contact with Europeans and Americans until the late eighteenth century. Long and hazardous routes around the Horn protected the Indians from European and Yankee seaborne traffic; vast distances and mountain walls limited contact by land. The Columbia River, which in Euro-American imagination might have been the great "River of the West," the fabled Northwest Passage, also proved to be a barrier rather than a highway. The Columbia is more than twelve hundred miles long. The Snake runs into it. It drains more than 250,000 square miles, carrying all the water west of the Continental Divide from British Columbia to parts of Utah, Wyoming, and even Nevada and snowmelt from the Rocky Mountains, the Cascades, the Bitterroots, and the Selkirks. No river in the Western Hemisphere empties more water into the Pacific. Today, with dams at every bend and on its tributaries, the river is a shadow of the force it once was (Richard White calls it a "virtual river"), but when it collides with the coastal breakers of the Pacific it still presents one of the world's great hazards for sailors. In the late eighteenth century the breakers were so huge that seamen searching for the River of the West often were unable to find the Columbia, let alone penetrate it. When Lewis and Clark arrived from the other direction they were bombarded with the thunder of crashing waves for twenty-four straight days and could not imagine how the Pacific got its name.[140] Chinook and Clatsop Indians at the mouth of the Columbia, however, moved easily across the waters in long, sturdy canoes. They traded inland with other Indian peoples and acquired items from half a continent away at the busy portage market at The Dalles.[141] Northwest Coast people were not isolated, but they were isolated, for a time, from direct contact with Europeans.

Many Europeans who traveled to the Northwest Coast at this time recorded detailed accounts of the Native peoples most involved in the maritime trade: Chinooks on the Columbia, Nootkas on the west coast of Vancouver, Haidas on the Queen Charlotte Islands, and Tlingits in southeastern Alaska. Euro-American observers rarely displayed much cultural sensitivity toward the coastal peoples, some of whom practiced ornamental head deformation as a mark of status and wore labrets in their lower lips. But seamen's journals provide valuable ethnographic information, and in some cases shipboard artists created invaluable visual records of the Native cultures of the Northwest. They also provide insights into the cataclysmic changes they themselves initiated.

Spain had sent occasional voyages up the Pacific Coast, and Indian accounts told of Spanish sailors shipwrecked on their shores, but in the last quarter of the eighteenth century Spain focused serious attention on the North in response to Russian activities in the area. When Spaniards sailed up the coast looking for Russians, the British set sail to find out what the Spaniards were up to.[142]

Russian interest in the Northwest Coast of America represented the culmination of an expansion eastward across Siberia that had begun in the seventeenth century. Vitus Bering, a Dane in the czar's service who explored the Asian shoreline northward and gave his name to the strait, reached the Aleutian Islands in 1741. A boatload of sailors from the companion ship commanded by Alexei Chirikov disappeared and was never seen again, but the expedition traded sea otter pelts from the Natives and sold them for nearly one thousand rubles each in Chinese markets. The profits to be made unleashed a rush of *promyshleniki* (Russian fur traders), mainly from Siberia, to the Aleutian chain. They threatened and abused the Natives, forcing the men to hunt for sea otter pelts by holding their women hostage. Much of the Russian "trade" actually involved Aleut and Kodiak kayakers harvesting otter furs for Russian ships. The Russians worked the Aleutian chain, exhausting one island after another. By 1762 they had reached the Alaska Peninsula.[143]

Spanish expeditions led by Juan Pérez in 1774 and by Bruno de Hezeta and Peruvian-born Juan Francisco de la Bodega y Quadra in 1775 sailed north from Monterey in response to rumors of Russians on the coast of what Spain regarded as part of Alta California.[144] Pérez sighted what is now Vancouver Island, and, at the north end of the Queen Charlotte Islands, twenty-one canoes came out to his ship. The Indians "sang and danced, and cast feathers in the air," and then traded pelts to the crew. They were, Pérez noted in his diary, "very adept at trading and commerce, judging by the briskness with which they dealt with us" and the scrutiny with which they examined trade goods. Heading back south, Pérez anchored off Nootka and traded with the inhabitants. According to José Mariano

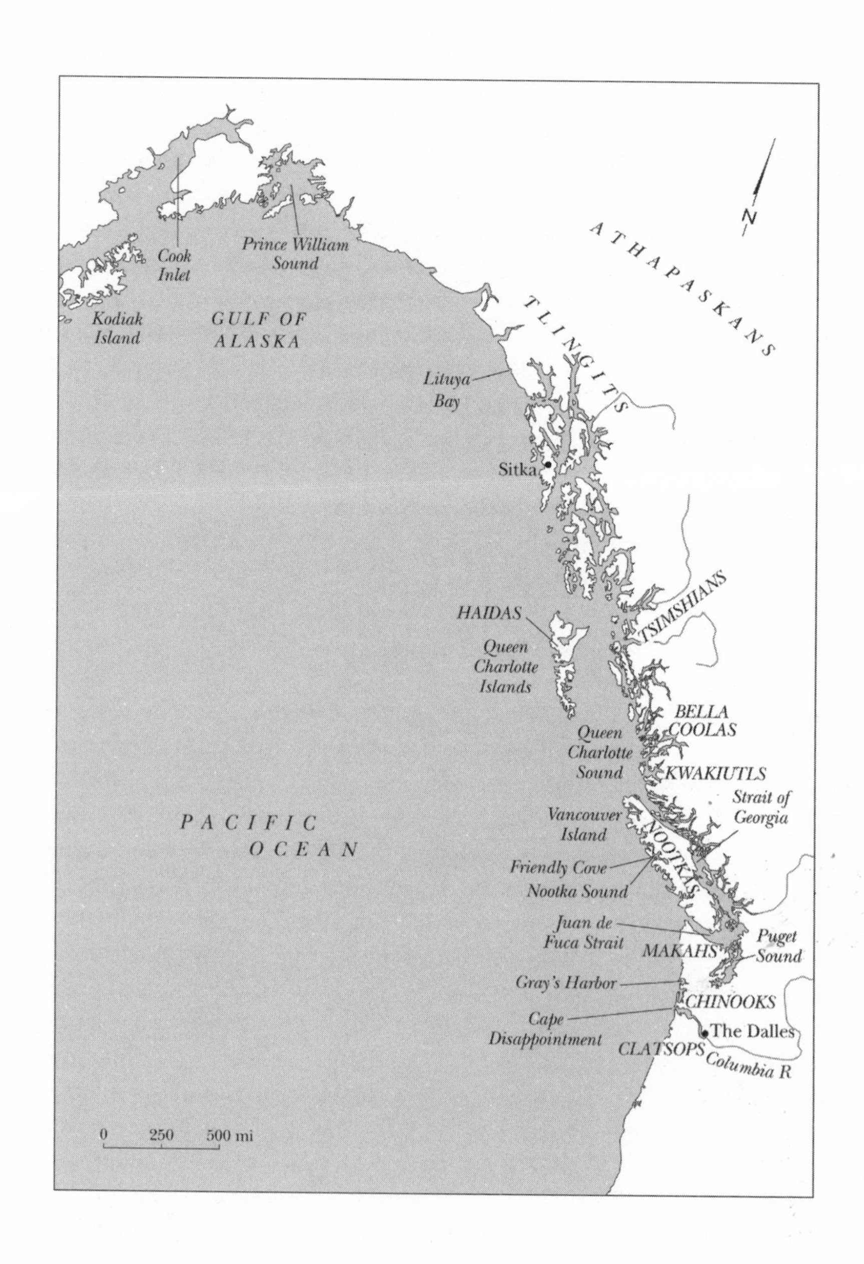

14. The Northwest Coast in the late eighteenth century

Moziño, a Spanish botanist who visited Nootka eighteen years later, the Indians had been terrified by the sight of Pérez's ship, "and even now they testify that they were seized with fright from the moment they saw on the horizon the giant 'machine' which little by little approached their coasts." Many hid in the mountains, but "the most daring took their canoes out to examine more closely the huge mass that had come out of the ocean." Beckoned aboard by the Spaniards, they "inspected with wonder all the new and extraordinary objects that were presented to them." The captain gave them some gifts; they gave him sea otter skins in return. [145] The Indians killed half a dozen crewmen from the Hezeta–Bodega y Quadra expedition near the mouth of the Quinault River, but Bodega y Quadra's ship pushed north to Alaska.[146]

It was time for Britain to assert its claims to the area and to search for a northwest passage at its western opening.[147] Sir Francis Drake may have sailed as far north as Oregon in 1579, but Capt. James Cook brought the Northwest Coast into the British orbit during his third and final voyage. In 1776 Cook left England with two ships, *Resolution* and *Discovery*; sailed around the Cape of Good Hope, past Australia and Tasmania, and on to New Zealand; and dropped anchor at Tahiti, where he let off a Tahitian who had been visiting London. Heading northward, on December 25, 1777, Cook saw and named Christmas Island, then sailed north and east to Hawaii, which he named the Sandwich Islands in honor of the first lord of the Admiralty. In early spring 1778 Cook reached the Northwest Coast of America. He missed the fog-shrouded Juan de Fuca Strait and sailed into Nootka Sound (also known as King George's Sound and, sometimes, as Friendly Cove) in March. Three canoes came out to meet the ship. A leader, perhaps the Nootka chief Maquinna (or his father), "stood up and made a long harangue, inviting us to land, as we guessed by his gestures." He wore an otter-skin robe and shook a rattle and while he spoke "kept strewing handfuls of feathers towards us." Some of his companions threw handfuls of red dust or powder. After the chief's oration, "of which we did not understand a word," another Indian sang with "softness and melody," and more than thirty canoes gathered around the ship, ready to trade. [148] Ship's artist John Webber made sketches of the Natives who came to trade. Cook pushed north past the Aleutians, saw Natives wearing Russian jackets and breeches, met Russian traders, traversed the Bering Strait, and entered the Arctic Ocean. He turned back when the ice pack prevented further progress. From the Aleutians the expedition sailed to Hawaii, where Cook was killed. Cook's voyages alarmed Spain, but Indian rebellions and the American Revolution precluded sending counterexpeditions to the Northwest Coast.[149]

Cook and his scurvy-ridden crew were the first British subjects to set foot on what became British Columbia. Cook recognized the possibilities of a lucrative sea otter trade, although he thought discovery of a northwest passage was an essential prerequisite for British involvement in it. The Indians of the coast seemed quite self-sufficient, he noted, but European trade would soon change that: "A trade with Foreigners would increase their wants by introducing new luxuries amongst them, in order to purchase which they would be the more assiduous in procuring skins," he wrote.[150] The expedition bought fifteen hundred beaver pelts as well as sea otter furs, which brought handsome profits in China. Cook's crew made it back to England with news of the killing to be made. John Ledyard, a young New Englander who had sailed with Cook, published his own account of the voyage in an effort to promote American participation in the trade: "Skins which did not cost the purchaser sixpence sterling sold in China for 100 dollars," he declared. William Sturgis, who made four voyages to the Northwest Coast and in later life lectured on the subject in Boston, said that the possibility of striking it rich produced "a rush into the trade by those who were without knowledge, experience, or sufficient capital for the purpose."[151]

An enormous commerce involving three continents was soon under way. At the trade's height, merchants from England and New England loaded ships with manufactured goods, sailed around the tip of South America and up to the Northwest Pacific Coast, and exchanged their goods for sea otter pelts. They then sailed across the Pacific, sold the pelts in China, loaded up with silks, spices, and tea, and sailed home. In China warm and glossy sea otter fur became a status symbol of the royal family, mandarins, and wealthy classes. In England and New England sea otters were the key to great fortunes. Indian villages became busy ports of call in an intercontinental trade network.[152]

James Hanna sailed to the coast of British Columbia in 1785 to trade for pelts. Despite a violent brush with Indians at Nootka, he returned the next year. Capt. Charles William Barkley reached Nootka in 1787, but Indians killed several of his crew members when they went ashore for water. The *King George* and the *Queen Charlotte*, under Capts. Nathaniel Portlock and George Dixon, veterans of Cook's voyage, left England in 1786. They sailed to Alaska, wintered in Hawaii, and revisited Alaska in 1787. Dixon circumnavigated the Queen Charlotte Islands and found a wealth of furs there. Smallpox had ravaged the coast several years earlier. In 1905 a Kaisun Indian told anthropologist John Swanton a story that may refer to the Haidas' encounter with Dixon's ship. When it came in sight "they thought it was the spirit of the 'Pestilence,'" and, dancing on the shore, waved their hands to try and get the ship to turn back. When the sailors landed, "they sent down to them their old men, who had only a few years to live, anyhow, expecting them to fall dead." But the newcomers began buying their furs, and then the younger people went down too and traded their otter-skin cloaks for axes and iron. Dixon's voyage opened the floodgates into the Haidas' world. Trading ships came every year during the next decade.[153]

The French, briefly, also tried to get in on the act. In 1786 Jean François de La Pérouse stopped off at Alaska's Lituya Bay and claimed the spot for Louis XVI before heading south to Monterey. Tlingit legend, recorded in the 1880s, recalled how a group of Chilkat people had met the Pérouse expedition while the Chilkats were traveling north in the spring to trade for copper. They were camped at Lituya Bay when two ships sailed into view. "The people believed they were great black birds with far reaching white wings, like their bird creator, Yehlh, when he assumed the form of a raven." As the ships came closer to shore and the sailors climbed the rigging to furl the sails, the Indians "thought the large birds had folded their wings and a flock of small black messengers were rising from their bodies and flying about." Despite their fear, a group of warriors put on their armor and launched a war canoe, but a blast of smoke from a ship's cannon overturned the canoe and sent them scrambling ashore. Finally, an old warrior who was nearly blind declared that his life was almost over, put on a robe of sea otter skins, and had his slaves paddle him out to the ships. He climbed aboard, and, though the black forms still looked like crows to his dim eyes, he exchanged his robe for a tin pan and food. When he returned to shore, his people touched and smelled him but would not eat the food. After much thought the old man decided the occupants of the ships were people, and the Indians visited the ships to trade.[154]

John Meares first appeared on the Northwest Coast in 1786. Meares, a British naval officer turned merchant adventurer, sailed under the Portuguese flag because he lacked the trading licenses required by the Pacific monopolies granted to Britain's East India Company and South Sea Company. Sailing in the *Nootka* from India, he arrived off the coast of Alaska late in the season, wintered at Prince William Sound, and lost a score of his crew to scurvy. He returned in 1788 with Chinese carpenters, intending to build vessels and a post at Nootka. Near Port Cox he traded with Indians who acknowledged Wickannish, chief of Clayoquot, as their chief and then proceeded to the land of the Makahs, against whom Wickannish warned him. Twenty or thirty Makahs with painted faces, dressed in sea otter cloaks, and well armed with spears and bows and arrows paddled out in canoes to meet the ship. Their chief, Tatooche, a "surly and forbidding" character, his face painted black and glittering with sand or powdered mica, informed Meares that the power of Wickannish ended here and that his territory stretched to the south and east. He would not allow his people to trade. The next day Tatooche and about four hundred men paddled their canoes around Meares's ship, singing. "Offended as we might be with these people," wrote Meares, "we could not but be charmed by their music." Sailing south to the mouth of the Quinault River, Meares's crew traded a couple of sea otter pelts from a man and boy who refused to leave their canoe and come aboard. Meares failed to find the mouth of the Columbia and declared, "No such river exists." Leaving what he called "Cape Disappointment," he headed back north and ran into trouble around Port San Juan (also known as Port Renfrow and "Poverty Cove"), where warriors from an Indian village repelled the ship's longboat, wounding most of its crew.[155] Meares later claimed, perhaps in an effort to boost British claims to the area, that Maquinna acknowledged British sovereignty and sold him a spot of ground at Friendly Cove in Nootka Sound, where he built a trading house, probably little more than a hut. Maquinna denied it and habitually referred to the captain as "Liar Meares."[156]

As other nations probed the coast of Alaska, Russia redoubled its efforts to secure the sea otter trade. Initially, preoccupied with events in Europe, the Russian state had left things in the hands of private companies. Grigorri Shelikov led the most successful company. In 1784 he established a settlement on Kodiak Island after subjugating the Alutiiq inhabitants. Back in Saint Petersburg in 1787–88 he petitioned the government to grant his company a monopoly and asked that missionaries be sent. Aleksandr Baranov, who became chief manager of Shelikov's North American business in 1790, continued Shelikov's paternalistic and often brutal policies. When the first group of Russian Orthodox missionaries arrived at Kodiak in 1794, they were shocked at what they saw, but their attempts to improve treatment of the Natives brought them into conflict with Baranov. In 1799 the state granted a monopoly to Shelikov's heirs in a charter that formed the Russian-American Company. The company took control of trading operations, but government regulations prohibiting abuse of the Natives were regularly ignored. Pushing southeast along the coast, Russians opened trade relations with the Tlingits in the late 1780s. In 1799 Baranov shifted the Russian-American Company's base of operations to a site a few miles north of present-day Sitka, where he established a fort named after the archangel Michael on land purchased from the Sitkan chief, Katlean.[157] But the powerful Tlingits, who numbered some ten thousand at the turn of the century, proved formidable customers and adversaries.[158]

When Scotsman Alexander Walker visited Prince William Sound in 1785 he reported that the Russian trade was extensive, expanding, and deadly for the Natives. The Russians, said Walker, employed twenty-five ships and about one thousand men and traded primarily in brandy.[159] In 1788 a Spanish expedition near Prince William Sound met Indians dressed in Russian clothing, Russians riding in Indian canoes, and an Indian who had been to Saint Petersburg and seen the czarina.[160]

In 1789 English and Spanish claims clashed in Nootka Sound. Capt. James Colnett reached Nootka and the Queen Charlotte Islands in 1787, wintered at Hawaii, traded at Prince William Sound in 1788, and then sailed for Canton. He returned the next year with two ships, intending to occupy Nootka. He brought with him thirty Chinese artisans, including carpenters, blacksmiths, bricklayers, tailors, cobblers, and a cook. Two other British ships made it to Nootka before him. American ships under John Kendrick and Robert Gray were also there. The Spanish had established an outpost at Nootka, and the commander, Esteban José Martínez, who had been second in command and pilot on the Pérez expedition in 1774, attempted to assert Spain's claims in the face of British and American competition. He seized two vessels and arrested Colnett, who was taken to Mexico and spent a year in captivity. It looked for a time as if Britain and Spain would go to war over the incident and the whole of Europe might be drawn into the fracas.[161]

War was averted, but the crisis did not stem the influx of sailors on the coast. Nootka was busier than ever from 1790 to 1792. By one count, in 1792, at the height of the maritime trade on the Northwest Coast, thirty-two vessels visited the area: eight Spanish, thirteen British, five American, four Portuguese, one French, and one ship sailing under the Swedish flag, with an unknown number of Russian vessels operating off the coast of Alaska. Spain established a settlement at Neah Bay in 1792.[162] The

Indian inhabitants came into contact with crews that included Russians, English, Scots, "Boston men," Spaniards, Portuguese, Hawaiians, Hindus, Filipinos, Malays, and Chinese. A Spanish pilot at Nootka said the Indians were "continually asking when we were going to leave, the eagerness with which they solicit this being noteworthy." In May 1792 George Vancouver's crew saw Clallam Indians on the shore of Juan de Fuca Strait. The Indians "seemed to view us with the utmost indifference and unconcern," wrote Vancouver. "They continued to fish before their huts as regardless of our being present, as if such vessels had been familiar to them, and unworthy of their attention."[163]

The world began to close in from land and sea. Scotsman Alexander Mackenzie, in the employ of the North West Company, became the first white man to cross the continent north of Mexico when he reached the Pacific in July 1793. He recorded and dated his feat on a rock near Elcho Harbor: "Alexander Mackenzie, from Canada, by land." But he was not the first white man to reach Elcho Harbor: George Vancouver had reached the same place by sea less than seven weeks before, and the Indians in the area greeted Mackenzie with what could only be described as a bad attitude.[164]

The United States emerged as top dog in the dog-eat-dog Northwest Coast trade. Spain's interest in the area was primarily strategic (to protect the Californias and Mexico from foreign penetration), and the California coast provided the bulk of Spanish sea otter skins.[165] Britain dominated the sea otter trade south of Alaska until 1788, when two American vessels, the *Columbia Rediviva* and the *Lady Washington,* captained by one-eyed Robert Gray and John Kendrick, reached Nootka, entering Friendly Cove just as Meares left for China. Gray became the first American to circumnavigate the globe, made a second voyage in 1790–93, and gave his vessel's name to the Columbia River after he crossed its bar in 1792.[166]

Americans began the practice of wintering on the Northwest Coast and edged out the British. They became better acquainted with the Indians, secured the winter trade, and were on the spot when the spring trade began. They extended the trade from sea otters to include fur seals and land animal furs, sold firearms, and encouraged trading on the vessel's deck rather than over the sides, with only chiefs allowed on board. According to one Spanish source, Kendrick "gained the friendship of the natives as no one else had, continually giving them presents, entertaining them with fireworks, speaking their language, wearing their clothes, and, in a word, adapting himself to all their customs." He bought land from Maquinna, gave the chief a swivel gun, traded firearms to the Indians, and taught them how to use them, "a lesson that could be harmful to all humanity." When Robert Haswell, formerly first officer of the *Columbia* and now commanding his own sloop, tried to trade with Indians on the northern shores of the Queen Charlotte Islands in April 1792, they demanded exorbitantly high prices for their sea otter skins, telling him that other captains "would be here soon, and they would give them what they had asked." British traders labored under South Sea Company and East India Company monopolies, and ships making the voyage to and from England had to keep an eye open for French naval vessels. American traders faced no such restraints, and, newly liberated from British imperial restraints, Yankee merchants flexed their economic muscles. By 1800 the Americans had transformed the Northwest Coast into what historian Frederic W. Howay called a "trade suburb of Boston." The next year, American vessels outnumbered British ships on the coast twenty-two to one, and, according to William Sturgis, the Indians had "the impression that Boston was our whole country." The Union Jack rarely flew on the Northwest Coast thereafter.[167]

Indians embraced the maritime trade. The new materials, tools, and goods contributed to an artistic florescence even as Indian cultures experienced the shock of contact. But did the merchandise of the Industrial Revolution revolutionize their societies? Indian people adjusted to the presence and plethora of foreign traders and quickly became shrewd dealers, to the chagrin of Euro-American traders seeking easy profits. Observers regularly commented on their commercial acumen, and captains sailing from England and Boston carried warnings of the hard bargaining they could expect when they reached the Northwest Coast. Indians might accept beads and trinkets as gifts, but once they got down to business they wanted metal goods and clothing. "As we advanced up the Sound, the price of everything became more exorbitant," wrote Alexander Walker. "The Natives totally despising Glasses, Beads, and other Bawbles, were only to be satisfied with Brass, Copper, or Iron[.] They were indeed in Possession of such a quantity of Beads, that they offered them to us in derision." Indians became discriminating consumers, examined the quality of the goods offered them, and drove up the price of furs. Maquinna was reported to be interested only in guns, blue cloth, and windowpanes. Traders regularly complained that Indians robbed them blind: "We were, more or less, the dupes of their cunning," said John Meares. Native chiefs learned to manipulate competition between different traders and to monopolize profitable roles as middlemen by preventing tribes further inland from dealing directly with Europeans. They obliged Europeans to participate in or at least tolerate a considerable amount of ceremonial as a prerequisite to trade and to accede to the custom of reciprocal gift giving. Many goods were acquired as prestige items to be given away at potlatches, although the new wealth was not easily absorbed into the Indians' economic structure. Northwest Coast Indians seem to have participated in the trade willingly, driven hard bargains, shaped the trade to their own purposes, and kept the transient maritime traders at arm's length.[168] If they developed a taste for brass and gold buttons, it meant only, as one old man reminded William Sturgis, that Indians and white people were "equally foolish."[169]

Maritime traders cultivated the friendship of Indian leaders, usually hereditary clan chiefs, for both political and commercial purposes. William Beresford, operating around Norfolk Sound, where the Indians "would come alongside at first light and sing for more than half an hour before they started trading," said that the chief had "always the entire management of all the trade belonging to his people" and made every effort to strike a good bargain.[170] Some chiefs acquired considerable wealth. In 1792, when the Spaniard Jacinto Caamaño met Cunneah, the septuagenarian Haida chief wore silk breeches ornamented with small gold flowers and two blue frock coats, one on top of the other. His coats and breeches were both decorated with Chinese coins so that he sounded "like a carriage mule, as he walked." At the same time, successful hunters who accumulated wealth seem to have threatened the status of hereditary clan chiefs with competitive potlatching.[171]

Wickannish controlled a trade network around the Clayoquot Sound region, a number of small islands with several villages scattered through them. In American eyes, only the Nootka chief Maquinna was more important than Wickannish.[172] Maquinna controlled a trading network on the east coast of Vancouver Island. He "held the highest position in the highest ranked household at Yuquot," a Nootka summer village site that had been occupied for at least eighteen hundred years and perhaps much longer and that now became the busiest trading spot on the Northwest Coast. John Meares estimated Maquinna was chief to ten thousand people. Maquinna quickly emerged as a key player in the intertribal and international rivalries on the coast and stamped his

20. Northwest Coast chief, Nachey or Tzachey, sketched by German-born Sigismund Bacstrom, a ship's surgeon who also sketched Hawaiian natives and Chinese soldiers during his voyage along the Pacific Coast–Canton trade route (Sigismund Bacstrom, "Drawings and Sketches Made during a Voyage around the World, 1791–1793," Beinecke Library, Yale University). The drawing shows "a trade hat, European in design, and the indications of brass buttons" (Vaughan and Holm, *Soft Gold*, 208–9).

presence in the journals of maritime traders as a man of influence and savvy who could not be ignored.[173]

Rival captains tried to outdo each other in cultivating Maquinna's friendship with gifts and deferential treatment. Bodega y Quadra was one of several sea captains who employed what one scholar describes as "dining room diplomacy." According to one report, Maquinna came aboard ship daily to dine with the captain. "He asks for anything he pleases and uses a spoon, fork and glass very [well?]. He asks for wine and sherry, coffee upon finishing if there is any, and chocolate in the mornings." James Colnett portrayed him as a "most miserable, cowardly wretch," completely under the Spaniards' thumb. George Vancouver was less impressed than others with Maquinna, but he nevertheless visited the chief at his winter village, Tahsis, in the fall of 1792 and staged a firework display to impress his guest when Maquinna came aboard ship with his relatives. Maquinna's commercial connections bolstered his own status. In 1803, by which time the maritime trade had moved away from Nootka, he gave away four hundred yards of cloth, one hundred looking glasses, one hundred muskets, and twenty kegs of gunpowder at a single potlatch. Some ship's captains regarded him as fickle and untrustworthy, which of course meant that he followed his own interests, not theirs. He was, noted one observer, "endowed with a clear and sagacious talent, and knew very well the rights of sovereignty"; a Spanish source said he "united the qualities of a legislator, judge and father of his subjects."[174]

No matter how Northwest Coast Indians endeavored to direct the tide, the floodgates of change had been opened. Indians became acquainted with "many things of which they had better have remained in ignorance."[175] They acquired alcohol, guns, and new diseases. Rapid decline of Indian populations and the massive slaughter of sea otters altered the Northwest world forever. Overhunting produced glutted markets, fluctuating prices, and depletion of the very source on which the trade rested. James Colnett estimated that the Northwest Coast produced "furs sufficient to Supply China, Corea, and Japan, and also Europe, and it would take with the present method of catching them two Centuries to destroy them so that they could any ways be miss'd."[176] He was wrong, of course.

Before the mid-eighteenth century, sea otters ranged from Baja California to Alaska. Well adapted to ocean life with webbed feet, insulating folds of fat, and thick fur, which they keep year-round in the cold Japan Current, sea otters are swift swimmers, able to remain at sea most of

21. Sketch of Maquinna wearing a conical hat displaying his prowess as a whale hunter. Sketch attributed to Spanish artist José Cardero. Portrait from [Espinosa y Tello], *A Spanish Voyage.* (Print courtesy, Rauner Special Collections, Dartmouth College) Among sea mammal hunters, a chief's power over his followers often stemmed from his reputation as a whaler. His feats and those of his ancestors were celebrated in feasts and masked dances as well as in designs on blankets and conical hats and testified to his ritual intercession with the spirit world as well as to his bravery and skill with a harpoon.

the time and to submerge for long periods. But they are also docile and playful mammals, and mothers will not abandon their young, whom they carry under their arms until the pups are able to swim. They made easy prey. On one occasion, the British bought almost three hundred skins in less than half an hour. They acquired 1,821 sea otter skins from the Queen Charlotte Islands in one month. Indians indicated that the area immediately around Cook's River "was drained of furs" as early as 1786.[177] In 1792 José Mariano Moziño, the official botanist accompanying Bodega y Quadra's expedition to Nootka Sound, noted that sea otters had become so scarce that it was "a very rare thing to encounter one in any part of the bay"; another Spanish observer that year said the otters were being destroyed by the "luxury of the Asiatics and the necessity and interest of the Indians." By the turn of the century the sea otter was on the way to becoming an endangered species.[178]

As Indian men devoted more energy to hunting and chiefs traded pelts for sheets of copper and other goods that could be given away for status at potlatch ceremonies, they spent less time laying in food supplies by whaling and salmon fishing. Before the end of the century, Northwest Coast Indians were going hungry during the winter months. In September 1794 Maquinna and other visiting chiefs charged Vancouver's crew high prices for a small supply of fish: the Indians were short of food either from a poor fishing season the preceding summer "or from their neglect and inattention in providing their usual supply for the winter."[179]

Despite the dominance of men like Maquinna, women were also active in the trade of matrilineal tribes such as the Haidas, Nootkas, and Tlingits with whom the maritime traders did the most business. Alexander Walker said the women at Nootka Sound "managed the traffic." William Sturgis recalled that "the management of the trade was in great measure intrusted to the women" and that men would examine a musket "and then leave their wives to make the purchase."[180] Although some Euro-American seafarers reported that Indian women displayed chastity before contact with the trade ships, Northwest Coast women quickly became renowned for trading sex. Sailors expressed a pronounced preference for Hawaiian women, but they were always eager customers for Northwest Coast women. In some Northwest societies high status women seem to have trafficked in the sexual services of their slave women.[181]

John Hoskins, a Bostonian on board the *Columbia* during its second voyage, reported that until the ship reached Vancouver Island, the women were "exceeding modest; nothing could even tempt them to come on board the ship." But at the southern end of Vancouver Island in 1791 he found venereal disease spreading through the village of Nittenat: the chief, Cassacan, explained he had caught it after sleeping with a slave girl he had formerly given to a ship's captain for several sheets of copper. At the Queen Charlotte Islands, the women crowded aboard ship and "were always ready and willing to gratify the amorous inclinations of any who wish it." Hoskins also noted that Cassacan's face bore the marks of smallpox. "Infamous Europeans, a scandal to the Christian name," he wrote. "Is it you, who bring and leave in a country with people you deem savages the most loathsome diseases? Oh, miserable inhabitants! You, by being in a state of nature, are considered as savages; but from your intercourse with men who dare call themselves civilized have you not become more wretched than the beasts of the forest?" Lewis and Clark found venereal disease rampant among the Natives of the lower Columbia.[182]

Involvement in a global trade brought demographic disaster to the Northwest Coast.[183] Alcohol made deadly inroads. Like many others, Alexander Walker acknowledged that "on our first acquaintance with these People they testified the utmost dislike to Spirits," but from continued intercourse with Europeans they acquired "a most infatuated pollution for Brandy and Rum, or any liquid that intoxicates." In areas where the Russians operated, claimed Walker, alcohol and diseases had cut the Native population by more than half.[184]

When George Vancouver sailed through Juan de Fuca Strait in 1792, he found grim evidence of diseases imported from the outside world, although it is unclear whether the epidemics came from direct contact with sailors or spread via other Indians inland. Smallpox had left its marks on many people, leaving some of them blind in one eye. Vancouver's crew found abandoned villages littered with bones and so many skeletons scattered along the beach that he called the Discovery Bay region "a general cemetery for the whole of the surrounding country." It was obvious that some disaster had struck the region, but they could not identify its cause.[185] On the coast of southeastern Alaska Nathaniel Portlock in 1787 found depopulated villages and adults and youths with pockmarked faces, though younger children bore no marks of disease.[186] Other diseases followed, with devastating consequences. From a conservative estimate of more than 180,000 in 1774, the population of the Northwest Coast had dropped to 35,000 or 40,000 a century later.[187]

Sailors accustomed to violence in their rigidly disciplined shipboard lives expected violence in dealing with Natives. Tensions escalated as traders competed aggressively for Indian customers and employed ruthless tactics to secure their trade. Isolated instances of violence occurred from the early years of the trade, but open hostilities erupted with increasing regularity.[188] After Americans began trading guns, firearms spread rapidly up and down the coast, and Indians became adept in their use. By 1792 everyone at Nootka was reported to have muskets.[189] Indian canoes that came alongside to trade did so more often under the watchful guns of a ship's crew. Indian war canoes more often made hostile demonstrations to keep the seamen away from their villages. In December 1790, at Clayoquot Sound on Vancouver Island, James Colnett's crew fired on Indian canoes to repel an apparent attempt to board the ship; Colnett then fired a cannon shot into the village of Opitsat as a warning against any future attempts. In March 1792 a Hawaiian crewman learned from the Indians that Wickannish was planning an attack on the *Columbia*. The crew stood to arms, and there were some tense moments. Then Gray dispatched John Boit with three well-armed boats to Opitsat. Seventeen-year-old Boit did not relish the task: "It was a Command I was no ways tenacious off [*sic*], and am grieved to think Capt. Gray shou'd let his passions go so far," he wrote. The village contained about two hundred houses, each one with elaborate animal crest carvings around the doorway. "This fine Village, the Work of Ages, was in a short time totally destroyed." In May, in Gray's Harbor, Indian canoes approached the ship in what seemed a threatening manner. The crew fired over their heads, but the Indians kept coming. One canoe, holding at least twenty men, got too close for comfort, "and with a Nine pounder, loaded with langerege and about 10 Musketts, loaded with Buck shot, we dash'd her all to pieces, and no doubt kill'd every soul in her." Three weeks later, Gray's men opened fire on another war canoe in Columbia Cove, killing or wounding twenty-five Indians. Trading continued, but it was punctuated with threats and skirmishes.[190]

The Tlingits, the most formidable warriors on the coast, had a record of unfortunate experiences in their dealings with the newcomers. They skirmished with the Russians in 1792 and caught George Vancouver off guard with an assault in August 1793. Vancouver blamed the attack on the evildoings of other traders who had sold the Natives defective muskets and "pursued a line of conduct diametrically opposite to the true principles of justice in their commercial dealings."[191] Tlingit relations with the Russians were continually tense. In 1802 Tlingits attacked and burned the Russian outpost at New Archangel. The Russians blamed foreign intrigues, but the Tlingits had a record of grievances.[192]

In 1803 Maquinna and the Indians of Nootka Sound attacked and captured the *Boston* and killed most of its crew. The attack was sparked by an insult from the ship's captain to the chief but appears to have been the culmination of a long series of injuries the Indians had experienced at the hands of "their Civilized Visitors." This "*Boston* massacre" was, in fact, an act of desperation. The Nootkas and Haidas had lost their status as middlemen when maritime traders began dealing with Tsimshian peoples on the coast who in turn developed their own middleman position between the maritime traders and interior fur producers. By the time of the attack, Nootka Sound had been hunted out, and trading ships neglected the once-thriving area. Maquinna and his people, who had formerly controlled a vibrant trade, were now bypassed by traders looking for new sources of furs.[193] The new world created by the trade in otter skins was crumbling around them.

Smallpox Used Them Up

While the repercussions of the American Revolution echoed beyond the Mississippi, the West experienced its own kind of revolution. The revolution did not begin in Lexington or Boston; it appears to have begun in the Valley of Mexico. It was not a struggle for liberty; it was a smallpox pandemic that reached from South America to the Saskatchewan, from Puget Sound to Hudson Bay. While rebels and redcoats killed each other by the hundreds in the East, smallpox killed Indian people by the thousands in the West.

The great smallpox epidemic of 1779–83 was certainly not the first epidemic to ravage the West, nor was it the only disease killing Indian people during the Revolutionary years. But it was more extensive than any before or since. Until recently, its extent and its impact on the course of American history have hardly been considered in histories of the United States or in histories of the disease.[194] William McNeill suggested that historians generally downplay the role of diseases in history because we want human experience to make sense. Unpredictable epidemics that bring colossal loss of life lie "beyond historical explanation"; in other words, they boggle the mind.[195] But the absence from American history of an event that killed tens of thousands of people at the time of the Revolution has another explanation. It happened in Indian country, country that was not yet "American." Evidence of its impact lies in French, Spanish, British, and Indian rather than American records. In a society that celebrates the achievements of pioneer ancestors, it raises the troubling possibility that "microbes, not men, determined the continent's history."[196]

Smallpox has been one of the great scourges of humanity. The virus enters the body through the respiratory tract. After an incubation period of ten to fourteen days, the victim suffers high fever and vomiting, followed by skin eruptions three or four days later. In patients who do not die, the pustules dry up in a week or ten days and then fall off, leaving pockmarks. The whole process takes less than a month, by which time "the patient is either dead or immune."[197] The disease is communicable until the lesions are completely healed and the scabs fall off.

Smallpox killed untold millions before its eradication in the 1970s. According to the World Health Organization, it accounted for an average of 10 percent of all recorded deaths in Asia and Europe.[198] It afflicted princes, pharaohs, and emperors. Like a biblical scourge, it swept away armies in midcampaign. It contributed to the collapse of empires and disrupted successions in royal lineages. It scarred Elizabeth I of England. William III, who had lost his parents to smallpox, watched his wife die of smallpox but survived himself, having had the disease as a child. George Washington had it as a young man. Smallpox victims often, literally, rotted to death. It was "the most terrible of all the ministers of death," wrote Thomas Babington Macauley in his *History of England,* "filling the churchyard with corpses, tormenting with constant fears all whom it had not yet stricken, leaving on those whose lives it spared the hideous traces of its power."[199] A photographer at the University of Birmingham in England died of smallpox in 1978 after having been exposed to the virus through a laboratory air conditioning vent; the virus and the victim were not even in the same room. Lingering dread of smallpox prompted the World Health Organization to vote to destroy the remaining samples of the virus, preserved in Atlanta and Moscow, rather than risk the horror of the virus escaping among a now-unvaccinated world population, but fear of unknown samples falling into terrorist hands delayed implementation of the decision. Recent events give a hint of the terror smallpox inspired.

Smallpox mortality rates seem to have ranged from 18 to 40 percent in the cities of eighteenth-century Britain; in the last two decades of the century it accounted for 10 percent of all deaths in London and 20 percent of deaths in Glasgow. In Sweden more than twenty-seven thousand people died from smallpox around the time of the American Revolution; in Russia more than eight hundred thousand died from it in the first decade of the nineteenth century. Death rates were generally lower in the less crowded and more healthy North American colonies, but in the hundred years before the Revolution the disease was absent for as long as five years on only two occasions.[200]

Smallpox plagued Boston, Philadelphia, Charleston, and other eastern cities during the Revolution. In 1777 George Washington implemented inoculation for the American army, but the disease continued to flare up, adding to the miseries of war for soldiers and civilians alike.[201] Smallpox raged at Onondaga in the winter of 1776–77. It hit Creeks and Cherokees in the fall of 1779, Chickamaugas in the spring of 1780. It struck Oneidas in December 1780 and Senecas in the winter of 1781–82.[202] Death tolls in the East paled in comparison with the horrors in the West.

Numerical data about the impact of smallpox need to be used carefully to avoid falling into what one critic calls the "high counter" trap and basing assertions about its impact on assumption rather than hard evidence.[203] Nevertheless, reported death rates convey a sense of the size and scope of this disaster. The epidemic killed an estimated eighteen thousand people in Mexico City between September and December 1779. Tumbrels passed through the streets every evening to collect the corpses.[204] From there it spread in all directions: to the silver-mining districts of northern Mexico, to Guatemala in 1780–81, Colombia in 1781–83, Ecuador in 1783.[205] A group of infected families from Sonora, headed for the region of modern-day Los Angeles, carried the disease to Baja California. Dominican priests watched it "spread like lightning through all the missions" and cause "havoc which only those who have seen it can believe." Some priests inoculated their congregations, but most watched helplessly as corpses lay in the fields and people died of starvation. Many Indians committed suicide, "and the poor little children, abandoned beside the dead, died without help." The epidemic spread along the main north-south mission trails. Indians fled the mission death traps into the mountains, carrying the disease to the non-Christian Indians who lived there.[206]

Smallpox spread north along the Camino Real and other trails from Mexico to New Spain's northern frontier. These trails were traveled most frequently during the dry (winter) season, when infectious diseases like smallpox have their highest incidence, and the trails conveyed not only people but also textiles, particularly cotton, which can harbor the smallpox virus.[207] Smallpox seems to have claimed its first victims from the very old, the very young, and women of childbearing age, and it threatened the viability of many frontier communities as functioning population centers.[208]

In New Mexico more than five thousand people died of smallpox in 1780–81. At Sandia the resident priest ticked off the names of the dead as they were carried to their graves and recorded the cause of death in the margin of his parish book. At San Juan the epidemic broke out in late January, peaked in mid-February, and killed one third of the population. At San Felipe 130 people died in February alone; at Santo Domingo 230 in February and the first week of March. The priest at Santa Clara wrote the words "Abundance of Smallpox" at the top of his register for 1781 and recorded 106 deaths. So many people died that Governor Anza urged reducing the number of missions in New Mexico.[209] At Pecos disease, combined with Comanche raids and drought, took a terrible toll: "These miserable wretches are tossed about like a ball in the hands of fortune," wrote Fray Domínguez. The population of Pecos fell from 449 in 1750 to 269 in 1776. The burial records are missing, but the population fell again from 235 to 138 between 1779 and 1789.[210] The ravages of the disease among nonmission populations are more difficult to ascertain but in some cases were even more devastating. Drought and disease working together may have toppled the Hopi population by nearly 90 percent, from 7,494 in 1775 to 798 in 1780. When Governor Anza visited the Hopis to recruit refugees that year, they told him they expected the epidemic to exterminate them.[211]

The epidemic from Mexico City may have followed, coincided, or connected with an epidemic that spread across Louisiana and the southern plains. Anza's military and diplomatic triumphs in securing peace with the Comanches occurred in the context of epidemic disease, which may suggest a more compelling explanation of Comanche willingness to make peace. Spanish peace envoys encountered a band of Comanches in 1785 who asked if any of the Spaniards were sick; two thirds of the Comanche people had recently died of smallpox, they said, "from which followed the total destruction of their nation."[212]

The disease spread far and fast along well-traveled trade routes. By the time of the American Revolution, ancient networks of commerce and communication had extended, enlarged, and proliferated throughout the West. These routes became the fissures by which epidemic became pandemic. Long before Europeans arrived, Indian peoples traded marine shells from the Pacific and Gulf Coasts, obsidian from the Rocky Mountains, copper from the shores of Lake Superior, feathers and exotic birds from Mexico, and turquoise from the Southwest. Hunting peoples traded with farming communities. In the century before the pandemic the infusion of new goods and the diffusion of horses generated unprecedented movement and interaction among the peoples of the West, creating conditions that allowed smallpox to race through two thirds of the continent in two to three years.

Horses had reached virtually every tribe on the plains by the second half of the eighteenth century, and the routes of exchange by which horses spread continued to pulse with activity. When smallpox broke out in 1779 it raced across the plains along roughly the same lines by which horses spread across the West. Shoshones told Lewis and Clark in 1805 that they could travel to Spanish trade sites in just ten days.[213] A Shoshone who became infected with smallpox while trading for horses could be back home before the symptoms erupted, and the Shoshones were major agents in the diffusion of horses through the Northwest.

As horses spread north across the West, manufactured goods filtered in via the Mandan and Hidatsa villages on the Missouri, from French traders operating among the Wichitas and Caddos, and from British and Yankee traders on the Northwest Coast. Indian middlemen shuttled between Indians and Europeans, between Indians and Indians. Traditional trading centers became the hubs of vast trading networks that connected Indian peoples across half a continent and more and tied them into commercial systems reaching from Europe to China. When the rival Hudson's Bay Company and North West Company built a string of trading posts stretching west to the Saskatchewan River, they created a series of stepping stones by which disease would leap from the northern plains back to the bay. When smallpox hit village farmers, they died in huge numbers; when it hit mobile hunters, they carried it to other groups. People who fled the dread disease infected allies and relatives who took them in.[214]

The Mandans, Hidatsas, and Arikaras held a commanding position on the Great Bend of the upper Missouri prior to 1780. An estimated twenty-four thousand Arikaras lived in numerous villages. They lost 75–80 percent of their population in the epidemic. Trader Jean-Baptiste Truteau, who was there in 1794–95, said that "in ancient times the Ricara nation was very large; it counted thirty-two populous villages, now depopulated and almost entirely destroyed by the smallpox, which broke out among them at three different times. A few families only, from each of the villages, escaped" and congregated in just a couple of villages. Once able to field four thousand warriors, the Arikaras were now reduced to about five hundred fighting men. Lewis and Clark found only about two thousand Arikaras, twelve hundred Mandans, and twenty-seven hundred

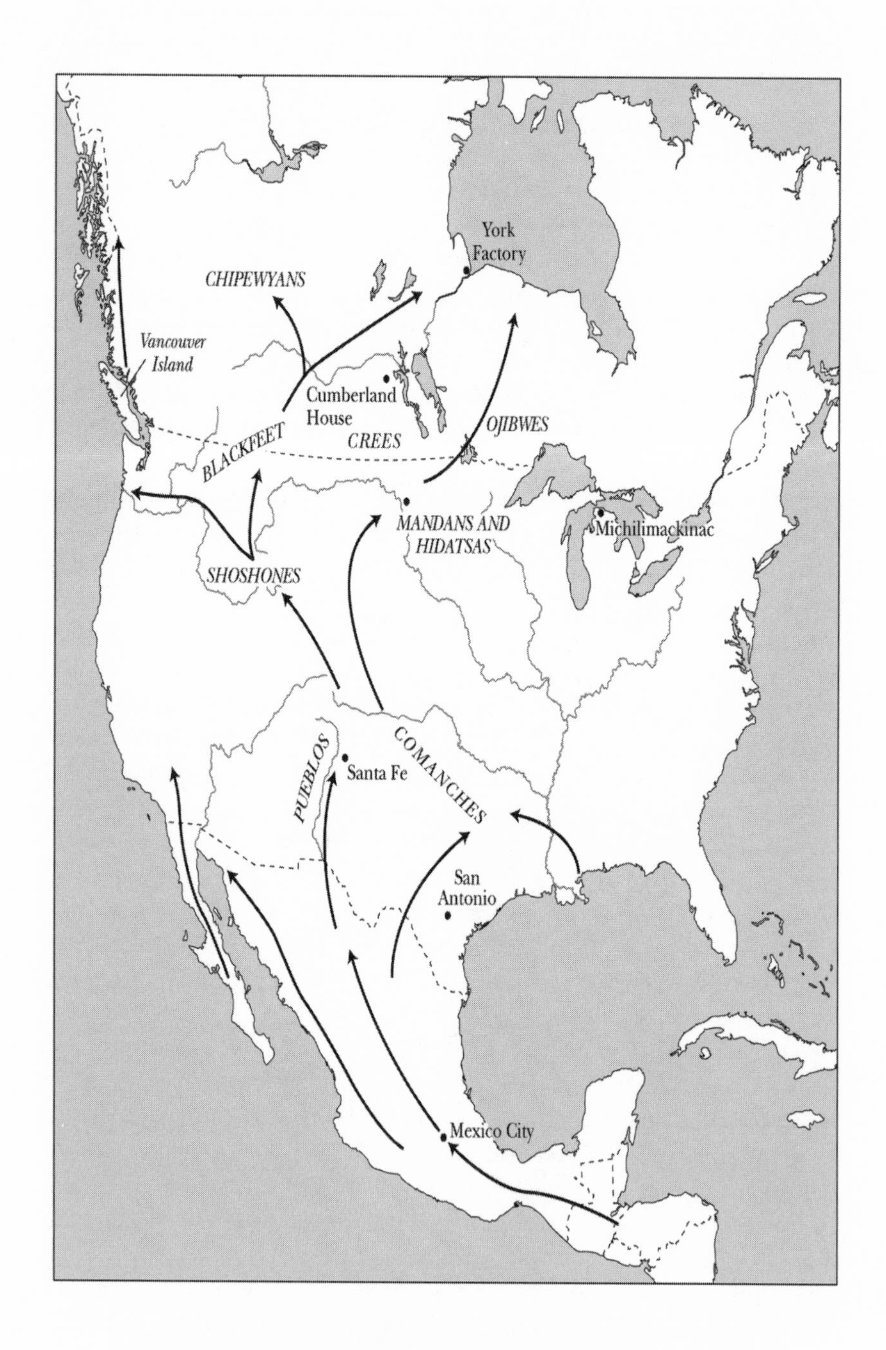

15. The smallpox pandemic, 1779–1784. (Adapted from Elizabeth A. Fenn, *Pox Americana: The Great North American Smallpox Epidemic of 1775–1782* [New York: Hill and Wang, 2001], 7.)

Hidatsas. The Mandans, who numbered about nine thousand people in the middle of the eighteenth century, told them that twenty-five years previously they had inhabited half a dozen villages but had been reduced to two by repeated attacks from the Sioux and smallpox. The survivors retreated north, opening the way for the Sioux to move west across the Missouri and establish themselves as the dominant power on the northern and central plains, where the U.S. army confronted them in the mid-nineteenth century.[215]

Once smallpox hit the Missouri River trading villages it spread quickly. An Ojibwe tradition recalls that an Ojibwe-Cree-Assiniboine war party contracted the disease during an attack on a Hidatsa village. It killed about two thousand Ojibwes.[216] From the Ojibwes, according to trader David Thompson, the epidemic spread "over all the Indians of the forest to it's [*sic*] northward extremity, and by the Sieux over the Indians of the Plains and crossed the Rocky Mountains."[217] Sioux winter counts referred to 1779–80 as Smallpox Used Them Up Winter and recorded its presence for several years after.[218] By the time Lewis and Clark met them in 1804, the Sicangu or Brulé Sioux had already experienced at least five major epidemics, their Oglala relatives had also experienced five, the Yanktonais at least four, and the Minniconjous at least three.[219] It killed between one third and half of the Assiniboines. Most of the survivors began to move away from the lower Assiniboine and Red River Valleys and migrated south closer to the Mandan trade centers.[220]

The Crows, regular visitors to the Hidatsa village, caught the disease, which, said François-Antoine Larocque in 1802, "raged among them for many years successively & as late as three years ago." They told him they had totaled two thousand lodges before the smallpox came but now numbered about twenty-four hundred people in three hundred lodges.[221] From the Crows it appears to have spread west to the Flatheads or Salish, although Shoshones just as likely transmitted it there. As many as half the population died. The Salish passed it on to the Pend d'Oreilles, Kalispels, Spokanes, Colvilles, and Columbia River peoples.[222] The Kutenais were hit hard: "The Small Pox almost entirely rooted them out," David Thompson wrote in 1807. The disease appears to have prompted the Kutenais' final retreat from the plains.[223]

Saukamappee recalled how his adopted people contracted the disease. A Blackfeet war party came upon a silent Shoshone encampment in the Red Deer Valley. The warriors ripped open the tipis but recoiled in horror at the rotting corpses and dying inhabitants they found inside.

Two days later smallpox broke out among the Blackfeet. According to trader Matthew Cocking, "most of them died on their return, the few that reached their own Parts communicated the Disorder to their Countrymen and since then it has run with great rapidity through the whole Country." "We had no belief that one man could give it to another, any more than a wounded man could give his wound to another," explained Saukamappee. In some villages, everyone died; in others, the survivors had all they could do just to feed their families. "Our hearts were low and dejected," Saukamappee remembered, "and we shall never be again the same people."[224] They never were. The most formidable military power on the northern plains was reduced to a shadow of its strength long before the Lewis and Clark expedition encountered it or the U.S. army confronted it. The Blackfeet dispatched peace emissaries to the Shoshones, but they couldn't find any; the country to the south was empty and silent.[225] Coming on the heels of increased pressures from other tribes, the smallpox epidemic seems to have completed the Shoshone withdrawal from the northern plains. Lewis and Clark found the Shoshones sheltering in the foothills of the Rockies, beset by enemies and eager for American allies and American trade.

The epidemic likely spread from the Shoshones and Nez Perces along Columbia River trade routes to the Pacific. Smallpox hit the coast in the late 1770s or early 1780s, though scholars disagree as to just when and how it got there. Maritime traders routinely placed the blame for its introduction on traders of other nations. It may even have reached the Tlingits from Kamchatka, where a huge pandemic that spread from Saint Petersburg to Siberia had raged in 1768–69.[226] Lewis and Clark saw evidence of smallpox in abandoned coastal villages and pockmarked faces. The disease had hit the Chinooks and Clatsops "about 28 or 30 years" before they arrived: "A woman who was badly marked with the Small Pox . . . made Signs that they all died with the disorder which marked her face, and which She was verry near dieing with when a Girl."[227]

From the Columbia it was a short step to the thriving trade communities farther up the coast. By one estimate the "great majority of the people" died around the Strait of Georgia and Puget Sound.[228] Englishman Nathaniel Portlock found far fewer Tlingits than he had expected when he arrived in the Sitka area in 1787. He "observed the oldest of the men to be very much marked with the small-pox, as was a girl who appeared to be about fourteen years old." The old man "endeavoured to describe the excessive torments" he had experienced. "He told me that the distemper carried off great numbers of the inhabitants, and that he himself had lost ten children by it; he had ten strokes tattooed on one of his arms, which I understood were marks for the number of children he had lost."[229]

By the time the epidemic hit the northern plains of western interior Canada it may well have come at the Indians from two directions. David Thompson believed the Sioux picked up the disease from the trading villages on the Missouri River and spread it north. William Tomison believed the disease arrived via the Shoshones. They may both have been right.[230] Trader John McDonnell said the epidemic killed one third of the Crees; Thompson estimated it killed more than half; Alexander Henry reckoned it carried off two thirds of the nation. In the mid-1700s six major groups of Crees inhabited the western parklands, plains, and boreal forests of western Canada—the Susuhana, Sturgeon, Pegogamaw, Athabaska, Missinipi, and Keskachewan/Beaver. They were all obliterated by the epidemic: "All references to named Cree groups in the west cease" after 1781.[231] Some thirty thousand Indians died on the Canadian plains. [232] Chipewyans, formerly the largest Athapaskan group in the central subarctic, lost about 90 percent of their population.[233]

"It destroyed with its pestilential breath whole families and tribes," wrote Alexander Mackenzie; the dead, the dying, and the suicides presented a "horrid scene."[234] Hudson's Bay Company traders journals in the winter of 1781–82 recorded Indians dying every day and employees burying the dead. "The smallpox is rageing all round Us with great Violence, sparing very few," reported William Walker from Hudson House, "the Indians lying Dead about the Barren Ground like rotten sheep, their Tents left standing and Wild beasts Devouring them." Bands of Indians who had come regularly to the posts were never heard from again. People fled from the afflicted, leaving them to starve. "It cuts me to the Heart to see the Miserable condition they are in and not being able to help them," wrote William Tomison at Cumberland House, his anguish no doubt increased by the realization that he had lost about one thousand beaver pelts because "my Debtors are all Dead."[235] Other traders went among the dead, taking beaver robes from the corpses.[236] At York Factory in the summer of 1782 Indians were dying of "a violent breaking out upon them all over their bodies and within the mouth and throat." By August most of the Indians who had formerly brought furs to the post were "now no more, having been carried off by that cruel disorder the Small Pox."[237] At the Churchill River Post at the end of 1783, Samuel Hearne "hardly expect[ed] a Skin of Trade" because smallpox and famine had "made such Havock."[238]

Smallpox seems to have been age-selective, laying its deadly hand on children in particular—nine out of every ten people who died of smallpox in eighteenth-century Britain were children. Children who survived the disease itself often died of starvation and neglect when smallpox claimed their parents. Deaths in the younger population reduced the number of individuals surviving to reproductive age and produced a decrease in births twenty or twenty-five years later. The survivors of the 1779–83 epidemic acquired immunity and were spared when another epidemic hit the plains in 1801, but their children were not. Once again there were fewer survivors at the reproductive age.[239] Fetal deaths are not usually factored into assessments of population decline, but smallpox is particularly deadly for pregnant women. Smallpox reduced the capacity of those couples who survived it to produce children. It probably produced infertility in males and left many women less able to carry fetuses to term.[240]

Smallpox left survivors heartbroken and dazed. Sometimes it left them pockmarked and blind. It eroded confidence in traditional healers and healing rituals. In fact, the common medical treatment of sweating in a lodge and then plunging into cold water often proved fatal to smallpox victims.[241] In one village numbed and scarred survivors sat, too weak to move more than two hundred yards from the stench of the lodges that contained the rotting corpses of their relatives. "They were in such a state of despair and despondence that they could hardly converse with us," reported a trader. "From what we could learn, three-fifths had died under this disease. . . . They informed us, that as far as they knew all the Indians were in the same dreadful state, as themselves."[242] Despair added to the death toll. As their world fell apart and loved ones rotted to death, many survivors lost the will to live and the will to reproduce: "Many put an end to their own existence to end the pain, and others for grief at the loss of their families," wrote William Tomison. An Oglala winter count by American Horse marks 1784 with the suicide of a smallpox victim: the man sat in his tipi, sang his death song, then shot himself.[243]

The impact of smallpox was not uniform, but with insufficient time between epidemics to allow for recovery, it sent populations spiraling downward in many areas. Northern plains winter counts record an epidemic of some sort occurring on average every 5.7 years in the eighteenth and nineteenth centuries.[244] Survivors had to regroup socially and politically as well as psychologically and emotionally. Sometimes small groups of survivors from larger stricken populations congregated to form new communities that cut across ethnic boundaries. Some communities tried to rebuild their populations by large-scale adoptions. Societies struggled to redefine their political structures and patterns of leadership. New villages were racked by internal discord as chiefs from different communities wrestled for authority. Trader Pierre-Antoine Tabeau, who lived among the Arikaras in 1803–4, said that their three remaining villages were "composed of ten different tribes and of as many chiefs without counting an infinity of others who have remained, after the disaster, captains without companies."[245]

Some areas of Europe took five or six generations to recover from the ravages of the Black Death in the fourteenth century.[246] The American West was still reeling from the impact of the 1779–83 epidemic and in some areas from another outbreak in 1801 when Lewis and Clark arrived. Lakota winter counts marked 1801–2 with the all-too-familiar symbol of a man's head and body covered with red blotches.[247] As Lewis and Clark headed up the Missouri, they passed abandoned villages and met remnants of formerly powerful tribes. Under their renowned chief, Black Bird, the Omahas had been a major power in the region during the last quarter of the eighteenth century, but Black Bird and as many as four hundred of his people perished in the 1801 epidemic. "I am told," wrote Clark, "whin this fatal malady was among them they Carried their franzey to verry extraordinary length, not only of burning their Village, but they put their *wives* & Children to D[e]ath with a view of their all going together to Some better Countrey." Tribal tradition recalls that surviving Omahas launched a suicidal assault against their Cheyenne, Pawnee, and Oto enemies, preferring to die than to live with the horror and pass their pockmarked faces on to their children. The once-powerful Omahas become "a wandering nation, deserted by the traders," and easy prey for well-armed and aggressive neighbors.[248]

Just as Lewis and Clark found people like the Arikaras much reduced by the twin assaults of smallpox and the Sioux, so their contemporaries, Peter Custis and Thomas Freeman, on an abortive expedition up the Red River, found the once-populous communities of the Caddo confederacy reduced by the attacks of smallpox and the Osages.[249] Custis and Freeman saw plenty of wildlife, but, as happened elsewhere across the continent, wildlife increased in areas that had been depopulated by disease. The abundance of game was testimony to an absence of Indian hunters rather than to untouched natural bounty.[250]

In 1803 American emissaries, in Paris to negotiate the purchase of the city of New Orleans, pulled off one of the biggest real estate deals in history. France transferred to the United States all its territorial claims west of the Mississippi to the Rocky Mountains, and the United States doubled in size. But the American West in 1803 was a very different place from what it had been just a generation earlier. It had felt the reverberations of revolution in the East. Missionaries and traders had reached the Pacific Coast. Balances of power had shifted between Indian nations as between European nations. And smallpox had ravaged the country. To Americans who had just won their independence from one empire, it seemed that God had cleared the way for His chosen people to build their own empire in the West, just as He had when the Pilgrims landed in Massachusetts Bay in 1620 in the wake of an epidemic that had depopulated the East Coast. The Revolution meant a new nation had its eyes on the West; smallpox cleared the West for occupation. George Washington crossing the Delaware is a more comfortable image of nation building than smallpox stalking Indian lodges, but they are two sides of the same coin in explaining how the West became "American."

Epilogue

The Slave in the Chariot

In March 1806, as Lewis and Clark prepared to depart the Pacific Coast for the long trek back east, they handed out to visiting Indians "certificates of good deportment" and lists of the names of the men in their expedition. They hoped that "through the medium of some civilized person who may see the same, it may be made known to the informed world" that the men of the expedition had made it across the continent and were on their way home. Yankee ships operating on the coast had been instructed to rendezvous with Lewis and Clark and transport their expeditionary notes back to the United States, but Lewis and Clark thought the chances of the government ever obtaining a report "through the medium of the savages and the traders of this coast" were slim. But in July Indians came on board the American ship *Lydia* and delivered papers that "Capt. Clark Had Left with them declaring them Citizens of America." The *Lydia* carried Clark's letter to Canton and handed it on to another vessel, which then carried it back to Philadelphia.[1] The United States was beginning to enfold the West in arms that reached around the globe.

The last twenty-five years of the eighteenth century determined the future of the American West. Dwindling resources, foreign diversions, and the formidable power of the Osages, Comanches, Apaches, and Quechan league stalled the Spanish colonial advance. Meanwhile, the combined impact of revolution in the East and pandemic in the West changed America forever. The revolution that secured American independence from the British Empire produced an expansive republic whose vision of its own empire reached, ultimately, to the Pacific, where American maritime traders demonstrated and dominated the commercial opportunities available.

It was a different kind of empire—in Jefferson's words, an "empire of liberty." Instead of struggling to hold expansive forces in check, as the

British had done, or trying to defend an exposed frontier with limited military resources and fluctuating Indian policies, as Spain continued to do, the United States government followed, harnessed, and built a new nation on western land hunger. Its citizens participated in the process of empire building and enjoyed the fruits of empire in a way colonial peoples had never done under older imperial systems. The British Empire, as Anthony Wallace observes, was hierarchical and authoritarian but "ethnically inclusive." The Jeffersonian state was "egalitarian, democratic, and ethnically exclusive." Citizenship was reserved to "free white persons." African Americans were regarded as forever excluded. Indians, on the other hand, were eligible for inclusion if they gave up the things that made them Indian and adopted white American ways of living and thinking. The first step in that process was to relinquish their land. The American Revolution furnished the vision, the ideology, and the methodology for the new republic to build a new Western Empire.[2]

While the new nation poised itself to embrace the West, portentous events in the Far West warned of things to come. According to Native tradition, volcanic activity in the Cascade Mountains in the late eighteenth century prompted a Spokane Indian to prophesy that a "different kind of man" would soon come from the East and that after that the world would "fall to pieces."[3]

Seen from the perspective of a modern world power, the story has an inevitability about it. The chronological coincidence of revolution in the East and pandemic in the West, followed within a generation by the acquisition of Louisiana Territory, set the stage for the United States to realize its destiny and build an ocean-to-ocean republic. Contrary to what Hollywood would have us believe, Elliott West reminds us, the nineteenth-century American West "was not a particularly dangerous place to live—unless, of course, you were Indian." White pioneers who arrived in the wake of smallpox and other epidemics engaged in "heroic baby-making," and most of their babies survived. The Indians' high mortality rates and low fertility and the invaders' low mortality rates and high fertility meant that the outcome of the "breeding contest for control of the new country" was not long in doubt.[4]

To judge by most history books, public television documentaries, and popular culture, the "winning of the West" is the *real* history of the West; what went before is just prelude. But American history is not as short as it seems we would like it to be. The West that Lewis and Clark saw was not a pristine wilderness; it was a landscape that had evolved over millions of years and an environment that had been shaped by Indian and animal life for thousands of years. Crops, technologies, and rituals from Mesoamerica; flora and fauna, plagues, and peoples from Europe; and indigenous pioneers had all altered the West long before Lewis and Clark arrived. They saw an ecosystem in which abundances and scarcities of wildlife were determined by the repercussions on animal populations of human disease that thinned the ranks of human predators and intertribal warfare that created buffer zones where game flourished. Lewis and Clark did not see an unchanging West, they saw "a snapshot of time and place."[5] The dog-nomads whom Coronado's soldiers encountered on the southern plains in 1541 were the latest in a succession of peoples who had inhabited the area over thousands of years. When the Choctaw Indians were removed from their Mississippi homelands and resettled west of Arkansas Territory in what eventually became Indian Territory before becoming part of the state of Oklahoma, they were transported up the Arkansas River and disembarked a little more than a mile upstream from the Caddoan mounds at Spiro.[6] Lewis and Clark embarked on their trek west within miles of the site of Cahokia. Tribal stories linked the people to earlier civilizations, the "ancient ones"; clan stories traced their ancestry back to the animals. American history, as Calvin Martin observes, "is radically redefined when it begins with the shape of a bear."[7]

If American history west of the Mississippi "begins" with Lewis and Clark, then Indian history and, by extension, the history of the United States seems pretty simple: "Indians owned the West and then they lost it." But the story was never simple. People built societies, and societies changed over time. The people who survived dealt effectively with challenges from environment, drought, disease, population growth and decline, new and closed opportunities. They balanced tradition and innovation, weighed war and peace, and endured encounters with Indian, Spanish, French, British, and, eventually, American neighbors and newcomers. Some communities collapsed, and some peoples "disappeared" to the extent that they amalgamated with other peoples and remade themselves. Lewis and Clark did not enter an unchanging world inhabited by people ripe for conquest and victimization. They traversed different ecological, cultural, and linguistic zones and stepped through complex intertribal relations. Nations like the Blackfeet, Lakotas, Osages, and Comanches had established, were in the process of establishing, or were trying to hold onto impressive regional and interregional hegemonies. Other less powerful or less fortunately situated peoples like the Shoshones, Crows, and Pawnees saw the coming of Americans as an opportunity rather than a harbinger of disaster. The fact that some of the people Lewis and Clark met had "never seen a white man" did not mean they had not seen change.

The Lewis and Clark expedition occurred just two hundred years ago. By the time Lewis and Clark headed out from St. Louis, many of the people who had previously inhabited the West were gone. Some had died only a couple of years before when another smallpox epidemic swept the Missouri Valley. Others had been gone for centuries, and places like Mesa Verde and Cahokia that had once bustled with activity were long silent. In other places Indian inhabitants remained where they had lived from time beyond memory; it was the Spanish, French, and English, who had competed for their trade, their lands, their allegiance, or their souls, who had come and gone.

But the land now claimed by the United States bore the imprints of previous imperial efforts that had included and often promoted cultural mixings. Long before it became "American," the West was a land of combined races and cultures. Indians and Europeans who had lived together for generations produced mixed communities and people of mixed descent. Indian and European cultures produced a new Hispanic culture in the Southwest. Franco-Indian families and communities persisted in the Great Lakes, Louisiana, and the Midwest. Multicultural individuals, many of them former captives, moved along intersecting Indian and European exchange networks and webs of kinship relations built by their experiences.[8] In 1806 Thomas Freeman and Peter Custis described the settlers living on the banks of the Cane River near Natchitoches as a "mixture of French, Spanish, Indian, and Negro blood."[9] Across large stretches of the West, Natives had absorbed newcomers into their families, communities, and ways of life even as they adjusted to the newcomers and the changes they brought.

Now came the Americans. The Osages remembered seeing them on the left bank of the Mississippi, "chopping trees and building and plowing and swearing." They had hair on their faces like French voyageurs, "and soon the Little Ones were calling them Heavy Eyebrows as well, but knowing them to be Long Knives."[10] Jefferson did little to allay Osage apprehensions. He told Osage and other delegates in Washington in 1806 that the United States had peaceful intentions, but "we are strong, we are numerous as the stars in the heaven, and we are all gun-men."

As James Ronda notes, the image of "an American nation armed and on the move" was not lost on the Indians.[11] When Zebulon Pike and a party of Americans ascended the Mississippi in 1806, Indians went out of their way to avoid meeting them, having "the idea of our being a very vindictive, ferocious, and warlike people."[12] Lewis and Clark brought the promise of a new power in the West. Indian people recognized the new power as more aggressive than its predecessors but saw little to suggest that the newcomers would last any longer than those who had come and gone before.

Each Indian community, village, band, nation, tribe, and confederacy constituted, as it were, the hub of a wheel whose spokes connected it to other communities, tribes, nations, and often to European colonies and powers that impinged upon its world. At first, the arrival of Lewis and Clark and the Americans meant adding just another spoke to the wheel. But the changes would run deeper than that. James Ronda notes that when Lewis and Clark arrived on the Pacific Coast in December 1805 they came at the wrong time and from the wrong direction as far as Native peoples were concerned—they were accustomed to trading with traders from the sea in the spring and fall. But Lewis and Clark "wanted to reshape the landscape of time. Days and months once measured in seasons and salmon runs were now to be calculated by calendars and journal entries."[13]

Lewis and Clark reshaped time in other ways. By their feat they created a new calendar: American history in the West unfolded after Lewis and Clark; anything that happened before was B.L.C. (before Lewis and Clark). Millennia became concentrated into one "pre-American" time frame, and with it a nation's sense of its own ancient experiences became stunted or lost entirely. Did the people who inhabited Cahokia for seven hundred years think there would be a time when Cahokia no longer existed? Did the Anasazi and Hohokam who irrigated the deserts of the Southwest know that their systems and the way of life they supported would ultimately fail? Could the people who lived for thousands of years on buffalo or salmon ever have imagined that the source of their life could disappear or become polluted? American expansion and occupation of the West occurred in the blink of an eye, historically speaking. In the late nineteenth century buffalo were exterminated to make way for cattle, Indians were dispossessed to make way for ranchers and farmers. At the end of the twentieth century buffalo started returning, the cattle industry struggled to survive, and farming communities on the northern plains experienced population decline, while Indian populations in reservation communities increased to reach precontact levels. At the beginning of the twenty-first century, the American West has an economy and a way of life that depend on oil and water. But gauged against the long span of human history in the West, this way of life is still a baby; its chances of surviving its infancy are not good. Automobiles and oil may not be that different from horses and buffalo.

In 1997–98 massive floods and snowstorms hit the American West. The western United States had not been singled out for special treatment: all over the world the climate anomaly known as El Niño disrupted weather patterns and caused chaos. In the wake of El Niño scientists and historians gained new understanding of how the global weather system affects human societies and how short-term climate shifts have shaped history. After about 3000 B.C. people began living in more sedentary and concentrated farming societies. Populations grew, and they became more vulnerable to short-term climate changes such as El Niño. In 2180 B.C., for example, devastating droughts, triggered ultimately by interactions between the atmosphere and the ocean on the other side of the world, struck the Nile Valley and toppled the Old Kingdom of ancient Egypt. Fifteen hundred years ago the civilization of the Moche warrior-priests in northern Peru collapsed under the impact of droughts followed by torrential rains and flooding. A drought cycle gave the coup de grâce to a Mayan civilization that placed great stress on the fragile Central American lowlands. Throughout history climate changes have had catastrophic impacts on human societies. Faced with such catastrophes people had to make innovations or move away. "The lesson," concludes Brian Fagan, "is simple: The ultimate equation of history balances the needs of the population and the carrying capacity of the land. When carrying capacity is exceeded and technology or social engineering cannot restore the balance, all humanity can do is disperse—if there is the space to do so."[14]

There is no American exceptionalism. Charting the creation and subsequent decline of both Cheyenne and settler society in nineteenth-century Colorado, Elliott West says simply: "Everything passes, . . . no one escapes."[15] It's a simple reminder of the human condition and a simple lesson from history. But it's a lesson lost in American history if we look on Jamestown, Santa Fe, the American Revolution, and the Lewis and Clark expedition as opening chapters in a story of nation building and progress, a story that, because it is our story, we assume will be different from everybody else's. It won't. The cycles of history will continue as they always have, and, ultimately, the only truly exceptional thing about American history will be that it happened in America. The clues to America's long history lie on the ground and in the traditions and memories of its Native peoples; so perhaps do the clues to its likely future. The histories of Chaco, Cahokia, Caddos, Cheyennes, and Comanches are not just pieces in a prelude to the American story, an ancient, distant, and separate Native heritage that can be dismissed with a nod of approval or disdain in a page or two of text in our history books. Their stories are our story; they made choices that made sense at the time they made them but with long-term consequences they could not foresee. The people of Chaco built an impressive society in the Southwest in the tenth and eleventh centuries, but they failed to change course. Misuse of farmland, desperate straits that forced out small farmers, a loss of community, and an inability to deal with a catastrophic climate shift brought about the collapse of the Chaco world. "The parallels to modern America," notes David Stuart, "seem obvious."[16]

It is said that a victorious Roman general who returned in triumph and was given a victory parade through the Imperial City was accompanied by a slave who stood behind and to one side of the general in his chariot. To prevent the military hero from getting carried away by all the accolades, the slave from time to time would lean forward and whisper in the general's ear, reminding him that all this was transitory, that his moment of glory would pass. Nations, no less than Roman generals, need such reminders, perhaps this nation more than most. In many ways a historian is the slave in the chariot. Amid the tumult of national celebrations, monumental moments, and icons of national identity, historians need to remember and remind us that history does indeed work in cycles. No one gets to be top dog forever. In looking back to Chaco and Cahokia in the eleventh century and to the Comanches and Cheyennes in the eighteenth century, we should see our future as clearly as Hamlet saw his in Yorick's skull.[17] Two hundred years after Lewis and Clark, the voices of children are as absent in dead and dying farming towns on the northern plains as they are in the ruins of Mesa Verde. Buffalo are making a comeback. In contrast, some areas of California, the Southwest, and the Colorado Front Range seem to be on the verge of population strangulation. The Ogallala Aquifer is being drawn steadily down, and, if predictions of global climate change are even close to accurate, the West faces environmental challenges that will dwarf those the Anasazi confronted.[18] Recent events have exposed dramatically the fragility of our own power and prosperity. To borrow a term from the archaeology of the Old West, the United States might better be seen as a phase rather than a final solution.

The American West remains one vast winter count; we are adding our symbols, but the spiraling calendar continues.

Notes

Abbreviations

HNAI	William Sturtevant, gen. ed. *Handbook of North American Indians.* Washington DC: Smithsonian Institution Press, 1978–. Vol. 4: *Indian-White Relations*, ed. Wilcomb Washburn (1988). Vol. 6: *Subarctic*, ed. June Helm (1981). Vol. 7: *Northwest Coast*, ed. Wayne Suttles (1990). Vol. 8: *California*, ed. Robert F. Heizer (1978). Vols. 9–10: *Southwest*, ed. Alfonso Ortiz (1979, 1983). Vol. 11: *Great Basin*, ed. Warren L. D'Azevedo (1986). Vol. 12: *Plateau*, ed. Deward E. Walker Jr. (1998). Vol. 13: *Plains*, ed. Raymond J. DeMallie (2001). Vol. 15: *Northeast*, ed. Bruce G. Trigger (1978).
Presidio and Militia	Thomas H. Naylor and Charles W. Polzer, comps. and eds. *The Presidio and Militia on the Northern Frontier of New Spain: A Documentary History.* 2 vols. in 3. Vol. 1, *1570–1700*, comp. and ed. Thomas H. Naylor and Charles W. Polzer. Vol. 2, pt. 1, *The Californias and Sinaloa-Sonora, 1700–1765*, comp. and ed. Thomas H. Naylor and Charles W. Polzer. Vol. 2, pt. 2, *The Central Corridor and the Texas Corridor, 1700–1765*, comp. and ed. Diana Hadley, Thomas H. Naylor, and Mardith K. Schuetz-Miller. Tucson: University of Arizona Press, 1986–97.

SANM	Spanish Archives of New Mexico, 1621–1821. Microfilm reels. State of New Mexico Records Center, Santa Fe.
SMV	Lawrence Kinnaird, trans. and ed., *Spain in the Mississippi Valley, 1765–1794: Translations of Materials from the Spanish Archives in the Bancroft Library, University of California, Berkeley.* American Historical Association, Annual Report for the Year 1945 (Washington DC: American Historical Association, 1946–49). Vols. 2–4, pt. 1: *The Revolutionary Period, 1765–1781*; pt. 2: *The Post-War Decade, 1782–1791*; pt. 3: *Problems of Frontier Defense, 1792–1794.*
WHC	*Collections of the State Historical Society of Wisconsin.* 1855–1931. 31 vols.
WHC, 16, 17, 18	Reuben G. Thwaites, ed., *The French Regime in Wisconsin.* Vol. 1: *1634–1727* (*WHC,* 16); vol. 2: *1727–1748* (*WHC,* 17); vol. 3: *1743–1760* (*WHC,* 18).

Prologue: Land and History in the American West

1. Gary E. Moulton, ed., *The Journals of the Lewis and Clark Expedition,* 13 vols. (Lincoln: University of Nebraska Press, 1983–2001), 2: 153–54; Biloine Whiting Young and Melvin L. Fowler, *Cahokia: The Great Native American Metropolis* (Urbana: University of Illinois Press, 2000), 3. On Jefferson's interest in and attitudes toward Indians, see Anthony F. C. Wallace, *Jefferson and the Indians: The Tragic Fate of the First Americans* (Cambridge: Harvard University Press, 1999).

2. Peter Nabokov, *A Forest of Time: American Indian Ways of History* (Cambridge: Cambridge University Press, 2002).

3. Quoted in Raymond J. DeMallie and Douglas R. Parks, "Tribal Traditions and Records," in *HNAI,* 13: 1070. Eric R. Wolff, *Europe and the People without History* (Berkeley: University of California Press, 1982).

4. Richard White, *The Organic Machine* (New York: Hill and Wang, 1995), ix; Richard White and John Findlay, *Power and Place in the North American West* (Center for the Study of the Pacific Northwest in association with the University of Washington Press, 1999).

5. Howard Meredith, *Dancing on Common Ground: Tribal Cultures and Al-*

liances on the Southern Plains (Lawrence: University Press of Kansas, 1995), chap. 2, quote at 12.

6. On winter counts, see Garrick Mallery, *Picture-Writing of the American Indians,* Tenth Annual Report of the Bureau of American Ethnology, 1888–89 (Washington DC: GPO, 1893; reprint, 2 vols., New York: Dover, 1972), 266–328; James H. Howard, *Dakota Winter Counts as a Source of Plains History,* Smithsonian Institution, Bureau of American Ethnology, Bulletin 173, Anthropological Papers no. 61 (Washington DC: GPO, 1960), 335–416; Melburn D. Thurman, "Plains Indian Winter Counts and the New Ethnohistory," *Plains Anthropologist* 27 (1982): 173–75; Ronald T. McCoy, "Winter Count: The Teton Chronicles to 1700," Ph.D. diss., Northern Arizona University, 1983, 163–64. "Winter count" is a literal translation of the Sioux name *waníyetu yawápi*; see DeMallie and Parks, "Tribal Traditions and Records," in *HNAI,* 13: 1068.

7. John McPhee, *Basin and Range* (New York: Farrar, Straus and Giroux, 1980), 81.

8. Dan Flores, *Caprock Canyonlands* (Austin: University of Texas Press, 1990), 7–8; Tim Flannery, *The Eternal Frontier: An Ecological History of North America and Its Peoples* (New York: Atlantic Monthly Press, 2001), "a comprehensive record" quote at 39; John McPhee, *Rising from the Plains* (New York: Farrar, Straus and Giroux, 1986), 136–37. Wyoming geologist David Love was McPhee's guide through the geology of the state.

9. James D. Keyser and Michael A. Klassen, *Plains Indian Rock Art* (Seattle: University of Washington Press, 2001), quote at 5; Polly Schaafsma, *The Rock Art of Utah: A Study from the Donald Scott Collection* (1971; reprint, Salt Lake City: University of Utah Press, 1994); Julie E. Francis and Lawrence L. Loendorf, *Ancient Visions: Petroglyphs and Pictographs from the Wind River and Bighorn Country, Wyoming and Montana* (Salt Lake City: University of Utah Press, 2002).

10. Willa Cather, *Later Novels* (New York: Library of America, 1990), 216.

11. For instance, Timothy A. Kohler, "News from the North American Southwest: Prehistory on the Edge of Chaos," *Journal of Archaeological Research* 1 (1993): 267–321, surveys the developments and debates emanating from the northern Mogollon and Anasazi areas of the Southwest over just five years.

12. Roger C. Echo-Hawk, "Ancient History in the New World: Integrating Oral Traditions and the Archaeological Record," *American Antiquity* 65 (2000): 267–90.

13. Calvin Luther Martin, *The Way of the Human Being* (New Haven CT: Yale University Press, 1999), 3, 6.

14. Nabokov, *A Forest of Time,* chap. 5; Keith H. Basso, *Wisdom Sits in Places:*

Landscape and Language among the Western Apache (Albuquerque: University of New Mexico Press, 1996), 34.

15. Quoted in Alfonso Ortiz, "Introduction," in *HNAI*, 9: 1.

16. Paula Gunn Allen, "Iyani: It Goes This Way," quoted in Robert M. Nelson, *Place and Vision: The Function of Landscape in Native American Fiction* (New York: Peter Lang, 1993), 1.

17. Ruth M. Underhill, *Papago Woman* (Prospect Heights IL: Waveland Press, 1979), 3.

18. Raymond J. DeMallie, ed., *The Sixth Grandfather: Black Elk's Teachings Given to John G. Neihardt* (Lincoln: University of Nebraska Press, 1984), 69.

19. Robin Ridington, "Northern Hunters," in Alvin M. Josephy, ed., *America in 1492: The World of the Indian Peoples before the Arrival of Columbus* (New York: Alfred A. Knopf, 1992), 32.

20. Ancient Pueblo people, explains Laguna writer Leslie Marmon Silko, saw themselves and the world they inhabited as part of a continuous story made up of "innumerable bundles of other stories" ("Landscape, History, and the Pueblo Imagination," *Antaeus* 57 [fall 1986]: 83–94, esp. 87–90); see also Leslie Marmon Silko, *Yellow Woman and a Beauty of the Spirit: Essays on Native American Life Today* (New York: Simon and Schuster, 1996), 30–36.

21. Alfred C. Bowers, *Hidatsa Social and Ceremonial Organization*, Smithsonian Institution, Bureau of American Ethnology, Bulletin 194 (Washington DC: GPO, 1963; reprint, Lincoln: University of Nebraska Press, 1992), 2.

22. George A. Dorsey, *The Pawnee Mythology* (1906; reprint, Lincoln: University of Nebraska Press, 1997), 136; Gene Weltfish, *The Lost Universe: The Way of Life of the Pawnee* (New York: Ballantine Books, 1971), 10, 16, 97–98, 200, 207, 243; Douglas R. Parks, ed., *Ceremonies of the Pawnee by James R. Murie* (Lincoln: University of Nebraska Press, 1989), 39–42; Douglas R. Parks and Waldo R. Wedel, "Pawnee Geography: Historical and Sacred," *Great Plains Quarterly* 5 (1985): 143–76; Richard White, "The Cultural Landscape of the Pawnees," *Great Plains Quarterly* 2 (1982): 31–40.

23. Personal observation and conversation with Charles Lamb and Weldon Johnson of the Colorado Indian Tribes Museum, September 1986; Jefferson Reid and Stephanie Whittlesey, *The Archaeology of Ancient Arizona* (Tucson: University of Arizona Press, 1997), 125–27.

24. N. Scott Momaday, *The Man Made of Words* (New York: St. Martin's Press, 1997), 114.

25. Richard White, *Remembering Ahanagran: Storytelling in a Family's Past* (New York: Hill and Wang, 1998), 50.

26. Luther Standing Bear, *Land of the Spotted Eagle* (1933; reprint, Lincoln: University of Nebraska Press, 1978), 248.

27. Elaine Jahner, "Writing into the Political Winds," ms.

28. O. E. Rölvaag, *Giants in the Earth: A Saga of the Prairie,* introduction by Lincoln Colcord (New York: Harper and Row, 1927), quote at xi.

29. White, *The Organic Machine,* 22.

30. See, for example, Daniel J. Gelo, " 'Comanche Land and Ever Has Been': A Native Geography of the Nineteenth-Century Comanchería," *Southwestern Historical Quarterly* 111 (2000): 273–307, quote at 300.

31. G. Malcolm Lewis, ed., *Cartographic Encounters: Perspectives on Native American Mapmaking and Map Use* (Chicago: University of Chicago Press, 1998), 5n3, 18–19; Susan C. Vehik, "Oñate's Expedition to the Southern Plains: Routes, Destinations, and Implications for Late Prehistoric Cultural Adaptations," *Plains Anthropologist* 31 (1986): 13–33.

32. Mark Warhus, *Another America: Native American Maps and the History of Our Land* (New York: St. Martin's Press, 1997); William C. Foster, *Spanish Expeditions into Texas, 1689–1768* (Austin: University of Texas Press, 1995); Donald J. Blakeslee, *Along Ancient Trails: The Mallet Expedition of 1739* (Niwot: University Press of Colorado, 1995); Ralph A. Smith, trans. and ed., "Account of the Journey of Bénard de La Harpe: Discovery Made by Him of Several Nations Situated in the West," *Southwestern Historical Quarterly* 62 (1958–59): 253; E. E. Rich, ed., *Observations on Hudson's Bay by James Isham* (Toronto: Champlain Society for the Hudson's Bay Record Society, 1949), 65, 102; G. Malcolm Lewis, "Indian Maps: Their Place in the History of Plains Cartography," *Great Plains Quarterly* 4 (1984): 91–108, Truteau quote at 96.

33. Warhus, *Another America,* 2–3, 154–57; D. W. Moodie and Barry Kaye, "The Ac Ko Mok Ki Map," *Beaver* (spring 1977): 5–15; Barbara Belyea, "Inland Journeys, Native Maps," *Cartographica* 33 (summer 1996): 1–16, reprinted in Lewis, ed., *Cartographic Encounters,* 135–55; Barbara Belyea, "Mapping the Marias: The Interface of Native and Scientific Cartographies," *Great Plains Quarterly* 17 (summer–fall 1997): 165–84; Theodore Binnema, "How Does a Map Mean? Old Swan's Map of 1801 and the Blackfoot World," in Theodore Binnema, Gerhard J. Ens, and R. C. MacLeod, eds., *From Rupert's Land to Canada* (Edmonton: University of Alberta Press, 2001), 201–24.

34. James P. Ronda, " 'A Chart in His Way': Indian Cartography and the Lewis and Clark Expedition," *Great Plains Quarterly* 4 (1984): 43–53; Moulton, ed., *The Journals,* 5: 88. On the use of maps to dispossess Indians, see J. B. Harley, "Victims of a Map: New England Cartography and the Native Americans," in Emerson Baker et al., eds., *American Beginnings: Exploration, Culture, and Cartography in the Land of Norumbega* (Lincoln: University of Nebraska Press, 1994). Early maps of the West are compiled in Carl I. Wheat, *Mapping the Transmississippi West 1540–1861. I: The Spanish Entrada to the Louisiana Purchase, 1540–1804* (San Francisco: Institute of Historical Cartography, 1957).

35. Barbara Belyea, "Amerindian Maps: The Explorer as Translator," *Journal of Historical Geography* 18 (1992): 267–77; Belyea, "Inland Journeys, Native

Maps"; Peter Nabokov, "Orientations from Their Side: Dimensions of Native American Cartographic Discourse," in Lewis, ed., *Cartographic Encounters,* 241–69; Warhus, *Another America,* 3–4.

36. Belyea, "Inland Journeys, Native Maps," 7.

37. Dan Flores, *The Natural West: Environmental History in the Great Plains and Rocky Mountains* (Norman: University of Oklahoma Press, 2001), 153–54.

38. See, for example, Tracey Neal Leavelle, "Geographies of Encounter: Christianity, Space, and Order in French and Indian North America," ms.

39. José Rabasa, *Writing Violence on the Northern Frontier: The Historiography of Sixteenth-Century New Mexico and Florida and the Legacy of Conquest* (Durham NC: Duke University Press, 2000), 20–21.

40. *Presidio and Militia,* 2, pt. 1: 2–7, 253; 2, pt. 2: 10–12, 17.

41. William Cronon, George Miles, and Jay Gitlin, eds., *Under an Open Sky: Rethinking America's Western Past* (New York: W. W. Norton, 1992), 6.

42. Quoted in Thomas Bailey and David Kennedy, *American Pageant* (Lexington KY: D. C. Heath, 1991), 284.

43. Wallace Stegner, "Thoughts in a Dry Land," in *Where the Bluebird Sings to the Lemonade Springs: Living and Writing in the West* (New York: Penguin, 1992), 45–46.

44. Jahner, "Writing into the Political Winds."

45. Flannery, *The Eternal Frontier,* 85–86.

46. Momaday, *The Man Made of Words,* 91.

47. See, for example, Timothy Egan, *Lasso the Wind: Away to the New West* (New York: Alfred A. Knopf, 1998).

48. Patricia Nelson Limerick, *Something in the Soil: Legacies and Reckonings in the New West* (New York: W. W. Norton, 2000), 192.

49. Richard White, *"It's Your Misfortune and None of My Own": A New History of the American West* (Norman: University of Oklahoma Press, 1991); Walter Nugent, *Into the West: The Story of Its People* (New York: Alfred A. Knopf, 1999). Clyde A. Milner II, Ann Butler, and David Rich Lewis, eds., *Major Problems in the History of the American West,* 2nd ed. (Lexington KY: D. C. Heath, 1997) devotes about 10 percent of the documents to the centuries before 1800.

50. Ray Allen Billington, *Westward Expansion: A History of the American Frontier* (New York: Macmillan, 1949); Bernard DeVoto, *The Course of Empire* (1952; reprint, Boston: Houghton Mifflin, 1980).

51. Henry David Thoreau, *The Maine Woods* (1864; reprint, New York: Penguin, 1988), 105–6.

52. Martin, *The Way of the Human Being,* 138.

53. Echo-Hawk, "Ancient History in the New World."

54. Reid and Whittlesey, *The Archaeology of Ancient Arizona,* 205–20.

55. Ralph Waldo Emerson, "History," in *Self-Reliance and Other Essays* (New York: Dover, 1993), 17.

56. White, *Remembering Ahanagran*, 40.

57. David E. Stuart, *Anasazi America: Seventeen Centuries on the Road from Center Place* (Albuquerque: University of New Mexico Press, 2000), offers explicit parallels between conditions leading to the collapse of Chacoan society and conditions in modern American society.

1. Pioneers

1. George C. Frison, *Prehistoric Hunters of the High Plains*, 2nd ed. (San Diego: Academic Press, 1991), 39–40.

2. Daniel T. Reff, ed., *History of the Triumphs of Our Holy Faith amongst the Most Barbarous and Fierce Peoples of the New World by Andrés Pérez de Ribas: An English Translation Based on the 1645 Spanish Original* (Tucson: University of Arizona Press, 1999), 98–99.

3. L. E. Huddleston, *Origins of the American Indians: European Concepts, 1492–1729* (Austin: University of Texas Press, 1967).

4. E. C. Pielou, *After the Ice Age: The Return of Life to Glaciated North America* (Chicago: University of Chicago Press, 1991), 2, 91–96; Tim Flannery, *The Eternal Frontier: An Ecological History of North America and Its Peoples* (New York: Atlantic Monthly Press, 2001), 149–50 (estimates of ice coverage).

5. Flannery, *The Eternal Frontier*, 146.

6. Pielou, *After the Ice Age*, 186–87, 193.

7. Donald K. Grayson, *The Desert's Past: A Natural Prehistory of the Great Basin* (Washington DC: Smithsonian Institution Press, 1993), 77, 85–96.

8. For a discussion of McNickle's life and works, see Dorothy R. Parker, *Singing an Indian Song: A Biography of D'Arcy McNickle* (Lincoln: University of Nebraska Press, 1992).

9. D'Arcy McNickle, *They Came Here First: The Epic of the American Indian* (Philadelphia: J. B. Lippincott, 1949), 15–19.

10. N. Scott Momaday, "The Becoming of the Native: Man in America before Columbus," in Alvin M. Josephy, ed., *America in 1492: The World of the Indian Peoples before the Arrival of Columbus* (New York: Alfred A. Knopf, 1992), 15.

11. N. Scott Momaday, *The Way to Rainy Mountain* (Albuquerque: University of New Mexico Press, 1969), 17.

12. Raymond J. DeMallie and Douglas R. Parks, "Tribal Traditions and Records," in *HNAI*, 13: 1065.

13. George A. Dorsey, *The Mythology of the Wichita* (1904; reprint, Norman: University of Oklahoma Press, 1995), 25–29.

14. Howard Harrod, *The Animals Came Dancing: Native American Sacred Ecology and Animal Kinship* (Tucson: University of Arizona Press, 2000), 38–40; Douglas R. Parks, ed., *Ceremonies of the Pawnee by James R. Murie* (Lincoln:

University of Nebraska Press, 1989), 38–39, 43–51; Gene Weltfish, *The Lost Universe: The Way of Life of the Pawnee* (New York: Ballantine Books, 1971), 78.

15. John J. Mathews, *The Osages: Children of the Middle Waters* (Norman: University of Oklahoma Press, 1961), 7–19; Garrick A. Bailey, *Changes in Osage Social Organization, 1673–1906*, University of Oregon Anthropological Papers no. 5 (1973), 10–13.

16. Aileen O'Bryan, *The Diné: Origin Myths of the Navaho Indians*, Smithsonian Institution, Bureau of American Ethnology, Bulletin 163 (Washington DC: GPO, 1956), 1–13; Ethelou Yazzie, ed., *Navajo History*, vol. 1 (Rough Rock AZ: Rough Rock Press, formerly Navajo Curriculum Center, 1971); Washington Matthews, comp. and trans., *Navaho Legends* (1897; reprint, Salt Lake City: University of Utah Press, 1994), 62–159; Paul Zolbrod, *Diné bahane': The Navajo Creation Story* (Albuquerque: University of New Mexico Press, 1984), 35; Jerrold E. Levy, *In the Beginning: The Navajo Genesis* (Berkeley: University of California Press, 1998), chaps. 3–4.

17. Harrod, *The Animals Came Dancing*, 23.

18. Robert H. Lowie, *The Crow Indians* (New York: Farrar and Rinehart, 1935), 122–31; Harrod, *The Animals Came Dancing*, 27–30.

19. Ella E. Clark, *Indian Legends from the Northern Rockies* (Norman: University of Oklahoma Press, 1966), 235–39.

20. Rebecca Tsosie, "Indigenous Rights and Archaeology," in Nina Swidler, Kurt E. Dongoske, Roger Anyon, and Alan S. Downer, eds., *Native Americans and Archaeologists: Stepping Stones to Common Ground* (Walnut Creek CA: Altamira Press, 1997), 66; Vine Deloria Jr., *Red Earth, White Lies: Native Americans and the Myth of Scientific Fact* (New York: Scribner's, 1995), chap. 4.

21. See, for example, Alan Lyle Bryan, ed., *New Evidence for the Pleistocene Peopling of the Americas* (Orono: University of Maine Center for the Study of Early Man, 1986).

22. David Hurst Thomas, *Exploring Native North America* (New York: Oxford University Press, 2000), 19–29; Jack L. Hofman and Russell W. Graham, "The Paleo-Indian Cultures of the Great Plains," in W. Raymond Wood, ed., *Archaeology on the Great Plains* (Lawrence: University Press of Kansas, 1998), 87–139. Radiocarbon dates for Clovis points in the West range from about 11,500 to about 10,900 B.P. Calibrating radiocarbon dates into calendar years produces an estimate of about 13,400 to 13,000 years ago, although calibrations of radiocarbon dates, and hence the age of Clovis points, remains an issue of some dispute (Robert L. Kelly, personal communication, May 3, 2002).

23. Thomas D. Dillehay, *The Settlement of the Americas: A New Prehistory* (New York: Basic Books, 2000).

24. D. J. Melzer et al., "On the Pleistocene Antiquity of Monte Verde, Southern Chile," *American Antiquity* 62 (1997): 659–63; Dillehay, *The Settle-*

ment of the Americas; Brian M. Fagan, *Ancient North America: The Archaeology of a Continent*, 3rd ed. (London: Thames and Hudson, 2000), 77n, 81. Stuart J. Fiedel, "Older than We Thought: Implications of Corrected Dates for Paleoindians," *American Antiquity* 64, no. 1 (1999): 95–115, disputes Dillehay.

25. David Hurst Thomas, *Skull Wars: Kennewick Man, Archaeology, and the Battle for Native American Identity* (New York: Basic Books, 2000); James C. Chatters, *Ancient Encounters: Kennewick Man and the First Americans* (New York: Simon and Schuster, 2001).

26. K. Fladmark, "Routes: Alternate Migration Corridors for Early Man in North America," *American Antiquity* 44 (1979): 55–69; E. James Dixon, *Bones, Boats, and Bison: Archaeology and the First Colonization of Western North America* (Albuquerque: University of New Mexico Press, 1999).

27. Robert N. Zeitlin and Judith Francis Zeitlin, "The Paleoindian and Archaic Cultures of Mesoamerica," in Richard E. W. Adams and Murdo J. MacLeod, eds., *The Cambridge History of the Native Peoples of the Americas*, vol. 2, *Mesoamerica* (Cambridge: Cambridge University Press, 2000), pt. 1: 51–53.

28. Roger C. Echo-Hawk, "Ancient History in the New World: Integrating Oral Traditions and the Archaeological Record in Deep Time," *American Antiquity* 65 (2000): 267–90, esp. 273–78; Roger C. Echo-Hawk, "Forging a New Ancient History for Native America," in Swidler et al., eds., *Native Americans and Archaeologists*, 88–102, esp. 96–100.

29. Harrod, *The Animals Came Dancing*, 43.

30. Frison, *Prehistoric Hunters*, 143–49.

31. George C. Frison and Lawrence C. Todd, *The Colby Mammoth Site: Taphonomy and Archaeology of a Clovis Kill in Northern Wyoming* (Albuquerque: University of New Mexico Press, 1986).

32. Pielou, *After the Ice Age*, 228–29.

33. See, for example, the essays in Paul S. Martin and Richard G. Klein, eds., *Quaternary Extinctions: A Prehistoric Revolution* (Tucson: University of Arizona Press, 1984). Tables listing the species that became extinct are at 361–64.

34. Donald J. Grayson, "Late Pleistocene Mammalian Extinctions in North America: Taxonomy, Chronology and Explanations," *Journal of World Prehistory* 5 (1991): 193–231, provides a full discussion of the various interpretations and the weight of evidence favoring climate change as the root cause of the extinctions. His review is updated in Donald J. Grayson, "The Archaeological Record of Human Impacts on Animal Populations," *Journal of World Prehistory* 15 (2001): 1–68. Grayson rejects the "overkill credo" as a statement of faith based on extinction patterns in island environments and lacking support in the archaeological and paleontological record in continental North America. Flannery, on the other hand, prefers the Clovis interpretation (*The Eternal Frontier*, chaps. 14–15).

35. John H. Blitz, "Adoption of the Bow in Prehistoric North America," *North American Archaeologist* 9 (1988): 123–45.

36. David S. Whitley, *The Art of the Shaman: Rock Art of California* (Salt Lake City: University of Utah Press, 2000), 39, 110.

37. Frison, *Prehistoric Hunters,* 140, 297–98.

38. Frison, *Prehistoric Hunters,* 139–43; Robin Ridington, "Northern Hunters," in Josephy, ed., *America in 1492,* 25.

39. Calvin Luther Martin, *The Way of the Human Being* (New Haven CT: Yale University Press, 1999); Ridington, "Northern Hunters," 21–47, quote at 25.

40. Harrod, *The Animals Came Dancing*; Adrian Tanner, *Bringing Home Animals: Religious Ideology and Mode of Production of the Mistassini Cree Hunters* (New York: St. Martin's Press, 1979), 108–81; Ridington, "Northern Hunters," 21–47. For a critique of the idea of the Indian as ecologist, see Shepard Krech III, *The Ecological Indian: Myth and History* (New York: W. W. Norton, 1999).

41. Levy, *In the Beginning,* 84–93; Joseph Bruchac, *The Wind Eagle and Other Abenaki Stories* (Greenfield Center NY: Bowman Books, 1985), 5–7.

42. Harrod, *The Animals Came Dancing,* 60–70.

43. Harrod, *The Animals Came Dancing,* 98–104.

44. George Bird Grinnell, *Pawnee, Blackfoot, and Cheyenne: History and Folklore of the Plains from the Writings of George Bird Grinnell* (New York: Scribner's, 1961), 121–24; Howard L. Harrod, *Renewing the World: Plains Indian Religion and Morality* (Tucson: University of Arizona Press, 1987), 44, 55, 132–33, 164–65.

45. Frank Gilbert Roe, *The North American Buffalo: A Critical Study of the Species in Its Wild State* (Toronto: University of Toronto Press, 1970; reprint, London: David and Charles, 1972), 204.

46. Liz Bryan, *The Buffalo People: Prehistoric Archaeology on the Canadian Plains* (Edmonton: University of Alberta Press, 1991), 32.

47. Flannery, *The Eternal Frontier,* 320.

48. Theodore Binnema, *Common and Contested Ground: A Human and Environmental History of the Northwestern Plains* (Norman: University of Oklahoma Press, 2001), chap. 1.

49. Dan Flores, "Bison Ecology and Bison Diplomacy: The Southern Plains 1800–1850," *Journal of American History* 78 (1991): 469; Tom D. Dillehay, "Late Quaternary Bison Population Changes of the Southern Plains," *Plains Anthropologist* 19 (1974): 180–96; Darrell Creel, "Bison Hides in Late Prehistoric Exchange in the Southern Plains," *American Antiquity* 56 (1991): 40–49; Jeffrey A. Huebner, "Late Prehistoric Bison Populations in Central and Southern Texas," *Plains Anthropologist* 36 (1991): 343–58.

50. Rolena Adorno and Patrick Charles Pautz, *Álvar Núñez Cabeza de Vaca: His Account, His Life, and the Expedition of Pánfilo de Narváez,* 3 vols. (Lincoln: University of Nebraska Press, 1999), 1: 147.

51. Dolores A. Gunnerson, "Man and Bison on the Plains in the Protohistoric Period," *Plains Anthropologist* 17 (1972): 1–10.

52. Charles A. Reher, "Buffalo Population and Other Deterministic Factors in a Model of Adaptive Process on the Shortgrass Plains," *Plains Anthropologist* 23 (1978): pt. 2: 23–39; Charles A. Reher, "Adaptive Process on the Shortgrass Plains," in Lewis R. Binford, ed., *For Theory Building in Archaeology* (New York: Academic Press, 1977), 13–40; John R. Bozell, "Culture, Environment, and Bison Populations on the Late Prehistoric and Early Historic Central Plains," *Plains Anthropologist* 40 (1995): 145–63.

53. Andrew C. Isenberg, *The Destruction of the Bison: An Environmental History, 1750–1920* (Cambridge: Cambridge University Press, 2000), 23–25.

54. Waldo R. Wedel, *Central Plains Prehistory: Holocene Environments and Culture Change in the Republican River Basin* (Lincoln: University of Nebraska Press, 1986), 123.

55. Binnema, *Common and Contested Ground*, 61.

56. Roe, *The North American Buffalo*, dismissed the notion of mass migrations of buffalo herds, but the evidence supports a pattern of seasonal dispersal and congregation; Binnema, *Common and Contested Ground*, chap. 2; Douglas B. Bamforth, "Historical Documents and Bison Ecology on the Great Plains," *Plains Anthropologist* 32 (1987): 1–16.

57. Leslie B. Davis and Michael Wilson, eds., "Bison Procurement and Utilization: A Symposium," *Plains Anthropologist* 23 (1978): pt. 2; Philip Duke, *Points in Time: Structure and Event in a Late Northern Plains Hunting Society* (Niwot: University Press of Colorado, 1999), 89, 97, 131; George C. Frison, "The Northwestern and Northern Plains Archaic," in Wood, ed., *Archaeology on the Great Plains*, 140–72; Frison, *Prehistoric Hunters*, 155–234.

58. Leland C. Bement, *Bison Hunting at Cooper Site: Where Lightning Bolts Drew Thundering Herds* (Norman: University of Oklahoma Press, 1999), esp. 37–39, 101, 176–77, 180 for the painted skull.

59. Joe Ben Wheat, *The Olson-Chubbock Site: A Paleo-Indian Bison Kill*, Memoirs of the Society for American Archaeology no. 26 (1972).

60. James D. Keyser and Michael A. Klassen, *Plains Indian Rock Art* (Seattle: University of Washington Press, 2001), chap. 6; Polly Schaafsma, *The Rock Art of Utah: A Study from the Donald Scott Collection* (1971; reprint, Salt Lake City: University of Utah Press, 1994), 147.

61. Frison, *Prehistoric Hunters*, 200–208; George C. Frison, "The Buffalo Pound in Northwestern Plains Prehistory, Site 48CA302," *American Antiquity* 36 (1971): 77–91.

62. Frison, *Prehistoric Hunters*, 226–27; Charles A. Reher and George C. Frison, "The Vore Site, 48CK302: A Stratified Buffalo Jump in the Wyoming Black Hills," *Plains Anthropologist* 25 (1980): pt. 2: 19 (skulls), quote at 136.

63. Thomas, *Exploring Native North America*, 52–55; Frison, *Prehistoric Hunt-*

ers, 219–20; Lawrence J. Burpee, ed., "An Adventurer from Hudson's Bay: The Journal of Matthew Cocking," *Proceedings and Transactions of the Royal Society of Canada*, 3rd series, 2 (1908): sec. 2: 108–11.

64. Peigan is the Canadian spelling, Piegan the American.

65. Brian O. K. Reeves, "Head-Smashed-In: 5500 Years of Bison Jumping in the Alberta Plains," *Plains Anthropologist* 23 (1978): pt. 2: 151–74; Thomas, *Exploring Native North America*, 52–61.

66. Joe Medicine Crow, "Notes on Crow Indian Buffalo Jump Traditions," *Plains Anthropologist* 23 (1978): pt. 2: 249–53.

67. Frison, "The Northwestern and Northern Plains Archaic," 149, 151–52.

68. Frison, *Prehistoric Hunters*, 298–325.

69. George C. Frison, ed., *The Mill Iron Site* (Albuquerque: University of New Mexico Press, 1996), 209–10; Frison, *Prehistoric Hunters*, chaps. 4, 7; Caroline R. Hudecek-Cuffe, *Engendering Northern Plains Paleoindian Archaeology: Decision-Making and Gender Roles in Subsistence and Settlement Strategies*, British Archaeological Report Series no. 699, Oxford University (1998), 47–48, 66–76; Douglas B. Bamforth, "The Technological Organization of Paleo-Indian Small-Group Bison Hunting on the Llano Estacado," *Plains Anthropologist* 30 (1985): 243–85.

70. Patrick M. Lubinski and Vicki Herren, "An Introduction to Pronghorn Biology, Ethnography, and Archaeology," and Linea Sundstrom, "Cheyenne Pronghorn Procurement and Ceremony," both in Jana V. Pastor and Patrick M. Lubinski, eds., *Pronghorn Past and Present: Archaeology, Ethnography, and Biology, Plains Anthropologist* 45 (memoir 32) (2000): 3–11, 119–32; Grayson, *The Desert's Past*, 38.

71. For an exception and an example of how feminist gender studies can restore the people behind the artifacts, see Janet D. Spector, *What This Awl Means: Feminist Archaeology at a Wahpeton Dakota Village* (Saint Paul: Minnesota Historical Society, 1993).

72. Hudecek-Cuffe, *Engendering Northern Plains Paleoindian Archaeology*; Marcel Kornfeld, ed., "Approaches to Gender Processes on the Great Plains," *Plains Anthropologist* 36 (1991): 1–7; Todd R. Guenther, "The Horse Creek Site: Some Evidence for Gender Roles in a Transitional Early to Middle Plains Archaic Base Camp," *Plains Anthropologist* 36 (1991): 9–23; M. Gero, "Genderlithics: Women's Roles in Stone Tool Production," in Joan M. Gero and Margaret W. Conkey, eds., *Engendering Archaeology: Women and Prehistory* (Oxford: Basil Blackwell, 1991), 163–93; Christine R. Szuter, "Gender and Animals: Hunting Technology, Ritual, and Subsistence," in Patricia L. Crown, ed., *Women and Men in the Prehispanic Southwest: Labor, Power, and Prestige* (Santa Fe NM: School of American Research Press, 2001), chap. 6; Alice Kehoe, "The Shackles of Tradition," in Patricia Albers and Beatrice Medicine, eds., *The*

Hidden Half: Studies of Plains Indian Women (Lanham MD: University Press of America, 1983), 66–69.

73. Jon L. Gibson, *The Ancient Mounds of Poverty Point: Place of Rings* (Gainesville: University Press of Florida, 2000).

74. Thomas, *Exploring Native North America*, 94–105.

75. Kenneth M. Ames and Herbert D. G. Maschner, *Peoples of the Northwest Coast: Their Archaeology and Prehistory* (London: Thames and Hudson, 1999), 13–15, 24–29.

76. Ames and Maschner, *Peoples of the Northwest Coast*, 17.

77. Ames and Maschner, *Peoples of the Northwest Coast*, 81, 88.

78. Julie K. Stein, *Exploring Coast Salish Prehistory: The Archaeology of San Juan Island* (Seattle: University of Washington Press, 2000).

79. Fagan, *Ancient North America*, 213–16, 223–31; Thomas, *Exploring Native North America*, chap. 6; Janine Bowechop, "The Makah Tribe and the Archaeological Community: A Thirty-Year Perspective," paper presented at the symposium "On the Threshold: Native American–Archaeologist Relations in the Twenty-First Century," Dartmouth College, May 2001; Gary Wessen, "Prehistory of the Ocean Coast of Washington," in *HNAI*, 7: 415–16, 419; Ann M. Renker and Erna Gunther, "Makah," in *HNAI*, 7: 425–26.

80. Ames and Maschner, *Peoples of the Northwest Coast*, chap. 8; Robert H. Ruby and John A. Brown, *The Chinook Indians: Traders of the Lower Columbia River* (Norman: University of Oklahoma Press, 1976), 21–22; Robert H. Ruby and John A. Brown, *Indian Slavery in the Pacific Northwest* (Spokane WA: Arthur H. Clark, 1993).

81. Gordon W. Hewes, "Fishing," in *HNAI*, 12: 620–40, quote at 620, map of fishing sites at 621.

82. Robert Boyd, ed., *Indians, Fire and the Land in the Pacific Northwest* (Corvallis: Oregon State University Press, 1999).

83. Richard D. Daugherty, "People of the Salmon," in Josephy, ed., *America in 1492*, 54–55; Richard White, *The Organic Machine* (New York: Hill and Wang, 1995), 15–18; Fagan, *Ancient North America*, 232–34; Ames and Maschner, *Peoples of the Northwest Coast*, 23, 83, 115, 127, 171. For descriptions and maps of The Dalles area as it was when Lewis and Clark passed through in 1805, see Gary E. Moulton, ed., *The Journals of the Lewis and Clark Expedition*, 13 vols. (Lincoln: University of Nebraska Press, 1983–2001), 1: map 78; 5: 328–33; 9: 242–43; 10: 155. Joseph Whitehouse noted Indian fishing stations the length of the Columbia and recorded the expedition's dependence on dried fish obtained from Indians; see Moulton, ed., *The Journals*, 11: 359, 362–67, 393, 400, 408, 430.

84. Theodore Stern, "Columbia River Trade Network," in *HNAI*, 12: 641–52, map at 642; Silvester L. Lahren Jr., "Kalispel," in *HNAI*, 12: 283; Hewes, "Fishing," in *HNAI*, 12: 623–24.

85. William L. Lang and Robert C. Carriker, eds., *Great River of the West: Essays on the Columbia River* (Seattle: University of Washington Press, 1999), 147.

86. Richard M. Pettigrew, "Prehistory of the Lower Columbia and Willamette Valley," in *HNAI*, 7: 523–25.

87. Franz Boas, *Folktales of the Salishan and Sahaptin Tribes*, American Folklore Society, memoir 11 (1917), 101; see also Clark, *Indian Legends from the Northern Rockies*, 82–86. I am grateful to my colleague Dan Runnels for the Beaver story and for many other insights into Native history on the Columbia.

88. Bill Reid and Robert Bringhurst, *The Raven Steals the Light* (Seattle: University of Washington Press, 1984), 19–23.

89. Sean L. Swezey and Robert F. Heizer, "Ritual Management of Salmonid Fish Resources in California," *Journal of California Anthropology* 4 (1977): 7–29, reprinted in Thomas C. Blackburn and Kat Anderson, eds., *Before the Wilderness: Environmental Management by Native Californians* (Menlo Park CA: Ballena Press, 1993), 299–327.

90. Moulton, ed., *The Journals*, 7: 142.

91. Judith Roche and Meg Hutchison, eds., *First Fish, First People: Salmon Tales of the North Pacific Rim* (Seattle: University of Washington Press, 1998); Robert Bringhurst, *A Story as Sharp as a Knife: The Classical Haida Mythtellers and Their World* (Vancouver: Douglas and McIntyre, 1999), 65, 120, 155, 288–89; White, *The Organic Machine*, 18–20.

92. Bringhurst, *A Story as Sharp as a Knife*, 120.

93. [Josef Espinosa y Tello], *A Spanish Voyage to Vancouver and the Northwest Coast of America*, trans. Cecil Jane (London: Argonaut Press, 1930), 106–7.

94. Fagan, *Ancient North America*, 234–35.

95. Karen Olsen Bruhns and Karen E. Stothert, *Women in Ancient America* (Norman: University of Oklahoma Press, 1999), 66–70; Thomas L. Jackson, "Pounding Acorn: Women's Production as Social and Economic Focus," in Gero and Conkey, eds., *Engendering Archaeology*, 301–25.

96. William F. Shipley, "Native Languages of California," in *HNAI*, 8: 80–90, provides lists of the region's languages.

97. Fagan, *Ancient North America*, 234–50; Blackburn and Anderson, eds., *Before the Wilderness.*

98. Helen McCarthy, "Managing Oaks and the Acorn Crop," in Blackburn and Anderson, eds., *Before the Wilderness*, 213–28.

99. Henry T. Lewis, "Patterns of Indian Burning in California: Ecology and Ethnohistory," and Jan Timbrook, John R. Johnson, and David D. Earle, "Vegetation Burning by the Chumash," both in Blackburn and Anderson, eds., *Before the Wilderness*, 55–116, 117–49; Herbert E. Bolton, trans. and ed., *Spanish Exploration in the Southwest, 1542–1706* (New York: Barnes and Noble, 1967), 24, 33, 80.

100. Rose Marie Beebe and Robert M. Senkewicz, eds., *Lands of Promise and Despair: Chronicles of Early California, 1535–1846* (Santa Clara and Berkeley: Santa Clara University and Heyday Books, 2001), 45.

101. Blackburn and Anderson, eds., *Before the Wilderness*, 15–54; Florence C. Shipek, "A Native American Adaptation to Drought: The Kumeyaay as Seen in the San Diego Mission Records, 1778–1798," *Ethnohistory* 28 (1981): 298; Florence C. Shipek, "An Example of Intensive Plant Husbandry: The Kumeyaay of Southern California," in David R. Harris and Gordon C. Hillman, eds., *Farming and Foraging: The Evolution of Plant Exploitation* (London: Unwin Hyman, 1989), 159–70; Florence C. Shipek, "Kumeyaay Plant Husbandry: Fire, Water, and Erosion Control Systems," in Blackburn and Anderson, eds., *Before the Wilderness*, 379–88. On plant husbandry more generally, see William E. Doolittle, *Cultivated Landscapes of North America* (New York: Oxford University Press, 2000), chaps. 2–3.

102. On shell beads, see Chester King, "Protohistoric and Historic Archaeology," in HNAI, 8: 58–62.

103. Grayson, *The Desert's Past*, 8, 34–40, 258; Martha C. Knack, *Boundaries Between: The Southern Paiutes, 1775–1995* (Lincoln: University of Nebraska Press, 2001), chap. 2; Fagan, *Ancient North America*, chap. 12; Catherine S. Fowler, "Subsistence," in HNAI, 11: 64–97, provides lists of the plants, animals, and fishes harvested by Great Basin peoples. Catherine S. Fowler and Lawrence E. Dawson, "Ethnographic Basketry," in HNAI, 11: 705–37, survey the various types of baskets developed.

104. Grayson, *The Desert's Past*, 258–71; John P. Marwitt, "Fremont Cultures," in HNAI, 11: 161–72.

105. Richard E. Hughes and James A. Bennyhoff, "Early Trade," in HNAI, 11: 238–55.

106. Frison, *Prehistoric Hunters*; L. Adrian Hannus, "Cultures of the Heartland: Beyond the Black Hills," in Karl H. Schlesier, ed., *Plains Indians, A.D. 500–1500: The Archaeological Past of Historical Groups* (Norman: University of Oklahoma Press, 1994), 179, 184–90; Blitz, "Adoption of the Bow."

107. Echo-Hawk, "Ancient History in the New World," 283–85; Schlesier, ed., *Plains Indians*, 308–81; Jeffrey R. Hanson, "The Late High Plains Hunters," in Wood, ed., *Archaeology on the Great Plains*, 456; Tanis C. Thorne, *The Many Hands of My Relations: French and Indians on the Lower Missouri* (Columbia: University of Missouri Press, 1996), 62.

108. Robert L. Kelly and Lawrence C. Todd, "Coming into the Country: Early Paleoindian Hunting and Mobility," *American Antiquity* 53 (1988): 231–44.

109. Patricia J. O'Brien, "The Central Lowland Plains: An Overview, A.D. 500–1500," in Schlesier, ed., *Plains Indians*, 201; Wedel, *Central Plains Prehistory*, 42–45.

110. Susan C. Vehik, "Cultural Continuity and Discontinuity in the Southern Prairies and Cross Timbers," in Schlesier, ed., *Plains Indians,* 239–63.

111. Vehik, "Cultural Continuity," 246–49; Timothy G. Baugh, "Holocene Adaptations in the Southern High Plains," in Schlesier, ed., *Plains Indians,* 279–80; Richard R. Drass, "The Southern Plains Villagers," in Wood, ed., *Archaeology on the Great Plains,* 418–22; Robert E. Bell and Robert L. Brooks, "Plains Village Tradition: Southern," in *HNAI,* 13: 213–15.

112. Vehik, "Cultural Continuity," 250–51; Baugh, "Holocene Adaptations," 283–85.

113. Drass, "The Southern Plains Villagers," 446–47.

114. Echo-Hawk, "Ancient History in the New World," quote at 274.

115. William W. Warren, *History of the Ojibwa People* (Saint Paul: Minnesota Historical Society, 1984), 76–82.

116. James V. Wright, "Prehistory of the Canadian Shield," in *HNAI,* 6: 86–96; Karl H. Schlesier, *The Wolves of Heaven: Cheyenne Shamanism, Ceremonies, and Prehistoric Origins* (Norman: University of Oklahoma Press, 1987), 43–44, 111, 164–66.

117. Schlesier, *The Wolves of Heaven,* 43–44, Cheyenne tradition quote at 51, Bent quote at 76; John Stands in Timber and Margot Liberty, *Cheyenne Memories* (Lincoln: University of Nebraska Press, 1972), 13.

118. J. Loring Haskell, *Southern Athapaskan Migration,* A.D. *200–1750* (Tsaile AZ: Navajo Community College Press, 1987); Richard J. Perry, "The Apachean Transition from the Subarctic to the Southwest," *Plains Anthropologist* 25 (1980): 279–96.

119. One, using glottochronology to estimate the time span in the divergence of Diné languages, hypothesizes that the ancestors of the Apaches and Navajos may have reached the Southwest as early as A.D. 575. See Jay W. Palmer, "Migrations of the Apachean Dineh," *North American Archaeologist* 13 (1992): 195–218.

120. Edward T. Hall, "Recent Clues to Athapascan Prehistory in the Southwest," *American Anthropologist* 46 (1944): 98–105; Perry, "The Apachean Transition"; Haskell, *Southern Athapaskan Migration.* David R. Wilcox, "The Entry of Athapaskans into the American Southwest," in David R. Wilcox and E. Bruce Masse, eds., *The Protohistoric Period in the North American Southwest,* A.D. *1450–1700,* Anthropological Research Papers no. 24, Arizona State University (1981), 213–56, surveys the literature on the subject's historiography and favors a high plains route and a relatively recent arrival in the Southwest, just before the Spanish invasion. See also, in the same volume, David A. Gregory, "Western Apache Archaeology: Problems and Approaches," 257–74; Thomas H. Naylor, "Athapaskans They Weren't: The Suma Rebels Executed at Casas Grandes in 1685," 275–81; David M. Brugge, "Comments on Athabaskans and Sumas," 282–90; and Curtis F. Schaafsma, "Early Apacheans in the South-

west: A Review," 291–320. See also Ronald H. Towner, ed., *The Archaeology of Navajo Origins* (Salt Lake City: University of Utah Press, 1996).

121. For example, Jack D. Forbes, *Apache, Navaho, and Spaniard* (Norman: University of Oklahoma Press, 1960), xii–xxi; Jack D. Forbes, "The Early Western Apache, 1300–1700," *Journal of the West* 5 (1966): 336–54.

122. Yazzie, ed., *Navajo History*, 1: 83; Robert A. Roessel Jr., *Dinétah: Navajo History*, vol. 2 (Rough Rock AZ: Navajo Curriculum Center, 1983), 101–9; Patrick Hogan, "Dinétah: A Reevaluation of Pre-Revolt Navajo Occupation in Northwest New Mexico," *Journal of Anthropological Research* 45 (1989): 53–66; Towner, ed., *The Archaeology of Navajo Origins*; Curtis F. Schaafsma, *Apaches de Navajo: Seventeenth-Century Navajos in the Chama Valley of New Mexico* (Salt Lake City: University of Utah Press, 2002).

123. Matthews, comp. and trans., *Navaho Legends*, 68; Levy, *In the Beginning*, 58.

124. Frank Waters, *Book of the Hopi* (New York: Penguin, 1977), 255–57.

125. Lawrence L. Loendorf, "A Dated Rock Art Panel of Shield Bearing Warriors in South Central Montana," *Plains Anthropologist* 35 (1990): 45–54; Julie E. Francis, "An Overview of Wyoming Rock Art," in Frison, *Prehistoric Hunters*, chap. 10, esp. 406–9; Keyser and Klassen, *Plains Indian Rock Art*, chap. 13; Julie E. Francis and Lawrence L. Loendorf, *Ancient Visions: Petroglyphs and Pictographs from the Wind River and Bighorn Country, Wyoming and Montana* (Salt Lake City: University of Utah Press, 2002), 132–48.

126. Kevin D. Black, "Archaic Continuity in the Colorado Rockies: The Mountain Tradition," *Plains Anthropologist* 36 (1991): 1–29; Bonnie L. Pitblado, "Peak to Peak in Paleoindian Time: Occupation of Southwest Colorado," *Plains Anthropologist* 43 (1998): 333–48.

127. Gary A. Wright, "The Shoshonean Migration Problem," *Plains Anthropologist* 23 (1978): 113–37.

128. Grayson, *The Desert's Past*, 258–71.

129. J. Richard Ambler and Mark Q. Sutton, "The Anasazi Abandonment of the San Juan Drainage and the Numic Expansion," *North American Archaeologist* 10 (1989): 39–53.

130. Momaday, *The Way to Rainy Mountain*, 8–9; M. Scott Momaday, *The Man Made of Words* (New York: St. Martin's Press, 1997), 122–23.

131. George E. Hyde, *Indians of the Woodlands: From Prehistoric Times to 1725* (Norman: University of Oklahoma Press, 1962), chap. 8; Thorne, *The Many Hands of My Relations*, 12–24; W. David Baird, *The Quapaw Indians: A History of the Downstream People* (Norman: University of Oklahoma Press, 1980), chap. 1; Garrick Bailey, ed., *The Osage and the Invisible World from the Works of Francis La Flesche* (Norman: University of Oklahoma Press, 1995), 27–28; Susan C. Vehik, "Dhegiha Origins and Plains Archeology," *Plains Anthropologist* 38 (1993): 231–52; Dale R. Henning, "The Adaptive Patterning

of the Dhegiha Sioux," *Plains Anthropologist* 38 (1993): 253–64; William E. Unrau, *The Kansa Indians: A History of the Wind People, 1673–1873* (Norman: University of Oklahoma Press, 1971), 12–24.

132. Linguistic evidence suggests that the major Siouan subgroups—Eastern, Central, and Western—may have separated around 500 B.C. Some scholars argue that the Siouans began to diverge around A.D. 700, when the people who eventually became Dakotas split off. The Chiwere and Dhegiha may have separated around A.D. 100. They seem to have been associated with the Oneota cultures that developed in southern Wisconsin and Minnesota between A.D. 1000 and 1200. Others insist that the groups did not reach the prairies until after 1600, that Dhegihan migrations occurred long after the Chiwere movements, and that they may have been associated with seventeenth-century population disruption in the Ohio Valley. The archaeological record does reveal that roughly similar climatic cycles prevailed between 1300 and again between 1500 and 1600, with increased rainfall in the West prompting population movements from the woodlands and generating geopolitical adjustments as peoples moved, met, and mingled. See Dale R. Henning, "The Oneota Tradition," in Wood, ed., *Archaeology on the Great Plains*, 360–64; Thorne, *The Many Hands of My Relations*, 14–16; Bailey, *Changes in Osage Social Organization*, 3.

133. George E. Hyde, *The Pawnee Indians* (Norman: University of Oklahoma Press, 1951), 7–13; David J. Wishart, *An Unspeakable Sadness: The Dispossession of the Nebraska Indians* (Lincoln: University of Nebraska Press, 1994), 4–5. The Pawnees eventually comprised four divisions. The Skiri or Skidi, also known as the Panimahas or Loups, spoke a distinct dialect from the "south bands"—the Chauri (Grand), the Kitahahki (Republican), and the Pitahawirata. See Douglas R. Parks, "Pawnee," in *HNAI*, 13: 515, 545–46.

134. R. Peter Winham and Edward J. Lueck, "Cultures of the Middle Missouri," in Schlesier, ed., *Plains Indians*, 161–62, citing Alfred W. Bowers, *Mandan Social and Ceremonial Organization* (Chicago: University of Chicago Press, 1950), 156–63, 347–65.

135. Prince Maximilian zu Wied, "Travels in the Interior of North America," in Reuben G. Thwaites, ed., *Early Western Travels, 1748–1846*, 32 vols. (Cleveland: Arthur H. Clark, 1904), 23: 306–7, quoted in Isenberg, *The Destruction of the Bison*, 15–16.

136. Winham and Lueck, "Cultures of the Middle Missouri," 162.

137. W. Raymond Wood and Alan S. Downer, "Notes on the Crow-Hidatsa Schism," *Plains Anthropologist* 22 (1977): 83–100; Leslie B. Davis, ed., "Symposium on the Crow-Hidatsa Separations," *Archaeology in Montana* 20, no. 3 (September–December 1979); Alfred W. Bowers, *Hidatsa Social and Ceremonial Organization* (1963; reprint, Lincoln: University of Nebraska Press, 1992),

10–25; George C. Frison, "Archaeological Evidence of the Crow Indians in Northern Wyoming: A Study of a Late Prehistoric Period Buffalo Economy," Ph.D. diss., University of Michigan, 1967, esp. 218ff., 233, 246; Reher and Frison, "The Vore Site," 32; Douglas R. Parks, *Traditional Narratives of the Arikara Indians,* 4 vols. (Lincoln: University of Nebraska Press, 1991), 3: 361–63.

138. The Crow migration story is related in Joseph Medicine Crow, *From the Heart of the Crow Country: The Crow Indians' Own Stories* (New York: Crown, 1992), 16–24, Arapooish's speech on the advantages of Crow country at xxi–xxii. Originally recorded in Washington Irving, *The Adventures of Captain Bonneville, U.S.A.* (1837; reprint, Norman: University of Oklahoma Press, 1961), 165, the speech is also reprinted in Colin G. Calloway, *Our Hearts Fell to the Ground: Plains Indian Views of How the West Was Lost* (Boston: Bedford Books, 1996), 77.

139. Patricia K. Galloway, *Choctaw Genesis, 1500–1700* (Lincoln: University of Nebraska Press, 1995), 324–37, 345.

140. Dawson A. Phelps, ed., "Extracts from the Journal of the Reverend Joseph Bullen, 1799 and 1800," *Journal of Mississippi History* 17 (1955): 264.

141. Donna L. Aikers, "Removing the Heart of the Choctaw People: Indian Removal from a Native Perspective," *American Indian Culture and Research Journal* 21 (1999): 67–69.

142. Blitz, "Adoption of the Bow," 133–37.

143. Douglas B. Bamforth, "Indigenous People, Indigenous Violence: Precontact Warfare on the North American Great Plains," *Man: The Journal of the Royal Anthropological Institute* 29 (1994): 95–115; P. Willey, *Prehistoric Warfare on the Great Plains: Skeletal Analysis of the Crow Creek Massacre Victims* (New York: Garland Publishing, 1990); Larry J. Zimmerman and Lawrence E. Bradley, "The Crow Creek Massacre: Initial Coalescent Warfare and Speculations about the Genesis of Extended Coalescent," and P. Willey and Thomas E. Emerson, "The Osteology and Archaeology of the Crow Creek Massacre," both in *Plains Anthropologist* 38 (1993): 215–26, 227–69.

144. Schlesier, *Wolves of Heaven,* 76–78, 135, 179–80.

145. McNickle, *They Came Here First,* 18.

2. Singing Up a New World

1. George A. Dorsey, *The Mythology of the Wichita* (1904; reprint, Norman: University of Oklahoma Press, 1995), 25, 28.

2. Roger Echo-Hawk, "Ancient History in the New World: Integrating Oral Traditions and the Archaeological Record in Deep Time," *American Antiquity* 65 (2000): 279, 286–87. George F. Will and George E. Hyde, *Corn among the Indians of the Upper Missouri* (1917; reprint, Lincoln: University of Nebraska

Press, 1964), 210–26, survey corn origin myths among the Pawnees, Arikaras, Wichitas, and Mandans.

3. Christine Hastorf and Sissel Johannessen, "Becoming Corn-Eaters in Prehistoric America," in Sissel Johannessen and Christine Hastorf, eds., *Corn and Culture in the Prehistoric New World* (Boulder CO: Westview Press, 1994), 136.

4. Alan R. Sandstrom, *Corn Is Our Blood: Culture and Ethnic Identity in a Contemporary Aztec Indian Village* (Norman: University of Oklahoma Press, 1991), 241, 247.

5. Ethelou Yazzie, ed., *Navajo History*, vol. 1 (Rough Rock AZ: Rough Rock Press, formerly Navajo Curriculum Center, 1971), 9.

6. Richard Ford, "Corn Is Our Mother," in Johannessen and Hastorf, eds., *Corn and Culture*, 513–25, quotes at 525.

7. Vorsila L. Bohrer, "Maize in Middle America and Southwestern United States Agricultural Traditions," in Johannessen and Hastorf, eds., *Corn and Culture*, 478, 481; Ford, "Corn Is Our Mother," 514.

8. Alfonso Ortiz, "Some Cultural Meanings of Corn in Aboriginal North America," in Johannessen and Hastorf, eds., *Corn and Culture*, 533 (cf. Ruth Underhill, *Singing for Power* [Berkeley: University of California Press, 1938], 43).

9. Brian Fagan, *Floods, Famines and Emperors: El Niño and the Fate of Civilizations* (New York: Basic Books, 1999), 70.

10. Calvin Luther Martin, *In the Spirit of the Earth: Rethinking History and Time* (Baltimore MD: Johns Hopkins University Press, 1992), 37; Robert J. Wenke, *Patterns in Prehistory: Humankind's First Three Million Years*, 3rd ed. (New York: Oxford University Press, 1990), chap. 6; T. Douglas Price and Anne Birgette Gebauer, eds., *Last Hunters, First Farmers: New Perspectives on the Prehistoric Transition to Agriculture* (Santa Fe NM: School of American Research Press, 1995), 3, 6; Jared Diamond, *Guns, Germs, and Steel: The Fates of Human Societies* (New York: W. W. Norton, 1997), chap. 5; José Jesús Sánchez-González, "Modern Variability and Patterns of Maize Movement in Mesoamerica," in Johannessen and Hastorf, eds., *Corn and Culture*, 136.

11. Ortiz, "Some Cultural Meanings of Corn," 527.

12. Linda S. Cordell, *Ancient Pueblo Peoples* (Washington DC: Smithsonian Books, 1994), 48.

13. Kent V. Flannery, ed., *Guilá Naquitz: Archaic Foraging and Early Agriculture in Oaxaca, Mexico* (New York: Academic Press, 1986), 3–18; Robert N. Zeitlin and Judith Francis Zeitlin, "The Paleoindian and Archaic Cultures of Mesoamerica," in Richard E. W. Adams and Murdo J. MacLeod, eds., *The Cambridge History of the Native Peoples of the Americas*, vol. 2, *Mesoamerica* (Cambridge: Cambridge University Press, 2000), pt. 1: 103–7; Richard I. Ford, ed., *Prehistoric Food Production in North America*, Anthropological Papers no.

75, Museum of Anthropology, University of Michigan, Ann Arbor (1985), 11–18; Wenke, *Patterns in Prehistory*, 226–31; David E. Stuart, *Anasazi America: Seventeen Centuries on the Road from Center Place* (Albuquerque: University of New Mexico Press, 2000), 37; Diamond, *Guns, Germs, and Steel*, chap. 6; Shirley Powell, "Anasazi Demographic Patterns and Organizational Responses: Assumptions and Interpretive Difficulties," in George J. Gumerman, ed., *The Anasazi in a Changing Environment* (Cambridge: Cambridge University Press, 1988), 186–88.

14. Paul E. Minnis, "Domesticating People and Plants in the Greater Southwest," in Ford, ed., *Prehistoric Food Production*, 309–39, describes the initial introduction of domesticated plants as "a monumental nonevent with little *immediate* impact" (310).

15. George R. Milner, *The Cahokia Chiefdom: The Archaeology of a Mississippian Society* (Washington DC: Smithsonian Institution Press, 1998), 174.

16. Martin, *In the Spirit of the Earth*, 37–57.

17. Flannery, ed., *Guilá Naquitz*, 7.

18. Jeff Bennetzen et al., "Genetic Evidence and the Origin of Maize," and Mary W. Eubanks, "An Interdisciplinary Perspective on the Origin of Maize," both in *Latin American Antiquity* 12 (2001): 84–86, 91–98; Zeitlin and Zeitlin, "The Paleoindian and Archaic Cultures," 96–101; Flannery, ed., *Guilá Naquitz*, 7–8; R. G. Matson, *The Origins of Southwestern Agriculture* (Tucson: University of Arizona Press, 1991), 207–9; Wenke, *Patterns in Prehistory*, 253–54.

19. R. Douglas Hurt, *Indian Agriculture in America: Prehistory to the Present* (Lawrence: University Press of Kansas, 1987), 3, 7; Gayle J. Fritz, "Are the First American Farmers Getting Younger?" *Current Anthropology* 35 (1994): 305–9, (3640 B.C. date at 306); Zeitlin and Zeitlin, "The Paleoindian and Archaic Cultures," 75–79, 96–97, (2750 B.C. date at 78); Walton C. Galinat, "Domestication and Diffusion of Maize," in Ford, ed., *Prehistoric Food Production*, 245–78; Sánchez-González, "Modern Variability and Patterns of Maize Movement," 135–56. On difficulties and controversies surrounding accelerator mass spectroscopic dating, see Austin Long and Gayle J. Fritz, "Validity of AMS Dates on Maize from the Tehuacán Valley," *Latin American Antiquity* 12 (2001): 87–90.

20. Diamond, *Guns, Germs, and Steel*, chap. 10, explains the importance of the major axes of the continents to the diffusion of crops. Matson, *The Origins of Southwestern Agriculture*, 208–9.

21. Quoted in Richard Wolkomir, "Bringing Ancient Ways to Our Farmers' Fields," *Winds of Change* (summer 1996): 30.

22. Galinat, "Domestication and Diffusion of Maize," 264–66; Cordell, *Ancient Pueblo Peoples*, 48–49; Patty Jo Watson and Mary C. Kennedy, "The Development of Horticulture in the Eastern Woodlands of North America: Women's Role," in Joan M. Gero and Margaret W. Conkey, eds., *Engendering*

Archaeology: Women and Prehistory (Oxford: Basil Blackwell, 1991), 255–75.

23. Hurt, *Indian Agriculture,* 24; Paul E. Minnis and Wayne J. Elisens, eds., *Biodiversity and Native America* (Norman: University of Oklahoma Press, 2000), 13. See also Gregory Cajete, ed., *A People's Ecology: Explorations in Sustainable Living* (Santa Fe NM: Clear Light, 1999).

24. Ford, ed., *Prehistoric Food Production,* 344–47; Flannery, ed., *Guilá Naquitz,* 6.

25. Mark D. Varien, *Sedentism and Mobility in a Social Landscape: Mesa Verde and Beyond* (Tucson: University of Arizona Press, 1999).

26. Karen Olsen Bruhns and Karen E. Stothert, *Women in Ancient America* (Norman: University of Oklahoma Press, 1999), 92, 94; Patricia L. Crown, ed., *Women and Men in the Prehispanic Southwest: Labor, Power, Prestige* (Santa Fe NM: School of American Research Press, 2001), 30.

27. Debra L. Martin, "Patterns of Diet and Disease: Health Profiles for the Prehistoric Southwest," and Linda S. Cordell, David E. Doyel, and Keith W. Kintigh, "Processes of Aggregation in the Prehistoric Southwest," both in George J. Gumerman, ed., *Themes in Southwest Prehistory* (Santa Fe NM: School of American Research Press, 1994), 87–108, 110; Charles F. Merbs, "Patterns of Health and Sickness in the Precontact Southwest," in David Hurst Thomas, ed., *Columbian Consequences,* vol. 1, *Archaeological and Historical Perspectives on the Spanish Borderlands West* (Washington DC: Smithsonian Institution Press, 1989), 41–56; John A. Williams, "Disease Profiles of Archaic and Woodland Populations in the Northern Plains," in Douglas W. Owsley and Richard L. Jantz, eds., *Skeletal Biology in the Great Plains: Migration, Warfare, Health, and Subsistence* (Washington DC: Smithsonian Institution Press, 1994), 91–108; Stuart, *Anasazi America,* 45.

28. Bohrer, "Maize in Middle America," 469–512; Karl Taube, "Lightning Celts and Corn Fetishes: The Formative Olmec and the Development of Maize Symbolism in Mesoamerica and the American Southwest," in John E. Clark and Mary E. Pye, eds., *Olmec Art and Archaeology in Mesoamerica* (New Haven CT: Yale University Press, 2000), 297–337; Cordell, *Ancient Pueblo Peoples,* 49–51; George P. Hammond and Agapito Rey, eds., *Don Juan de Oñate: Colonizer of New Mexico, 1595–1628,* 2 vols. (Albuquerque: University of New Mexico Press, 1953), 2: 673–74.

29. George J. Gumerman and Murray Gell-Mann, "Cultural Evolution in the Prehistoric Southwest," in Gumerman, ed., *Themes in Southwest Prehistory,* 17; Cordell, *Ancient Pueblo Peoples,* 38.

30. Jeffrey S. Dean, "Dendrochronology and Paleoenvironmental Reconstruction on the Colorado Plateaus," in Gumerman, ed., *The Anasazi in a Changing Environment,* 122–23.

31. Matson, *The Origins of Southwestern Agriculture,* 245, 307.

32. Sánchez-González, "Modern Variability and Patterns of Maize Move-

ment," 147–48; Karen R. Adams, "A Regional Synthesis of *Zea mays* in the Prehistoric American Southwest," in Johannessen and Hastorf, eds., *Corn and Culture*, 273–302; Matson, *The Origins of Southwestern Agriculture*, 209–10, 310; W. H. Wills, "Archaic Foraging and the Beginning of Food Production in the American Southwest," in Price and Gebauer, eds., *Last Hunters, First Farmers*, 215; Michael S. Berry, "The Age of Maize in the Greater Southwest: A Critical Review," in Ford, ed., *Prehistoric Food Production*, 279–307.

33. Timothy A. Kohler, "News from the North American Southwest: Prehistory of the Edge of Chaos," *Journal of Archaeological Research* 1 (1993): 274–75.

34. Wills, "Archaic Foraging," 217, 223, 242; W. H. Wills and Bruce B. Huckell, "Economic Implications of Changing Land-Use Patterns in the Late Archaic," in Gumerman, ed., *Themes in Southwest Prehistory*, 33–52.

35. Linda S. Cordell and Bruce D. Smith, "Indigenous Farmers," in Bruce G. Trigger and Wilcomb E. Washburn, eds., *The Cambridge History of the Native Peoples of the Americas*, vol. 1, *North America* (Cambridge: Cambridge University Press, 1996), pt. 1: 213.

36. Peter Nabokov and Robert Easton, *Native American Architecture* (New York: Oxford University Press, 1989), 348.

37. Some scholars suspect that notions of cultural traditions may have outlived their usefulness, obscuring what may in fact have been social and economic interactions rather than shared culture. Cordell and Smith, "Indigenous Farmers," 210, 213–14; Gumerman and Gell-Mann, "Cultural Evolution"; Joseph A. Tainter and Fred Plog, "Strong and Weak Patterning in Southwestern Prehistory: The Formation of Puebloan Archaeology," in Gumerman, ed., *Themes in Southwest Prehistory*, 165–81.

38. Jefferson Reid and Stephanie Whittlesey, *The Archaeology of Ancient Arizona* (Tucson: University of Arizona Press, 1997), 70–73; W. Bruce Masse, "The Quest for Subsistence Sufficiency and Civilization in the Sonoran Desert," in Patricia L. Crown and W. James Judge, eds., *Chaco and Hohokam: Prehistoric Regional Settlements in the American Southwest* (Santa Fe NM: School of American Research Press, 1991), 196.

39. George J. Gumerman, ed., *Exploring the Hohokam: Prehistoric Desert Peoples of the American Southwest* (Albuquerque: University of New Mexico Press, 1991), xv–xvi, 1–7.

40. Daniel E. Doyel, "Hohokam Cultural Evolution in the Phoenix Basin," in Gumerman, ed., *Exploring the Hohokam*, 231–78. Emil Haury, *The Hohokam: Desert Farmers and Craftsmen* (Tucson: University of Arizona Press, 1976), suggested Mesoamerican origins; Matson, *The Origins of Southwestern Agriculture*, 205–7 and passim discusses models of migration and in situ development in relation to the origins of agriculture.

41. Masse, "The Quest for Subsistence Sufficiency," 197, 204–8; Shepard Krech III, *The Ecological Indian: Myth and History* (New York: W. W. Norton,

1999), 45–49; Gary Paul Nabhan, "Native American Management and Conservation of Biodiversity in the Sonoran Desert Bioregion," in Minnis and Elisens, eds., *Biodiversity and Native America,* 29–43; Suzanne K. Fish and Gary P. Nabhan, "The Desert as Context: The Hohokam Environment," in Gumerman, ed., *Exploring the Hohokam,* 29–60, esp. 41, 51–52; Robert E. Grasser and Scott M. Kwatkowski, "Food for Thought: Recognizing Patterns in Hohokam Subsistence," in Gumerman, ed., *Exploring the Hohokam,* 417–59; Reid and Whittlesey, *The Archaeology of Ancient Arizona,* 76–79.

42. David Hurst Thomas, *Exploring Native North America* (New York: Oxford University Press, 2000), 147.

43. Masse, "The Quest for Subsistence Sufficiency," 210–14; Krech, *The Ecological Indian,* 46, 49–53; Jill Neitzel, "Hohokam Material Culture and Behavior: The Dimensions of Organizational Change," in Gumerman, ed., *Exploring the Hohokam,* 180–82, 194–98; Paul R. Fish and Suzanne K. Fish, "Hohokam Political and Social Organization," in Gumerman, ed., *Exploring the Hohokam,* 157. William E. Doolittle, *Cultivated Landscapes of Native North America* (New York: Oxford University Press, 2000), chap. 10 discusses canal irrigation in the Southwest.

44. Krech, *The Ecological Indian,* 53; Fish and Fish, "Hohokam Political and Social Organization," 155–59; Doyel, "Hohokam Cultural Evolution," 265–66.

45. Fish and Fish, "Hohokam Political and Social Organization," 162–63, Cushing quote at 158–59.

46. Doyel, "Hohokam Cultural Evolution," 249, 251; Fish and Fish, "Hohokam Political and Social Organization," 156.

47. Nabokov and Easton, *Native American Architecture,* 355; Stephen Plog, *Ancient Peoples of the Ancient Southwest* (London: Thames and Hudson, 1997), 84–87; David R. Wilcox, "Hohokam Social Complexity," in Crown and Judge, eds., *Chaco and Hohokam,* 264–65, 271; Masse, "The Quest for Subsistence Sufficiency," 217–18; David A. Gregory, "Form and Function in Hohokam Settlement Patterns," in Crown and Judge, eds., *Chaco and Hohokam,* 184; Doyel, "Hohokam Cultural Evolution," 251–53; Patricia L. Crown, "The Role of Exchange and Interaction in Salt-Gila Basin Prehistory," in Gumerman, ed., *Exploring the Hohokam,* 383–415.

48. Wilcox, "Hohokam Social Complexity," 266–68, 275; Doyel, "Hohokam Cultural Evolution," 255. Father Pedro Font visited Casa Grande in 1775 and wrote a description of its ruins, together with an account of its origins and history as related to him by Gila River Pimas: "It all reduces itself to fables, confusedly mixed with some Catholic truths," Font wrote. Herbert E. Bolton, ed., *Anza's California Expeditions,* 5 vols. (Berkeley: University of California Press, 1930), 4: 34–41, quote at 34.

49. Crown and Judge, eds., *Chaco and Hohokam,* 8, 222.

50. Nabokov and Easton, *Native American Architecture,* 354; Krech, *The Ecological Indian,* 43.

51. Krech, *The Ecological Indian,* chap. 2.

52. Thomas, *Exploring Native North America,* 141–42.

53. Reid and Whittlesey, *The Archaeology of Ancient Arizona,* chap. 5.

54. Cordell, *Ancient Pueblo Peoples,* 18–19, 59.

55. Hurt, *Indian Agriculture,* 16; Matson, *The Origins of Southwestern Agriculture,* 207–16.

56. Cordell, *Ancient Pueblo Peoples,* 60–61, 66–68; Reid and Whittlesey, *The Archaeology of Ancient Arizona,* chap. 6; Nabokov and Easton, *Native American Architecture,* 353.

57. Stuart, *Anasazi America,* 47.

58. Cordell, *Ancient Pueblo Peoples,* 82.

59. Nabokov and Easton, *Native American Architecture,* 356–57, 371.

60. For broader consideration of the transition and its implications for sociopolitical organization, see Gary M. Feinman, Kent G. Lightfoot, and Steadman Upham, "Political Hierarchies and Organizational Strategies in the Puebloan Southwest," *American Antiquity* 65 (2000): 449–70.

61. Plog, *Ancient Peoples,* 93–95; Deborah L. Nichols and F. E. Smiley, eds., "A Summary of Prehistoric Research on Northern Black Mesa," in Deborah L. Nichols and F. E. Smiley, eds., *Excavations on Black Mesa, 1982: A Descriptive Report,* Research Papers no. 39, Southern Illinois University at Carbondale Center for Archaeological Investigations (1984), 89–107; Deborah L. Nichols and F. E. Smiley, "An Overview of Northern Black Mesa," in A. L. Christenson and W. J. Perry, eds., *Excavations on Black Mesa,* Research Papers no. 46, Southern Illinois University at Carbondale Center for Archaeological Investigations (1985). Shirley Powell and George J. Gumerman, *People of the Mesa: The Archaeology of Black Mesa, Arizona* (Carbondale: Southern Illinois University Press, 1987), provide a brief and illustrated overview of the archaeological work at Black Mesa.

62. Frank McNitt, ed., *Navaho Expedition: Journal of a Military Reconnaissance from Santa Fe, New Mexico to the Navaho Country Made in 1849 by Lieutenant James H. Simpson* (Norman: University of Oklahoma Press, 1964), 39–56.

63. Crown and Judge, eds., *Chaco and Hohokam,* chap. 2. On Navajo workers at Chaco, see Joe Watkins, *Indigenous Archaeology: American Indian Values and Scientific Practice* (Walnut Creek CA: Altamira Press, 2000), 95. *American Antiquity* 66 (January 2001) features essays on Chaco in a special issue.

64. Cordell, *Ancient Pueblo Peoples,* 96.

65. Kendrick Frazier, *People of Chaco: A Canyon and Its Culture* (rev. ed., New York: W. W. Norton, 1999), 153–59; Crown and Judge, eds., *Chaco and Hohokam,* 65–68.

66. Frazier, *People of Chaco,* 65–66, 228–29; Thomas C. Windes and Peter J.

McKenna, "Going against the Grain: Wood Production in Chacoan Society," *American Antiquity* 66 (January 2001): 119–40; William Lumpkin, "Reflections on Chacoan Architecture," in David Grant Noble, ed., *New Light on Chaco Canyon* (Santa Fe NM: School of American Research Press, 1984), 20; Cordell, *Ancient Pueblo Peoples,* 96. See also Nabokov and Easton, *Native American Architecture,* 361.

67. Frazier, *People of Chaco,* 76–77.

68. Noble, ed., *New Light on Chaco Canyon,* 19.

69. Frazier, *People of Chaco,* 44, 49, 153–56; see also Francis Jennings, *The Founders of America* (New York: W. W. Norton, 1993), 54. George H. Pepper began archaeological work at Pueblo Bonito in 1896 and published his findings twenty-four years later. George H. Pepper, *Pueblo Bonito* (1920; reprint, Albuquerque: University of New Mexico Press, 1996). Stephen H. Lekson, *The Chaco Meridian: Centers of Political Power in the Southwest* (Walnut Creek CA: Altamira Press, 1999), 21, estimates the total population of Chaco Canyon at between twenty-five hundred and three thousand, with a small number of people, "hundreds, at most," living in each great house.

70. Lynne Sebastian, *The Chaco Anasazi: Sociopolitical Evolution in the Prehistoric Southwest* (Cambridge: Cambridge University Press, 1992), 56; Frazier, *People of Chaco,* chap. 5; Doolittle, *Cultivated Landscapes,* 335–38.

71. Frazier, *People of Chaco,* chap. 7; Brian M. Fagan, *Ancient North America: The Archaeology of a Continent,* 3rd ed. (London: Thames and Hudson, 2000), 324.

72. Crown and Judge, eds., *Chaco and Hohokam.*

73. Noble, ed., *New Light on Chaco Canyon,* 52; Frazier, *People of Chaco,* 201, 233; R. Gwinn Vivian, "Chacoan Roads: Morphology," and "Chacoan Roads: Function," both in *Kiva: The Journal of Southwestern Anthropology and History* 63, no. 1 (fall 1997): 7–34, 35–67; Lekson, *The Chaco Meridian,* 114–15; Stuart, *Anasazi America,* 108.

74. Noble, ed., *New Light on Chaco Canyon,* 56–57; Frazier, *People of Chaco,* 52–53, 151, 183–85; Crown and Judge, eds., *Chaco and Hohokam,* 295, 301, 307; H. Wolcott Toll, "Material Distributions and Exchange in the Chaco System," in Crown and Judge, eds., *Chaco and Hohokam,* 77–107. On the organization of production in Chaco, see the special edition of *American Antiquity* 66 (January 2001), especially Colin Renfrew, "Production and Consumption in a Sacred Economy: The Material Correlates of High Devotional Expression at Chaco Canyon," 14–25; Timothy Earle, "Economic Support of Chaco Canyon Society," 26–35; and Frances Joan Mathien, "The Organization of Turquoise Production and Consumption by the Prehistoric Chacoans," 103–18.

75. Christy G. Turner II and Jacqueline A. Turner, *Man Corn: Cannibalism and Violence in the Prehistoric American Southwest* (Salt Lake City: University of Utah Press, 1999), esp. chap. 5.

76. Frazier, *People of Chaco*, chap. 10; Plog, *Ancient Peoples*, 100–101.

77. Cordell, *Ancient Pueblo Peoples*, 90–91.

78. Cordell, *Ancient Pueblo Peoples*, 84, 93, 115–24; Crown and Judge, eds., *Chaco and Hohokam*, 303, 305; Stuart, *Anasazi America*, chap. 6, quote at 119; Sebastian, *The Chaco Anasazi*, 149.

79. Cordell, *Ancient Pueblo Peoples*, 126–28; Crown and Judge, eds., *Chaco and Hohokam*, 26; Stuart, *Anasazi America*, 131–32.

80. Willa Cather, *Later Novels* (New York: Library of America, 1990), 221, quoted in Thomas, *Exploring Native North America*, 116.

81. Fagan, *Ancient North America*, 336.

82. Lekson, *The Chaco Meridian*, 102–3.

83. Cordell, *Ancient Pueblo Peoples*, 130–32. See the various articles on environmental change, agricultural production, population movement, and settlement patterns in the special issue of *Kiva: The Journal of Southwestern Anthropology and History* 66 (fall 2000) edited by Mark D. Varien.

84. Cordell, *Ancient Pueblo Peoples*, 131–32; David R. Wilcox and Jonathan Haas, "The Scream of the Butterfly: Competition and Conflict in the Prehistoric Southwest," in Gumerman, ed., *Themes in Southwest Prehistory*, 211–38; J. Richard Ambler and Mark Q. Sutton, "The Anasazi Abandonment of the San Juan Drainage and the Numic Expansion," *North American Archaeologist* 10 (1989): 39–53; Jonathan Haas and Winifred Creamer, "The Role of Warfare in the Pueblo III Period," in Michael A. Adler, ed., *The Prehistoric Pueblo World, A.D. 1150–1350* (Tucson: University of Arizona Press, 1996), 205–13; Steven A. LeBlanc, *Prehistoric Warfare in the American Southwest* (Salt Lake City: University of Utah Press, 1998); William D. Lipe, "The Depopulation of the Northern San Juan: Conditions in the Turbulent 1200s," *Journal of Anthropological Archaeology* 14 (1995): 143–69, esp. 156–58; Turner and Turner, *Man Corn*; Stuart, *Anasazi America*, 127–28, 135–36, 138, 142; Kristin A. Kuckelman, Ricky R. Lightfoot, and Debra L. Martin, "Changing Patterns of Violence in the Northern San Juan Region," *Kiva: The Journal of Southwestern Anthropology and History* 66 (fall 2000): 147–66. The Crow Canyon Archaeological Center conducted excavations at Castle Rock pueblo from 1990 to 1994. Kristin A. Kuckelman, ed., *The Archaeology of Castle Rock Pueblo: A Thirteenth-Century Village in Southwestern Colorado*, a fully electronic site report, is available at www.crowcanyon.org. On rock art, see Polly Schaafsma, *Warrior, Shield, and Star: Imagery and Ideology of Pueblo Warfare* (Santa Fe NM: Western Edge Press, 2000).

85. The recent literature on abandonment, migration, and mobility in the Southwest is substantial: Katherine A. Spielmann, ed., *Migration and Reorganization: The Pueblo IV Period in the American Southwest*, Anthropological Research Papers no. 51, Arizona State University (1998); Mark D. Varien, *Sedentism and Mobility in a Social Landscape: Mesa Verde and Beyond* (Tucson: University of

Arizona Press, 1999); Andrew I. Duff and Richard H. Wilhusen, "Prehistoric Population Dynamics in the Northern San Juan Region, A.D. 950–1300," *Kiva: The Journal of Southwestern Anthropology and History* 66 (fall 2000): 167–90; Margaret C. Nelson, *Mimbres during the Twelfth Century: Abandonment, Continuity, and Reorganization* (Tucson: University of Arizona Press, 1999); Frazier, *People of Chaco*, chap. 11; Paul R. Fish, Suzanne K. Fish, George J. Gumerman, and J. Jefferson Reid, "Toward an Explanation for Southwestern 'Abandonments,"' in Gumerman, ed., *Themes in Southwest Prehistory*, 135–63; Lipe, "The Depopulation," 162–64; Miriam T. Stark, Jeffery J. Clark, and Mark D. Elson, "Causes and Consequences of Migration in the 13th Century Tonto Basin," *Journal of Anthropological Archaeology* 14 (1995): 212–26; the various essays in Adler, ed., *The Prehistoric Pueblo World*; Steadman Upham, "Adaptive Diversity and Southwestern Abandonment," *Journal of Anthropological Research* 40 (1984): 235–56; Steadman Upham, "Nomads of the Desert West: A Shifting Continuum in Prehistory," *Journal of World Prehistory* 8 (1994): 143–67; Scott Rushforth and Steadman Upham, *A Hopi Social History: Anthropological Perspectives on Sociocultural Persistence and Change* (Austin: University of Texas Press, 1992), chap. 3.

86. Rushforth and Upham, *A Hopi Social History*, 15, 52–67.

87. Tessie Naranjo, "Thoughts on Migration by Santa Clara Pueblo," *Journal of Anthropological Archaeology* 14 (1995): 247–50.

88. Stephen H. Lekson and Catherine M. Cameron, "The Abandonment of Chaco Canyon, the Mesa Verde Migrations, and the Reorganization of the Pueblo World," *Journal of Anthropological Archaeology* 14 (1995): 194–95; T. J. Ferguson and E. Richard Hart, *A Zuni Atlas* (Norman: University of Oklahoma Press, 1985), 126.

89. Catherine M. Cameron, guest ed., "Migration and the Movement of Southwestern Peoples," *Journal of Anthropological Archaeology* 14 (1995): esp. 104–24.

90. Carroll L. Riley, *Rio del Norte: People of the Upper Rio Grande from Earliest Times to the Pueblo Revolt* (Salt Lake City: University of Utah Press, 1995), 107–12.

91. Leo W. Simmons, ed., *Sun Chief: The Autobiography of a Hopi Indian* (New Haven CT: Yale University Press, 1942), 422.

92. Paul Horgan, *Great River: The Rio Grande in North American History* (Hanover NH: University Press of New England for Wesleyan University Press, 1984), 22.

93. Stephen H. Lekson, "Was Casas a Pueblo?" in Curtis F. Schaafsma and Carroll L. Riley, eds., *The Casas Grandes World* (Salt Lake City: University of Utah Press, 1999), 90–91. White House in Canyon de Chelly was a Chacoan outlier great house, but the White House mentioned in the origin stories of several Puebloan groups may refer to various places. See R. Gwinn Vivian

and Bruce Hilpert, *The Chaco Handbook: An Encyclopedic Guide* (Salt Lake City: University of Utah Press, 2002), 269–70.

94. Cordell and Smith, "Indigenous Farmers," 228; Cordell, *Ancient Pueblo Peoples,* 140–42; Plog, *Ancient Peoples,* 172–77. Lekson, *The Chaco Meridian,* 160, calls Casas Grandes the "most wonderful city ever built in the Pueblo Southwest." The seminal work on Casas Grandes was C. C. Di Peso, J. B. Rinaldo, and G. J. Fenner, *Casas Grandes: Fallen Trading Center of the Gran Chichimeca,* 3 vols. (Dragoon: Amerind Foundation; Flagstaff AZ: Northland Press, 1974). More recent research and interpretations are presented in Schaafsma and Riley, eds., *The Casas Grandes World.*

95. Lekson, *The Chaco Meridian.*

96. Riley, *Rio del Norte,* 112–13.

97. Randall H. McGuire, E. Charles Adams, Ben A. Nelson, and Katherine A. Spielmann, "Drawing the Southwest to Scale: Perspectives on Macroregional Relations," in Gumerman, ed., *Themes in Southwest Prehistory,* 252–53.

98. Hopis believe that Homol'ovi I was home to the Sand and Water clan people and that the Tobacco, Rabbit, Sun, and several other clans lived in Homol'ovi II, which had approximately one thousand rooms and was a major center in a network that exchanged ceramics, shells, and obsidian across large areas of the Southwest. Archaeological interpretation of ceramics seems to indicate that Homol'ovi III "was settled by immigrants from the upper Little Colorado River with strong Mogollon connections" and Homol'ovi IV was built by the Anasazi. In time, the people of the Water, Sand, and other clans trekked north to the mesas, which "were fixed by prophecy and historical circumstance" to be the Hopi homeland. See Reid and Whittlesey, *The Archaeology of Ancient Arizona,* 199–201, 203–4. Harold Courlander, *The Fourth World of the Hopis: The Epic Story of the Hopi Indians as Preserved in Their Legends and Traditions* (Albuquerque: University of New Mexico Press, 1971), contains accounts of the wanderings of different clans and groups.

99. Plog, *Ancient Peoples,* 122, 157–58; Rushforth and Upham, *A Hopi Social History,* 68–69; E. Charles Adams, "The Pueblo III–Pueblo IV Transition in the Hopi Area, Arizona," in Adler, ed., *The Prehistoric Pueblo World,* 48–58; Simmons, ed., *Sun Chief,* 421.

100. Elsie Clew Parsons, *Pueblo Indian Religion,* 2 vols. (1939; reprint, Lincoln: University of Nebraska Press, 1996), 1: 171–72, 178, 218.

101. Matson, *The Origins of Southwestern Agriculture,* 214; Cordell, *Ancient Pueblo Peoples,* 51–54.

102. Simmons, ed., *Sun Chief,* 58–59.

103. Frank Waters, *Book of the Hopi* (New York: Penguin, 1977), 258.

104. Quoted in Plog, *Ancient Peoples,* 170–71.

105. Sekaquaptewa cited in John D. Loftin, *Religion and Hopi Life in the Twentieth Century* (Bloomington: Indiana University Press, 1991), 4–5, 7.

106. Plog, *Ancient Peoples,* 166. Life expectancy at Chaco was higher, however, than that for laborers in the cities of northern England during the Industrial Revolution.

107. J. O. Brew, "Hopi Prehistory and History to 1850," in *HNAI,* 9: 514.

108. Rina Swentzell, quoted in Lekson and Cameron, "The Abandonment of Chaco Canyon," 195.

109. Roger G. Kennedy, *Hidden Cities: The Discovery and Loss of Ancient North American Civilization* (New York: Penguin, 1994); Robert E. Bieder, *Science Encounters the American Indian, 1820–1880: The Early Years of American Ethnology* (Norman: University of Oklahoma Press, 1986), 108–19.

110. Hastorf and Johannessen, "Becoming Corn-Eaters," 428–43; Hurt, *Indian Agriculture,* 3–4, 11; Bruce D. Smith, *Rivers of Change: Essays on Early Agriculture in Eastern North America* (Washington DC: Smithsonian Institution Press, 1992), chap. 11; Bruce D. Smith, "Seed Plant Domestication in Eastern North America," in Price and Gebauer, eds., *Last Hunters, First Farmers,* 193–213; Bruce D. Smith, "Origins of Agriculture in Eastern North America," *Science* 246 (1989): 1566–71.

111. Cordell and Smith, "Indigenous Farmers," 236, 247–48; Hurt, *Indian Agriculture,* 11.

112. Cordell and Smith, "Indigenous Farmers," 250, 260; Hastorf and Johannessen, "Becoming Corn-Eaters," 431–33.

113. Bruce D. Smith, "Agricultural Chiefdoms of the Eastern Woodlands," in Trigger and Washburn, eds., *The Cambridge History,* 1, pt. 1: 268.

114. Patricia K. Galloway, ed., *The Southeastern Ceremonial Complex: Artifacts and Analysis* (Lincoln: University of Nebraska Press, 1989); Thomas E. Emerson, "Cahokian Elite Ideology and the Mississippian Cosmos," in Timothy E. Pauketat and Thomas E. Emerson, eds., *Cahokia: Domination and Ideology in the Mississippian World* (Lincoln: University of Nebraska Press, 1997), chap. 10.

115. Designated a World Heritage Site by UNESCO in 1982, Cahokia has been described as the "largest and most complex expression of Precolumbian Native American civilization in North America," as "one of the great urban centers of the world" in its time, and even as "North America's Rome." See Pauketat and Emerson, eds., *Cahokia,* 1; *Cahokia, City of the Sun* (Collinsville IL: Cahokia Mounds Museum Society, 1999), 24; Biloine Whiting Young and Melvin L. Fowler, *Cahokia: The Great Native American Metropolis* (Urbana: University of Illinois Press, 2000), ix, 273. Milner, *The Cahokia Chiefdom,* offers a more restrained assessment.

116. Young and Fowler, *Cahokia,* 112–13; Milner, *The Cahokia Chiefdom,* chap. 2, describes the geography of the region and provides maps detailing the location of rivers and wetlands.

117. Pauketat and Emerson, eds., *Cahokia,* 21–26.

118. Pauketat and Emerson, eds., *Cahokia,* 31–32.

119. Robert L. Hall, "Cahokia Identity and Interaction Models of Cahokia Mississippian," in Thomas E. Emerson and R. Barry Lewis, eds., *Cahokia and the Hinterlands: Middle Mississippian Cultures of the Midwest* (Urbana: University of Illinois Press, 1991), 23; Timothy R. Pauketat, *The Ascent of Chiefs: Cahokia and Mississippian Politics in North America* (Tuscaloosa: University of Alabama Press, 1994), 48–51; Milner, *The Cahokia Chiefdom*, chap. 4; Lynda Norene Shaffer, *Native Americans before 1492: The Moundbuilding Centers of the Eastern Woodlands* (London: E. M. Sharpe, 1992), 56–57; Neal H. Lopinot, "Cahokian Food Production Reconsidered," and Lucretia S. Kelly, "Patterns of Faunal Exploitation at Cahokia," both in Pauketat and Emerson, eds., *Cahokia*, chaps. 3–4; Peter Peregrine, "A Graph-Theoretic Approach to the Evolution of Cahokia," *American Antiquity* 56, no. 1 (1996): 66.

120. Pauketat, *The Ascent of Chiefs*; Pauketat and Emerson, eds., *Cahokia*; Thomas E. Emerson, *Cahokia and the Archaeology of Power* (Tuscaloosa: University of Alabama Press, 1997), 260–62; Milner, *The Cahokia Chiefdom*, 129–37; James M. Collins and Michael L. Chalfant, "A Second Terrace Perspective on Monks Mound," *American Antiquity* 58, no. 2 (1993): 319–32; Young and Fowler, *Cahokia*, chap. 17.

121. Brackenridge quoted in Pauketat and Emerson, eds., *Cahokia*, 11; Kennedy, *Hidden Cities*, 12.

122. Shaffer, *Native Americans before 1492*, 53–54; Alvin M. Josephy, *America in 1492: The World of the Indian Peoples before the Arrival of Columbus* (New York: Random House, 1991), diagram at 139; Young and Fowler, *Cahokia*, chaps. 14–15. See also Melvin L. Fowler and E. C. Krupp, "Sky Watchers, Sacred Space, Cosmology and Community Organization at Ancient Cahokia," *Wisconsin Archaeologist* 77 (1996): 151–58.

123. Young and Fowler, *Cahokia*, chap. 9; Milner, *The Cahokia Chiefdom*, 129–36.

124. Milner, *The Cahokia Chiefdom*, 12–13, 144–50. Native historian Jack Forbes indicts non-Native scholars who assume that mound-building societies must have been hierarchical. Making assumptions on the basis of Old World historical experiences, "they see social hierarchy in every grave with gift offerings, just as every executed person becomes a human sacrifice" (Jack Forbes, "The Urban Tradition among Native Americans," *American Indian Culture and Research Journal* 22, no. 4 [1998]: 15–42, quote at 22).

125. Milner, *The Cahokia Chiefdom*, 1. Young and Fowler, *Cahokia*, provide an accessible survey of the evolution of Cahokia archaeology, including the personality and professional conflicts involved.

126. To Patricia O'Brien, for example, Cahokia meets the criteria for a state and an urban center; to Timothy Pauketat and Thomas Emerson, Cahokia can never be considered a state, even at its height, and qualifies as a complex chiefdom, a centralized polity without a formal bureaucracy. See Pa-

tricia J. O'Brien, "Cahokia: The Political Capital of the 'Ramey' State?" *North American Archaeologist* 10 (1989): 275–92; Pauketat and Emerson, eds., *Cahokia*, 3; Emerson, *Cahokia and the Archaeology of Power*, 251; Emerson quote in Young and Fowler, *Cahokia*, 317.

127. Thomas Hall and Christopher Chase-Dunn, "World-Systems in North America: Networks, Rise and Fall and Pulsations of Trade in Stateless Systems," *American Indian Culture and Research Journal* 22, no. 1 (1998): 39. James B. Griffen dismisses estimates of Cahokia's population at thirty thousand as "gross overestimates" and part of what he calls the Cahokia ascendancy myth ("Cahokia Interaction with Contemporary Southeastern and Eastern Societies," *Midcontinental Journal of Archaeology* 18, no. 1 [1993]: 3–17). Milner, *The Cahokia Chiefdom*, chap. 6, suggests that while the regional population may have been in the tens of thousands, Cahokia itself probably held only several thousand people even at its height. See also Timothy R. Pauketat and Neal H. Lopinot, "Cahokian Population Dynamics," in Pauketat and Emerson, eds., *Cahokia*, 103–23.

128. Emerson and Lewis, eds., *Cahokia and the Hinterlands*; Peregrine, "A Graph-Theoretic Approach," 67, 73; Hall and Chase-Dunn, "World-Systems," 40–42; Young and Fowler, *Cahokia*, chap. 19.

129. Patricia O'Brien, "The World-System of Cahokia within the Middle Mississippian Tradition," *Review* 15, no. 3 (1992): 389–417.

130. J. Daniel Rogers and Bruce D. Smith, eds., *Mississippian Communities and Households* (Tuscaloosa: University of Alabama Press, 1995), 36; Milner, *The Cahokia Chiefdom*, 171–72; Pauketat and Emerson, eds., *Cahokia*, 269, 278; Young and Fowler, *Cahokia*, 310–15.

131. Hall, "Cahokia Identity," 23.

132. Pauketat and Emerson, eds., *Cahokia*, 23–24.

133. Antoine Le Page Du Pratz, *The History of Louisiana*, translated from the French (London, 1774; reprint, New Orleans: J. S. W. Harmanson, 1947).

134. Thomas, *Exploring Native North America*, 163–71; Philip Phillips and James A. Brown, *Pre-Columbian Shell Engravings from the Craig Mound at Spiro, Oklahoma*, 6 vols. in 2 pts. (Cambridge: Peabody Museum of Archaeology and Ethnology, Harvard University, 1978–84), 1: 1–22. Howard Meredith, *Dancing on Common Ground: Tribal Cultures and Alliances on the Southern Plains* (Lawrence: University Press of Kansas, 1995), 29–31, identifies Spiro as Dit-the.

135. Timothy K. Perttula, "Caddoan Area Archaeology since 1990," *Journal of Archaeological Research* 4 (1996): 295–348.

136. George A. Dorsey, *Traditions of the Caddo* (1905; reprint, Lincoln: University of Nebraska Press, 1997), 7–8; Vynola Beaver Newkumet and Howard L. Meredith, *Hasinai: A Traditional History of the Caddo Confederacy*

(College Station: Texas A & M University Press, 1988), 4–9, 31–33; John R. Swanton, *Source Material on the History and Ethnology of the Caddo Indians* (1942; reprint, Norman: University of Oklahoma Press, 1996), 127–32; Timothy K. Perttula, *The Caddo Nation: Archaeological and Ethnohistoric Perspectives* (Austin: University of Texas Press, 1992), 13–15.

137. Fagan, *Ancient North America*, 141, 144.

138. David LaVere, *The Caddo Chiefdoms: Caddo Economics and Politics, 700–1835* (Lincoln: University of Nebraska Press, 1998), 11–12; Cecile Elkins Carter, *Caddo Indians: Where We Come From* (Norman: University of Oklahoma Press, 1995), 14–19, 74–75.

139. LaVere, *The Caddo Chiefdoms*, 12.

140. LaVere, *The Caddo Chiefdoms*, 12–13; Perttula, *The Caddo Nation*, 96; Ann M. Early, "The Caddos of the Trans-Mississippi South," in Bonnie G. McEwan, ed., *Indians of the Greater Southeast: Historical Archaeology and Ethnohistory* (Gainesville: University Press of Florida, 2000), 12–26.

141. LaVere, *The Caddo Chiefdoms*, 14–15; Herbert E. Bolton, *The Hasinais: Southern Caddoans as Seen by the Earliest Europeans* (Norman: University of Oklahoma Press, 1987), 82–84; Swanton, *Source Material on the History and Ethnology of the Caddo Indians*, 170–73.

142. LaVere, *The Caddo Chiefdoms*, 15–19; Bolton, *The Hasinais*, 74–79; Swanton, *Source Material*, 170–73; Mattie Austin Hatcher, trans., "Descriptions of the Tejas or Asinai Indians, 1691–1722," *Southwestern Historical Quarterly* 30 (1926–27): 212–13, 216–18.

143. LaVere, *The Caddo Chiefdoms*, 19–20.

144. LaVere, *The Caddo Chiefdoms*, 22–26; Perttula, "Caddoan Area Archaeology," 311–12, 320; Meredith, *Dancing on Common Ground*, 28–32.

145. LaVere, *The Caddo Chiefdoms*, 26–28.

146. LaVere, *The Caddo Chiefdoms*, 29; Perttula, *The Caddo Nation*, 84–86.

147. LaVere, *The Caddo Chiefdoms*, 29.

148. Meredith, *Dancing on Common Ground*, 31.

149. LaVere, *The Caddo Chiefdoms*, 30–31; Perttula, "Caddoan Area Archaeology," 319.

150. LaVere, *The Caddo Chiefdoms*, 31–32.

151. Waldo R. Wedel, *Central Plains Prehistory: Holocene Environments and Culture Change in the Republican Valley* (Lincoln: University of Nebraska Press, 1986), chaps. 7, 9; Richard White, *The Roots of Dependency: Subsistence, Environment, and Social Change among the Choctaws, Pawnees, and Navajos* (Lincoln: University of Nebraska Press, 1983), 147–48.

152. Mary J. Adair, "Corn and Culture History in the Central Plains," in Johannessen and Hastorf, eds., *Corn and Culture*, 330; White, *The Roots of Dependency*, 157, 172–73; Gene Weltfish, *The Lost Universe: The Way of Life of the Pawnee* (New York: Basic Books, 1965), 97–99; Douglas R. Parks, ed.,

Ceremonies of the Pawnee by James R. Murie (Lincoln: University of Nebraska Press, 1989), 11–16; Will and Hyde, *Corn among the Indians,* 249–50. The Quaker-Pawnee encounter is described in Richard White, "The Cultural Landscape of the Pawnees," *Great Plains Historical Quarterly* 2 (1982): 31–40.

153. Weltfish, *The Lost Universe,* 102; Wedel, *Central Plains Prehistory,* 163–64; White, *The Roots of Dependency,* 159. Will and Hyde, *Corn among the Indians,* 299–317, list varieties grown by the different tribes.

154. Melvin R. Gilmore, *Prairie Smoke* (Saint Paul: Minnesota Historical Society Press, 1987), 175–76; Weltfish, *The Lost Universe,* 124.

155. Raymond Wood, "Plains Village Tradition: Middle Missouri," in *HNAI,* 13: 186–95.

156. Will and Hyde, *Corn among the Indians,* 216; Virginia Bergman Peters, *Women of the Earth Lodges: Tribal Life on the Plains* (New Haven CT: Archon Books, 1995), 29–30.

157. Battiste Good, "Battiste Good's Winter Count," in Garrick Mallery, *Picture-Writing of the American Indians,* Tenth Annual Report of the Bureau of American Ethnology, 1888–89 (Washington DC: GPO, 1893; reprint, 2 vols., New York: Dover, 1972), 1: 294, 297–300, 303–5, 311, 316, 318.

158. Will and Hyde, *Corn among the Indians,* 218–20.

159. Alfred W. Bowers, *Hidatsa Social and Ceremonial Organization* (1963; reprint, Lincoln: University of Nebraska Press, 1992), 202–4; Will and Hyde, *Corn among the Indians,* 244, 247–48, 268–76.

160. Peters, *Women of the Earth Lodges,* 116.

161. Elliott Coues, ed., *New Light on the History of the Greater Northwest: The Manuscript Journals of Alexander Henry and David Thompson, 1799–1814,* 2 vols. (1897; reprint, Minneapolis: Ross and Haines, 1965), 1: 384–85.

162. Will and Hyde, *Corn among the Indians,* 146.

163. Quoted in James P. Ronda, ed., *Revealing America: Image and Imagination in the Exploration of North America* (Lexington MA: D. C. Heath, 1996), 36.

164. Hurt, *Indian Agriculture,* 34; Sagard quoted in W. Vernon Kinetz, *The Indians of the Western Great Lakes, 1615–1760* (Ann Arbor: University of Michigan Press, 1965), 16–17, 30; Reuben G. Thwaites, ed., *The Jesuit Relations and Allied Documents: Travels and Explorations of the Jesuit Missionaries in New France 1610–1791,* 73 vols. (Cleveland: Burrows Brothers, 1896–1901), 10: 103.

165. Nicolas de La Salle, *Relation of the Discovery of the Mississippi River,* trans. Melville B. Anderson (Chicago: Caxton Club, 1898), 7.

166. Emma Helen Blair, trans. and ed., *The Indian Tribes of the Upper Mississippi Valley and Region of the Great Lakes,* 2 vols. (1911; reprint, Lincoln: University of Nebraska Press, 1996), 1: 102.

167. Marc Simmons, *Coronado's Land: Daily Life in Colonial New Mexico* (Albuquerque: University of New Mexico Press, 1991), 66–67, 121.

168. Pierre Margry, ed., *Découvertes et établissements des français dans l'ouest et dans le sud de l'Amérique Septentrionale (1614–1754)*, 6 vols. (Paris: Imprimerie D. Jouaust, 1876–86), 3: 462; William C. Foster, ed., *The La Salle Expedition to Texas: The Journal of Henri Joutel, 1684–1687* (Austin: Texas State Historical Association, 1998), 270–71, 277, 280; William C. Foster, ed., *Texas and Northeastern Mexico, 1630–1690 by Juan Bautista Chapa*, trans. Ned F. Brierley (Austin: University of Texas Press, 1997), 166.

169. See, for example, Daniel H. Usner Jr., *Indians, Settlers, and Slaves in a Frontier Exchange Economy* (Chapel Hill: University of North Carolina Press, 1992).

170. See, for example, Rolena Adorno and Patrick Charles Pautz, *Álvar Núñez Cabeza de Vaca: His Account, His Life, and the Expedition of Pánfilo de Narváez*, 3 vols. (Lincoln: University of Nebraska Press, 1999), 1: 57–59, 61, 71; 2: 86–89.

171. *WHC*, 17: 33.

172. Colin G. Calloway, *The American Revolution in Indian Country* (Cambridge: Cambridge University Press, 1995), 51, 289; Walter Lowrie and Matthew St. Clair Clarke, eds., *American State Papers: Indian Affairs*, 2 vols. (Washington DC: Gales and Seaton, 1832–34), 1: 490.

3. Sons of the Sun and People of the Earth

1. Johann Huizinga, *The Waning of the Middle Ages* (1927; reprint, New York: Doubleday, 1956), 9.

2. Anthony Pagdon, *Lords of All the World: Ideologies of Empire in Spain, Britain and France, c. 1500–c. 1800* (New Haven CT: Yale University Press, 1995), 1, Hakluyt quote at 11, Robertson quote at 104; Colin G. Calloway, *New Worlds for All: Indians, Europeans, and the Remaking of America* (Baltimore MD: Johns Hopkins University Press, 1997).

3. For example, Dennis Reinhartz and Gerald D. Saxon, eds., *The Mapping of the Entradas into the Greater Southwest* (Norman: University of Oklahoma Press, 1998).

4. José Rabasa, *Writing Violence on the Northern Frontier: The Historiography of Sixteenth-Century New Mexico and Florida and the Legacy of Conquest* (Durham NC: Duke University Press, 2000), quote at 14.

5. Quoted in Albert L. Hurtado and Peter Iverson, eds., *Major Problems in American Indian History: Documents and Essays* (Lexington MA: D. C. Heath, 1994), 83–84.

6. Patricia Seed, *Ceremonies of Possession in Europe's Conquest of the New World, 1492–1640* (Cambridge: Cambridge University Press, 1995), chap. 3, quote at 70.

7. Pagdon, *Lords of All the World*, chaps. 1–3.

8. John Francis Bannon, ed., *Bolton and the Spanish Borderlands* (Norman: University of Oklahoma Press, 1964), 34–35, 51, 306. On Potosí, see Jack Weatherford, *Indian Givers: How the Indians of the Americas Transformed the World* (New York: Ballantine Books, 1990), 1–5.

9. George P. Hammond and Agapito Rey, eds., *Narratives of the Coronado Expedition 1540–1542* (Albuquerque: University of New Mexico Press, 1940), 131.

10. Rolena Adorno and Patrick Charles Pautz, *Álvar Núñez Cabeza de Vaca: His Account, His Life, and the Expedition of Pánfilo de Narváez*, 3 vols. (Lincoln: University of Nebraska Press, 1999), 1: 99, 103, 107; Cyclone Covey, trans. and ed., *Cabeza de Vaca's Adventures in the Unknown Interior of America* (Albuquerque: University of New Mexico Press, 1993), 56–60.

11. Beatriz Pastor Bodmer, *The Armature of Conquest: Spanish Accounts of the Discovery of America, 1492–1589*, trans. Lydia Longstreth Hunt (Stanford CA: Stanford University Press, 1992), chap. 3.

12. Adorno and Pautz, *Álvar Núñez Cabeza de Vaca*, 1: 55, 59.

13. Adorno and Pautz, *Álvar Núñez Cabeza de Vaca*, 2: chap. 6.

14. David A. Howard, *Conquistador in Chains: Cabeza de Vaca and the Indians of the Americas* (Tuscaloosa: University of Alabama Press, 1997), 9. On the Indian groups of the Gulf Coast at the time of Cabeza de Vaca's arrival, see Adorno and Pautz, *Álvar Núñez Cabeza de Vaca*, 2: 237–44.

15. Adorno and Pautz, *Álvar Núñez Cabeza de Vaca*, 1: 209, 211; Covey, trans. and ed., *Cabeza de Vaca's Adventures*, 106.

16. Adorno and Pautz, *Álvar Núñez Cabeza de Vaca*, 1: 147.

17. Adorno and Pautz, *Álvar Núñez Cabeza de Vaca*, 2: 320. On the identity of the Jumanos, see "All Change on the Southern Plains," in chap. 6, this volume. Daniel T. Reff, *Disease, Depopulation, and Culture Change in Northwestern New Spain, 1518–1764* (Salt Lake City: University of Utah Press, 1991), 46–47, questions the inference that the meeting with the Jumanos occurred in the La Junta area.

18. Adorno and Pautz, *Álvar Núñez Cabeza de Vaca*, 1: 159; Covey, trans. and ed., *Cabeza de Vaca's Adventures*, 65.

19. Adorno and Pautz, *Álvar Núñez Cabeza de Vaca*, 1: 165; 2: 297–300.

20. Adorno and Pautz, *Álvar Núñez Cabeza de Vaca*, 1: 231n1, 235; 2: 339, 343.

21. Silvia Spitta, "Shamanism and Christianity: The Transcultural Semiotics of Cabeza de Vaca's *Naufragios*," in Silvia Spitta, *Between Two Waters: Narratives of Transculturation in Latin America* (Houston TX: Rice University Press, 1995), 29–54; Haniel Long quoted in Covey, trans. and ed., *Cabeza de Vaca's Adventures*, 149; Stanford Lomakema, "The Effect of Americanization on Hopi Culture and Health," lecture, Dartmouth College, Oct. 20, 1998.

22. Spitta, "Shamanism and Christianity," 34; Pastor Bodmer, *The Armature of Conquest*, 129–51.

23. Adorno and Pautz, *Álvar Núñez Cabeza de Vaca*, 1: 237.

24. Adorno and Pautz, *Álvar Núñez Cabeza de Vaca*, 3: 325–81, esp. 334–38 on Guzmán and Indian slavery.

25. Adorno and Pautz, *Álvar Núñez Cabeza de Vaca*, 1: 239–45, quotes at 239; 2: 347–49.

26. Adorno and Pautz, *Álvar Núñez Cabeza de Vaca*, 1: 249, 251.

27. Bernard DeVoto, *The Course of Empire* (1952; reprint, Boston: Houghton Mifflin, 1980), 19.

28. José Rabasa, "Allegory and Ethnography in Cabeza de Vaca's Naufragios and Commentaries," in William B. Taylor and Franklin Pease G.Y., eds., *Violence, Resistance, and Survival in the Americas: Native Americans and the Legacy of Conquest* (Washington DC: Smithsonian Institution Press, 1994), 40–66; Rabasa, *Writing Violence*, chap. 1.

29. Cynthia Radding, "Cultural Boundaries between Adaptation and Defiance: The Mission Communities of Northwestern New Spain," in Nicholas Griffiths and Fernando Cervantes, eds., *Spiritual Encounters: Interactions between Christianity and Native Religions in Colonial America* (Lincoln: University of Nebraska Press, 1999), 120.

30. On Cabeza de Vaca's life, see Adorno and Pautz, *Álvar Núñez Cabeza de Vaca*, 1: 293–413.

31. Rangel's figures, cited in Charles Hudson, *Knights of Spain, Warriors of the Sun: Hernando de Soto and the South's Ancient Chiefdoms* (Athens: University of Georgia Press, 1997), 244.

32. Gloria A. Young and Michael P. Hoffman, eds., *The Expedition of Hernando de Soto West of the Mississippi, 1541–1543: Proceedings of the De Soto Symposia, 1988 and 1990* (Fayetteville: University of Arkansas Press, 1993).

33. David H. Dye, "Reconstruction of the de Soto Expedition Route in Arkansas: The Mississippi Alluvial Plain," Phyllis A. Morse, "The Parkin Site and Its Role in Determining the Route of the de Soto Expedition," and George Sabo III, "Indians and Spaniards in Arkansas: Symbolic Action in the Sixteenth Century," all in Young and Hoffman, eds., *The Expedition of Hernando de Soto*, 36–53, 58–67, 198–203. Pacaha may have been Capaha or Quapaw, but evidently it was not a Quapaw or Siouan word; more likely it was Tunican. See Robert L. Rankin, "Language Affiliations of Some de Soto Place Names in Arkansas," in Young and Hoffman, eds., *The Expedition of Hernando de Soto*, 213–17, 220.

34. The Tulas may have been a Caddoan people, but the evidence is inconclusive. See Cecile Elkins Carter, *Caddo Indians: Where We Come From* (Norman: University of Oklahoma Press, 1995), 21. Wallace Chafe, "Caddo Names in the de Soto Documents," in Young and Hoffman, eds., *The Expedition of*

Hernando de Soto, 225, concludes that Tula is not a Caddoan word and was probably the name given to the town by one of De Soto's Muskogean guides.

35. Hudson, *Knights of Spain,* 322; Ann M. Early, "Finding the Middle Passage: The Spanish Journey from the Swamplands to Caddo Country," in Young and Hoffman, eds., *The Expedition of Hernando de Soto,* 71–72.

36. Hudson, *Knights of Spain,* 328–29.

37. Sabo, "Indians and Spaniards in Arkansas," 204.

38. Frank R. Schambach, "The End of the Trail: Reconstruction of the Route of Hernando de Soto's Army through Southwest Arkansas and East Texas," in Young and Hoffman, eds., *The Expedition of Hernando de Soto,* 78–105.

39. Schambach, "The End of the Trail," 86–96; Hudson, *Knights of Spain,* 355–56, 359–63; Carter, *Caddo Indians,* 24–25. Naguatex is commonly regarded as a Spanish pronunciation of the Caddoan name Namidish or Nawidish, meaning "place of the salt" or "people of the salt," but there is disagreement on this. See Wallace Chafe, "Caddo Names in the de Soto Documents," in Young and Hoffman, eds., *The Expedition of Hernando de Soto,* 222–23, cf. Schambach, "The End of the Trail," 89–90.

40. Nancy Adele Kenmotsu, James E. Bruseth, and James E. Corbin, "Moscoso and the Route in Texas: A Reconstruction," in Young and Hoffman, eds., *The Expedition of Hernando de Soto,* 106–30; Schambach, "The End of the Trail," 100.

41. Hudson, *Knights of Spain,* 418.

42. David Ewing Duncan, *Hernando de Soto: A Savage Quest in the Americas* (New York: Crown, 1995), 388.

43. See Russell Thornton, Jonathan Warren, and Tim Miller, "Depopulation in the Southeast after 1492," in John W. Verano and Douglas H. Ubelaker, eds., *Disease and Demography in the Americas* (Washington DC: Smithsonian Institution Press, 1992), 187–95; Hudson, *Knights of Spain,* 418–26; Ann F. Ramenofsky and Patricia Galloway, "Disease and the Soto Entrada," in Patricia K. Galloway, ed., *The Hernando de Soto Expedition: History, Historiography, and "Discovery" in the Southeast* (Lincoln: University of Nebraska Press, 1997), 259–79, identify nineteen diseases that could have been introduced by the invading Spaniards and suggest that ten of them, including smallpox, tuberculosis, typhoid fever, and whooping cough, probably were. For discussion of the impact of the De Soto expedition west of the Mississippi, see Barbara A. Burnett and Katherine A. Murray, "Death, Drought, and de Soto: The Bioarchaeology of Depopulation," and Timothy K. Perttula, "The Long-Term Effects of the de Soto Entrada on Aboriginal Caddoan Populations," in Young and Hoffman, eds., *The Expedition of Hernando de Soto,* 227–36, 237–53. On the dangers of assuming that disease caused depopulation and for a critique of the premises, methodology, and conclusions of those he calls the

"High Counters," see David Henige, *Numbers from Nowhere: The American Indian Contact Population Debate* (Norman: University of Oklahoma Press, 1998).

44. Jay K. Johnson, "From Chiefdom to Tribe in Northeast Mississippi: The de Soto Expedition as a Window on a Culture in Transition," in Galloway, ed., *The Hernando de Soto Expedition*, 295–312.

45. Hudson, *Knights of Spain*, 423–44, 432–33; Michael P. Hoffman, "Identification of Ethnic Groups Contacted by the de Soto Expedition in Arkansas," in Young and Hoffman, eds., *The Expedition of Hernando de Soto*, 133–34.

46. Cleve Hallenbeck, *The Journey of Fray Marcos de Niza* (Dallas TX: Southern Methodist University Press, 1987), 2.

47. *Presidio and Militia*, 2, pt. 1: 253; 2, pt. 2: 17.

48. Hammond and Rey, eds., *Narratives*, 66, 75–77, 178, 198–99; Hallenbeck, *The Journey of Fray Marcos de Niza*; Edmund J. Ladd, "Zuni on the Day the Men in Metal Arrived," in Richard Flint and Shirley Cushing Flint, eds., *The Coronado Expedition to Tierra Nueva: The 1540–1542 Route across the Southwest* (Niwot: University Press of Colorado, 1997), 227–28; Dedra S. McDonald, "Intimacy and Empire: Indian-African Interaction in Spanish Colonial New Mexico, 1500–1800," *American Indian Quarterly* 22 (1998): 134–35.

49. Hammond and Rey, eds., *Narratives*, 79. Marcos has been branded a liar for claiming there were great riches in Cíbola, but his own report contains no mention of gold. For discussion of the veracity of Marcos's claims and his reputation as the "Lying Monk," see Hallenbeck, *The Journey of Fray Marcos de Niza*, 41–95, and William K. Hartmann, "Pathfinder for Coronado: Reevaluating the Mysterious Journey of Marcos de Niza," in Flint and Flint, eds., *The Coronado Expedition*, 73–101.

50. Hammond and Rey, eds., *Narratives*, 200.

51. "Muster Roll of the Expedition," in Hammond and Rey, eds., *Narratives*, 87–108; Flint and Flint, eds., *The Coronado Expedition*, xvii, 5–6; Richard Flint, "Armas de la Tierra: The Mexican Indian Component of Coronado Expedition Material Culture," in Flint and Flint, eds., *The Coronado Expedition*, 57–70.

52. Inga Clendinnen, " 'Fierce and Unnatural Cruelty': Cortés and the Conquest of Mexico," *Representations* 33 (1991): 92–94.

53. Rabasa, *Writing Violence*, 27.

54. Hammond and Rey, eds., *Narratives*, 168–70, 172; Ladd, "Zuni on the Day the Men in Metal Arrived," 231–33.

55. Hammond and Rey, eds., *Narratives*, 174, 177; Cheryl J. Foote and Sandra K. Schackel, "Indian Women of New Mexico, 1535–1680," in Joan M. Jensen and Darlis A. Miller, eds., *New Mexico Women: Intercultural Perspectives* (Albuquerque: University of New Mexico Press, 1986), 17–40.

56. Hammond and Rey, eds., *Narratives*, 177–78.

57. Hammond and Rey, eds., *Narratives*, 213–15.

58. Frank Waters, *Book of the Hopi* (New York: Penguin, 1977), 251–52; Edward H. Spicer, *Cycles of Conquest: The Impact of Spain, Mexico, and the United States on the Indians of the Southwest, 1533–1960* (Tucson: University of Arizona Press, 1962), 189.

59. Hammond and Rey, eds., *Narratives*, 258–59; Elinore M. Barrett, *Conquest and Catastrophe: Changing Rio Grande Settlement Patterns in the Sixteenth and Seventeenth Centuries* (Albuquerque: University of New Mexico Press, 2002), 12.

60. Hammond and Rey, eds., *Narratives*, 217, 324–25.

61. Hammond and Rey, eds., *Narratives*, 218, 233. Explanation of the Acoma greeting is provided by Velma Garcia-Mason, "Acoma Pueblo," in *HNAI*, 9: 455–56.

62. Hammond and Rey, eds., *Narratives*, 256–57; Peter Nabokov and Robert Easton, *Native American Architecture* (New York: Oxford University Press, 1989), 351.

63. Mildred M. Wedel, "The Man They Called Turco," in Don G. Wyckoff and Jack L. Hofman, eds., *Pathways to Plains Prehistory: Anthropological Perspectives on Plains Natives and Their Pasts*, Oklahoma Anthropological Society, memoir 3 (1982), 153–62, identifies the Turk as a Wichita from Quivira. Carroll Riley identifies the Turk as Pawnee ("The Teya Indians of the Southwestern Plains," in Flint and Flint, eds., *The Coronado Expedition*, 320).

64. Hammond and Rey, eds., *Narratives*, 219, 221, 290.

65. Carroll L. Riley, *Rio del Norte: People of the Upper Rio Grande from Earliest Times to the Pueblo Revolt* (Salt Lake City: University of Utah Press, 1995), 170.

66. Hammond and Rey, eds., *Narratives*, 223–27, 333–34, 355–58; David J. Weber, *The Spanish Frontier in North America* (New Haven CT: Yale University Press, 1992), 99.

67. Hammond and Rey, eds., *Narratives*, 228–30, 333.

68. Hammond and Rey, eds., *Narratives*, 233–34. On the pueblos of Arenal, Moho, and other sites in the Tiguex region, see Barrett, *Conquest and Catastrophe*, 26–28.

69. The identity of the Querechos has been complicated by debates over the route taken by Coronado's army and the locations of its encounters with the Indians. See Judith A. Habïcht-Mauche, "Coronado's Querechos and Teyas in the Archaeological Record of the Texas Panhandle," *Plains Anthropologist* 37 (1992): 247–59.

70. Hammond and Rey, eds., *Narratives*, 235–36.

71. Hammond and Rey, eds., *Narratives*, 186–87, 237, 261, 292, 311. John Miller Morris, *El Llano Estacado: Exploration and Imagination on the High Plains of Texas and New Mexico, 1536–1860* (Austin: Texas State Historical Association, 1997), 87–89, 118–21, discusses Castañeda's reactions and the words he used to describe the plains.

72. Dan Flores, *Horizontal Yellow: Nature and History in the Near Southwest* (Albuquerque: University of New Mexico Press, 1999), 170; Felix D. Almaráz Jr., "An Uninviting Land: El Llano Estacado, 1534–1824," in Ralph H. Vigil, Frances W. Kaye, and John R. Wunder, eds., *Spain and the Plains: Myths and Realities of the Spanish Exploration and Settlement on the Great Plains* (Niwot: University of Colorado Press, 1994), 74; Morris, *El Llano Estacado.*

73. Morris, *El Llano Estacado,* 64–65.

74. Hammond and Rey, eds., *Narratives,* 186, 261–62, 310–11.

75. The Spaniards came to use the name Tejas for the Hasinai confederacy of the Caddos, but it is not clear that the people Coronado met were Caddo. Linguist Nancy Hickerson thinks that the Indians called Teyas by the Spaniards may have been the same people they called Jumanos after the 1580s. John R. Swanton, *Source Material on the History and Ethnology of the Caddo Indians* (1942; reprint, Norman: University of Oklahoma Press, 1996), 35; Nancy Parrott Hickerson, *The Jumanos: Hunters and Traders of the South Plains* (Austin: University of Texas Press, 1994), 23–27; Habïcht-Mauche, "Coronado's Querechos and Teyas"; Riley, "The Teya Indians," 320–43.

76. Hammond and Rey, eds., *Narratives,* 188, 239–40.

77. Hammond and Rey, eds., *Narratives,* 241. Another account said the Turk confessed he led them astray "in order to kill them all so that they would not go to his country" (Hammond and Rey, eds., *Narratives,* 363).

78. Hammond and Rey, eds., *Narratives,* 266.

79. Quoted in Weber, *The Spanish Frontier,* 41.

80. Carroll L. Riley, *The Kachina and the Cross: Indians and Spaniards in the Early Southwest* (Salt Lake City: University of Utah Press, 1999), 36.

81. Riley, *The Kachina and the Cross,* 32.

82. Riley, *Rio del Norte,* 226.

83. Riley, *The Kachina and the Cross,* 33; Weber, *The Spanish Frontier,* 79.

84. "Gallegos' Relation of the Chamuscado-Rodríguez Expedition" and "Brief and True Account of the Discovery of New Mexico by Nine Men Who Set out from Santa Bárbara in the Company of Three Franciscan Friars," both in George P. Hammond and Agapito Rey, eds., *The Rediscovery of New Mexico* (Albuquerque: University of New Mexico Press, 1966), 94–95, 141–44. For lists and maps of the many pueblos recorded by this and other Spanish expeditions, see Albert H. Schroeder, "Pueblos Abandoned in Historic Times," in *HNAI,* 9: 236–54; for Pueblo population and settlement at this time, see Barrett, *Conquest and Catastrophe,* chap. 1.

85. "Gallegos' Relation," 108.

86. Riley, *Rio del Norte,* 233; Riley, *The Kachina and the Cross,* 33.

87. "Report of Antonio de Espejo," in Hammond and Rey, eds., *The Rediscovery of New Mexico,* 213–31, quote at 219.

88. "Report of Antonio de Espejo," 224.

89. "Report of Antonio de Espejo," 225–26.

90. "Castaño de Sosa's 'Memoria': Report on the Exploratory Expedition to New Mexico Undertaken on July 27, 1590, by Gaspar Castaño de Sosa while He Was Lieutenant Governor and Captain General of New León," in Hammond and Rey, eds., *The Rediscovery of New Mexico*, 269–77, quotes at 278, 282.

91. Riley, *Rio del Norte*, 245–46.

92. "Conquistador Statue Stirs Hispanic Pride and Indian Rage," *New York Times*, 9 February 1999, A10.

93. Donald Chipman, "The Oñate-Zaldívar Families of Northern New Spain," *New Mexico Historical Review* 52 (1977): 297–310.

94. Marc Simmons, *The Last Conquistador: Juan de Oñate and the Settling of the Far Southwest* (Norman: University of Oklahoma Press, 1991).

95. Riley, *The Kachina and the Cross*, 44–45; David H. Snow, *New Mexico's First Colonists: The 1597–1600 Enlistments for New Mexico under Juan de Oñate, Adelante and Gobernador* (Albuquerque: Hispanic Genealogical Research Center of New Mexico, 1998), 1–6.

96. Riley, *The Kachina and the Cross*, 45. On Zaldívar and his role in subsequent events, see also Nancy P. Hickerson, "The *Servicios* of Vicente de Zaldívar: New Light on the Jumano War of 1601," *Ethnohistory* 43 (1996): 127–44. On the establishment of the trail and the functioning of the supply route, see Max L. Moorehead, *New Mexico's Royal Road: Trade and Travel on the Chihuahua Trail* (Norman: University of Oklahoma Press, 1958), chaps. 1–2.

97. John L. Kessell, *Spain in the Southwest: A Narrative History of Colonial New Mexico, Arizona, Texas, and California* (Norman: University of Oklahoma Press, 2002), 75–76.

98. Quoted in Alfonso Ortiz, *The Pueblo* (New York: Chelsea House, 1994), 35.

99. Elinore M. Barrett, "The Geography of the Rio Grande Pueblos in the Seventeenth Century," *Ethnohistory* 49 (2002): 124, 126–31; Barrett, *Conquest and Catastrophe*, 54–58.

100. George P. Hammond and Agapito Rey, eds., *Don Juan de Oñate: Colonizer of New Mexico, 1595–1628*, 2 vols. (Albuquerque: University of New Mexico Press, 1953), 1: 337–62.

101. Alfonso Ortiz, "San Juan Pueblo," in *HNAI*, 9: 281–82.

102. Andrew L. Knaut, *The Pueblo Revolt of 1680* (Norman: University of Oklahoma Press, 1995), 48; H. Allen Anderson, "The Encomienda in New Mexico, 1598–1680," *New Mexico Historical Review* 60 (1985): 353–77; Spicer, *Cycles of Conquest*, 167.

103. Frederick W. Hodge, George P. Hammond, and Agapito Rey, eds., *Fray Alonso de Benavides' Revised Memorial of 1634* (Albuquerque: University of New Mexico Press, 1945), 47–48.

104. Hammond and Rey, eds., *Don Juan de Oñate,* 1: 354–56.

105. Indian testimonies are in Hammond and Rey, eds., *Don Juan de Oñate,* 1: 464–67. Garcia-Mason, "Acoma Pueblo," 457, mentions the oral history.

106. Hammond and Rey, eds., *Don Juan de Oñate,* 1: 435, 456.

107. Hammond and Rey, eds., *Don Juan de Oñate,* 1: 470.

108. Hammond and Rey, eds., *Don Juan de Oñate,* 1: 427, 462, 471–76, 614–15.

109. Hammond and Rey, eds., *Don Juan de Oñate,* 1: 427.

110. Hammond and Rey, eds., *Don Juan de Oñate,* 1: 477; George P. Hammond and Agapito Rey, eds., *New Mexico in 1602: Juan de Montoya's Relation of the Discovery of New Mexico* (Albuquerque: Quivira Society, 1938), "pacified and intimidated" quote at 48; Rabasa, *Writing Violence,* "theater of terror" quote at 107. Historian John Kessell raises doubts about whether the Acoma sentences were actually carried out, since Spanish strategy often involved sentencing Indians to death only to have the friars intercede and secure mercy. However, brutality against the Acomas in the trial was included in the list of charges later brought against Oñate; see Kessell, *Spain in the Southwest,* 84, 95.

111. Jack D. Forbes, *Apache, Navaho, and Spaniard* (Norman: University of Oklahoma Press, 1960), 94.

112. Hammond and Rey, eds., *Don Juan de Oñate,* 2: 656.

113. Hammond and Rey, eds., *Don Juan de Oñate,* 2: 619–22, 701.

114. Hammond and Rey, eds., *Don Juan de Oñate,* 2: 608–18, quotes at 609–10.

115. Hammond and Rey, eds., *Don Juan de Oñate,* 2: 698.

116. Hammond and Rey, eds., *Don Juan de Oñate,* 2: 673–76, 693–95.

117. Hammond and Rey, eds., *Don Juan de Oñate,* 2: 672–89.

118. Riley, *The Kachina and the Cross,* 87, 90, 92, 95, 100, 131–33.

119. Spicer, *Cycles of Conquest,* 157, 303–4, 388–92.

120. Spicer, *Cycles of Conquest,* 159, 302; Riley, *The Kachina and the Cross,* 93; Anderson, "The Encomienda in New Mexico."

121. Knaut, *The Pueblo Revolt,* 54.

122. Ramón A. Gutiérrez, *When Jesus Came, the Corn Mothers Went Away: Marriage, Sexuality, and Power in New Mexico, 1500–1846* (Stanford CA: Stanford University Press, 1991).

123. Riley, *The Kachina and the Cross,* 96–97.

124. Baker H. Morrow, trans. and ed., *A Harvest of Reluctant Souls: The Memorial of Fray Alonso de Benavides, 1630* (Niwot: University of Colorado Press, 1996), xi, 43, 85, 104; Hodge, Hammond, and Rey, eds., *Fray Alonso de Benavides' Revised Memorial,* 45, shaman quote at 66, 80, 85, 89, 99.

125. John L. Kessell, *Kiva, Cross, and Crown: The Pecos Indians and New Mexico, 1540–1840,* 2nd ed. (Albuquerque: University of New Mexico Press, 1987), 110–11, 127–28. There were actually four churches built at Pecos,

two before the revolt of 1680 and two after the reconquest of 1692; Frances Levine, *Our Prayers Are in This Place: Pecos Identity over the Centuries* (Albuquerque: University of New Mexico Press, 1999), 18–19.

126. Waters, *Book of the Hopi*, 254; Spicer, *Cycles of Conquest*, 190–91.

127. Richard E. W. Adams and Murdo J. MacLeod, eds., *The Cambridge History of the Native Peoples of the Americas*, vol. 2, *Mesoamerica* (Cambridge: Cambridge University Press, 2000), pt. 1: 18.

128. Gutiérrez, *When Jesus Came*, 93. Similar accommodations and survivals occurred throughout the Americas. Highland Mayas, for example, withstood the onslaught of Spanish acculturation not only by holding onto land and language but also by retaining their own principles of community organization and their own sense of identity. "Daily chores and the seasonal round followed a Maya, not a Spanish rhythm," explains W. George Lovell. "Even time itself, the days and months that make up a year, ticked on with a Maya pulse" ("The Highland Maya," in Adams and MacLeod, eds., *The Cambridge History*, 2, pt. 2: 412.

129. Ortiz, *The Pueblo*, 50.

130. Knaut, *The Pueblo Revolt*, 81; Riley, *Rio del Norte*, 5.

131. Spicer, *Cycles of Conquest*, 22–24.

132. Daniel T. Reff, ed., *History of the Triumphs of Our Holy Faith amongst the Most Barbarous and Fierce Peoples of the New World by Andrés Pérez de Ribas: An English Translation Based on the 1645 Spanish Original* (Tucson: University of Arizona Press, 1999), 27–46; Robert H. Jackson, *From Savages to Subjects: Missions in the History of the American Southwest* (Armonk NY: M. E. Sharpe, 2000) provides an overview of different missionary encounters.

133. Reff, ed., *History of the Triumphs*, 97.

134. Reff, ed., *History of the Triumphs*, 627–28.

135. Reff, ed., *History of the Triumphs*, 42–43, 122–23, 539, 673. For broader discussion of the impact of European epidemics in the region, see Reff, *Disease, Depopulation, and Culture Change.*

136. Andrés Pérez de Ribas gave a count of eighteen thousand "baptized and properly instructed" in 1600 and a count of forty thousand baptized by 1604, although, of course, it was in a missionary's interest to inflate the baptismal head count. See Reff, ed., *History of the Triumphs*, 169, 191.

137. Spicer, *Cycles of Conquest*, 47–48; Reff, ed., *History of the Triumphs*, 327, 337, 341; Evelyn Hu-DeHart, *Missionaries, Miners, and Indians: Spanish Contact with the Yaqui Nation of Northwestern New Spain 1533–1820* (Tucson: University of Arizona Press, 1981), chaps. 2–3.

138. Reff, ed., *History of the Triumphs*, book 5; Hu-DeHart, *Missionaries, Miners, and Indians*, 29–39; Spicer, *Cycles of Conquest*, 48–49; Edward H. Spicer, *The Yaquis: A Cultural History* (Tucson: University of Arizona Press, 1980),

13–32; Christopher Vecsey, *On the Padres' Trail* (Notre Dame IN: University of Notre Dame Press, 1996), 76–81, quote at 76.

139. Thomas E. Sheridan, comp. and ed., *Empire of Sand: The Seri Indians and the Struggle for Spanish Sonora, 1645–1803* (Tucson: University of Arizona Press, 1999), 3–6; Charles DiPeso and Daniel Matson, eds., "The Seri Indians in 1692 as Described by Adam Gilg, S.J.," *Arizona and the West* 7 (1965): 33–56, quote at 43; Spicer, *Cycles of Conquest*, 312–14.

140. Spicer, *Cycles of Conquest*, 105–7; Sheridan, comp. and ed., *Empire of Sand*, 1, 17–20, 31–33, 36–70.

141. This discussion of Pueblo-Plains exchange relies heavily on the essays in Katherine A. Spielmann, ed., *Farmers, Hunters, and Colonists: Interaction between the Southwest and the Southern Plains* (Tucson: University of Arizona Press, 1991).

142. Timothy G. Baugh, "Ecology and Exchange: The Dynamics of Plains-Pueblo Interaction," Christopher Lintz, "Texas Panhandle–Pueblo Interactions from the Thirteenth through the Sixteenth Century," and David R. Wilcox, "Changing Contexts of Pueblo Adaptations, A.D. 1250–1600," all in Spielmann, ed., *Farmers, Hunters, and Colonists*, 107–27, 89–106, 144–46.

143. Scott Rushforth and Steadman Upham, *A Hopi Social History* (Austin: University of Texas Press, 1992), 30; Hammond and Rey, eds., *The Rediscovery of New Mexico*, 26, 224. Forbes, *Apache, Navaho, and Spaniard*, 57, identified them as "undoubtedly Navajos."

144. Curtis F. Schaafsma, *Apaches de Navajo: Seventeenth-Century Navajos in the Chama Valley of New Mexico* (Salt Lake City: University of Utah Press, 2002), 241–46; Frank McNitt, *Navajo Wars: Military Campaigns, Slave Raids and Reprisals* (Albuquerque: University of New Mexico Press, 1972), 5–6; Morrow, trans. and ed., *A Harvest of Reluctant Souls*, 62. Edward T. Hall, *West of the Thirties: Discoveries among the Navajo and Hopi* (New York: Doubleday, 1994), 106, says the Spanish called them Apaches de Nabajo—Apaches with knives—because of the stone knives they carried.

145. Hammond and Rey, eds., *Don Juan de Oñate*, 1: 398–405; also in Hammond and Rey, eds., *New Mexico in 1602*, 50–58.

146. Hammond and Rey, eds., *Don Juan de Oñate*, 1: 484.

147. C. Lange, "Relations of the Southwest with the Plains and Great Basin," in *HNAI*, 9: 201–6.

148. Hammond and Rey, eds., *Don Juan de Oñate*, 2: 628; see also Forbes, *Apache, Navaho, and Spaniard*, 99.

149. Kessell, *Kiva, Cross, and Crown*, 134–35.

150. Kessell, *Kiva, Cross, and Crown*, 136; Forbes, *Apache, Navaho, and Spaniard*, 26.

151. George E. Hyde, *Indians of the High Plains: From the Prehistoric Period to the Coming of Europeans* (Norman: University of Oklahoma Press, 1959),

12, and Frank R. Secoy, *Changing Military Patterns of the Great Plains Indians* (1953; reprint, Lincoln: University of Nebraska Press, 1992), 12, suggest Plains Apaches; Forbes, *Apache, Navaho, and Spaniard,* 101, suggests Tonkawas; cf. Hammond and Rey, eds., *Don Juan de Oñate,* 2: 752, and F. Todd Smith, *The Wichita Indians: Traders of Texas and the Southern Plains, 1540–1845* (College Station: Texas A & M University Press, 2000), 13, who treat them as Iscanis. Douglas R. Parks, "Enigmatic Groups," in *HNAI,* 13: 965, favors Iscani over Apache, Tonkawa, Kansa, or Osage. In Karl H. Schlesier's opinion, the Escanxaques "represent the penultimate stage in the fate of a unique Plains Caddoan tradition that had lasted as an independent unit for nearly a thousand years until, decimated and displaced, its groups were subsumed, as were other originally independent groups, in that cauldron of survivors on the Red River during the eighteenth century called the Wichitas" ("Commentary: A History of Ethnic Groups on the Great Plains, A.D. 150–1550," in Karl H. Schlesier, ed., *Plains Indians* A.D. *500–1500: The Archaeological Past of Historical Groups* [Norman: University of Oklahoma Press, 1994], 360). On Oñate's route, the Indian settlements, and the various subdivisions of Wichitas, who were sometimes in conflict, see Susan C. Vehik, "Oñate's Expedition to the Southern Plains: Routes, Destinations, and Implications for Late Prehistoric Cultural Adaptations," *Plains Anthropologist* 31 (1986): 13–33.

152. Hammond and Rey, eds., *Don Juan de Oñate,* 2: 754.

153. Hammond and Rey, eds., *Don Juan de Oñate,* 2: 755, 841–59, 865, 932; Smith, *The Wichita Indians,* 13–14.

154. Forbes, *Apache, Navaho, and Spaniard,* 116–21.

155. Forbes, *Apache, Navaho, and Spaniard,* 27; Hammond and Rey, eds., *Narratives,* 294.

156. Hammond and Rey, eds., *Narratives,* 257–58; Bandelier's report of 1890, pp. 116–30, cited in Russell J. Barber and Frances F. Berdan, *The Emperor's Mirror: Understanding Cultures through Primary Sources* (Tucson: University of Arizona Press, 1988), 251.

157. Timothy G. Baugh, "Ecology and Exchange: The Dynamics of Plains-Pueblo Interaction," in Spielmann, ed., *Farmers, Hunters, and Colonists,* 121.

158. Frances Levine, "Economic Perspectives on the Comanchero Trade," in Spielmann, ed., *Farmers, Hunters, and Colonists,* 156.

159. Riley, *The Kachina and the Cross,* 10.

4. Rebellions and Reconquests

1. Susan M. Deeds, "Indigenous Rebellions on the Northern Mexican Mission Frontier: From First-Generation to Later Colonial Responses," in Donna J. Guy and Thomas E. Sheridan, eds., *Contested Ground: Comparative Frontiers on the Northern and Southern Edges of the Spanish Empire* (Tucson: University of

Arizona Press, 1998), 32–51; Cynthia Radding, *Wandering Peoples: Colonialism, Ethnic Spaces, and Ecological Frontiers in Northwestern New Mexico, 1700–1850* (Durham NC: Duke University Press, 1997), 39–40; *Presidio and Militia*, 2, pt. 2: 13, 43; Oakah L. Jones Jr., *Nueva Vizcaya: Heartland of the Spanish Frontier* (Albuquerque: University of New Mexico Press, 1988), chap. 5 and table 3. Jack D. Forbes, *Apache, Navaho, and Spaniard* (Norman: University of Oklahoma Press, 1960), 202–3, cites Spanish use of the term "epidemic."

2. Steve J. Stern, ed., *Resistance, Rebellion, and Consciousness in the Andean Peasant World, 18th to 20th Centuries* (Madison: University of Wisconsin Press, 1987), 11; Roberto Mario Salmon, *Indian Revolts in Northern New Spain: A Synthesis of Resistance (1680–1786)* (Lanham MD: University Press of America, 1991).

3. Joe S. Sando, *Pueblo Nations: Eight Centuries of Pueblo Indian History* (Santa Fe NM: Clear Light, 1992), 63.

4. David J. Weber, *What Caused the Pueblo Revolt of 1680?* (Boston: Bedford Books, 1999).

5. Daniel T. Reff, ed., *History of the Triumphs of Our Holy Faith amongst the Most Barbarous and Fierce Peoples of the New World by Andrés Pérez de Ribas: An English Translation Based on the 1645 Spanish Original* (Tucson: University of Arizona Press, 1999), 96, 124–25, 343, 505, 573, 594; Daniel T. Reff, "The 'Predicament of Culture' and Spanish Missionary Accounts of the Tepehuan and Pueblo Revolts," *Ethnohistory* 42 (1995): 63–90; Cynthia Radding, "Cultural Boundaries between Adaptation and Defiance: The Mission Communities of Northwestern New Spain," in Nicholas Griffiths and Fernando Cervantes, eds., *Spiritual Encounters: Interactions between Christianity and Native Religions in Colonial America* (Lincoln: University of Nebraska Press, 1999), 1116–35.

6. *Presidio and Militia*, 1: 34–35. On the war, see Philip Wayne Powell, *Soldiers, Indians, and Silver: The Northward Advance of New Spain, 1550–1600* (Los Angeles: University of California Press, 1952); Thomas D. Hall, *Social Change in the Southwest, 1350–1880* (Lawrence: University Press of Kansas, 1989), 63–73; and Reff, ed., *History of the Triumphs*, 698–701. On the development and role of presidios, see Max L. Moorehead, *The Presidio: Bastion of the Spanish Borderlands* (Norman: University of Oklahoma Press, 1975, 1991).

7. Reff, ed., *History of the Triumphs*, 158–62.

8. Reff, ed., *History of the Triumphs*, 505–10.

9. Reff, ed., *History of the Triumphs*, 236–43.

10. *Presidio and Militia*, 1: 149–53; Charles Wilson Hackett, ed., *Historical Documents Relating to New Mexico, Nueva Vizcaya, and Approaches Thereto, to 1773*, 3 vols. (Washington DC: Carnegie Institute, 1923–27), 2: 36–37, 101–15; Reff, ed., *History of the Triumphs*, book 10 and estimate at 140; Edward H. Spicer, *Cycles of Conquest: The Impact of Spain, Mexico, and the United States*

on the Indians of the Southwest, 1533–1960 (Tucson: University of Arizona Press, 1962), 26–28, 86; Charlotte M. Gradie, *The Tepehuan Revolt of 1616: Militarism, Evangelism, and Colonialism in Seventeenth-Century Nueva Vizcaya* (Salt Lake City: University of Utah Press, 2000).

11. *Presidio and Mission*, 1: 297–300, 379; Spicer, *Cycles of Conquest*, 29–33; Jones, *Nueva Vizcaya*, 99, 102–3; Salmon, *Indian Revolts*, 23–29.

12. William C. Foster, ed., *Texas and Northeastern Mexico, 1630–1690 by Juan Bautista Chapa*, trans. Ned F. Brierley (Austin: University of Texas Press, 1997), 52–56, 62–68, 74–85, 91–92.

13. Andrew Knaut, *The Pueblo Revolt of 1680: Conquest and Resistance in Seventeenth-Century New Mexico* (Norman: University of Oklahoma Press, 1995), chaps. 6–7.

14. Daniel T. Reff, *Disease, Depopulation, and Culture Change in Northwestern New Spain, 1518–1764* (Salt Lake City: University of Utah Press, 1991); Daniel T. Reff, "The Jesuit Mission Frontier in Comparative Perspective: The Reduction of the Río de la Plata and the Missions of Northwestern New Mexico, 1588–1700," in Guy and Sheridan, eds., *Contested Ground*, 16–31.

15. Reff, "The 'Predicament of Culture,'" 70–71.

16. John L. Kessell, *Kiva, Cross, and Crown: The Pecos Indians and New Mexico, 1540–1840* (Albuquerque: University of New Mexico Press, 1977), 163, 170.

17. J. Manuel Espinosa, trans. and ed., *The Pueblo Indian Revolt of 1696 and the Franciscan Missions in New Mexico: Letters of the Missionaries and Related Documents* (Norman: University of Oklahoma Press, 1988), 24–25.

18. Forbes, *Apache, Navaho, and Spaniard*, 136–37; Ralph Emerson Twitchell, trans. and ed., *The Spanish Archives of New Mexico*, 2 vols. (1914; reprint, New York: Arno Press, 1976), 2: 279–80.

19. Charles Wilson Hackett, ed., *Revolt of the Pueblo Indians of New Mexico and Otermín's Attempted Reconquest 1680–1682*, trans. Charmion Clair Shelby, 2 vols. (Albuquerque: University of New Mexico Press, 1942), 2: 245–46, 266, 299; Carroll L. Riley, *Rio del Norte: People of the Upper Rio Grande from Earliest Times to the Pueblo Revolt* (Salt Lake City: University of Utah Press, 1995), 266; Carroll L. Riley, *The Kachina and the Cross: Indians and Spaniards in the Early Southwest* (Salt Lake City: University of Utah Press, 1999), 214.

20. Frank D. Reeve, "Seventeenth Century Navaho-Spanish Relations," *New Mexico Historical Review* 32 (1957): 36–52; Curtis F. Schaafsma, "Pueblo and Apachean Alliance Formation in the Seventeenth Century," in Robert W. Preucel, ed., *Archaeologies of the Pueblo Revolt: Identity, Meaning, and Renewal in the Pueblo World* (Albuquerque: University of New Mexico Press, 2002), chap. 13; Forbes, *Apache, Navajo, and Spaniard*, 154–55; Hackett, ed., *Historical Documents*, 3: 111.

21. Kessell, *Kiva, Cross, and Crown*, 159, 222; Twitchell, trans. and ed., *The*

Spanish Archives, 2: 22; Ramón A. Gutiérrez, *When Jesus Came, the Corn Mothers Went Away: Marriage, Sexuality, and Power in New Mexico, 1500–1846* (Stanford CA: Stanford University Press, 1991), 112–13.

22. Forbes, *Apache, Navaho, and Spaniard*, 151.

23. Hackett, ed., *Historical Documents*, 3: 302; James E. Ivey, " 'The Greatest Misfortune of All': Famine in the Province of New Mexico, 1667–1672," *Journal of the Southwest* 36 (1994): 76–100.

24. Twitchell, trans. and ed., *The Spanish Archives*, 2: 269; Albert H. Schroeder, "Shifting for Survival," in David J. Weber, ed., *New Spain's Far Northern Frontier: Essays on Spain in the American West, 1540–1821* (Dallas TX: Southern Methodist University Press, 1979, 1988), 237–56.

25. Reeve, "Seventeenth Century Navaho-Spanish Relations," 46–47; Hackett, ed., *Historical Documents*, 3: 187.

26. Forbes, *Apache, Navaho, and Spaniard*, 160–61, 173; Hackett, ed., *Historical Documents*, 3: 272.

27. Ana María Alonso, *Thread of Blood: Colonialism, Revolution, and Gender on Mexico's Northern Frontier* (Tucson: University of Arizona Press, 1995), 21–25.

28. Reeve, "Seventeenth Century Navaho-Spanish Relations," 49–50.

29. Laura Bayer with Floyd Montoya and the Pueblo of Santa Ana, *Santa Ana: The People of the Pueblo, and the History of Tamaya* (Albuquerque: University of New Mexico Press, 1994), 61.

30. John L. Kessell, Rick Hendricks, and Meredith D. Dodge, eds., *By Force of Arms: The Journals of Don Diego de Vargas, New Mexico, 1691–93* (Albuquerque: University of New Mexico Press, 1992), 3, 5, 40n3; Reff, *Disease, Depopulation, and Culture Change*, 229; Elinore M. Barrett, "The Geography of the Rio Grande Pueblos in the Seventeenth Century," *Ethnohistory* 49 (2002): 123–69; Elinore M. Barrett, *Conquest and Catastrophe: Changing Rio Grande Pueblo Settlement Patterns in the Sixteenth and Seventeenth Centuries* (Albuquerque: University of New Mexico Press, 2002), chaps. 2–4.

31. Gutiérrez, *When Jesus Came*, 114.

32. Hackett, ed., *Historical Documents*, 3: 141; Gutiérrez, *When Jesus Came*, 127–28; Frank Waters, *Book of the Hopi* (New York: Penguin, 1977), 253.

33. Sando, *Pueblo Nations*, 62.

34. For fuller discussions of the power and meaning of ceramic designs during the era of the Pueblo Revolt, see Jeanette L. Mobley-Tanaka, "Crossed Cultures, Crossed Meanings: The Manipulation of Ritual Imagery in Early Historic Pueblo Resistance," Barbara J. Mills, "Acts of Resistance: Zuni Ceramics, Social Identity, and the Pueblo Revolt," and Patricia W. Capone and Robert W. Preucel, "Ceramic Semiotics: Women, Pottery, and Social Meanings at Kotyiti Pueblo," all in Preucel, ed., *Archaeologies of the Pueblo Revolt*.

35. France V. Scholes, "Church and State in New Mexico, 1610–1650,"

New Mexico Historical Review 11 (1936): 25; Riley, *The Kachina and the Cross,* 156–90; Hackett, ed., *Historical Documents,* 3: 66–74, 129–279; Christopher Vecsey, *On the Padres' Trail* (Notre Dame IN: University of Notre Dame Press, 1996), 130–31, 134.

36. Gutiérrez, *When Jesus Came,* 113, 123.

37. Hackett, ed., *Revolt of the Pueblo Indians,* 2: 291, 309.

38. Kessell, Hendricks, and Dodge, eds., *By Force of Arms,* 11.

39. Sando, *Pueblo Nations,* 6; Alfonso Ortiz, "Popay's Leadership: A Pueblo Perspective," *El Palacio* 86 (1980–81): 19–20.

40. Hackett, ed., *Revolt of the Pueblo Indians,* 2: Tupatú quote at 237; Espinosa, trans. and ed., *The Pueblo Indian Revolt,* 34.

41. Fray Angélico Chávez, "Pohé-Yemo's Representative and the Pueblo Revolt of 1680," *New Mexico Historical Review* 42 (1967): 85–106.

42. Hackett, ed., *Revolt of the Pueblo Indians,* 1: 338, 354–55; Dedra S. McDonald, "Intimacy and Empire: Indian-African Interaction in Spanish Colonial New Mexico, 1500–1800," *American Indian Quarterly* 22 (1998): 142–43.

43. Knaut, *The Pueblo Revolt,* 81.

44. Twitchell, trans. and ed., *The Spanish Archives,* 2: 52; Hackett, ed., *Revolt of the Pueblo Indians,* 2: 234.

45. Ortiz, "Popay's Leadership," 20; Gutiérrez, *When Jesus Came,* 162.

46. Kessell, Hendricks, and Dodge, eds., *By Force of Arms,* 16.

47. David J. Weber,*The Spanish Frontier in North America* (New Haven CT: Yale University Press, 1992), 134.

48. Hackett, ed., *Revolt of the Pueblo Indians,* 2: 246; Twitchell, trans. and ed., *The Spanish Archives,* 2: 63; Gutiérrez, *When Jesus Came,* 132–33; Franklin Folsom, *Red Power on the Rio Grande* (1973; reprint, Albuquerque: University of New Mexico Press, 1996), 32. Pueblo people still commemorate this event each year with foot races along the routes taken by the runners. Peter Nabokov, *Indian Running* (Santa Barbara CA: Capra Press, 1981).

49. Twitchell, trans. and ed., *The Spanish Archives,* 2: 47.

50. Hackett, ed., *Revolt of the Pueblo Indians,* 2: 3; "List and Memorial of the Religious Whom the Indians of New Mexico Killed," in Hackett, ed., *Historical Documents,* 3: 335.

51. Ekkehart Malotki, ed., *Hopi Ruin Legends: Kiqötutuwutsi,* narrated by Michael Lomatuway'ma, Lorena Lomatuway'ma, and Sidney Namingha Jr. (Lincoln: University of Nebraska Press, published for Northern Arizona University, 1993), 295n4.

52. Henry R. Voth, *The Traditions of the Hopi,* Field Columbian Museum Publication no. 96, Anthropological Series no. 8 (1905); Harold Courlander, *The Fourth World of the Hopis: The Epic Story of the Hopi Indians as Preserved in Their Legends and Traditions* (Albuquerque: University of New Mexico Press,

1971), 160–63; Waters, *Book of the Hopi,* 254; Scott Rushforth and Steadman Upham, *A Hopi Social History* (Austin: University of Texas Press, 1992), 102. Andrew Wiget, "Truth and the Hopi: An Historiographic Study of Documented Oral Tradition Concerning the Coming of the Spanish," *Ethnohistory* 29 (1982): 181–99, provides a critique of the Hopi oral tradition and, on p. 188, the description of Fray Trujillo.

53. Hackett, ed., *Revolt of the Pueblo Indians,* 1: 19; Hackett, ed., *Historical Documents,* 3: 327–35. On the experiences of the women, see Salomé Hernández, "*Nueva Mexicanas* as Refugees and Reconquest Settlers, 1680–1696," in Joan M. Jensen and Darlis A. Miller, eds., *New Mexico Women: Intercultural Perspectives* (Albuquerque: University of New Mexico Press, 1986), 41–69.

54. Twitchell, trans. and ed., *The Spanish Archives,* 2: 14; Hackett, ed., *Revolt of the Pueblo Indians,* 1: 20.

55. Twitchell, trans. and ed., *The Spanish Archives,* 2: 18, 43–44, 64; Hackett, ed., *Revolt of the Pueblo Indians,* 2: 247–48.

56. Gutiérrez, *When Jesus Came,* 135.

57. Hackett, ed., *Historical Documents,* 3: 354–55; Vecsey, *On the Padres' Trail,* 137–38.

58. Sando, *Pueblo Nations,* 67; Barrett, *Conquest and Catastrophe,* 94. Hopi and Sandia traditions seem to disagree on whether the Sandias abandoned their pueblo; see Elizabeth A. Brandt, "Sandia Pueblo," *HNAI,* 9: 345. On the resettling of Sandia, see SANM, series 2, reel 1, no. 848; Twitchell, trans. and ed., *The Spanish Archives,* 2: 220–25; Eleanor B. Adams and Angélico Chávez, trans. and eds., *The Missions of New Mexico, 1776: A Description by Fray Francisco Atanasio Domínguez with Other Contemporary Documents* (Albuquerque: University of New Mexico Press, 1956), 138; and Hackett, ed., *Historical Documents,* 3: 389–90, 472.

59. *HNAI,* 9: 185–86, 338–39, 353–54; Hackett, ed., *Historical Documents,* 3: 292, 297–98; John L. Kessell, Rick Hendricks, and Meredith D. Dodge, eds., *Remote beyond Compare: Letters of Don Diego de Vargas to His Family from New Spain and New Mexico, 1675–1706* (Albuquerque: University of New Mexico Press, 1989), 175, 179; Kessell, Hendricks, and Dodge, eds., *By Force of Arms,* 175–76.

60. Hackett, ed., *Revolt of the Pueblo Indians,* 1: 24–25, 61; 2: 4, 232–49; Twitchell, trans. and ed., *The Spanish Archives,* 2: 51–68; Hackett, ed., *Historical Documents,* 3: 355.

61. Sando, *Pueblo Nations,* 67; Ortiz, "Popay's Leadership," 21. I am grateful to Justin McHorse of Taos for bringing this interpretation to my attention.

62. Reff, "The 'Predicament of Culture.' "

63. Bayer, *Santa Ana,* 65–66.

64. Hackett, ed., *Historical Documents*, 2: 211; Hackett, ed., *Revolt of the Pueblo Indians*, 1: 188–89; 2: 21.

65. Radding, *Wandering Peoples*, 9, 32–40: Salmon, *Indian Revolts*.

66. *Presidio and Militia*, 2, pt. 1: 260–64.

67. *Presidio and Militia*, 1: 483; Forbes, *Apache, Navaho, and Spaniard*, 190–99.

68. Radding, *Wandering Peoples*, 280–81.

69. Radding, *Wandering Peoples*, 281.

70. Spicer, *Cycles of Conquest*, 96–99; Oakah L. Jones Jr., *Pueblo Warriors and Spanish Conquest* (Norman: University of Oklahoma Press, 1966), 24–29; Radding, *Wandering Peoples*, 281.

71. Jones, *Nueva Vizcaya*, 107.

72. Hackett, ed., *Historical Documents*, 2: 219–23; Jones, *Nueva Vizcaya*, 107–8.

73. Forbes, *Apache, Navaho, and Spaniard*, 200–202.

74. *Presidio and Militia*, 1: 507–8.

75. *Presidio and Militia*, 1: 529–31.

76. *Presidio and Militia*, 1: 485.

77. *Presidio and Militia*, 1: 548–58, "100 nations" quote at 556; Hackett, ed., *Historical Documents*, 2: 219; Forbes, *Apache, Navaho, and Spaniard*, 201–6.

78. Fernández fought against the Sumas and their allies in the 1680s. In the 1690s he was presidial commander at Janos and fought against Apaches, against Pimas in 1695, Tarahumaras in 1697, and Pima Bajos in 1701. *Presidio and Militia*, 1: 507; Forbes, *Apache, Navaho, and Spaniard*, 207–9.

79. Spicer, *Cycles of Conquest*, 87–88.

80. Quoted in Evelyn Hu-DeHart, *Missionaries, Miners, and Indians: Spanish Contact with the Yaqui Nation of Northwestern New Spain, 1533–1820* (Tucson: University of Arizona Press, 1981), 56.

81. Forbes, *Apache, Navaho, and Spaniard*, 209–11; *Presidio and Militia*, 1: 575–78; Hackett, ed., *Historical Documents*, 2: 229–31.

82. Foster, ed., *Texas and Northeastern Mexico*, 139–41.

83. Forbes, *Apache, Navaho, and Spaniard*, 218–20.

84. Hackett, ed., *Historical Documents*, 2: 11, 401, 447.

85. Hackett, ed., *Historical Documents*, 2: 393–405, 429–33.

86. Hackett, ed., *Historical Documents*, 2: 379.

87. Herbert E. Bolton, ed., *Kino's Historical Memoir of Pimería Alta, 1683–1711*, 2 vols. (Cleveland: Arthur H. Clark, 1919), 1: quotes at 63, 195; Rufus Kay Wyllys, ed., "Padre Luis Velarde's Relación of Pimería Alta, 1716," *New Mexico Historical Review* 6 (1931): 111–57, "cruel to himself" quote at 153.

88. Spicer, *Cycles of Conquest*, 118–25; Radding, *Wandering Peoples*, 282–83.

89. Bolton, ed., *Kino's Historical Memoir*, 1: 140–43; Wyllys, ed., "Padre Luis Velarde's Relación," 142–46.

90. Bolton, ed., *Kino's Historical Memoir,* 1: 148–49; *Presidio and Militia,* 1: 583–84.

91. *Presidio and Militia,* 1: 486, 583–84.

92. *Presidio and Militia,* 1: 585–86.

93. The campaign journal is printed, in both Spanish and English, in *Presidio and Militia,* 1: 583–718.

94. *Presidio and Militia,* 1: 599, 624–26.

95. *Presidio and Militia,* 1: 638.

96. *Presidio and Militia,* 1: 653–54.

97. Spicer, *Cycles of Conquest,* 96; Jack D. Forbes, *Warriors of the Colorado: The Yumas of the Quechan Nation and Their Neighbors* (Norman: University of Oklahoma Press, 1965), 117.

98. Spicer, *Cycles of Conquest,* 34–35.

99. Alonso, *Thread of Blood,* chap. 1; Salmon, *Indian Revolts*; Eric Van Young, "The Indigenous Peoples of Western Mexico from the Spanish Invasion to the Present," in Richard E. W. Adams and Murdo J. MacLeod, eds., *The Cambridge History of the Native Peoples of the Americas,* vol. 2, *Mesoamerica* (Cambridge: Cambridge University Press, 2000), pt. 1: quote at 159.

100. Quoted in Forbes, *Apache, Navaho, and Spaniard,* 230.

101. Forbes, *Apache, Navaho, and Spaniard,* 193.

102. Espinosa, trans. and ed., *The Pueblo Indian Revolt,* 35.

103. Kessell, *Kiva, Cross, and Crown,* 303. The volumes of the Vargas project, edited by John L. Kessell, Rick Hendricks, and Meredith D. Dodge and published by the University of New Mexico Press, are *Remote beyond Compare: Letters of Don Diego de Vargas to His Family from New Spain and New Mexico, 1675–1706* (1989); *By Force of Arms: The Journals of Don Diego de Vargas, New Mexico, 1691–93* (1992); *To the Royal Crown Restored: The Journals of Don Diego de Vargas, New Mexico, 1692–94* (1995); and *Blood on the Boulders: The Journals of Don Diego de Vargas, New Mexico, 1694–97,* 2 vols. (1998). *That Disturbances Cease: The Journals of Don Diego de Vargas, New Mexico, 1697–1700* (2000), unlike the previous volumes, focuses almost exclusively on the Hispanic community rather than on Spanish-Indian relations, in particular, the dispute between Vargas and Governor Rodríguez Cubero. The final volume of the project is *A Settling of Accounts: The Journals of Don Diego de Vargas, New Mexico, 1700–1704* (2002).

104. Espinosa, trans. and ed., *The Pueblo Indian Revolt,* 38; Twitchell, trans. and ed., *The Spanish Archives,* 2: 276–77.

105. Mark T. Lycett, "Transformations of Place: Occupational History and Differential Persistence in Seventeenth-Century New Mexico," in Preucel, ed., *Archaeologies of the Pueblo Revolt,* chap. 4.

106. *Presidio and Militia,* 2, pt. 2: 154, 232.

107. Twitchell, trans. and ed., *The Spanish Archives,* 2: 277.

108. Twitchell, trans. and ed., *The Spanish Archives*, 2: 277.

109. Espinosa, trans. and ed., *The Pueblo Indian Revolt*, 240n1; Sando, *Pueblo Nations*, 67.

110. Sando, *Pueblo Nations*, 69.

111. Vargas's official account of the campaign, "Armed Reconnaissance and Ritual Repossession by Diego de Vargas of Santa Fe and Twelve Pueblos of the Tewa, Tano, and Taos Indians, 9 Aug.–16. Oct. 1692," is in Kessell, Hendricks, and Dodge, eds., *By Force of Arms*, 357–490.

112. Kessell, Hendricks, and Dodge, eds., *Remote beyond Compare*, 55; Kessell, Hendricks, and Dodge, eds., *By Force of Arms*, 188. On the role of Pueblo allies in the reconquest, see Jones, *Pueblo Warriors and Spanish Conquest*, chap. 2.

113. Kessell, Hendricks, and Dodge, eds., *By Force of Arms*, 382–85.

114. Kessell, Hendricks, and Dodge, eds., *By Force of Arms*, 395–97.

115. Kessell, Hendricks, and Dodge, eds., *By Force of Arms*, 398, 401–2; Kessell, Hendricks, and Dodge, eds., *Remote beyond Compare*, 56–57.

116. Kessell, Hendricks, and Dodge, eds., *By Force of Arms*, 403–4, 406–7. Palm straw or yucca fiber headbands and saltwater shells were traditional items of formal costume (485n52).

117. Kessell, Hendricks, and Dodge, eds., *By Force of Arms*, 408–13.

118. Kessell, Hendricks, and Dodge, eds., *By Force of Arms*, 411–12, 116n52.

119. Rushforth and Upham, *A Hopi Social History*, 103; Waters, *Book of the Hopi*, 258–59.

120. Kessell, Hendricks, and Dodge, eds., *By Force of Arms*, 461; cf. Kessell, Hendricks, and Dodge, eds., *Remote beyond Compare*, 57.

121. John L. Kessell, Rick Hendricks, and Meredith D. Dodge, eds., *To the Royal Crown Restored: The Journals of Don Diego de Vargas, New Mexico, 1692–94* (Albuquerque: University of New Mexico Press, 1995), 181–220, quotes at 182, 216–17.

122. Kessell, Hendricks, and Dodge, eds., *By Force of Arms*, quote at 460; Kessell, Hendricks, and Dodge, eds., *To the Royal Crown Restored*, 373–553; Hernández, "*Nueva Mexicanas* as Refugees."

123. Kessell, Hendricks, and Dodge, eds., *To the Royal Crown Restored*, 402.

124. Espinosa, trans. and ed., *The Pueblo Indian Revolt*, 71.

125. Kessell, Hendricks, and Dodge, eds., *Remote beyond Compare*, 62; Kessell, Hendricks, and Dodge, eds., *To the Royal Crown Restored*, 529–33; Espinosa, trans. and ed., *The Pueblo Indian Revolt*, 42–43; John L. Kessell, Rick Hendricks, and Meredith D. Dodge, eds., *Blood on the Boulders: The Journals of Don Diego de Vargas, New Mexico, 1694–97*, 2 vols. (Albuquerque: University of New Mexico Press, 1998), 1: 36, 53, 94.

126. Kessell, Hendricks, and Dodge, eds., *Blood on the Boulders*, 1: 27; Espinosa, trans. and ed., *The Pueblo Indian Revolt*, 44–46, 78.

127. Kessell, Hendricks, and Dodge, eds., *Blood on the Boulders,* 1: 32–33, 185.

128. Summaries of the campaigns are contained in Vargas's reports to Conde de Galvé; Kessell, Hendricks, and Dodge, eds., *Blood on the Boulders,* 1: 242–54, 358–87; and Rick Hendricks, "Pueblo-Spanish Warfare in Seventeenth-Century New Mexico: The Battles of Black Mesa, Kotyiti, and Astialakwa," in Preucel, ed., *Archaeologies of the Pueblo Revolt,* chap. 12.

129. Kessell, Hendricks, and Dodge, eds., *Blood on the Boulders,* 1: 112–13.

130. Kessell, Hendricks, and Dodge, eds., *Blood on the Boulders,* 1: 192–95, 202.

131. Kessell, Hendricks, and Dodge, eds., *Blood on the Boulders,* 1: 229–30.

132. Kessell, Hendricks, and Dodge, eds., *Blood on the Boulders,* 1: 290–301.

133. Kessell, Hendricks, and Dodge, eds., *Blood on the Boulders,* 1: 323–27, 332.

134. Kessell, Hendricks, and Dodge, eds., *Blood on the Boulders,* 1: 378–89, 416–17.

135. Kessell, Hendricks, and Dodge, eds., *Blood on the Boulders,* 1: 405–6; Espinosa, trans. and ed., *The Pueblo Indian Revolt,* 46, 240n1.

136. Kessell, Hendricks, and Dodge, eds., *Blood on the Boulders,* 2: 641–71.

137. Kessell, Hendricks, and Dodge, eds., *Blood on the Boulders,* 1: 603–4; 2: 674; Kessell, Hendricks, and Dodge, eds., *Remote beyond Compare,* 62; Espinosa, trans. and ed., *The Pueblo Indian Revolt,* 163–236.

138. Kessell, Hendricks, and Dodge, eds., *Blood on the Boulders,* 2: 728–29, 733–35, 870–74; Espinosa, trans. and ed., *The Pueblo Indian Revolt,* 50, 243–45.

139. Espinosa, trans. and ed., *The Pueblo Indian Revolt,* 239; Kessell, Hendricks, and Dodge, eds., *Blood on the Boulders,* 2: 849; Preucel, ed., *Archaeologies of the Pueblo Revolt,* 9.

140. Kessell, Hendricks, and Dodge, eds., *Blood on the Boulders,* 2: 723–24, 897–98, 908, 937; Espinosa, trans. and ed., *The Pueblo Indian Revolt,* 50, 57.

141. Espinosa, trans. and ed., *The Pueblo Indian Revolt,* 239; Kessell, Hendricks, and Dodge, eds., *Blood on the Boulders,* 2: 736–37, 740–41, 751–52, 754, 757, 802, 898.

142. Kessell, Hendricks, and Dodge, eds., *Blood on the Boulders,* 2: 641, 677, 780, 788, 915–16.

143. Kessell, Hendricks, and Dodge, eds., *Blood on the Boulders,* 2: 840.

144. Kessell, Hendricks, and Dodge, eds., *Blood on the Boulders,* 2: 821–23, 882.

145. Kessell, Hendricks, and Dodge, eds., *Blood on the Boulders,* 2: 792, 796.

146. Kessell, Hendricks, and Dodge, eds., *Blood on the Boulders,* 2: 843–46, 887–89; Espinosa, trans. and ed., *The Pueblo Indian Revolt,* 279.

147. Espinosa, trans. and ed., *The Pueblo Indian Revolt*, 280; Kessell, Hendricks, and Dodge, eds., *Blood on the Boulders*, 2: 846.

148. Kessell, Hendricks, and Dodge, eds., *Blood on the Boulders*, 2: 985–90.

149. Kessell, Hendricks, and Dodge, eds., *Blood on the Boulders*, 2: 1001–5.

150. Kessell, Hendricks, and Dodge, eds., *Blood on the Boulders*, 2: 1008; Kessell, *Kiva, Cross, and Crown*, 288–97.

151. Kessell, Hendricks, and Dodge, eds., *Blood on the Boulders*, 2: 1017–22, 1026, 1028, 1030–35.

152. Espinosa, trans. and ed., *The Pueblo Indian Revolt*, 55; Kessell, Hendricks, and Dodge, eds., *Blood on the Boulders*, 2: 1050–55.

153. Kessell, Hendricks, and Dodge, eds., *Blood on the Boulders*, 2: 1056.

154. Rushforth and Upham, *A Hopi Social History*, 102; Ronald H. Towner, ed., *The Archaeology of Navajo Origins* (Salt Lake City: University of Utah Press, 1996), 88, 167–69; Curtis F. Schaafsma, *Apaches de Navajo: Seventeenth-Century Navajos in the Chama Valley of New Mexico* (Salt Lake City: University of Utah Press, 2002), 283–96.

155. On the investigations of Vargas as governor, the complaints brought against him by colonists, and his dispute with Governor Rodríguez Cubero, see John L. Kessell, Rick Hendricks, Meredith D. Dodge, and Larry D. Miller, eds., *That Disturbances Cease: The Journals of Don Diego de Vargas, New Mexico, 1697–1700* (Albuquerque: University of New Mexico Press, 2000).

156. Kessell, *Kiva, Cross, and Crown*, 293; Forbes, *Apache, Navaho, and Spaniard*, 279; *Presidio and Militia*, 2, pt. 2: 13; Radding, *Wandering Peoples*, 40.

157. E. Charles Adams, "The View from the Hopi Mesas," in David R. Wilcox and E. Bruce Masse, eds., *The Protohistoric Period in the North American Southwest*, A.D. *1450–1700*, Anthropological Research Papers no. 24, Arizona State University (1981), 321–35, esp. 325–26, 331.

158. Harold Courlander, ed., *Big Falling Snow: A Tewa-Hopi Indian's Life and Times and the History and Traditions of His People* (Albuquerque: University of New Mexico Press, 1978), viii–ix, 1.

159. Rushforth and Upham, *A Hopi Social History*, 97–106; Waters, *Book of the Hopi*, 258–66; Spicer, *Cycles of Conquest*, 192–95. The oral account of the attack is in Malotki, ed., *Hopi Ruin Legends*, 275–410, quote at 391; see also Courlander, *The Fourth World*, 177–84. Peter Whiteley, "Re-imagining Awat'ovi," in Preucel, ed., *Archaeologies of the Pueblo Revolt*, chap. 10, sees the attack not simply as a rejection of Christianity but as part of a systematic Hopi reforming of their culture and society, with significant influence from Rio Grande refugees.

160. Malotki, ed., *Hopi Ruin Legends*, 399–401.

161. Dennis Gilpin, "Early Navajo Occupation West of the Chuska Mountains," in Towner, ed., *The Archaeology of Navajo Origins*, 171.

162. David M. Brugge, *Navajos in the Catholic Church Records of New Mexico, 1694–1875* (Tsaile AZ: Navajo Community College Press, 1985), 29.

163. Spicer, *Cycles of Conquest*, 165, 193–94; Lansing B. Bloom, "A Campaign against the Moqui Pueblos under Governor Phelix Martínez, 1716," *New Mexico Historical Review* 6 (1931): 158–226; SANM, series 2, reel 5, archive 250.

164. E. Charles Adams, "Passive Resistance: Hopi Responses to Spanish Contact and Conquest," and Hartman H. Lomawaima, "Hopification, a Strategy for Cultural Preservation," both in David Hurst Thomas, ed., *Columbian Consequences*, vol. 1, *Archaeological and Historical Perspectives on the Spanish Borderlands West* (Washington DC: Smithsonian Institution Press, 1989), 77–99, 93–99.

165. T. J. Ferguson, "Dowa Yalanne: The Architecture of Zuni Resistance and Social Change during the Pueblo Revolt," in Preucel, ed., *Archaeologies of the Pueblo Revolt*, chap. 2; Robert W. Preucel, "The Emergence of Modern Zuni Culture and Society: A Summary of Zuni Tribal History A.D. 1450 to 1700," in Wilcox and Masse, eds., *The Protohistoric Period*, 336–53, Cushing quote at 346.

166. Elizabeth A. H. John, *Storms Brewed in Other Men's Worlds: The Confrontation of Indians, Spanish, and French in the Southwest, 1540–1795* (Lincoln: University of Nebraska Press, 1975), 115–16. Doubting the influx of Pueblo refugees after the 1696 revolt, Schaafsma, *Apaches de Navajo*, 283–96, asserts that other models must be found for Pueblo influence on post-1700 Navajo culture, as does Towner, ed., *The Archaeology of Navajo Origins*, 169.

167. Brugge, *Navajos in the Catholic Church Records*, 41.

168. Hackett, ed., *Historical Documents*, 3: 367, 382; John, *Storms*, 226–27, 232–35; Brugge, *Navajos in the Catholic Records*, 42; Rick Hendricks and John P. Wilson, eds. and trans., *The Navajos in 1705: Roque Madrid's Campaign Journal* (Albuquerque: University of New Mexico Press, 1996), quotes at 20, 26; Frank D. Reeve, "Navaho-Spanish Wars, 1680–1720," *New Mexico Historical Review* 33 (1958): 205–31; Frank D. Reeve, "The Navaho-Spanish Peace: 1720s-1770s," *New Mexico Historical Review* 34 (1959): 9–40; Frank McNitt, *Navajo Wars: Military Campaigns, Slave Raids, and Reprisals* (Albuquerque: University of New Mexico Press, 1972), 19–25; W. W. Hill, "Some Navaho Culture Changes during Two Centuries (with a Translation of the Early Eighteenth Century Rabal Manuscript)," *Smithsonian Miscellaneous Collections* 100 (1940): 395–413. The Rabal document is also reprinted in Robert A. Roessel Jr., *Dinétah: Navajo History*, vol. 2 (Rough Rock AZ: Navajo Curriculum Center, 1983), 67–77.

169. Hill, "Some Navaho Culture Changes," 395–413; Ronald H. Towner and Byron P. Johnson, *The San Rafael Survey: Reconstructing Eighteenth Century Navajo Population Dynamics in the Dinétah Using Archaeological and Dendrochrono-*

logical Data (Tucson: Arizona State Museum and the University of Arizona, 1998), 19–51.

170. Steven A. LeBlanc, *Prehistoric Warfare in the American Southwest* (Salt Lake City: University of Utah Press, 1999), 45; Robert Ryal Miller, trans. and ed., "New Mexico in Mid-Eighteenth Century: A Report Based on Governor Vélez Cachupín's Inspection," *Southwestern Historical Quarterly* 79 (1975): 175; *Presidio and Militia,* 2, pt. 1: 292–93; Jones, *Pueblo Warriors and Spanish Conquest.*

171. Espinosa, trans. and ed., *The Pueblo Indian Revolt,* 2.

172. Espinosa, trans. and ed., *The Pueblo Indian Revolt,* 253, 255, 290.

173. Kessell, Hendricks, and Dodge, eds., *To the Royal Crown Restored,* xi.

174. Florence Hawley Ellis, "Laguna Pueblo," in *HNAI,* 9: 438.

175. Kessell, Hendricks, and Dodge, eds., *By Force of Arms,* 12.

176. Weber, *The Spanish Frontier,* 136.

177. Oakah L. Jones Jr., *Los Paisanos: Spanish Settlers on the Frontier of New Spain,* 2nd ed. (Norman: University of Oklahoma Press, 1979), 119–29, 240.

178. John L. Kessell, "Spaniards and Pueblos: From Crusading Intolerance to Pragmatic Accommodation," in Thomas, ed., *Columbian Consequences,* 1: 127–38.

179. Kessell, Hendricks, and Dodge, eds., *Blood on the Borders,* 2: 1113, 1121.

180. Malcolm Ebright, "Advocates for the Oppressed: Indians, Genízaros and Their Spanish Advocates in New Mexico, 1700–1786," *New Mexico Historical Review* 71 (1996): 305–39.

181. Charles R. Cutter, *The Legal Culture of Northern New Spain, 1700–1810* (Albuquerque: University of New Mexico Press, 1995), 31–32.

182. Marc Simmons, *Coronado's Land: Essays on Daily Life in Colonial New Mexico* (Albuquerque: University of New Mexico Press, 1991), 3–4; Marc Simmons, *Spanish Pathways: Readings in the History of Hispanic New Mexico* (Albuquerque: University of New Mexico Press, 2001), 1–2, 98; Riley, *The Kachina and the Cross,* 134–39.

183. Jones, *Los Paisanos,* chaps. 5–6; Frances Leon Quintana, *Pobladores: Hispanic Americans of the Ute Frontier* (Notre Dame IN: University of Notre Dame Press, 1971), 12.

184. John Miller Morris, *El Llano Estacado: Exploration and Imagination on the High Plains of Texas and New Mexico, 1536–1860* (Austin: Texas State Historical Association, 1997), 157–62; Charles L. Kenner, *The Comanchero Frontier: A History of New Mexican–Plains Indian Relations* (Norman: University of Oklahoma Press, 1969), chap. 5.

185. Donald E. Chipman, *Spanish Texas, 1519–1821* (Austin: University of Texas Press, 1992), 54–55; Richard J. Morrissey, "The Northward Expansion of Cattle Ranching in New Spain, 1550–1600," *Agricultural History* 25 (1951):

115–21; Sandra L. Myers, "The Ranching Frontier: Spanish Institutional Backgrounds of the Plains Cattle Industry," in Weber, ed., *New Spain's Far Northern Frontier,* 79–93. Anglo-Americans who entered the Southwest in the nineteenth century brought their own heritage of open-range cattle herding that reached back to colonial South Carolina, but they soon adopted Hispanic customs and practices; Terry G. Jordan, *Trails to Texas* (Lincoln: University of Nebraska Press, 1981); Simmons, "The Rise of Cattle Ranching," in *Spanish Pathways,* 115–20.

186. Riley, *Rio del Norte,* 258–61; Riley, *The Kachina and the Cross,* 210–12.

187. Spicer, *Cycles of Conquest,* 422–30, 449–50, quote at 430.

188. Rayna Green, "Visualizing History: Locating History in Native American Art," lecture, Hood Museum of Art, Dartmouth College, May 9, 2001.

189. Spicer, *Cycles of Conquest,* 300.

190. Jones, *Los Paisanos,* 130–32; Riley, *The Kachina and the Cross,* 126–29.

191. Alfred Barnaby Thomas, trans. and ed., *After Coronado: Spanish Exploration Northeast of New Mexico, 1696–1727* (Norman: University of Oklahoma Press, 1935), 13–14; James F. Brooks, *Captives and Cousins: Slavery, Kinship, and Community in the Southwest Borderlands* (Chapel Hill: University of North Carolina Press, 2002), 33, 71.

192. Russell M. Magnaghi, "The Genízaro Experience in Spanish New Mexico," in Ralph H. Vigil, Frances W. Kaye, and John R. Wunder, eds., *Spain and the Plains: Myths and Realities of the Spanish Exploration and Settlement on the Great Plains* (Niwot: University of Colorado Press, 1994), 114–30; Russell M. Magnaghi, "Plains Indians in New Mexico: The Genízaro Experience," *Great Plains Quarterly* 10 (1990): 86–95; Hall, *Social Change,* 116–17; Albert H. Schroeder and Omer C. Stewart, "Indian Servitude in the Southwest," in *HNAI,* 4: 410–13; Brooks, *Captives and Cousins,* 123–38.

193. Gutiérrez, *When Jesus Came,* 150–52, 194–206; Adrian Bustamante, " 'The Matter Was Never Resolved': The Caste System in Colonial New Mexico, 1693–1823," *New Mexico Historical Review* 66 (1991): 143–63.

194. Hackett, ed., *Revolt of the Pueblo Indians,* 2: 235; Twitchell, trans. and ed., *The Spanish Archives,* 2: 53.

195. *Presidio and Militia,* 2, pt. 2: 244.

196. Spicer, *Cycles of Conquest,* 235–36, and maps at 237, 286.

197. Hackett, ed., *Historical Documents,* 2: 49–58, 233, 277–78, 235–91, passim.

198. Vynola Beaver Newkumet and Howard L. Meredith, *Hasinai: A Traditional History of the Caddo Confederacy* (College Station: Texas A & M University Press, 1988), 74; Herbert E. Bolton, "The Names Texas and Hasinai," in Herbert E. Bolton, *The Hasinais: Southern Caddoans as Seen by the Earliest Europeans* (Norman: University of Oklahoma Press, 1987), 53–69; John R. Swanton, ed., *Source Material on the History and Ethnology of the Caddo Indians* (1942; reprint,

Norman: University of Oklahoma Press, 1996), 4–5; Mattie Austin Hatcher, trans., "Descriptions of the Tejas or Asinai Indians, 1691–1722," *Southwestern Historical Quarterly* 30 (1926–27): 286.

199. Swanton, ed., *Source Material*, 17, 45–50; F. Todd Smith, *The Caddo Indians: Tribes at the Convergence of Empires, 1542–1854* (College Station: Texas A & M University Press, 1995), 27–35. Francisco Casañas de Jesus Maria's letter, reprinted in Spanish in Swanton at 241–63, is produced in English in Hatcher, trans., "Descriptions," 206–18, 283–304, disease at 294–95, 303. Massanet's observations on the Indians, the Tejas mission, and its abandonment are in *Presidio and Militia*, 2, pt. 2: 330–58.

200. Kessell, Hendricks, and Dodge, eds., *Blood on the Borders*, 2: 652–55.

201. *Presidio and Militia*, 2, pt. 2: 14.

202. Twitchell, trans. and ed., *The Spanish Archives*, 2: 189; Thomas, trans. and ed., *After Coronado*, 19.

203. John, *Storms*, 228–30; Thomas, trans. and ed., *After Coronado*, 16–22, 59–77; Charles Wilson Hackett, ed., *Pichardo's Treatise on the Limits of Louisiana and Texas*, 4 vols. (Austin: University of Texas Press, 1931–46), 3: 182.

204. Thomas, trans. and ed., *After Coronado*, 196.

205. T. N. Campbell, "Coahuiltecans and Their Neighbors," in *HNAI*, 10: 345–46; Robert H. Jackson, *From Savages to Subjects: Missions in the History of the American Southwest* (Armonk NY: M. E. Sharpe, 2000), 58, 90, 92, 95–96; *Letters and Memorials of the Father Presidente Fray Benito Fernández de Santa Ana, 1736–1754* (San Antonio TX: Old Spanish Missions Historical Research Library, 1981), 21, 22–23, complaint about insufficient soldiers at 25.

206. Twitchell, trans. and ed., *The Spanish Archives*, 2: 189; Thomas, trans. and ed., *After Coronado*, 31, 132, 143–44; Hackett, ed., *Pichardo's Treatise*, 1: 191–94. On identification of the Paloma Apaches, see Morris E. Opler, "The Apachean Culture Pattern and Its Origins," in *HNAI*, 10: 389.

207. Hackett, ed., *Pichardo's Treatise*, 3: 197. A Quadruple Alliance of European powers was formed in 1718 to oppose the Italian policy of Philip V of Spain. England declared war on Spain in December 1718, France in January 1719. Spain yielded to the terms of the Quadruple Alliance the next year.

208. *Presidio and Militia*, 2, pt. 2: 361–62, 401; Chipman, *Spanish Texas*, 118–19.

209. Thomas, trans. and ed., *After Coronado*, 33, 146–47.

210. *Presidio and Militia*, 2, pt. 2: 362, 398–438; Chipman, *Spanish Texas*, 120–23, 186.

211. Valero ordered the presidio built at El Cuartelejo but later took the advice of Valverde's council of war and changed his recommendation to La Jicarilla. Thomas, trans. and ed., *After Coronado*, 34–35, 150, 154–62; Hackett, ed., *Pichardo's Treatise*, 3: 201–18.

212. Thomas, trans. and ed., *After Coronado,* 37–38, 133–39, 162–67, 182–87; Twitchell, trans. and ed., *The Spanish Archives,* 2: 190–91; Hackett, ed., *Pichardo's Treatise,* 1: 195–98; *Presidio and Militia,* 2, pt. 2: 266–76.

213. Thomas, trans. and ed., *After Coronado,* 245–60.

214. Thomas H. Naylor and Charles W. Polzer, comps. and eds., *Pedro de Rivera and the Military Regulations for Northern New Spain, 1724–1729: A Documentary History of His Frontier Inspection and the Reglamento de 1729* (Tucson: University of Arizona Press, 1988).

5. Calumet and Fleur-de-lys

1. Donald Jackson, ed., *Black Hawk: An Autobiography* (Urbana: University of Illinois Press, 1990), 41–43.

2. Reuben G. Thwaites, ed., *The Jesuit Relations and Allied Documents: Travels and Explorations of the Jesuit Missionaries in New France 1610–1791,* 73 vols. (Cleveland: Burrows Brothers, 1896–1901), 8: 10–11.

3. Arthur T. Adams, ed., *The Explorations of Pierre Esprit Radisson* (Minneapolis: Ross and Haines, 1961), 128; D. Peter MacLeod, "The Anishinabeg Point of View: The History of the Great Lakes Region to 1800 in Nineteenth-Century Mississauga, Odawa, and Ojibwa Historiography," *Canadian Historical Review* 73 (1992): 195–201, esp. 206–7.

4. Colin G. Calloway, ed., *The World Turned Upside Down: Indian Voices from Early America* (Boston: Bedford Books, 1994), 33–34.

5. Cornelius J. Jaenen, ed., *The French Regime in the Upper Country of Canada during the Seventeenth Century* (Toronto: Champlain Society, 1996), 90–92; Bernard DeVoto, *The Course of Empire* (Boston: Houghton Mifflin, 1952), 55.

6. Bruce G. Trigger, *The Children of Aataentsic: A History of the Huron People to 1660,* 2 vols. (Montreal: McGill-Queens University Press, 1976), 213.

7. Pierre de Charlevoix, *Journal of a Voyage to North-America,* 2 vols. (London, 1761; reprint, New York: Readex Microprint, 1966), 1: 151; see also Thwaites, ed., *The Jesuit Relations,* 1: 249. Charlevoix provided a long discussion (151–67) on beaver; Gordon M. Sayre examines beaver in the literature of New France in *Les Sauvages Américains: Representations of Native Americans in French and English Colonial Literature* (Chapel Hill: University of North Carolina Press, 1997), chap. 5.

8. Emma Helen Blair, trans. and ed., *The Indian Tribes of the Upper Mississippi Valley and Region of the Great Lakes,* 2 vols. (1911; reprint, Lincoln: University of Nebraska Press, 1996), 1: 307; *WHC,* 16: 33; Louise Phelps Kellogg, ed., *Early Narratives of the Northwest, 1634–1699* (New York: Scribner's, 1917), 73.

9. Quoted in Sayre, *Les Sauvages Américains,* 9.

10. Galinée in Pierre Margry, ed., *Découvertes et établissements des français dans l'ouest et dans le sud de l'Amérique Septentrionale (1614–1754),* 6 vols. (Paris:

Imprimerie D. Jouaust, 1876–86), 1: 117–19; English translation in Kellogg, ed., *Early Narratives*, 172–73; Edmund B. O'Callaghan and Berthold Fernow, eds., *Documents Relative to the Colonial History of the State of New York*, 15 vols. (Albany NY: Weed, Parson, 1853–87), 9: spiritual and perilous quote at 77; le Beau in W. Vernon Kinetz, *The Indians of the Western Great Lakes, 1615–1760* (Ann Arbor: University of Michigan Press, 1965), 50; John McPhee, *The Survival of the Bark Canoe* (New York: Farrar, Straus and Giroux, 1975), 55.

11. McPhee, *The Survival of the Bark Canoe*, 57.

12. Quoted in Carolyn Gilman, *Where Two Worlds Meet: The Great Lakes Fur Trade* (Saint Paul: Minnesota Historical Society, 1982), 30.

13. Joseph L. Peyser, trans. and ed., *Letters from New France: The Upper Country 1686–1783* (Urbana: University of Illinois Press, 1992), 32; Margry, ed., *Découvertes et établissements*, 1: 82. On Colbert's and the king's concerns, see W. J. Eccles, *Canada under Louis XIV, 1663–1701* (New York: Oxford University Press, 1964), 105–6, 163–64.

14. Helen Hornbeck Tanner, ed., *Atlas of Great Lakes Indian History* (Norman: University of Oklahoma Press, 1987), 6–8 and map, 2; R. Cole Harris, ed., *Historical Atlas of Canada*, vol. 1, *From the Beginning to 1800* (Toronto: University of Toronto Press, 1987), pl. 36.

15. Thwaites, ed., *The Jesuit Relations*, 56: 171–73.

16. Thwaites, ed., *The Jesuit Relations*, 12: 117–24; 8: 77.

17. Kellogg, ed., *Early Narratives*, 136–37; Pierre de Charlevoix, *Journal of a Voyage to North-America*, 2 vols. (London, 1761; reprint, New York: Readex Microprint, 1966), 2: 135.

18. David M. Young, *Chicago Maritime: An Illustrated History* (DeKalb: Northern Illinois University Press, 2001), 17.

19. Sayre, *Les Sauvages Américains*, 114.

20. Marquette's journal of the voyage is in Thwaites, ed., *The Jesuit Relations*, 59: 87–183, quotes at 91–93. It is reprinted in Kellogg, ed., *Early Narratives*, 227–57, and in Alan Greer, ed., *The Jesuit Relations: Natives and Missionaries in Seventeenth-Century North America* (Boston: Bedford Books, 2000), 190. See also Jaenen, ed., *The French Regime*, 149–52, on Joliet.

21. Young, *Chicago Maritime*, 3, 11–12.

22. Tracy Neal Leavelle, "Geographies of Encounter: Christianity, Space, and Order in French and Indian North America," ms.

23. Trigger, *The Children of Aataentsic*, 30; Thwaites, ed., *The Jesuit Relations*, 8: 115. A fifth group, the Ataronchoron, appears not to have been recognized as a distinct tribe in the political organization of the confederacy and may have been a division of the Attignawantan. Georges E. Sioui, *Huron-Wendate: The Heritage of the Circle* (Vancouver: University of British Columbia Press/East Lansing: Michigan State University Press, 1999), presents an indigenous perspective on Huron history and society.

24. Trigger, *The Children of Aataentsic,* 165.

25. Thwaites, ed., *The Jesuit Relations,* 8: 115; Harris, ed., *Historical Atlas,* 1: pl. 34; Trigger, *The Children of Aataentsic,* 32, 166.

26. Trigger, *The Children of Aataentsic,* 166; Thwaites, ed., *The Jesuit Relations,* 8: 115.

27. Trigger, *The Children of Aataentsic,* 62–65, 168–76. For maps depicting Huron trade patterns, see Harris, ed., *Historical Atlas,* 1: pls. 33, 35.

28. Trigger, *The Children of Aataentsic,* 236–37, 243.

29. George M. Wrong, ed., *The Long Journey to the Country of the Huron by Father Gabriel Sagard* (Toronto: Champlain Society, 1939), 79; Nancy Bonvillain, *The Huron* (New York: Chelsea House, 1989), 42; Sioui, *Huron-Wendate,* 5.

30. Jaenen, ed., *The French Regime,* 107–16; Trigger, *The Children of Aataentsic,* 261–64, 473–76. Brulé was murdered at the Huron village at Toanché in 1633, possibly an assassination prompted by his dealings with the Iroquois. But Champlain had no desire to sever trade connections with the Hurons, so he pardoned the killers rather than seeking revenge or compensation for the killing, as was customary in Huron society.

31. Trigger, *The Children of Aataentsic,* 296–305, 308–30, 336–37; William H. Goetzmann and Glyndwr Williams, *The Atlas of North American Exploration: From the Norse Voyages to the Race to the Pole* (Norman: University of Oklahoma Press, 1998), 58–59.

32. Trigger, *The Children of Aataentsic,* 364, 432.

33. Trigger, *The Children of Aataentsic,* 350–58; Thwaites, ed., *The Jesuit Relations,* 8: 57.

34. Wrong, ed., *The Long Journey,* 102; Trigger, *The Children of Aataentsic,* 376–95.

35. Bruce G. Trigger, "The Mohawk-Mahican War (1624–28): The Establishment of a Pattern," *Canadian Historical Review* 52 (1971): 276–86.

36. Margry, ed., *Découvertes et établissements,* 1: 49–51; Jaenen, ed., *The French Regime,* 116–20; Goetzmann and Williams, *The Atlas,* 60. Nicollet had spent two years among the Algonkins and eight years with the Nipissings and had remained in Indian country during the English occupation of Quebec.

37. Peyser, trans. and ed., *Letters from New France,* 21, 24; Bruce G. Trigger, *Natives and Newcomers: Canada's "Heroic Age" Reconsidered* (Montreal: McGill-Queens University Press, 1985), 227.

38. Trigger, *The Children of Aataentsic,* 406–8; Thwaites, ed., *The Jesuit Relations,* 8: 135.

39. Thwaites, ed., *The Jesuit Relations,* 8: 169; 10: 87–115.

40. Thwaites, ed., *The Jesuit Relations,* 17: 145.

41. Thwaites, ed., *The Jesuit Relations,* 10: 29; 15: 37.

42. Thwaites, ed., *The Jesuit Relations*, 8: 93–94, 127; Kinetz, *The Indians*, 69.

43. Leavelle, "Geographies of Encounter."

44. Denys Delâge, *Bitter Feast: Amerindians and Europeans in Northeastern North America, 1600–1664* (Vancouver: University of British Columbia Press, 1993), 168. Inside the settlement at Sainte Marie they had their own blacksmith and carpentry store. A small farm with chickens, calves, and hogs provided the French with a diet similar to what they had eaten in France or Quebec. Many of the mission's necessities were manufactured on the spot, but items such as glassware were imported from France. The Jesuits needed a place where they could shut themselves off from the outer world and dedicate themselves to their prayers and plans for the mission. The hospital was open to all the Indians of the community, but only Christian Indians were admitted to the inner court of the settlement. Trigger, *The Children of Aataentsic*, 572–88, 669–72, 685. Harris, ed., *Historical Atlas*, 1: pl. 34, provides a plan of the mission. Frenchmen in outposts in seventeenth-century coastal Maine endeavored to insulate their communities and retain the trappings of French culture and class status even as they struggled to adjust to life on the frontier. Alaric Faulkner and Gretchen F. Faulkner, "Fort Pentagoet and Castin's Habitation: French Ventures in Acadian Maine," in Emerson W. Baker, Edwin A. Churchill, Richard S. D'Abatie, Kristine L. Jones, Victor A. Konrad, and Harald E. L. Prins, *American Beginnings: Exploration, Culture, and Cartography in the Land of Norumbega* (Lincoln: University of Nebraska Press, 1994), 217–40.

45. Susan Sleeper-Smith, *Indian Women and French Men: Rethinking Cultural Encounter in the Western Great Lakes* (Amherst: University of Massachusetts Press, 2001), 21–36.

46. Nicholas Griffiths and Fernando Cervantes, eds., *Spiritual Encounters: Interactions between Christianity and Native Religions in Colonial America* (Lincoln: University of Nebraska Press, 1999). On the Huron, see William B. Hart's essay in the same volume, " 'The Kindness of the Blessed Virgin': Faith, Succor, and the Cult of Mary among Christian Hurons and Iroquois in Seventeenth-Century New France," 65–90.

47. Thwaites, ed., *The Jesuit Relations*, 8: 91.

48. John Webster Grant, *Moon of Wintertime: Missionaries and the Indians of Canada in Encounter since 1534* (Toronto: University of Toronto Press, 1984), 250.

49. Trigger, *The Children of Aataentsic*, 47, 49, 85–90; Kinetz, *The Indians*, 90–99, 105–17; Thwaites, ed., *The Jesuit Relations*, 1: 265–67, 277; 10: 143–47, 275–305.

50. Thwaites, ed., *The Jesuit Relations*, 8: 141; 13: 127.

51. Thwaites, ed., *The Jesuit Relations*, 13: 171.

52. Thwaites, ed., *The Jesuit Relations*, 10: 19; 13: 133.

53. Thwaites, ed., *The Jesuit Relations,* 1: 25.

54. Carl O. Sauer, *Seventeenth Century North America* (Berkeley CA: Turtle Island, 1980), 115; Harris, ed., *Historical Atlas,* 1: pl. 35, charts the flow of the epidemics along the St. Lawrence and through Huronia and the Great Lakes.

55. Thwaites, ed., *The Jesuit Relations,* 8: 87–89.

56. Thwaites, ed., *The Jesuit Relations,* 10: 37.

57. Thwaites, ed., *The Jesuit Relations,* 13: 85–267; 14: 1, 9–11, 39–41, 53, 107; 15: 19–23, 43–47.

58. Trigger, *The Children of Aataentsic,* 500–501, 526–46, 588–602; Thwaites, ed., *The Jesuit Relations,* 12: 85–87; 14: 53; 15: 37–51; 17: 21, 227–29; 19: 89–93; 35: 131.

59. Trigger, *The Children of Aataentsic,* 589. See also Sioui, *Huron-Wendate,* 84–88.

60. Trigger, *The Children of Aataentsic,* xxvii–xxvii.

61. Grant, *Moon of Wintertime,* 565.

62. Thwaites, ed., *The Jesuit Relations,* 19: 77–79; Trigger, *The Children of Aataentsic,* 701–2. The Jesuits had hoped that the settlement of Ossossané, where the family of a chief named Chihwatenha provided a core of model Christians, would become a center of Huron Christianity.

63. Thwaites, ed., *The Jesuit Relations,* 10: 13; 17: 133.

64. Trigger, *The Children of Aataentsic,* 546–47, 613, chap. 10; Delâge, *Bitter Feast,* 167, 194–96, 218–24; Peyser, trans. and ed., *Letters from New France,* 25.

65. Brian J. Given, *A Most Pernicious Thing: Gun Trading and Native Warfare in the Early Contact Period* (Ottawa: Carleton University Press, 1994); Patrick M. Malone, *A Skulking War of War: Technology and Tactics among the New England Indians* (Lanham MD: Madison Books, 1991).

66. George Hunt in 1940 explained the Iroquois wars as an attempt to destroy the Hurons and divert their trade to Iroquois hands, but scholars have subsequently revised his thesis of economic motivation as the sole driving force behind Iroquois aggression. George T. Hunt, *The Wars of the Iroquois: A Study in Intertribal Relations* (Madison: University of Wisconsin Press, 1940). José Antonio Brandao, *"Yor Fyre Shall Burn No More": Iroquois Policy toward New France and Its Native Allies to 1701* (Lincoln: University of Nebraska Press, 1997), provides a thorough reassessment of the "beaver wars" thesis.

67. Trigger, *The Children of Aataentsic,* chap. 9.

68. Trigger, *The Children of Aataentsic,* 725–29, discusses Iroquois motives for dispersing the Hurons.

69. Daniel K. Richter, *The Ordeal of the Longhouse: The Peoples of the Iroquois League in the Era of European Colonization* (Chapel Hill: University of North Carolina Press, 1992), 74. Huron author Georges Sioui explains the Iroquois assault as a defensive measure in a broader war of cultural survival against Eu-

ropeans and their diseases. George E. Sioui, *For an Amerindian Autohistory: An Essay on the Foundations of a Social Ethic* (Montreal: McGill-Queens University Press, 1992), 39–60.

70. Richter, *The Ordeal of the Longhouse*, 59; Blair, trans. and ed., *The Indian Tribes*, 1: 146.

71. Richter, *The Ordeal of the Longhouse*, 50–74, quote at 61.

72. Wrong, ed., *The Long Journey*, 159.

73. Richter, *The Ordeal of the Longhouse*, 61; Trigger, *The Children of Aataentsic*, 751–53.

74. Trigger, *The Children of Aataentsic*, 760.

75. Trigger, *The Children of Aataentsic*, 762–66. Keith F. Otterbein, "Huron vs. Iroquois: A Case Study in Inter-Tribal Warfare," *Ethnohistory* 26 (1976): 141–52, analyzes the Iroquois campaign of 1649 based on the report of Father Paul Ragueneau in Thwaites, ed., *The Jesuit Relations*, 34: 123–37.

76. Trigger, *The Children of Aataentsic*, 778–82.

77. Delâge, *Bitter Feast*, 179; Trigger, *The Children of Aataentsic*, 739; Thwaites, ed., *The Jesuit Relations*, 34: 103; 35: Ragueneau quote at 21–23.

78. Thwaites, ed., *The Jesuit Relations*, 34: 19; 35: 25.

79. Thwaites, ed., *The Jesuit Relations*, 35: 79–101.

80. Trigger, *The Children of Aataentsic*, 801–20; Thwaites, ed., *The Jesuit Relations*, 35: 207–15; 54: 81.

81. Trigger, *The Children of Aataentsic*, 789–97. For identification of the Tobacco Hurons, see Louise Phelps Kellogg, *The French Régime in Wisconsin and the Northwest* (1925; reprint, New York: Cooper Square, 1968), 56, and Kellogg, ed., *Early Narratives*, 119. See also Harris, ed., *Historical Atlas*, 1: pl. 35.

82. Richter, *The Ordeal of the Longhouse*, 65; Thwaites, ed., *The Jesuit Relations*, 41: 133; 45: 207; 51: 123, 187.

83. Trigger, *The Children of Aataentsic*, 820–25; WHC, 16: 14–21; Thwaites, ed., *The Jesuit Relations*, 54: 167–71; 56: 115–17; Richard White, *The Middle Ground: Indians, Empires, and Republics in the Great Lakes Region, 1650–1815* (Cambridge: Cambridge University Press, 1991), 8–9; Adams, ed., *The Explorations*, 131–33.

84. Blair, trans. and ed., *The Indian Tribes*, 1: 364.

85. Kellogg, *The French Régime*, 100; White, *The Middle Ground*, 1–5, 10–14, 41–48; Thwaites, ed., *The Jesuit Relations*, 54: 191–93; 56: 115–17. Harris, ed., *Historical Atlas*, 1: pls. 35, 37, and Tanner, ed., *Atlas*, map 6, show the dislocations of Indian groups throughout the Great Lakes region during the sixty years or so of Iroquois warfare and indicate the tribal compositions of the refugee communities.

86. Thwaites, ed., *The Jesuit Relations*, 51: 47; 54: 191, 229; 55: 97, 169; 56: 115; WHC, 16: 15–21; Kellogg, ed., *Early Narratives*, 155; Tanner, ed., *Atlas*, 31; Blair, trans. and ed., *The Indian Tribes*, 1: 187–90.

87. Thwaites, ed., *The Jesuit Relations,* 54: 231.

88. Sleeper-Smith, *Indian Women and French Men.*

89. Martin Fournier, *Pierre-Esprit Radisson: Aventurer et commerçant* (Sillery, Quebec: Septentrion, 2001), 43–44, 79–82.

90. Adams, ed., *The Explorations,* 97. Other documents relating to Radisson are reproduced in Jaenen, ed., *The French Regime,* 121–45. On Radisson, his travels, and his writings, see Fournier, *Pierre-Esprit Radisson.*

91. Quoted in DeVoto, *The Course of Empire,* 111.

92. Peyser, trans. and ed., *Letters from New France,* 27.

93. White, *The Middle Ground,* 105–6; Thwaites, ed., *The Jesuit Relations,* 51: 21; 55: 207.

94. Kellogg, ed., *Early Narratives,* 107, 109–10, 156; Kellogg, *The French Régime,* 153–54; DeVoto, *The Course of Empire,* 108; Thwaites, ed., *The Jesuit Relations,* 50: 273, 279–81; 51: 47, 53; 54: 13, 165–69; *WHC,* 16: 64, 77–78.

95. Thwaites, ed., *The Jesuit Relations,* 54: 12, 129–37; 55: 101, 133, 143, 157–61, 171; 56: 115–17; 57: 203, 207; *WHC,* 16: 63–64; Kinetz, *The Indians,* 226–34, 245, 379–80; Tanner, ed., *Atlas,* 36–37.

96. Thwaites, ed., *The Jesuit Relations,* 56: 91.

97. Henry Reed Stiles, ed., *Joutel's Journal of La Salle's Last Voyage 1684–1687* (Albany NY: Joseph McDonough, 1906), 199.

98. *WHC,* 16: 3–10; Thwaites, ed., *The Jesuit Relations,* 54: 15, 223, 235; 55: 103, 183; 56: 123–25; Tanner, ed., *Atlas,* 30, 36–37.

99. Martha Royce Blaine, *The Ioway Indians* (Norman: University of Oklahoma Press, 1979), 17–18; Thwaites, ed., *The Jesuit Relations,* 60: 203.

100. Thwaites, ed., *The Jesuit Relations,* 57: 283; 58: 277; 61: 149, 155.

101. O'Callaghan and Fernow, eds., *Documents,* 9: 160–61, 201.

102. Helen H. Tanner, "The Rocks and Fields of Illinois Indian History," *Meeting Ground: The Newsletter of the D'Arcy McNickle Center for American Indian History* 41–43 (1999–2001): 6; Charles Callender, "Illinois," in *HNAI,* 15: 673–80; Thwaites, ed., *The Jesuit Relations,* 50: 289.

103. Thwaites, ed., *The Jesuit Relations,* 58: 97; 60: 159; Wayne C. Temple, *Indian Villages of the Illinois Country* (Springfield: Illinois State Museum, 1966), 18–20; Emily J. Blasingham, "The Depopulation of the Illinois Indians," *Ethnohistory* 3 (1956): 193–224, 361–411, Kaskaskia figures at 363–64.

104. Margry, ed., *Découvertes et établissements,* 1: 505–13, 521; O'Callaghan and Fernow, eds., *Documents,* 9: 163; Tanner, ed., *Atlas,* 5; Eric Hinderaker, *Elusive Empires: Constructing Colonialism in the Ohio Valley, 1673–1800* (Cambridge: Cambridge University Press, 1997), 11–14; Blasingham, "The Depopulation," 374.

105. Writing in 1690, l'Abbé Jean Cavelier, brother of La Salle, cited main-

taining the Ottawa beaver trade and defeating the Iroquois as "absolument nécessaires" if the colony of Canada were to survive. Margry, ed., *Découvertes et établissements,* 3: 588.

106. Nicolas de La Salle, *Relation of the Discovery of the Mississippi River,* trans. Melville B. Anderson (Chicago: Caxton Club, 1898), 67; White, *The Middle Ground,* 29–33; Kellogg, *The French Régime,* 219–42. Abenaki scholar Frederick Wiseman, "The Last Alliance: The Wabanaki and the Great Council Fire," ms., argues that an alliance stretched from the Mi'kmaqs of Nova Scotia to the Potawatomis of the western Great Lakes that preceded French contact and most likely the Iroquois confederacy. Therefore, to suggest that the French constructed the alliance in response to Iroquois aggression perpetuates a Franco-centered and Iroquois-centered interpretation of Algonkian history.

107. WHC, 16: 152, quoted in Kellogg, *The French Régime,* 253.

108. Colin G. Calloway, "Army Allies or Tribal Survival: The 'Other Indians' in the 1876 Campaign," in Charles E. Rankin, ed., *Legacy: New Perspectives on the Battle of the Little Bighorn* (Helena: Montana Historical Society Press, 1996), 63–81.

109. White, *The Middle Ground,* chap. 2; Sleeper-Smith, *Indian Women and French Men,* 38–40. On similar implications of kinship terms in the South, see Patricia Galloway, " 'The Chief Who Is Your Father': Choctaw and French Views of the Diplomatic Relation," in Peter H. Wood, Gregory A. Waselkov, and M. Thomas Hatley, eds., *Powhatan's Mantle: Indians in the Colonial Southeast* (Lincoln: University of Nebraska Press, 1989), 254–78.

110. Vine Deloria Jr. and Raymond J. DeMallie, eds., *Documents of American Indian Diplomacy: Treaties, Agreements, and Conventions, 1775–1979,* 2 vols. (Norman: University of Oklahoma Press, 1999), 1: 7.

111. Thwaites, ed., *The Jesuit Relations,* 58: 97–99; 59: 129–31.

112. Blair, trans. and ed., *The Indian Tribes,* 1: 184–86; also WHC, 16: 27.

113. Dean Snow, *The Iroquois* (Cambridge MA: Blackwell, 1994), 120; Jacques Le Sueur, "History of the Calumet and of the Dance," *Contributions from the Museum of the American Indian, Heye Foundation* 12, no. 5 (1952): 1–22; Donald J. Blakeslee, "Origin and Spread of the Calumet Ceremony," *American Antiquity* 46 (1981): 759–68; Tanis C. Thorne, *The Many Hands of My Relations: French and Indians on the Lower Missouri* (Columbia: University of Missouri Press, 1996), chap. 1.

114. Howard Meredith, *Dancing on Common Ground: Tribal Cultures and Alliances on the Southern Plains* (Lawrence: University Press of Kansas, 1995).

115. Sleeper-Smith, *Indian Women and French Men,* 46.

116. W. J. Eccles, *Essays on New France* (Toronto: Oxford University Press, 1987), 53.

117. O'Callaghan and Fernow, eds., *Documents,* 9: 448–51, 478–79.

118. Sleeper-Smith, *Indian Women and French Men,* 38–40; O'Callaghan and Fernow, eds., *Documents,* 9: 672, 737.

119. White, *The Middle Ground,* 34.

120. O'Callaghan and Fernow, eds., *Documents,* 9: 331, 358–69; Thwaites, ed., *The Jesuit Relations,* 63: 269–77.

121. *WHC,* 16: 166–67; Tanner, ed., *Atlas,* 31, 34–35; Leroy V. Eid, "The Ojibwa-Iroquois War: The War the Five Nations Did Not Win," *Ethnohistory* 26 (1979): 297–324; Peter Schmalz, "The Role of the Ojibwa in the Conquest of Southern Ontario, 1650–1751," *Ontario History* 76 (1984): 326–52.

122. Milo Milton Quaife, ed., *The Western Country in the 17th Century: The Memoirs of Lamothe Cadillac and Pierre Liette* (Chicago: R. R. Donnelley and Sons, 1947), 69.

123. On Iroquois losses, see, for example, O'Callaghan and Fernow, eds., *Documents,* 3: 800–809, 840–44; 4: 644, 689, 693, 701; 9: 460–61, 513–14, 520–24.

124. O'Callaghan and Fernow, eds., *Documents,* 9: 722–24. On the growing crisis within the Iroquois confederacy and Iroquois attempts to secure peace in the West by playing off their ties with the British and French, see Richter, *The Ordeal of the Longhouse,* chap. 8. Gilles Havard, *The Great Peace of Montreal of 1701: French-Native Diplomacy in the Seventeenth Century,* trans. Phyllis Aronoff and Howard Scott (Montreal: McGill-Queens University Press, 2001), sees the treaty as a triumph of French diplomacy. For an Abenaki perspective on the peace that restores the Algonkian tribes as active players, see Wiseman, "The Last Alliance."

125. Thorne, *The Many Hands of My Relations,* 25–26, 35.

126. Gary Clayton Anderson, *Kinsmen of Another Kind: Dakota-White Relations in the Upper Mississippi Valley, 1650–1862* (Lincoln: University of Nebraska Press, 1984), 29.

127. Blair, trans. and ed., *The Indian Tribes,* 1: 159–63.

128. Anderson, *Kinsmen of Another Kind,* chap. 1, population figures at 19. For the first Jesuit report, see Kellogg, ed., *Early Narratives,* 24. For the Assiniboine split and the first documentary reference, see Arthur J. Ray, *Indians in the Fur Trade: Their Role as Hunters, Trappers, and Middlemen in the Lands Southwest of Hudson Bay, 1660–1870* (Toronto: University of Toronto Press, 1974), 4–11; Thwaites, ed., *The Jesuit Relations,* 18: 231.

129. Anderson, *Kinsmen of Another Kind,* chap. 3.

130. Adams, ed., *The Explorations,* 134–35.

131. Adams, ed., *The Explorations,* 136–39.

132. Adams, ed., *The Explorations,* 147.

133. Thwaites, ed., *The Jesuit Relations,* 51: 53; Kellogg, ed., *Early Narratives,* 109, 132.

134. Kellogg, ed., *Early Narratives*, 329–34; Margry, ed., *Découvertes et établissements*, 6: 20–25, 50–51; Jaenen, ed., *The French Regime*, 184–91.

135. O'Callaghan and Fernow, eds., *Documents*, 9: 418.

136. O'Callaghan and Fernow, eds., *Documents*, 9: 570; Margry, ed., *Découvertes et établissements*, 6: 59, 83; *WHC*, 16: 178.

137. Anderson, *Kinsmen of Another Kind*, 19, 25–28, 36, 47; Gary Clayton Anderson, "Early Dakota Migration and Intertribal Warfare: A Revision," *Western Historical Quarterly* 11 (1980): 17–36. For a list of twenty-two Sioux villages at this time, based on information from Le Sueur, see Raymond J. DeMallie, "Sioux until 1850," in *HNAI*, 13: 723–24.

138. Quoted in Anthony Pagdon, *Lords of All the World: Ideologies of Empire in Spain, Britain and France, c. 1500–c. 1800* (New Haven CT: Yale University Press, 1995), 149.

139. Denonville quoted in Eccles, *Essays on New France*, 54.

140. Peyser, trans. and ed., *Letters from New France*, 60–68; O'Callaghan and Fernow, eds., *Documents*, 9: 586.

141. Sleeper-Smith, *Indian Women and French Men*, 42–43.

142. Kellogg, ed., *Early Narratives*, 322.

143. Jefferson to Robert R. Livingston, April 18, 1802, in Merrill D. Peterson, ed., *The Portable Thomas Jefferson* (New York: Viking, 1975), 485.

144. Patricia Seed, *Ceremonies of Possession in Europe's Conquest of the New World, 1492–1640* (Cambridge: Cambridge University Press, 1995), 62.

145. Margry, ed., *Découvertes et établissements*, 1: 96–99; Jaenen, ed., *The French Regime*, 67–74; O'Callaghan and Fernow, eds., *Documents*, 9: 803–4; Kellogg, ed., *Early Narratives*, 217–20; Thwaites, ed., *The Jesuit Relations*, 55: 105–15.

146. Eccles, *Essays on New France*, 98, 164–65; William W. Warren, *History of the Ojibway People* (1885; reprint, Saint Paul: Minnesota Historical Society Press, 1984), 130–32; MacLeod, "The Anishinabeg Point of View," 207–8.

147. Leavelle, "Geographies of Encounter."

148. For an overview of French efforts to do so, see John Anthony Caruso, *The Mississippi Valley Frontier: The Age of French Exploration and Settlement* (New York: Bobbs-Merrill, 1966).

149. For example, Margry, ed., *Découvertes et établissements*, 2: 168.

150. Goetzmann and Williams, *The Atlas*, 68–69; DeVoto, *The Course of Empire*, 160, 163.

151. Quaife, ed., *The Western Country*, 73–76.

152. Thwaites, ed., *The Jesuit Relations*, 59: 87–183; Kellogg, ed., *Early Narratives*, 227–57.

153. Thwaites, ed., *The Jesuit Relations*, 59: 115–37, quotes at 117, 131.

154. Hyde, *Indians of the Woodlands*, 177, 180, 184, 191; Thwaites, ed., *The Jesuit Relations*, 54: 191; 59: 127.

155. Thwaites, ed., *The Jesuit Relations,* 59: 141.

156. Thwaites, ed., *The Jesuit Relations,* 59: 145.

157. Thwaites, ed., *The Jesuit Relations,* 59: 155–61.

158. A copy of Marquette's map is in Sara Jones Tucker, comp., *Indian Villages of the Illinois Country,* pt. 1, *Atlas* (Springfield: Illinois State Museum, 1942), pl. 5.

159. Thwaites, ed., *The Jesuit Relations,* 59: 165–211.

160. Robert S. Weddle et al., eds. and trans., *La Salle, the Mississippi, and the Gulf: Three Primary Documents* (College Station: Texas A & M University Press, 1987), 29–30.

161. Glenn R. Conrad, "Reluctant Imperialist: France in North America," in Patricia K. Galloway, ed., *La Salle and His Legacy: Frenchmen and Indians in the Lower Mississippi Valley* (Jackson: University Press of Mississippi, 1982), 102.

162. Margry, ed., *Découvertes et établissements,* 1: 337–38; Peyser, trans. and ed., *Letters from New France,* 34; Jaenen, ed., *The French Regime,* 160–61; W. J. Eccles, *The Canadian Frontier, 1534–1760* (Albuquerque: University of New Mexico Press, 1974), 109.

163. The "official relation" of La Salle's activities from 1679 to 1681 is in Margry, ed., *Découvertes et établissements,* 1: 433–544.

164. Tonti's memoir on La Salle's voyages is in Margry, ed., *Découvertes et établissements,* 1: 573–616, identities of the Indian contingent at 593–95; an English translation is in Kellogg, ed., *Early Narratives,* 286–334. The account of Nicolas de La Salle (no relation) is in Margry, ed., *Découvertes et établissements,* 1: 547–70.

165. Willard H. Rollings, "Living in a Graveyard: Native Americans in Colonial Arkansas," in Jeannie Whayne, comp., *Cultural Encounters in the Early South: Indians and Europeans in Arkansas* (Fayetteville: University of Arkansas Press, 1995), 38–42.

166. Dan F. Morse, "The Seventeenth-Century Michigamea Village Location in Arkansas," in John A. Walthall and Thomas E. Emerson, eds., *Calumet and Fleur-de-Lys: Archaeology of Indian and French Contact in the Midcontinent* (Washington DC: Smithsonian Institution Press, 1992), 55–74.

167. W. David Baird, *The Quapaw Indians: A History of the Downstream People* (Norman: University of Oklahoma Press, 1980), chap. 1; Margry, ed., *Découvertes et établissements,* 3: 442–44; William C. Foster, ed., *The La Salle Expedition to Texas: The Journal of Henri Joutel, 1684–1687,* trans. Johanna S. Warren (Austin: Texas State Historical Association, 1998), 270–71, 277, 280; Alan Gallay, *The Indian Slave Trade: The Rise of the English Empire in the American South, 1670–1717* (New Haven CT: Yale University Press, 2002), 112.

168. Margry, ed., *Découvertes et établissements,* 1: 553–54; 2: 184; La Salle, *Relation,* 19–23.

169. George Sabo III analyzes calumet ceremonies among the Quapaws

and Caddos and their role in establishing relations with La Salle and other strangers in "Rituals of Encounter: Interpreting Native American Views of European Explorers," in Whayne, comp., *Cultural Encounters*, 76–87; "Rituals of Encounter: Interpreting Native American Views of European Explorers," *Arkansas Historical Quarterly* 51 (1992): 54–68; "Encounters and Images: European Contact and Caddo Indians," *Historical Reflections* 21 (1995): 217–42; and "The Quapaw Indians of Arkansas, 1673–1803," in Bonnie G. McEwan, ed., *Indians of the Greater Southeast: Historical Archaeology and Ethnohistory* (Gainesville: University Press of Florida, 2000), 178–203. See also Robert L. Hall, "Calumet Ceremonialism and the Honored Child," in Robert L. Hall, *An Archaeology of the Soul: North American Indian Belief and Ritual* (Urbana: University of Illinois Press, 1997), 49–58. On the use of the calumet among Central Siouan peoples, see Thorne, *The Many Hands of My Relations*; on limited understanding on the part of French and Quapaws, see Joseph Patrick Key, "'Masters of This Country': The Quapaws and Environmental Change in Arkansas, 1673–1833," Ph.D. diss., University of Arkansas, 2001, 15; and Gallay, *The Indian Slave Trade*, 105–10.

170. Margry, ed., *Découvertes et établissements*, 2: 191–93.

171. Margry, ed., *Découvertes et établissements*, 3: 15–28, 44–48. John Gilmeary Shea, ed., *The Expedition of Don Diego de Peñalosa . . . from Santa Fe to the River Mischipi and Quivira in 1662, as Described by Father Nicholas de Freytas, O.S.F. With an Account of Peñalosa's Projects to Aid the French to Conquer the Mining Country in Northern Mexico; and His Connection with Cavelier de La Salle* (New York: J. G. Shea, 1882; reprint, Chicago: Rio Grande Press, 1964) appears to be a fake, probably written by Peñalosa himself and based on accounts of previous expeditions, especially those of Oñate.

172. Margry, ed., *Découvertes et établissements*, 2: 382–83; O'Callaghan and Fernow, eds., *Documents*, 9: 225.

173. Peter H. Wood, "La Salle: Discovery of a Lost Explorer," *American Historical Review* 89 (1984): 294–323, reconstructs La Salle's purposes and geographical reasoning. Robert S. Weddle, *The Wreck of the Belle, the Ruin of La Salle* (College Station: Texas A & M University Press, 2001) provides an excellent examination of La Salle's motivations and actions.

174. Henri Joutel's account of the expedition and the experiences of the colonists from 1684 to 1687 is in Margry, ed., *Découvertes et établissements*, 3: 89–534, and, in its most recent translation, Foster, ed., *The La Salle Expedition.*

175. John R. Swanton, *Source Material on the History and Ethnology of the Caddo Indians* (1942; reprint, Norman: University of Oklahoma Press, 1996), 3–4, 6–14, Douay quote at 39; F. Todd Smith, *The Caddo Indians: Tribes at the Convergence of Empires, 1542–1854* (College Station: Texas A & M University Press, 1995) chap. 1; Cecile Elkins Carter, *Caddo Indians: Where We Come From* (Norman: University of Oklahoma Press, 1995), 4; Timothy K. Pert-

tula, "European Contact and Its Effects on Aboriginal Caddoan Populations between A.D. 1520 and A.D. 1680," in David Hurst Thomas, ed., *Columbian Consequences*, vol. 3, *The Spanish Borderlands in Pan-American Perspective* (Washington DC: Smithsonian Institution Press, 1991), 501–18; Timothy K. Perttula, *The Caddo Nation: Archaeological and Ethnohistoric Perspectives* (Austin: University of Texas Press, 1992), 71–89, 217–22, 226; Daniel A. Hickerson, "Historical Processes, Epidemic Disease, and the Formation of the Hasinai Confederacy," *Ethnohistory* 44 (1997): 36–38; Ann M. Early, "The Caddos of the Trans-Mississippi South," in McEwan, ed., *Indians of the Greater Southeast*, 122–41.

176. Hickerson, "Historical Processes," 38–40; Daniel A. Hickerson, "Trade, Mediation, and Political Status in the Hasinai Confederacy," *Research in Economic Anthropology* 17 (1996): 149–68; David La Vere, *The Caddo Chiefdoms: Caddo Economics and Politics, 700–1835* (Lincoln: University of Nebraska Press, 1998), 36–37, 48; Margry, ed., *Découvertes et établissements*, 3: 305, 357–58; Foster, ed., *The La Salle Expedition*, 178–80, 182, 204–6; Swanton, *Source Material*, 39, 192–94; Charles Wilson Hackett, ed., *Pichardo's Treatise on the Limits of Louisiana and Texas*, 4 vols. (Austin: University of Texas Press, 1931–46), 2: 137–39.

177. Vynola Beaver Newkumet and Howard L. Meredith, *Hasinai: A Traditional History of the Caddo Confederacy* (College Station: Texas A & M University Press, 1988), 74–75.

178. Carter, *Caddo Indians*, 67.

179. Foster, ed., *The La Salle Expedition*, 211–15; Weddle et al., eds. and trans., *La Salle, the Mississippi, and the Gulf*, 231, 235–36, 238–39, 251. Many years later, Jean-Bernard Bossu met Rutel's son among the Quapaws; the son told him the Caddos had adopted his father and given him a wife because he had helped defeat their enemies with his gun and taught them how to sail and row their canoes! Seymour Feiler, trans. and ed., *Jean-Bernard Bossu's Travels in the Interior of North America 1751–1762* (Norman: University of Oklahoma Press, 1962), 67.

180. As Daniel Hickerson, "Historical Processes," 40, points out, "Military alliance may have been expected, even assumed, of the friends and neighbors of the Hasinai."

181. La Vere, *The Caddo Chiefdoms*, 41–47.

182. Sabo, "Rituals of Encounter," 81–87; Margry, ed., *Découvertes et établissements*, 3: 404–6, 416–19, 445–47; Stiles, ed., *Joutel's Journal*, 165–66, 171–74.

183. Margry, ed., *Découvertes et établissements*, 3: 447–61; Foster, ed., *The La Salle Expedition*, 268–81; Baird, *The Quapaw Indians*, 25; Sayre, *Les Sauvages Américains*, 267–68.

184. Robert S. Weddle, *Wilderness Manhunt: The Spanish Search for La Salle*

(Austin: University of Texas Press, 1973), 139–42; Charles Wilson Hackett, ed., *Historical Documents Relating to New Mexico, Nueva Vizcaya, and Approaches Thereto, to 1773*, 3 vols. (Washington DC: Carnegie Institute, 1923–27), 2: 470–72; Hackett, ed., *Pichardo's Treatise*, 1: 145, 159–63; William C. Foster, ed., *Texas and Northeastern Mexico, 1630–1690 by Juan Bautista Chapa*, trans. Ned F. Brinkley (Austin: University of Texas Press, 1997), 104–13, 116–21, 128–36, 135–39.

185. Margry, ed., *Découvertes et établissements*, 3: 609–21 provides extracts from the Talon interrogations; see the full text in Weddle et al., eds. and trans., *La Salle, the Mississippi, and the Gulf*, 225–58; see also Robert S. Weddle, "The Talon Interrogations: A Rare Perspective," in Weddle et al., eds. and trans., *La Salle, the Mississippi, and the Gulf*, 209–24.

186. Richebourg Gaillaird McWilliams, trans. and ed., *Iberville's Gulf Journals* (University: University of Alabama Press, 1981), 4–8. Documents relating to Iberville's enterprises are in Margry, ed., *Découvertes et établissements*, 4. On the "Le Moyne clan," see Jay Gitlin, "On the Boundaries of Empire: Connecting the West to Its Imperial Past," in William Cronon, George Miles, and Jay Gitlin, eds., *Under an Open Sky: Rethinking America's Western Past* (New York: W. W. Norton, 1992), 76.

187. Elizabeth A. H. John, *Storms Brewed in Other Men's Worlds: The Confrontation of Indians, Spanish, and French in the Southwest, 1540–1795* (Lincoln: University of Nebraska Press, 1975), 196–98.

188. McWilliams, trans. and ed., *Iberville's Gulf Journals*, 44, 58–59, 61–62, 67–69, 71–73, 126, quotes at 46, 67; Richebourg Gaillaird McWilliams, trans. and ed., *Fleur de Lys and Calumet: Being the Pénicaut Narrative of French Adventure in Louisiana* (Baton Rouge: Louisiana State University Press, 1953), 5–6, 28–29.

189. Bienville's journal of his overland journey is in McWilliams, trans. and ed., *Iberville's Gulf Journals*, 146–56.

190. McWilliams, trans. and ed., *Iberville's Gulf Journals*, 117–20; Patricia Galloway, "Henri de Tonti du Village des Chactas: The Beginning of the French Alliance," in Galloway, ed., *La Salle and His Legacy*, 146–75.

191. E. Wagner Stearn and Allen E. Stearn, *The Effect of Smallpox on the Destiny of the American Indian* (Boston: Bruce Humphries, 1945), 33; Kellogg, ed., *Early Narratives*, 359; Baird, *The Quapaw Indians*, 27.

192. McWilliams, trans. and ed., *Iberville's Gulf Journals*, 63, 122.

193. Daniel H. Usner Jr., "A Population History of American Indians in the Eighteenth-Century Lower Mississippi Valley," in Daniel H. Usner Jr., *American Indians in the Lower Mississippi Valley: Social and Economic Histories* (Lincoln: University of Nebraska Press, 1998), 33–55.

194. Margry, ed., *Découvertes et établissements*, 6: 59–87; WHC, 16: 173–200. The narrative of André-Joseph Pénicaut, a young carpenter with a gift for In-

dian languages who participated in Le Sueur's expedition up the Mississippi, is in McWilliams, trans. and ed., *Fleur de Lys and Calumet*, 32–54.

195. Thwaites, ed., *The Jesuit Relations*, 8: 223.

196. David La Vere, "Between Kinship and Capitalism: French and Spanish Rivalry in the Colonial Louisiana-Texas Indian Trade," *Journal of Southern History* 64 (1988): 197–98.

197. Hackett, ed., *Pichardo's Treatise*, 4: 310–15; *Presidio and Militia*, 2, pt. 2: 365–84; La Vere, "Between Kinship and Capitalism," 206.

198. Daniel H. Usner Jr., *Indians, Settlers, and Slaves in a Frontier Exchange Economy: The Lower Mississippi Valley before 1783* (Chapel Hill: University of North Carolina Press, 1992), 32–33, 36, 46–54, 93, 200.

199. Margry, ed., *Découvertes et établissements*, 6: 309–15. Padouca was a Dhegiha and Chiwere Siouan name meaning "enemy" and referred to Plains Apaches until the mid-eighteenth century, after which it referred increasingly to Comanches. Morris W. Foster and Martha McCollough, "Plains Apache," in *HNAI*, 13: 938–39; Thomas W. Kavanagh, "Comanche," in *HNAI*, 13: 903.

200. La Harpe's journal and accompanying letters are printed in French in Margry, ed., *Découvertes et établissements*, 6: 241–306, and in English by Ralph A. Smith, trans. and ed., "Account of the Journey of Bénard de La Harpe: Discovery Made by Him of Several Nations Situated in the West," *Southwestern Historical Quarterly* 62 (1958–59): 75–86, 246–59, 371–85, 525–41.

201. John, *Storms*, chap. 4; Perttula, *The Caddo Nation*, 180, 231; La Vere, "Between Kinship and Capitalism."

202. Hackett, ed., *Pichardo's Treatise*, 1: 219–24.

203. The Padoucas were still more likely Plains Apaches than Comanches at this date as they practiced horticulture and pottery. See Donald J. Blakeslee, *Along Ancient Trails: The Mallet Expedition of 1739* (Niwot: University of Colorado Press, 1995), 35–36.

204. "Journal of the Voyage of Monsieur de Bourgmont . . . to the Padoucas," in Frank Norall, *Bourgmont, Explorer of the Missouri 1698–1725* (Lincoln: University of Nebraska Press, 1988), 150–59. The Kansas who accompanied Bourgmont were actually heading out onto the plains for their annual summer buffalo hunt. See Garrick A. Bailey and Gloria A. Young, "Kansa," in *HNAI*, 13: 463.

205. Richard N. Ellis and Charlie R. Steen, eds., "An Indian Delegation in France, 1725," *Journal of the Illinois State Historical Society* 67 (1974): 385–405.

206. Gary E. Moulton, ed., *The Journals of the Lewis and Clark Expedition*, 13 vols. (Lincoln: University of Nebraska Press, 1983–2001), 2: 404n6.

207. The Mallets kept a journal of their expedition, but it was lost. Governor Bienville wrote a brief summary of the journal, which is published in

Margry, ed., *Découvertes et établissements,* 6: 455–62, and, in both French and English, in Blakeslee, *Along Ancient Trails,* 46–52, 215–20.

208. As in the case of the Mallet expedition, only excerpts survive from Fabry's journal of the expedition; they were published in Margry, ed., *Découvertes et établissements,* 6: 468–71, and translated, with accompanying documents, in Blakeslee, *Along Ancient Trails,* 227–44.

209. Jaenen, ed., *The French Regime,* 7, 275.

210. John Joseph Mathews, *The Osages: Children of the Middle Waters* (Norman: University of Oklahoma Press, 1961), 97–102.

211. Warren, *History of the Ojibway People,* 132–33.

212. Mathews, *The Osages,* 116–17, 132.

6. The Coming of the Centaurs

1. Tim Flannery, *The Eternal Frontier: An Ecological History of North America and Its Peoples* (New York: Atlantic Monthly Press, 2001), 293; Dan Flores, *Horizontal Yellow: Nature and History in the Near Southwest* (Albuquerque: University of New Mexico Press, 1999), 99.

2. See, for example, Frank Gilbert Roe, *The Indian and the Horse* (Norman: University of Oklahoma Press, 1955), 330–31, 376–79.

3. Frank Raymond Secoy, *Changing Military Patterns of the Great Plains Indians* (1953; reprint, Lincoln: University of Nebraska Press, 1992), 45–46.

4. Alfred W. Crosby, *The Columbian Exchange: Biological and Cultural Consequences of 1492* (Westport CT: Greenwood Press, 1972), 80–83.

5. Roe, *The Indian and the Horse,* chap. 2, quote at 85.

6. Sandra L. Myers, "The Ranching Frontier: Spanish Institutional Backgrounds of the Plains Cattle Industry," in David J. Weber, ed., *New Spain's Northern Frontier: Essays on Spain in the American West* (Dallas TX: Southern Methodist University Press, 1988), 79–93; D. E. Worcester, "The Spread of Spanish Horses among the Plains Indian Tribes," *Pacific Historical Review* 14 (1945): 225; Peter Iverson, *When Indians Became Cowboys: Native Peoples and Cattle Ranching in the American West* (Norman: University of Oklahoma Press, 1994).

7. Jack D. Forbes, "The Appearance of the Mounted Indian in Northern Mexico and the Southwest, to 1680," *Southwestern Journal of Anthropology* 15 (1959): 189–212.

8. Loretta Fowler, "The Great Plains from the Arrival of the Horse to 1885," in Bruce G. Trigger and Wilcomb E. Washburn, eds., *The Cambridge History of the Native Peoples of the Americas,* vol. 1, *North America* (Cambridge: Cambridge University Press, 1996), pt. 2: 8; John C. Ewers, *The Horse in Blackfoot Indian Culture, with Comparative Material from Other Tribes* (1955; reprint, Washington DC: Smithsonian Institution Press, 1969), 1–19.

9. Isaac Joslin Cox, ed., *The Journeys of René-Robert Cavelier, Sieur de La Salle,* 2 vols. (New York: Allerton, 1922), 1: 47–50, 55, 60, 240, 249, 255, 290–92, 298; Timothy K. Perttula, *The Caddo Nation: Archaeological and Ethnohistoric Perspectives* (Austin: University of Texas Press, 1992), 200. On the question of whether the Caddos adopted the Spanish or Apache style of horse armor, see Secoy, *Changing Military Patterns,* 13–14, 17–18, 21–22.

10. Pierre Margry, ed., *Découvertes et établissements des français dans l'ouest et dans le sud de l'Amérique Septentrionale (1614–1754),* 6 vols. (Paris: Imprimerie D. Jouaust, 1876–86), 2: 201–2.

11. John Joseph Mathews, *The Osages: Children of the Middle Waters* (Norman: University of Oklahoma Press, 1961), 126–28.

12. Tanis C. Thorne, *The Many Hands of My Relations: French and Indians on the Lower Missouri* (Columbia: University of Missouri Press, 1996), 44.

13. Worcester, "The Spread of Spanish Horses," 409; "Journal of the Voyage of Monsieur de Bourgmont . . . to the Padoucas," in Frank Norall, *Bourgmont, Explorer of the Missouri 1698–1725* (Lincoln: University of Nebraska Press, 1988), 127, 130–32.

14. James Taylor Carson, "Horses and the Economy and Culture of the Choctaw Indians, 1690–1840," *Ethnohistory* 42 (1995): 495–513.

15. Barbara Belyea, ed., *A Year Inland: The Journal of a Hudson's Bay Company Winterer* (Waterloo, Ontario: Wilfrid Laurier University Press, 2000), 255.

16. Francis Haines, "Horses for Western Indians," *American West* 3 (spring 1966): 4–15, 92.

17. Gary E. Moulton, ed., *The Journals of the Lewis and Clark Expedition,* 13 vols. (Lincoln: University of Nebraska Press, 1983–2001), 3: 101, 232, 292; 10: 69; 11: 116. Alan J. Osborn, "Ecological Aspects of Equestrian Adaptations in Aboriginal North America," *American Anthropologist* 85 (1983): 563–91, emphasizes the impact of winter—and forage quality and quantity—on horse populations and distribution.

18. Ewers, *The Horse in Blackfoot Indian Culture*; Roe, *The Indian and the Horse.*

19. Ewers, *The Horse in Blackfoot Indian Culture,* 240–42; Symmes C. Oliver, "Ecology and Cultural Continuity as Contributing Factors in the Social Organization of the Plains Indians," *University of California Publications in American Archaeology and Ethnology* 48, no. 1 (1962): 1–90, quote at 64.

20. David W. Penney, "The Horse as Symbol: Equine Representations in Plains Pictographic Art," in Evan M. Maurer, ed., *Visions of the People: A Pictorial History of Plains Indian Life* (Minneapolis: Minneapolis Institute of Arts, 1992), 69–79.

21. Charles A. Reher and George C. Frison, "The Vore Site 48CK302: A Stratified Buffalo Jump in the Wyoming Black Hills," *Plains Anthropologist* 25 (1980): pt. 2: 40–43, 47–49; John R. Bozell, "Culture, Environment, and

Bison Populations on the Late Prehistoric and Early Historic Central Plains," *Plains Anthropologist* 40 (1995): 145–63.

22. Lawrence J. Burpee, ed., "An Adventurer from Hudson's Bay: The Journal of Matthew Cocking from York Factory to the Blackfoot Country, 1772–73," *Proceedings and Transactions of the Royal Society of Canada*, 3rd series, 2 (1908): sec. 2: 108–11; Arthur S. Morton, ed., *Journal of Duncan McGillivray of the North West Company, at Fort George on the Saskatchewan, 1794–95* (Toronto: Macmillan, 1929), 43–44.

23. Francis Haines, *The Buffalo: The Story of American Bison and Their Hunters from Prehistoric Times to the Present* (1970; reprint, Norman: University of Oklahoma Press, 1995), 45; Tom McHugh, *The Time of the Buffalo* (New York: Alfred A. Knopf, 1972), 76–80; "Journal of the Voyage of Monsieur de Bourgmont," 159.

24. Ewers, *The Horse in Blackfoot Indian Culture*, 169, 304–5; John C. Ewers, *The Blackfeet, Raiders of the Northwestern Plains* (Norman: University of Oklahoma Press, 1958), 79.

25. Ewers, *The Horse in Blackfoot Indian Culture*, 142, 315–16; Haines, *The Buffalo*, 46; Margot Liberty, "Hell Came with Horses: Plains Indian Women in the Equestrian Era," *Montana: The Magazine of Western History* 32 (summer 1982): 10–29; Alan M. Klein, "The Political Economy of Gender: A 19th Century Plains Indian Case Study," in Patricia Albers and Beatrice Medicine, eds., *The Hidden Half: Studies of Plains Indian Women* (Lanham MD: University Press of America, 1983), 143–65.

26. Frank B. Linderman, *Pretty-Shield, Medicine Woman of the Crows* (Lincoln: University of Nebraska Press, 1972), 83.

27. Ewers, *The Horse in Blackfoot Indian Culture*, 306–9; Roe, *The Indian and the Horse*, 20–24; Ralph A. Smith, trans. and ed., "Account of the Journey of Bénard de La Harpe: Discovery Made by Him of Several Nations Situated in the West," *Southwestern Historical Quarterly* 62 (1958–59): 379; "Journal of the Voyage of Monsieur de Bourgmont," 136–37; Lawrence J. Burpee, ed., *Journals and Letters of Pierre Gaultier de Varennes de La Vérendrye and His Sons* (Toronto: Champlain Society, 1927), 317–18; Elliott Coues, ed., *New Light on the Early History of the Greater Northwest: The Manuscript Journals of Alexander Henry and David Thompson*, 2 vols. (1879; reprint, Minneapolis: Ross and Haines, 1965), 2: 518; E. E. Rich, ed., *Cumberland House Journals and Inland Journals, 1775–82*, 1st series (London: Hudson's Bay Record Society, 1952), 330; Morton, ed., *Journal of Duncan McGillivray*, 69; Burpee, ed., "An Adventurer from Hudson's Bay," 111; Theodore Binnema, *Common and Contested Ground: A Human and Environmental History of the Northwestern Plains* (Norman: University of Oklahoma Press, 2001), 49.

28. Herbert E. Bolton, ed., *Athanase de Mézières and the Texas-Louisiana Frontier 1768–1780*, 2 vols. (Cleveland: Arthur H. Clark, 1914), 2: 280.

29. Ewers, *The Horse in Blackfoot Indian Culture,* 150–51. See also McHugh, *The Time of the Buffalo,* chap. 8.

30. Dolores A. Gunnerson, "Man and Bison on the Plains in the Protohistoric Period," *Plains Anthropologist* 17 (1972): 6.

31. Belyea, ed., *A Year Inland,* 88, 99, quote at 107.

32. Arthur J. Ray, *Indians in the Fur Trade: Their Role as Hunters, Trappers, and Middlemen in the Lands Southwest of Hudson Bay, 1660–1870* (Toronto: University of Toronto Press, 1974), 162; Frank Gilbert Roe, *The North American Buffalo: A Critical Study of the Species in Its Wild State* (Toronto: University of Toronto Press, 1970; reprint, London: David and Charles, 1972), 608–9; Burpee, ed., "An Adventurer from Hudson's Bay," 107; Coues, ed., *New Light,* 2: 724; Morton, ed., *Journal of Duncan McGillivray,* 47; Annie Heloise Abel, ed., *Tabeau's Narrative of Loisel's Expedition to the Upper Missouri* (Norman: University of Oklahoma Press, 1939), 72; Andrew C. Isenberg, *The Destruction of the Bison: An Environmental History, 1750–1920* (Cambridge: Cambridge University Press, 2000), 65–66, 81; Bolton, ed., *Athanase de Mézières,* 1: 219.

33. Elliott West, "Called out People: The Cheyennes and the Central Plains," *Montana: The Magazine of Western History* 48 (summer 1998): 7.

34. Leonard Crow Dog asserted that this aspect of the story was fabricated by white missionaries. Leonard Crow Dog and Richard Erdoes, *Crow Dog: Four Generations of Sioux Medicine Men* (New York: HarperCollins, 1995), 4–5.

35. On White Buffalo Calf Woman, see Jeffrey Ostler, " 'They Regard Their Passing as Wakan': Interpreting Western Sioux Explanations for the Bison's Decline," *Western Historical Quarterly* 30 (1999): 479–80; Lee Irwin, *The Dream Seekers: Native American Visionary Traditions of the Great Plains* (Norman: University of Oklahoma Press, 1994), 43.

36. A nineteenth-century Piegan named Medicine Weasel who killed a white buffalo trembled so much he could not hold his knife steady to skin it; James Willard Schultz, *My Life as an Indian* (1935; reprint, Greenwich NY: Fawcett Books, n.d.), 45–46. See also Ronald T. McCoy, "Winter Count: The Teton Chronicles to 1700," Ph.D. diss., Northern Arizona University, 1983, 163–64.

37. Oliver, "Ecology and Cultural Continuity," 1–90; Isenberg, *The Destruction of the Bison,* 43–44, 69–70, 77.

38. Dan Flores, "Bison Ecology and Bison Diplomacy: The Southern Plains 1800–1850," *Journal of American History* 78 (1991): 467.

39. Patricia C. Albers, "Symbiosis, Merger, and War: Contrasting Forms of Intertribal Relationship among Historic Plains Indians," in John H. Moore, ed., *The Political Economy of North American Indians* (Norman: University of Oklahoma Press, 1993), 94–132; Terry L. Anderson and Steven LaCombe, "Institutional Change in the Indian Horse Culture," in Linda Barrington, ed., *The Other Side of the Frontier: Economic Explorations into Native American History*

(Boulder CO: Westview Press, 1999), 103–23; Thomas Biolsi, "Ecological and Cultural Factors in Plains Indian Warfare," in R. Brian Ferguson, ed., *Warfare, Culture and Environment* (New York: Academic Press, 1984), 141–68, esp. 155–58; W. W. Newcomb Jr., "A Re-examination of the Causes of Plains Warfare," *American Anthropologist* 52 (1950): 317–30.

40. Elliott West, *The Contested Plains: Indians, Goldseekers, and the Rush to Colorado* (Lawrence: University Press of Kansas, 1998), 333, 336.

41. N. Scott Momaday, *The Way to Rainy Mountain* (Albuquerque: University of New Mexico Press, 1969), 6–7; N. Scott Momaday, "The Centaur Complex," in *The Man Made of Words* (New York: St. Martin's Press, 1997), 77.

42. Gary Clayton Anderson, *The Indian Southwest, 1580–1830: Ethnogenesis and Reinvention, 1580–1830* (Norman: University of Oklahoma Press, 1999), 7. An overview of population shifts is given in Albert H. Schroeder, "Shifting for Survival in the Spanish Southwest," *New Mexico Historical Review* 43 (1968): 291–310, reprinted in Weber, ed., *New Spain's Northern Frontier,* 237–55.

43. Anderson, *The Indian Southwest,* chap. 1; Nancy Parrott Hickerson, *The Jumanos: Hunters and Traders of the South Plains* (Austin: University of Texas Press, 1994). Hickerson argues that the Teyas of early Spanish records were most likely Jumanos (24–27). See also Frederick W. Hodge, George P. Hammond, and Agapito Rey, eds., *Fray Alonso de Benavides' Revised Memorial of 1634* (Albuquerque: University of New Mexico Press, 1945), 66.

44. Charles Wilson Hackett, ed., *Pichardo's Treatise on the Limits of Louisiana and Texas,* 4 vols. (Austin: University of Texas Press, 1931–46), 1: 137–39; Anderson, *The Indian Southwest,* 27–28. On Sabeata and his role operating between the French, Spanish, and Caddos, see Elizabeth A. H. John, *Storms Brewed in Other Men's Worlds: The Confrontation of Indians, Spanish, and French in the Southwest, 1540–1795* (Lincoln: University of Nebraska Press, 1975), 175–94; Hickerson, *The Jumanos,* 127–31, 182–99; and Charles J. Kelley, "Juan Sabeata and Diffusion in Aboriginal Texas," *American Anthropologist* 57 (1955): 981–95.

45. Anderson, *The Indian Southwest,* chaps. 3–4; Hickerson, *The Jumanos,* chap. 16; John C. Ewers, "The Influence of Epidemics on the Indian Populations and Cultures of Texas," *Plains Anthropologist* 18 (1973): 104–15; John, *Storms,* 194.

46. George E. Hyde, *Indians of the High Plains: From Prehistoric Times to the Coming of Europeans* (Norman: University of Oklahoma Press, 1959), 10, 14n.

47. LaVerne Harrell Clark, *They Sang for Horses: The Impact of the Horse on Navajo and Apache Folklore* (Tucson: University of Arizona Press, 1966), 43, 85–90, 110–15.

48. Forbes, "The Appearance of the Mounted Indian," 200; Worcester, "The Spread of Spanish Horses," 226.

49. Secoy, *Changing Military Patterns*, 6–10, 12–14, 17–18, 20–27; John, *Storms*, 151.

50. Anderson, *The Indian Southwest*, 95–96.

51. James H. Gunnerson, *An Introduction to Plains Apache Archaeology—The Dismal River Aspect*, Smithsonian Institution, Bureau of American Ethnology, Bulletin 173, Anthropological Papers no. 58 (Washington DC: GPO, 1960), 131–260, identified the Dismal River people, who supplemented hunting with agriculture and exchange with the Pueblos, as Plains Apaches in the final phase of their high plains domination, ca. 1700. Anderson, *The Indian Southwest*, chap. 5.

52. Secoy, *Changing Military Patterns*, 23; Charles Wilson Hackett, ed., *Historical Documents Relating to New Mexico, Nueva Vizcaya, and Approaches Thereto, to 1773*, 3 vols. (Washington DC: Carnegie Institute, 1923–27), 3: 186–87, 244.

53. John L. Kessell, Rick Hendricks, and Meredith D. Dodge, eds., *Blood on the Boulders: The Journals of Don Diego de Vargas, New Mexico, 1694–97*, 2 vols. (Albuquerque: University of New Mexico Press, 1998), 1: 220.

54. Petition to the Cabildo, November 26, 1703, SANM, no. 91, cited in John, *Storms*, 151.

55. John, *Storms*, 235, 237, 25–56; Anderson, *The Indian Southwest*, 110; Ernest Wallace and E. Adamson Hoebel, *The Comanches: Lords of the South Plains* (Norman: University of Oklahoma Press, 1952), 288; Alfred Barnaby Thomas, trans. and ed., *After Coronado: Spanish Exploration Northeast of New Mexico, 1696–1727* (Norman: University of Oklahoma Press, 1935), 80–98, 114–15; SANM, series 2, reel 4, frames 1032, 1069; reel 6, frames 93, 104.

56. Thomas F. Schiltz, *Apaches in Texas* (El Paso: Texas Western Press, 1987), 7.

57. David M. Brugge, *Navajos in the Catholic Church Records of New Mexico 1694–1875* (Tsaile AZ: Navajo Community College Press, 1985), 21–22.

58. Hyde, *Indians of the High Plains*, 41–42; John R. Swanton, *Source Material on the History and Ethnology of the Caddo Indians* (1942; reprint, Norman: University of Oklahoma Press, 1996), 269–70.

59. John, *Storms*, 267; Anderson, *The Indian Southwest*, 126 and chap. 5.

60. Hyde, *Indians of the High Plains*, chap. 2; Jack Forbes, *Apache, Navaho, and Spaniard* (Norman: University of Oklahoma Press, 1960), xxii; Frank R. Secoy, "The Identity of the Padouca: An Ethno-historical Analysis," *American Anthropologist* 53 (1951): 525–42; Thomas W. Kavanagh, *The Comanches: A History, 1706–1875* (Lincoln: University of Nebraska Press, 1996), 65–66; Mathews, *The Osages*, 126, 138. See also Morris W. Foster and Martha McCollough, "Plains Apache," in *HNAI*, 13: 938–39; and Thomas W. Kavanagh, "Comanche," in *HNAI*, 13: 903.

61. John, *Storms*, 271–72; Anderson, *The Indian Southwest*, chap. 6; Thomas

D. Hall, *Social Change in the Southwest, 1350–1880* (Lawrence: University Press of Kansas, 1988), 103–5, mutual predation at 128.

62. Kristine L. Jones, "Comparative Raiding Economies, North and South," in Donna J. Guy and Thomas E. Sheridan, eds., *Contested Ground: Comparative Frontiers on the Northern and Southern Edges of the Spanish Empire* (Tucson: University of Arizona Press, 1998), 96–114. See also William L. Merrill, "Cultural Creativity and Raiding Bands in Eighteenth-Century Northern New Spain," in William B. Taylor and Franklin Pease G.Y., eds., *Violence, Resistance, and Survival in the Americas: Native Americans and the Legacy of Conquest* (Washington DC: Smithsonian Institution Press, 1994), 124–52.

63. *Presidio and Militia,* 2, pt. 1: 303, 306–7; Keith H. Basso, ed., *Western Apache Raiding and Warfare: From the Notes of Grenville Goodwin* (Tucson: University of Arizona Press, 1971).

64. Donald Worcester, *The Apaches* (Norman: University of Oklahoma Press, 1979), 22.

65. Martha C. Knack, *Boundaries Between: The Southern Paiutes, 1777–1795* (Lincoln: University of Nebraska Press, 2001), 30–31. Demitri B. Shimkin, "The Introduction of the Horse," in *HNAI,* 11: 517–24, surveys its impact in the Great Basin.

66. Ewers, *The Horse in Blackfoot Indian Culture,* 3.

67. John, *Storms,* 117–21, 231, quote at 119.

68. Ned Blackhawk, "Violence over the Land: Colonial Encounters in the American Great Basin," Ph.D. diss., University of Washington, 1999; Sondra Jones, " 'Redeeming' the Indian: The Enslavement of Indian Children in New Mexico and Utah," *Utah Historical Quarterly* 67 (1999): 220–41. Jones finds that Paiute and other parents did on occasion barter their children into slavery and that Ute raids for Paiute and Goshute captives did not begin in earnest until after the Spanish established contact with the Western Utes in 1776 (223–25n).

69. Kavanagh, *The Comanches,* 63–65; John, *Storms,* 231. Wallace and Hoebel, *The Comanches,* 4, say that Komantcia meant "enemy" or "anyone who wants to fight me all the time," and the interpretation has stuck, but James A. Goss insists it is "just plain wrong" and that Kumantsi is a term for distinguishing people who are related but different, "other" relatives. He warns against the dangers of carelessly applying outsiders' names for Native peoples and discusses the absurdity of the "naming game" (James A. Goss, "The Yamparika—Shoshones, Comanches, or Utes—or Does It Matter?" in Richard O. Clemmer, L. Daniel Myers, and Mary Elizabeth Rudden, eds., *Julian Steward and the Great Basin: The Making of an Anthropologist* [Salt Lake City: University of Utah Press, 1999], 79–80, 77).

70. Daniel J. Gelo, " 'Comanche Land and Ever Has Been': A Native Geography of the Nineteenth-Century Comanchería," *Southwestern Historical Quar-*

terly 111 (2000): 274; W. P. Clark, *The Indian Sign Language* (1885; reprint, Lincoln: University of Nebraska Press, 1982), 118–20.

71. Wallace and Hoebel, *The Comanches*, 35, 46; Daniel J. Gelo, trans. and ed., *Comanche Vocabulary: Trilingual Edition*, comp. Manuel García Rejón (Austin: University of Texas Press, 1995), xviii, 32, 61; Joseph B. Casagrande, "Comanche Linguistic Acculturation II," *International Journal of American Linguistics* 20 (1954): 220. "Automobile" in modern Comanche is *navukuw·*? "without its horse" (Casagrande, "Comanche Linguistic Acculturation II," 233).

72. Dan Flores, *Caprock Canyonlands* (Austin: University of Texas Press, 1990), 83–84; Flores, "Bison Ecology and Bison Diplomacy," 471, 481. William R. Brown Jr., "Comanchería Demography, 1805–1830," *Panhandle-Plains Historical Review* 59 (1986): 1–17, provides buffalo estimates at 9–12. Pekka Hämäläinen, "The Comanche Empire: A Study of Indigenous Power, 1700–1875," Ph.D. diss., University of Helsinki, 2001, emphasizes the role of Comanches as pastoralists, as does Gerald Betty, " 'Skillful in the Management of the Horse': The Comanches as Southern Plains Pastoralists," *Heritage of the Great Plains* 30 (spring–summer 1997): 5–13. Bolton, ed., *Athanase de Mézières*, 2: 175.

73. Pekka Hämäläinen, "The Western Comanche Trade Center: Rethinking the Plains Indian Trade System," *Western Historical Quarterly* 29 (1998): 488; Martha A. Works, "Creating Trading Places on the New Mexican Frontier," *Geographical Review* 82 (1992): 268–81.

74. The Spanish officer's report is in Thomas, trans. and ed., *After Coronado*, 194. Secoy, *Changing Military Patterns*, 31; John, *Storms*, 265–66; Hämäläinen, "The Comanche Empire," chap. 2; Hämäläinen, "The Western Comanche Trade Center," 489.

75. Wallace and Hoebel, *The Comanches*, 288; John, *Storms*, 256; Bolton, ed., *Athanase de Mézières*, 1: 24–25.

76. Hämäläinen, "The Western Comanche Trade Center," 489; Hämäläinen, "The Comanche Empire," 64.

77. Map of the Domínguez–Vélez de Escalante expedition by don Bernardo de Miera y Pacheco, 1778, in Ted J. Warner, ed., *The Domínguez-Escalante Journal* (Salt Lake City: University of Utah Press, 1995), 144–45, quoted in Kavanagh, *The Comanches*, 90.

78. Howard Meredith, *Dancing on Common Ground: Tribal Cultures and Alliances on the Southern Plains* (Lawrence: University Press of Kansas, 1995), esp. chap. 7; Hämäläinen, "The Comanche Empire."

79. Hämäläinen, "The Western Comanche Trade Center," 485–513; Hämäläinen, "The Comanche Empire," chaps. 3–4; Works, "Creating Trading Places," 273–78; Eleanor B. Adams and Angélico Chávez, trans. and eds., *The Missions of New Mexico, 1776: A Description by Fray Francisco Atanasio Dominguez*

with Other Contemporary Documents (Albuquerque: University of New Mexico Press, 1956), 252–53. See also Anderson, *The Indian Southwest*; Kavanagh, *The Comanches*, 127–31.

80. Charles L. Kenner, *The Comanchero Frontier: A History of New Mexican–Plains Indian Relations* (Norman: University of Oklahoma Press, 1969), 38.

81. Hämäläinen, "The Western Comanche Trade Center," 492; Cheryl Foote, "Spanish-Indian Trade along New Mexico's Northern Frontier in the Eighteenth Century," *Journal of the West* 44, no. 2 (1985): 22–33.

82. Hackett, ed., *Historical Documents*, 3: 401.

83. Foote, "Spanish-Indian Trade," 22, 33; Anderson, *The Indian Southwest*, 205–7, 220–26, 235; James L. Brooks, *Captives and Cousins: Slavery, Kinship, and Community in the Southwest Borderlands* (Chapel Hill: University of North Carolina Press, 2002).

84. Anderson, *The Indian Southwest*, chap. 10.

85. Hall, *Social Change*, 119; Kavanagh, *The Comanches*, 54–55, 102, Marín quote at 125. See also John C. Ewers, ed., *Report on the Indian Tribes of Texas in 1828 by José Francisco Ruiz* (New Haven CT: Yale University Press, 1972), 10–12 for the role and power of Comanche war chiefs.

86. Bolton, ed., *Athanase de Mézières*, 1: 297; Kavanagh, *The Comanches*, 71, 102; Hackett, ed., *Pichardo's Treatise*, 3: 299–308.

87. This brief description of Comanche divisions and bands is drawn, modified, and simplified from Hämäläinen, "The Western Comanche Trade Center," 493–94; Wallace and Hoebel, *The Comanches*, 22–31; Anderson, *The Indian Southwest*, 218–19; and Kavanagh, *The Comanches*, 121–24, 478–83.

88. Joseph Jablow, *The Cheyenne in Plains Indian Trade Relations, 1795–1840* (1951; reprint, Lincoln: University of Nebraska Press, 1994), 15, 24, 67–68.

89. Catherine Price, "The Comanche Threat to Texas and New Mexico in the Eighteenth Century and the Development of Spanish Indian Policy," *Journal of the West* 44, no. 2 (1985): 39; SANM, series 1 (English translations), reel 4, archive 1328 (report of Comanche attack on Pecos in 1748).

90. Hämäläinen, "The Comanche Empire," chap. 5.

91. Robert Ryal Miller, trans. and ed., "New Mexico in Mid-Eighteenth Century: A Report Based on Governor Vélez Cachupín's Inspection," *Southwestern Historical Quarterly* 79 (1975): 166–81, quote at 169; SANM, series 1 (English translations), reel 3, archives 1098, 1100, 1129.

92. Alfred Barnaby Thomas, ed., *The Plains Indians and New Mexico, 1751–1778* (Norman: University of Oklahoma Press, 1940), 68–74; Stanley Noyes, *Los Comanches: The Horse People, 1751–1845* (Albuquerque: University of New Mexico Press, 1993), 5–10, 49–59; John, *Storms*, 321–22. Vélez Cachupín's account of his campaign is in SANM, series 2, reel 8, archive 1049.

93. Thomas, ed., *The Plains Indians*, 134–35.

94. Odie B. Faulk, "The Comanche Invasion of Texas, 1743–1836," *Great*

Plains Journal 9 (1969): 10–50, esp. 13–19; Lesley Byrd Simpson, ed., *The San Sabá Papers: A Documentary Account of the Founding and Destruction of San Sabá Mission* (1959; reprint, Dallas TX: Southern Methodist University Press, 2000); Bolton, ed., *Athanase de Mézières,* 1: 49; Hackett, ed., *Pichardo's Treatise,* 2: 236–37; *Presidio and Militia,* 2, pt. 2: 511–12; Anderson, *The Indian Southwest,* 88–89, 152–53, 162; John, *Storms,* 349–52.

95. Eleanor B. Adams, ed., "Bishop Tamarón's Visitation of New Mexico, 1760," *New Mexico Historical Review* 28 (1953): 211–12, 215–16.

96. Adams, ed., "Bishop Tamarón's Visitation," 217; Adams and Chávez, trans. and eds., *The Missions of New Mexico,* 251; Anderson, *The Indian Southwest,* 209; Thomas, ed., *The Plains Indians,* 151.

97. Thomas, ed., *The Plains Indians,* 38–43.

98. Thomas, ed., *The Plains Indians,* 47–48, 169–75; John, *Storms,* 477–80; Anderson, *The Indian Southwest,* 211; Noyes, *Los Comanches,* 63–64.

99. Alfred B. Thomas, ed., "Governor Mendinueta's Proposals for the Defense of New Mexico, 1772–1778," *New Mexico Historical Review* 6 (1931): 21–39.

100. John, *Storms,* 590–91; Secoy, *Changing Military Patterns,* chap. 7; Hall, *Social Change,* 113.

101. Bolton, ed., *Athanase de Mézières,* 1: 218–19.

102. Wallace and Hoebel, *The Comanches,* 31; Anderson, *The Indian Southwest,* 216–17, 219; Hämäläinen, "The Comanche Empire," 149, 198–99.

103. Pekka Hämäläinen, "The First Phase of Destruction: Killing the Southern Plains Buffalo, 1790–1840," *Great Plains Quarterly* 21 (2001): 101–14. On horse numbers, see Hämäläinen, "The Comanche Empire," 148–51.

104. Ella E. Clark, *Indian Legends from the Northern Rockies* (Norman: University of Oklahoma Press, 1988), 202–5.

105. Much of the information that follows was originally published in Colin G. Calloway, "Snake Frontiers: The Eastern Shoshones in the Eighteenth Century," *Annals of Wyoming* 63 (summer 1991): 82–92.

106. Hyde, *Indians of the High Plains,* 127n; Demitri B. Shimkin, "Eastern Shoshone," in *HNAI,* 11: 305, 334; Robert F. Murphy and Yolanda Murphy, "Northern Shoshone and Bannock," in *HNAI,* 11: 287; Burpee, ed., *Journals and Letters,* 21, 412n; Virginia Trenholm and Maurine Carley, *The Shoshonis, Sentinels of the Rockies* (Norman: University of Oklahoma Press, 1964), 19.

107. Calloway, "Snake Frontiers," 85; Shimkin, "Eastern Shoshone," 309; James Mooney, *Calendar History of the Kiowa Indians,* Seventeenth Annual Report of the Bureau of American Ethnology, 1895–96 (Washington DC: GPO, 1898; reprint, Washington DC: Smithsonian Institution Press, 1979), 160; Clark, *Indian Legends,* 168.

108. George C. Frison, *Prehistoric Hunters of the High Plains* (New York:

Academic Press, 1978), 51, 64–67, 80–81, 246, 369, 405–10, 424; George C. Frison, "Shoshonean Antelope Procurement in the Upper Green River Basin, Wyoming," *Plains Anthropologist* 16 (1971): 254–84; Davis S. Gebhard, *The Rock Art of Dinwoody* (Santa Barbara: Art Galleries, University of California, 1969), 21–22; Mark E. Miller and George W. Gill, "A Late Prehistoric Bundle Burial from Southern Wyoming," *Plains Anthropologist* 25 (1980): 235–46; Gary A. Wright, "The Shoshonean Migration Problem," *Plains Anthropologist* 23 (1978): 113–37.

109. Ewers, *The Horse in Blackfoot Indian Culture,* 6–7; D. B. Shimkin, "Wind River Shoshone Geography," *American Anthropologist* 40 (1938): 415; Clark Wissler, "The Influence of the Horse in the Development of Plains Culture," *American Anthropologist* 16 (1914): 13, 24; Roe, *The Indian and the Horse,* 126–28, 308; Haines, "Horses for Western Indians," 12; Francis Haines, "The Northward Spread of Horses to the Plains Indians," *American Anthropologist* 40 (1938): 435–36.

110. Sylvester L. Lahren Jr., "Kalispel," in *HNAI,* 12: 283; Theodore Stern, "Columbia River Trade Network," in *HNAI,* 12: 645.

111. Murphy and Murphy, "Northern Shoshone and Bannock," 289–91; Shimkin, "Eastern Shoshone," 309; Moulton, ed., *The Journals,* 5: 119–20.

112. Hyde, *Indians of the High Plains,* x, 117, 134; Secoy, *Changing Military Patterns,* 33.

113. For another Indian account of how the Blackfeet obtained their first horses and guns, see James Willard Schultz (Apikuni), *Why Gone Those Times: Blackfoot Tales* (Norman: University of Oklahoma Press, 1974), 129–40. In the winter of 1877–78 Red Eagle told Schultz how the Blackfeet got their first guns from the Crees and then turned them against the Crows and other enemies. Red Eagle said, "This is the story of the gun as my grandfather told it to me—and as his father told it to him."

114. Richard Glover, ed., *David Thompson's Narrative, 1784–1812* (Toronto: Champlain Society, 1962), 240–42; John C. Ewers, "Intertribal Warfare as the Precursor of Indian-White Warfare on the Northern Great Plains," *Western Historical Quarterly* 6 (1975): 401; Colin G. Calloway, ed., *Our Hearts Fell to the Ground: Plains Indian Views of How the West Was Lost* (Boston: Bedford Books, 1996), 43–44.

115. James D. Keyser and Michael A. Klassen, *Plains Indian Rock Art* (Seattle: University of Washington Press, 2001), 222–23. See also James D. Keyser, "The Plains Indian War Complex and the Rock Art of Writing-on-Stone, Alberta, Canada," *Journal of Field Archaeology* 6 (spring 1979): 41–48, for horse-related changes in warfare.

116. Burpee, ed., *Journals and Letters,* 21, 412; Hyde, *Indians of the High Plains,* 131; Burpee, ed., "An Adventurer from Hudson's Bay," 103, 106.

117. Robert H. Ruby and John A. Brown, *The Cayuse Indians* (Norman:

University of Oklahoma Press, 1972), 7–14, 19; Theodore Stern, "Cayuse, Umatilla, and Walla Walla," in *HNAI*, 12: 396.

118. Alvin M. Josephy, *The Nez Perce Indians and the Opening of the Northwest* (New Haven CT: Yale University Press, 1965), 28–33; Francis Haines, *The Nez Perces: Tribesmen of the Columbia Plateau* (Norman: University of Oklahoma Press, 1955), 18–23; Moulton, ed., *The Journals*, 5: 223–25n, 313–16, quote at 313; Stern, "Cayuse, Umatilla, and Walla Walla," 396.

119. Hyde, *Indians of the High Plains*, 119; Secoy, *Changing Military Patterns*, 38; Frison, *Prehistoric Hunters*, 67; George C. Frison, "Crow Pottery in Northern Wyoming," *Plains Anthropologist* 21 (1976): 29–44.

120. Hugh A. Dempsey, *The Amazing Death of Calf Shirt and Other Blackfoot Stories: Three Hundred Years of Blackfoot History* (Norman: University of Oklahoma Press, 1994), 27; Ewers, *The Horse in Blackfoot Indian Culture*, 16–18. I am grateful to Russel Barsh for suggesting the possibility of a longer tribal memory relating to horses (personal communication, spring 1999).

121. Belyea, ed., *A Year Inland*, 199; Coues, ed., *New Light*, 2: 526.

122. Coues, ed., *New Light*, 2: 529, 724, 747; Edward Umfreville, *The Present State of Hudson's Bay* (London, 1790), 200; Glover, ed., *David Thompson's Narrative*, 50, 269.

123. Secoy, *Changing Military Patterns*, 47; Glover, ed., *David Thompson's Narrative*, 240, 242–43.

124. Binnema, *Common and Contested Ground*, chaps. 5–8, examines the context and complexities of these contests.

125. Ewers, *The Blackfeet*, 23–28; Ray, *Indians in the Fur Trade*, passim; R. Cole Harris, ed., *Historical Atlas of Canada*, vol. 1 (Toronto: University of Toronto Press, 1987), pls. 57, 60, 61, 62; Hugh A. Dempsey, "Blackfeet," in *HNAI*, 12: 607.

126. Fur trade scholars have long argued that Indian customers did not react to market forces in the same way as Europeans, but trade accounts suggest that Indians trading at York Factory may indeed have responded to higher prices by buying more goods and expending more effort rather than purchasing similar amounts with less effort. Ray, *Indians in the Fur Trade*, 68; cf. Ann M. Carlos and Frank D. Lewis, "Trade, Consumption, and the Native Economy: Lessons from York Factory, Hudson Bay," *Journal of Economic History* 61 (2001): 1037–64.

127. Binnema, *Common and Contested Ground*, 178–92; Ray, *Indians in the Fur Trade*, chaps. 1–3; John S. Milloy, *The Plains Cree: Trade, Diplomacy and War, 1790 to 1870* (Winnipeg: University of Manitoba Press, 1988), chap. 1, Cree profits at 19. David G. Mandlebaum, *The Plains Cree*, Anthropological Papers of the American Museum of Natural History no. 37 (1940), pt. 2: 155–316, presented what became the standard interpretation of western migration in Cree history. Dale Russell argues that the interpretation gathered authority

through repetition and that the actual evidence is slim: Crees were in the West early and did not make a transition from being a forest people to a plains people but rather continued to live in the parklands of Saskatchewan. Dale R. Russell, *Eighteenth-Century Western Cree and Their Neighbours* (Hull, Quebec: Canadian Museum of Civilization, 1991).

128. Belyea, ed., *A Year Inland,* 370.

129. Belyea, ed., *A Year Inland,* esp. 39–40, 104–8, 180–81, 275, 315, 344, 376–77.

130. Burpee, ed., "An Adventurer from Hudson's Bay," 119.

131. Ray, *Indians in the Fur Trade,* 102–4, 125–26, 131–34. Ray traces the movement of Cree and Assiniboine peoples southwestward to take advantage of new opportunities in the fur trade. Russell, *Eighteenth-Century Western Cree,* argues that fur trade records give a distorted impression of movement since the newly arrived traders made written note of people who were already there.

132. Trudy Nicks, "The Iroquois and the Fur Trade in Western Canada," in Carol M. Judd and Arthur J. Ray, eds., *Old Trails and New Directions: Papers of the Third North American Fur Trade Conference* (Toronto: University of Toronto Press, 1980), 85–101; Jan Grabowski and Nicole St.-Onge, "Montreal Iroquois *Engagés* in the Western Fur Trade, 1800–1821," in Theodore Binnema, Gerhard J. Ens, and R. C. MacLeod, eds., *From Rupert's Land to Canada* (Edmonton: University of Alberta Press, 2001), 23–58.

133. Colin G. Calloway, *Crown and Calumet: British-Indian Relations, 1783–1815* (Norman: University of Oklahoma Press, 1987), 153–57, 175–77; Ray, *Indians in the Fur Trade,* chap. 6. According to North West Company trader Duncan McGillivray, alcohol consumption nearly doubled during the peak years of competition between 1799 and 1804 ("Some Account of the Trade Carried on by the Northwest Company," in *Dominion of Canada: Report of the Public Archives of Canada* [1928], 62–63).

134. Glover, ed., *David Thompson's Narrative,* 240, 258, 269.

135. See, for example, Alice M. Johnson, ed., *Saskatchewan Journals and Correspondence: Edmonton House 1795–1800; Chesterfield House 1800–1802* (London: Hudson's Bay Record Society, 1967), 274, 276, 278, 306.

136. "François-Antoine Larocque's 'Yellowstone Journal,'" in W. Raymond Wood and Thomas D. Thiessen, eds., *Early Fur Trade on the Northern Plains: Canadian Traders among the Mandan and Hidatsa Indians, 1738–1818* (Norman: University of Oklahoma Press, 1985), 189; Moulton, ed., *The Journals,* 3: 436; 5: 91; 6: 316; 10: 235.

137. Clark, *Indian Legends,* 206.

138. Secoy, *Changing Military Patterns,* 16–17, 60–62.

139. Calloway, "Snake Frontiers," 88–90; Coues, ed., *New Light,* 2: 526, 726.

140. Hyde, *Indians of the High Plains,* 181–85.

141. Moulton, ed., *The Journals,* 8: 128–35.

142. Burpee, ed., *Journals and Letters,* 155, 157, 332.

143. John McDonnell, "Some Account of the Red River, . . ." in L. R. Masson, ed., *Les Bourgeois de la Compagnie du Nord-Ouest: Récits de voyages, lettres et rapports inédits relatifs au nord-ouest canadien,* 2 vols. (1889–90; reprint, New York: Antiquarian Press, 1960), 1: 273.

144. A. P. Nasatir, ed., *Before Lewis and Clark: Documents Illustrating the History of the Missouri, 1785–1804,* 2 vols. (1952; reprint, Lincoln: University of Nebraska Press, 1990), 1: 58; Burpee, ed., *Journals and Letters,* 108, 337; Annie Heloise Abel, ed., "Description of the Upper Missouri, by Jean-Baptiste Truteau," *Mississippi Valley Historical Review* 8 (1921): 173.

145. Ewers, *The Horse in Blackfoot Indian Culture,* 4–5; Burpee, ed., *Journals and Letters,* 108, 337.

146. Abel, ed., *Tabeau's Narrative,* 154, 158.

147. Moulton, ed., *The Journals,* 3: 422.

148. For information on the exchange network that centered on the upper Missouri, see Wood and Thiessen, eds., *Early Fur Trade*; Moulton, ed., *The Journals,* 3: 386–445; Nasatir, ed., *Before Lewis and Clark*; "Truteau's Journal," *American Historical Review* 19 (1914): 299–33; Abel, ed., *Tabeau's Narrative*; John C. Ewers, "The Indian Trade of the Upper Missouri before Lewis and Clark," in John C. Ewers, *Indian Life on the Upper Missouri* (Norman: University of Oklahoma Press, 1968), 14–34; and Roy W. Meyer, *The Village Indians of the Upper Missouri* (Lincoln: University of Nebraska Press, 1977). On the place of the upper Missouri exchange center in the trade networks that crisscrossed the West, see William R. Swagerty, "Indian Trade in the Trans-Mississippi West to 1870," in *HNAI,* 4: 351–74.

149. James P. Ronda, *Finding the West: Explorations with Lewis and Clark* (Albuquerque: University of New Mexico Press, 2001), 69.

150. Preston Holder, *The Hoe and the Horse on the Plains: A Study of Cultural Development among North American Indians* (Lincoln: University of Nebraska Press, 1970) provides a general, though dated, discussion of farming and nomadism on the plains.

151. Joseph Medicine Crow, *From the Heart of the Crow Country: The Crow Indians' Own Stories* (New York: Crown, 1992), 100–101; Clark, *Indian Legends,* 312–14.

152. Coues, ed., *New Light,* 1: 398–99; John C. Ewers, *Five Indian Tribes of the Upper Missouri, by Edwin Thompson Denig* (Norman: University of Oklahoma Press, 1961), 144; "François-Antoine Larocque's 'Yellowstone Journal,'" 213.

153. Medicine Crow, *From the Heart of the Crow Country,* 103–4.

154. "François-Antoine Larocque's 'Yellowstone Journal,'" 207, 213.

155. Medicine Crow, *From the Heart of the Crow Country,* 102.

156. "Charles Mckenzie's Narratives," in Wood and Thiessen, eds., *Early Fur Trade,* 245.

157. Medicine Crow, *From the Heart of the Crow Country,* 102–3.

158. Peter Nabokov, *Two Leggings: The Making of a Crow Warrior* (1967; reprint, Lincoln: University of Nebraska Press, 1982), 162.

159. "François-Antoine Larocque's 'Yellowstone Journal,'" 213.

160. Colin G. Calloway, " 'The Only Way Open to Us': The Crow Struggle for Survival in the Nineteenth Century," *North Dakota History* 53 (summer 1986): 25–34.

161. Medicine Crow, *From the Heart of the Crow Country,* 109.

162. Erminie Voegelin, "Kiowa-Crow Mythological Affiliations," *American Anthropologist* 35 (1933): 470–74.

163. Mooney, *Calendar History,* 152–64; Momaday, *The Way to Rainy Mountain,* 4, 6–7.

164. John Stands in Timber and Margot Liberty, *Cheyenne Memories* (Lincoln: University of Nebraska Press, 1972), 13; John H. Moore, *The Cheyenne* (Cambridge MA: Blackwell, 1996), 13–15; George E. Hyde, *The Life of George Bent, Written from His Letters* (Norman: University of Oklahoma Press, 1968), 3.

165. Moore, *The Cheyenne,* 17, 21–29; Glover, ed., *David Thompson's Narrative,* 195–96.

166. Moore, *The Cheyenne,* 28–29. Moore provides more detailed discussion of the various bands and their identification in early records and maps in *The Cheyenne Nation: A Social and Demographic History* (Lincoln: University of Nebraska Press, 1987), chap. 3.

167. Stands in Timber and Liberty, *Cheyenne Memories,* 40, 117.

168. Quoted in West, "Called out People," 14.

169. Abel, ed., *Tabeau's Narrative,* 152.

170. Moore, *The Cheyenne,* 30–32.

171. West, "Called out People," 8.

172. Stands in Timber and Liberty, *Cheyenne Memories,* 115; Hyde, *The Life of George Bent,* 13.

173. George Bird Grinnell, *The Cheyenne Indians: Their History and Ways of Life,* 2 vols. (1923; reprint, Lincoln: University of Nebraska Press, 1972), 1: 11; Abel, ed., *Tabeau's Narrative,* 98, 153–55; Virginia Cole Trenholm, *The Arapahoes* (Norman: University of Oklahoma Press, 1970), 28.

174. Elliott West, *The Way to the West: Essays on the Central Plains* (Albuquerque: University of New Mexico Press, 1995), 15; West, "Called out People," 2–15; Abel, ed., *Tabeau's Narrative,* 152–53; Jablow, *The Cheyenne in Plains Indian Trade Relations.*

175. West, "Called out People," 14.

176. Secoy, *Changing Military Patterns,* 67; Hyde, *Indians of the High Plains,* 6–12.

177. Gary Clayton Anderson, "Early Dakota Migration and Intertribal War: A Revision," *Western Historical Quarterly* 11 (1980): 17–36; Richard White, "The Winning of the West: The Expansion of the Western Sioux in the Eighteenth and Nineteenth Centuries," *Journal of American History* 65 (1978): 321–23; George E. Hyde, *Red Cloud's Folk: A History of the Oglala Sioux Indians* (Norman: University of Oklahoma Press, 1937), 11.

178. Burpee, ed., *Journals and Letters,* 134–35, 282; Alexander Henry, *Travels and Adventures in the Years 1760–1776* (Chicago: R. R. Donnelley and Sons, 1921), 197; Norman Gelb, ed., *Jonathan Carver's Travels through America, 1766–1768* (New York: John Wiley and Sons, 1993), 81.

179. Hyde, *Red Cloud's Folk,* 4. On the complexities of such relations, see Susan R. Sharrock, "Crees, Cree-Assiniboines, and Assiniboines: Interethnic Social Organization on the Far Northern Plains," *Ethnohistory* 21 (1974): 95–122, esp. 101–6.

180. McCoy, "Winter Count," 125–27; Garrick Mallery, *Picture-Writing of the American Indians,* Tenth Annual Report of the Bureau of American Ethnology, 1888–89 (Washington DC: GPO, 1893; reprint, 2 vols., New York: Dover, 1972), 1: 295–305.

181. Gelb, ed., *Jonathan Carver's Travels,* 151–52; "The Narrative of Peter Pond," in Charles M. Gates, ed., *Five Fur Traders of the Northwest* (Saint Paul: Minnesota Historical Society, 1965), 58.

182. George Bird Grinnell, *The Fighting Cheyennes* (1915; reprint, Norman: University of Oklahoma Press, 1956), 37; "Journal of Jean Baptiste Truteau," *South Dakota Historical Collections* 7 (1914): 472–74.

183. Hyde, *Red Cloud's Folk,* 23. Another winter count, by Cloud Shield, places the event in 1776. (The counts are in the tenth and fourteenth reports of the Bureau of American Ethnology.)

184. Douglas Bamforth, "Indigenous People, Indigenous Violence: Precontact Warfare on the North American Great Plains," *Man: The Journal of the Royal Anthropological Institute* 29 (1994): 100–102; D. Owsley, H. Berryman, and W. Bass, "Demographic and Osteological Evidence for Warfare at the Larson Site, South Dakota," *Plains Anthropologist* 22 (1977): 119–31.

185. George E. Hyde, *The Pawnee Indians* (Norman: University of Oklahoma Press, 1951), 86; Abel, ed., *Tabeau's Narrative,* 123–24, 128, 130–31.

186. White, "The Winning of the West," 327; McDonnell, "Some Account of the Red River," 1: 268; Moulton, ed., *The Journals,* 8: 319.

187. Moulton, ed., *The Journals,* 3: 418; Zebulon Montgomery Pike, *An Account of Expeditions to the Sources of the Mississippi, and through the Western Parts of Louisiana, . . . and a Tour through the Interior Parts of New Spain* (Philadelphia:

C. and A. Conrad, 1810; reprint, New York: Readex Microprint, 1966), appendix to pt. 1: 62.

188. Isenberg, *The Destruction of the Bison,* 33, 39, 42, 47, 53, 59–62.

189. Flores, "Bison Ecology and Bison Diplomacy"; Isenberg, *The Destruction of the Bison,* 81–85; West, *The Way to the West,* 51–83; Hämäläinen, "The First Phase of Destruction."

7. People In Between and People on the Edge

1. Pekka Hämäläinen, "The Comanche Empire: A Study of Indigenous Power, 1700–1875," Ph.D. diss., University of Helsinki, 2001; Willard H. Rollings, *The Osage: An Ethnohistorical Study of Hegemony on the Prairie-Plains* (Columbia: University of Missouri Press, 1992). On the importance of imperial competition in frontier history and intercultural relations, see Jeremy Adelman and Stephen Aron, "From Borderlands to Borders: Empires, Nation-States, and the Peoples in Between in North American History," *American Historical Review* 104 (1999): 814–41. On Adelman and Aron's lack of attention to Indian agency, see the rejoinder by John R. Wunder and Pekka Hämäläinen, "Of Lethal Places and Lethal Essays," *American Historical Review* 104 (1999): 1229–34.

2. Thomas F. Schiltz and Donald E. Worcester, "The Spread of Firearms among the Indian Tribes on the Northern Frontier of New Spain," *American Indian Quarterly* 11 (1987): 1–10; Frank R. Secoy, *Changing Military Patterns of the Great Plains Indians* (1953; reprint, Lincoln: University of Nebraska Press, 1992), 92.

3. Daniel K. Richter, *The Ordeal of the Longhouse: The Peoples of the Iroquois League in the Era of European Colonization* (Chapel Hill: University of North Carolina Press, 1992), chap. 8; Gilles Havard, *The Great Peace of Montreal of 1701* (Montreal: McGill-Queens University Press, 2001).

4. Donald J. Blakeslee, *Along Ancient Trails: The Mallet Expedition of 1739* (Niwot: University of Colorado Press, 1995); William C. Foster, *Spanish Expeditions into Texas, 1698–1768* (Austin: University of Texas Press, 1995), 1–4, 9–11, 217–20. Foster provides detailed routes for the expeditions.

5. For example, Ralph A. Smith, trans. and ed., "Account of the Journey of Bénard de La Harpe: Discovery Made by Him of Several Nations Situated in the West," *Southwestern Historical Quarterly* 62 (1958–59): 374–75.

6. Robert P. Wiegers, "A Proposal for Indian Slave Trading in the Mississippi Valley and Its Impact on the Osage," *Plains Anthropologist* 33 (1988): 187–202; Russell M. Magnaghi, "Intertribal Slaving on the Great Plains in the Eighteenth Century," in Russell M. Magnaghi, ed., *From the Mississippi to the Pacific: Essays in Honor of John Francis Bannon, S.J.* (Marquette: Northern

Michigan University Press, 1982), 43–55; Ron Welburn, "The Other Middle Passage: The Bermuda-Barbados Trade in Native American Slaves," in Ron Welburn, *Roanoke and Wampum: Topics in Native American Heritage and Literatures* (New York: Peter Lang, 2001), 25–32; Alan Gallay, *The Indian Slave Trade: The Rise of the English Empire in the American South, 1670–1717* (New Haven CT: Yale University Press, 2002), 7. For a guide to the sources and literature on Indian slavery, see Russell M. Magnaghi, *Indian Slavery, Labor, Evangelization, and Captivity in the Americas: An Annotated Bibliography* (Lanham MD: Scarecrow Press, 1998).

7. Gallay, *The Indian Slave Trade*; F. Todd Smith, *The Caddo Indians: Tribes at the Convergence of Empires, 1542–1854* (College Station: Texas A & M University Press, 1995), 37; W. David Baird, *The Quapaw Indians: A History of the Downstream People* (Norman: University of Oklahoma Press, 1980), 27–28; Alexander Moore, ed., *Nairne's Muskhogean Journals: The 1708 Expedition to the Mississippi River* (Jackson: University of Mississippi Press, 1988), 47; Dunbar Rowland, A. G. Sanders, and Patricia Kay Galloway, eds., *Mississippi Provincial Archives, French Dominion*, vols. 4–5 (Baton Rouge: Louisiana State University Press, 1984), 5: 76; Richebourg Gaillaird McWilliams, trans. and ed., *Iberville's Gulf Journals* (University: University of Alabama Press, 1981), 172; Daniel H. Usner Jr., "A Population History of American Indians in the Eighteenth-Century Lower Mississippi Valley," in Daniel H. Usner Jr., *American Indians in the Lower Mississippi Valley: Social and Economic Histories* (Lincoln: University of Nebraska Press, 1998), 33–55.

8. Records relating to "Panis" must be used with caution, since the term sometimes referred to the Taovayas, Wichitas, Yscanis, and Tawakonis and was therefore synonymous with "Wichita" rather than "Pawnee." See Herbert E. Bolton, ed., *Athanase de Mézières and the Texas-Louisiana Frontier 1768–1780*, 2 vols. (Cleveland: Arthur H. Clark, 1914), 2: 81n, 85n. It may also have been used to refer to Indian slaves from anywhere on the plains.

9. Mildred M. Wedel, "The Identity of La Salle's Pana Slave," *Plains Anthropologist* 18 (1973): 203–17.

10. Quoted in Havard, *The Great Peace*, 156.

11. Wiegers, "A Proposal," 189–92; Richebourg Gaillaird McWilliams, trans. and ed., *Fleur de Lys and Calumet: Being the Pénicaut Narrative of French Adventure in Louisiana* (Baton Rouge: Louisiana State University Press, 1953), 122; *WHC*, 16: 331–32.

12. William J. Eccles, "La Mer de L'Ouest: Outpost of Empire," in William J. Eccles, *Essays on New France* (Oxford: Oxford University Press, 1987), 104; William J. Eccles, *France in America* (New York: Harper and Row, 1972), 77; *WHC*, 17: 418.

13. Brett Rushforth, "'A Little Flesh We Offer You': French-Indian Al-

liance and the Origins of Panis Slavery," *William and Mary Quarterly* (forthcoming), examines the development of Panis slavery in the context of growing French dependence on Indians as trade partners and military allies.

14. L. R. Bailey, *Indian Slave Trade in the Southwest: A Study of Slave-Taking and the Traffic in Indian Captives* (Los Angeles: Westernlore Press, 1966); James F. Brooks, *Captives and Cousins: Slavery, Kinship, and Community in the Southwest Borderlands* (Chapel Hill: University of North Carolina Press, 2002).

15. Nicolas de La Salle, *Relation of the Discovery of the Mississippi River,* trans. Melville B. Anderson (Chicago: Caxton Club, 1898), 65; George E. Hyde, *The Pawnee Indians* (Norman: University of Oklahoma Press, 1951), 46–47, 56; Bailey, *Indian Slave Trade,* 23; David M. Brugge, "Some Plains Indians in the Church Records of New Mexico," *Plains Anthropologist* 10 (1965): 181–90; David M. Brugge, *Navajos in the Catholic Church Records of New Mexico, 1694–1875* (Tsaile AZ: Navajo Community College Press, 1985), 20.

16. George E. Hyde, *Indians of the High Plains: From Prehistoric Times to the Coming of Europeans* (Norman: University of Oklahoma Press, 1959), 41–42; John R. Swanton, *Source Material on the History and Ethnology of the Caddo Indians* (1942; reprint, Norman: University of Oklahoma Press, 1996), 269–70.

17. Bailey, *Indian Slave Trade,* 19. Brooks, *Captives and Cousins,* 146, lists nine hundred Apache baptisms for the whole century.

18. Fritz Leo Hoffmann, trans., *Diary of the Alarcón Expedition into Texas, 1718–1719, by Fray Francisco Céliz* (Berkeley: Quivira Society, 1935), 77, 83.

19. Ned Blackhawk, "Violence over the Land: Colonial Encounters in the American Great Basin," Ph.D. diss., University of Washington, 1999; Sondra Jones, " 'Redeeming' the Indian: The Enslavement of Indian Children in New Mexico and Utah," *Utah Historical Quarterly* 67 (1999): 220–41.

20. Thomas D. Hall, *Social Change in the Southwest, 1350–1880* (Lawrence: University Press of Kansas, 1988), 101, citing Frances L. Swadesh, *Los Primeros Pobladores: Hispanic Americans of the Ute Frontier* (Notre Dame IN: University of Notre Dame Press, 1974), 47; Ralph Emerson Twitchell, trans. and ed., *The Spanish Archives of New Mexico,* 2 vols. (1914; reprint, New York: Arno Press, 1976), 2: 233; SANM, series 1, reel 1, archives 28, 36; reel 3, archives 1100, 1129; series 2, reel 11, frame 520; Lesley Poling-Kempes, *Valley of Shining Stone: The Story of Abiquiu* (Tucson: University of Arizona Press, 1997), 36, 38–42; Blackhawk, "Violence over the Land," 92–95; Brooks, *Captives and Cousins,* 125, 150–59.

21. Bailey, *Indian Slave Trade,* 25–27; Wiegers, "A Proposal," 191–94.

22. Blakeslee, *Along Ancient Trails,* 20; Stephen Webre, "The Problem of Indian Slavery in Spanish Louisiana, 1769–1803," *Louisiana History* 25 (1984): 117–35; *SMV,* 2: 167–79.

23. Charles Wilson Hackett, ed., *Historical Documents Relating to New Mex-*

ico, Nueva Vizcaya, and Approaches Thereto, to 1773, 3 vols. (Washington DC: Carnegie Institute, 1923–27), 3: 487.

24. James F. Brooks, "Served Well by Plunder: *La Gran Ladronería* and Producers of History astride the Rio Grande," *American Quarterly* 52 (2000): 36.

25. Oakah L. Jones Jr., "Rescue and Ransom of Spanish Captives from the *indios bárbaros* on the Northern Frontier of New Spain," *Colonial Latin American Historical Review* 4 (1995): 129–48; James F. Brooks, " 'This Evil Extends Especially . . . to the Feminine Sex': Negotiating Captivity in the New Mexico Borderlands," *Feminist Studies* 22 (1996): 279–309; Brooks, *Captives and Cousins*; SANM, series 2, reel 11, frames 344, 723.

26. Bolton, ed., *Athanase de Mézières*, 1: 51.

27. Morris S. Arnold, *The Rumble of a Distant Drum: The Quapaws and Old World Newcomers, 1673–1804* (Fayetteville: University of Arkansas Press, 2000), 21–28; Rowland, Sanders, and Galloway, eds., *Mississippi Provincial Archives*, 5: 76.

28. Daniel H. Usner Jr., "French-Natchez Borderlands in Colonial Louisiana," in Usner Jr., *American Indians*, 16–32; Seymour Feiler, trans. and ed., *Jean-Bernard Bossu's Travels in the Interior of North America 1751–1762* (Norman: University of Oklahoma Press, 1962), 37, 39. The speech of the Stung Serpent to Le Page Du Pratz is in Colin G. Calloway, ed., *The World Turned Upside Down: Indian Voices from Early America* (Boston: Bedford Books, 1994), 91. Documents relating to the beginning of the war are reprinted in Gail Alexander Buzhardt and Margaret Hawthorne, eds., *Rencontres sur le Mississippi, 1682–1763* (Jackson: University of Mississippi Press, 1993), 41–48.

29. Rowland, Sanders, and Galloway, eds., *Mississippi Provincial Archives*, 4: 32, 37–38.

30. Rowland, Sanders, and Galloway, eds., *Mississippi Provincial Archives*, 4: 112.

31. Rowland, Sanders, and Galloway, eds., *Mississippi Provincial Archives*, 4: 81.

32. Rowland, Sanders, and Galloway, eds., *Mississippi Provincial Archives*, 4: 105; 5: 48–49, 76, 122; Feiler, trans. and ed., *Jean-Bossu's Travels*, 173; Buzhardt and Hawthorne, eds., *Rencontres sur le Mississippi*, 166–69.

33. Dunbar Rowland and A. G. Sanders, eds., *Mississippi Provincial Archives, French Dominion*, vols. 1–3 (Jackson: Mississippi Department of Archives and History, 1927–32), 1: 211, 228–29; 3: 538; Rowland, Sanders, and Galloway, eds., *Mississippi Provincial Archives*, 4: 259; *WHC*, 17: 161–62.

34. Patricia Galloway, *Choctaw Genesis, 1500–1700* (Lincoln: University of Nebraska Press, 1995), 2–3, 198; Richard White, *The Roots of Dependency: Subsistence, Environment, and Social Change among the Choctaws, Navajos, and Pawnees* (Lincoln: University of Nebraska Press, 1983), 5, 37.

35. Galloway, *Choctaw Genesis*, 27, 264–66, 338–60.

36. Rowland and Sanders, eds., *Mississippi Provincial Archives*, 3: 526–27; White, *The Roots of Dependency*, Bienville quote at 5.

37. White, *The Roots of Dependency*, chap. 3; Rowland, Sanders, and Galloway, eds., *Mississippi Provincial Archives*, 4–5: passim, quotes at 5: 97, 128; Buzhardt and Hawthorne, eds., *Rencontres sur le Mississippi*, 171, 177–85.

38. Neil Schmitz, *White Robe's Dilemma: Tribal History in American Literature* (Amherst: University of Massachusetts Press, 2001), 138.

39. Reuben G. Thwaites, ed., *The Jesuit Relations and Allied Documents: Travels and Explorations of the Jesuit Missionaries in New France 1610–1791*, 73 vols. (Cleveland: Burrows Brothers, 1896–1901), 44: 247.

40. For the sources of Fox-French conflict, see R. David Edmunds and Joseph L. Peyser, *The Fox Wars: The Mesquakie Challenge to New France* (Norman: University of Oklahoma Press, 1993).

41. Milo Milton Quaife, ed., *The Western Country in the 17th Century: The Memoirs of Lamothe Cadillac and Pierre Liette* (Chicago: R. R. Donnelley and Sons, 1947), 67.

42. Quoted in Eric Hinderaker, *Elusive Empires: Constructing Colonialism in the Ohio Valley, 1673–1800* (Cambridge: Cambridge University Press, 1997), 49.

43. Edmunds and Peyser, *The Fox Wars*, 61–85; WHC, 16: 267–89, 293–95, 301–7, 310, 327, 341–44.

44. WHC, 16: 393–94, 396–98, 417, 450–51, 456–69; 17: xii–xii, 1–7.

45. WHC, 17: 7–17, 77–80.

46. WHC, 16: 476–77; 17: 21–22, 31–34.

47. The following account is based on the "Réaume Narrative," translated and reprinted in Lenville J. Stelle, "History and Archaeology: The 1730 Mesquakie Fort," in John A. Walthall and Thomas E. Emerson, eds., *Calumet and Fleur-de-Lys: Archaeology of Indian and French Contact in the Midcontinent* (Washington DC: Smithsonian Institution Press, 1992), 265–307, "Réaume Narrative" at 301–4; Edmunds and Peyser, *The Fox Wars*, chap. 5; WHC, 17: 59–70, 87–102, 109–30, 148–55, 167–68. See also Schmitz, *White Robe's Dilemma*, 38–42, for discussion of Fox stories of the disaster.

48. WHC, 17: 182–83.

49. Edmunds and Peyser, *The Fox Wars*, 191–203; WHC, 17: 188–91, 200–203, 206–10, 215–33, 255–60, 263, 275.

50. Lucy Eldersveld Murphy, "Autonomy and the Economic Roles of Indian Women of the Fox-Wisconsin River Region, 1763–1832," in Nancy Shoemaker, ed., *Negotiators of Change: Historical Perspectives on Native American Women* (New York: Routledge, 1995), 80–82; Lucy Eldersveld Murphy, *A Gathering of Peoples: Indians, Métis, and Mining in the Western Great Lakes, 1737–1832* (Lincoln: University of Nebraska Press, 2000), chap. 3.

51. Stelle, "History and Archaeology," 304.

52. SANM, series 1, reel 4, archive 1328; Herbert E. Bolton, "French Intrusions into New Mexico, 1749–1752," in John Francis Bannon, ed., *Bolton and the Spanish Borderlands* (Norman: University of Oklahoma Press, 1964), 150–71; Bolton, ed., *Athanase de Mézières,* 1: 59–60; Charles Wilson Hackett, ed., *Pichardo's Treatise on the Limits of Louisiana and Texas,* 4 vols. (Austin: University of Texas Press, 1931–46), 3: 299–333.

53. Blakeslee, *Along Ancient Trails,* 203–9, 245–48; Hackett, ed., *Pichardo's Treatise,* 3: 334–63.

54. Alfred B. Thomas, ed., *The Plains Indians and New Mexico, 1751–1778* (Albuquerque: University of New Mexico Press, 1940), 82–110.

55. David La Vere, "Friendly Persuasions: Gifts and Reciprocity in Comanche-Euroamerican Relations," *Chronicles of Oklahoma* 71 (1993): 322–37.

56. Robert Ryal Miller, trans. and ed., "New Mexico in Mid-Eighteenth Century: A Report Based on Governor Vélez Cachupín's Inspection," *Southwestern Historical Quarterly* 79 (1975): 172–73.

57. Elizabeth A. H. John, *Storms Brewed in Other Men's Worlds: The Confrontation of Indians, Spanish, and French in the Southwest, 1540–1795* (Lincoln: University of Nebraska Press, 1975), 215, 304–5, 318–19; Elizabeth Ann Harper [John], "The Taovayas Indians in Frontier Trade and Diplomacy, 1719–1768," *Chronicles of Oklahoma* 31 (1953): 268–89; Smith, *The Caddo Indians,* chaps. 3–4; F. Todd Smith, *The Wichita Indians: Traders of Texas and the Southern Plains, 1540–1845* (College Station: Texas A & M University Press, 2000), 15–28; Hackett, ed., *Pichardo's Treatise,* 3: 299–370; *WHC,* 18: 87–88. On Osage dominance, see Rollings, *The Osage.*

58. Foster, *Spanish Expeditions,* 229, 262–63, 265–89.

59. Russell M. Magnaghi, trans. and ed., "Texas as Seen by Governor Winthuysen, 1741–1744," *Southwestern Historical Quarterly* 88 (1984): 167–80.

60. Hackett, ed., *Pichardo's Treatise,* 4: 1–118, quotes at 16, 76.

61. Eccles, *Essays on New France,* 85, 103.

62. Susan Sleeper-Smith, *Indian Women and French Men: Rethinking Cultural Encounter in the Western Great Lakes* (Amherst: University of Massachusetts Press, 2001).

63. Steve J. Stern, ed., *Resistance, Rebellion and Consciousness in the Andean Peasant World: 18th to 20th Centuries* (Madison: University of Wisconsin Press, 1987), 34.

64. Marguerite Eyer Wilbur, trans. and ed., *The Indian Uprising in Lower California 1734–1737 as Described by Father Sigismundo Taraval* (Los Angeles: Quivira Society, 1931).

65. Jack D. Forbes, *Warriors of the Colorado: The Yumans of the Quechan Nation and Their Neighbors* (Norman: University of Oklahoma Press, 1965), 130; *Presidio and Militia,* 2, pt. 1: 444; Roberto Mario Salmon, *Indian Revolts in*

Northern New Spain: A Synthesis of Resistance (1680–1786) (Lanham MD: University Press of America, 1991), chap. 5.

66. *Presidio and Militia,* 2, pt. 1: 313–26; Evelyn Hu-DeHart, *Missionaries, Miners, and Indians: Spanish Contact with the Yaqui Nation of Northwestern New Spain, 1533–1820* (Tucson: University of Arizona Press, 1981), 59–87, quote at 60; Edward Spicer, *Cycles of Conquest: The Impact of Spain, Mexico, and the United States on the Indians of the Southwest, 1533–1960* (Tucson: University of Arizona Press, 1962), 51–53; Edward Spicer, *The Yaquis: A Cultural History* (Tucson: University of Arizona Press, 1980), 32–57; John D. Meredith, "The Yaqui Rebellion of 1740: A Jesuit Account and Its Implications," *Ethnohistory* 22 (1975): 223–61; Cynthia Radding, "Cultural Boundaries between Adaptation and Defiance: The Mission Communities of Northwestern New Spain," in Nicholas Griffiths and Fernando Cervantes, eds., *Spiritual Encounters: Interactions between Christianity and Native Religions in Colonial America* (Lincoln: University of Nebraska Press, 1999), 127. Hu-DeHart, *Missionaries, Miners, and Indians,* 81, 125n32 discusses and dismisses the casualty figures.

67. Thomas Sheridan, comp. and ed., *Empire of Sand: The Seri Indians and the Struggle for Spanish Sonora, 1645–1803* (Tucson: University of Arizona Press, 1999), 13–15, chaps. 2–4; *Presidio and Militia,* 2, pt. 1: 443–79; José Luis Mirafuentes Galván, "Colonial Expansion and Indian Resistance in Sonora: The Seri Uprisings in 1748 and 1750," in William B. Taylor and Franklin Pease G.Y., eds., *Violence, Resistance, and Survival in the Americas: Native Americans and the Legacy of Conquest* (Washington DC: Smithsonian Institution Press, 1994), 101–23; Spicer, *Cycles of Conquest,* 107–10.

68. Russell C. Ewing, "The Pima Outbreak in November, 1751," *New Mexico Historical Review* 8 (1938): 337–46; Lawrence Kinnaird, ed., *The Frontiers of New Spain: Nicolas de Lafora's Description 1766–1768* (Berkeley: Quivira Society, 1958), quote at 128; Spicer, *Cycles of Conquest,* 129–32; *Presidio and Militia,* 2, pt. 1: 407–8; Salmon, *Indian Revolts,* 75–80; Radding, "Cultural Boundaries," 129.

69. For example, "Reports on the American Colonies, 1721–1762," in *Collections of the Michigan Pioneer and Historical Society* (1874–1929), 19: 2–8. See also Charles Morse Stotz, *Outposts of the War for Empire: The French and the English in Western Pennsylvania, 1749–1764* (Pittsburgh: Historical Society of Western Pennsylvania and University of Pittsburgh Press, 1985), 5–10.

70. William J. Eccles, "Sovereignty Association, 1500–1783," in Eccles, *Essays on New France,* 156–81; Fred Anderson, *Crucible of War: The Seven Years' War and the Fate of Empire in British North America, 1754–1766* (New York: Alfred A. Knopf, 2000), 16–21; Francis Jennings, *The Ambiguous Iroquois Empire: The Covenant Chain Confederation of Indian Tribes with English Colonies from Its Beginnings to the Lancaster Treaty of 1744* (New York: W. W. Norton, 1984);

Francis Jennings, *Empire of Fortune: Crowns, Colonies and Tribes in the Seven Years War in America* (New York: W. W. Norton, 1988), quote at 126.

71. Michael N. McConnell, *A Country Between: The Upper Ohio Valley and Its Peoples, 1724–1774* (Lincoln: University of Nebraska Press, 1992), chaps. 1–5; Richard White, *The Middle Ground: Indians, Empires, and Republics in the Great Lakes Region, 1650–1815* (Cambridge: Cambridge University Press, 1991), chap. 5.

72. White, *The Middle Ground*, 222–227; McConnell, *A Country Between*, 51–60.

73. McConnell, *A Country Between*, 85.

74. The proceedings of the Treaty of Lancaster are reprinted in Donald H. Kent, ed., *Pennsylvania Treaties, 1737–1756* (Frederick MD: University Publications of America, 1984), 77–110.

75. Kent, ed., *Pennsylvania Treaties*, 173, 177–85; Hinderaker, *Elusive Empires*, 18, 42–44; "Christopher Gist's First and Second Journals," in Lois Mulkearn, ed., *George Mercer Papers Relating to the Ohio Company of Virginia* (Pittsburgh: University of Pittsburgh Press, 1954), 19.

76. R. David Edmunds, "Old Briton," in R. David Edmunds, ed., *American Indian Leaders: Studies in Diversity* (Lincoln: University of Nebraska Press, 1980), 1–20; Andrew Gallup, ed., *The Céleron Expedition to the Ohio Country, 1749: The Reports of Pierre-Joseph Céleron and Father Bonnecamps* (Bowie MD: Heritage Books, 1997); *WHC*, 18: 36–58, 69, 104–8, 128–31; Miami report in James Sullivan et al., eds., *The Papers of Sir William Johnson*, 15 vols. (Albany: University of the State of New York, 1921–1965), 9: 82; Kent, ed., *Pennsylvania Treaties*, 225–32, 237, 246–47, 262–65, "lost People" quote at 265; Joseph L. Peyser, trans. and ed., *On the Eve of Conquest: The Chevalier De Raymond's Critique of New France in 1754* (East Lansing: Michigan State University Press, 1997), 18–25; Mulkearn, ed., *George Mercer Papers*, 21–22; "Proceedings of George Croghan and Andrew Montour at the Ohio, May 1751," in Reuben G. Thwaites, ed., *Early Western Travels, 1748–1846*, 32 vols. (Cleveland: Arthur H. Clark, 1904–7), 1: 58–69; White, *The Middle Ground*, 228–34.

77. Mulkearn, ed., *George Mercer Papers*, 7–8, 18.

78. "Christopher Gist's First and Second Journals," 9–10, 39.

79. The Treaty of Logstown is reprinted in Mulkearn, ed., *George Mercer Papers*, 127–39, 273–84, quote at 129; McConnell, *A Country Between*, 95–99; Jennings, *Empire of Fortune*, 43.

80. White, *The Middle Ground*, 237; Hinderaker, *Elusive Empires*, 39, 43–44, 139.

81. *The Journal of Major George Washington, Sent by Hon. Robert Dinwiddie . . . to the Commandant of the French Forces on Ohio* (Williamsburg, 1754; facsimile reprint, Williamsburg VA: Colonial Williamsburg Foundation, 1959), quote at 13; Mulkearn, ed., *George Mercer Papers*, 74–76.

82. French documents relating to Washington's expedition, including the terms of surrender, are reproduced in Joseph L. Peyser, trans. and ed., *Letters from New France: The Upper Country 1686–1783* (Urbana: University of Illinois Press, 1992), 196–210; the terms of surrender, plus a plan of Fort Duquesne in 1754, are also in *Pennsylvania Archives,* 1st series, 2 (1853): 146–47.

83. Jennings, *Empire of Fortune,* 123.

84. Hinderaker, *Elusive Empires,* 32–33, 39, 44–45.

85. *Pennsylvania Archives,* 1st series, 3 (1853): 539.

86. On the mixing of Indian and European warfare, see Ian K. Steele, *Warpaths: Invasions of North America* (New York: Oxford University Press, 1994), pt. 3; and Armstrong Starkey, *European and Native American Warfare, 1675–1815* (Norman: University of Oklahoma Press, 1998), 92–103.

87. Quoted in *The Journal of Major George Washington,* 7; also in Kent, ed., *Pennsylvania Treaties,* 309. See also Mulkearn, ed., *George Mercer Papers,* 76.

88. Mulkearn, ed., *George Mercer Papers,* 96.

89. Edmund B. O'Callaghan and Berthold Fernow, eds., *Documents Relative to the Colonial History of the State of New York,* 15 vols. (Albany NY: Weed, Parson, 1853–87), 7: 18; Samuel Johnson, "Observations on the Present State of Affairs, 1756," in Donald J. Greene, ed., *Samuel Johnson: Political Writings,* Yale Edition of the Works of Samuel Johnson, vol. 10 (New Haven CT: Yale University Press, 1977), 188. I am grateful to Elijah Gould for bringing this quotation to my attention.

90. Brian Leigh Dunnigan, ed., *Memoir on the Late War in North America between France and England by Pierre Pouchot,* trans. Michael Cardy (Youngstown NY: Old Fort Niagara Association, 1994), 57.

91. *Pennsylvania Archives,* 1st series, 2 (1853): 176.

92. Wilbur R. Jacobs, ed., *The Appalachian Indian Frontier: The Edmund Atkin Report and Plan of 1755* (1954; reprint, Lincoln: University of Nebraska Press, 1967).

93. Shingas related his account of the exchange with Braddock to a captive: Beverley W. Bond Jr., ed., "The Captivity of Charles Stuart, 1755–57," *Mississippi Valley Historical Review* 13 (1926–27): 63–64. References to Osages and Otos at the battle are in Zebulon Montgomery Pike, *An Account of Expeditions to the Sources of the Mississippi, and through the Western Parts of Louisiana, . . . and a Tour through the Interior Parts of New Spain* (Philadelphia: C. and A. Conrad, 1810; reprint, New York: Readex Microprint, 1966), appendix to pt. 2: 13–14; and John Joseph Mathews, *The Osages: Children of the Middle Waters* (Norman: University of Oklahoma Press, 1961), 224–25.

94. Charles Henry Lincoln, ed., *Manuscript Records of the French and Indian War in the Library of the American Antiquarian Society* (1909; reprint, Bowie MD: Heritage Books, 1992), 174–77. Anderson provides an account of the battle (*Crucible of War,* 94–97). Sources relating to the campaign are available in

Winthrop Sargent, *The History of an Expedition against Fort Du Quesne, in 1755; under Major-General Edward Braddock . . . Edited from the Original Manuscripts* (Philadelphia: Lippincott, Grambo, for the Historical Society of Pennsylvania, 1855), and Paul E. Kopperman, *Braddock at the Monongahela* (Pittsburgh: University of Pittsburgh Press, 1977).

95. Sullivan et al., eds., *The Papers of Sir William Johnson,* 9: 310, 328, 364; *Pennsylvania Archives,* 1st series, 2 (1853): 535, 574.

96. *Pennsylvania Archives,* 1st series, 2 (1853): 443–45, 450, 475–76, 494, 528, 548.

97. Edward P. Hamilton, ed., *Adventure in the Wilderness: The American Journals of Louis Antoine de Bougainville, 1756–1760* (Norman: University of Oklahoma Press, 1964), 259; Dunnigan, ed., *Memoir on the Late War,* 171; Anderson, *Crucible of War,* 150–51.

98. Hamilton, ed., *Adventure in the Wilderness,* 170.

99. Hamilton, ed., *Adventure in the Wilderness,* 37, 51, 148–49, 170.

100. D. Peter MacLeod, "Microbes and Muskets: Smallpox and the Participation of the Amerindian Allies of New France in the Seven Years' War," *Ethnohistory* 39 (1992): 45, fig. 1; Hamilton, ed., *Adventure in the Wilderness,* 150; O'Callaghan and Berthold Fernow, eds., *Documents,* 10: 607–8, 610. On the experiences of the Iroquois from the St. Lawrence communities, see D. Peter MacLeod, *The Canadian Iroquois in the Seven Years War* (Toronto: Dundurn Press, 1996).

101. O'Callaghan and Berthold Fernow, eds., *Documents,* 10: 608; Hamilton, ed., *Adventure in the Wilderness,* Bougainville quote at 118, 151; Jennings, *Empire of Fortune,* 189–90, 217–18.

102. *Pennsylvania Archives,* 1st series, 2 (1853): 607, 619, 767–75; 3 (1853): 199–200.

103. "A Treaty between Virginia and the Catawbas and Cherokees, 1756," *Virginia Magazine of History and Biography* 13 (January 1906): 225–64; *Pennsylvania Archives,* 1st series, 2 (1853): 580; Sullivan et al., eds., *The Papers of Sir William Johnson,* 9: 364, quote at 842.

104. Hamilton, ed., *Adventure in the Wilderness,* 172.

105. Ian K. Steele, *Betrayals: Fort William Henry and the "Massacre"* (New York: Oxford University Press, 1990); Steele, *Warpaths,* quote at 204.

106. O'Callaghan and Berthold Fernow, eds., *Documents,* 10: 249–50; Hamilton, ed., *Adventure in the Wilderness,* Bougainville quote at 193; MacLeod, "Microbes and Muskets," 42–64; Helen H. Tanner, *Atlas of Great Lakes Indian History* (Norman: University of Oklahoma Press, 1987), 46–47, 172–73.

107. Dunnigan, ed., *Memoir on the Late War,* 121; R. David Edmunds, *The Potawatomis: Keepers of the Fire* (Norman: University of Oklahoma Press, 1978), 49–56.

108. Andrew J. Blackbird, *History of the Ottawa and Chippewa Indians of Michigan* (Ypsilanti MI: Ypsilanti Printing House, 1887), 9–10; Helen Jaskoski, "Andrew Blackbird's Smallpox Story," in Alan R. Viele, ed., *Native American Perspectives on Literature and History* (Norman: University of Oklahoma Press, 1994), 25–35. Tanner, *Atlas,* 170, map 32 shows a smallpox epidemic in the Ottawas' homeland at the northern end of Lake Michigan in 1757–58.

109. D. Peter MacLeod, "The Anishinabeg Point of View: The History of the Great Lakes Region to 1800 in Nineteenth-Century Mississauga, Odawa, and Ojibwa Historiography," *Canadian Historical Review* 73 (1992): 202–3.

110. *Pennsylvania Archives,* 1st series, 3 (1853): 456–70, quote at 465; Sylvester K. Stevens et al., eds., *The Papers of Henry Bouquet,* 6 vols. (Harrisburg: Pennsylvania Historical Commission, 1972–94), 2: 187–93, quote at 191.

111. Post had two Indian wives, marrying a Wampanoag and then a Delaware woman in turn. "Journal of Christian Frederick Post, from Philadelphia to the Ohio," in Thwaites, ed., *Early Western Travels,* 1: 175–291; James H. Merrell, *Into the American Woods: Negotiators on the Pennsylvania Frontier* (New York: W. W. Norton, 1999), 85, 242. Walter T. Champion Jr., "Christian Frederick Post and the Winning of the West," *Pennsylvania Magazine of History and Biography* 104 (1980): 308–25, assesses the Moravian's role in the Treaty of Easton and securing an Indian alliance.

112. *Pennsylvania Archives,* 1st series, 3 (1853): 534–35; "Journal of Christian Frederick Post," 214–16; the Delawares' speech is reproduced in Calloway, ed., *The World Turned Upside Down,* 133–34.

113. *Pennsylvania Archives,* 1st series, 3 (1853): 548–49.

114. A German farmer-turned-interpreter who had lived among the Mohawks, was adopted by them, and developed a facility in Iroquoian languages, Weiser played a pivotal role as negotiator and intermediary in tribal relations with the colonial governments of Pennsylvania, Maryland, and Virginia. Merrell, *Into the American Woods*; Paul A. W. Wallace, *Conrad Weiser, 1696–1760, Friend of Colonist and Mohawk* (Philadelphia: University of Pennsylvania Press, 1945).

115. Sullivan et al., eds., *The Papers of Sir William Johnson,* 10: 43–48, 54, 396; McConnell, *A Country Between,* 132–35, 142–46.

116. O'Callaghan and Berthold Fernow, eds., *Documents,* 10: Montcalm quote at 876; Stevens et al., eds., *The Papers of Henry Bouquet,* 2: 610–14, quote at 613.

117. Post's second journal, in Thwaites, ed., *Early Western Travels,* 1: 274, 278; also quoted in Randolph C. Downes, *Council Fires on the Upper Ohio: A Narrative of Indian Affairs in the Upper Ohio Valley until 1795* (Pittsburgh: University of Pittsburgh Press, 1940), 93–95.

118. O'Callaghan and Berthold Fernow, eds., *Documents,* 10: 948, quote at 1132. See also Sullivan et al., eds., *The Papers of Sir William Johnson,* 10: 163.

119. Dunnigan, ed., *Memoir on the Late War,* 415–16; Sullivan et al., eds., *The Papers of Sir William Johnson,* 10: 55; Hamilton, ed., *Adventure in the Wilderness,* 246.

120. For French accounts of the siege, see Dunnigan, ed., *Memoir on the Late War,* 200–231, 503–28; O'Callaghan and Berthold Fernow, eds., *Documents,* 10: 977–92.

121. Sullivan et al., eds., *The Papers of Sir William Johnson,* 10: 136.

122. White, *The Middle Ground,* 255–56.

123. Anderson, *Crucible of War,* 344–68, sees Wolfe's victory as the fortuitous outcome of Wolfe's wish for a heroic death rather than a brilliantly planned and executed assault.

124. Peter Cunningham, ed., *The Letters of Horace Walpole, Earl of Orford,* 9 vols. (London: Bickers and Son, 1880), 3: 259.

125. *Pennsylvania Archives,* 1st series, 3 (1853): 744–52; 4 (1853): 48–49; Stevens et al., eds., *The Papers of Henry Bouquet,* 5: 150–56; "George Croghan's Journal, 1760–61," in Thwaites, ed., *Early Western Travels,* 1: 104, full journal at 100–125. Jon William Parmenter, "Pontiac's War: Forging New Links in the Anglo-Iroquois Covenant Chain, 1758–1766," *Ethnohistory* 44 (1997): 617–54, traces the diplomatic efforts, and achievements, of the western tribes.

126. Anderson, *Crucible of War,* 504–7.

127. Stevens et al., eds., *The Papers of Henry Bouquet,* 2: 98–100, 143–44, 149, 215–16, 562, 566.

128. Duane H. King and E. Raymond Evans, eds., "Memoirs of the Grant Campaigns against the Cherokees in 1761," *Journal of Cherokee Studies* 2, no. 3 (summer 1977); Tom Hatley, *The Dividing Paths: Cherokees and South Carolinians through the Era of Revolution* (New York: Oxford University Press, 1993), chap. 10. Little Carpenter's talks with Grant are in Edith Mays, comp., *Amherst Papers, 1756–1763: The Southern Sector: Despatches from South Carolina, Virginia and His Majesty's Superintendent of Indian Affairs* (Bowie MD: Heritage Books, 1999), 260–63, quote at 261, 293–300, which also contains many other documents on the Cherokee War.

129. Amherst to Grant, February 27, 1761, in Mays, comp., *Amherst Papers,* 202.

130. "Gladwin Manuscripts," in *Collections of the Michigan Pioneer and Historical Society* (1874–1929), 27: 653–54.

131. "Bouquet Papers," in *Collections of the Michigan Pioneer and Historical Society* (1874–1929), 19: 183–84; Sullivan et al., eds., *The Papers of Sir William Johnson,* 10: 659–60.

132. Anderson, *Crucible of War,* 284–85, 328–29; McConnell, *A Country Between,* 166–67. On Fort Pitt, see Stotz, *Outposts of the War for Empire,* 127–40.

133. McConnell, *A Country Between*, 150.

134. Colin G. Calloway, *The Western Abenakis of Vermont 1600–1800: War, Migration, and the Survival of an Indian People* (Norman: University of Oklahoma Press, 1990), chap. 10; David Jaffee, *People of the Wachusett: Greater New England in History and Memory, 1630–1860* (Ithaca NY: Cornell University Press, 1999), pt. 3.

135. Mulkearn, ed., *George Mercer Papers*, xv, 395, appendix 29.

136. McConnell, *A Country Between*, 123–24, 239; Hinderaker, *Elusive Empires*, 157.

137. Minavavana's speech is in Alexander Henry, *Travels and Adventures in the Years 1760–1776* (Chicago: R. R. Donnelley and Sons, 1921), 43–45; reprinted in Calloway, ed., *The World Turned Upside Down*, 136–37.

138. William R. Nester, *"Haughty Conquerors": Amherst and the Great Indian Uprising of 1763* (Westport CT: Praeger, 2000), 50–52; Wilbur R. Jacobs, *Wilderness Politics and Indian Gifts: The Northern Colonial Frontier, 1748–1763* (1950; reprint, Lincoln: University of Nebraska Press, 1966), 180–85; White, *The Middle Ground*, 256–68; Hinderaker, *Elusive Empires*, 147–49; "Bouquet Papers," 139, Campbell quote and need for secrecy at 153; Sullivan et al., eds., *The Papers of Sir William Johnson*, 3: 185–86, 345, 530–31, 733; 10: Johnson quote at 652.

139. Gregory Evans Dowd, *War under Heaven: Pontiac, the Indian Nations, and the British Empire* (Baltimore MD: Johns Hopkins University Press, 2002).

140. Sullivan et al., eds., *The Papers of Sir William Johnson*, 10: 521–29.

141. "Bouquet Papers," 77–79, 83, 86–88; McConnell, *A Country Between*, 171–75; Thomas S. Abler, "Guyasuta," in *American National Biography*, 24 vols. (New York: American Council of Learned Societies and Oxford University Press, 1999), 5: 750–51; Parmenter, "Pontiac's War," 624; Seneca warriors' quote in Sullivan et al., eds., *The Papers of Sir William Johnson*, 3: 698.

142. Gregory Evans Dowd, *A Spirited Resistance: The North American Indian Struggle for Unity* (Baltimore MD: Johns Hopkins University Press, 1992), 33–36; Gregory Evans Dowd,"Thinking and Believing: Nativism and Unity in the Ages of Pontiac and Tecumseh," *American Indian Quarterly* 16 (1992): 309–35; Sullivan et al., eds., *The Papers of Sir William Johnson*, 10: 965.

143. Dowd, *War under Heaven*.

144. Fred Anderson points out parallels between the conflict called Pontiac's War and colonial protests against the Stamp Act in 1766, both representing efforts to defend local autonomy within the empire (*Crucible of War*, xx–xxi).

145. On the massive and recurrent rebellions in Peru, for example, see Luis Miguel Glave, "The 'Republic of Indians' in Revolt (c. 1680–1790)," in Frank Salomon and Stuart B. Schwartz, eds., *The Cambridge History of the Native Peoples of the Americas*, vol. 3, *South America* (Cambridge: Cambridge University

Press, 2000), pt. 2: 502–57; Stern, ed., *Resistance, Rebellion and Consciousness*, pts. 1–2; Ward Stavig, *The World of Tupac Amaru: Conflict, Community, and Identity in Colonial Peru* (Lincoln: University of Nebraska Press, 1999).

146. "Gladwin Manuscripts," 632–34, reports of French involvement at 648–64; Minavavana's speech in Henry, *Travels and Adventures*, 43–45, reprinted in Calloway, ed., *The World Turned Upside Down*, 136–37; Gregory Evans Dowd, "The French King Wakes up in Detroit; 'Pontiac's War' in Rumor and History," *Ethnohistory* 37 (1990): 254–78; Dowd, *A Spirited Resistance*, chap. 2. See also McConnell, *A Country Between*, chap. 8; Sleeper-Smith, *Indian Women and French Men*, chap. 4.

147. "Bouquet Papers," 196–97.

148. "Bouquet Papers," 209–18; "Gladwin Manuscripts," 636–39, 668–69; Stotz, *Outposts of the War for Empire*, 52. The circumstances of the capture of Michilimackinac were related by trader Alexander Henry, who survived the attack, and by William Warren, who "learned [it] verbally from the old French traders and half-breeds, who learned it from the lips of those who were present." William Warren, *History of the Ojibway People* (1885; reprint, Saint Paul: Minnesota Historical Society Press, 1984), 201–9.

149. O'Callaghan and Berthold Fernow, eds., *Documents*, 7: 532.

150. *An Historical Account of the Expedition against the Ohio Indians in the Year 1764 under the Command of Henry Bouquet* (Dublin: John Milliken, 1769), vi.

151. Arman Francis Lucier, comp., *Pontiac's Conspiracy and Other Indian Affairs: Notices Abstracted from Colonial Newspapers, 1763–1765* (Bowie MD: Heritage Books, 2000), 143; Stevens et al., eds., *The Papers of Henry Bouquet*, 6: 261–62; also quoted in Francis Parkman, *The Conspiracy of Pontiac*, 2 vols. (New York: E. P. Dutton, 1908), 2: 15.

152. Nester, *Haughty Conquerors*, 114–17, quote at 114; Sullivan et al., eds., *The Papers of Sir William Johnson*, 10: 733.

153. "Journal of William Trent," in John W. Harpster, ed., *Pen Pictures of Early Western Pennsylvania* (Pittsburgh: University of Pittsburgh Press, 1938), 103–4; Bernard Knollenberg, "General Amherst and Germ Warfare," *Mississippi Valley Historical Review* 41 (1954–55): 489–94; Donald K. Kent's rejoinder is in *Mississippi Valley Historical Review* 41 (1954–55): 762–63. Elizabeth A. Fenn, "Biological Warfare in Eighteenth-Century North America: Beyond Jeffery Amherst," *Journal of American History* 86 (2000): 1552–80, weighs the evidence against Amherst, traces the long-standing debate about whether he ordered germ warfare, and considers the broader context for the application of such tactics. Philip Ranlet, "The British, the Indians, and Smallpox: What Actually Happened at Fort Pitt in 1763," *Pennsylvania History* 67 (2000): 427–41, and Ron Welburn, "Amherst and Indians, Then and Today: A Cautionary Review," in Welburn, *Roanoke and Wampum*, 35–50, also review the evidence.

154. "Bouquet Papers," 219–22.

155. Sullivan et al., eds., *The Papers of Sir William Johnson,* 4: 348, 365, 367–72; Parmenter, "Pontiac's War," 624–25.

156. "Bouquet Papers," 237; Lucier, comp., *Pontiac's Conspiracy,* 79–82.

157. Clarence Edwin Carter, ed., *The Correspondence of General Thomas Gage with the Secretaries of State, and the War Office and the Treasury, 1763–1775,* 2 vols. (New Haven CT: Yale University Press, 1933), 2: 3–4.

158. The proclamation is in Sullivan et al., eds., *The Papers of Sir William Johnson,* 10: 977–85. Carter, ed., *The Correspondence,* 2: "all just Cause" quote at 2. Jack M. Sosin, *Whitehall and the Wilderness: The Middle West in British Colonial Policy, 1760–1775* (Lincoln: University of Nebraska Press, 1961), chap. 3, traces the evolution of the proclamation line through British politics and imperial machinery.

159. Carter, ed., *The Correspondence,* 1: 3.

160. On the Paxton Boys' massacre, see Merrell, *Into the American Woods,* 285–88; *Pennsylvania Archives,* 1st series, 4 (1853): 147–49, 151–55; Lucier, comp., *Pontiac's Conspiracy,* 138–39, 164–73, 176–85; and Benjamin Franklin, "A Narrative of the Late Massacres in Lancaster County," in Leonard W. Larabee, ed., *The Papers of Benjamin Franklin,* 36 vols. (New Haven CT: Yale University Press, 1959–2001), 11: 47–69. Gage quote in "Bouquet Papers," 294.

161. "Gladwin Manuscripts," 671–72.

162. Sullivan et al., eds., *The Papers of Sir William Johnson,* 4: 466–81; Lucier, comp., *Pontiac's Conspiracy,* 195–98; Carter, ed., *The Correspondence,* 2: 19; Nester, *Haughty Conquerors,* 190–93.

163. *An Historical Account,* 2.

164. "Bouquet Papers," 271–75; Lucier, comp., *Pontiac's Conspiracy,* 244–45; Carter, ed., *The Correspondence,* 1: 37–40, quote at 39.

165. *An Historical Account,* 17–21, quotes at 19–20; "Bouquet Papers," 279–82.

166. *An Historical Account,* 25–37; Carter, ed., *The Correspondence,* 1: 45–46. Ohio Indians captured hundreds of colonists in the war years; Matthew C. Ward, "Redeeming the Captives: Pennsylvania Captives among the Ohio Indians, 1755–1765," *Pennsylvania Magazine of History and Biography* 125 (2001): 161–89.

167. "Bouquet Papers," 291.

168. Peyser, trans. and ed., *Letters from New France,* 214.

169. *Journal of Captain Thomas Morris* (New York: Readex Microprint, 1966), 7–8. Morris's journal is also reprinted in Thwaites, ed., *Early Western Travels,* 1: 301–28, quotes at 305–6. Thomas King's account is in Sullivan et al., eds., *The Papers of Sir William Johnson,* 11: 369–72.

170. Bernard DeVoto, *The Course of Empire* (Boston: Houghton Mifflin, 1952), 233.

171. *Pennsylvania Colonial Records,* 9: 259–60; Shawnees quoted in Downes, *Council Fires,* 122; Parmenter, "Pontiac's War," 636. The July 1765 treaty with Johnson is in O'Callaghan and Berthold Fernow, eds., *Documents,* 7: 750–58.

172. "George Croghan's Journal, 1765," in Thwaites, ed., *Early Western Travels,* 1: 126–73, quotes at 157, 170; Sullivan et al., eds., *The Papers of Sir William Johnson,* 4: 848; 11: 577, 629, Fraser quote at 743, 839, 889–901; O'Callaghan and Berthold Fernow, eds., *Documents,* 7: 787–78, Johnson's meeting with Pontiac at 854–67; Parmenter, "Pontiac's War," 636–39.

173. Pike, *An Account of Expeditions,* appendix to pt. 1: 58.

174. White, *The Middle Ground,* 269–71; Steele, *Warpaths,* 246–47; Parmenter, "Pontiac's War," 638–39; Nester, *Haughty Conquerors,* 223.

175. *Pennsylvania Archives,* 1st series, 4 (1853): 182–92; O'Callaghan and Berthold Fernow, eds., *Documents,* 7: 634–41. See also Peter Marshall, "Colonial Protest and Imperial Retrenchment: Indian Policy, 1764–1768," *Journal of American Studies* 5 (1971): 1–17.

176. See, for example, *Pennsylvania Archives,* 1st series, 4 (1853): 251–52, 255, 283–85.

177. Sosin, *Whitehall and the Wilderness.*

178. Dowd, *War under Heaven,* chap. 8.

179. Woody Holton, *Forced Founders: Indians, Debtors, Slaves, and the Making of the American Revolution in Virginia* (Chapel Hill: University of North Carolina Press, 1999), chap. 1, esp. 7–8, 29–31; Washington to Crawford, quoted in Anderson, *Crucible of War,* 740.

180. Carter, ed., *The Correspondence,* 1: 11, 61, 91, 142–43; Howard H. Peckham, ed., *George Croghan's Journal of His Trip to Detroit in 1767 with His Correspondence Relating Thereto* (Ann Arbor: University of Michigan Press, 1939), 16–17, 23–26, 33–35; White, *The Middle Ground,* chaps. 7–8; McConnell, *A Country Between,* chap. 8; Jennings, *Empire of Fortune,* chaps. 20–21.

181. Peter Marshall, "Sir William Johnson and the Treaty of Fort Stanwix, 1768," *Journal of American Studies* 1 (1967): 149–79; Carter, ed., *The Correspondence,* 2: 71, 85, quote at 98. The proceedings and deed of the Treaty of Fort Stanwix, October 24–November 6, 1768, are in O'Callaghan and Berthold Fernow, eds., *Documents,* 8: 111–34.

182. Gage quotes in Sullivan et al., eds., *The Papers of Sir William Johnson,* 6: 212; 12: 710; White, *The Middle Ground,* 339–51.

183. Carter, ed., *The Correspondence,* 1: 333, 335–36.

184. John Mack Faragher, *Daniel Boone: The Life and Legend of an American Pioneer* (New York: Henry Holt, 1992), 89–93.

185. White, *The Middle Ground,* 340.

186. Arthur J. Ray, *Indians in the Fur Trade: Their Role as Hunters, Trappers, and Middlemen in the Lands Southwest of Hudson Bay, 1660–1870* (Toronto: University of Toronto Press, 1974).

187. William L. McDowell Jr., ed., *Colonial Records of South Carolina: Documents Relating to Indian Affairs, 1754–1765* (Columbia: University of South Carolina Press, 1970), 109–10.

188. Rowland, Sanders, and Galloway, eds., *Mississippi Provincial Archives*, 5: 294–301.

189. John, *Storms*, 338–39.

190. Lesley Byrd Simpson, ed., *The San Sabá Papers: A Documentary Account of the Founding and Destruction of San Sabá Mission* (1959; reprint, Dallas TX: Southern Methodist University Press, 2000); Bolton, ed., *Athanase de Mézières*, 1: 49; Hackett, ed., *Pichardo's Treatise*, 2: 236–37; *Presidio and Militia*, 2, pt. 2: 511–12; Gary Clayton Anderson, *The Indian Southwest, 1580–1830: Ethnogenesis and Reinvention, 1580–1830* (Norman: University of Oklahoma Press, 1999), 88–89, 152–53, 162; John, *Storms*, 349–52.

191. John, *Storms*, 362–69, 380–81.

192. Hinderaker, *Elusive Empires*, 176–77.

193. Emily J. Blasingham, "The Depopulation of the Illinois Indians," *Ethnohistory* 3 (1956): 370, 391.

194. Arrell M. Gibson, *The Kickapoos: Lords of the Middle Border* (Norman: University of Oklahoma Press, 1963), 32.

195. Sleeper-Smith, *Indian Women and French Men*, 56, 63; Murphy, *A Gathering of Peoples.*

196. Carter, ed., *The Correspondence*, 1: 199.

197. Jay Gitlin, "On the Boundaries of Empire: Connecting the West to Its Imperial Past," in William Cronon, George Miles, and Jay Gitlin, eds., *Under an Open Sky: Rethinking America's Western Past* (New York: W. W. Norton, 1992), 71–89, esp. 77–78. The British Indian Department likewise came to incorporate and rely upon individuals whose identities and loyalties could not always be described as simply "British." Calloway, *Crown and Calumet*, chap. 2.

198. William R. Swagerty, "History of the United States Plains until 1850," in *HNAI*, 13: 257.

199. Kinnaird, ed., *The Frontiers of New Spain*, 76–80, 94, 106, 185, 215–17. Lafora listed the following tribes in Texas alone: "Adaes, Ais, Ainais, Nacogdoches, Neches, Nazones, Nabidachos, Naconomes, Tojuanes, Anames, Eruipiames, Cujanes, Mayeyes, Pampopas, Pasúas, Cocas, Coapites, Copanes, Carancaguaces, Tacames, Taranames, Atastagonias, Pelones, Salinas, Parchinas, Annas, Pacaos, Pajaloce, Petalac, Orcoquizaes, Vidais, Atacapás, Apilusas, Borridos, Tancahues, Taguaconas, . . . Taquayas and Yscanis."

200. On frontier conditions in the 1760s and the role of Gálvez and Rubí in bringing about reform of military regulations in 1772, see Joseph P. Park, "Spanish Indian Policy in Northern Mexico, 1765–1810," *Arizona and the West* 4 (1962): 325–44, reprinted in David J. Weber, ed., *New Spain's Northern*

Frontier: Essays on Spain in the American West (Dallas TX: Southern Methodist University Press, 1988), 217–34, and David J. Weber, *The Spanish Frontier in North America* (New Haven CT: Yale University Press, 1992), 204–20.

201. For discussion of the various bands of Apaches and the sometimes confusing ways in which the Spanish identified them, see Max L. Moorehead, *The Apache Frontier: Jacobo Ugarte and Spanish-Indian Relations in Northern New Spain, 1769–1791* (Norman: University of Oklahoma Press, 1968), chaps. 8–9.

202. Cynthia Radding, *Wandering Peoples: Colonialism, Ethnic Spaces, and Ecological Frontiers in Northwestern Mexico, 1700–1850* (Durham NC: Duke University Press, 1997), 44–45; Jack S. Williams and Robert L. Hoover, *Arms of the Apachería: A Comparison of Apachean and Spanish Fighting Techniques in the Later Eighteenth Century* (Greeley: University of Northern Colorado Museum of Anthropology, 1983).

203. Bolton, ed., *Athanase de Mézières*, 1: 18–28, 67–71, 89; *SMV*, 2: xviii, 59–62, 154–55; Kathleen DuVal, "The Education of Fernando de Leyba: Quapaws and Spaniards on the Border of Empires," *Arkansas Historical Quarterly* 60 (2001): 1–29; La Vere, "Friendly Persuasions," 329.

204. Bolton, ed., *Athanase de Mézières*, 1: 71–72, first wife at 83–84n104, 92–97, 113–14, 127–30, 135–36, 148–50, 206–27, Cadodacho expedition quote at 210, 1771 treaty at 256–48, Brazos expedition at 282–306; Smith, *The Wichita Indians*, 45–91; John, *Storms*, chaps. 10–11; Anderson, *The Indian Southwest*, 101–2, 166–70.

205. Bolton, ed., *Athanase de Mézières*, 1: 96–97, 115; John, *Storms*, 518.

206. Bolton, ed., *Athanase de Mézières*, 1: 303, 311.

207. Bolton, ed., *Athanase de Mézières*, 1: 331.

208. Thomas, ed., *The Plains Indians*, 161–63; Bolton, ed., *Athanase de Mézières*, 1: 76–77; Hackett, ed., *Pichardo's Treatise*, 1: 392.

209. Rollings, *The Osage*, 98–100; Garrick A. Bailey, *The Osage and the Invisible World, from the Works of Francis La Flesche* (Norman: University of Oklahoma Press, 1995), 27–28.

210. Rollings, *The Osage*, 67–81, population figures at 69n; Bolton, ed., *Athanase de Mézières*, 1: 304; A. P. Nasatir, ed., *Before Lewis and Clark: Documents Illustrating the History of the Missouri, 1785–1804*, 2 vols. (1952; reprint, Lincoln: University of Nebraska Press, 1990), 1: 51–52.

211. Smith, trans. and ed., "Account of the Journey," 382–84.

212. Mathews, *The Osages*, 134. On gun parts as archaeological evidence, see Carl H. Chapman, "The Little Osage and Missouri Indian Village Sites, ca. 1727–1777 A.D.," *Missouri Archaeologist* 21 (1959): 1–67, cited in Garrick A. Bailey, *Changes in Osage Social Organization, 1673–1906*, University of Oregon Anthropological Papers no. 5 (1973), 34.

213. Pierre Margry, ed., *Découvertes et établissements des français dans l'ouest et*

dans le sud de l'Amérique Septentrionale (1614–1754), 6 vols. (Paris: Imprimerie D. Jouaust, 1876–86), 6: 313–14.

214. Rollings, *The Osage,* 82–95, 100–123, 282; Wiegers, "A Proposal," 197–99; Mathews, *The Osages,* 126–29, 137–38, captive paint and straps at 156.

215. Garrick A. Bailey, "Osage," in *HNAI,* 13: 484.

216. Rollings, *The Osage,* 124–30, 146–48, 189–90.

217. Rollings, *The Osage,* 130–33; Sullivan et al., eds., *The Papers of Sir William Johnson,* 6: 391, 393.

218. Rollings, *The Osage,* 134–35; Gilbert C. Din and A. P. Nasatir, *The Imperial Osages: Spanish-Indian Diplomacy in the Mississippi Valley* (Norman: University of Oklahoma Press, 1983), chap. 3.

219. Din and Nasatir, *The Imperial Osages,* 70; Bolton, ed., *Athanase de Mézières,* 1: 166–68.

220. Rollings, *The Osage,* 136–38.

221. Draft to Piernas, New Orleans, August 21, 1772, quoted in Din and Nasatir, *The Imperial Osages,* 82.

222. Bolton, ed., *Athanase de Mézières,* 2: 24–26.

223. *SMV,* 1: 204–7, 214–18; A. P. Nasatir, "Ducharme's Invasion of Missouri: An Incident in the Anglo-Spanish Rivalry for the Indian Trade of Upper Louisiana," *Missouri Historical Review* 24 (1929–30): 3–25, 238–60, 420–39.

224. Douglas A. Hurt, "Brothers of Influence: Auguste and Pierre Chouteau and the Osages before 1804," *Chronicles of Oklahoma* 78 (2000): 260–77; Bailey, *Changes in Osage Social Organization.*

8. The Killing Years

1. For an overview of the impact of the conflict, see Colin G. Calloway, *The American Revolution in Indian Country: Crisis and Diversity in Native American Communities* (Cambridge: Cambridge University Press, 1995).

2. *WHC,* 18: 412–14, 424; Louis Houck, ed., *The Spanish Regime in Missouri,* 2 vols. (Chicago: R. R. Donnelley and Sons, 1909), 1: 175–76.

3. *SMV,* 2, pt. 1: 298.

4. Max M. Mintz, *Seeds of Empire: The American Revolutionary Conquest of the Iroquois* (New York: New York University Press, 1999); Barbara Graymont, *The Iroquois in the American Revolution* (Syracuse NY: Syracuse University Press, 1972); Frederick Cook, ed., *Journals of the Military Expedition of Major General John Sullivan against the Six Nations* (Auburn NY: Knapp, Peck and Thompson, 1887); Calloway, *The American Revolution,* chap. 5.

5. On the Delawares in the Revolution and the schisms within the nation, see C. A. Weslager, *The Delaware Indians* (New Brunswick NJ: Rutgers

University Press, 1972), chap. 13; Gregory Evans Dowd, *A Spirited Resistance: The North American Indian Struggle for Unity 1745–1815* (Baltimore MD: Johns Hopkins University Press, 1992), 65–89; Reuben G. Thwaites and Louise P. Kellogg, eds., *Frontier Defense on the Upper Ohio, 1777–1778* (Madison: Wisconsin State Historical Society, 1912), 27–29, 95–97, 100–101, 215–20; George Morgan Letterbooks, 3 vols., Carnegie Library, Pittsburgh, passim, esp. 1: 18–22, 46, 49–51; 3: 149–51, 162–65. John Heckewelder, *A Narrative of the Mission of the United Brethren among the Delaware and Mohegan Indians* (Philadelphia: McCarty and Davis, 1820) provides a firsthand, pro-American account of developments in Delaware country.

6. Robert L. Scribner et al., eds., *Revolutionary Virginia, the Road to Independence: A Documentary Record,* 7 vols. (Charlottesville: University Press of Virginia, 1973–83), 7: 770.

7. Julian P. Boyd, ed., *The Papers of Thomas Jefferson,* 29 vols. (Princeton NJ: Princeton University Press, 1950–2002), 3: 259, 276.

8. For fuller treatments of Shawnee experiences in the Revolution, with full documentation, see Colin G. Calloway, "'We Have Always Been the Frontier': The American Revolution in Shawnee Country," *American Indian Quarterly* 16 (1992): 39–52; and Calloway, *The American Revolution,* chap. 6.

9. "Journal of Daniel Boone," *Ohio Archaeological and Historical Publications* 13 (1904): 276.

10. David A. Armour and Keith R. Widder, *At the Crossroads: Michilimackinac during the American Revolution,* rev. ed. (Mackinac Island MI: Mackinac Island State Park Commission, 1986), 54–56; *Collections of the Michigan Pioneer and Historical Society* (1874–1929), 10: 261–63; *WHC,* 11: 111, 133; 18: 355–58.

11. Paul L. Stevens, "Wabasha Visits Governor Carleton, 1776: New Light on a Legendary Episode of Dakota-British Diplomacy on the Great Lakes Frontier," *Michigan Historical Review* 16 (1990): 21–48; Gary Clayton Anderson, *Kinsmen of Another Kind: Dakota-White Relations in the Upper Mississippi Valley, 1650–1862* (Lincoln: University of Nebraska Press, 1984), 65; Papers of Sir Frederick Haldimand, British Museum, Additional Manuscripts 21757: 284–92, 332; 21771: 108–9; *WHC,* 11: 147–48; 18: 413–14.

12. Papers of Sir Frederick Haldimand, 21756: 12–13; *WHC,* 11: 132.

13. Bert Anson, *The Miami Indians* (Norman: University of Oklahoma Press, 1970), 84, 91; Richard White, *The Middle Ground: Indians, Empires, and Republics in the Great Lakes Region, 1650–1815* (Cambridge: Cambridge University Press, 1991), 399; *Collections of the Michigan Pioneer and Historical Society* (1874–1929), 9: 383, 395–96; 19: 411, 423, 497, 537. *Collections of the Illinois Historical Society* (1903), vol. 1, contains documents relating to "Clark's Conquest of the Illinois" and "Letters from the Canadian Archives" relating to the contest in the area.

14. R. David Edmunds, *The Potawatomis: Keepers of the Fire* (Norman: University of Oklahoma Press, 1978), 99–115; *Collections of the Michigan Pioneer and Historical Society* (1874–1929), 9: 392–96, 454; 10: 349–51, 380–81, 453–55; Houck, ed., *The Spanish Regime,* 1: 175.

15. Arrell M. Gibson, *The Kickapoos* (Norman: University of Oklahoma Press, 1963), 35–40.

16. Papers of Sir Frederick Haldimand, 21756: 22; SMV, 2, pt. 1: 398; WHC, 11: 126, 163; 18: 365, 412–15.

17. Abraham P. Nasatir, "The Anglo-Spanish Frontier in Illinois Country during the Revolution, 1779–1783," *Journal of the Illinois State Historical Society* 21 (1928): 343–50; Don Rickey, "The British-American Attack on St. Louis, May 26, 1780," *Missouri Historical Review* 55 (1960): 35–45; Lawrence Kinnaird, "The Western Fringe of Revolution," *Western Historical Quarterly* 7 (1976): 268–69; Lawrence Kinnaird, "The Spanish Expedition against Fort St. Joseph in 1781: A New Interpretation," *Mississippi Valley Historical Review* 19 (1932): 173–91; SMV, 1: 431–34; WHC, 18: 412–15; Houck, *The Spanish Regime,* 1: 167, 175–77.

18. Stanley Faye, "Illinois Indians on the Lower Mississippi, 1771–1782," *Journal of the Illinois State Historical Society* 35 (1942): 57–72.

19. The Treaty of Sycamore Shoals is reprinted in Colin G. Calloway, ed., *Revolution and Confederation,* vol. 18 of Alden T. Vaughan, gen. ed., *Early American Indian Documents: Treaties and Laws* (Frederick MD: University Publications of America, 1993), 203–5.

20. See, for example, Eric Hinderaker, *Elusive Empires: Constructing Colonialism in the Ohio Valley, 1673–1800* (Cambridge: Cambridge University Press, 1997), 195–99, 215–25; John Mack Faragher, *Daniel Boone: The Life and Legend of an American Pioneer* (New York: Henry Holt, 1992), chaps. 3–4; Stephen Aron, *How the West Was Lost: The Transformation of Kentucky from Daniel Boone to Henry Clay* (Baltimore MD: Johns Hopkins University Press, 1996), chap. 2.

21. Calloway, *The American Revolution,* chap. 7.

22. Richard White, *The Roots of Dependency: Subsistence, Environment, and Social Change among the Choctaws, Pawnees, and Navajos* (Lincoln: University of Nebraska Press, 1983), 81, 87–88, 107. See also Greg O'Brien, *Choctaws in a Revolutionary Age, 1750–1830* (Lincoln: University of Nebraska Press, 2002).

23. David H. Corkran, *The Creek Frontier, 1540–1783* (Norman: University of Oklahoma Press, 1967), 316–25.

24. Calloway, *The American Revolution,* chap. 8.

25. Calloway, " 'We Have Always Been the Frontier,"' 44–45; Helen Hornbeck Tanner, "The Glaize in 1792: A Composite Indian Community," *Ethnohistory* 25 (1978): 15–39.

26. White, *The Middle Ground,* chaps. 9–11; John Fitzpatrick, ed., *Writings of Washington,* 39 vols. (Washington DC: Carnegie Institute, 1931–44), 27: 486.

27. SMV, 3, pt. 2: 117.

28. All the treaties are reprinted in Calloway, ed., *Revolution and Confederation.*

29. "At a Council Held at Wakitunikee, May 18, 1785," British Museum, Miscellaneous American Papers, Additional Manuscripts, 24322; also in *Collections of the Michigan Pioneer and Historical Society* (1874–1929), 25: 691–93.

30. Excerpts from the treaty proceedings at Fort Finney are reprinted in Calloway, ed., *Revolution and Confederation,* 340–51.

31. Colin G. Calloway, ed., *The World Turned Upside Down: Indian Voices from Early America* (Boston: Bedford Books, 1994), 175–76.

32. John Sugden, *Blue Jacket, Warrior of the Shawnees* (Lincoln: University of Nebraska Press, 2000), presents the Shawnee war chief as the leading force in the defense of the Ohio country.

33. Hinderaker, *Elusive Empires,* 227–31.

34. Calloway, ed., *The World Turned Upside Down,* 181–83.

35. Colin G. Calloway, *Crown and Calumet: British-Indian Relations, 1783–1815* (Norman: University of Oklahoma Press, 1987), 224–27.

36. R. David Edmunds, *The Shawnee Prophet* (Lincoln: University of Nebraska Press, 1983); John Sugden, *Tecumseh: A Life* (New York: Henry Holt, 1998).

37. Calloway, *The American Revolution,* chap. 8.

38. Talk of the Chickasaw Chiefs at Silver Bluffs, represented by Wolf's Friend, McHenry Papers, William L. Clements Library, University of Michigan, Ann Arbor.

39. Gilbert C. Din and A. P. Nasatir, *The Imperial Osages: Spanish-Indian Diplomacy in the Mississippi Valley* (Norman: University of Oklahoma Press, 1983), 222.

40. Jerry Eugene Clark, "Shawnee Indian Migration: A System Analysis," Ph.D. diss., University of Kentucky, 1974, 52–53; Vernon Kinetz and Erminie Voegelin, eds., "Shawnese Traditions: C. C. Trowbridge's Account," *Occasional Contributions from the Museum of Anthropology of the University of Michigan* 9 (June 1939): xiv; Houck, ed., *The Spanish Regime,* 2: 50–94; SMV, 3, pt. 2: 186; Louis Vincent, "Journal de mes voyages," William L. Clements Library, University of Michigan, Ann Arbor. For continuing Shawnee migration to the region, see George E. Lankford, "Shawnee Convergence: Immigrant Indians in the Ozarks," *Arkansas Historical Quarterly* 58 (1999): 390–413.

41. William G. McLoughlin, *Cherokee Renascence in the New Republic* (Princeton NJ: Princeton University Press, 1986), 56; Robert A. Myers, "Cherokee Pioneers in Arkansas: The St. Francis Years, 1785–1813," *Arkansas Historical Quarterly* 56 (1997): 127–57.

42. SMV, 3, pt. 2: 57, 157, 186, 203–8, 210, 255, 280, 332, 406; Din and Nasatir, *The Imperial Osages,* 176, 190, 192; 196n, 198, 207, 305, 318; Willard

H. Rollings, *The Osage: An Ethnohistorical Study of Hegemony on the Prairie Plains* (Columbia: University of Missouri Press, 1992), chaps. 3–6. Spaniards often loosely employed the term "Abenaki" to refer to Indians from New England or the Northeast in general.

43. Joseph P. Key, "'Masters of This Country': The Quapaws and Environmental Change in Arkansas, 1673–1833," Ph.D. diss., University of Arkansas, 2001, 152.

44. Elizabeth A. H. John, ed., *Views from the Apache Frontier: Report on the Northern Provinces of New Spain by José Cortés, 1799* (Norman: University of Oklahoma Press, 1989), 43; Elizabeth A. H. John, *Storms Brewed in Other Men's Worlds: The Confrontation of Indians, Spanish, and French in the Southwest, 1540–1795* (Lincoln: University of Nebraska Press, 1975), 590–91.

45. "An Account of the Indian Tribes in Louisiana [1803]," in Clarence E. Carter, ed., *Territorial Papers of the United States*, 28 vols. (Washington DC: GPO, 1934–75), 9: 64; Gary E. Moulton, ed., *The Journals of the Lewis and Clark Expedition*, 13 vols. (Lincoln: University of Nebraska Press, 1983–2001), 2: 107–9, 112, 140, 180n3.

46. Juan Gassiot, quoted in David J. Weber, *The Spanish Frontier in North America* (New Haven CT: Yale University Press, 1992), 271, 273.

47. John, *Storms*, 504.

48. Steve J. Stern, ed., *Resistance, Rebellion, and Consciousness in the Andean Peasant World, 18th to 20th Centuries* (Madison: University of Wisconsin Press, 1987), death toll at 35. Ward Stavig, *The World of Tupac Amaru: Conflict, Community, and Identity in Colonial Peru* (Lincoln: University of Nebraska Press, 1999), provides background on the rebellion.

49. James F. Brooks, "Served Well by Plunder: *La Gran Ladronería* and Producers of History Astride the Rio Grande," *American Quarterly* 52 (2000): 36, 55n42 lists 1,674 Spanish subjects killed in the Provincias Internas; Governor Felipe Barri listed 1,763 people killed in Nueva Vizcaya during the same period, with similar losses of property and livestock; Oakah L. Jones Jr., *Nueva Vizcaya: Heartland of the Spanish Frontier* (Albuquerque: University of New Mexico Press, 1988), 192.

50. See, for example, Herbert E. Bolton, ed., *Athanase de Mézières and the Texas-Louisiana Frontier 1768–1780*, 2 vols. (Cleveland: Arthur H. Clark, 1914), 2: 141–86, 221–23; Thomas Sheridan, comp. and ed., *Empire of Sand: The Seri Indians and the Struggle for Spanish Sonora, 1645–1803* (Tucson: University of Arizona Press, 1999), 432–36.

51. Bolton, ed., *Athanase de Mézières*, 2: quotes at 133, councils of war at 147–70; Max L. Moorehead, *The Presidio: Bastion of the Spanish Borderlands* (Norman: University of Oklahoma Press, 1975, 1991), chap. 4.

52. Donald E. Worcester, trans. and ed., *Instructions for Governing the Interior Provinces of New Spain, 1786 by Bernardo de Gálvez* (Berkeley: Quivira Society;

Albuquerque: University of New Mexico Press, 1951), 13, 17–18; John, *Storms*, 431–42; Catherine Price, "The Comanche Threat to Texas and New Mexico in the Eighteenth Century and the Development of Spanish Indian Policy," *Journal of the West* 44, no. 2 (1985): 35, 40–42.

53. Richard W. Slatta, "Spanish Colonial Military Strategy and Ideology," in Donna J. Guy and Thomas E. Sheridan, eds., *Contested Ground: Comparative Frontiers on the Northern and Southern Edges of the Spanish Empire* (Tucson: University of Arizona Press, 1998), 86–87; Worcester, trans. and ed., *Instructions*, 37.

54. Bolton, ed., *Athanase de Mézières*, 2: 185–238.

55. Bolton, ed., *Athanase de Mézières*, 1: 84.

56. Bolton, ed., *Athanase de Mézières*, 2: 277, 269–72; John, *Storms*, 636–37.

57. Bolton, ed., *Athanase de Mézières*, 2: 279.

58. Bolton, ed., *Athanase de Mézières*, 2: 222–23.

59. "Report of the Indian Tribes Who Receive Presents at St. Louis," November 15, 1777, in Houck, ed., *The Spanish Regime*, 1: 142–44, estimated Big Osages at 800 warriors, Little Osages at 350–400; Mézières reported the Big Osages at 800 men (2: 144); A. P. Nasatir, ed., "An Account of Spanish Louisiana, 1785," *Missouri Historical Review* 24 (1930): 533, gives a warrior count of 400–450 for the Big Osages and about 250 for the Little Osages. Some turn-of-the-century estimates confirm the 1,200 total, although some place the warrior count of the Big Osages alone at 1,200; A. P. Nasatir, ed., *Before Lewis and Clark: Documents Illustrating the History of the Missouri, 1785–1804*, 2 vols. (1952; reprint, Lincoln: University of Nebraska Press, 1990), 2: 539, 706n, cf. 694, 760.

60. Rollings, *The Osage*, 137–38, 149–53, 169–70; Din and Nasatir, *The Imperial Osages*, 247; Houck, ed., *The Spanish Regime*, 2: 100–103; Nasatir, ed., *Before Lewis and Clark*, 1: 154, 156–59, 198.

61. Bolton, ed., *Athanase de Mézières*, 2: 131, 143–47.

62. *SMV*, 3, pt. 2: 409.

63. Houck, ed., *The Spanish Regime*, 1: 163–65.

64. Rollings, *The Osage*, 180–88.

65. Rollings, *The Osage*, 138–42; *SMV*, 3, pt. 2: 369.

66. Rollings, *The Osage*, 42–43, 180, 190.

67. Rollings, *The Osage*, 162–66; Garrick A. Bailey, *Changes in Osage Social Organization, 1673–1906*, University of Oregon Anthropological Papers no. 5 (1973), leader of southern band identified as Big Foot at 52.

68. Bolton, ed., *Athanase de Mézières*, 2: 248–51; *SMV*, 1: Qui Te Sain at 392; 3, pt. 2: xxxi, 172, 256, 407; Din and Nasatir, *The Imperial Osages*, 137–39.

69. Din and Nasatir, *The Imperial Osages*, 159–60; *SMV*, 3, pt. 2: 258.

70. *SMV*, 3, pt. 2: xxxi–xxxii, 184, 201, 285–87, 316, 369, 414–17; Din and Nasatir, *The Imperial Osages*, 170–216; Gary Clayton Anderson, *The Indian*

Southwest, 1580–1830: Ethnogenesis and Reinvention, 1580–1830 (Norman: University of Oklahoma Press, 1999), 176; Houck, ed., *The Spanish Regime*, 1: 250–51, 253–57; John, *Storms*, 458, 495, 702–3; Rollings, *The Osage*, 171–72.

71. *SMV*, 3, pt. 2: 312.

72. John J. Mathews, *The Osages: Children of the Middle Waters* (Norman: University of Oklahoma Press, 1961), 265, 279–81.

73. Douglas A. Hurt, "Brothers of Influence: Auguste and Pierre Chouteau and the Osages before 1804," *Chronicles of Oklahoma* 78 (2000): 260–77; William E. Foley and C. David Rice, *The First Chouteaus: River Barons of Early St. Louis* (Urbana: University of Illinois Press, 1983).

74. Rollings, *The Osage*, 173–77, 191–94; Din and Nasatir, *The Imperial Osages*, chaps. 9–11; Nasatir, ed., *Before Lewis and Clark*, 1: 172–73; *SMV*, 2: 331–32, 406; 3: Chickasaw quote at 118–20, 148–49. The Osage delegates who died were Lafond, Soldat Du Chene, and La Vent (The Wind).

75. Moulton, ed., *The Journals*, 2: 266, 267n3; 3: 391; Mathews, *The Osages*, 354–55, quote at 354.

76. Rollings, *The Osage*, 213–15; Donald Jackson, ed., *The Letters of the Lewis and Clark Expedition with Related Documents, 1783–1854*, 2 vols. (Urbana: University of Illinois Press, 1978), 1: quote at 200. See also the depiction of the Osages, "An Account of the Indian Tribes in Louisiana, [1803]," in Carter, ed., *Territorial Papers*, 9: 64.

77. Dan L. Flores, ed., *Jefferson and Southwestern Exploration: The Freeman and Custis Accounts of the Red River Expedition of 1806* (Norman: University of Oklahoma Press, 1984), 164–65.

78. Bolton, ed., *Athanase de Mézières*, 1: 218; 2: 126, 174; Donald C. Cutter, trans. and ed., *The Defenses of Northern New Spain: Hugo O'Conor's Report to Teodoro de Croix, July 22, 1777* (Dallas TX: Southern Methodist University Press/De Golyer Library, 1994), 92.

79. Thomas W. Kavanagh, *The Comanches: A History, 1706–1875* (Lincoln: University of Nebraska Press, 1999), 83–84, 86; Pekka Hämäläinen, "The Comanche Empire: A Study of Indigenous Power, 1700–1875," Ph.D. diss., University of Helsinki, 2001, chap. 5; Ross Frank, *From Settler to Citizen: New Mexican Economic Development and the Creation of Vecino Society, 1750–1820* (Berkeley: University of California Press, 2000), chap. 1.

80. John, *Storms*, 474; Anderson, *Indian Southwest*, 212.

81. John, *Storms*, 590–91; Thomas D. Hall, *Social Change in the Southwest, 1350–1880* (Lawrence: University Press of Kansas, 1988), 133; Frank R. Secoy, *Changing Military Patterns of the Great Plains Indians* (1953; reprint, Lincoln: University of Nebraska Press, 1992), chap. 7; Pekka Hämäläinen, "The Western Comanche Trade Center: Rethinking the Plains Indian Trade System," *Western Historical Quarterly* 29 (1998): 502–3.

82. Elizabeth A. H. John, ed., "Inside the Comanchería, 1785: The Diary

of Pedro Vial and Francisco Xavier Chaves," trans. Adán Benavides Jr., *Southwestern Historical Quarterly* 98 (1994): 37–38.

83. John, *Storms*, 557–72. For brief appreciations of Anza's remarkable career, see Herbert E. Bolton, "Juan Bautista de Anza, Borderlands Frontiersman," in John Francis Bannon, ed., *Bolton and the Spanish Borderlands* (Norman: University of Oklahoma Press, 1964), 281–87; and Patricia Nelson Limerick, "Historical Lessons on Anza Day," in Patricia Nelson Limerick, *Something in the Soil: Legacies and Reckonings in the New West* (New York: W. W. Norton, 2000), 110–25. John L. Kessell, *Spain in the Southwest: A Narrative History of Colonial New Mexico, Arizona, Texas, and California* (Norman: University of Oklahoma Press, 2002), 292–303, provides a concise summary of Anza's war and peace with the Comanches.

84. Juan Bautista de Anza, "Diary of the Expedition . . . against the Comanche Nation," in Alfred Barnaby Thomas, ed., *Forgotten Frontiers: A Study of the Spanish Indian Policy of Don Juan Bautista de Anza, 1777–1787* (Norman: University of Oklahoma Press, 1932), 122–39. Cuerno Verde has been identified as a leader of the Cuchanec, or Buffalo Eater, band, but Kavanagh, *The Comanches*, 92–93, 123, 482, suggests he was more likely a Yupe and points out that there may have been three Comanche leaders called Cuerno Verde. Hämäläinen, "The Comanche Empire," 118, identifies him as a Kotsoteka.

85. John, ed., "Inside the Comanchería, 1785," 27–56; Armando Represa, *La España ilustrado en el lejano oeste: Viajes y exploraciones por las provincias y territorios hispánicos de Norteamérica en el siglo XVIII* (Valladolid: Junta de Castilla y León, Consejería de Cultura y Bienestar Social, 1990), Iron Shirt quote at 22–23. I am grateful to Kathryn Ritcheske for locating and translating this work at the De Golyer Library, Southern Methodist University, Dallas TX.

86. "An Account of the Events Concerning the Comanche Peace 1785–1786," in Thomas, ed., *Forgotten Frontiers*, 294–321, quotes at 295, 297; Max L. Moorehead, *The Apache Frontier: Jacobo Ugarte and Spanish-Indian Relations in Northern New Spain, 1761–1791* (Norman: University of Oklahoma Press, 1968), chap. 7; Kavanagh, *The Comanches*, 110–11; Price, "The Comanche Threat," 42–43; Charles L. Kenner, *The Comanchero Frontier: A History of New Mexican–Plains Indian Relations* (Norman: University of Oklahoma Press, 1969), 51–52, chap. 3. The treaties with the Eastern Comanches in October 1785 and with Ecueracapa in February 1786 are reprinted in Vine Deloria and Raymond J. DeMallie, eds., *Documents of American Indian Diplomacy: Treaties, Agreements, and Conventions, 1775–1979*, 2 vols. (Norman: University of Oklahoma Press, 1999), 1: 131–34. Ecueracapa was sometimes erroneously identified as Cota de Malla (Coat of Mail), but there is confusion in the records, and this name may have belonged to another chief, an Eastern Comanche of considerable influence. Moorehead, *The Apache Frontier*,

154n10; Kavanagh, *The Comanches*, 105, 111, 119–21, 24. Hämäläinen, "The Comanche Empire," 118, identifies Ecueracapa as a Kotsoteka.

87. Worcester, trans. and ed., *Instructions*, 36, 40–42, 49–50, quotes at 41, 72.

88. Frank, *From Settler to Citizen*, chap. 4; Marc Simmons, *Spanish Pathways: Readings in the History of Hispanic New Mexico* (Albuquerque: University of New Mexico Press, 2001), 119.

89. Felix D. Almaráz Jr., "An Uninviting Land: El Llano Estacado, 1534–1824," in Ralph H. Vigil, Frances W. Kaye, and John R. Wunder, eds., *Spain and the Plains: Myths and Realities of the Spanish Exploration and Settlement on the Great Plains* (Niwot: University of Colorado Press, 1994), 82.

90. Bolton, ed., *Athanase de Mézières*, 2: 181–82.

91. "An Account of the Events," 305–21; Alfred B. Thomas, ed., "An Eighteenth Century Comanche Document," *American Anthropologist*, n.s. 31 (1929): 289–98, provides a list of the Comanche chiefs who met at Pecos in the spring of 1786 and of Comanches who participated in a campaign against the Apaches that same year, as does Kavanagh, *The Comanches*, 117. For assistance provided by Ecueracapa's Comanches in the "eternal war," see Moorehead, *The Apache Frontier*, 164–69.

92. Kavanagh, *The Comanches*, 116–18; Hämäläinen, "The Western Comanche Trade Center," 504; Anderson, *Indian Southwest*, quote at 232.

93. SANM, series 1, reel 4, archive 1333; Dan Flores, *Caprock Canyonlands* (Austin: University of Texas Press, 1990), 85; Frances Levine, *Our Prayers Are in This Place: Pecos Pueblo Identity over the Centuries* (Albuquerque: University of New Mexico Press, 1999), xxi, chap. 6; Hämäläinen, "The Comanche Empire," 89.

94. Hämäläinen, "The Western Comanche Trade Center," 508.

95. John, *Storms*, 762.

96. William B. Griffen, *Apaches at War and Peace: The Janos Presidio, 1750–1858* (Norman: University of Oklahoma Press, 1988), 28–52; Jones, *Nueva Vizcaya*, 190–95; Cynthia Radding, *Wandering Peoples: Colonialism, Ethnic Spaces, and Ecological Frontiers in Northwestern New Mexico, 1700–1850* (Durham NC: Duke University Press, 1997).

97. Marc Simmons, *Coronado's Land: Daily Life in Colonial New Mexico* (Albuquerque: University of New Mexico Press, 1991), 51–54; Moorehead, *The Presidio*, 71–72; Max L. Moorehead, "Spanish Deportation of Hostile Apaches: The Policy and the Practice," *Arizona and the West* 17 (1975): 205–20; SANM, series 2, reel 12, frame 132. Zebulon Pike saw shackled Apache prisoners bound for transportation in 1807; Zebulon Montgomery Pike, *An Account of Expeditions to the Sources of the Mississippi, and through the Western Parts of Louisiana, . . . and a Tour through the Interior Parts of New Spain* (Philadelphia: C. and A. Conrad, 1810; reprint, New York: Readex Microprint, 1966), 254.

Katsi Cook, personal communication, Dartmouth College, February 2001 (Cuban descendants).

98. Jack S. Williams and Robert L. Hoover, *Arms of the Apachería: A Comparison of Apache and Spanish Fighting Techniques in the Later Eighteenth Century* (Greeley: University of Northern Colorado Museum of Anthropology, 1983); Moorehead, *The Apache Frontier*, chaps. 5–6.

99. Cutter, trans. and ed., *The Defenses*, 34–45, 68, 71–73; Slatta, "Spanish Colonial Military Strategy," 89.

100. John, *Storms*, 535, 633.

101. Moorehead, *The Apache Frontier*, 174–82. The treaty with the Navajos is in Deloria and DeMallie, eds., *Documents of American Indian Diplomacy*, 1: 133–34.

102. Worcester, trans. and ed., *Instructions*, 34, 43.

103. Moorehead, *The Apache Frontier*, 182–86, 192–99, 273–76.

104. George P. Hammond, ed., "The Zuñiga Journal, Tucson to Santa Fe: The Opening of a Spanish Trade Route, 1788–1795," *New Mexico Historical Review* 6 (1931): 40–65, figures at 46–47.

105. Moorehead, *The Apache Frontier*, chaps. 9–10, three-hundred-day campaign at 255.

106. Griffen, *Apaches at Peace and War*, 53–86, Janos figures at 73; Simmons, *Coronado's Land*, 56–60; SANM, series 2, reel 12, frame 643; Moorehead, *The Presidio*, chap. 10, esp. 260–61.

107. Jones, *Nueva Vizcaya*, 215; John, ed., *Views from the Apache Frontier*, 30, 71–72, "They scale" quote at 72, "as old as the nations themselves" quote at 76.

108. Juan Agustín de Morfí, "Account of Disorders in New Mexico, 1778," reprinted in Simmons, *Coronado's Land*, 156–57.

109. Oakah L. Jones Jr., *Pueblo Warriors and Spanish Conquest* (Norman: University of Oklahoma Press, 1966); Jones, 15–29, also discusses the Tlaxcalans and Opatas as allies. Radding, *Wandering Peoples*, 255–63; Cutter, trans. and ed., *The Defenses*, 85; John, ed., *Views from the Apache Frontier*, 26–27.

110. "Indian and Mission Affairs, 1773," reprinted in Simmons, *Coronado's Land*, 124–25.

111. Eleanor B. Adams and Angélico Chávez, trans. and eds., *The Missions of New Mexico, 1776: A Description by Fray Francisco Atanasio Domínguez with Other Contemporary Documents* (Albuquerque: University of New Mexico Press, 1956), 283–85, 302; Frank Waters, *Book of the Hopi* (New York: Penguin, 1977), 265.

112. Ted J. Warner, ed., *The Domínguez-Escalante Journal: Their Expedition through Colorado, Utah, Arizona, and New Mexico in 1776*, trans. Angélico Chávez (Salt Lake City: University of Utah Press, 1995), 130–38; Morfí, "Account of Disorders," 147.

113. John, *Storms*, 572, 593–601.

114. On Spanish efforts to establish a route to California, see Joseph P. Sánchez, *Explorers, Traders, and Slavers: Forging the Old Spanish Trail, 1678–1850* (Salt Lake City: University of Utah Press, 1997); Jack D. Forbes, *Warriors of the Colorado: The Yumas of the Quechan Nation and Their Neighbors* (Norman: University of Oklahoma Press, 1965), chap. 5, for Taravel, see 128, 149–50; William H. Goetzmann and Glyndwr Williams, *The Atlas of North American Exploration* (Norman: University of Oklahoma Press, 1992), 126–27. Herbert E. Bolton, ed., *Anza's California Expeditions*, 5 vols. (Berkeley: University of California Press, 1930), contains diaries by Garcés and other fathers as well as by Anza. Virginia M. Bouvier, *Women and the Conquest of California, 1542–1840: Codes of Silence* (Tucson: University of Arizona Press, 2001), 58–67, discusses the role and experiences of the women in Anza's colonizing expedition.

115. Elliott Coues, trans. and ed., *On the Trail of a Spanish Pioneer: The Diary and Itinerary of Francisco Garcés in His Travels through Sonora, Arizona, and California, 1775–1776*, 2 vols. (New York: F. P. Harper, 1900), quote at 116; Julio C. Montané Martí, ed., *Diario íntimo de fray Pedro Font y diario de fray Tomás Eixarch* (Hermosillo: Universidad de Sonora, 2000), 128.

116. Warner, ed., *The Domínguez-Escalante Journal*, quote at 80; Martha C. Knack, *Boundaries Between: The Southern Paiutes, 1775–1995* (Lincoln: University of Nebraska Press, 2001), 31–34; Ronald H. Towner, ed., *The Archaeology of Navajo Origins* (Salt Lake City: University of Utah Press, 2002), 6.

117. Bolton, ed., *Anza's California Expeditions*, 2: 33–44, 157–68; 3: 311–81, quote at 318; 4: 69–87.

118. Mark Santiago, *Massacre at the Yuma Crossing: Spanish Relations with the Quechans, 1779–1782* (Tucson: University of Arizona Press, 1998); Forbes, *Warriors of the Colorado*, 80, chap. 6.

119. Nasatir, ed., *Before Lewis and Clark*, 1: 77, 83–84, 93–94, 145, 175–79; Calloway, *Crown and Calumet*, 30, 132–37, 142–43; John, *Storms*, 512; Bolton, ed., *Athanase de Mézières*, 2: Russian quote at 182.

120. Nasatir, ed., *Before Lewis and Clark*, 1: 84–87, 151–53, 156, 186–94, 217–30, 243–53.

121. "Journal of Jean Baptiste Truteau on the Upper Missouri, 'Première Partie,' June 7, 1794–March 26, 1795," *American Historical Review* 19 (1914): 299–333, quotes (in French) at 306–7, 232. Truteau's journal is translated and reprinted together with part 2 in Nasatir, ed., *Before Lewis and Clark*, 1: 259–311, quotes at 264, 282.

122. Nasatir, ed., *Before Lewis and Clark*, 1: 87–108; MacKay's journals are in Nasatir, ed., *Before Lewis and Clark*, 1: 356–64, quote at 363; 2: 490–95. MacKay's instructions to Evans and extracts from Evans's journal are in Nasatir, ed., *Before Lewis and Clark*, 2: 410–15, 495–99.

123. Nasatir, ed., *Before Lewis and Clark,* 1: 111, 335–41; 2: 385, 387, 391–92, 407, 425, 433, 439.

124. Nasatir, ed., *Before Lewis and Clark,* 2: viii, 592.

125. John, *Storms,* 765–66.

126. Carlos A. Schwantes, *The Pacific Northwest: An Interpretive History,* rev. ed. (Lincoln: University of Nebraska Press, 1996), 41–42. The title of this section is taken from J. S. Holliday, *The World Rushed In: The California Gold Rush Experience* (New York: Simon and Schuster, 1981).

127. Moulton, ed., *The Journals,* 6: quote at 339; Thomas Vaughan and Bill Holm, eds., *Soft Gold: The Fur Trade and Cultural Exchange on the Northwest Coast of America* (Portland: Oregon Historical Society Press, 1982).

128. Moulton, ed., *The Journals,* 6: 17, 27, 32, 41, 49, 205; 9: 250; 11: 361, 380–81, 386, 389–90, 395. As early as 1787, Nathaniel Portlock met Indians who "spoke several English words very plainly." William Beresford, *A Voyage round the World; but More Particularly to the North-West Coast of America; Performed in 1785, 1786, 1787, and 1788, in the "King George" and "Queen Charlotte," Captains Portlock and Dixon* (London: John Stockdale and George Goulding, 1789), 218.

129. William L. Preston, "Portents of Plague from California's Protohistoric Period," *Ethnohistory* 49 (2002): 69–121.

130. Rose Marie Beebe and Robert M. Senkewicz, eds., *Lands of Promise and Despair: Chronicles of Early California, 1535–1846* (Santa Clara and Berkeley: Santa Clara University and Heyday Books, 2001), 46–53, 179; *English Account of the Portola Expedition which Discovered San Francisco Bay, by Miguel Costansó,* introduction by Michael Mathes (1790; Fairfield WA: Ye Galleon Press, 2000), quote at 15.

131. Christopher Vecsey, *On the Padres' Trail* (Notre Dame IN: University of Notre Dame Press, 1996), 222–25; Rebecca Allen, *Native Americans at Mission Santa Cruz, 1791–1834: Interpreting the Archaeological Record* (Los Angeles: University of California, Institute of Archaeology, 1998), 1–2, 8–9; Bouvier, *Women and the Conquest of California,* 37.

132. Robert H. Jackson, *From Savages to Subjects: Missions in the History of the American Southwest* (Armonk NY: M. E. Sharpe, 2000), 93–94; Florence C. Shipek, "A Native American Adaptation to Drought: The Kumeyaay as Seen in the San Diego Mission Records 1770–1798," *Ethnohistory* 28 (1981): 295–312.

133. Donald C. Cutter, *California in 1792: A Spanish Naval Visit* (Norman: University of Oklahoma Press, 1990), 131.

134. Malcolm Margolin, ed., *Monterey in 1786: The Journals of Jean François de La Pérouse* (Berkeley CA: Heyday Books, 1989), 33, 81–82; W. Kaye Lamb, ed., *George Vancouver: A Voyage of Discovery to the North Pacific Ocean and round the World, 1791–1795,* 4 vols. (London: Hakluyt Society, 1984), 2: 721.

135. Florence C. Shipek, "California Indian Reactions to the Franciscans," *Americas* 41 (1985): 480–92; Vicki L. Ruiz, "Interpreting Voice and Locating Power," in Clyde A. Milner II, ed., *A New Significance: Re-Envisioning the History of the American West* (New York: Oxford University Press, 1996), 97.

136. Albert L. Hurtado, "Sexuality in California's Franciscan Missions: Cultural Perceptions and Sad Realities," *California History* 71 (1992): 371–85; Bouvier, *Women and the Conquest of California*, chaps. 3, 5–7, quote at 52; Robert H. Jackson and Edward Castillo, *Indians, Franciscans, and Spanish Colonization: The Impact of the Mission System on California Indians* (Albuquerque: University of New Mexico Press, 1995); Beebe and Senkewicz, eds., *Lands of Promise*, 155–61, 186–92.

137. Robert H. Jackson, *Indian Population Decline: The Missions of Northwestern New Spain, 1687–1840* (Albuquerque: University of New Mexico Press, 1994); Jackson, *From Savages to Subjects*, 86–87, 93–94, 104–5.

138. Vecsey, *On the Padres' Trail*, 379–93. For an overview of "The Indian versus the Spanish Mission," see Sherburne F. Cook, *The Conflict between the California Indian and White Civilization* (Berkeley: University of California Press, 1976), pt. 1.

139. Kenneth M. Ames and Herbert D. G. Maschner, *Peoples of the Northwest Coast: Their Archaeology and Prehistory* (London: Thames and Hudson, 1999), 10.

140. Moulton, ed., *The Journals*, 6: 103–4. For discussion of the Columbia, see Timothy Egan, *The Good Rain: Across Time and Terrain in the Pacific Northwest* (New York: Vintage, 1991); Richard White, *The Organic Machine* (New York: Hill and Wang, 1995), "virtual river" quote at 106–8; and William L. Lang and Robert C. Carriker, eds., *Great River of the West: Essays on the Columbia River* (Seattle: University of Washington Press, 1999).

141. Robert H. Ruby and John A. Brown, *The Chinook Indians: Traders of the Lower Columbia River* (Norman: University of Oklahoma Press, 1976), chap. 1.

142. Erna Gunther, *Indian Life on the Northwest Coast of North America, as Seen by the Early Explorers and Fur Traders during the Last Decades of the Eighteenth Century* (Chicago: University of Chicago Press, 1972), 4–17.

143. Raisa V. Makarova, *Russians on the Pacific 1743–1799*, trans. and ed. Richard A. Pierce and Alton S. Donnelly (Kingston, Ontario: Limestone Press, 1975). Stephen Haycox surveys the literature on Russian expansion for American historians who have generally ignored it in "In Search of the Great Bear: A Historiography of Russian Exploration in Alaska and California," in Carlos A. Schwantes, ed., *Encounters with a Distant Land: Exploration and the Great Northwest* (Moscow: University of Idaho Press, 1994), 37–56.

144. Warren L. Cook, *Flood Tide of Empire: Spain and the Pacific Northwest, 1543–1819* (New Haven CT: Yale University Press, 1973), chap. 3; Herbert

K. Beals, trans. and ed., *For Honor and Country: The Diary of Bruno de Hezeta* (Portland: Oregon Historical Society Press, 1985).

145. Herbert K. Beals, trans. and ed., *Juan Pérez on the Northwest Coast: Six Documents of His Expedition in 1774* (Portland: Oregon Historical Society Press, 1980), 77; Iris Higbie Wilson, trans. and ed., *Noticias de Nutka: An Account of Nootka Sound in 1792 by José Mariano Moziño* (Seattle: University of Washington Press, 1970), 66.

146. Beals, trans. and ed., *For Honor and Country*, 77–78; Cook, *Flood Tide of Empire*, 72–83.

147. For overviews of British ambitions and activities in the area, see Barry Gough, *Distant Dominion: Britain and the Northwest Coast of North America, 1579–1809* (Vancouver: University of British Columbia Press, 1980). Barry Gough, *The Northwest Coast: British Navigation, Trade, and Discoveries to 1812* (Vancouver: University of British Columbia Press, 1992) reprints segments of *Distant Dominion.*

148. Robert Welsch, ed., *Captain Cook: Voyages of Discovery, Compiled by John Barrow from the Authorized 18th Century Admiralty Editions and Documents* (Chicago: Academy Publishers, 1993); J. G. Beaglehole, ed., *The Journals of Captain James Cook on His Voyages of Discovery*, 4 vols. (Cambridge: Cambridge University Press for the Hakluyt Society, 1967), quotes at 3, pt. 1: 295–96, 298–99. Scotsman Alexander Walker provides evidence that this chief may have been Maquinna and that the name may have been a title handed down from father to son; Robin Fisher and J. M. Bumsted, *An Account of a Voyage to the Northwest Coast of America in 1785 and 1786 by Alexander Walker* (Seattle: University of Washington Press; Vancouver: Douglas and McIntyre, 1982), 17, 63, 236n135.

149. Welsch, ed., *Captain Cook*, 382; Cook, *Flood Tide of Empire*, 88–100.

150. Beaglehole, ed., *The Journals*, 3, pt. 1: 371–72.

151. John Ledyard, *A Journal of Captain Cook's Last Voyage to the Pacific Ocean, and in Quest of a Northwest Passage, Performed in the Years 1776–79* (Hartford CT: Nathaniel Patten, 1783), 70; Mary Malloy, ed., *"A Most Remarkable Enterprise": Lectures on the Northwest Coast Trade and Northwest Coast Indian Life by Captain William Sturgis* (Marstons Mills MA: Parnassus Imprints, 2000), 18.

152. The most complete account of the trade is James R. Gibson, *Otter Skins, Boston Ships, and China Goods: The Maritime Fur Trade of the Northwest Coast, 1785–1841* (Montreal: McGill-Queens University Press; Seattle: University of Washington Press, 1992).

153. Beresford, *A Voyage*; Gunther, *Indian Life*, 120–21, Swanton quote at 121.

154. Quoted in Gunther, *Indian Life*, 141–42.

155. John Meares, *Voyages Made in the Years 1788 and 1789, from China to*

the North West Coast of America . . . (London, 1790), 153–54; Gunther, *Indian Life,* 56–58.

156. Cook, *Flood Tide of Empire,* 138, 142; Wilson, trans. and ed., *Noticias de Nutka,* 88.

157. Sergei Kan, *Memory Eternal: Tlingit Culture and Russian Orthodox Christianity through Two Centuries* (Seattle: University of Washington Press, 1999), 34–58; Gunther, *Indian Life,* 174.

158. Gibson, *Otter Skins,* 13–18.

159. Beresford, *A Voyage,* 99–105; Fisher and Bumsted, *An Account,* 148.

160. Jim McDowell, *José Narváez, the Forgotten Explorer, Including His Narrative of a Voyage on the Northwest Coast in 1788* (Spokane WA: Arthur H. Clark, 1998), 122, 147.

161. Frederic W. Howay, ed., *The Journal of Captain James Colnett aboard the Argonaut* (Toronto: Champlain Society, 1940), 53–169; William R. Manning, *The Nootka Sound Controversy,* Annual Report of the American Historical Association (Washington DC, 1904); Cook, *Flood Tide of Empire,* chaps. 5–10.

162. Cook, *Flood Tide of Empire,* chap. 8, figures on vessels at 551. Counts of ships differ slightly: Lamb, ed., *George Vancouver,* 4: 1550–51, also provides lists of vessels on the coast in 1792; Gibson, *Otter Skins,* 299–310, lists vessels that actually were trading and hunting on the coast for every year from 1785 to 1841; [Josef Espinosa y Tello], *A Spanish Voyage to Vancouver and the Northwest Coast of America,* trans. Cecil Jane (London: Argonaut Press, 1930), 90, reported twenty-two vessels in 1792 but did not include Spanish ships in that count.

163. Cook, *Flood Tide of Empire,* 286; Lamb, ed., *George Vancouver,* 2: 512.

164. Lamb, ed., *George Vancouver,* 3: 931n1; W. Kaye Lamb, ed., *The Journals and Letters of Sir Alexander Mackenzie* (Cambridge: Cambridge University Press for the Hakluyt Society, 1970), 375–76.

165. Gibson, *Otter Skins,* 18–21.

166. John Scofield, *Hail, Columbia: Robert Gray, John Hendrick, and the Pacific Fur Trade* (Portland: Oregon Historical Society Press, 1993); Frederic W. Howay, ed., *Voyages of the "Columbia" to the Northwest Coast* (Portland: Oregon Historical Society Press, 1990), originally published in *Collections of the Massachusetts Historical Society* 79 (1941). The original logs of Haswell, Boit, and Hoskins are in the Massachusetts Historical Society. Many of the records of this aspect of far western history are in the East, since journals and logs were deposited in the communities from which the ships sailed, not in the communities with which they traded.

167. Wilson, trans. and ed., *Noticias de Nutka,* Spanish source at 70–71; "Haswell's Second Log," in Howay, ed., *Voyages,* 323; Scofield, *Hail, Columbia;* Frederic W. Howay, "Early Days of the Maritime Fur Trade on the Northwest Coast," *Canadian Historical Review* 4 (1923): 26–44, quote at 41–42; Gibson,

Otter Skins, chap. 3. Briton C. Busch and Barry M. Gough, eds., *Fur Traders from New England: The Boston Men in the North Pacific, 1787–1800* (Spokane WA: Arthur H. Clark, 1997), 122–23 reprints a list of American vessels engaged in the northwestern sea otter trade. Mary Malloy, *"Boston Men" on the Northwest Coast: The American Maritime Fur Trade 1788–1844* (Kingston, Ontario: Limestone Press, 1998), 25–26. Malloy traces the emergence of Yankee dominance of the trade and provides an updated and complete list of American vessels in the maritime trade (61–173). Sturgis quote in Malloy, ed., *A Most Remarkable Enterprise,* 13.

168. Robin Fisher, *Contact and Conflict: Indian-European Relations in British Columbia, 1774–1890* (Vancouver: University of British Columbia Press, 1977), chap. 7; Gibson, *Otter Skins,* chap. 6; Douglas Cole and David Darling, "History of the Early Period," in *HNAI,* 7: 119–34; Beresford, *A Voyage,* 218–19, 227, 249–50; Fisher and Bumsted, *An Account,* 43; [Espinosa y Tello], *A Spanish Voyage,* 90; Meares, *Voyages Made,* 119–20, 148, and appendix 1, "Instructions of the Merchants Proprietors." Malloy, *"Boston Men" on the Northwest Coast,* questions the degree of "Indian control" in the trade.

169. Malloy, ed., *A Most Remarkable Enterprise,* 32.

170. Beresford, *A Voyage,* 187.

171. Gibson, *Otter Skins,* 114–15, 270–71. The description of Cunneah is in Gunther, *Indian Life,* 135. Cf. Peter Puget, "The Vancouver Expedition: Peter Puget's Journal of the Exploration of Puget Sound, May 7–June 11, 1792," *Pacific Northwest Quarterly* 30 (1939): 189.

172. Malloy, *"Boston Men" on the Northwest Coast,* 178.

173. On Maquinna, see, for example, Fisher and Bumsted, *An Account,* 15–17, 50–51, 62–63, passim; Lamb, ed., *George Vancouver,* 2: 661–62n, 670–73; 4: 1401–5; Meares, *Voyages Made,* 229, passim; *Dictionary of Canadian Biography,* 14 vols. (Toronto: University of Toronto Press, 1966–), 4: 567–69. According to Ames and Maschner, evidence for structures at Yuquot date to A.D. 1; other sources suggest occupation for four thousand years (*Peoples of the Northwest Coast,* 159).

174. Cook, *Flood Tide of Empire,* 335–40, quotes at 336–37; Howay, ed., *The Journal of Captain James Colnett,* 208; Lamb, ed., *George Vancouver,* 2: 671–73; [Espinosa y Tello], *A Spanish Voyage,* 23; Gibson, *Otter Skins,* 270. John Jewitt spent more than a year as a captive of Maquinna after the ship *Boston* was destroyed in 1803; John R. Jewitt, *A Journal Kept at Nootka Sound* (1807; reprint, Boston: Charles E. Goodspeed, 1931). Jewitt produced a later and more elaborate account of his experiences: *The Captive of Nootka, or the Adventures of John R. Jewitt* (Philadelphia: Lippincott, Grambo, 1854).

175. [Espinosa y Tello], *A Spanish Voyage,* 115.

176. Howay, ed., *The Journal of Captain James Colnett,* 280.

177. Beresford, *A Voyage,* 114–15.

178. Egan, *The Good Rain*, 131; Gibson, *Otter Skins*, 175–87; Wilson, trans. and ed., *Noticias de Nutka*, 48; [Espinosa y Tello], *A Spanish Voyage*, 97.

179. Cook, *Flood Tide of Empire*, 313; Lamb, ed., *George Vancouver*, 4: quote at 1399.

180. Gibson, *Otter Skins*, 115–16; Fisher and Bumsted, *An Account*, 47; Malloy, *A Most Remarkable Enterprise*, 16.

181. Mary C. Wright, "Economic Development and Native American Women in the Early Nineteenth Century," *American Quarterly* 33 (1981): 525–36, esp. 534–35.

182. "John Hoskins' Narrative," in Howay, ed., *Voyages*, 196, 200; Gibson, *Otter Skins*, 235–39, 272–73; Moulton, ed., *The Journals*, 6: 65, 74–76, 239, 241, 416, 418.

183. Robert Boyd, *The Coming of the Spirit of Pestilence: Introduced Infectious Diseases and Population Decline among the Northwest Coast Indians, 1774–1874* (Seattle: University of Washington Press, 1999); Gibson, *Otter Skins*, 273–77.

184. Gibson, *Otter Skins*, 224–26; Fisher and Bumsted, *An Account*, 80, 148.

185. Lamb, ed., *George Vancouver*, 2: 516–17, 528, 538–40, 559. Thomas Manby, "Voyage of H.M.S. *Discovery* to the Northwest Coast of America," Beinecke Rare Book and Manuscript Library, Yale University, pt. 2: 18–21; Puget, "The Vancouver Expedition," 215. I am grateful to Elizabeth Fenn for bringing the Manby and Puget sources to my attention.

186. Beresford, *A Voyage*, 271–73.

187. Boyd, *The Coming of the Spirit of Pestilence*, 3.

188. Malloy, *"Boston Men" on the Northwest Coast*, 44–46; F. W. Howay, "Indian Attacks upon Maritime Traders of the North-West Coast, 1785–1805," *Canadian Historical Review* 6 (1925): 287–309; Gibson, *Otter Skins*, 153–74.

189. Gibson, *Otter Skins*, 220–24; [Espinosa y Tello], *A Spanish Voyage*, 18; Cook, *Flood Tide of Empire*, 341.

190. Howay, ed., *The Journal of Captain James Colnett*, 201; "Boit's Log," in Howay, ed., *Voyages*, 390–91, 395, 401; Scofield, *Hail, Columbia*, 244–56. Indians carried reports of Gray's attacks to Spanish ships; [Espinosa y Tello], *A Spanish Voyage*, 22–23.

191. Lamb, ed., *George Vancouver*, 3: 1016.

192. Kan, *Memory Eternal*, 58–65, describes the attack and its place in Russian and Tlingit memories.

193. Fisher and Bumsted, *An Account*, 189; Jewitt, *A Journal*, 1, 22; Gibson, *Otter Skins*, 135; Cole and Darling, "History," 125.

194. Bruce G. Trigger and Wilcomb E. Washburn, eds., *The Cambridge History of the Native Peoples of the Americas*, vol. 1, *North America* (Cambridge: Cambridge University Press, 1996), for instance, mentions the 1779–83 smallpox epidemic only a couple of times in its two thick parts and gives no impression of its pandemic character or the depth and range of its repercussions. Epi-

demiological overviews generally fail to recognize the pandemic nature of the 1779–83 epidemic. See, for example, F. Fenner, D. A. Henderson, I. Arita, Z. Jezek, and I. D. Ladnyi, *Smallpox and Its Eradication* (Geneva: World Health Organization, 1988), 212, table 5.1. Elizabeth A. Fenn has completed the first full-length scholarly treatment of the pandemic: *Pox Americana: The Great North American Smallpox Epidemic of 1775–1782* (New York: Hill and Wang, 2001).

195. William H. McNeill, *Plagues and Peoples* (New York: Doubleday, 1977), 3–4.

196. Georges E. Sioui, *For an Amerindian Autohistory* (Montreal: McGill-Queens University Press, 1992), 40.

197. Alfred W. Crosby, *The Columbian Exchange: Biological and Cultural Consequences of 1492* (Westport CT: Greenwood Press, 1972), 46.

198. Fenner et al., *Smallpox,* vii.

199. On smallpox in history, see Fenner et al., *Smallpox,* chap. 5; Donald R. Hopkins, *Princes and Peasants: Smallpox in History* (Chicago: University of Chicago Press, 1983), who quotes Macauley at 38; and Joel N. Shurkin, *The Invisible Fire: The Story of Mankind's Victory over the Ancient Scourge of Smallpox* (New York: G. P. Putnam's Sons, 1979), who quotes him at 15. McNeill examines the impact of smallpox and other epidemics in *Plagues and Peoples.*

200. Fenner et al., *Smallpox,* 231; John Duffy, *Epidemics in Colonial America* (Baton Rouge: Louisiana State University Press, 1953), 20–21, 51, 57, 104.

201. Fenn, *Pox Americana,* chaps. 2–4.

202. Anthony Wallace, *The Death and Rebirth of the Seneca* (New York: Alfred A. Knopf, 1970), 195.

203. David P. Henige, *Numbers from Nowhere: The American Indian Contact Population Debate* (Norman: University of Oklahoma Press, 1998) takes issue with scholars who, in his view, inflate precontact population estimates based on a misreading of the data.

204. Donald B. Cooper, *Epidemic Disease in Mexico City, 1716–1813* (Austin: University of Texas Press, 1965), 68; Fenn, *Pox Americana,* 138–40.

205. W. George Lovell, *Conquest and Survival in Colonial Guatemala: A Historical Geography of the Cuchumatan Highlands, 1500–1821* (Montreal: McGill-Queens University Press, 1992), 154–60; Juan A. Villamarin and Judith E. Villamarin, "Epidemic Disease in the Sabana de Bogotá, 1536–1810," in Noble David Cook and W. George Lovell, eds., *"Secret Judgments of God": Old World Disease in Colonial Spanish America* (Norman: University of Oklahoma Press, 1992), 128–29; Suzanne Austin Alchon, "Disease, Population, and Public Health in Eighteenth-Century Quito," in Cook and Lovell, eds., *Secret Judgments of God,* 167, 178–79. It seems likely that these were southern outbreaks of the pandemic.

206. Robert H. Jackson, "The 1781–1782 Smallpox Epidemic in Baja

California," *Journal of California and Great Basin Anthropology* 3 (1981): 138–43; Fenn, *Pox Americana*, 151–56; Luis Sales, O.P., *Observations on California, 1772–1790*, ed. Charles N. Rudkin (Los Angeles: Dawson's Bookshop, 1956), 60, 168–69.

207. Daniel T. Reff, *Disease, Depopulation, and Culture Change in Northwestern New Spain, 1518–1764* (Salt Lake City: University of Utah Press, 1991), 119–23. In laboratory conditions, the smallpox virus has been shown to remain active and infectious for up to seventeen months if wrapped in raw cotton. F. O. MacCallum and J. R. McDonald, "Survival of the Variola Virus in Raw Cotton," *Bulletin of the World Health Organization* 16 (1957): 247–54.

208. Thomas L. Pearcy, "The Smallpox Outbreak of 1779–1782: A Brief Comparative Look at Twelve Borderland Communities," *Journal of the West* 36 (January 1997): 26–37.

209. Marc Simmons, "New Mexico's Smallpox Epidemic of 1780–81," *New Mexico Historical Review* 41 (1966): 319–26; S. D. Aberle, J. H. Watkins, and E. H. Pitney, "The Vital History of San Juan Pueblo," *Human Biology* 12 (1940): 168, 183.

210. John L. Kessell, *Kiva, Cross, and Crown: The Pecos Indians and New Mexico, 1540–1840*, 2nd ed. (Albuquerque: University of New Mexico Press, 1987), 342, 347–48, quote at 347, 490–91; Frances Levine and Anna LaBauve, "Examining the Complexity of Historic Population Decline: A Case Study of Pecos Pueblo, New Mexico," *Ethnohistory* 44 (1997): 75–112; Levine, *Our Prayers*, chap. 4; Albert H. Schroeder, "Pecos Pueblo," in *HNAI*, 9: 432.

211. Fenn, *Pox Americana*, 163; Thomas, ed., *Forgotten Frontiers*, 244–45.

212. John, ed., "Inside the Comanchería, 1785," quote at 37–38; Fenn, *Pox Americana*, 214–15.

213. Laura Peers, "Trade and Change on the Columbia Plateau, 1750–1840," *Columbia: The Magazine of Northwest History* 10 (winter 1996–97): 6; Moulton, ed., *The Journals*, 5: 91.

214. John F. Taylor, "Sociocultural Effects of Epidemics on the Northern Plains, 1734–1850," *Western Canadian Journal of Anthropology* 7, no. 4 (1977): 60.

215. Alfred Bowers, *Hidatsa Social and Ceremonial Organization*, Smithsonian Institution, Bureau of American Ethnology, Bulletin 194 (Washington DC: GPO, 1963; reprint, Lincoln: University of Nebraska Press, 1992), 214–15, 486; "Journal of Jean Baptiste Truteau," in Nasatir, ed., *Before Lewis and Clark*, 1: "in ancient times" quote at 299; Annie Heloise Abel, ed., *Tabeau's Narrative of Loisel's Expedition to the Upper Missouri* (Norman: University of Oklahoma Press, 1939), 123–24; Moulton, ed., *The Journals*, 1 (atlas): maps 25, 28–29; 3: 161, 163, 197, 201–2, 205–7, 233, 312, 401–5; Richard White, "The Winning of the West: The Expansion of the Western Sioux in the Eighteenth and Nineteenth Centuries," *Journal of American History* 65 (1978): 325;

W. Raymond Wood and Lee Irwin, "Mandan," in *HNAI*, 13: 350–52. Truteau said the Arikaras once inhabited thirty-two villages; Tabeau said eighteen; Truteau found them in two villages; Tabeau and Lewis and Clark in three. Tabeau provided a list of the ten Arikara divisions and their chiefs (Abel, ed., *Tabeau's Narrative*, 125). Ann F. Ramenofsky examines the history of smallpox epidemics on the middle Missouri as one of the test cases in *Vectors of Death: The Archaeology of European Contact* (Albuquerque: University of New Mexico Press, 1987), 102–35.

216. William Warren, *History of the Ojibway People* (1885; reprint, St. Paul: Minnesota Historical Society Press, 1984), 261–62; E. Wagner Stearn and Allen E. Stearn, *The Effect of Smallpox on the Destiny of the Amerindian* (Boston: Bruce Humphries, 1945), 48; Russel Thornton, *American Indian Holocaust and Survival: A Population History since 1492* (Norman: University of Oklahoma Press, 1987), 81.

217. Richard Glover, ed., *David Thompson's Narrative, 1784–1812* (Toronto: Champlain Society, 1962), 236.

218. Garrick Mallery, *Picture-Writing of the American Indians*, Tenth Annual Report of the Bureau of American Ethnology, 1888–89 (Washington DC: GPO, 1893; reprint, 2 vols., New York: Dover, 1972), 1: 308; Linda Sundstrom, "Smallpox Used Them Up: References to Epidemic Disease in Northern Plains Winter Counts, 1714–1920," *Ethnohistory* 44 (1997): 305–29; Ronald T. McCoy, "Winter Count: The Teton Chronicles," Ph.D. diss., Northern Arizona University, 1983, 217–24, 227.

219. Sundstrom, "Smallpox Used Them Up."

220. Raymond J. DeMallie and David Reed Miller, "Assiniboine," in *HNAI*, 13: 574.

221. "François-Antoine Larocque's 'Yellowstone Journal,'" in W. Raymond Wood and Thomas D. Thiessen, eds., *Early Fur Trade on the Northern Plains: Canadian Traders among the Mandan and Hidatsa Indians, 1738–1818* (Norman: University of Oklahoma Press, 1985), 206.

222. James A. Teit, *The Salishan Tribes of the Western Plateaus*, Forty-fifth Annual Report of the Bureau of American Ethnology (Washington DC: GPO, 1930), 315; Peers, "Trade and Change," 7.

223. Barbara Belya, ed., *Columbia Journals: David Thompson* (Seattle: University of Washington Press, 1994), 70; Theodore Binnema, *Common and Contested Ground: A Human and Environmental History of the Northwestern Plains* (Norman: University of Oklahoma Press, 2001), 128.

224. Glover, ed., *David Thompson's Narrative*, quotes at 246. William Tomison and Matthew Cocking attributed the epidemic to the Shoshones; E. E. Rich, ed., *Cumberland House Journals and Inland Journals, 1775–82*, 2nd series (London: Hudson's Bay Record Society, 1952), 281, 298.

225. Glover, ed., *David Thompson's Narrative*, 247–48.

226. Cole Harris, "Voices of Disaster: Smallpox around the Strait of Georgia in 1782," *Ethnohistory* 41 (1994): 591–626; Robert Boyd, "Smallpox in the Pacific Northwest: The First Epidemics," B.C. *Studies* 101 (1994): 5–40; Robert Boyd, "Commentary on Early Contact-Era Smallpox in the Pacific Northwest," *Ethnohistory* 43 (1996): 307–28; Boyd, *The Coming of the Spirit of Pestilence,* chap. 2. Boyd suggests the possibility of the Kamchatka-Tlingit route. Fenn, *Pox Americana,* chap. 8, esp. 253, finds the preponderance of evidence points up the Columbia to the Shoshones.

227. Moulton, ed., *The Journals,* 6: 81, 285–87; 7: 65, 86.

228. Harris, "Voices of Disaster," 609.

229. Beresford, *A Voyage,* 271–72, quoted in both Boyd, *The Coming of the Spirit of Pestilence,* 23–24, and Fenn, *Pox Americana,* 227.

230. Jody F. Decker, "Tracing Historical Diffusion Patterns: The Case of the 1780–82 Smallpox Epidemic among the Indians of Western Canada," *Native Studies Review* 4, nos. 1–2 (1988): 1–24; Rich, ed., *Cumberland House Journals,* 281.

231. John McDonnell, "Some Account of the Red River," in L. R. Masson, ed., *Les Bourgeois de la Compagnie du Nord-Ouest,* 2 vols. (1889–90; reprint, New York: Antiquarian Press, 1960), 1: 277–78; John S. Milloy, *The Plains Cree: Trade, Diplomacy and War, 1790 to 1870* (Winnipeg: University of Manitoba Press, 1988), 45, 71; Glover, ed., *David Thompson's Narrative,* 92; Dale R. Russell, *Eighteenth-Century Western Cree and Their Neighbours* (Hull, Quebec: Canadian Museum of Civilization, 1991), quote at 216.

232. Jody F. Decker, "Depopulation of the Northern Plains Natives," *Social Science and Medicine* 33, no. 4 (1991): 381–93. Decker estimates that 21,500 died among Plains groups, minus the Plains Cree (381), and reports a 50 percent mortality rate among a Plains Cree population of about 15,000 (386–87).

233. J. B. Tyrrell, ed., *A Journey from Prince Wales's Fort in Hudson's Bay to the Northern Ocean in the Years 1769, 1770, 1771, and 1772, by Samuel Hearne* (Toronto: Champlain Society, 1911), 200–201; Arthur J. Ray, *Indians in the Fur Trade: Their Role as Hunters, Trappers, and Middlemen in the Lands Southwest of Hudson Bay, 1660–1870* (Toronto: University of Toronto Press, 1974), chap. 5.

234. Lamb, ed., *The Journals and Letters,* 74.

235. Rich, ed., *Cumberland House Journals,* "The smallpox is rageing" quote at 225–26, "It cuts me to the Heart" quote at 232, "my Debtors are all Dead" quote at 238, 265, 270, 281.

236. Glover, ed., *David Thompson's Narrative,* 236. Fenn, *Pox Americana,* chap. 6, traces the impact of the epidemic in the Hudson's Bay Company territory.

237. Decker, "Tracing Historical Diffusion Patterns," 13; Rich, ed., *Cumberland House Journals,* quote at 297.

238. E. E. Rich, ed., *Moose Fort Journals, 1783–85* (London: Hudson's Bay Record Society, 1954), 225–26.

239. Ann M. Palkovich, "Demography and Disease Patterns in a Protohistoric Plains Group: A Study of the Morbridge Site (39WW1)," *Plains Anthropologist* 26 (1981): pt. 2: 71–84; Decker, "Depopulation," 483, 490.

240. Russell Thornton, Tim Miller, and Jonathan Warren, "American Indian Population Recovery Following Smallpox Epidemics," *American Anthropologist* 93, no. 1 (1991): 33, 42n9; David E. Stannard, "The Consequences of Contact: Toward an Interdisciplinary Theory of Native Responses to Biological and Cultural Invasion," in David Hurst Thomas, ed., *Columbian Consequences,* vol. 3, *The Spanish Borderlands in Pan-American Perspective* (Washington DC: Smithsonian Institution Press, 1991), 532–33.

241. John F. Taylor, "Sociocultural Effects of Epidemics on the Northern Plains, 1734–1850," *Western Canadian Journal of Anthropology* 7, no. 4 (1977): 58; Glover, ed., *David Thompson's Narrative,* 236, 246.

242. Glover, ed., *David Thompson's Narrative,* 236.

243. Stannard, "The Consequences of Contact," 529; Tomison quoted in Decker, "Tracing Historical Diffusion Patterns," 21; Sundstrom, "Smallpox Used Them Up"; McCoy, "Winter Count," 227. See also, Lamb, ed., *The Journals and Letters,* 74.

244. Sundstrom, "Smallpox Used Them Up."

245. Taylor, "Sociocultural Effects," 63; Abel, ed., *Tabeau's Narrative,* 124.

246. McNeill, *Plagues and Peoples,* 150; Philip Ziegler, *The Black Death* (Harmondsworth: Pelican, 1976).

247. Mallery, "Picture Writing," 266–328; "Lone Dog's Winter Count" is reproduced in Calloway, ed., *Our Hearts Fell to the Ground,* 31–36.

248. Moulton, ed., *The Journals,* 2: 479; 3: 399; 9: 38, 358, 394; 10: 27–28; John M. O'Shea and John Ludwickson, *Archaeology and Ethnohistory of the Omaha Indians: The Big Village Site* (Lincoln: University of Nebraska Press, 1992), 25–31. The tradition of the Omaha suicide attack is recounted in Alice C. Fletcher and Francis La Flesche, *The Omaha Tribe,* 2 vols. (1911; reprint, Lincoln: University of Nebraska Press, 1972), 1: 86–87. A belief that mutilation that occurred during life would be replicated in the afterworld may have added to the horror. Taylor, "Sociocultural Effects," 62.

249. Flores, ed., *Jefferson,* 167–70.

250. Dan Flores, *The Natural West: Environmental History in the Great Plains and Rocky Mountains* (Norman: University of Oklahoma Press, 2001), 47.

EPILOGUE

1. Gary E. Moulton, ed., *The Journals of the Lewis and Clark Expedition*, 13 vols. (Lincoln: University of Nebraska Press, 1983–2001), 6: 429–31; John R. Jewitt, *A Journal Kept at Nootka Sound* (1807; reprint, Boston: Charles E. Goodspeed, 1931), xvi; Mary Malloy, *"Boston Men" on the Northwest Coast: The American Maritime Fur Trade 1788–1844* (Kingston, Ontario: Limestone Press, 1998), 53, 169.

2. Eric Hinderaker, *Elusive Empires: Constructing Colonialism in the Ohio Valley, 1673–1800* (Cambridge: Cambridge University Press, 1997), 185–86, 260–70; Anthony F. C. Wallace, *Jefferson and the Indians: The Tragic Fate of the First Americans* (Cambridge: Harvard University Press, 1999), quote at 18; Colin G. Calloway, *The American Revolution in Indian Country* (Cambridge: Cambridge University Press, 1995), 292–301.

3. Christopher L. Miller, *Prophetic Worlds: Indians and Whites on the Columbia Plateau* (New Brunswick NJ: Rutgers University Press, 1985), 1, 42–43, quote on title page.

4. Elliott West, *The Way to the West: Essays on the Central Plains* (Albuquerque: University of New Mexico Press, 1995), 90–92.

5. Dan Flores, *The Natural West: Environmental History in the Great Plains and Rocky Mountains* (Norman: University of Oklahoma Press, 2001), 189–93, quote at 193; Paul S. Martin and Christine R. Szuter, "War Zones and Game Sinks in Lewis and Clark's West," *Conservation Biology* 13 (winter 1999): 36–45.

6. Philip Phillips and James A. Brown, *Pre-Columbian Shell Engravings from the Craig Mound at Spiro, Oklahoma*, 6 vols. in 2 pts. (Cambridge: Peabody Museum of Archaeology and Ethnology, Harvard University, 1978–84), 1: 1.

7. Calvin Martin, *The Way of the Human Being* (New Haven CT: Yale University Press, 1999), 76.

8. James F. Brooks, *Captives and Cousins: Slavery, Kinship, and Community in the Southwest Borderlands* (Chapel Hill: University of North Carolina Press, 2002).

9. Dan L. Flores, ed., *Jefferson and Southwestern Exploration: The Freeman and Custis Accounts of the Red River Expedition of 1806* (Norman: University of Oklahoma Press, 1984), 118.

10. John Joseph Mathews, *The Osages: Children of the Middle Waters* (Norman: University of Oklahoma Press, 1961), 259.

11. Quoted and discussed in James P. Ronda, *Jefferson's West: A Journey with Lewis and Clark* (N.p.: Thomas Jefferson Foundation, 2000), 55.

12. Zebulon Montgomery Pike, *An Account of Expeditions to the Sources of the Mississippi, and through the Western Parts of Louisiana, . . . and a Tour through the*

Interior Parts of New Spain (Philadelphia: C. and A. Conrad, 1810; reprint, New York: Readex Microprint, 1966), 12.

13. James P. Ronda, *Finding the West: Explorations with Lewis and Clark* (Albuquerque: University of New Mexico Press, 2001), 100–101.

14. Brian Fagan, *Floods, Famines and Emperors: El Niño and the Fate of Civilizations* (New York: Basic Books, 1999), quote at 97.

15. Elliott West, *The Contested Plains: Indians, Goldseekers, and the Rush to Colorado* (Lawrence: University Press of Kansas, 1998), 337.

16. David E. Stuart, *Anasazi America: Seventeen Centuries on the Road from Center Place* (Albuquerque: University of New Mexico Press, 2000), xiii.

17. Cf. Ronald J. Mason, "Archaeology and Native North American Oral Tradition," *American Antiquity* 65 (2000): 248 (for Yorick's skull analogy).

18. Flores, *The Natural West*, chap. 9.

Selected Bibliography

This bibliography represents a selection of the sources consulted and the literature available. Readers should consult the notes for additional items and more specific references, particularly older journal articles.

Primary Sources

Abel, Annie Heloise, ed. "Description of the Upper Missouri, by Jean-Baptiste Trudeau." *Mississippi Valley Historical Review* 8 (1921): 149–79.

———, ed. *Tabeau's Narrative of Loisel's Expedition to the Upper Missouri.* Norman: University of Oklahoma Press, 1939.

Adams, Arthur T., ed. *The Explorations of Pierre Esprit Radisson.* Minneapolis: Ross and Haines, 1961.

Adams, Eleanor B., and Angélico Chávez, trans. and eds. *The Missions of New Mexico, 1776: A Description by Fray Francisco Atanasio Domínguez with Other Contemporary Documents.* Albuquerque: University of New Mexico Press, 1956.

Adorno, Rolena, and Patrick Charles Pautz. *Álvar Núñez Cabeza de Vaca: His Account, His Life, and the Expedition of Pánfilo de Narváez.* 3 vols. Lincoln: University of Nebraska Press, 1999.

Beaglehole, J. G., ed. *The Journals of Captain James Cook on His Voyages of Discovery.* 4 vols. Cambridge: Cambridge University Press for the Hakluyt Society, 1967.

Beals, Herbert K., trans. and ed. *For Honor and Country: The Diary of Bruno de Hezeta.* Portland: Oregon Historical Society Press, 1985.

Beebe, Rose Marie, and Robert M. Senkewicz, eds. *Lands of Promise and Despair: Chronicles of Early California, 1535–1846.* Santa Clara and Berkeley: Santa Clara University and Heyday Books, 2001.

Belyea, Barbara, ed. *Columbia Journals: David Thompson.* Seattle: University of Washington Press, 1994.

———, ed. *A Year Inland: The Journal of a Hudson's Bay Company Winterer.* Waterloo, Ontario: Wilfrid Laurier University Press, 2000.

Blair, Emma Helen, trans. and ed. *The Indian Tribes of the Upper Mississippi Valley and Region of the Great Lakes.* 2 vols. 1911. Reprint, Lincoln: University of Nebraska Press, 1996.

Bolton, Herbert E., ed. *Anza's California Expeditions.* 5 vols. Berkeley: University of California Press, 1930.

———, ed. *Athanase de Mézières and the Texas-Louisiana Frontier 1768–1780.* 2 vols. Cleveland: Arthur H. Clark, 1914.
———, ed. *Kino's Historical Memoir of Pimería Alta, 1683–1711.* 2 vols. Cleveland: Arthur H. Clark, 1919.
Burpee, Lawrence J., ed. "An Adventurer from Hudson's Bay: The Journal of Matthew Cocking." *Proceedings and Transactions of the Royal Society of Canada,* 3rd series, 2 (1908): sec. 2.
Calloway, Colin G., ed. *Our Hearts Fell to the Ground: Plains Indian Views of How the West Was Lost.* Boston: Bedford Books, 1996.
———, ed. *The World Turned Upside Down: Indian Voices from Early America.* Boston: Bedford Books, 1994.
Charlevoix, Pierre de. *Journal of a Voyage to North-America.* 2 vols. London, 1761. Reprint, New York: Readex Microprint, 1966.
Clayton, Lawrence A., Vernon James Knight Jr., and Edward C. Moore, eds. *The De Soto Chronicles: The Expedition of Hernando de Soto to North America in 1539–1543.* 2 vols. Tuscaloosa: University of Alabama Press, 1993.
Coues, Elliott, ed. *New Light on the History of the Greater Northwest: The Manuscript Journals of Alexander Henry and David Thompson, 1799–1814.* 2 vols. 1897. Reprint, Minneapolis: Ross and Haines, 1965.
———, trans. and ed. *On the Trail of a Spanish Pioneer: The Diary and Itinerary of Francisco Garcés in His Travels through Sonora, Arizona, and California, 1775–1776.* 2 vols. New York: F. P. Harper, 1900.
Cox, Isaac Joslin, ed. *The Journeys of René-Robert Cavelier, Sieur de La Salle.* 2 vols. New York: Allerton, 1922.
Cutter, Donald C., trans. and ed. *The Defenses of Northern New Spain: Hugo O'Conor's Report to Teodoro de Croix, July 22, 1777.* Dallas TX: Southern Methodist University Press/De Golyer Library, 1994.
Dunnigan, Brian Leigh, ed. *Memoir on the Late War in North America between France and England by Pierre Pouchot.* Trans. Michael Cardy. Youngstown NY: Old Fort Niagara Association, 1994.
Espinosa, J. Manuel, trans. and ed. *The Pueblo Indian Revolt of 1696 and the Franciscan Missions in New Mexico: Letters of the Missionaries and Related Documents.* Norman: University of Oklahoma Press, 1988.
[Espinosa y Tello, Josef]. *A Spanish Voyage to Vancouver and the Northwest Coast of America.* Trans. Cecil Jane. London: Argonaut Press, 1930.
Feiler, Seymour, trans. and ed. *Jean-Bernard Bossu's Travels in the Interior of North America 1751–1762.* Norman: University of Oklahoma Press, 1962.
Fisher, Robin, and J. M. Bumsted. *An Account of a Voyage to the Northwest Coast of America in 1785 and 1786 by Alexander Walker.* Seattle: University of Washington Press; Vancouver: Douglas and McIntyre, 1982.
Flores, Dan L., ed. *Jefferson and Southwestern Exploration: The Freeman and Custis*

Accounts of the Red River Expedition of 1806. Norman: University of Oklahoma Press, 1984.

Foster, William C., ed. *The La Salle Expedition to Texas: The Journal of Henri Joutel, 1684–1687.* Trans. Johanna S. Warren. Austin: Texas State Historical Association, 1998.

———, ed. *Texas and Northeastern Mexico, 1630–1690 by Juan Bautista Chapa.* Trans. Ned F. Brierley. Austin: University of Texas Press, 1997.

Gelb, Norman, ed. *Jonathan Carver's Travels through America, 1766–1768.* New York: John Wiley and Sons, 1993.

Glover, Richard, ed. *David Thompson's Narrative, 1784–1812.* Toronto: Champlain Society, 1962.

Greer, Alan, ed. *The Jesuit Relations: Natives and Missionaries in Seventeenth-Century North America.* Boston: Bedford Books, 2000.

Gunther, Erna, ed. *Indian Life on the Northwest Coast of North America, as Seen by the Early Explorers and Fur Traders during the Last Decades of the Eighteenth Century.* Chicago: University of Chicago Press, 1972.

Hackett, Charles Wilson, ed. *Historical Documents Relating to New Mexico, Nueva Vizcaya, and Approaches Thereto, to 1773.* 3 vols. Washington DC: Carnegie Institute, 1923–27.

———, ed. *Pichardo's Treatise on the Limits of Louisiana and Texas.* 4 vols. Austin: University of Texas Press, 1931–46.

———, ed. *Revolt of the Pueblo Indians of New Mexico and Otermín's Attempted Reconquest 1680–1682.* Trans. Charmion Clair Shelby. 2 vols. Albuquerque: University of New Mexico Press, 1942.

Hallenbeck, Cleve. *The Journey of Fray Marcos de Niza.* Dallas TX: Southern Methodist University Press, 1987.

Hamilton, Edward P., ed. *Adventure in the Wilderness: The American Journals of Louis Antoine de Bougainville, 1756–1760.* Norman: University of Oklahoma Press, 1964.

Hammond, George P., and Agapito Rey, eds. *Don Juan de Oñate: Colonizer of New Mexico, 1595–1628.* 2 vols. Albuquerque: University of New Mexico Press, 1953.

———, eds. *Narratives of the Coronado Expedition 1540–1542.* Albuquerque: University of New Mexico Press, 1940.

———, eds. *New Mexico in 1602: Juan de Montoya's Relation of the Discovery of New Mexico.* Albuquerque: Quivira Society, 1938.

———, eds. *The Rediscovery of New Mexico.* Albuquerque: University of New Mexico Press, 1966.

Hendricks, Rick, and John P. Wilson, eds. and trans. *The Navajos in 1705: Roque Madrid's Campaign Journal.* Albuquerque: University of New Mexico Press, 1996.

Henry, Alexander. *Travels and Adventures in the Years 1760–1776.* Chicago: R. R. Donnelley and Sons, 1921.

Hodge, Frederick W., George P. Hammond, and Agapito Rey, eds. *Fray Alonso de Benavides' Revised Memorial of 1634.* Albuquerque: University of New Mexico Press, 1945.

Hoffmann, Fritz Leo, trans. *Diary of the Alarcón Expedition into Texas, 1718–1719, by Fray Francisco Céliz.* Los Angeles: Quivira Society, 1935.

Houck, Louis, ed. *The Spanish Regime in Missouri.* 2 vols. Chicago: R. R. Donnelley and Sons, 1909.

Howay, F. W., ed. *The Journal of Captain James Colnett aboard the Argonaut.* Toronto: Champlain Society, 1940.

———, ed. *Voyages of the "Columbia" to the Northwest Coast.* 1941. Reprint, Portland: Oregon Historical Society Press, 1990.

Jackson, Donald, ed. *The Letters of the Lewis and Clark Expedition with Related Documents, 1783–1854.* 2 vols. Urbana: University of Illinois Press, 1978.

Jacobs, Wilbur R., ed. *The Appalachian Indian Frontier: The Edmund Atkin Report and Plan of 1755.* 1954. Reprint, Lincoln: University of Nebraska Press, 1967.

Jaenen, Cornelius J., ed. *The French Regime in the Upper Country of Canada during the Seventeenth Century.* Toronto: Champlain Society, 1996.

John, Elizabeth A. H., ed. "Inside the Comanchería, 1785: The Diary of Pedro Vial and Francisco Xavier Chaves." Trans. Adán Benavides Jr. *Southwestern Historical Quarterly* 98 (1994): 27–56.

———, ed. *Views from the Apache Frontier: Report on the Northern Provinces of New Spain by José Cortés, 1799.* Norman: University of Oklahoma Press, 1989.

Johnson, Alice M., ed. *Saskatchewan Journals and Correspondence: Edmonton House 1795–1800; Chesterfield House 1800–1802.* London: Hudson's Bay Record Society, 1967.

"Journal of Jean Baptiste Truteau on the Upper Missouri, 'Première Partie,' June 7, 1794–March 26, 1795." *American Historical Review* 19 (1914): 299–333.

Kellogg, Louise Phelps, ed. *Early Narratives of the Northwest, 1634–1699.* New York: Scribner's, 1917.

Kessell, John L., Rick Hendricks, and Meredith D. Dodge, eds. *Blood on the Boulders: The Journals of Don Diego de Vargas, New Mexico, 1694–97.* 2 vols. Albuquerque: University of New Mexico Press, 1998.

———, eds. *By Force of Arms: The Journals of Don Diego de Vargas, New Mexico, 1691–93.* Albuquerque: University of New Mexico Press, 1992.

———, eds. *Remote beyond Compare: Letters of Don Diego de Vargas to His Family from New Spain and New Mexico, 1675–1706.* Albuquerque: University of New Mexico Press, 1989.

———, eds. *To the Royal Crown Restored: The Journals of Don Diego de Vargas, New Mexico, 1692–94.* Albuquerque: University of New Mexico Press, 1995.

Kessell, John L., Rick Hendricks, Meredith D. Dodge, and Larry D. Miller, eds. *That Disturbances Cease: The Journals of Don Diego de Vargas, New Mexico, 1697–1700.* Albuquerque: University of New Mexico Press, 2000.

Kinetz, W. Vernon, ed. *The Indians of the Western Great Lakes, 1615–1760.* Ann Arbor: University of Michigan Press, 1965.

Kinnaird, Lawrence, ed. *The Frontiers of New Spain: Nicolas de Lafora's Description 1766–1768.* Berkeley: Quivira Society, 1958.

———, trans. and ed. *Spain in the Mississippi Valley, 1765–1794: Translations of Materials from the Spanish Archives in the Bancroft Library, University of California, Berkeley.* Vols. 2–4. American Historical Association, Annual Report for the Year 1945. Washington DC: American Historical Association, 1946–49.

Lamb, W. Kaye, ed. *George Vancouver: A Voyage of Discovery to the North Pacific Ocean and round the World, 1791–1795.* 4 vols. London: Hakluyt Society, 1984.

———, ed. *The Journals and Letters of Sir Alexander Mackenzie.* Cambridge: Cambridge University Press for the Hakluyt Society, 1970.

La Salle, Nicolas de. *Relation of the Discovery of the Mississippi River.* Trans. Melville B. Anderson. Chicago: Caxton Club, 1898.

Lowrie, Walter, and Matthew St. Clair Clarke, eds. *American State Papers: Indian Affairs.* Washington DC: Gales and Seaton, 1832.

Malloy, Mary, ed. *"A Most Remarkable Enterprise": Lectures on the Northwest Coast Trade and Northwest Coast Indian Life by Captain William Sturgis.* Marstons Mills MA: Parnassus Imprints, 2000.

Margolin, Malcolm, ed. *Monterey in 1786: The Journals of Jean François de La Pérouse.* Berkeley CA: Heyday Books, 1989.

Margry, Pierre, ed. *Découvertes et établissements des français dans l'ouest et dans le sud de l'Amérique Septentrionale (1614–1754).* 6 vols. Paris: Imprimerie D. Jouaust, 1876–86.

Masson, L. R., ed. *Les Bourgeois de la Compagnie du Nord-Ouest: Récits de voyages, lettres et rapports inédits relatifs au nord-ouest Canadien.* 2 vols. 1889–90. Reprint, New York: Antiquarian Press, 1960.

McGillivray, Duncan. "Some Account of the Trade Carried on by the Northwest Company." In *Dominion of Canada: Report of the Public Archives of Canada,* 1928. 56–73.

McWilliams, Richebourg Gaillaird, trans. and ed. *Fleur de Lys and Calumet: Being the Pénicaut Narrative of French Adventure in Louisiana.* Baton Rouge: Louisiana State University Press, 1953.

———, trans. and ed. *Iberville's Gulf Journals.* University: University of Alabama Press, 1981.

Meares, John. *Voyages Made in the Years 1788 and 1789, from China to the North West Coast of America . . .* London, 1790.

Mooney, James. *Calendar History of the Kiowa Indians.* Seventeenth Annual Report of the Bureau of American Ethnology, 1895–96. Washington DC: GPO, 1898; reprint, Washington DC: Smithsonian Institution Press, 1979.

Morrow, Baker H., trans. and ed. *A Harvest of Reluctant Souls: The Memorial of Fray Alonso de Benavides, 1630.* Niwot: University of Colorado Press, 1996.

Morton, Arthur S., ed. *Journal of Duncan McGillivray of the North West Company, at Fort George on the Saskatchewan, 1794–95.* Toronto: Macmillan, 1929.

Moulton, Gary E., ed. *The Journals of the Lewis and Clark Expedition.* 13 vols. Lincoln: University of Nebraska Press, 1983–2001.

Mulkearn, Lois, ed. *George Mercer Papers Relating to the Ohio Company of Virginia.* Pittsburgh: University of Pittsburgh Press, 1954.

Nasatir, A. P., ed. *Before Lewis and Clark: Documents Illustrating the History of the Missouri, 1785–1804.* 2 vols. 1952. Reprint, Lincoln: University of Nebraska Press, 1990.

Naylor, Thomas H., and Charles W. Polzer, comps. and eds. *Pedro de Rivera and the Military Regulations for Northern New Spain, 1724–1729: A Documentary History of His Frontier Inspection and the Reglamento de 1729.* Tucson: University of Arizona Press, 1988.

———, comps. and eds. *The Presidio and Militia on the Northern Frontier of New Spain: A Documentary History.* 2 vols. in 3. Tucson: University of Arizona Press, 1986–97.

O'Callaghan, Edmund B., and Berthold Fernow, eds. *Documents Relative to the Colonial History of the State of New York.* 15 vols. Albany NY: Weed, Parson, 1853–87.

Peckham, Howard H., ed. *George Croghan's Journal of His Trip to Detroit in 1767 with His Correspondence Relating Thereto.* Ann Arbor: University of Michigan Press, 1939.

Peyser, Joseph L., trans. and ed. *Letters from New France: The Upper Country 1686–1783.* Urbana: University of Illinois Press, 1992.

Pike, Zebulon Montgomery. *An Account of Expeditions to the Sources of the Mississippi, and through the Western Parts of Louisiana, . . . and a Tour through the Interior Parts of New Spain.* Philadelphia: C. and A. Conrad, 1810. Reprint, New York: Readex Microprint, 1966.

Post, Frederick. "Journal of Christian Frederick Post, from Philadelphia to the Ohio." In Reuben G. Thwaites, ed. *Early Western Travels, 1748–1846.* Vol. 23. Cleveland: Arthur H. Clark, 1904–7.

Pratz, Antoine Le Page du. *The History of Louisiana.* Translated from the French. London, 1774. Reprint, New Orleans: J. S. W. Harmanson, 1947.

Quaife, Milo Milton, ed. *The Western Country in the 17th Century: The Memoirs of Lamothe Cadillac and Pierre Liette.* Chicago: R. R. Donnelley and Sons, 1947.

Reff, Daniel T., ed. *History of the Triumphs of Our Holy Faith amongst the Most Barbarous and Fierce Peoples of the New World by Andrés Pérez de Ribas: An English Translation Based on the 1645 Spanish Original.* Tucson: University of Arizona Press, 1999.

Rich, E. E., ed. *Cumberland House Journals and Inland Journals, 1775–82.* London: Hudson's Bay Record Society, 1952.

———, ed. *Moose Fort Journals, 1783–85.* London: Hudson's Bay Record Society, 1954.

———, ed. *Observations on Hudson's Bay by James Isham.* Toronto: Champlain Society for the Hudson's Bay Record Society, 1949.

Rowland, Dunbar, and A. G. Sanders, eds. *Mississippi Provincial Archives, French Dominion.* Vols. 1–3. Jackson: Mississippi Department of Archives and History, 1927–32.

Rowland, Dunbar, A. G. Sanders, and Patricia Kay Galloway, eds. *Mississippi Provincial Archives, French Dominion.* Vols. 4–5. Baton Rouge: Louisiana State University Press, 1984.

Sheridan, Thomas E., comp. and ed. *Empire of Sand: The Seri Indians and the Struggle for Spanish Sonora, 1645–1803.* Tucson: University of Arizona Press, 1999.

Simpson, Lesley Byrd, ed. *The San Sabá Papers: A Documentary Account of the Founding and Destruction of San Sabá Mission.* 1959. Reprint, Dallas TX: Southern Methodist University Press, 2000.

Smith, Ralph A., trans. and ed. "Account of the Journey of Bénard de La Harpe: Discovery Made by Him of Several Nations Situated in the West." *Southwestern Historical Quarterly* 62 (1958–59): 75–86, 246–59, 371–85, 525–41.

[Smith, William]. *An Historical Account of the Expedition against the Ohio Indians in the Year 1764 under the Command of Henry Bouquet.* Dublin: John Milliken, 1769.

Spanish Archives of New Mexico, 1621–1821. Microfilm reels. State of New Mexico Records Center, Santa Fe.

Stands in Timber, John, and Margot Liberty. *Cheyenne Memories.* Lincoln: University of Nebraska Press, 1972.

Stevens, Sylvester K., et al., eds. *The Papers of Henry Bouquet.* 6 vols. Harrisburg: Pennsylvania Historical Commission, 1972–94.

Stiles, Henry Reed, ed. *Joutel's Journal of La Salle's Last Voyage 1684–1687.* Albany NY: Joseph McDonough, 1906.

Sullivan, James, et al., eds. *The Papers of Sir William Johnson.* 15 vols. Albany: University of the State of New York, 1921–65.

Swanton, John R. *Source Material on the History and Ethnology of the Caddo Indians.* 1942. Reprint, Norman: University of Oklahoma Press, 1996.

Thomas, Alfred Barnaby, ed. *Forgotten Frontiers: A Study of the Spanish Indian*

Policy of Don Juan Bautista de Anza, 1777–1787. Norman: University of Oklahoma Press, 1932.

———, ed. *The Plains Indians and New Mexico, 1751–1778.* Albuquerque: University of New Mexico Press, 1940.

———, trans. and ed. *After Coronado: Spanish Exploration Northeast of New Mexico, 1696–1727.* Norman: University of Oklahoma Press, 1935.

Thwaites, Reuben G., ed. *The Jesuit Relations and Allied Documents: Travels and Explorations of the Jesuit Missionaries in New France 1610–1791.* 73 vols. Cleveland: Burrows Brothers, 1896–1901.

Thwaites, Reuben G., and Louise P. Kellogg, eds. *Frontier Defense on the Upper Ohio, 1777–1778.* Madison: Wisconsin State Historical Society, 1912.

Twitchell, Ralph Emerson, trans. and ed. *The Spanish Archives of New Mexico.* 2 vols. 1914. Reprint, New York: Arno Press, 1976.

Warner, Ted J., ed. *The Domínguez-Escalante Journal: Their Expedition through Colorado, Utah, Arizona, and New Mexico in 1776.* Trans. Angélico Chávez. Salt Lake City: University of Utah Press, 1995.

Weddle, Robert S., et al., eds. and trans. *La Salle, the Mississippi, and the Gulf: Three Primary Documents.* College Station: Texas A & M University Press, 1987.

Wilson, Iris Higbie, trans. and ed. *Noticias de Nutka: An Account of Nootka Sound in 1792 by José Mariano Moziño.* Seattle: University of Washington Press, 1970.

Wood, W. Raymond, and Thomas D. Thiessen, eds. *Early Fur Trade on the Northern Plains: Canadian Traders among the Mandan and Hidatsa Indians, 1738–1818.* Norman: University of Oklahoma Press, 1985.

Worcester, Donald E., trans. and ed. *Instructions for Governing the Interior Provinces of New Spain, 1786 by Bernardo de Gálvez.* Berkeley: Quivira Society, 1951; Albuquerque: University of New Mexico Press, 1951.

Wrong, George M., ed. *The Long Journey to the Country of the Huron by Father Gabriel Sagard.* Toronto: Champlain Society, 1939.

Secondary Sources

Adams, Richard E. W., and Murdo J. MacLeod, eds. *The Cambridge History of the Native Peoples of the Americas.* Vol. 2, *Mesoamerica.* Cambridge: Cambridge University Press, 2000.

Adler, Michael A., ed. *The Prehistoric Pueblo World,* A.D. *1150–1350.* Tucson: University of Arizona Press, 1996.

Albers, Patricia, and Beatrice Medicine, eds. *The Hidden Half: Studies of Plains Indian Women.* Lanham MD: University Press of America, 1983.

Alonso, Ana María. *Thread of Blood: Colonialism, Revolution, and Gender on Mexico's Northern Frontier.* Tucson: University of Arizona Press, 1995.

American Antiquity 66 (January 2001). Special issue on Chaco Canyon.
Ames, Kenneth M., and Herbert D. G. Maschner. *Peoples of the Northwest Coast: Their Archaeology and Prehistory*. London: Thames and Hudson, 1999.
Anderson, Fred. *Crucible of War: The Seven Years' War and the Fate of Empire in British North America, 1754–1766*. New York: Alfred A. Knopf, 2000.
Anderson, Gary Clayton. *The Indian Southwest, 1580–1830: Ethnogenesis and Reinvention, 1580–1830*. Norman: University of Oklahoma Press, 1999.
———. *Kinsmen of Another Kind: Dakota-White Relations in the Upper Mississippi Valley, 1650–1862*. Lincoln: University of Nebraska Press, 1984.
Anson, Bert. *The Miami Indians*. Norman: University of Oklahoma Press, 1970.
Arnold, Morris S. *The Rumble of a Distant Drum: The Quapaws and Old World Newcomers, 1673–1804*. Fayetteville: University of Arkansas Press, 2000.
Aron, Stephen. *How the West Was Lost: The Transformation of Kentucky from Daniel Boone to Henry Clay*. Baltimore MD: Johns Hopkins University Press, 1996.
Bailey, Garrick A. *Changes in Osage Social Organization, 1673–1906*. University of Oregon Anthropological Papers no. 5, 1973.
———, ed. *The Osage and the Invisible World from the Works of Francis La Flesche*. Norman: University of Oklahoma Press, 1995.
Bailey, L. R. *Indian Slave Trade in the Southwest: A Study of Slave-Taking and the Traffic in Indian Captives*. Los Angeles: Westernlore Press, 1966.
Baird, W. David. *The Quapaw Indians: A History of the Downstream People*. Norman: University of Oklahoma Press, 1980.
Bamforth, Douglas B. "Historical Documents and Bison Ecology on the Great Plains." *Plains Anthropologist* 32 (1987): 1–16.
Bannon, John Francis, ed. *Bolton and the Spanish Borderlands*. Norman: University of Oklahoma Press, 1964.
Barrett, Elinore M. *Conquest and Catastrophe: Changing Rio Grande Settlement Patterns in the Sixteenth and Seventeenth Centuries*. Albuquerque: University of New Mexico Press, 2002.
———. "The Geography of the Rio Grande Pueblos in the Seventeenth Century." *Ethnohistory* 49 (2002): 123–69.
Basso, Keith H. *Wisdom Sits in Places: Landscape and Language among the Western Apache*. Albuquerque: University of New Mexico Press, 1996.
Bayer, Laura, with Floyd Montoya and the Pueblo of Santa Ana. *Santa Ana: The People of the Pueblo, and the History of Tamaya*. Albuquerque: University of New Mexico Press, 1994.
Belyea, Barbara. "Amerindian Maps: The Explorer as Translator." *Journal of Historical Geography* 18 (1992): 267–77.
———. "Mapping the Marias: The Interface of Native and Scientific Cartographies." *Great Plains Quarterly* 17 (summer–fall 1997): 165–84.

Bement, Leland C. *Bison Hunting at Cooper Site: Where Lightning Bolts Drew Thundering Herds.* Norman: University of Oklahoma Press, 1999.

Betty, Gerald. "'Skillful in the Management of the Horse': The Comanches as Southern Plains Pastoralists." *Heritage of the Great Plains* 30 (spring–summer 1997): 5–13.

Billington, Ray Allen. *Westward Expansion: A History of the American Frontier.* New York: Macmillan, 1949.

Binnema, Theodore. *Common and Contested Ground: A Human and Environmental History of the Northwestern Plains.* Norman: University of Oklahoma Press, 2001.

Biolsi, Thomas. "Ecological and Cultural Factors in Plains Indian Warfare." In R. Brian Ferguson, ed. *Warfare, Culture and Environment.* New York: Academic Press, 1984.

Blackburn, Thomas C., and Kat Anderson. *Before the Wilderness: Environmental Management by Native Californians.* Menlo Park CA: Ballena Press, 1993.

Blackhawk, Ned. "Violence over the Land: Colonial Encounters in the American Great Basin." Ph.D. diss., University of Washington, 1999.

Blakeslee, Donald J. *Along Ancient Trails: The Mallet Expedition of 1739.* Niwot: University of Colorado Press, 1995.

Blasingham, Emily J. "The Depopulation of the Illinois Indians." *Ethnohistory* 3 (1956): 193–224.

Bolton, Herbert Eugene. *The Hasinais: Southern Caddoans as Seen by the Earliest Europeans.* Norman: University of Oklahoma Press, 1987.

Bouvier, Virginia M. *Women and the Conquest of California, 1542–1840: Codes of Silence.* Tucson: University of Arizona Press, 2001.

Bowers, Alfred. *Hidatsa Social and Ceremonial Organization.* Smithsonian Institution, Bureau of American Ethnology, Bulletin 194. Washington DC: GPO, 1963. Reprint, Lincoln: University of Nebraska Press, 1992.

———. *Mandan Social and Ceremonial Organization.* Chicago: University of Chicago Press, 1950.

Boyd, Robert. *The Coming of the Spirit of Pestilence: Introduced Infectious Diseases and Population Decline among the Northwest Coast Indians, 1774–1874.* Seattle: University of Washington Press, 1999.

Brooks, James L. *Captives and Cousins: Slavery, Kinship, and Community in the Southwest Borderlands.* Chapel Hill: University of North Carolina Press, 2002.

———. "Served Well by Plunder: *La Gran Ladronería* and Producers of History astride the Rio Grande." *American Quarterly* 52 (2000): 23–58.

———. "'This Evil Extends Especially . . . to the Feminine Sex': Negotiating Captivity in the New Mexico Borderlands." *Feminist Studies* 22 (1996): 279–309.

Brown, William R., Jr. "Comanchería Demography, 1805–1830." *Panhandle-Plains Historical Review* 59 (1986): 1–17.

Brugge, David M. *Navajos in the Catholic Church Records of New Mexico, 1694–1875*. Tsaile AZ: Navajo Community College Press, 1985.

Bruhns, Karen Olsen, and Karen E. Stothert. *Women in Ancient America*. Norman: University of Oklahoma Press, 1999.

Bryan, Liz. *The Buffalo People: Prehistoric Archaeology on the Canadian Plains*. Edmonton: University of Alberta Press, 1991.

Busch, Briton C., and Barry M. Gough, eds. *Fur Traders from New England: The Boston Men in the North Pacific, 1787–1800*. Spokane WA: Arthur H. Clark, 1997.

Calloway, Colin G. *The American Revolution in Indian Country: Crisis and Diversity in Native American Communities*. Cambridge: Cambridge University Press, 1995.

———. *Crown and Calumet: British-Indian Relations, 1783–1815*. Norman: University of Oklahoma Press, 1987.

———. *New Worlds for All: Indians, Europeans, and the Remaking of America*. Baltimore MD: Johns Hopkins University Press, 1997.

———. " 'The Only Way Open to Us': The Crow Struggle for Survival in the Nineteenth Century." *North Dakota History* 53 (1986): 25–34.

———. "Snake Frontiers: The Eastern Shoshones in the Eighteenth Century." *Annals of Wyoming* 63 (summer 1991): 82–92.

———. " 'We Have Always Been the Frontier': The American Revolution in Shawnee Country." *American Indian Quarterly* 16 (1992): 39–52.

Carter, Cecile Elkins. *Caddo Indians: Where We Come From*. Norman: University of Oklahoma Press, 1995.

Chatters, James C. *Ancient Encounters: Kennewick Man and the First Americans*. New York: Simon and Schuster, 2001.

Chipman, Donald E. *Spanish Texas, 1519–1821*. Austin: University of Texas Press, 1992.

Clark, Ella E. *Indian Legends from the Northern Rockies*. Norman: University of Oklahoma Press, 1966.

Clark, LaVerne Harrell. *They Sang for Horses: The Impact of the Horse on Navajo and Apache Folklore*. Tucson: University of Arizona Press, 1966.

Cook, Noble David, and W. George Lovell, eds. *"Secret Judgments of God": Old World Disease in Colonial Spanish America*. Norman: University of Oklahoma Press, 1992.

Cook, Sherburne F. *The Conflict between the California Indian and White Civilization*. Berkeley: University of California Press, 1976.

Cook, Warren L. *Flood Tide of Empire: Spain and the Pacific Northwest, 1543–1819*. New Haven CT: Yale University Press, 1973.

Cordell, Linda S. *Ancient Pueblo Peoples.* Washington DC: Smithsonian Institution Press, 1994.

Cronon, William, George Miles, and Jay Gitlin, eds. *Under an Open Sky: Rethinking America's Western Past.* New York: W. W. Norton, 1992.

Crosby, Alfred W. *The Columbian Exchange: Biological and Cultural Consequences of 1492.* Westport CT: Greenwood Press, 1972.

Crow, Joseph Medicine. *From the Heart of the Crow Country: The Crow Indians' Own Stories.* New York: Crown, 1992.

Crown, Patricia L. *Women and Men in the Prehispanic Southwest: Labor, Prestige, and Power.* Santa Fe NM: School of American Research Press, 2001.

Crown, Patricia L., and W. James Judge. *Chaco and Hohokam: Prehistoric Regional Settlements in the American Southwest.* Santa Fe NM: School of American Research Press, 1991.

Cutter, Charles R. *The Legal Culture of Northern New Spain, 1700–1810.* Albuquerque: University of New Mexico Press, 1995.

Cutter, Donald C. *California in 1792: A Spanish Naval Visit.* Norman: University of Oklahoma Press, 1990.

Davis, Leslie B., ed. "Symposium on the Crow-Hidatsa Separations." *Archaeology in Montana* 20, no. 3 (September–December 1979).

Davis, Leslie B., and Michael Wilson, eds. "Bison Procurement and Utilization: A Symposium." *Plains Anthropologist* 23 (1978): pt. 2.

D'Azevedo, Warren L., ed. *Great Basin.* Vol. 11, *Handbook of North American Indians.* William Sturtevant, gen. ed. Washington DC: Smithsonian Institution Press, 1986.

Decker, Jody F. "Depopulation of the Northern Plains Natives." *Social Science and Medicine* 33, no. 4 (1991): 381–93.

———. "Tracing Historical Diffusion Patterns: The Case of the 1780–82 Smallpox Epidemic among the Indians of Western Canada." *Native Studies Review* 4, nos. 1–2 (1988): 1–24.

Delâge, Denys. *Bitter Feast: Amerindians and Europeans in Northeastern North America, 1600–1664.* Vancouver: University of British Columbia Press, 1993.

DeMallie, Raymond J., ed. *Plains.* Vol. 13, *Handbook of North American Indians.* William Sturtevant, gen. ed. Washington DC: Smithsonian Institution Press, 2001.

DeVoto, Bernard. *The Course of Empire.* 1952. Reprint, Boston: Houghton Mifflin, 1980.

Diamond, Jared. *Guns, Germs, and Steel: The Fates of Human Societies.* New York: W. W. Norton, 1997.

Dillehay, Thomas D. *The Settlement of the Americas: A New Prehistory.* New York: Basic Books, 2000.

Din, Gilbert C., and A. P. Nasatir. *The Imperial Osages: Spanish-Indian Diplomacy in the Mississippi Valley.* Norman: University of Oklahoma Press, 1983.

Dixon, E. James. *Bones, Boats, and Bison: Archaeology and the First Colonization of Western North America.* Albuquerque: University of New Mexico Press, 1999.

Dobyns, Henry F. "Puebloan Historic Demographic Trends." *Ethnohistory* 49 (2002): 171–204.

Dowd, Gregory Evans. *A Spirited Resistance: The North American Indian Struggle for Unity, 1745–1815.* Baltimore MD: Johns Hopkins University Press, 1992.

———. *War under Heaven: Pontiac, the Indian Nations, and the British Empire.* Baltimore MD: Johns Hopkins University Press, 2002.

Downes, Randolph C. *Council Fires on the Upper Ohio: A Narrative of Indian Affairs in the Upper Ohio Valley until 1795.* Pittsburgh: University of Pittsburgh Press, 1940.

Duke, Philip. *Points in Time: Structure and Event in a Late Northern Plains Hunting Society.* Niwot: University of Colorado Press, 1999.

Duncan, David Ewing. *Hernando de Soto: A Savage Quest in the Americas.* New York: Crown, 1995.

DuVal, Kathleen. "The Education of Fernando de Leyba: Quapaws and Spaniards on the Border of Empires." *Arkansas Historical Quarterly* 60 (2001): 1–29.

Early, Ann M. "The Caddos of the Trans-Mississippi South." In Bonnie G. McEwan, ed. *Indians of the Greater Southeast: Historical Archaeology and Ethnohistory.* Gainesville: University Press of Florida, 2000.

Ebright, Malcolm. "Advocates for the Oppressed: Indians, Genízaros and Their Spanish Advocates in New Mexico, 1700–1786." *New Mexico Historical Review* 71 (1996): 305–39.

Eccles, William J. *The Canadian Frontier, 1534–1760.* Albuquerque: University of New Mexico Press, 1974.

———. *Essays on New France.* Toronto: Oxford University Press, 1987.

———. *France in America.* New York: Harper and Row, 1972.

Echo-Hawk, Roger C. "Ancient History in the New World: Integrating Oral Traditions and the Archaeological Record." *American Antiquity* 65 (2000): 267–90.

Edmunds, R. David. *The Potawatomis: Keepers of the Fire.* Norman: University of Oklahoma Press, 1978.

———, ed. *American Indian Leaders: Studies in Diversity.* Lincoln: University of Nebraska Press, 1980.

Edmunds, R. David, and Joseph L. Peyser. *The Fox Wars: The Mesquakie Challenge to New France.* Norman: University of Oklahoma Press, 1993.

Eid, Leroy V. "The Ojibwa-Iroquois War: The War the Five Nations Did Not Win." *Ethnohistory* 26 (1979): 297–324.

Emerson, Thomas E. *Cahokia and the Archaeology of Power.* Tuscaloosa: University of Alabama Press, 1997.

Emerson, Thomas E., and R. Barry Lewis, eds. *Cahokia and the Hinterlands:*

Middle Mississippian Cultures of the Midwest. Urbana: University of Illinois Press, 1991.

Ewers, John C. *The Blackfeet, Raiders of the Northwestern Plains.* Norman: University of Oklahoma Press, 1958.

———. *The Horse in Blackfoot Indian Culture, with Comparative Material from Other Tribes.* 1955. Reprint, Washington DC: Smithsonian Institution Press, 1969.

———. *Indian Life on the Upper Missouri.* Norman: University of Oklahoma Press, 1968.

———. "The Influence of Epidemics on the Indian Populations and Cultures of Texas." *Plains Anthropologist* 18 (1973): 104–15.

———. "Intertribal Warfare as the Precursor of Indian-White Warfare on the Northern Great Plains." *Western Historical Quarterly* 6 (1975): 397–410.

Fagan, Brian M. *Ancient North America: The Archaeology of a Continent.* 3rd ed. London: Thames and Hudson, 2000.

———. *Floods, Famines and Emperors: El Niño and the Fate of Civilizations.* New York: Basic Books, 1999.

Faragher, John Mack. *Daniel Boone: The Life and Legend of an American Pioneer.* New York: Henry Holt, 1992.

Faulk, Odie B. "The Comanche Invasion of Texas, 1743–1836." *Great Plains Journal* 9 (1969): 10–50.

Fenn, Elizabeth A. "Biological Warfare in Eighteenth-Century North America: Beyond Jeffery Amherst." *Journal of American History* 86 (2000): 1552–80.

———. *Pox Americana: The Great North American Smallpox Epidemic of 1775–1782.* New York: Hill and Wang, 2001.

Fisher, Robin. *Contact and Conflict: Indian-European Relations in British Columbia, 1774–1890.* Vancouver: University of British Columbia Press, 1977.

Flannery, Tim. *The Eternal Frontier: An Ecological History of North America and Its Peoples.* New York: Atlantic Monthly Press, 2001.

Fletcher, Alice C., and Francis La Flesche. *The Omaha Tribe.* 2 vols. 1911. Reprint, Lincoln: University of Nebraska Press, 1972.

Flint, Richard, and Shirley Cushing Flint, eds. *The Coronado Expedition to Tierra Nueva: The 1540–1542 Route across the Southwest.* Niwot: University of Colorado Press, 1997.

Flores, Dan. "Bison Ecology and Bison Diplomacy: The Southern Plains 1800–1850." *Journal of American History* 78 (1991): 469.

———. *Caprock Canyonlands.* Austin: University of Texas Press, 1990.

———. *Horizontal Yellow: Nature and History in the Near Southwest.* Albuquerque: University of New Mexico Press, 1999.

———. *The Natural West: Environmental History in the Great Plains and Rocky Mountains.* Norman: University of Oklahoma Press, 2001.

Foley, William E., and C. David Rice. *The First Chouteaus: River Barons of Early St. Louis.* Urbana: University of Illinois Press, 1983.

Folsom, Franklin. *Red Power on the Rio Grande.* 1973. Reprint, Albuquerque: University of New Mexico Press, 1996.

Forbes, Jack D. *Apache, Navaho, and Spaniard.* Norman: University of Oklahoma Press, 1960.

———. *Warriors of the Colorado: The Yumans of the Quechan Nation and Their Neighbors.* Norman: University of Oklahoma Press, 1965.

Ford, Richard I., ed. *Prehistoric Food Production in North America.* Anthropological Papers no. 75, Museum of Anthropology, University of Michigan, Ann Arbor, 1985.

Foster, William C. *Spanish Expeditions into Texas, 1689–1768.* Austin: University of Texas Press, 1995.

Francis, Julie E., and Loendorf, Lawrence L. *Ancient Visions: Petroglyphs and Pictographs from the Wind River and Bighorn Country, Wyoming and Montana.* Salt Lake City: University of Utah Press, 2002.

Frank, Ross. *From Settler to Citizen: New Mexican Economic Development and the Creation of Vecino Society, 1750–1820.* Berkeley: University of California Press, 2000.

Frazier, Kendrick. *People of Chaco: A Canyon and Its Culture.* Rev. ed. New York: W. W. Norton, 1999.

Frison, George C. *Prehistoric Hunters of the High Plains.* 2nd ed. San Diego: Academic Press, 1991.

Galloway, Patricia K. *Choctaw Genesis, 1500–1700.* Lincoln: University of Nebraska Press, 1995.

———, ed. *The Hernando de Soto Expedition: History, Historiography, and "Discovery" in the Southeast.* Lincoln: University of Nebraska Press, 1997.

———, ed. *La Salle and His Legacy: Frenchmen and Indians in the Lower Mississippi Valley.* Jackson: University of Mississippi Press, 1982.

Gelo, Daniel J. " 'Comanche Land and Ever Has Been': A Native Geography of the Nineteenth-Century Comanchería." *Southwestern Historical Quarterly* 111 (2000): 273–307.

Gero, Joan M., and Margaret W. Conkey, eds. *Engendering Archaeology: Women and Prehistory.* Oxford: Basil Blackwell, 1991.

Gibson, Arrell M. *The Kickapoos: Lords of the Middle Border.* Norman: University of Oklahoma Press, 1963.

Gibson, James R. *Otter Skins, Boston Ships, and China Goods: The Maritime Fur Trade of the Northwest Coast, 1785–1841.* Montreal: McGill-Queens University Press; Seattle: University of Washington Press, 1992.

Goetzmann, William H., and Glyndwr Williams. *The Atlas of North American Exploration: From the Norse Voyages to the Race to the Pole.* Norman: University of Oklahoma Press, 1998.

Grant, John Webster. *Moon of Wintertime: Missionaries and the Indians of Canada in Encounter since 1534*. Toronto: University of Toronto Press, 1984.

Grayson, Donald K. *The Desert's Past: A Natural Prehistory of the Great Basin.* Washington DC: Smithsonian Institution Press, 1993.

Griffen, William B. *Apaches at War and Peace: The Janos Presidio, 1750–1858.* Norman: University of Oklahoma Press, 1988.

Gumerman, George J., ed. *The Anasazi in a Changing Environment.* Cambridge: Cambridge University Press, 1988.

———, ed. *Exploring the Hohokam: Prehistoric Desert Peoples of the American Southwest.* Albuquerque: University of New Mexico Press, 1991.

———, ed. *Themes in Southwest Prehistory.* Santa Fe NM: School of American Research Press, 1994.

Gutiérrez, Ramón A. *When Jesus Came, the Corn Mothers Went Away: Marriage, Sexuality, and Power in New Mexico, 1500–1846.* Stanford CA: Stanford University Press, 1991.

Guy, Donna J., and Thomas E. Sheridan, eds. *Contested Ground: Comparative Frontiers on the Northern and Southern Edges of the Spanish Empire.* Tucson: University of Arizona Press, 1998.

Haines, Francis. *The Buffalo: The Story of American Bison and Their Hunters from Prehistoric Times to the Present.* 1970. Reprint, Norman: University of Oklahoma Press, 1995.

Hall, Robert L. *An Archaeology of the Soul: North American Indian Belief and Ritual.* Urbana: University of Illinois Press, 1997.

Hall, Thomas D. *Social Change in the Southwest, 1350–1880.* Lawrence: University Press of Kansas, 1988.

Hämäläinen, Pekka. "The Comanche Empire: A Study of Indigenous Power, 1700–1875." Ph.D. diss., University of Helsinki, 2001.

———. "The First Phase of Destruction: Killing the Southern Plains Buffalo, 1790–1840." *Great Plains Quarterly* 21 (2001): 101–14.

———. "The Western Comanche Trade Center: Rethinking the Plains Indian Trade System." *Western Historical Quarterly* 29 (1998): 485–513.

Harper [John], Elizabeth Ann. "The Taovayas Indians in Frontier Trade and Diplomacy, 1719–1768." *Chronicles of Oklahoma* 31 (1953): 268–89.

Harris, R. Cole, ed. *Historical Atlas of Canada.* Vol. 1, *From the Beginning to 1800.* Toronto: University of Toronto Press, 1987.

Harrod, Howard L. *The Animals Came Dancing: Native American Sacred Ecology and Animal Kinship.* Tucson: University of Arizona Press, 2000.

———. *Renewing the World: Plains Indian Religion and Morality.* Tucson: University of Arizona Press, 1987.

Haynes, Gary. *The Early Settlement of North America: The Clovis Era.* Cambridge: Cambridge University Press, 2002.

Heizer, Robert F., ed. *California.* Vol. 8, *Handbook of North American Indians.*

William Sturtevant, gen. ed. Washington DC: Smithsonian Institution Press, 1978.

Helm, June, ed. *Subarctic*. Vol. 6, *Handbook of North American Indians*. William Sturtevant, gen. ed. Washington DC: Smithsonian Institution Press, 1981.

Hickerson, Daniel A. "Historical Processes, Epidemic Disease, and the Formation of the Hasinai Confederacy." *Ethnohistory* 44 (1997): 31–52.

———. "Trade, Mediation, and Political Status in the Hasinai Confederacy." *Research in Economic Anthropology* 17 (1996): 149–68.

Hickerson, Nancy Parrott. *The Jumanos: Hunters and Traders of the South Plains*. Austin: University of Texas Press, 1994.

Hinderaker, Eric. *Elusive Empires: Constructing Colonialism in the Ohio Valley, 1673–1800*. Cambridge: Cambridge University Press, 1997.

Holder, Preston. *The Hoe and the Horse on the Plains: A Study of Cultural Development among North American Indians*. Lincoln: University of Nebraska Press, 1970.

Horgan, Paul. *Great River: The Rio Grande in North American History*. Hanover NH: University Press of New England for Wesleyan University Press, 1984.

Howard, David A. *Conquistador in Chains: Cabeza de Vaca and the Indians of the Americas*. Tuscaloosa: University of Alabama Press, 1997.

Hu-DeHart, Evelyn. *Missionaries, Miners, and Indians: Spanish Contact with the Yaqui Nation of Northwestern New Spain 1533–1820*. Tucson: University of Arizona Press, 1981.

Hudson, Charles. *Knights of Spain, Warriors of the Sun: Hernando de Soto and the South's Ancient Chiefdoms*. Athens: University of Georgia Press, 1997.

Hunt, George T. *The Wars of the Iroquois: A Study in Intertribal Relations*. Madison: University of Wisconsin Press, 1940.

Hurt, Douglas A. "Brothers of Influence: Auguste and Pierre Chouteau and the Osages before 1804." *Chronicles of Oklahoma* 78 (2000): 260–77.

Hurt, R. Douglas. *Indian Agriculture in America: Prehistory to the Present*. Lawrence: University Press of Kansas, 1987.

Hurtado, Albert L. "Sexuality in California's Franciscan Missions: Cultural Perceptions and Sad Realities." *California History* 71 (1992): 371–85.

Hyde, George E. *Indians of the High Plains: From the Prehistoric Period to the Coming of Europeans*. Norman: University of Oklahoma Press, 1959.

———. *The Pawnee Indians*. Norman: University of Oklahoma Press, 1951.

Isenberg, Andrew C. *The Destruction of the Bison: An Environmental History, 1750–1920*. Cambridge: Cambridge University Press, 2000.

Ivey, James. " 'The Greatest Misfortune of All': Famine in the Province of New Mexico, 1667–1672." *Journal of the Southwest* 36 (1994): 76–100.

Jablow, Joseph. *The Cheyenne in Plains Indian Trade Relations, 1795–1840*. 1951. Reprint, Lincoln: University of Nebraska Press, 1994.

Jackson, Robert H. *From Savages to Subjects: Missions in the History of the American Southwest*. Armonk NY: M. E. Sharpe, 2000.

———. *Indian Population Decline: The Missions of Northwestern New Spain, 1687–1840.* Albuquerque: University of New Mexico Press, 1994.

Jackson, Robert H., and Edward Castillo. *Indians, Franciscans, and Spanish Colonization: The Impact of the Mission System on California Indians.* Albuquerque: University of New Mexico Press, 1995.

Jensen, Joan M., and Darlis A. Miller, eds. *New Mexico Women: Intercultural Perspectives.* Albuquerque: University of New Mexico Press, 1986.

Johannessen, Sissel, and Christine Hastorf, eds. *Corn and Culture in the Prehistoric New World.* Boulder CO: Westview Press, 1994.

John, Elizabeth A. H. *Storms Brewed in Other Men's Worlds: The Confrontation of Indians, Spanish, and French in the Southwest, 1540–1795.* Lincoln: University of Nebraska Press, 1975.

Jones, Oakah L., Jr. *Los Paisanos: Spanish Settlers on the Frontier of New Spain.* 2nd ed. Norman: University of Oklahoma Press, 1979.

———. *Nueva Vizcaya: Heartland of the Spanish Frontier.* Albuquerque: University of New Mexico Press, 1988.

———. *Pueblo Warriors and Spanish Conquest.* Norman: University of Oklahoma Press, 1966.

———. "Rescue and Ransom of Spanish Captives from the *indios bárbaros* on the Northern Frontier of New Spain." *Colonial Latin American Historical Review* 4 (1995): 129–48.

Josephy, Alvin M., ed. *America in 1492: The World of the Indian Peoples before the Arrival of Columbus.* New York: Random House, 1991.

———. *The Nez Perce Indians and the Opening of the Northwest.* New Haven CT: Yale University Press, 1965.

Journal of Anthropological Archaeology 14 (June 1995). Catherine M. Cameron, guest ed. Special issue on migration and movement in the Southwest.

Kavanagh, Thomas W. *The Comanches: A History, 1706–1875.* Lincoln: University of Nebraska Press, 1999.

Kennedy, Roger G. *Hidden Cities: The Discovery and Loss of Ancient North American Civilization.* New York: Penguin, 1994.

Kenner, Charles L. *The Comanchero Frontier: A History of New Mexican–Plains Indian Relations.* Norman: University of Oklahoma Press, 1969.

Kessell, John L. *Kiva, Cross, and Crown: The Pecos Indians and New Mexico, 1540–1840.* 2nd ed. Albuquerque: University of New Mexico Press, 1987.

———. *Spain in the Southwest: A Narrative History of Colonial New Mexico, Arizona, Texas, and California.* Norman: University of Oklahoma Press, 2002.

Key, Joseph Patrick. "'Masters of This Country': The Quapaws and Environmental Change in Arkansas, 1673–1833." Ph.D. diss., University of Arkansas, 2001.

Keyser, James D., and Michael A. Klassen. *Plains Indian Rock Art.* Seattle: University of Washington Press, 2001.

Kiva: The Journal of Southwestern Anthropology and History 66 (fall 2000). Mark D. Varien, ed. Special issue on environmental change, agriculture, and population movement.

Knaut, Andrew L. *The Pueblo Revolt of 1680: Conquest and Resistance in Seventeenth-Century New Mexico.* Norman: University of Oklahoma Press, 1995.

Krech, Shepard, III. *The Ecological Indian: Myth and History.* New York: W. W. Norton, 1999.

Lang, William L., and Robert C. Carriker, eds. *Great River of the West: Essays on the Columbia River.* Seattle: University of Washington Press, 1999.

Lankford, George E. "Shawnee Convergence: Immigrant Indians in the Ozarks." *Arkansas Historical Quarterly* 58 (1999): 390–413.

La Vere, David. "Between Kinship and Capitalism: French and Spanish Rivalry in the Colonial Louisiana-Texas Indian Trade." *Journal of Southern History* 64 (1988): 197–218.

———. *The Caddo Chiefdoms: Caddo Economics and Politics, 700–1835.* Lincoln: University of Nebraska Press, 1998.

———. "Friendly Persuasions: Gifts and Reciprocity in Comanche-Euroamerican Relations." *Chronicles of Oklahoma* 71 (1993): 322–37.

LeBlanc, Steven A. *Prehistoric Warfare in the American Southwest.* Salt Lake City: University of Utah Press, 1998.

Lekson, Stephen H. *The Chaco Meridian: Centers of Political Power in the Southwest.* Walnut Creek CA: Altamira Press, 1999.

Levine, Frances. *Our Prayers Are in This Place: Pecos Identity over the Centuries.* Albuquerque: University of New Mexico Press, 1999.

Levy, Jerrold E. *In the Beginning: The Navajo Genesis.* Berkeley: University of California Press, 1998.

Lewis, G. Malcolm, ed. *Cartographic Encounters: Perspectives on Native American Mapmaking and Map Use.* Chicago: University of Chicago Press, 1998.

———. "Indian Maps: Their Place in the History of Plains Cartography." *Great Plains Quarterly* 4 (1984): 91–108.

Lowie, Robert H. *The Crow Indians.* New York: Farrar and Rinehart, 1935.

MacLeod, D. Peter. "The Anishinabeg Point of View: The History of the Great Lakes Region to 1800 in Nineteenth-Century Mississauga, Odawa, and Ojibwa Historiography." *Canadian Historical Review* 73 (1992): 195–201.

Magnaghi, Russell M. *Indian Slavery, Labor, Evangelization, and Captivity in the Americas: An Annotated Bibliography.* Lanham MD: Scarecrow Press, 1998.

———. "Plains Indians in New Mexico: The Genízaro Experience." *Great Plains Quarterly* 10 (1990): 86–95.

Makarova, Raisa V. *Russians on the Pacific 1743–1799.* Trans. and ed. Richard A. Pierce and Alton S. Donnelly. Kingston, Ontario: Limestone Press, 1975.

Malloy, Mary. *"Boston Men" on the Northwest Coast: The American Maritime Fur Trade 1788–1844*. Kingston, Ontario: Limestone Press, 1998.

Martin, Paul S., and Richard G. Klein, eds. *Quaternary Extinctions: A Prehistoric Revolution*. Tucson: University of Arizona Press, 1984.

Martin, Paul S., and Christine R. Szuter. "War Zones and Game Sinks in Lewis and Clark's West." *Conservation Biology* 13 (winter 1999): 36–45.

Mathews, John J. *The Osages: Children of the Middle Waters*. Norman: University of Oklahoma Press, 1961.

Matson, R. G. *The Origins of Southwestern Agriculture*. Tucson: University of Arizona Press, 1991.

McConnell, Michael N. *A Country Between: The Upper Ohio Valley and Its Peoples, 1724–1774*. Lincoln: University of Nebraska Press, 1992.

McCoy, Ronald T. "Winter Count: The Teton Chronicles to 1700." Ph.D. diss., Northern Arizona University, 1983.

McDonald, Dedra S. "Intimacy and Empire: Indian-African Interaction in Spanish Colonial New Mexico, 1500–1800." *American Indian Quarterly* 22 (winter–spring 1998): 134–35.

McNitt, Frank. *Navajo Wars: Military Campaigns, Slave Raids and Reprisals*. Albuquerque: University of New Mexico Press, 1972.

McPhee, John. *Basin and Range*. New York: Farrar, Straus and Giroux, 1980.

———. *Rising from the Plains*. New York: Farrar, Straus and Giroux, 1986.

———. *The Survival of the Bark Canoe*. New York: Farrar, Straus and Giroux, 1975.

Meredith, Howard. *Dancing on Common Ground: Tribal Cultures and Alliances on the Southern Plains*. Lawrence: University Press of Kansas, 1995.

Merrell, James H. *Into the American Woods: Negotiators on the Pennsylvania Frontier*. New York: W. W. Norton, 1999.

Meyer, Roy W. *The Village Indians of the Upper Missouri*. Lincoln: University of Nebraska Press, 1977.

Milloy, John S. *The Plains Cree: Trade, Diplomacy and War, 1790 to 1870*. Winnipeg: University of Manitoba Press, 1988.

Milner, George R. *The Cahokia Chiefdom: The Archaeology of a Mississippian Society*. Washington DC: Smithsonian Institution Press, 1998.

Minnis, Paul E., and Wayne J. Elisens, eds. *Biodiversity and Native America*. Norman: University of Oklahoma Press, 2000.

Momaday, N. Scott. *The Man Made of Words*. New York: St. Martin's Press, 1997.

———. *The Way to Rainy Mountain*. Albuquerque: University of New Mexico Press, 1969.

Moodie, D. W., and Barry Kaye. "The Ac Ko Mok Ki Map." *Beaver* (spring 1977): 5–15.

Moore, John H. *The Cheyenne*. Cambridge MA: Basil Blackwell, 1996.

———. *The Cheyenne Nation: A Social and Demographic History.* Lincoln: University of Nebraska Press, 1987.

Moorehead, Max L. *The Apache Frontier: Jacobo Ugarte and Spanish-Indian Relations in Northern New Spain, 1769–1791.* Norman: University of Oklahoma Press, 1968.

———. *New Mexico's Royal Road: Trade and Travel on the Chihuahua Trail.* Norman: University of Oklahoma Press, 1958.

———. *The Presidio: Bastion of the Spanish Borderlands.* Norman: University of Oklahoma Press, 1975, 1991.

———. "Spanish Deportation of Hostile Apaches: The Policy and the Practice." *Arizona and the West* 17 (1975): 205–20.

Morris, John Miller. *El Llano Estacado: Exploration and Imagination on the High Plains of Texas and New Mexico, 1536–1860.* Austin: Texas State Historical Association, 1997.

Nabokov, Peter. *A Forest of Time: American Indian Ways of History.* Cambridge: Cambridge University Press, 2002.

———. *Two Leggings: The Making of a Crow Warrior.* 1967. Reprint, Lincoln: University of Nebraska Press, 1982.

Nabokov, Peter, and Robert Easton. *Native American Architecture.* New York: Oxford University Press, 1989.

Naranjo, Tessie. "Thoughts on Migration by Santa Clara Pueblo." *Journal of Anthropological Archaeology* 14 (1995): 247–50.

Nelson, Margaret C. *Mimbres during the Twelfth Century: Abandonment, Continuity, and Reorganization.* Tucson: University of Arizona Press, 1999.

Newkumet, Vynola Beaver, and Howard L. Meredith. *Hasinai: A Traditional History of the Caddo Confederacy.* College Station: Texas A & M University Press, 1988.

Noble, David Grant, ed. *New Light on Chaco Canyon.* Santa Fe NM: School of American Research Press, 1984.

Norall, Frank. *Bourgmont, Explorer of the Missouri 1698–1725.* Lincoln: University of Nebraska Press, 1988.

Noyes, Stanley. *Los Comanches: The Horse People, 1751–1845.* Albuquerque: University of New Mexico Press, 1993.

Ortiz, Alfonso. *The Pueblo.* New York: Chelsea House, 1994.

———, ed. *Southwest.* Vols. 9–10, *Handbook of North American Indians.* William Sturtevant, gen. ed. Washington DC: Smithsonian Institution Press, 1979, 1983.

O'Shea, John M., and John Ludwickson. *Archaeology and Ethnohistory of the Omaha Indians: The Big Village Site.* Lincoln: University of Nebraska Press, 1992.

Owsley, Douglas W., and Richard L. Jantz, eds. *Skeletal Biology in the Great Plains: Migration, Warfare, Health, and Subsistence.* Washington DC: Smithsonian Institution Press, 1994.

Pagdon, Anthony. *Lords of All the World: Ideologies of Empire in Spain, Britain and France, c. 1500–c. 1800.* New Haven CT: Yale University Press, 1995.

Parks, Douglas R., ed. *Ceremonies of the Pawnee by James R. Murie.* Lincoln: University of Nebraska Press, 1989.

Parks, Douglas R., and Waldo R. Wedel. "Pawnee Geography: Historical and Sacred." *Great Plains Quarterly* 5 (1985): 143–76.

Pauketat, Timothy R. *The Ascent of Chiefs: Cahokia and Mississippian Politics in North America.* Tuscaloosa: University of Alabama Press, 1994.

Pauketat, Timothy R., and Thomas E. Emerson, eds. *Cahokia: Domination and Ideology in the Mississippian World.* Lincoln: University of Nebraska Press, 1997.

Perttula, Timothy K. *The Caddo Nation: Archaeological and Ethnohistoric Perspectives.* Austin: University of Texas Press, 1992.

Peters, Virginia Bergman. *Women of the Earth Lodges: Tribal Life on the Plains.* New Haven CT: Archon Books, 1995.

Plog, Stephen. *Ancient Peoples of the Ancient Southwest.* London: Thames and Hudson, 1997.

Poling-Kempes, Lesley. *Valley of Shining Stone: The Story of Abiquiu.* Tucson: University of Arizona Press, 1997.

Powell, Philip Wayne. *Soldiers, Indians, and Silver: The Northward Advance of New Spain, 1550–1600.* Los Angeles: University of California Press, 1952.

Powell, Shirley, and George J. Gumerman. *People of the Mesa: The Archaeology of Black Mesa, Arizona.* Carbondale: Southern Illinois University Press, 1987.

Preucel, Robert W., ed. *Archaeologies of the Pueblo Revolt: Identity, Meaning, and Renewal in the Pueblo World.* Albuquerque: University of New Mexico Press, 2002.

Price, Catherine. "The Comanche Threat to Texas and New Mexico in the Eighteenth Century and the Development of Spanish Indian Policy." *Journal of the West* 44, no. 2 (1985): 34–45.

Price, T. Douglas, and Anne Birgette Gebauer, eds. *Last Hunters, First Farmers: New Perspectives on the Prehistoric Transition to Agriculture.* Santa Fe NM: School of American Research Press, 1995.

Rabasa, José. *Writing Violence on the Northern Frontier: The Historiography of Sixteenth-Century New Mexico and Florida and the Legacy of Conquest.* Durham NC: Duke University Press, 2000.

Radding, Cynthia. *Wandering Peoples: Colonialism, Ethnic Spaces, and Ecological Frontiers in Northwestern New Mexico, 1700–1850.* Durham NC: Duke University Press, 1997.

Ramenofsky, Ann F. *Vectors of Death: The Archaeology of European Contact.* Albuquerque: University of New Mexico Press, 1987.

Ray, Arthur J. *Indians in the Fur Trade: Their Role as Hunters, Trappers, and*

Middlemen in the Lands Southwest of Hudson Bay, 1660–1870. Toronto: University of Toronto Press, 1974.

Reff, Daniel T. *Disease, Depopulation, and Culture Change in Northwestern New Spain, 1518–1764.* Salt Lake City: University of Utah Press, 1991.

———. "The 'Predicament of Culture' and Spanish Missionary Accounts of the Tepehuan and Pueblo Revolts." *Ethnohistory* 42 (1995): 63–90.

Reid, Jefferson, and Stephanie Whittlesey. *The Archaeology of Ancient Arizona.* Tucson: University of Arizona Press, 1997.

Richter, Daniel K. *The Ordeal of the Longhouse: The Peoples of the Iroquois League in the Era of European Colonization.* Chapel Hill: University of North Carolina Press, 1992.

Riley, Carroll L. *The Kachina and the Cross: Indians and Spaniards in the Early Southwest.* Salt Lake City: University of Utah Press, 1999.

———. *Rio del Norte: People of the Upper Rio Grande from Earliest Times to the Pueblo Revolt.* Salt Lake City: University of Utah Press, 1995.

Roe, Frank Gilbert. *The Indian and the Horse.* Norman: University of Oklahoma Press, 1955.

———. *The North American Buffalo: A Critical Study of the Species in Its Wild State.* Toronto: University of Toronto Press, 1970.

Rollings, Willard H. *The Osage: An Ethnohistorical Study of Hegemony on the Prairie-Plains.* Columbia: University of Missouri Press, 1992.

Ronda, James P. " 'A Chart in His Way': Indian Cartography and the Lewis and Clark Expedition." *Great Plains Quarterly* 4 (1984): 43–53.

———. *Finding the West: Explorations with Lewis and Clark.* Albuquerque: University of New Mexico Press, 2001.

———. *Jefferson's West: A Journey with Lewis and Clark.* N.p.: Thomas Jefferson Foundation, 2000.

———. *Lewis and Clark among the Indians.* Lincoln: University of Nebraska Press, 1984.

———, ed. *Revealing America: Image and Imagination in the Exploration of North America.* Lexington MA: D. C. Heath, 1996.

Ruby, Robert H., and John A. Brown. *The Cayuse Indians.* Norman: University of Oklahoma Press, 1972.

———. *The Chinook Indians: Traders of the Lower Columbia River.* Norman: University of Oklahoma Press, 1976.

———. *Indian Slavery in the Pacific Northwest.* Spokane WA: Arthur H. Clark, 1993.

Rushforth, Scott, and Steadman Upham. *A Hopi Social History: Anthropological Perspectives on Sociocultural Persistence and Change.* Austin: University of Texas Press, 1992.

Russell, Dale R. *Eighteenth-Century Western Cree and Their Neighbours.* Hull, Quebec: Canadian Museum of Civilization, 1991.

Sabo, George, III. "Encounters and Images: European Contact and Caddo Indians." *Historical Reflections* 21 (1995): 217–42.

———. "The Quapaw Indians of Arkansas, 1673–1803." In Bonnie G. McEwan, ed. *Indians of the Greater Southeast: Historical Archaeology and Ethnohistory.* Gainesville: University Press of Florida, 2000.

———. "Rituals of Encounter: Interpreting Native American Views of European Explorers." *Arkansas Historical Quarterly* 51 (1992): 54–68.

Salmon, Roberto Mario. *Indian Revolts in Northern New Spain: A Synthesis of Resistance (1680–1786).* Lanham MD: University Press of America, 1991.

Salomon, Frank, and Stuart B. Schwartz, eds. *The Cambridge History of the Native Peoples of the Americas.* Vol. 3, *South America.* Cambridge: Cambridge University Press, 2000.

Sánchez, Joseph P. *Explorers, Traders, and Slavers: Forging the Old Spanish Trail, 1678–1850.* Salt Lake City: University of Utah Press, 1997.

Sando, Joe S. *Pueblo Nations: Eight Centuries of Pueblo Indian History.* Santa Fe NM: Clear Light Publishers, 1992.

Santiago, Mark. *Massacre at the Yuma Crossing: Spanish Relations with the Quechans, 1779–1782.* Tucson: University of Arizona Press, 1998.

Schaafsma, Curtis F. *Apaches de Navajo: Seventeenth-Century Navajos in the Chama Valley.* Salt Lake City: University of Utah Press, 2002.

Schaafsma, Curtis F., and Carroll L. Riley, eds. *The Casas Grandes World.* Salt Lake City: University of Utah Press, 1999.

Schaafsma, Polly. *The Rock Art of Utah: A Study from the Donald Scott Collection.* 1971. Reprint, Salt Lake City: University of Utah Press, 1994.

Schiltz, Thomas F., and Donald E. Worcester. "The Spread of Firearms among the Indian Tribes on the Northern Frontier of New Spain." *American Indian Quarterly* 11 (1987): 1–10.

Schlesier, Karl H., ed. *Plains Indians, A.D. 500–1500: The Archaeological Past of Historical Groups.* Norman: University of Oklahoma Press, 1994.

———. *The Wolves of Heaven: Cheyenne Shamanism, Ceremonies, and Prehistoric Origins.* Norman: University of Oklahoma Press, 1987.

Scofield, John. *Hail, Columbia: Robert Gray, John Hendrick, and the Pacific Fur Trade.* Portland: Oregon Historical Society Press, 1993.

Sebastian, Lynne. *The Chaco Anasazi: Sociopolitical Evolution in the Prehistoric Southwest.* Cambridge: Cambridge University Press, 1992.

Secoy, Frank R. *Changing Military Patterns of the Great Plains Indians.* 1953. Reprint, Lincoln: University of Nebraska Press, 1992.

Seed, Patricia. *Ceremonies of Possession in Europe's Conquest of the New World, 1492–1640.* Cambridge: Cambridge University Press, 1995.

Simmons, Marc. *Coronado's Land: Daily Life in Colonial New Mexico.* Albuquerque: University of New Mexico Press, 1991.

———. *The Last Conquistador: Juan de Oñate and the Settling of the Far Southwest.* Norman: University of Oklahoma Press, 1991.

———. "New Mexico's Smallpox Epidemic of 1780–81." *New Mexico Historical Review* 41 (1966): 319–26.

———. *Spanish Pathways: Readings in the History of Hispanic New Mexico.* Albuquerque: University of New Mexico Press, 2001.

Sleeper-Smith, Susan. *Indian Women and French Men: Rethinking Cultural Encounter in the Western Great Lakes.* Amherst: University of Massachusetts Press, 2001.

Smith, F. Todd. *The Caddo Indians: Tribes at the Convergence of Empires, 1542–1854.* College Station: Texas A & M University Press, 1995.

———. *The Wichita Indians: Traders of Texas and the Southern Plains, 1540–1845.* College Station: Texas A & M University Press, 2000.

Sosin, Jack M. *Whitehall and the Wilderness: The Middle West in British Colonial Policy, 1760–1775.* Lincoln: University of Nebraska Press, 1961.

Spicer, Edward H. *Cycles of Conquest: The Impact of Spain, Mexico, and the United States on the Indians of the Southwest, 1533–1960.* Tucson: University of Arizona Press, 1962.

———. *The Yaquis: A Cultural History.* Tucson: University of Arizona Press, 1980.

Spielmann, Katherine A., ed. *Farmers, Hunters, and Colonists: Interaction between the Southwest and the Southern Plains.* Tucson: University of Arizona Press, 1991.

———, ed. *Migration and Reorganization: The Pueblo IV Period in the American Southwest.* Anthropological Research Papers no. 51, Arizona State University, Tempe, 1998.

Steele, Ian K. *Warpaths: Invasions of North America.* New York: Oxford University Press, 1994.

Stuart, David E. *Anasazi America: Seventeen Centuries on the Road from Center Place.* Albuquerque: University of New Mexico Press, 2000.

Sundstrom, Linda. "Smallpox Used Them Up: References to Epidemic Disease in Northern Plains Winter Counts, 1714–1920." *Ethnohistory* 44 (1997): 305–43.

Suttles, Wayne, ed. *Northwest Coast.* Vol. 7, *Handbook of North American Indians.* William Sturtevant, gen. ed. Washington DC: Smithsonian Institution Press, 1990.

Tanner, Helen Hornbeck, ed. *Atlas of Great Lakes Indian History.* Norman: University of Oklahoma Press, 1987.

Thomas, David Hurst. *Exploring Native North America.* New York: Oxford University Press, 2000.

———. *Skull Wars: Kennewick Man, Archaeology, and the Battle for Native American Identity.* New York: Basic Books, 2000.

———, ed. *Columbian Consequences.* Vol. 1, *Archaeological and Historical Perspectives on the Spanish Borderlands West*; vol. 3, *The Spanish Borderlands in Pan-American Perspective.* Washington DC: Smithsonian Institution Press, 1989, 1991.

Thorne, Tanis C. *The Many Hands of My Relations: French and Indians on the Lower Missouri.* Columbia: University of Missouri Press, 1996.

Towner, Ronald H. *The Archaeology of Navajo Origins.* Salt Lake City: University of Utah Press, 1996.

Trenholm, Virginia Cole. *The Arapahoes.* Norman: University of Oklahoma Press, 1970.

Trenholm, Virginia, and Maurine Carley. *The Shoshonis, Sentinels of the Rockies.* Norman: University of Oklahoma Press, 1964.

Trigger, Bruce G. *The Children of Aataentsic: A History of the Huron People to 1660.* 2 vols. Montreal: McGill-Queens University Press, 1976.

———, ed. *Northeast.* Vol. 15, *Handbook of North American Indians.* William Sturtevant, gen. ed. Washington DC: Smithsonian Institution Press, 1978.

Trigger, Bruce G., and Wilcomb E. Washburn, eds. *The Cambridge History of the Native Peoples of the Americas.* Vol. 1, *North America.* Cambridge: Cambridge University Press, 1996.

Turner, Christy G., II, and Jacqueline A. Turner. *Man Corn: Cannibalism and Violence in the Prehistoric American Southwest.* Salt Lake City: University of Utah Press, 1999.

Unrau, William E. *The Kansa Indians: A History of the Wind People, 1673–1873.* Norman: University of Oklahoma Press, 1971.

Usner, Daniel H., Jr. *American Indians in the Lower Mississippi Valley: Social and Economic Histories.* Lincoln: University of Nebraska Press, 1998.

———. *Indians, Settlers, and Slaves in a Frontier Exchange Economy: The Lower Mississippi Valley before 1783.* Chapel Hill: University of North Carolina Press, 1992.

Varien, Mark D. *Sedentism and Mobility in a Social Landscape: Mesa Verde and Beyond.* Tucson: University of Arizona Press, 1999.

Vaughan, Thomas, and Bill Holm, eds. *Soft Gold: The Fur Trade and Cultural Exchange on the Northwest Coast of America.* Portland: Oregon Historical Society Press, 1982.

Vecsey, Christopher. *On the Padres' Trail.* Notre Dame IN: University of Notre Dame Press, 1996.

Verano, John W., and Douglas H. Ubelaker, eds. *Disease and Demography in the Americas.* Washington DC: Smithsonian Institution Press, 1992.

Vigil, Ralph H., Frances W. Kaye, and John R. Wunder, eds. *Spain and the Plains: Myths and Realities of the Spanish Exploration and Settlement on the Great Plains.* Niwot: University of Colorado Press, 1994.

Walker, Deward E., Jr., ed. *Plateau.* Vol. 12, *Handbook of North American Indians.* William Sturtevant, gen. ed. Washington DC: Smithsonian Institution Press, 1998.

Wallace, Anthony F. C. *Jefferson and the Indians: The Tragic Fate of the First Americans.* Cambridge: Harvard University Press, 1999.

Wallace, Ernest, and E. Adamson Hoebel. *The Comanches: Lords of the South Plains.* Norman: University of Oklahoma Press, 1952.

Walthall, John A., and Thomas E. Emerson, eds. *Calumet and Fleur-de-Lys: Archaeology of Indian and French Contact in the Midcontinent.* Washington DC: Smithsonian Institution Press, 1992.

Warhus, Mark. *Another America: Native American Maps and the History of Our Land.* New York: St. Martin's Press, 1997.

Warren, William W. *History of the Ojibway People.* 1885. Reprint, St. Paul: Minnesota Historical Society Press, 1984.

Washburn, Wilcomb, ed. *Indian-White Relations.* Vol. 4, *Handbook of North American Indians.* William Sturtevant, gen. ed. Washington DC: Smithsonian Institution Press, 1988.

Waters, Frank. *Book of the Hopi.* New York: Penguin, 1977.

Weber, David J. *The Spanish Frontier in North America.* New Haven CT: Yale University Press, 1992.

———. *What Caused the Pueblo Revolt of 1680?* Boston: Bedford Books, 1999.

———, ed. *New Spain's Northern Frontier: Essays on Spain in the American West.* Dallas TX: Southern Methodist University Press, 1988.

Weddle, Robert S. *Wilderness Manhunt: The Spanish Search for La Salle.* Austin: University of Texas Press, 1973.

———. *The Wreck of the Belle, the Ruin of La Salle.* College Station: Texas A & M University Press, 2001.

Wedel, Waldo R. *Central Plains Prehistory: Holocene Environments and Culture Change in the Republican River Basin.* Lincoln: University of Nebraska Press, 1986.

Weltfish, Gene. *The Lost Universe: The Way of Life of the Pawnee.* New York: Ballantine Books, 1971.

West, Elliott. "Called out People: The Cheyennes and the Central Plains." *Montana: The Magazine of Western History* 48 (summer 1998): 2–15.

———. *The Contested Plains: Indians, Goldseekers, and the Rush to Colorado.* Lawrence: University Press of Kansas, 1998.

———. *The Way to the West: Essays on the Central Plains.* Albuquerque: University of New Mexico Press, 1995.

Whayne, Jeannie, comp. *Cultural Encounters in the Early South: Indians and Europeans in Arkansas.* Fayetteville: University of Arkansas Press, 1995.

White, Richard. "The Cultural Landscape of the Pawnees." *Great Plains Quarterly* 2 (1982): 31–40.

———. *"It's Your Misfortune and None of My Own": A New History of the American West.* Norman: University of Oklahoma Press, 1991.

———. *The Middle Ground: Indians, Empires, and Republics in the Great Lakes Region, 1650–1815.* Cambridge: Cambridge University Press, 1991.

———. *The Organic Machine.* New York: Hill and Wang, 1995.

———. *The Roots of Dependency: Subsistence, Environment, and Social Change among the Choctaws, Pawnees, and Navajos.* Lincoln: University of Nebraska Press, 1983.

———. "The Winning of the West: The Expansion of the Western Sioux in the Eighteenth and Nineteenth Centuries." *Journal of American History* 65 (1978): 319–43.

Whitley, David S. *The Art of the Shaman: Rock Art of California.* Salt Lake City: University of Utah Press, 2000.

Wiegers, Robert P. "A Proposal for Indian Slave Trading in the Mississippi Valley and Its Impact on the Osage." *Plains Anthropologist* 33, no. 122 (1988): 187–202.

Wiget, Andrew. "Truth and the Hopi: An Historiographic Study of Documented Oral Tradition Concerning the Coming of the Spanish." *Ethnohistory* 29 (1982): 181–99.

Wilcox, David R., and E. Bruce Masse, eds. *The Protohistoric Period in the North American Southwest, A.D. 1450–1700.* Anthropological Research Papers no. 24, Arizona State University, Tempe, 1981.

Will, George F., and George E. Hyde. *Corn among the Indians of the Upper Missouri.* 1917. Reprint, Lincoln: University of Nebraska Press, 1964.

Willey, P. *Prehistoric Warfare on the Great Plains: Skeletal Analysis of the Crow Creek Massacre Victims.* New York: Garland, 1990.

Wood, Peter H. "La Salle: Discovery of a Lost Explorer." *American Historical Review* 89 (1984): 294–323.

Wood, W. Raymond, ed. *Archaeology on the Great Plains.* Lawrence: University Press of Kansas, 1998.

Worcester, Donald E. *The Apaches.* Norman: University of Oklahoma Press, 1979.

Yazzie, Ethelou, ed. *Navajo History.* Vol. 1. Rough Rock AZ: Rough Rock Press, formerly Navajo Curriculum Center, 1971.

Young, Biloine Whiting, and Melvin L. Fowler. *Cahokia: The Great Native American Metropolis.* Urbana: University of Illinois Press, 2000.

Young, Gloria A., and Michael P. Hoffman, eds. *The Expedition of Hernando de Soto West of the Mississippi, 1541–1543: Proceedings of the De Soto Symposia, 1988 and 1990.* Fayetteville: University of Arkansas Press, 1993.

Zolbrod, Paul. *Diné bahane': The Navajo Creation Story.* Albuquerque: University of New Mexico Press, 1984.

Index

Page references for illustrations appear in italics.